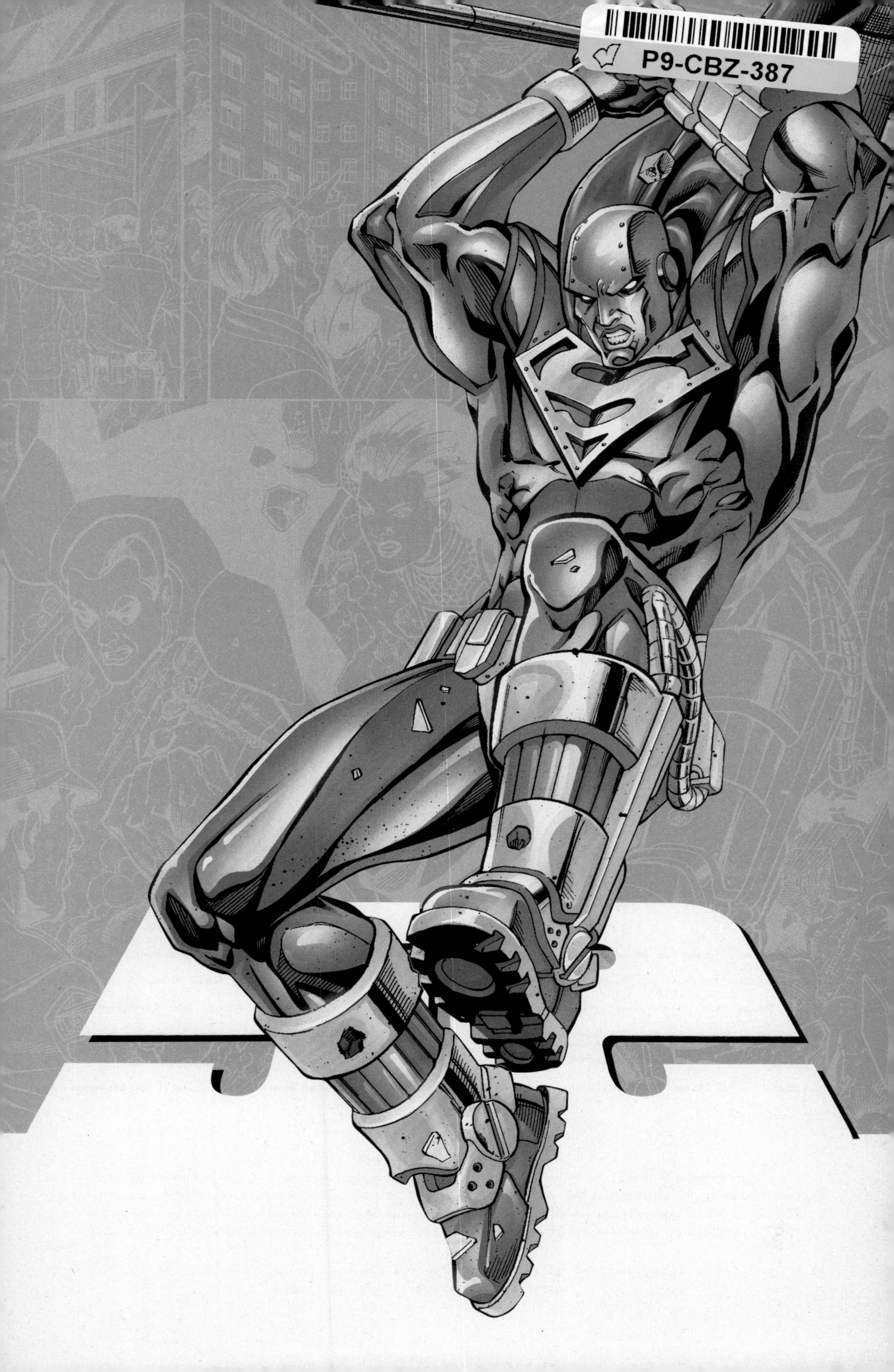

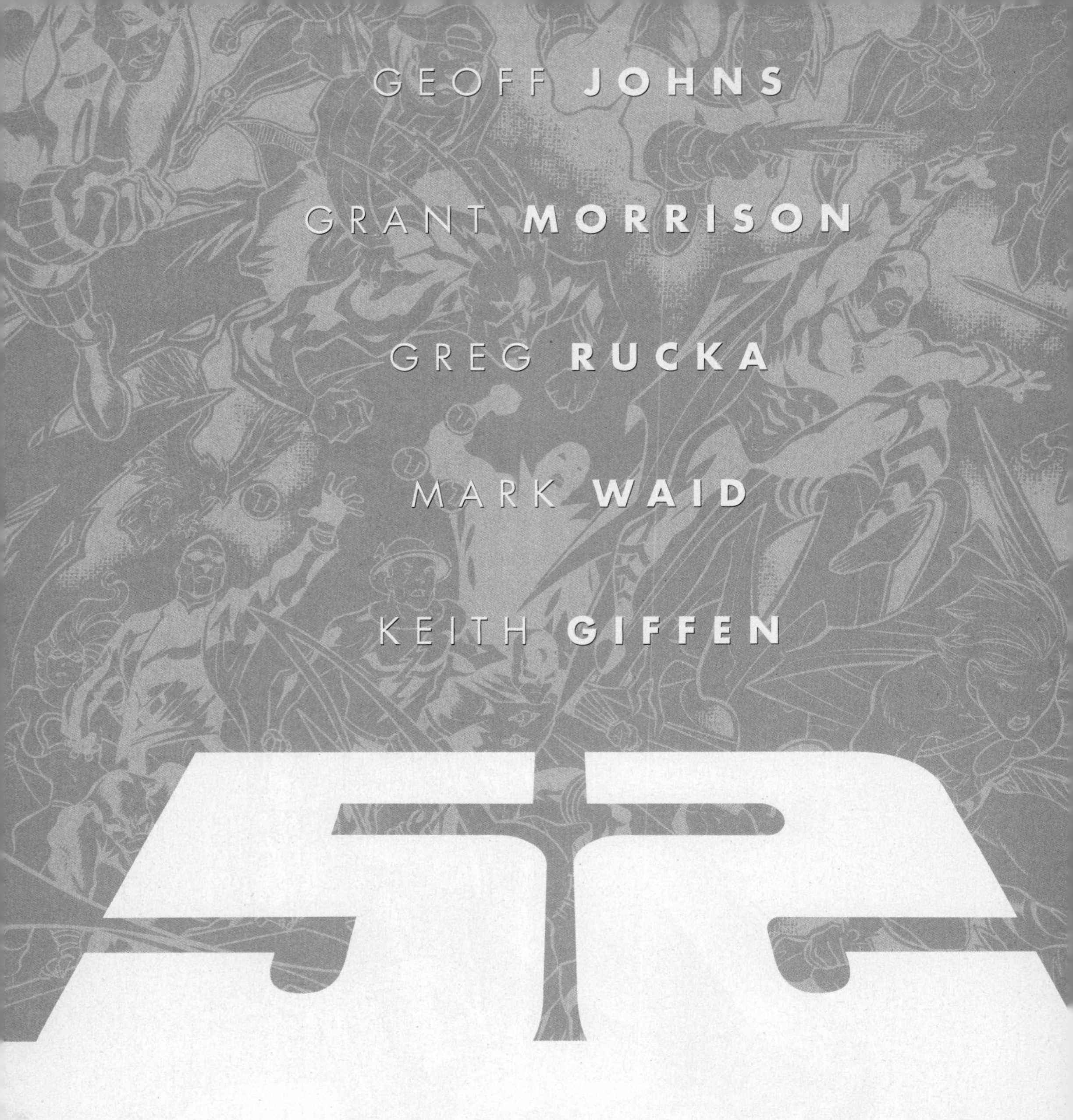

GEOFF **JOHNS**

GRANT **MORRISON**

GREG **RUCKA**

MARK **WAID**

KEITH **GIFFEN**

Dan DiDio Senior VP-Executive Editor **Michael Siglain** Editor-original series **Jeanine Schaefer** Associate Editor-original series **Harvey Richards** Assistant Editor-original series

Anton Kawasaki Editor-collected edition **Robbin Brosterman** Senior Art Director **Paul Levitz** President & Publisher **Georg Brewer** VP-Design & DC Direct Creative

Richard Bruning Senior VP-Creative Director **Patrick Caldon** Executive VP-Finance & Operations **Chris Caramalis** VP-Finance **John Cunningham** VP-Marketing

Terri Cunningham VP-Managing Editor **Alison Gill** VP-Manufacturing **David Hyde** VP-Publicity **Hank Kanalz** VP-General Manager, WildStorm **Jim Lee** Editorial Director-WildStorm **Paula Lowitt** Senior

VP-Business & Legal Affairs **MaryEllen McLaughlin** VP-Advertising & Custom Publishing **John Nee** SeniorVP-Business Development **Gregory Noveck** Senior VP-Creative Affairs

Sue Pohja VP-Book Trade Sales **Steve Rotterdam** Senior VP-Sales & Marketing **Cheryl Rubin** Senior VP-Brand Management **Jeff Trojan** VP-Business Development, DC Direct **Bob Wayne** VP-Sales

Cover by J.G. Jones with Alex Sinclair

52: VOLUME FOUR

DC Comics, 1700 Broadway, New York, NY 10019. A Warner Bros. Entertainment Company. Printed in Canada. First Printing.
ISBN:1-4012-1486-X ISBN 13: 978-1-4012-1486-9

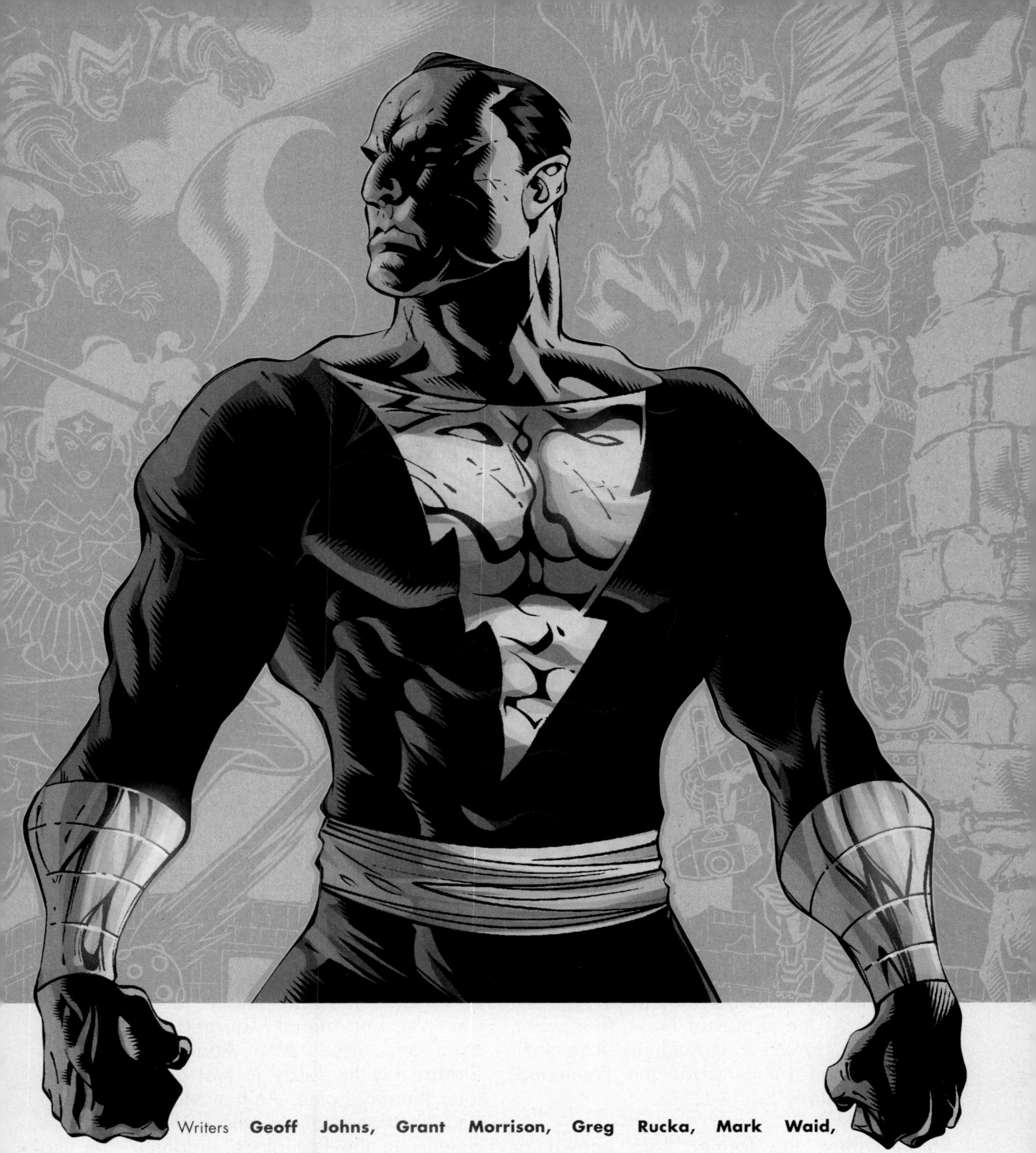

Writers **Geoff Johns, Grant Morrison, Greg Rucka, Mark Waid,**

Art Breakdowns **Keith Giffen** Pencils **Eddy Barrows, Chris Batista, Joe Bennett, Giuseppe Camuncoli, Jamal Igle, Dan Jurgens, Justiniano, Mike McKone, Patrick Olliffe, Darick Robertson** Inks **Eddy Barrows, Belardino Brabo, Drew Geraci, Dan Green, Jack Jadson, Andy Lanning, Patrick Olliffe, Rodney Ramos, Norm Rapmund, Darick Robertson, Lorenzo Ruggiero, Walden Wong** Colors **David Baron, Hi-Fi, Pete Pantazis, Alex Sinclair** Letters **Jared K. Fletcher, Rob Leigh, Ken Lopez** Original Covers **J.G. Jones** with **Alex Sinclair**

In the wake of the INFINITE CRISIS, the DC Universe is left without its three biggest icons — Superman, Batman and Wonder Woman.

But it is *not* a world without heroes...

In Metropolis, fame-seeking Booster Gold takes advantage of Superman's absence — using his robot sidekick Skeets's knowledge of the future to help prevent crimes and catastrophes. But a new, mysterious hero known as Supernova has been stealing some of Booster's thunder. When both heroes try and stop a giant creature from causing a nuclear explosion in the middle of the city, Booster performs a courageous act...and is seemingly killed in action. Skeets then finds Booster's ancestor Daniel Carter, to gain access to time traveler Rip Hunter's lab — but the now-sinister robot traps Daniel in a time loop and sets out to locate Hunter himself.

Elsewhere in Metropolis, Lex Luthor's Everyman Project, which gives ordinary people super-abilities, is in full swing. A newly powered Natasha Irons, niece to John Henry Irons (a.k.a. Steel), joins Luthor's new super-team: Infinity, Inc. — but John Henry learns that the super-powers that Luthor is giving people can be turned off at any moment. At the stroke of New Year's Eve, dozens of powered individuals lose their abilities when Luthor gives the command, resulting in many lost lives.

Ralph Dibny, the former hero known as Elongated Man, continues to search for a way to bring his dead wife Sue back to life by any means possible — exploring the realms of magic, the afterlife, and the mysterious place known as Nanda Parbat, an Asian mountain haven where there is no death.

Black Adam and his new family — wife Isis, brother-in-law Osiris, and Osiris's new friend, the talking crocodile Sobek — continue their reign. But when Amanda Waller deploys her Suicide Squad against them and forces Osiris to kill one of her agents, the leaked footage of the incident tarnishes the prince's reputation.

Noble scientist Will Magnus, creator of the Metal Men, finds himself on Oolong Island — where a community of the smartest criminal minds of the world have been gathered to wield an unlimited budget by the diabolical Chang Tzu, and unleash their weapon, the Four Horsemen of Apokolips, upon Black Adam.

With the low point of her Gotham City life behind her, former police officer Renee Montoya teams up with the enigmatic Vic Sage, a.k.a. The Question. But Sage has been stricken with a cancer that is slowly killing him. Before the sickness can completely overcome him, Renee makes a desperate attempt to take Sage back to Nanda Parbat to save his life. But Sage dies right outside the haven's gates before they can enter.

In the farthest reaches of space, Adam Strange, Starfire and Animal Man are trying to find their way home. Forging an unlikely alliance with Lobo, the space heroes end up on the run from Lady Styx — whose forces are on a crusade towards conquering the universe. The trio finally faces her and triumphs, but Animal Man gets injected by a toxin and dies. After Adam Strange and Starfire lay his body to rest and depart on their journey home, Animal Man awakens to find the strange aliens who had given him his powers in the first place suddenly standing over him.

The robot Skeets eventually finds Rip Hunter and corners the time-traveller and Supernova in the Bottle City of Kandor, where Supernova reveals himself to be Booster Gold — having faked his death. Booster and Hunter trap Skeets in the Phantom Zone...for now.

Natasha Irons works undercover to expose Luthor's plan — which was to give himself powers. When Luthor finally acquires them, Natasha faces the villain — but loses to Luthor's newly enhanced strength...

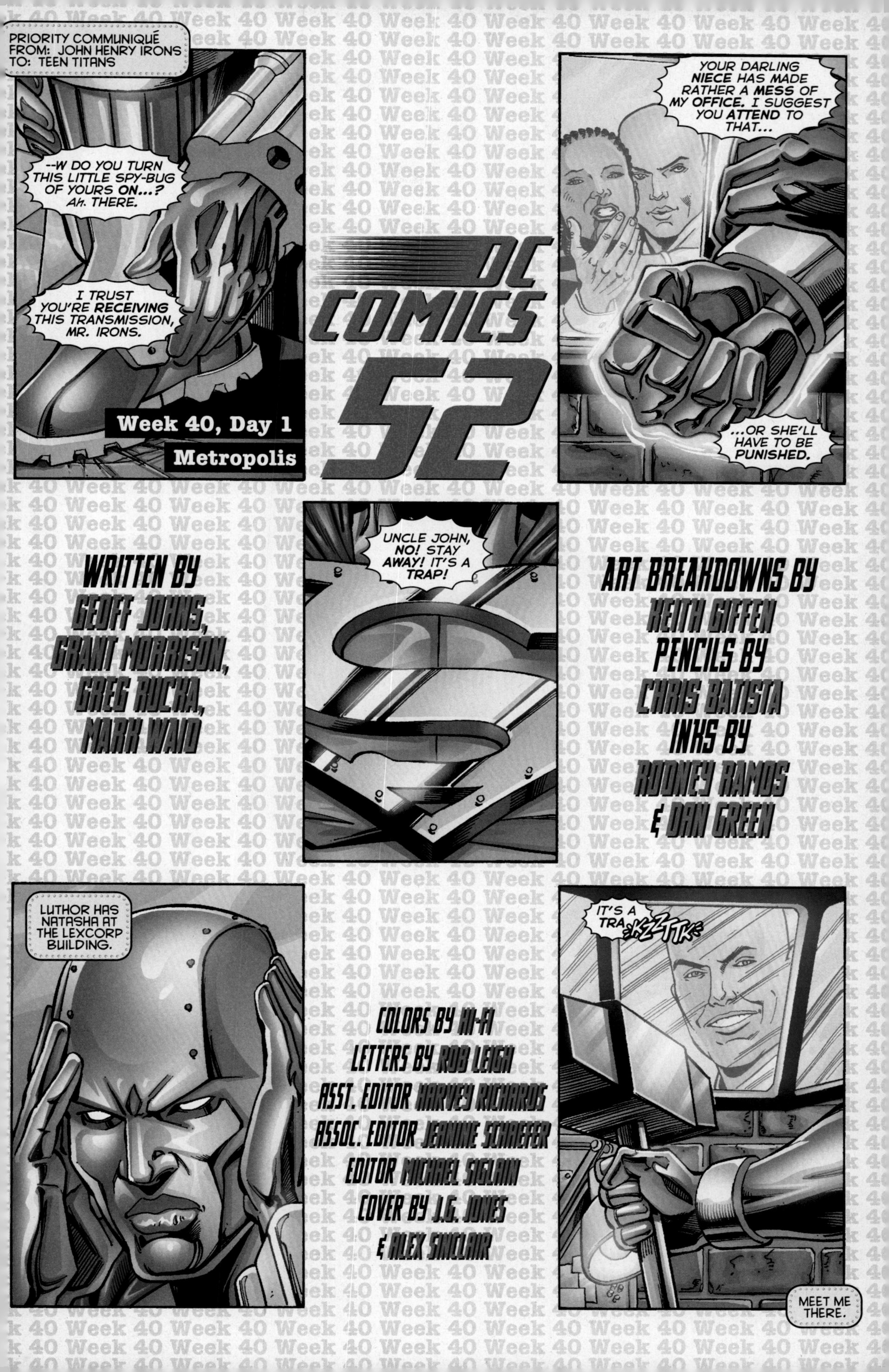
PRIORITY COMMUNIQUÉ
FROM: JOHN HENRY IRONS
TO: TEEN TITANS
--W DO YOU TURN THIS LITTLE SPY-BUG OF YOURS ON...? Ah. THERE.
I TRUST YOU'RE RECEIVING THIS TRANSMISSION, MR. IRONS.
Week 40, Day 1
Metropolis
YOUR DARLING NIECE HAS MADE RATHER A MESS OF MY OFFICE. I SUGGEST YOU ATTEND TO THAT...
...OR SHE'LL HAVE TO BE PUNISHED.
DC COMICS
52
WRITTEN BY
GEOFF JOHNS,
GRANT MORRISON,
GREG RUCKA,
MARK WAID
UNCLE JOHN, NO! STAY AWAY! IT'S A TRAP!
ART BREAKDOWNS BY
KEITH GIFFEN
PENCILS BY
CHRIS BATISTA
INKS BY
RODNEY RAMOS
& DAN GREEN
LUTHOR HAS NATASHA AT THE LEXCORP BUILDING.
COLORS BY HI-FI
LETTERS BY ROB LEIGH
ASST. EDITOR HARVEY RICHARDS
ASSOC. EDITOR JEANINE SCHAEFER
EDITOR MICHAEL SIGLAIN
COVER BY J.G. JONES
& ALEX SINCLAIR
IT'S A TRA-KZZTTK-
MEET ME THERE.

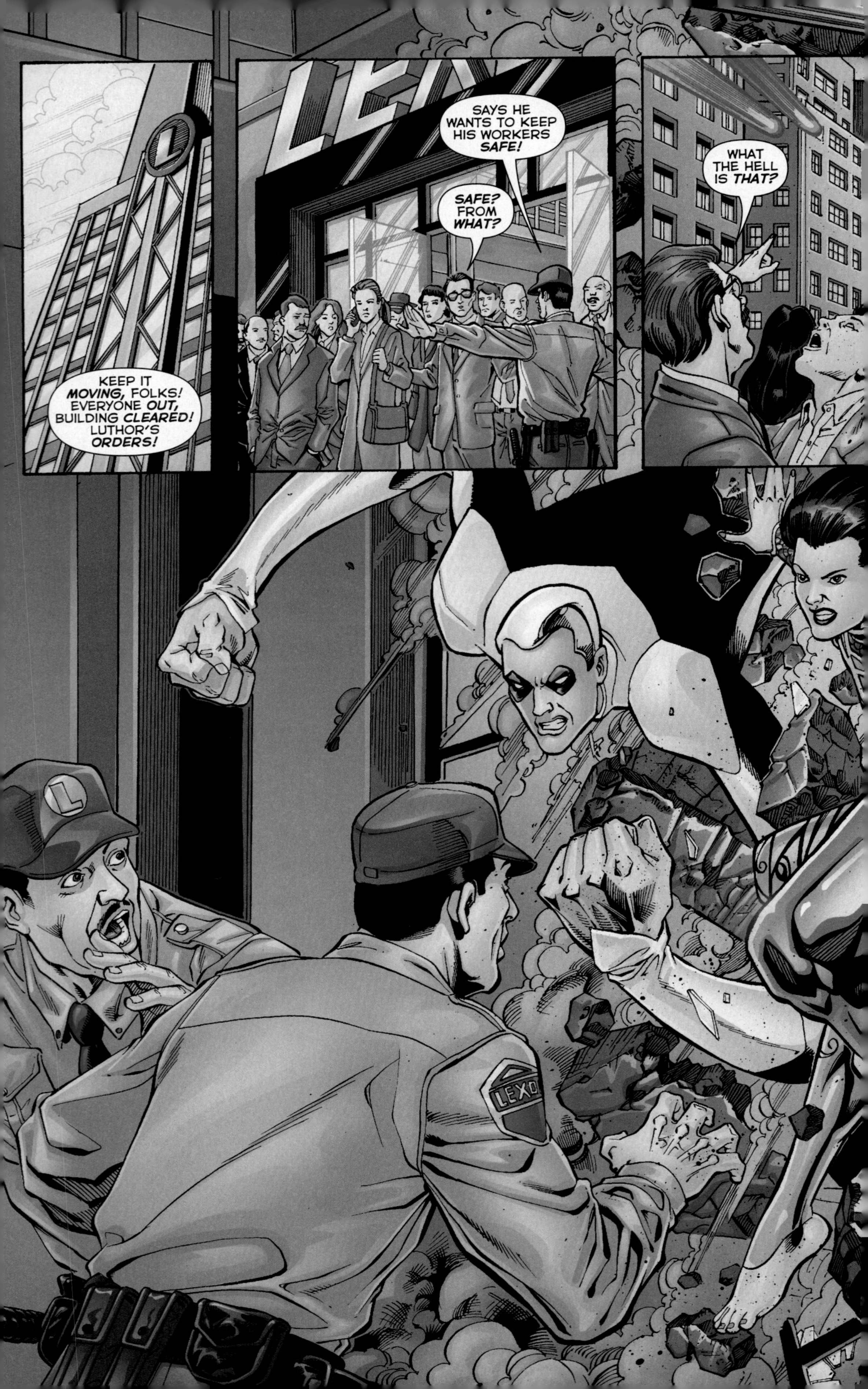
KEEP IT MOVING, FOLKS! EVERYONE OUT, BUILDING CLEARED! LUTHOR'S ORDERS!
SAYS HE WANTS TO KEEP HIS WORKERS SAFE!
SAFE? FROM WHAT?
WHAT THE HELL IS THAT?
LEXO

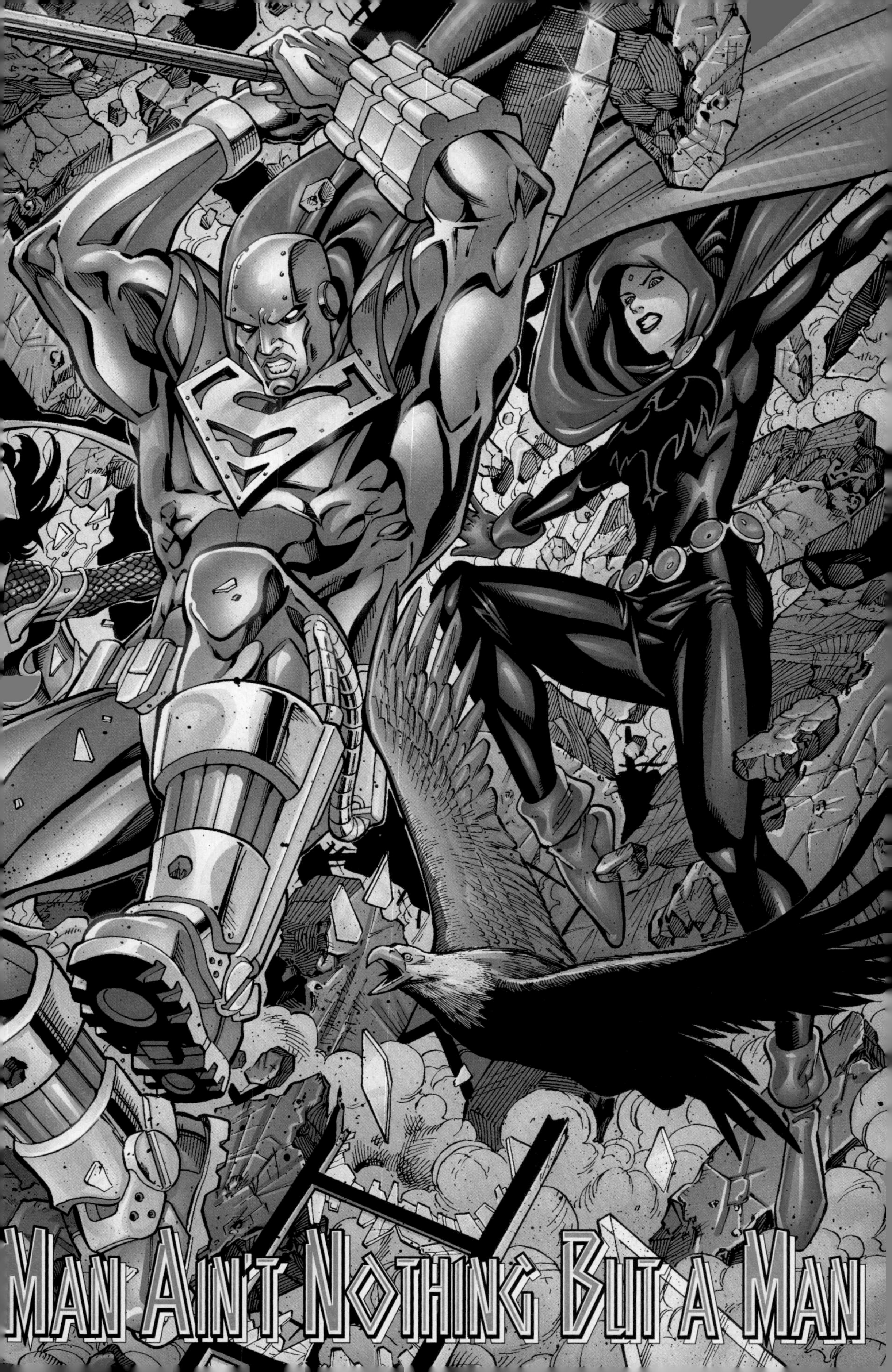
MAN AIN'T NOTHING BUT A MAN

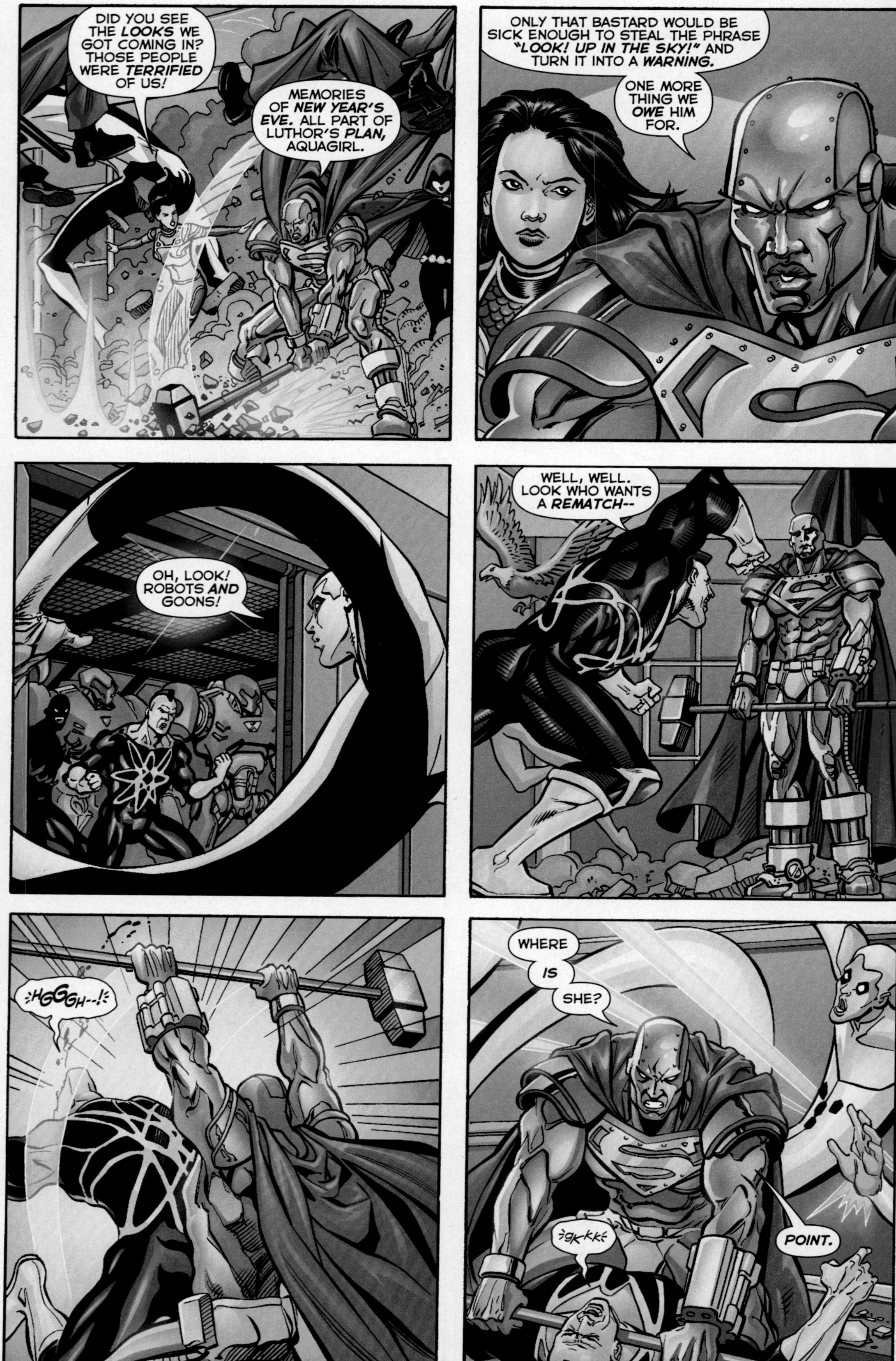

DID YOU SEE THE LOOKS WE GOT COMING IN? THOSE PEOPLE WERE TERRIFIED OF US!
MEMORIES OF NEW YEAR'S EVE. ALL PART OF LUTHOR'S PLAN, AQUAGIRL.
ONLY THAT BASTARD WOULD BE SICK ENOUGH TO STEAL THE PHRASE "LOOK! UP IN THE SKY!" AND TURN IT INTO A WARNING.
ONE MORE THING WE OWE HIM FOR.
OH, LOOK! ROBOTS AND GOONS!
WELL, WELL. LOOK WHO WANTS A REMATCH--
HGGGH--!
WHERE
IS
SHE?
GKKK
POINT.

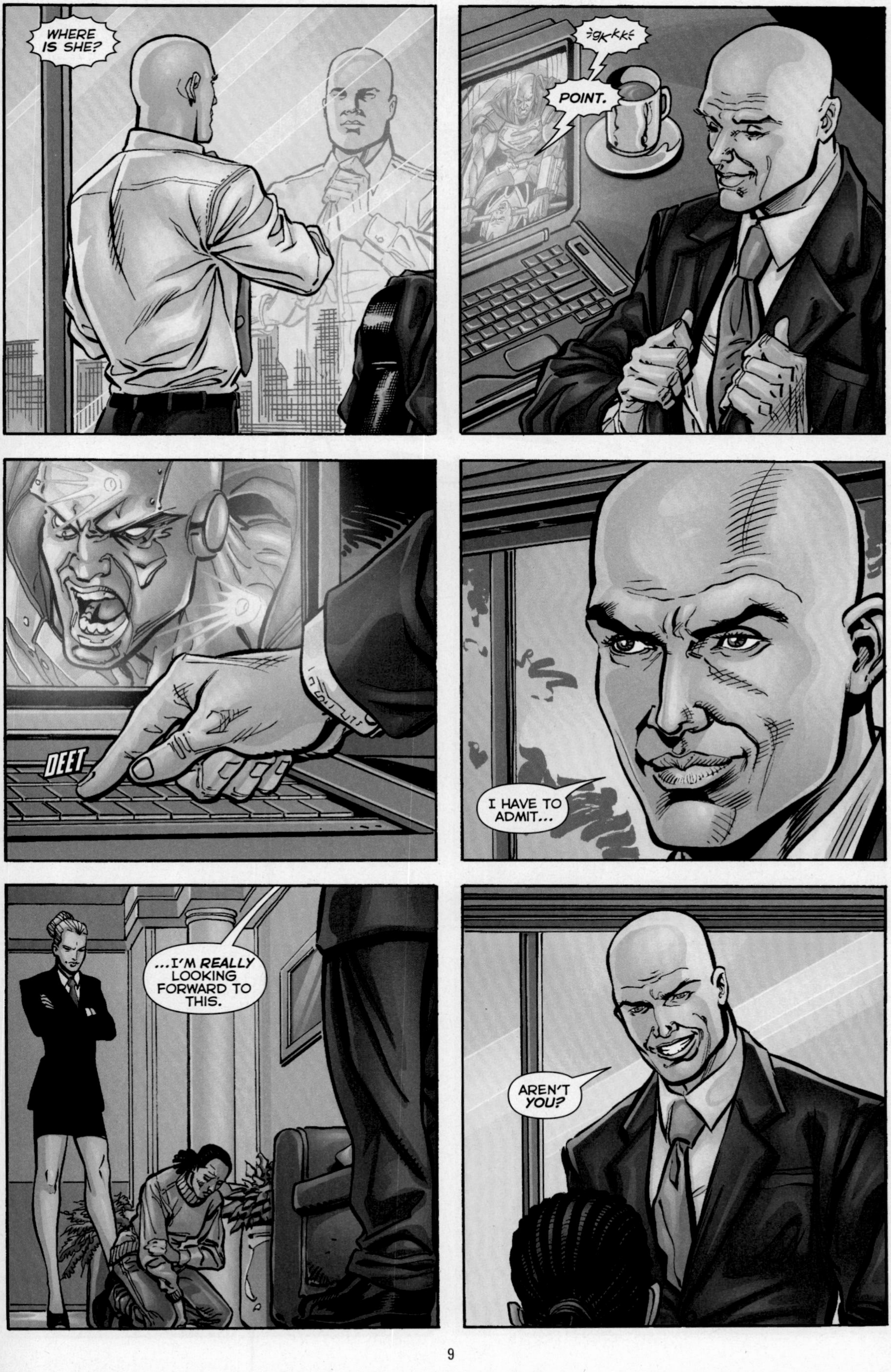
WHERE IS SHE?
GKKK
POINT.
DEET
I HAVE TO ADMIT...
...I'M REALLY LOOKING FORWARD TO THIS.
AREN'T YOU?

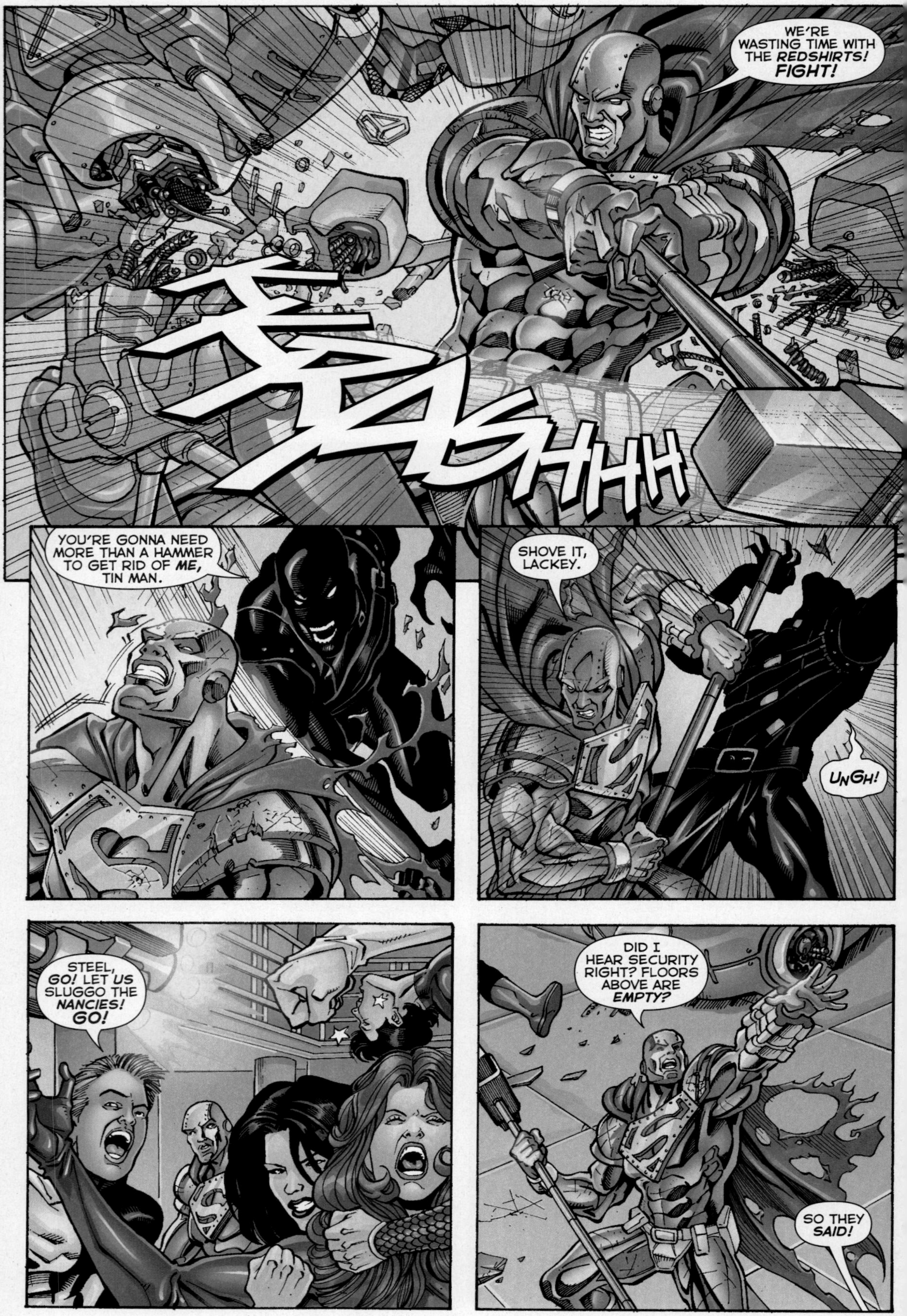

WE'RE WASTING TIME WITH THE REDSHIRTS! FIGHT!
KRASHHHH
YOU'RE GONNA NEED MORE THAN A HAMMER TO GET RID OF ME, TIN MAN.
SHOVE IT, LACKEY.
UNGH!
STEEL, GO! LET US SLUGGO THE NANCIES! GO!
DID I HEAR SECURITY RIGHT? FLOORS ABOVE ARE EMPTY?
SO THEY SAID!

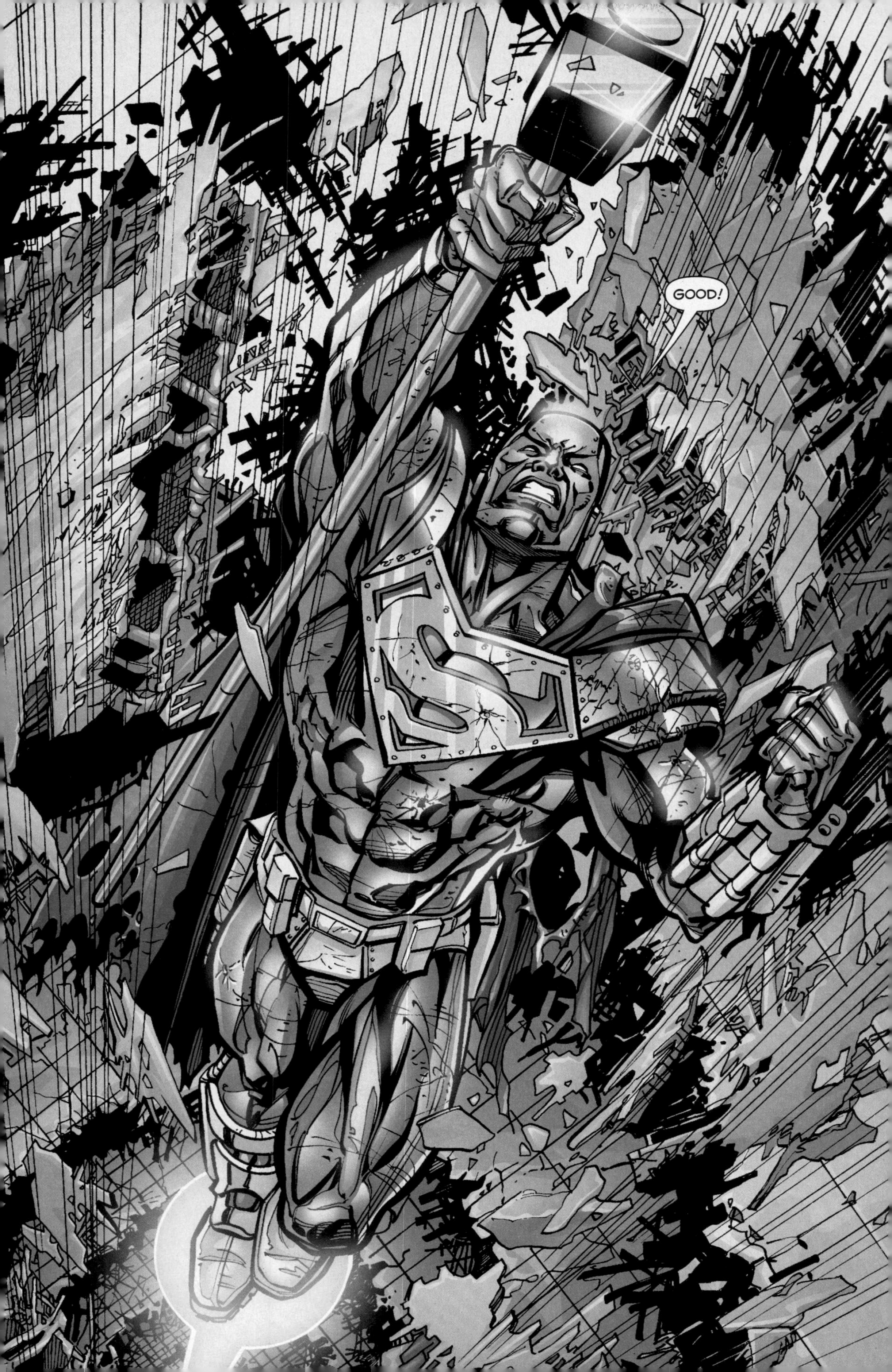
GOOD!

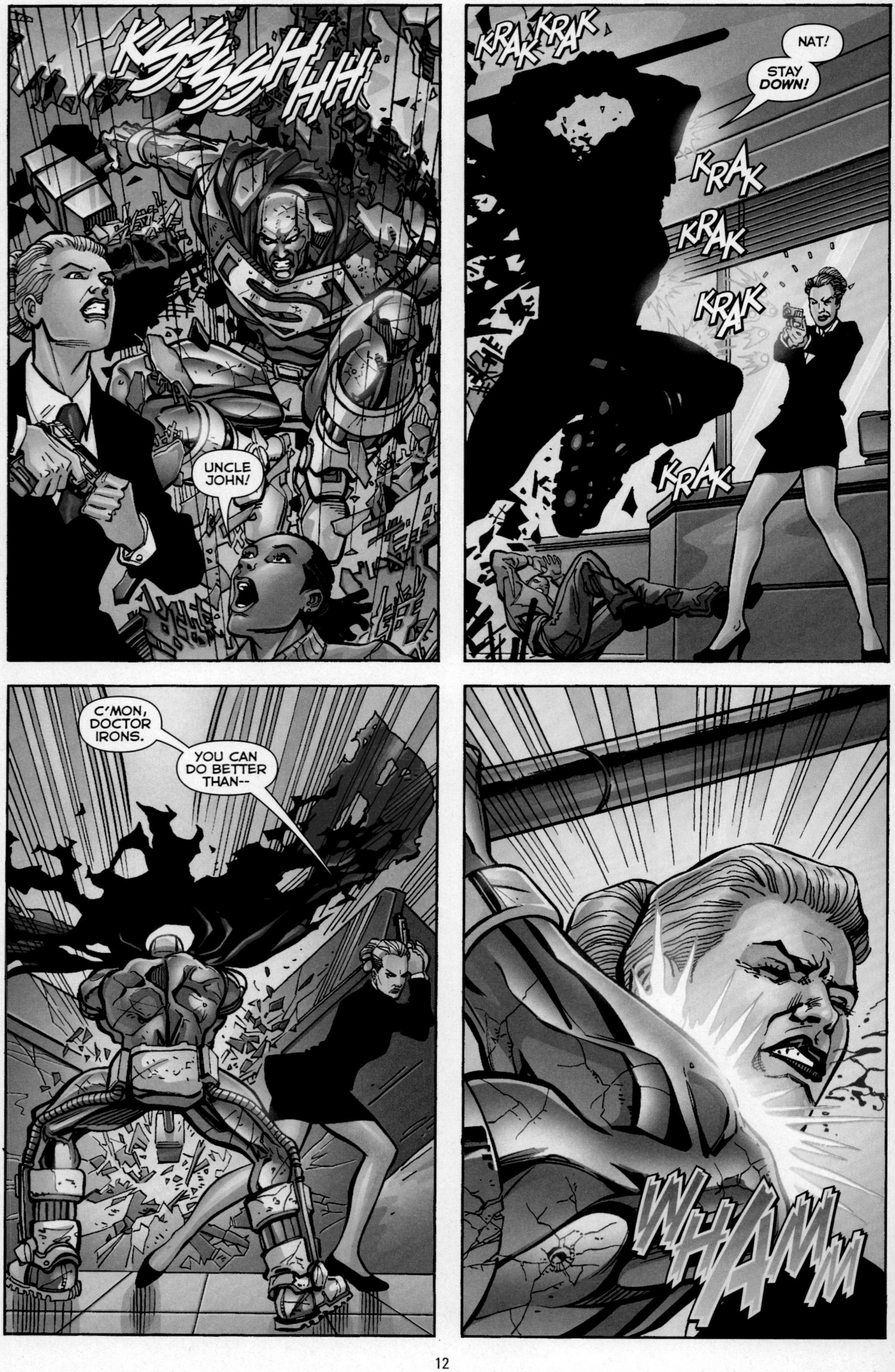

KSSSSHHH
UNCLE JOHN!
KRAK KRAK
NAT!
STAY DOWN!
KRAK
KRAK
KRAK
KRAK
C'MON, DOCTOR IRONS.
YOU CAN DO BETTER THAN--
WHAMM

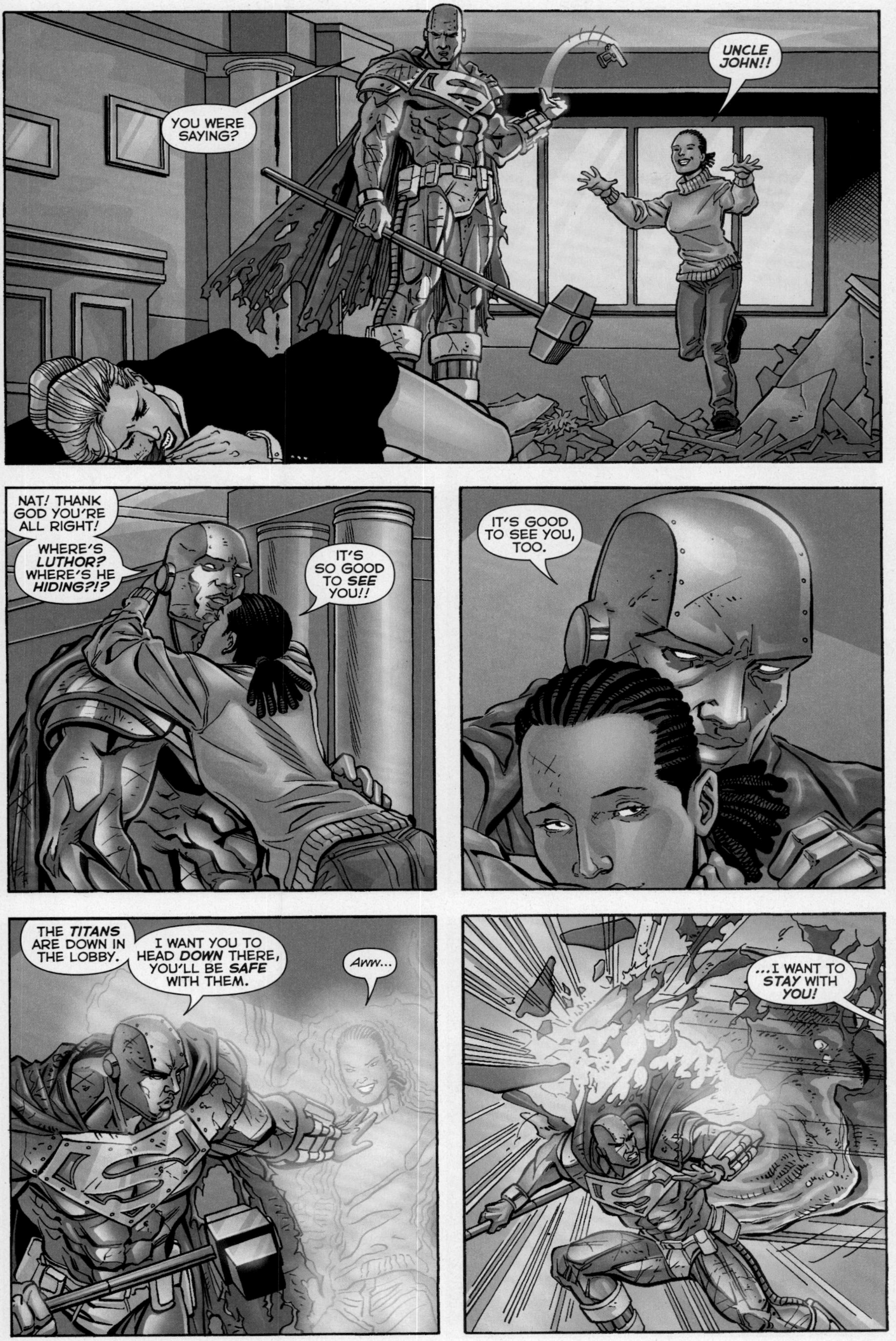
YOU WERE SAYING?
UNCLE JOHN!!
NAT! THANK GOD YOU'RE ALL RIGHT!
WHERE'S LUTHOR? WHERE'S HE HIDING?!?
IT'S SO GOOD TO SEE YOU!!
IT'S GOOD TO SEE YOU, TOO.
THE TITANS ARE DOWN IN THE LOBBY.
I WANT YOU TO HEAD DOWN THERE, YOU'LL BE SAFE WITH THEM.
Aww...
...I WANT TO STAY WITH YOU!

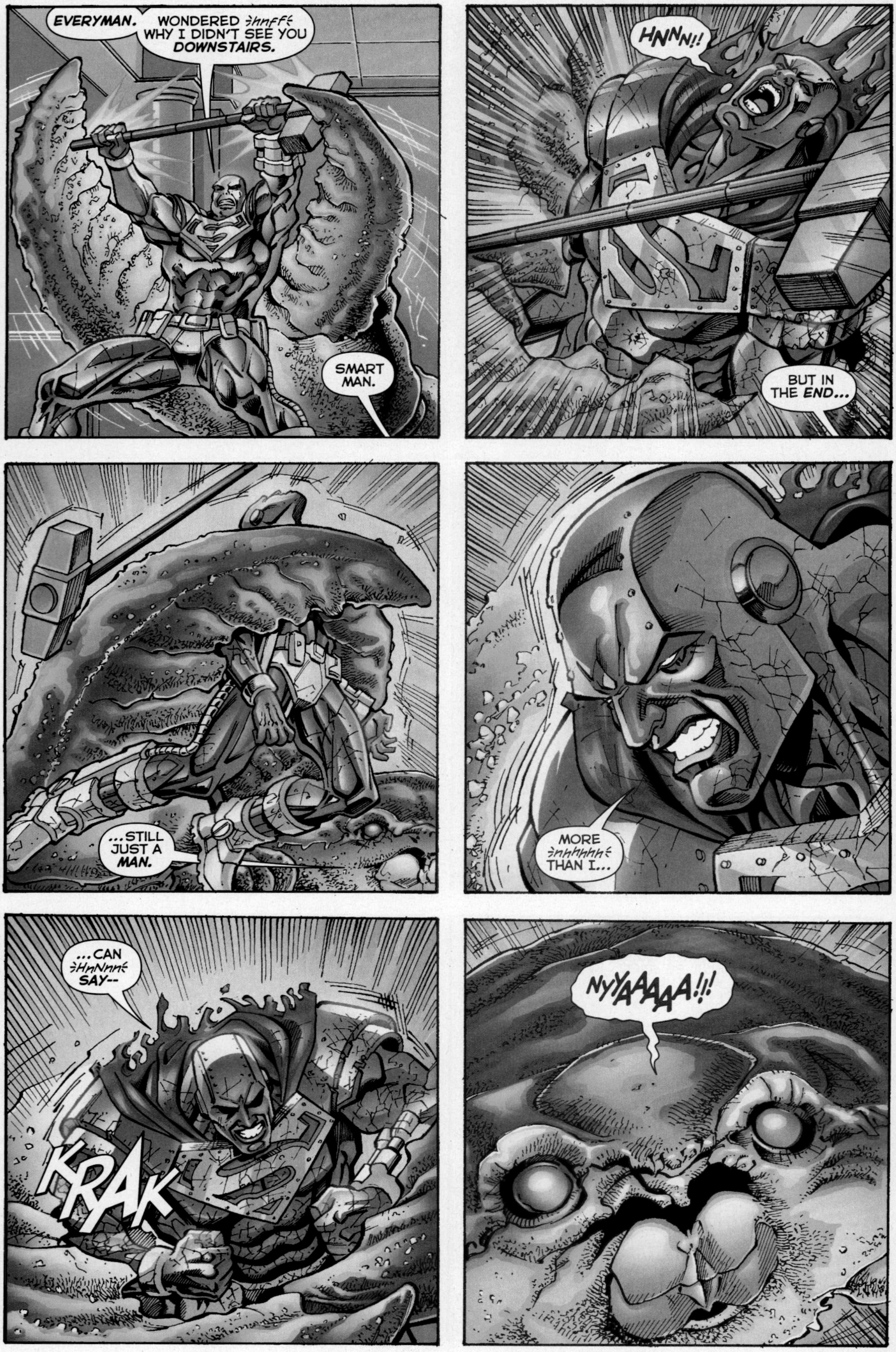
EVERYMAN.
WONDERED *hnff* WHY I DIDN'T SEE YOU DOWNSTAIRS.
SMART MAN.
HNNN!!
BUT IN THE END...
...STILL JUST A MAN.
MORE *hhhhhh* THAN I...
...CAN *HnNnn* SAY--
KRAK
NYYAAAAA!!!

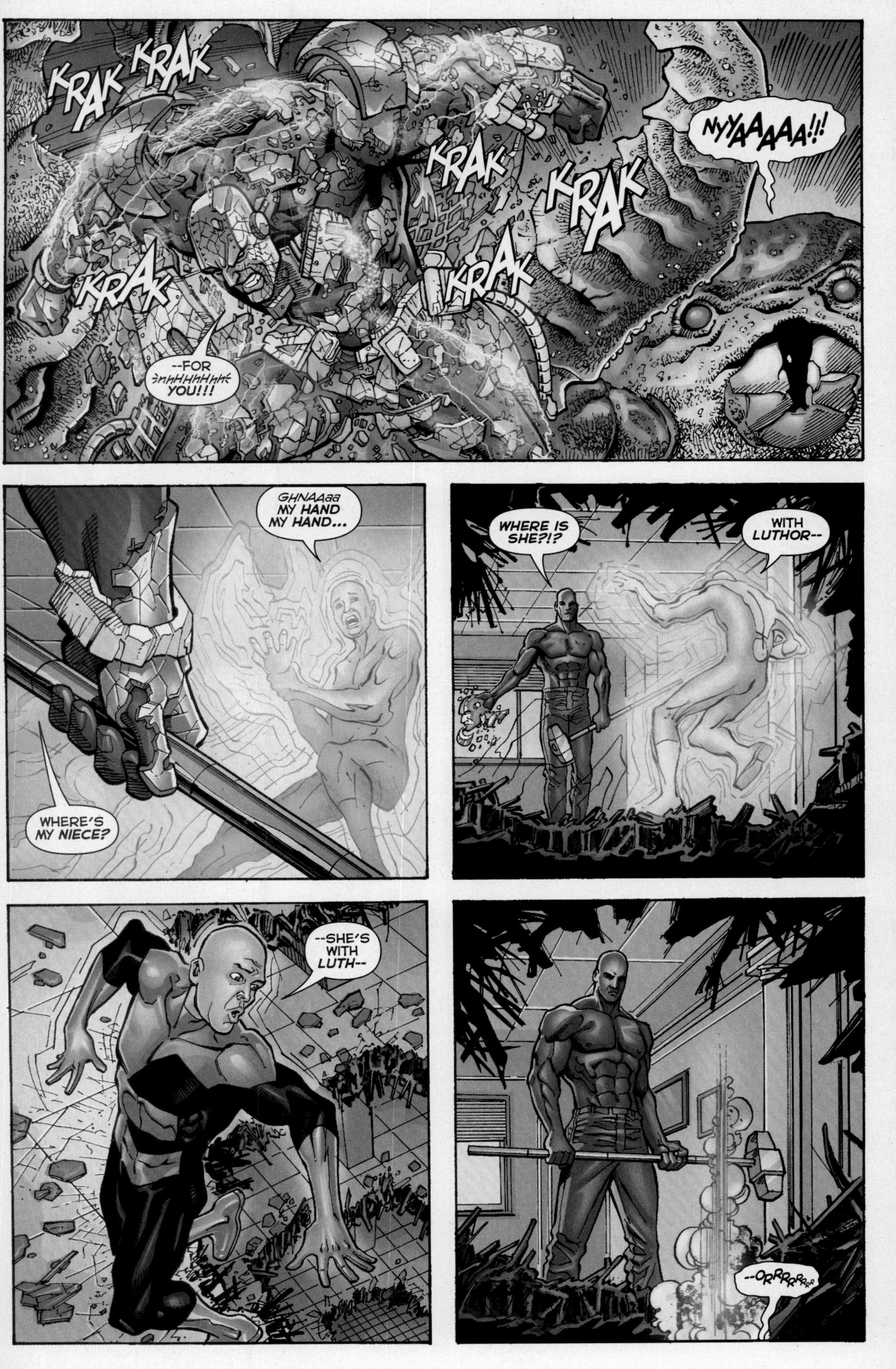
KRAK KRAK
NYYAAAAA!!!
KRAK
KRAK
KRAK
KRAK
--FOR
NNHHHHHH
YOU!!!
GHNAAaa
MY HAND
MY HAND...
WHERE'S
MY NIECE?
WHERE IS
SHE?!?
WITH
LUTHOR--
--SHE'S
WITH
LUTH--
--ORRRRRRR

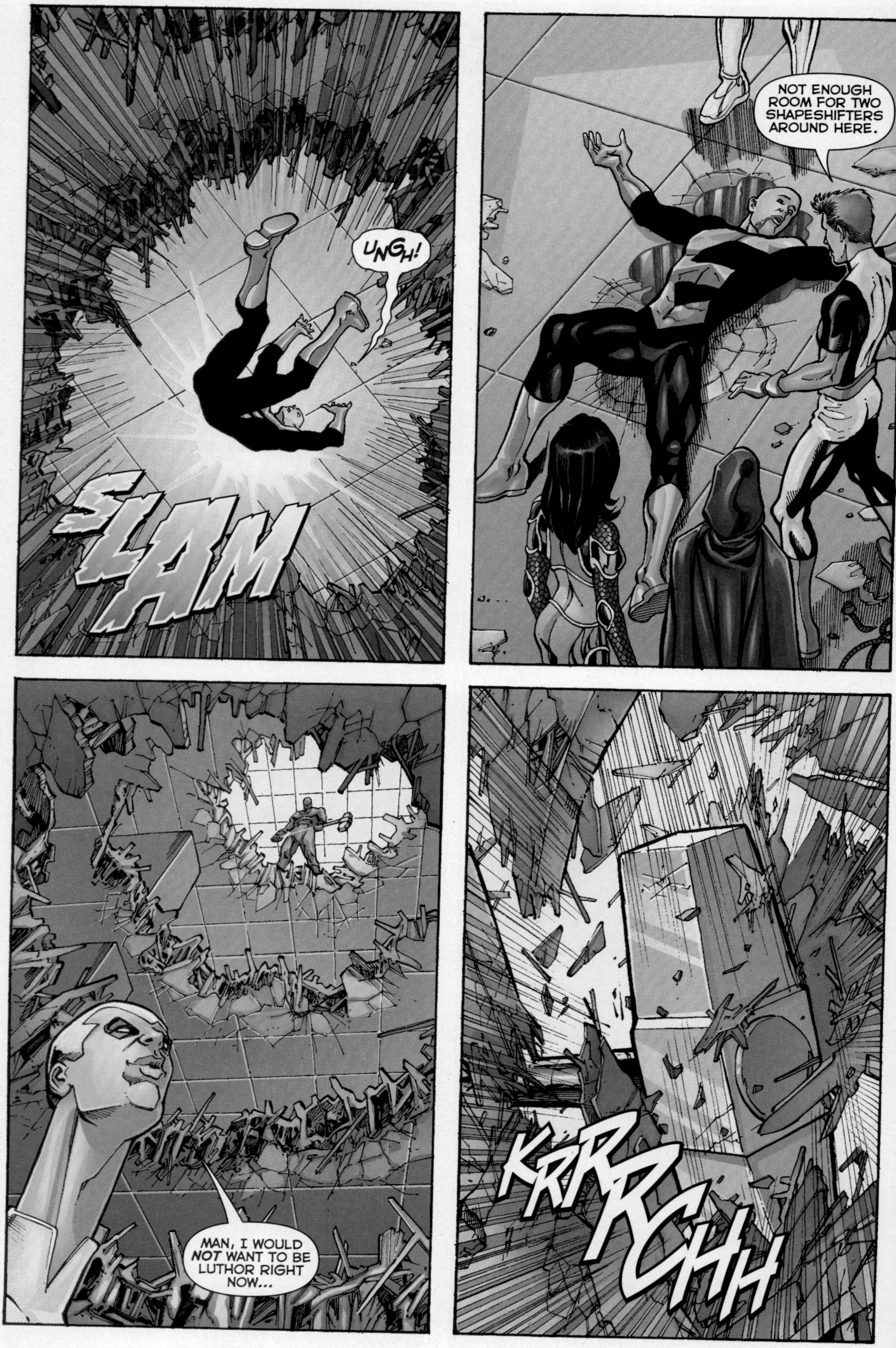
UNGH!
SLAM
NOT ENOUGH ROOM FOR TWO SHAPESHIFTERS AROUND HERE.
MAN, I WOULD NOT WANT TO BE LUTHOR RIGHT NOW...
KRRRCHH

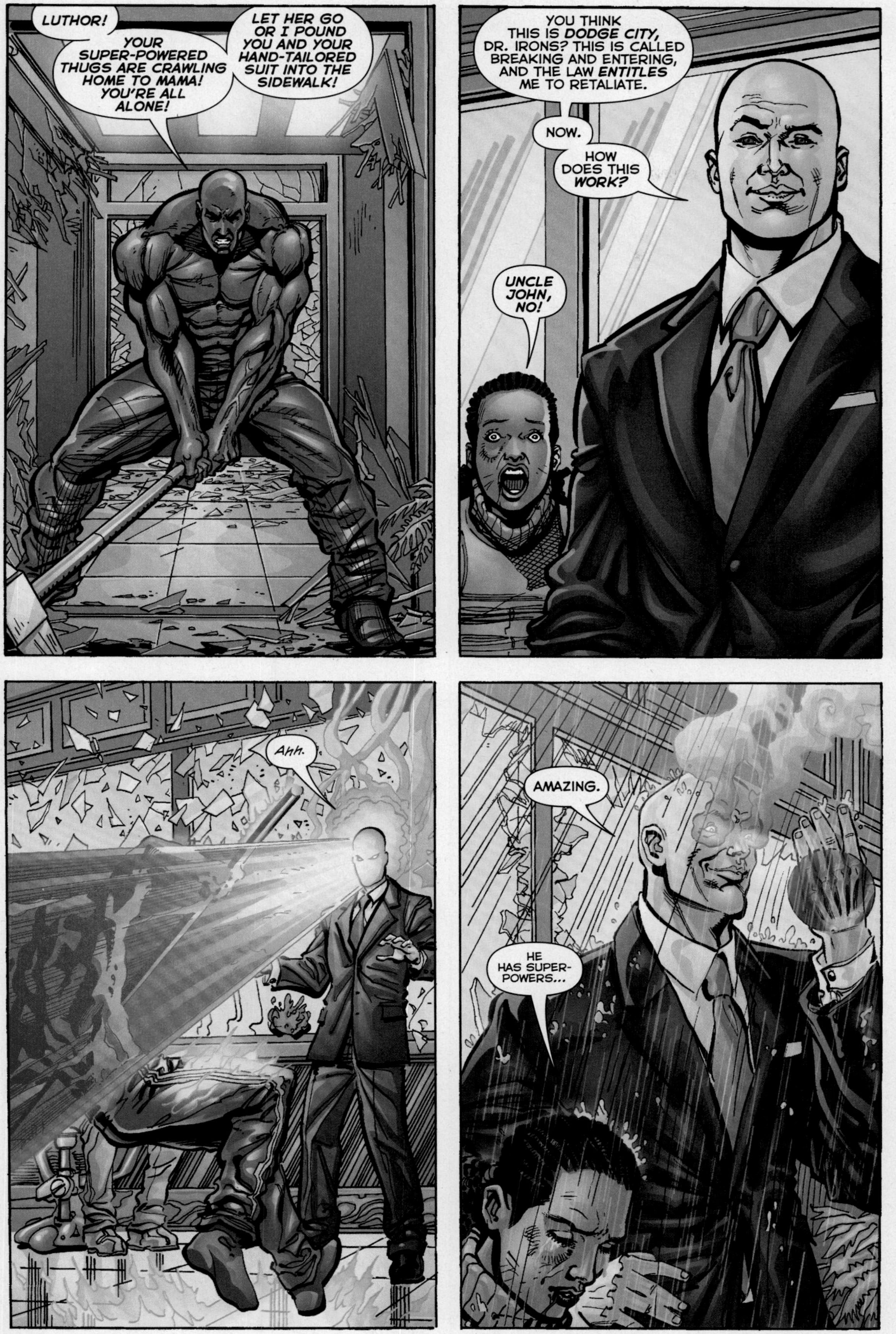
LUTHOR!
YOUR SUPER-POWERED THUGS ARE CRAWLING HOME TO MAMA! YOU'RE ALL ALONE!
LET HER GO OR I POUND YOU AND YOUR HAND-TAILORED SUIT INTO THE SIDEWALK!
YOU THINK THIS IS *DODGE CITY,* DR. IRONS? THIS IS CALLED BREAKING AND ENTERING, AND THE LAW *ENTITLES* ME TO RETALIATE.
NOW.
HOW DOES THIS *WORK?*
UNCLE JOHN, NO!
Ahh.
AMAZING.
HE HAS SUPER-POWERS...

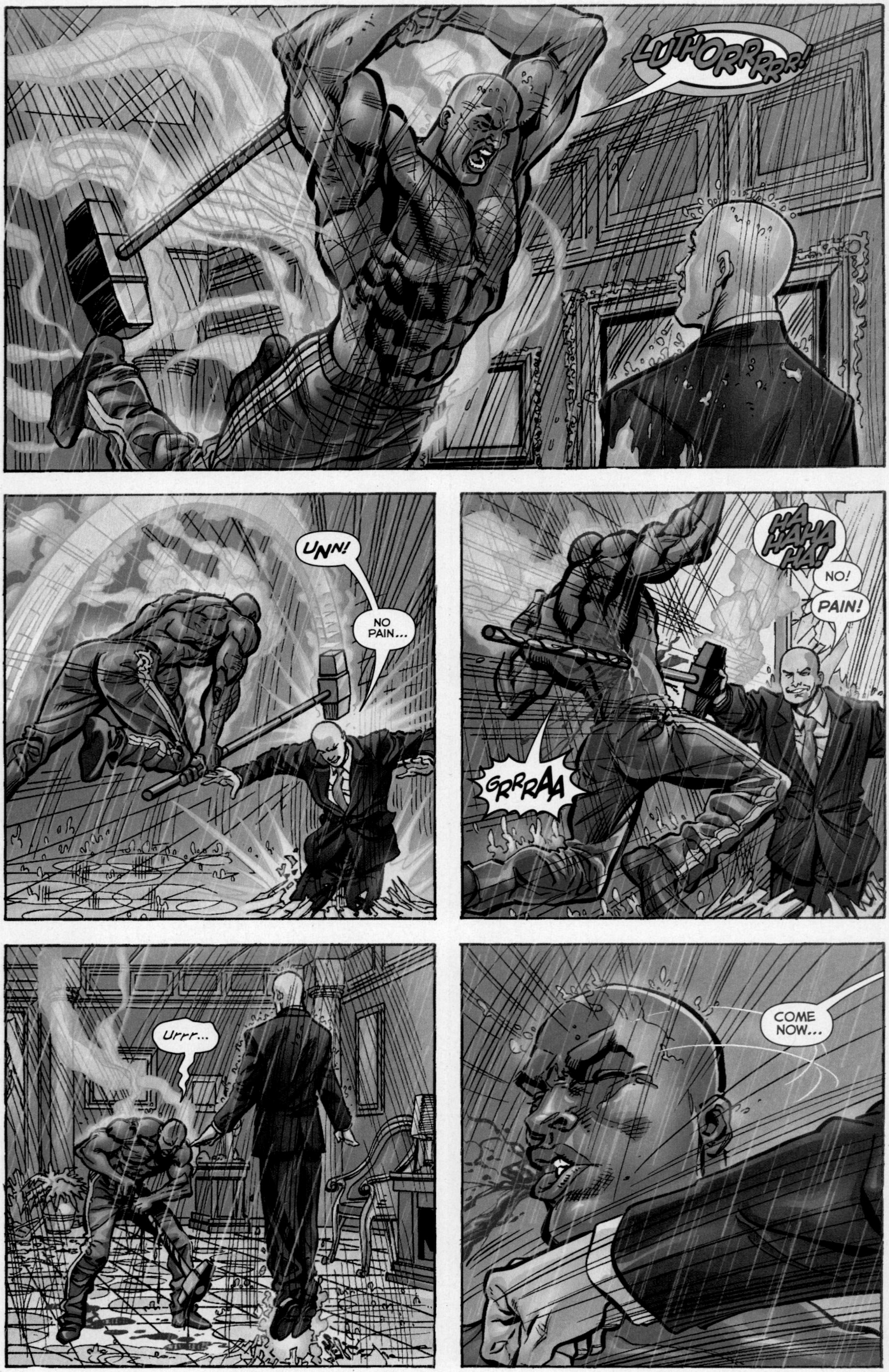
LUTHORRRRR!
UNN!
NO PAIN...
HA HAHA HA!
NO!
PAIN!
GRRRAA
Urrr...
COME NOW...

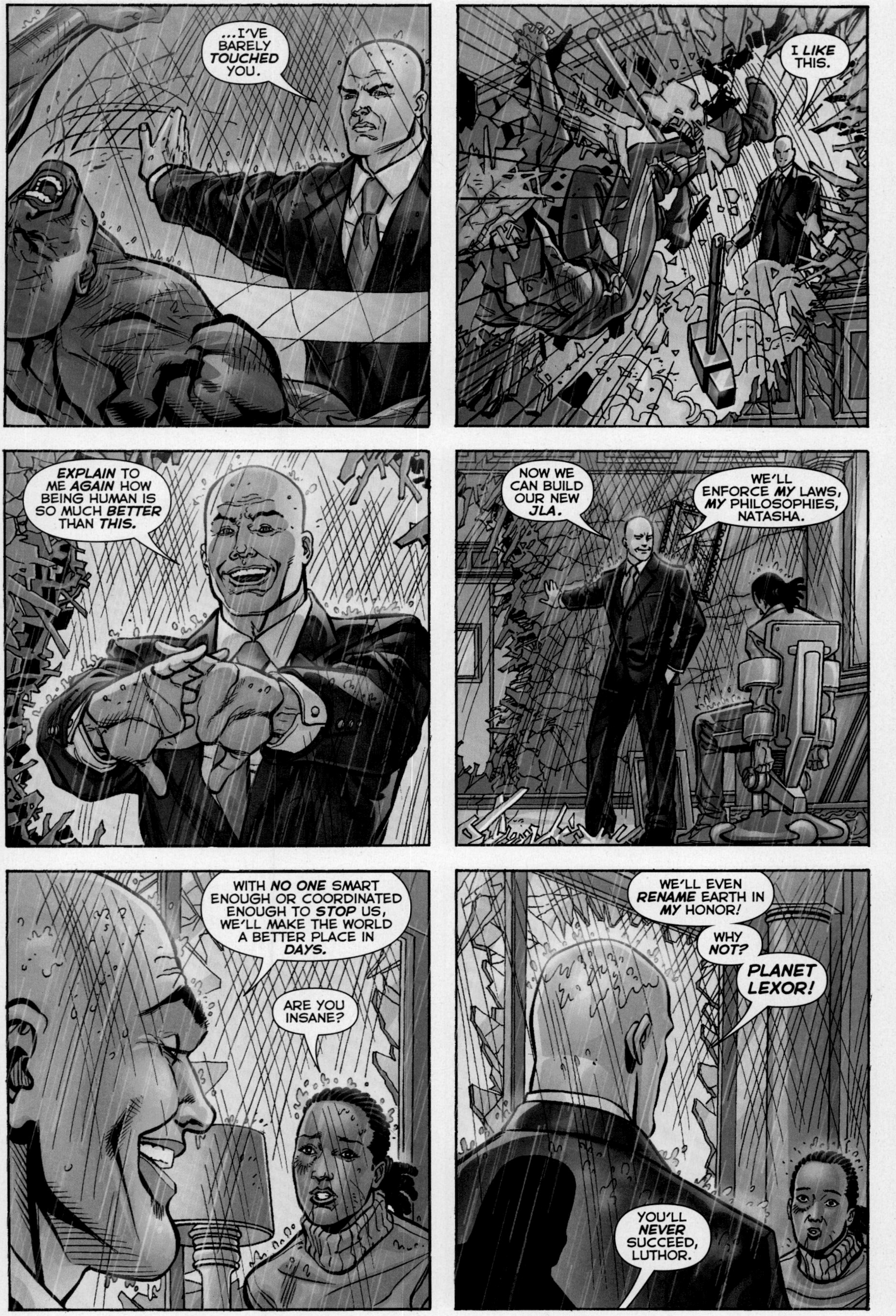
...I'VE BARELY TOUCHED YOU.
I LIKE THIS.
EXPLAIN TO ME AGAIN HOW BEING HUMAN IS SO MUCH BETTER THAN THIS.
NOW WE CAN BUILD OUR NEW JLA.
WE'LL ENFORCE MY LAWS, MY PHILOSOPHIES, NATASHA.
WITH NO ONE SMART ENOUGH OR COORDINATED ENOUGH TO STOP US, WE'LL MAKE THE WORLD A BETTER PLACE IN DAYS.
ARE YOU INSANE?
WE'LL EVEN RENAME EARTH IN MY HONOR!
WHY NOT?
PLANET LEXOR!
YOU'LL NEVER SUCCEED, LUTHOR.

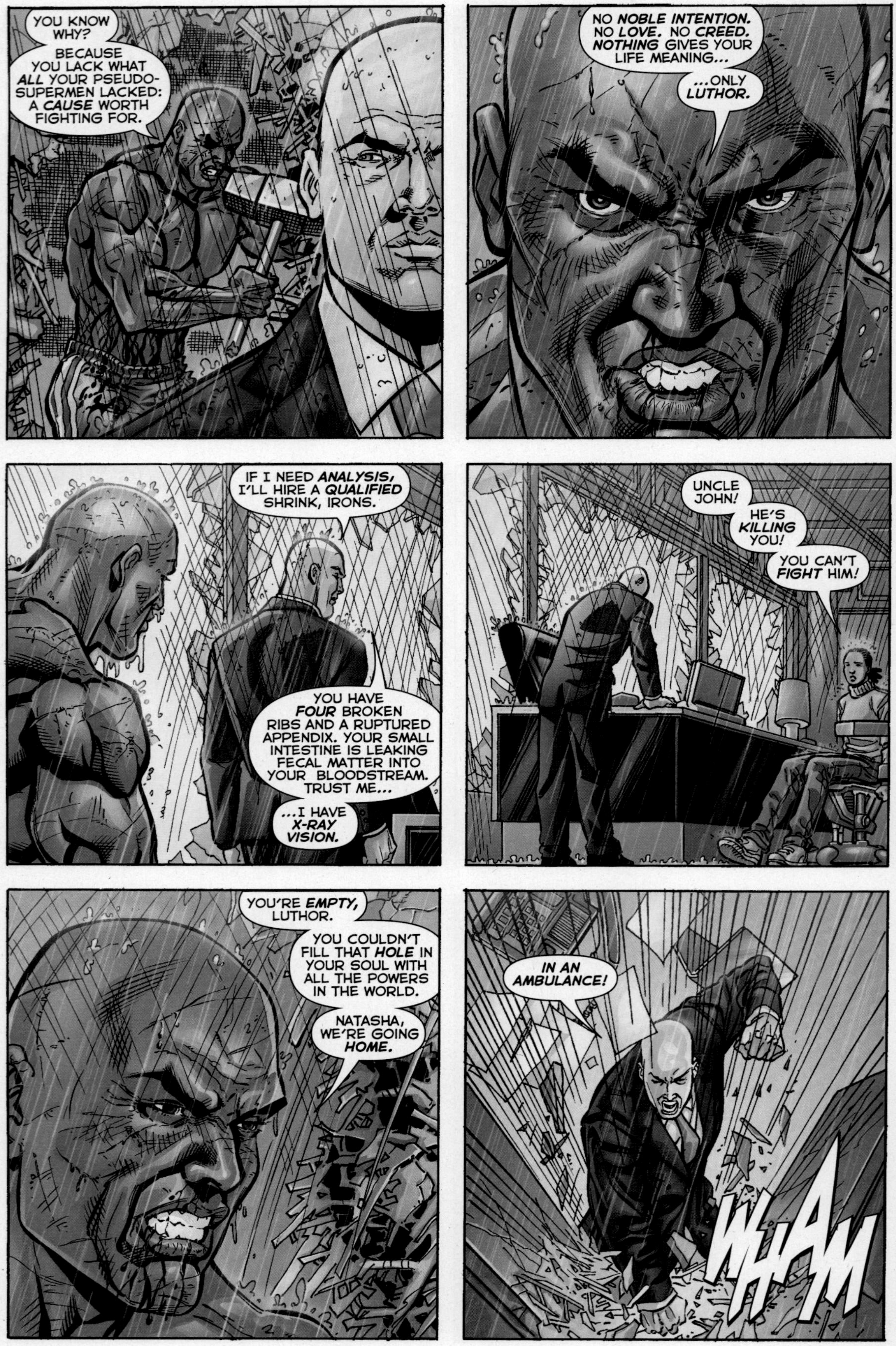
YOU KNOW WHY?
BECAUSE YOU LACK WHAT ALL YOUR PSEUDO-SUPERMEN LACKED: A CAUSE WORTH FIGHTING FOR.
NO NOBLE INTENTION. NO LOVE. NO CREED. NOTHING GIVES YOUR LIFE MEANING...
...ONLY LUTHOR.
IF I NEED ANALYSIS, I'LL HIRE A QUALIFIED SHRINK, IRONS.
YOU HAVE FOUR BROKEN RIBS AND A RUPTURED APPENDIX. YOUR SMALL INTESTINE IS LEAKING FECAL MATTER INTO YOUR BLOODSTREAM. TRUST ME...
...I HAVE X-RAY VISION.
UNCLE JOHN!
HE'S KILLING YOU!
YOU CAN'T FIGHT HIM!
YOU'RE EMPTY, LUTHOR.
YOU COULDN'T FILL THAT HOLE IN YOUR SOUL WITH ALL THE POWERS IN THE WORLD.
NATASHA, WE'RE GOING HOME.
IN AN AMBULANCE!
WHAM

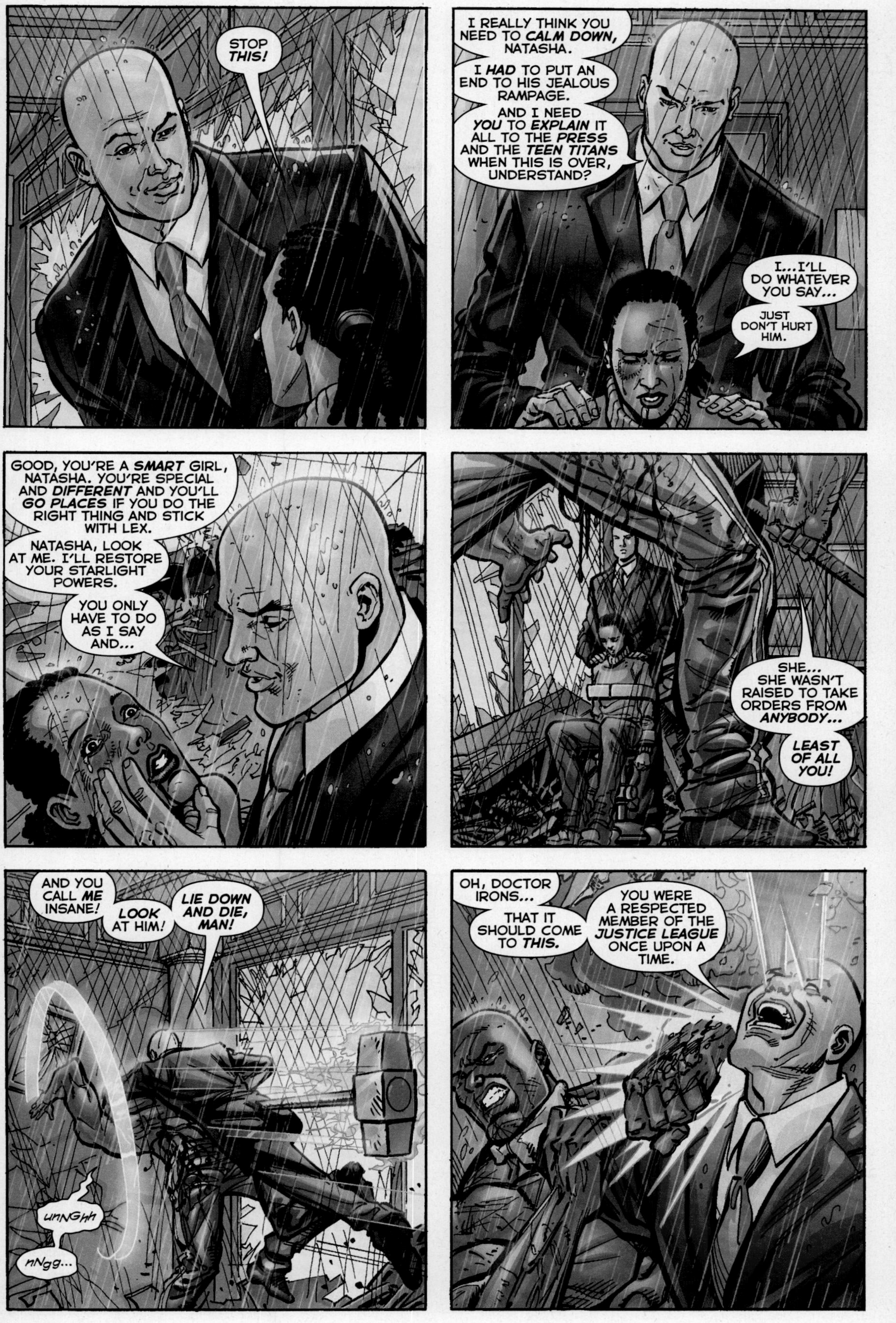
STOP THIS!
I REALLY THINK YOU NEED TO CALM DOWN, NATASHA.
I HAD TO PUT AN END TO HIS JEALOUS RAMPAGE.
AND I NEED YOU TO EXPLAIN IT ALL TO THE PRESS AND THE TEEN TITANS WHEN THIS IS OVER, UNDERSTAND?
I...I'LL DO WHATEVER YOU SAY...
JUST DON'T HURT HIM.
GOOD, YOU'RE A SMART GIRL, NATASHA. YOU'RE SPECIAL AND DIFFERENT AND YOU'LL GO PLACES IF YOU DO THE RIGHT THING AND STICK WITH LEX.
NATASHA, LOOK AT ME. I'LL RESTORE YOUR STARLIGHT POWERS.
YOU ONLY HAVE TO DO AS I SAY AND...
SHE... SHE WASN'T RAISED TO TAKE ORDERS FROM ANYBODY...
LEAST OF ALL YOU!
AND YOU CALL ME INSANE!
LOOK AT HIM!
LIE DOWN AND DIE, MAN!
unnGhh
nNgg...
OH, DOCTOR IRONS...
THAT IT SHOULD COME TO THIS.
YOU WERE A RESPECTED MEMBER OF THE JUSTICE LEAGUE ONCE UPON A TIME.

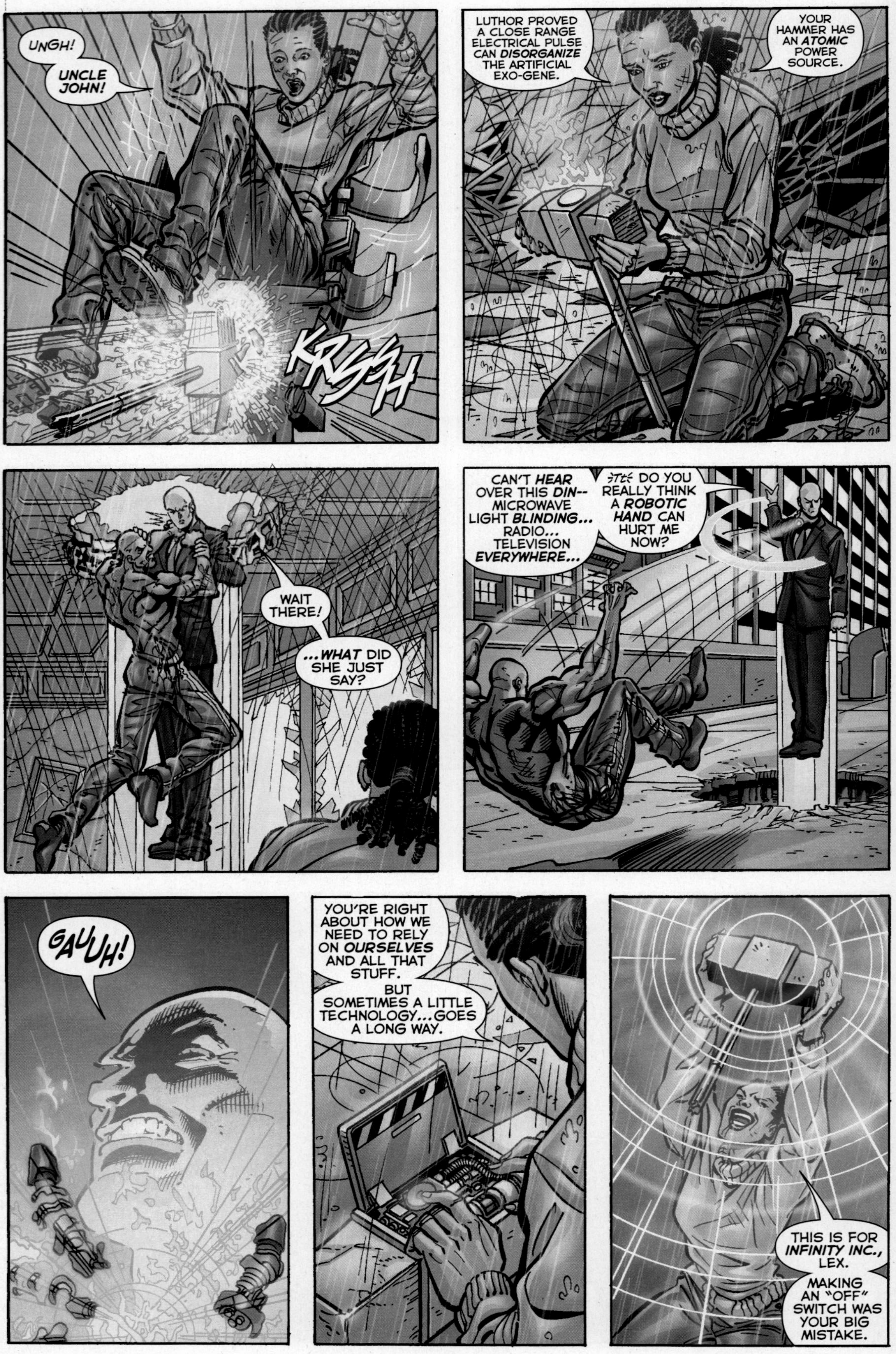
UNGH!
UNCLE JOHN!
KRSSH
LUTHOR PROVED A CLOSE RANGE ELECTRICAL PULSE CAN DISORGANIZE THE ARTIFICIAL EXO-GENE.
YOUR HAMMER HAS AN ATOMIC POWER SOURCE.
WAIT THERE!
...WHAT DID SHE JUST SAY?
CAN'T HEAR OVER THIS DIN-- MICROWAVE LIGHT BLINDING... RADIO... TELEVISION EVERYWHERE...
DO YOU REALLY THINK A ROBOTIC HAND CAN HURT ME NOW?
GAUUH!
YOU'RE RIGHT ABOUT HOW WE NEED TO RELY ON OURSELVES AND ALL THAT STUFF.
BUT SOMETIMES A LITTLE TECHNOLOGY...GOES A LONG WAY.
THIS IS FOR INFINITY INC., LEX.
MAKING AN "OFF" SWITCH WAS YOUR BIG MISTAKE.

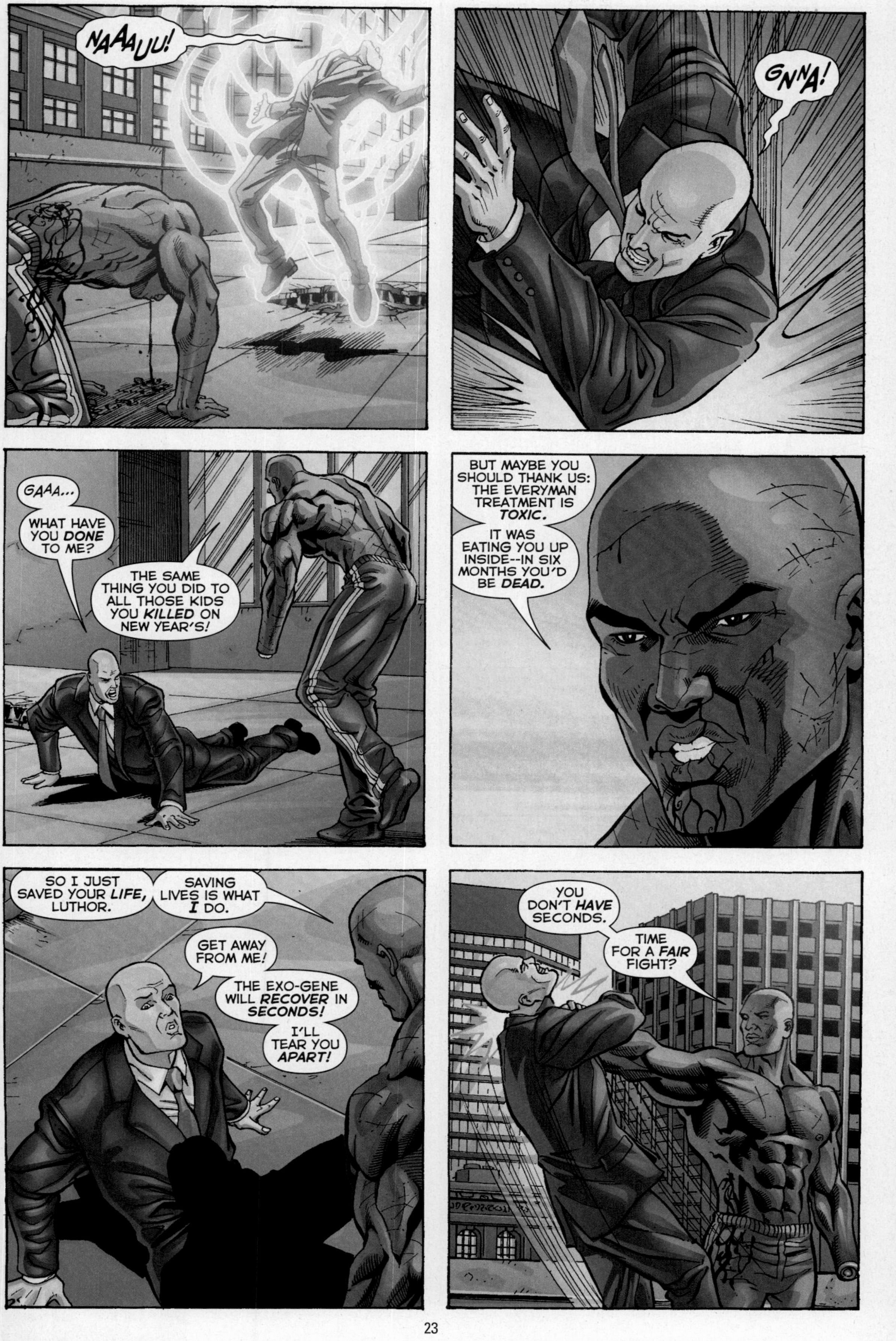
NAAAUU!
GNNA!
GAAA...
WHAT HAVE YOU DONE TO ME?
THE SAME THING YOU DID TO ALL THOSE KIDS YOU KILLED ON NEW YEAR'S!
BUT MAYBE YOU SHOULD THANK US: THE EVERYMAN TREATMENT IS TOXIC.
IT WAS EATING YOU UP INSIDE--IN SIX MONTHS YOU'D BE DEAD.
SO I JUST SAVED YOUR LIFE, LUTHOR.
SAVING LIVES IS WHAT I DO.
GET AWAY FROM ME!
THE EXO-GENE WILL RECOVER IN SECONDS!
I'LL TEAR YOU APART!
YOU DON'T HAVE SECONDS.
TIME FOR A FAIR FIGHT?

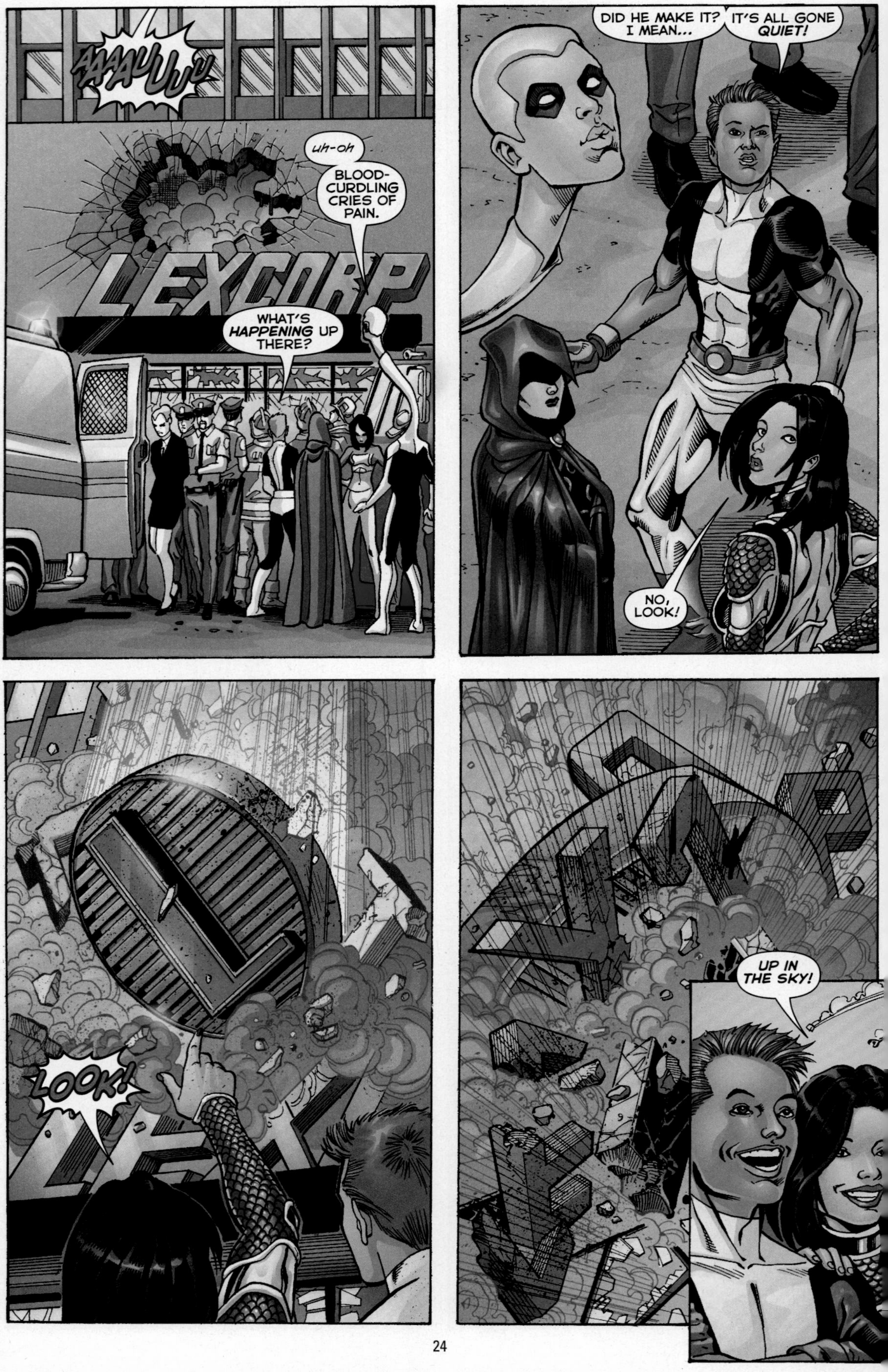

AAAAUUUU
uh-oh
BLOOD-CURDLING CRIES OF PAIN.
LEXCORP
WHAT'S HAPPENING UP THERE?
DID HE MAKE IT? I MEAN...
IT'S ALL GONE QUIET!
NO, LOOK!
LOOK!
UP IN THE SKY!

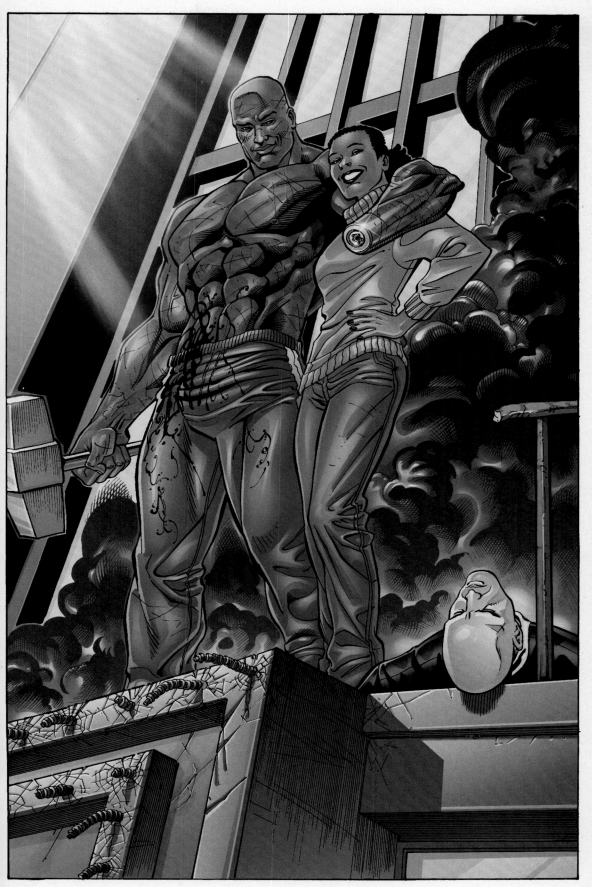

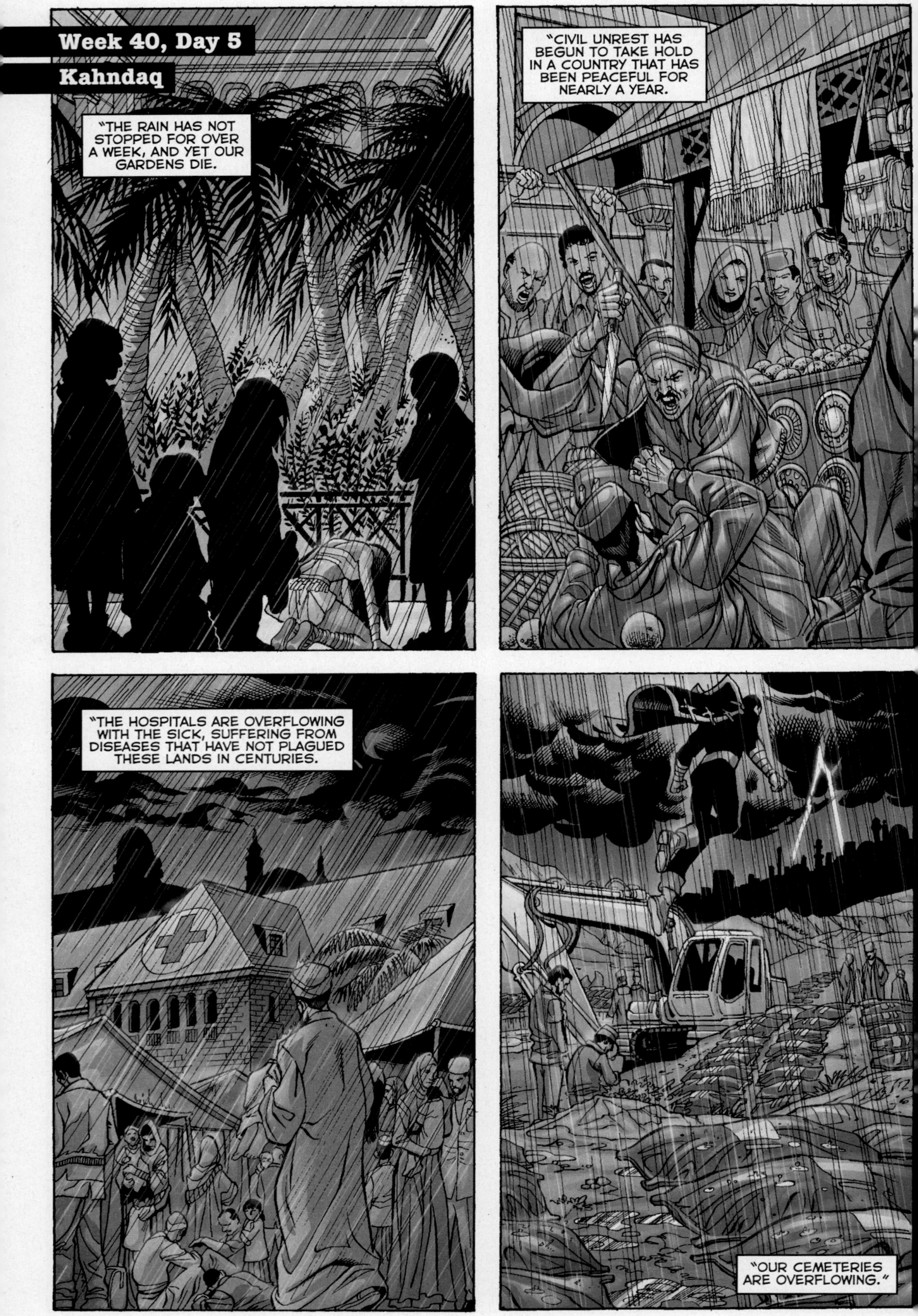
Week 40, Day 5
Kahndaq
"THE RAIN HAS NOT STOPPED FOR OVER A WEEK, AND YET OUR GARDENS DIE.
"CIVIL UNREST HAS BEGUN TO TAKE HOLD IN A COUNTRY THAT HAS BEEN PEACEFUL FOR NEARLY A YEAR.
"THE HOSPITALS ARE OVERFLOWING WITH THE SICK, SUFFERING FROM DISEASES THAT HAVE NOT PLAGUED THESE LANDS IN CENTURIES.
"OUR CEMETERIES ARE OVERFLOWING."

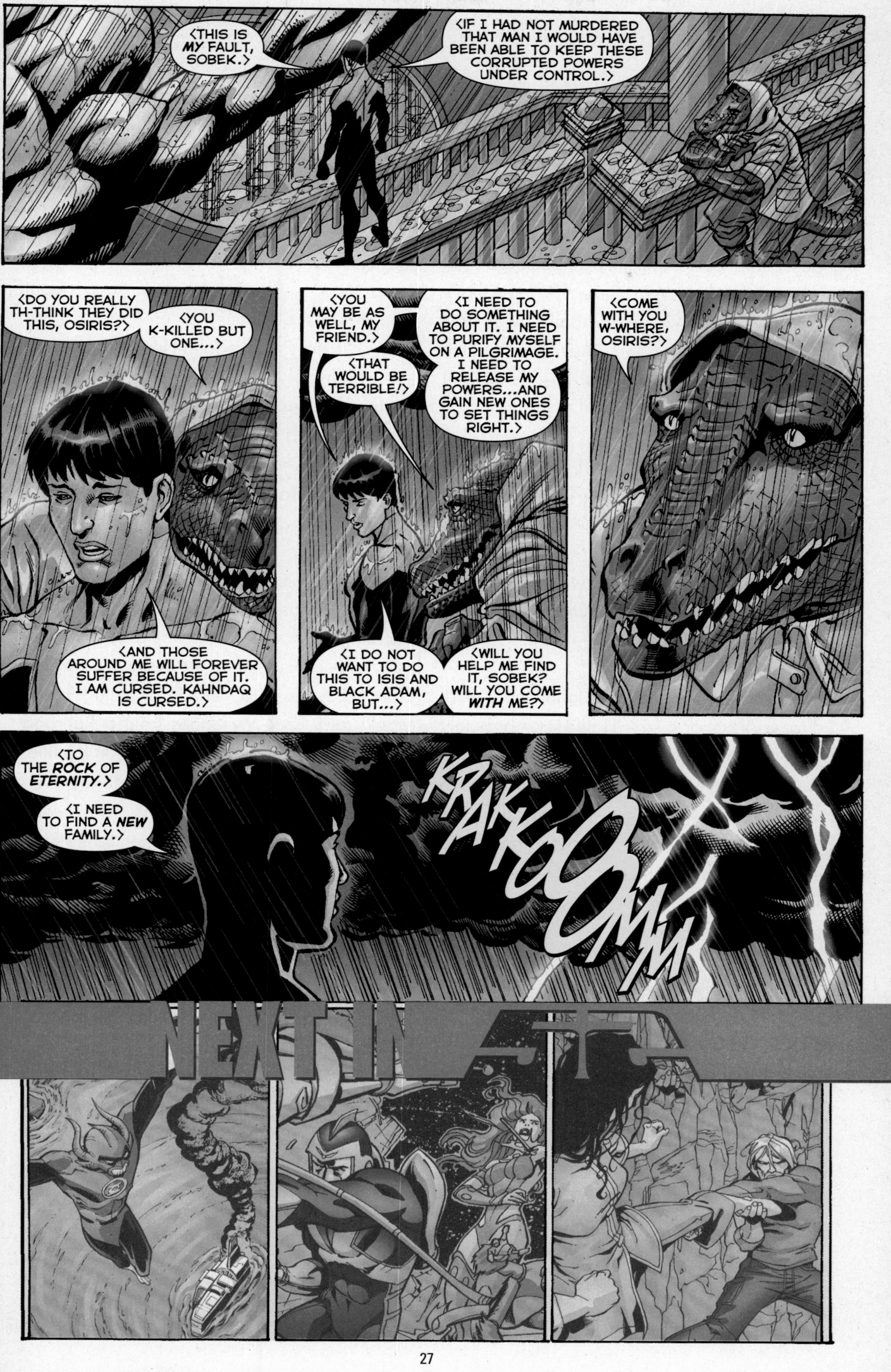
<THIS IS MY FAULT, SOBEK.>
<IF I HAD NOT MURDERED THAT MAN I WOULD HAVE BEEN ABLE TO KEEP THESE CORRUPTED POWERS UNDER CONTROL.>
<DO YOU REALLY TH-THINK THEY DID THIS, OSIRIS?>
<YOU K-KILLED BUT ONE...>
<AND THOSE AROUND ME WILL FOREVER SUFFER BECAUSE OF IT. I AM CURSED. KAHNDAQ IS CURSED.>
<YOU MAY BE AS WELL, MY FRIEND.>
<THAT WOULD BE TERRIBLE!>
<I NEED TO DO SOMETHING ABOUT IT. I NEED TO PURIFY MYSELF ON A PILGRIMAGE. I NEED TO RELEASE MY POWERS...AND GAIN NEW ONES TO SET THINGS RIGHT.>
<I DO NOT WANT TO DO THIS TO ISIS AND BLACK ADAM, BUT...>
<WILL YOU HELP ME FIND IT, SOBEK? WILL YOU COME WITH ME?>
<COME WITH YOU W-WHERE, OSIRIS?>
<TO THE ROCK OF ETERNITY.>
<I NEED TO FIND A NEW FAMILY.>
KRAKKOOOMMM
NEXT IN 52

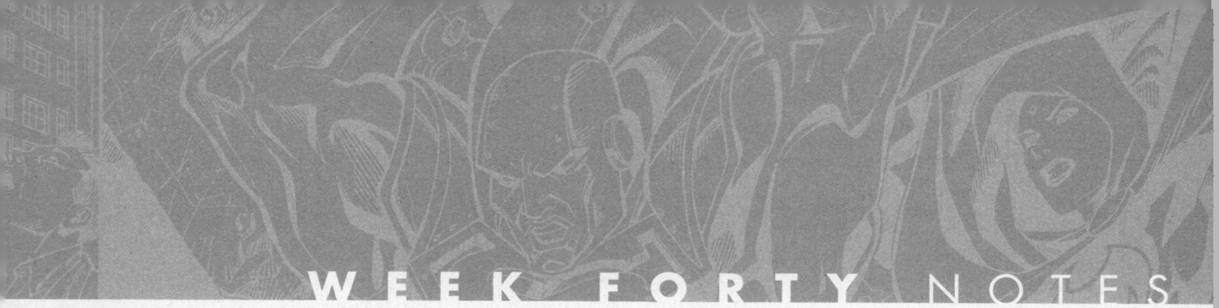

WEEK FORTY NOTES

KEITH GIFFEN

I guess you could call this our all-out-action prologue to World War Three. At least that's the way I see it. I've got to admit, I was kind of surprised to see the Luthor/John Henry storyline hit its climax this early — I shouldn't have been, but I was.

I think I mentioned in an earlier commentary that I deliberately sat out the weekly conference calls wherein the Big Four hammered out upcoming plotlines. I wanted to approach each script fresh, wanted to be as surprised as the readers by unfolding events. Guess I got what I wanted.

Oh, and cutting away when John Henry started to work Luthor over? Hated it. Absolutely hated it until I realized that nothing the Big Four could have put on the page would have been as satisfying to me as the "fill in the gaps" mental movie playing out in my head. Retribution's personal. Ask four readers what John Henry did to Luthor and you're likely to get four different answers.

In hindsight, pretty slick and oh, so satisfying.

MIKE SIGLAIN

Week 40 is, essentially, the end of our John Henry Irons/Lex Luthor story line, and as you can see by J.G.'s beautiful cover, it represents the fall of Lex Luthor.

The title of this issue — "Man Ain't Nothing But a Man" — comes from the song about John Henry, the famous African-American folk hero. His story — like John Henry Irons' story — is both an inspirational and moral one, about man versus technology. The title is taken from this quotation, "A man, he ain't nothing but a man/Before I'd let that steam drill beat me down/Oh, I'd die with the hammer in my hand."

From the very beginning, the writers wanted the title of this issue to be a line from the song. Deciding upon which line would be the tricky part. At various times the issue was called "The Measure of a Man," "Nothing but a Man," and "Got My Shoes from a Railroad Man." We went round and round on the title, and in the end I decided on an amended version of one of the suggestions, and here's why: storywise, in the end, when everything is stripped away from Steel, and it's just him going up against a technologically enhanced Luthor, John Henry "ain't nothing but a man" who'd "die with the hammer in [his] hand" before letting Luthor win. That pretty much says it all, so "Man Ain't Nothing but a Man" became our title.

This issue also contained Grant Morrison's wink and nod to the Silver Age.

(CONTINUED)

WEEK FORTY NOTES

(CONTINUED)

Many readers out there got the reference, but for those of you who didn't, Planet Lexor refers to a planet that was named in honor of Luthor, where Lex is the hero and Superman is the villain. It's a world where Superman has no powers, due to the fact that the planet revolves around a red sun. In SUPERMAN #164, by Edmond Hamilton and Curt Swan, we get the first appearance of Lexor — though it isn't officially named at the time — and, as in 52 week 40, we get to see Lex take down someone with an "S" on his chest in a story that revolves around technology. But unlike week 40, in SUPERMAN #164, hero and villain work together to help save an entire planet. Plus, Lex and Superman take off their shirts and duke it out. It was a different time back then. Anyway...

I'd be remiss if I didn't mention the stunning art team who worked on this issue. Chris Batista had just finished Week 31 for me, and he had the choice of doing an earlier issue or jumping on the big Steel vs. Luthor issue. It was a no-brainer, and as you can see, Chris did an amazing job. The writers and Giffen gave him a lot to work with, including a double page spread and two splash pages, and he didn't let them down. Just look at the intensity and brutality of those fight scenes.

SCRIPT EXCERPT

52 WEEK FORTY — PAGES TWO AND THREE

PANEL ONE
Exterior, LexCorp building. Day.

> **SECURITY (off-panel):** Keep it MOVING, folks! Everyone OUT, building CLEARED! Luthor's ORDERS!

PANEL TWO
LexCorp security officers are exiting, pushing a crowd of workers in front of them – everybody out of the pool.

> **SECURITY:** Says he wants to keep his workers SAFE!

> **WORKER:** SAFE? From WHAT?

PANEL THREE
The startled crowd looks up in fear, a little windblown, as colorful streaks blur like comets or meteors just over their heads, arrowing towards the building.

SUPERPANEL ACROSS SPREAD
Interior, LexCorp lobby. Steel backed by the Titans (Beast Boy [in winged form], Raven, Aquagirl, and Offspring – fliers carrying non-fliers) explode in through the doors.

> **TITLE:** MAN AIN'T NOTHING BUT A MAN

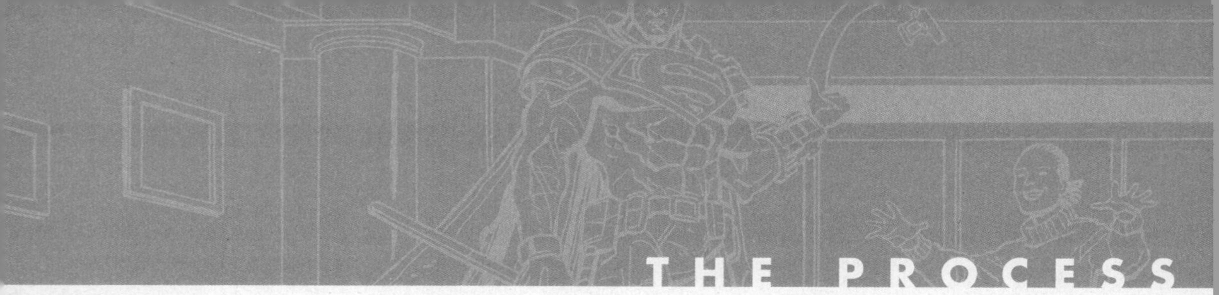

THE PROCESS

BREAKDOWNS BY **KEITH GIFFEN**

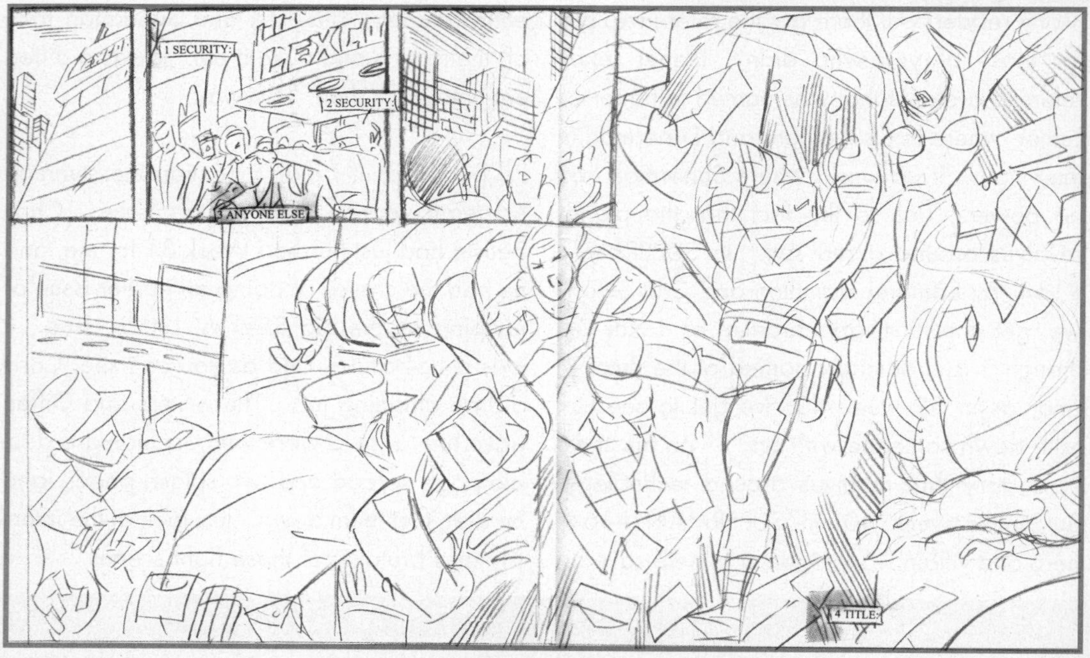
1 SECURITY:
2 SECURITY:
3 ANYONE ELSE
4 TITLE:

PENCILS & INKS BY **CHRIS BATISTA & RODNEY RAMOS**

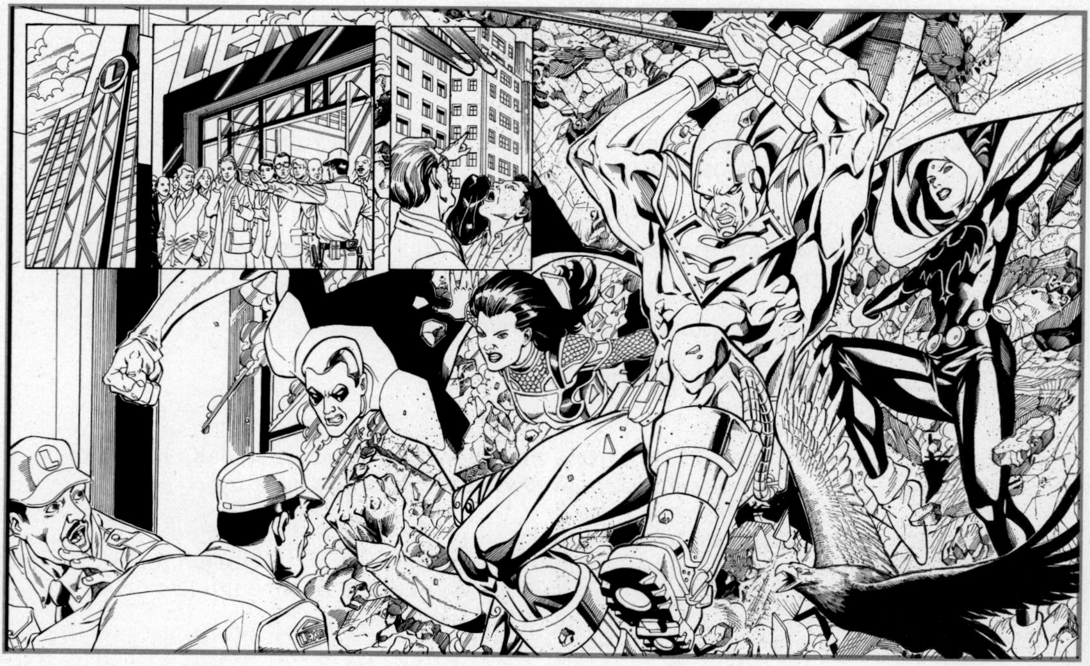

DC COMICS 52

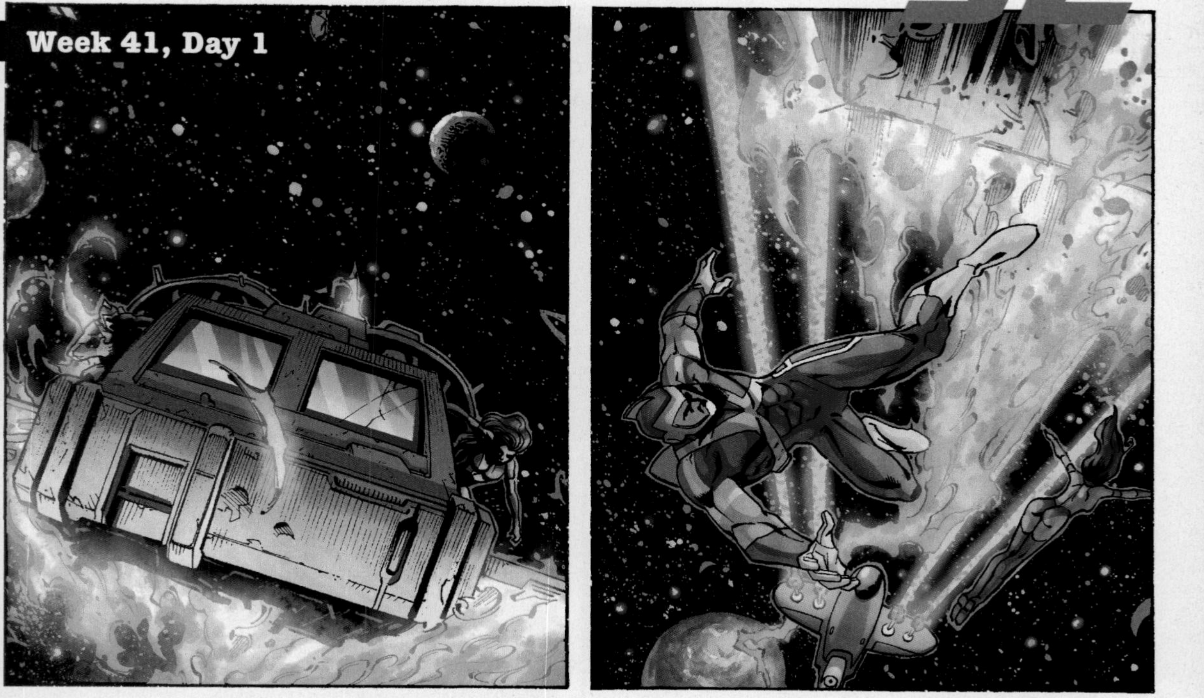

Week 41, Day 1

WRITTEN BY GEOFF JOHNS, GRANT MORRISON, GREG RUCKA, MARK WAID

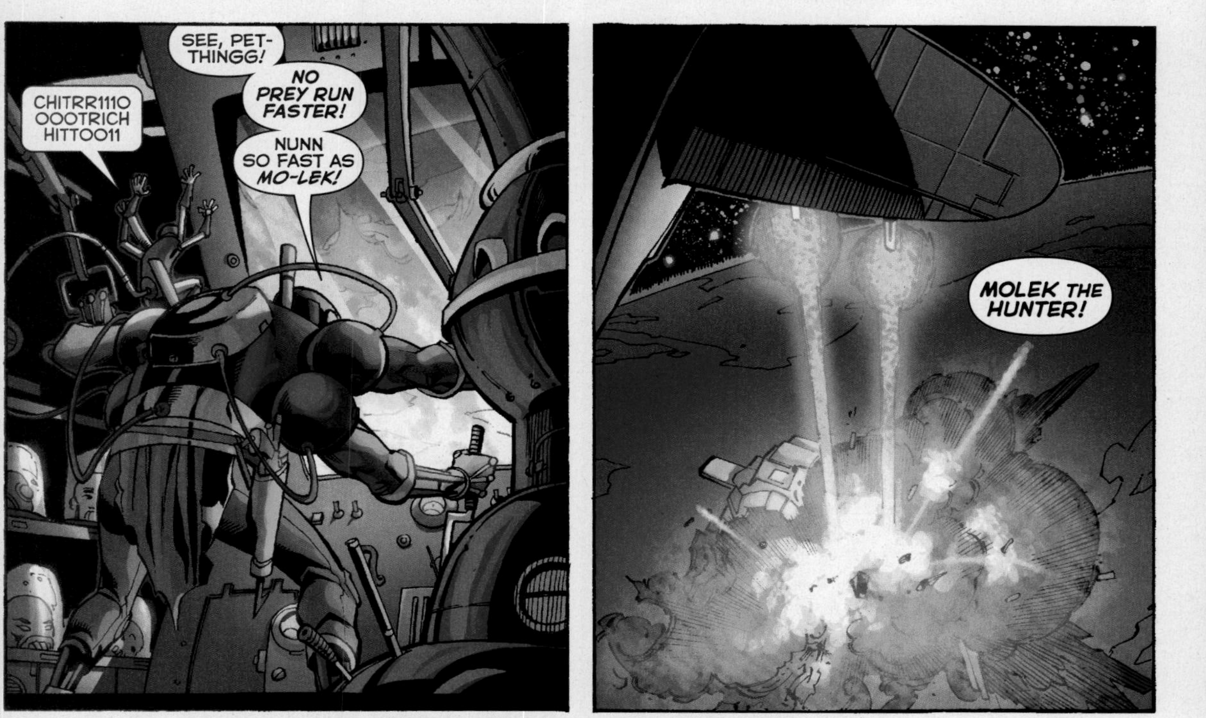

SEE, PET-THINGG!
CHITRR1110 OOOTRICH HITTOO11
NO PREY RUN FASTER!
NUNN SO FAST AS MO-LEK!
MOLEK THE HUNTER!

ART BREAKDOWNS BY KEITH GIFFEN
PENCILS BY GIUSEPPE CAMUNCOLI • INKS BY RODNEY RAMOS

COLORS BY ALEX SINCLAIR • LETTERS BY ROB LEIGH
ASSISTANT EDITOR HARVEY RICHARDS • ASSOCIATE EDITOR JEANINE SCHAEFER

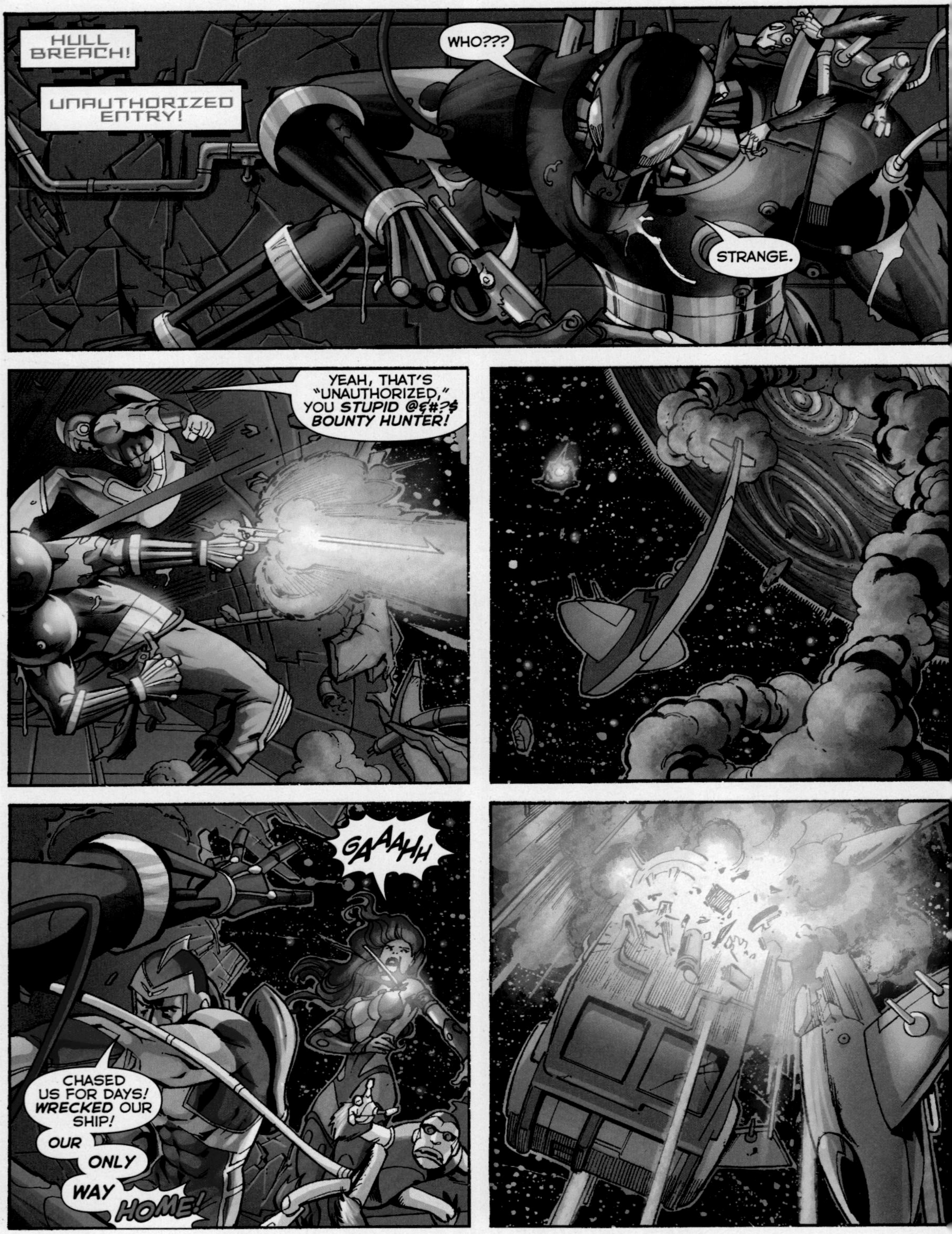
HULL BREACH!
UNAUTHORIZED ENTRY!
WHO???
STRANGE.
YEAH, THAT'S "UNAUTHORIZED," YOU STUPID @€#?$ BOUNTY HUNTER!
GAAAHH
CHASED US FOR DAYS! WRECKED OUR SHIP!
OUR ONLY WAY HOME!

EDITOR MICHAEL SIGLAIN • COVER BY J.G. JONES & ALEX SINCLAIR

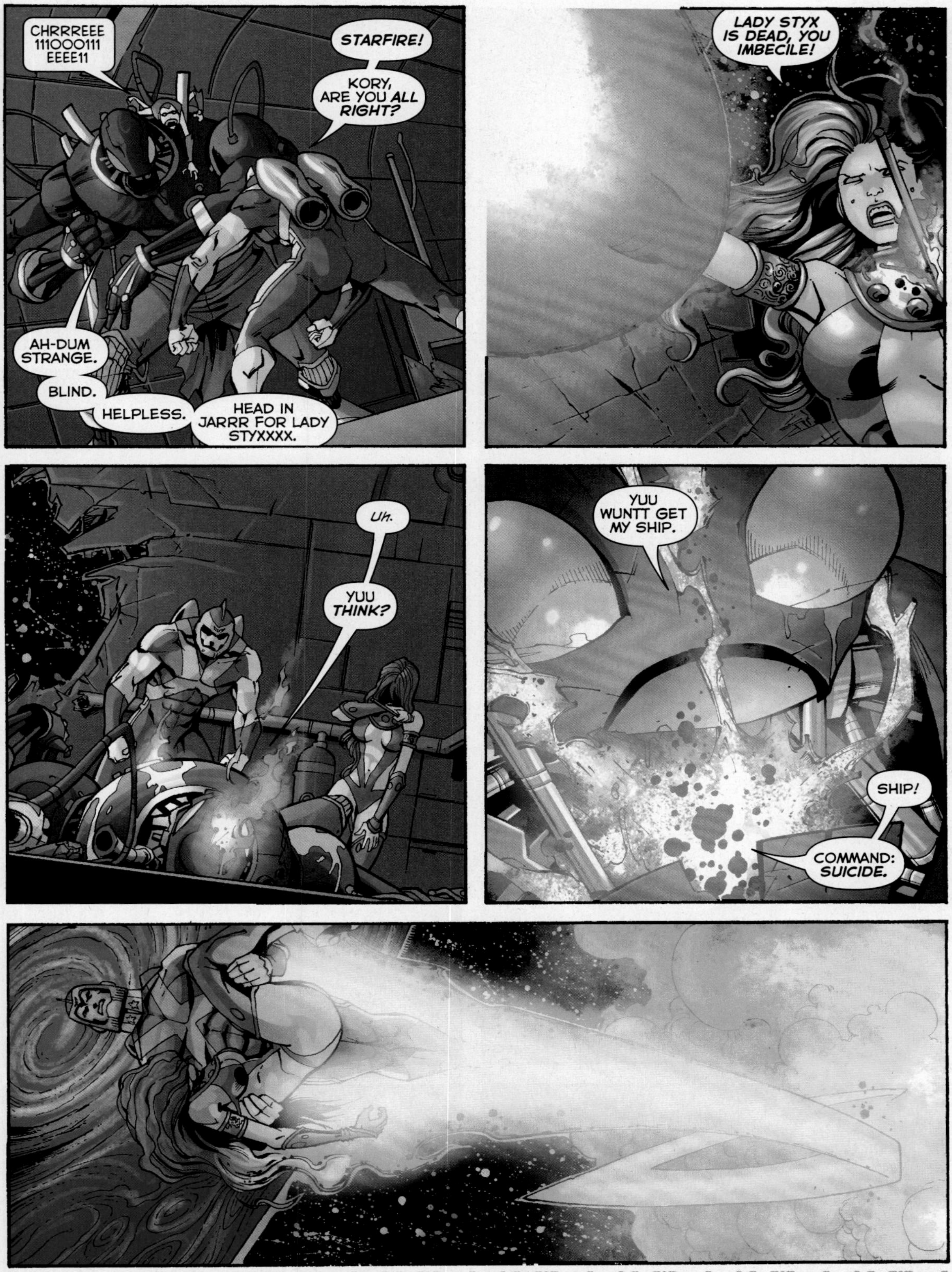
CHRRREEE 111000111 EEEE11
STARFIRE!
KORY, ARE YOU ALL RIGHT?
AH-DUM STRANGE.
BLIND.
HELPLESS.
HEAD IN JARRR FOR LADY STYXXXX.
LADY STYX IS DEAD, YOU IMBECILE!
Uh.
YUU THINK?
YUU WUNTT GET MY SHIP.
SHIP!
COMMAND: SUICIDE.

Week 41

MIRACLES & WONDERS

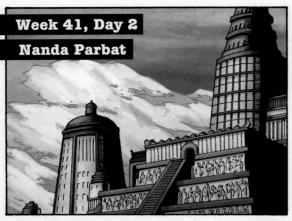

PONDERING THE INSOLUBLE?

HOW YOUR FLOWER CAN *CONTINUE* TO *LIVE* AFTER ALMOST *FOUR* MONTHS WITHOUT FOOD, WATER, OR SOIL?

WONDERING WHAT KEEPS IT GOING, MAYBE?

OR JUST ASKING WHY IT, LIKE *YOU*, IS STILL *ALIVE*...

...AND CHARLIE *ISN'T*.

I WAS... REMEMBERING WHEN ISIS GAVE IT TO ME.

I THINK SHE KNEW CHARLIE WAS SICK, TOT. I THINK SHE KNEW THERE WAS NOTHING SHE COULD DO FOR HIM.

I CAN'T SPEAK TO THAT. *WHERE* HAVE YOU BEEN?

I WAS ON THE MOUNTAIN. WITH THE MONKS.

YOU JUST WALKED OFF, RENEE. YOU LEFT WITHOUT A *WORD*. NOT TO *ME*, NOT TO *RICHARD*.

WHERE *IS* RICHARD?

AT THAT *ICE CAVE* OF HIS. HE WANTS YOU TO *MEET* HIM THERE...

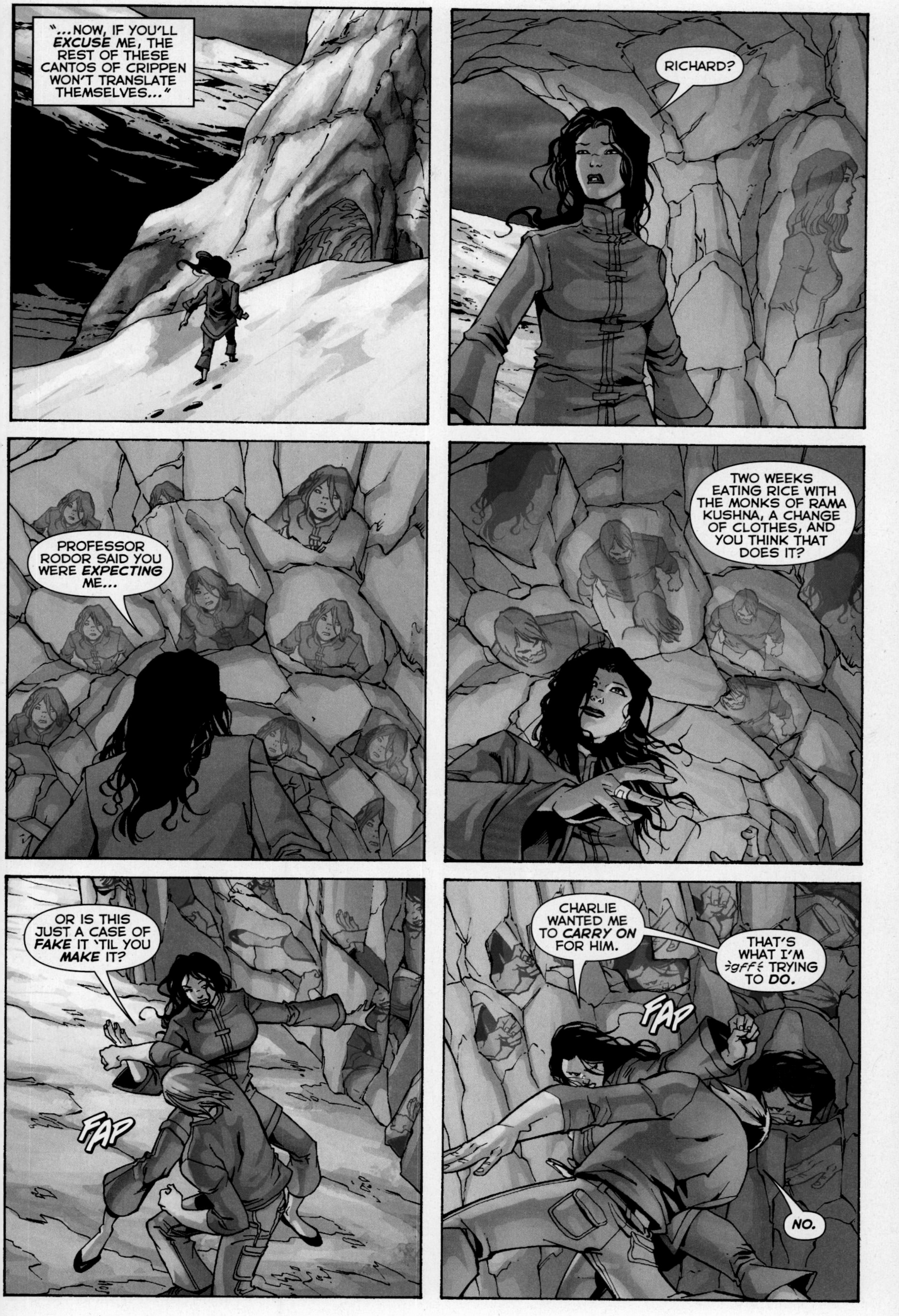
"...NOW, IF YOU'LL EXCUSE ME, THE REST OF THESE CANTOS OF CRIPPEN WON'T TRANSLATE THEMSELVES..."
RICHARD?
PROFESSOR RODOR SAID YOU WERE EXPECTING ME...
TWO WEEKS EATING RICE WITH THE MONKS OF RAMA KUSHNA, A CHANGE OF CLOTHES, AND YOU THINK THAT DOES IT?
OR IS THIS JUST A CASE OF FAKE IT 'TIL YOU MAKE IT?
FAP
CHARLIE WANTED ME TO CARRY ON FOR HIM.
THAT'S WHAT I'M gff TRYING TO DO.
FAP
NO.

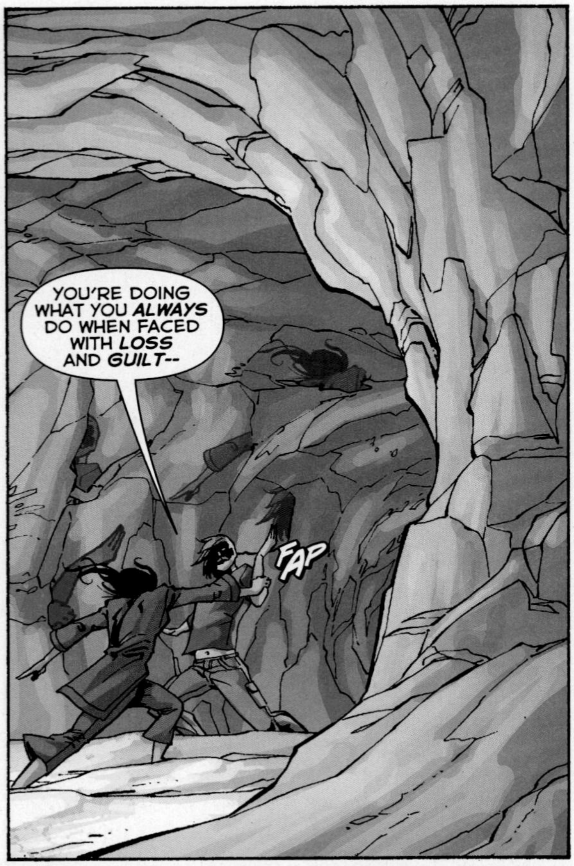
YOU'RE DOING WHAT YOU ALWAYS DO WHEN FACED WITH LOSS AND GUILT--
FAP

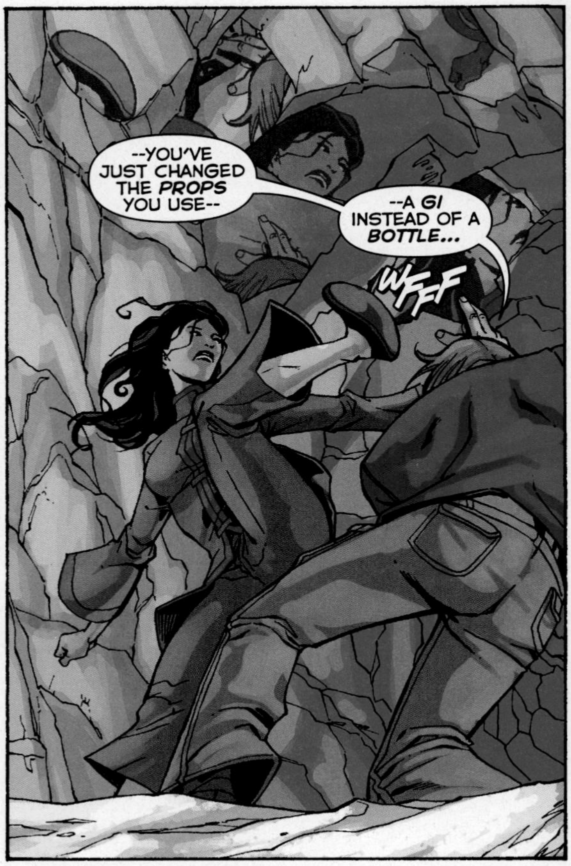
--YOU'VE JUST CHANGED THE PROPS YOU USE--
--A GI INSTEAD OF A BOTTLE...
WFFF

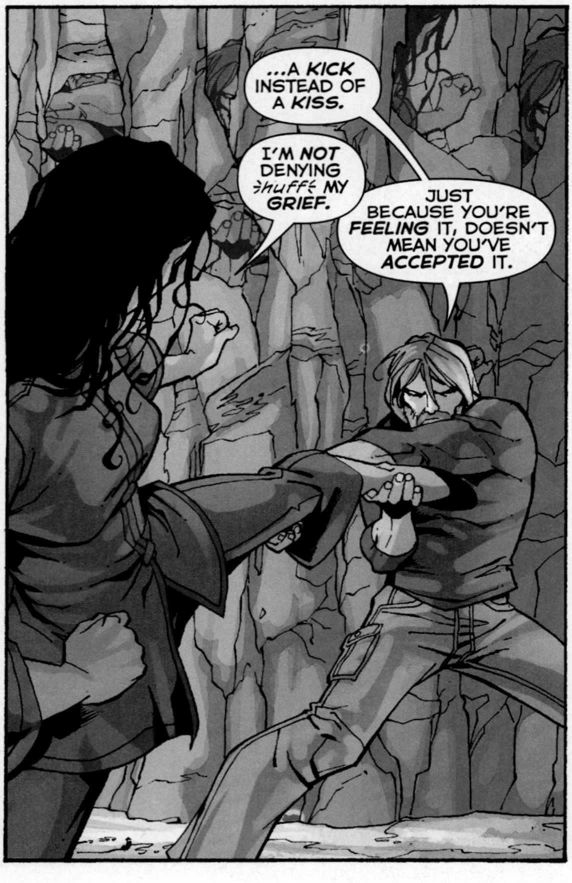
...A KICK INSTEAD OF A KISS.
I'M NOT DENYING huff MY GRIEF.
JUST BECAUSE YOU'RE FEELING IT, DOESN'T MEAN YOU'VE ACCEPTED IT.

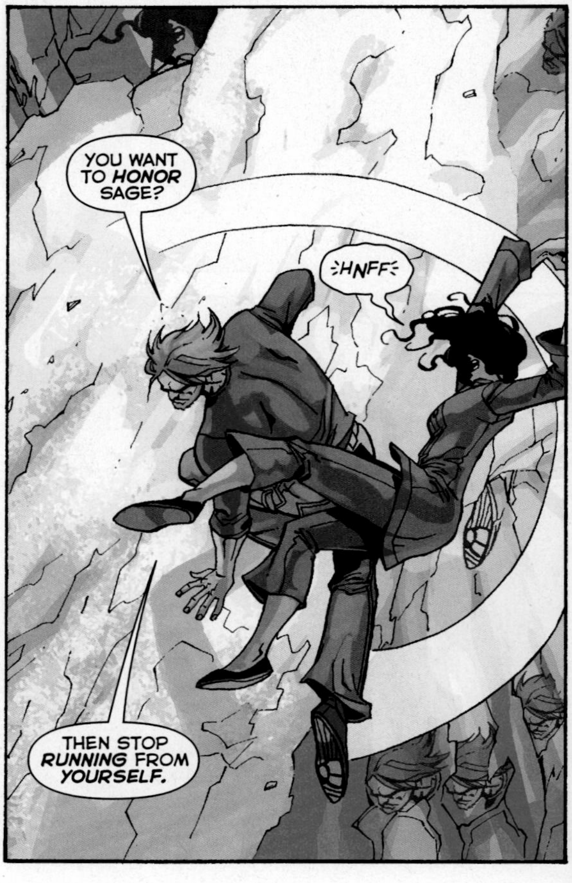
YOU WANT TO HONOR SAGE?
HNFF
THEN STOP RUNNING FROM YOURSELF.

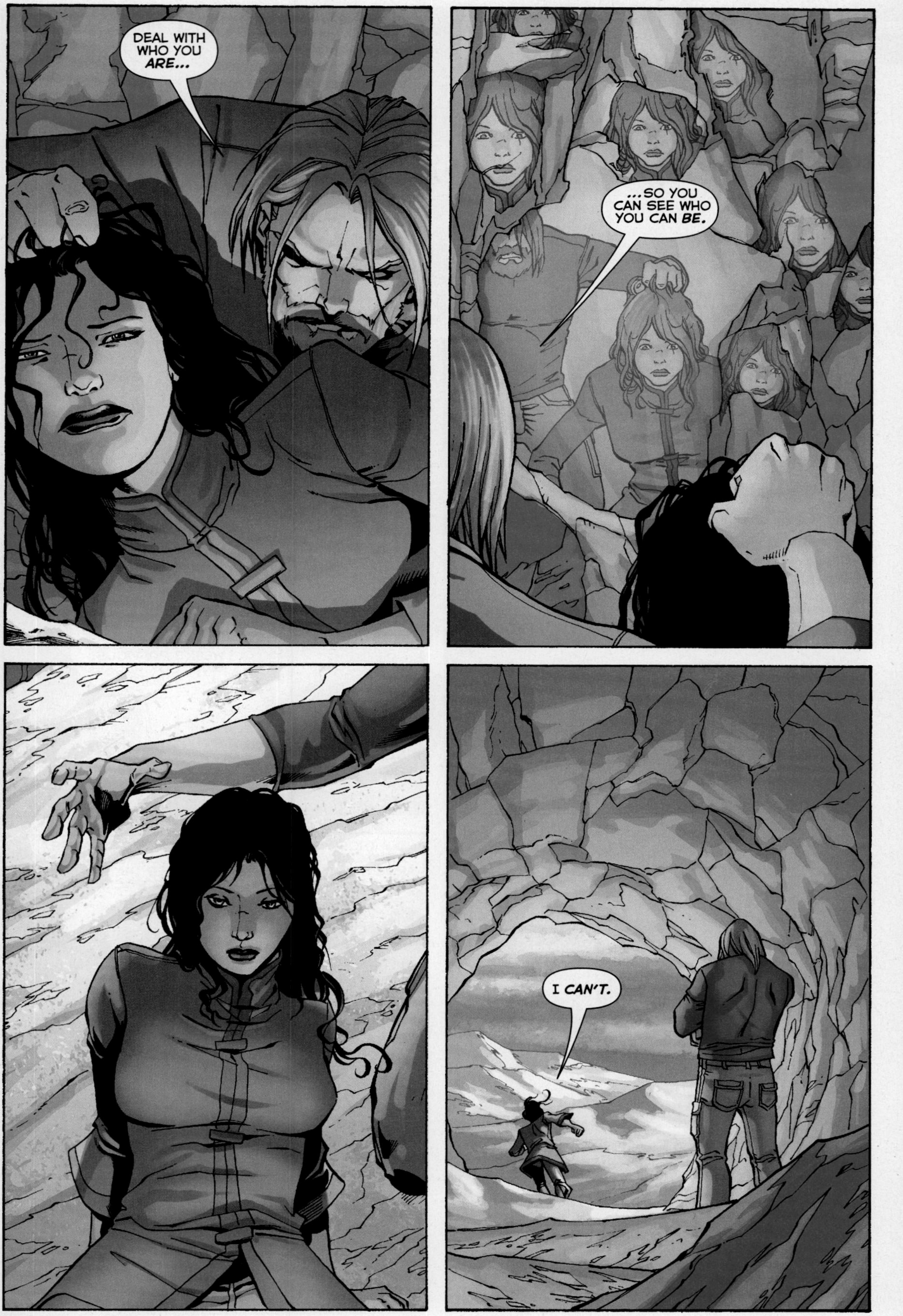
DEAL WITH WHO YOU *ARE...*
...SO YOU CAN SEE WHO YOU CAN *BE.*
I *CAN'T.*

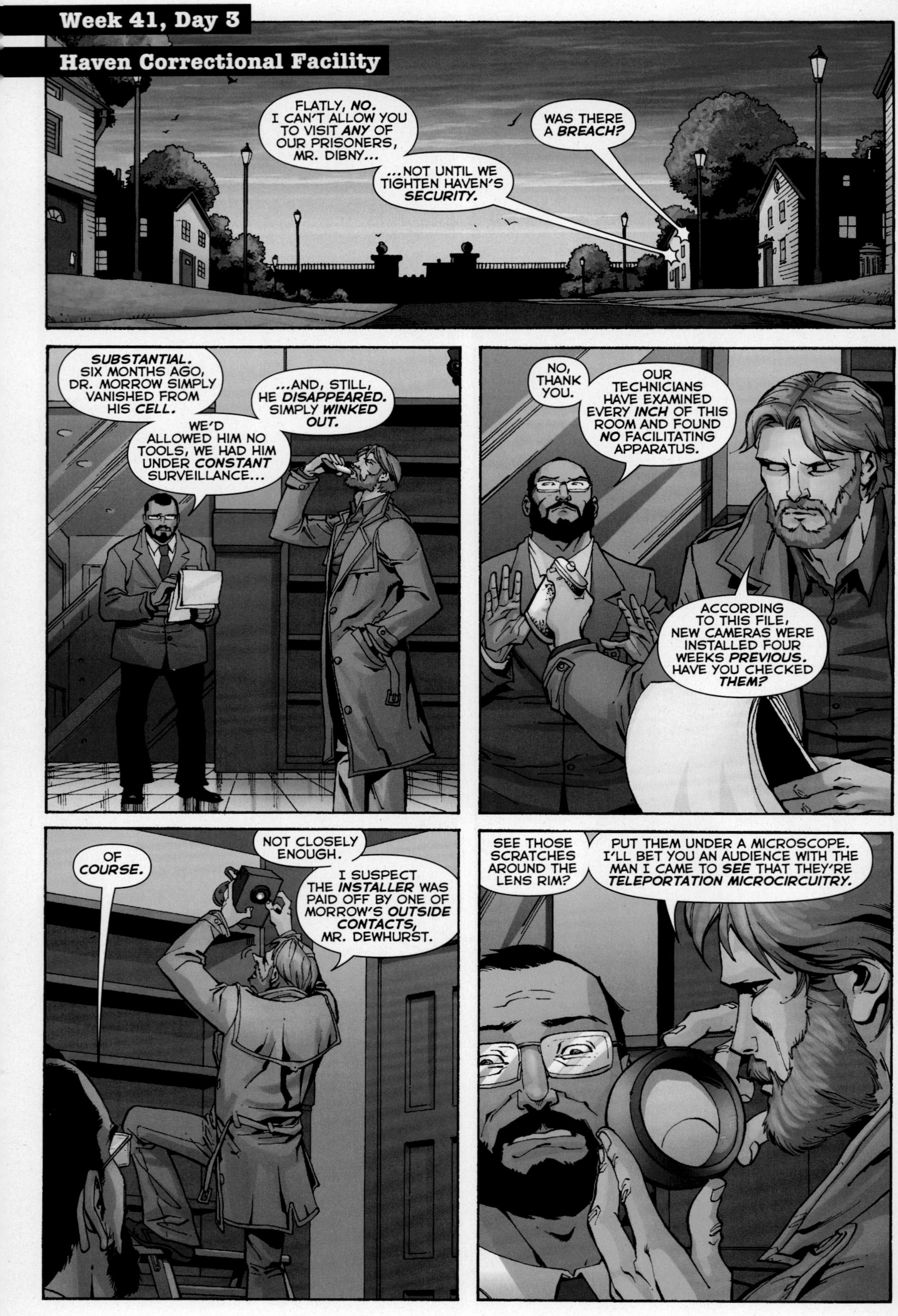
Week 41, Day 3
Haven Correctional Facility
FLATLY, NO. I CAN'T ALLOW YOU TO VISIT ANY OF OUR PRISONERS, MR. DIBNY...
...NOT UNTIL WE TIGHTEN HAVEN'S SECURITY.
WAS THERE A BREACH?
SUBSTANTIAL. SIX MONTHS AGO, DR. MORROW SIMPLY VANISHED FROM HIS CELL.
WE'D ALLOWED HIM NO TOOLS, WE HAD HIM UNDER CONSTANT SURVEILLANCE...
...AND, STILL, HE DISAPPEARED. SIMPLY WINKED OUT.
NO, THANK YOU.
OUR TECHNICIANS HAVE EXAMINED EVERY INCH OF THIS ROOM AND FOUND NO FACILITATING APPARATUS.
ACCORDING TO THIS FILE, NEW CAMERAS WERE INSTALLED FOUR WEEKS PREVIOUS. HAVE YOU CHECKED THEM?
OF COURSE.
NOT CLOSELY ENOUGH.
I SUSPECT THE INSTALLER WAS PAID OFF BY ONE OF MORROW'S OUTSIDE CONTACTS, MR. DEWHURST.
SEE THOSE SCRATCHES AROUND THE LENS RIM?
PUT THEM UNDER A MICROSCOPE. I'LL BET YOU AN AUDIENCE WITH THE MAN I CAME TO SEE THAT THEY'RE TELEPORTATION MICROCIRCUITRY.

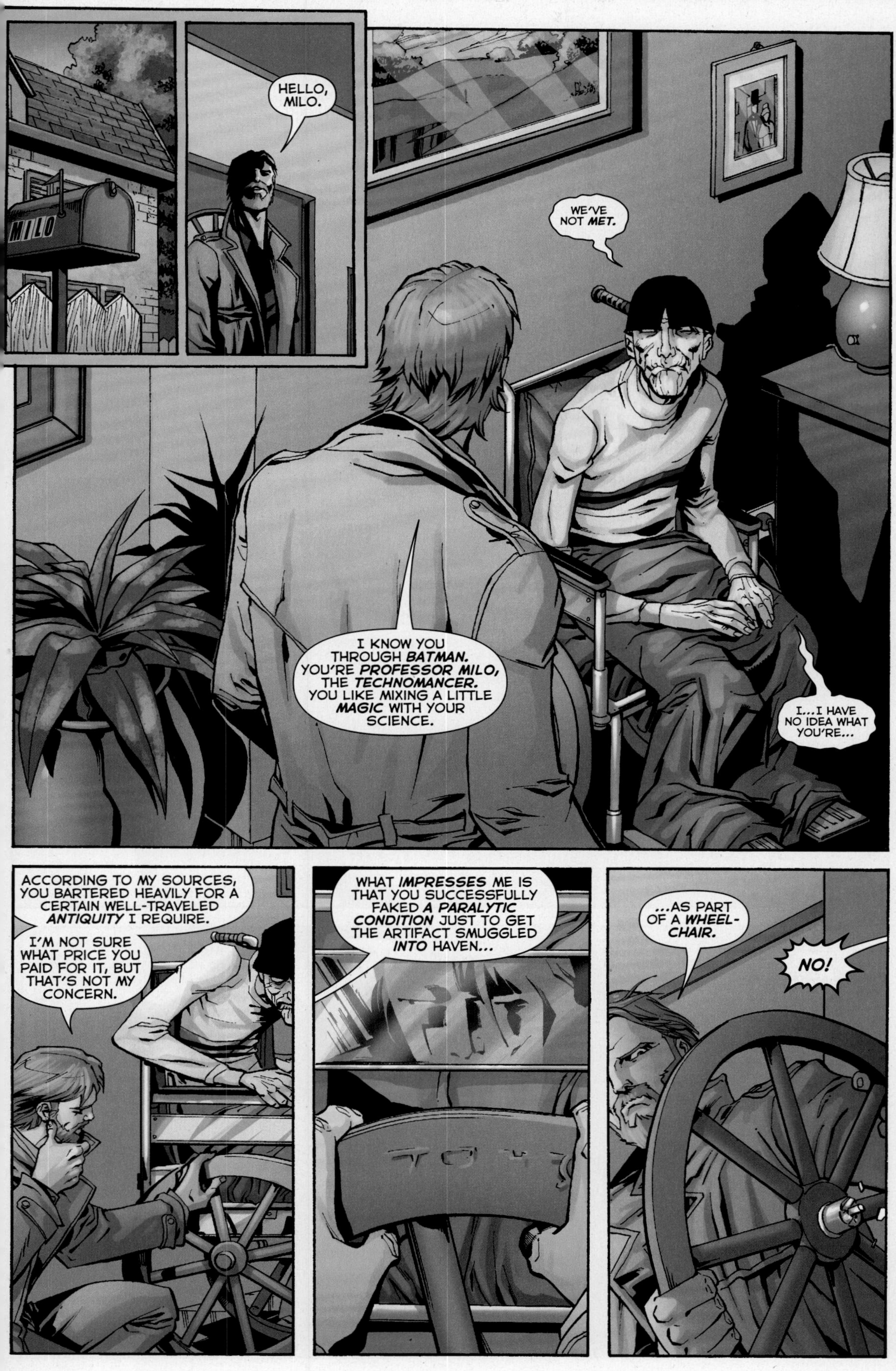
MILO
HELLO, MILO.
WE'VE NOT MET.
I KNOW YOU THROUGH BATMAN. YOU'RE PROFESSOR MILO, THE TECHNOMANCER. YOU LIKE MIXING A LITTLE MAGIC WITH YOUR SCIENCE.
I...I HAVE NO IDEA WHAT YOU'RE...
ACCORDING TO MY SOURCES, YOU BARTERED HEAVILY FOR A CERTAIN WELL-TRAVELED ANTIQUITY I REQUIRE.
I'M NOT SURE WHAT PRICE YOU PAID FOR IT, BUT THAT'S NOT MY CONCERN.
WHAT IMPRESSES ME IS THAT YOU SUCCESSFULLY FAKED A PARALYTIC CONDITION JUST TO GET THE ARTIFACT SMUGGLED INTO HAVEN...
...AS PART OF A WHEEL-CHAIR.
NO!

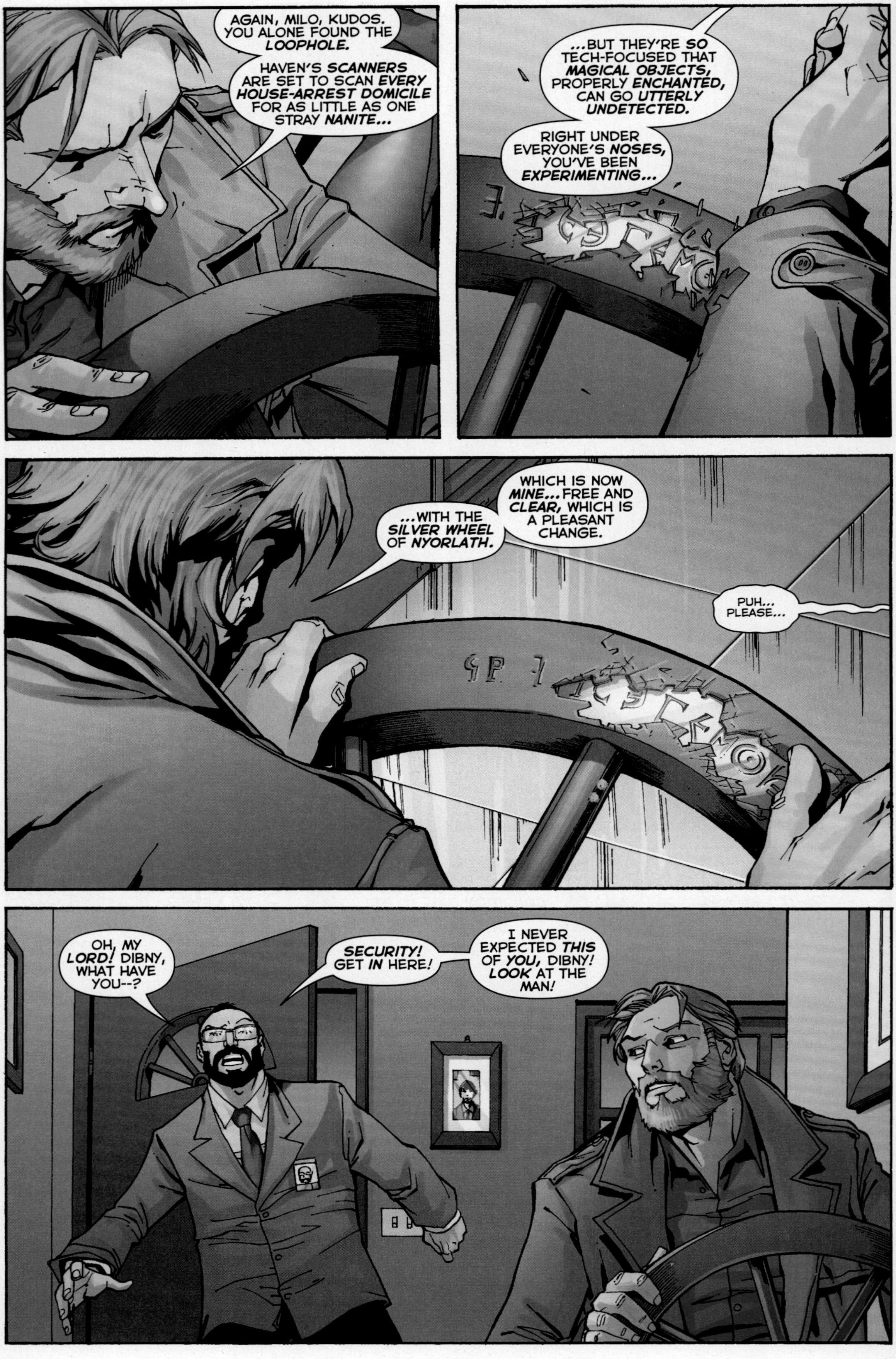
AGAIN, MILO, KUDOS. YOU ALONE FOUND THE LOOPHOLE.
HAVEN'S SCANNERS ARE SET TO SCAN EVERY HOUSE-ARREST DOMICILE FOR AS LITTLE AS ONE STRAY NANITE...
...BUT THEY'RE SO TECH-FOCUSED THAT MAGICAL OBJECTS, PROPERLY ENCHANTED, CAN GO UTTERLY UNDETECTED.
RIGHT UNDER EVERYONE'S NOSES, YOU'VE BEEN EXPERIMENTING...
...WITH THE SILVER WHEEL OF NYORLATH.
WHICH IS NOW MINE... FREE AND CLEAR, WHICH IS A PLEASANT CHANGE.
PUH... PLEASE...
OH, MY LORD! DIBNY, WHAT HAVE YOU--?
SECURITY! GET IN HERE!
I NEVER EXPECTED THIS OF YOU, DIBNY! LOOK AT THE MAN!

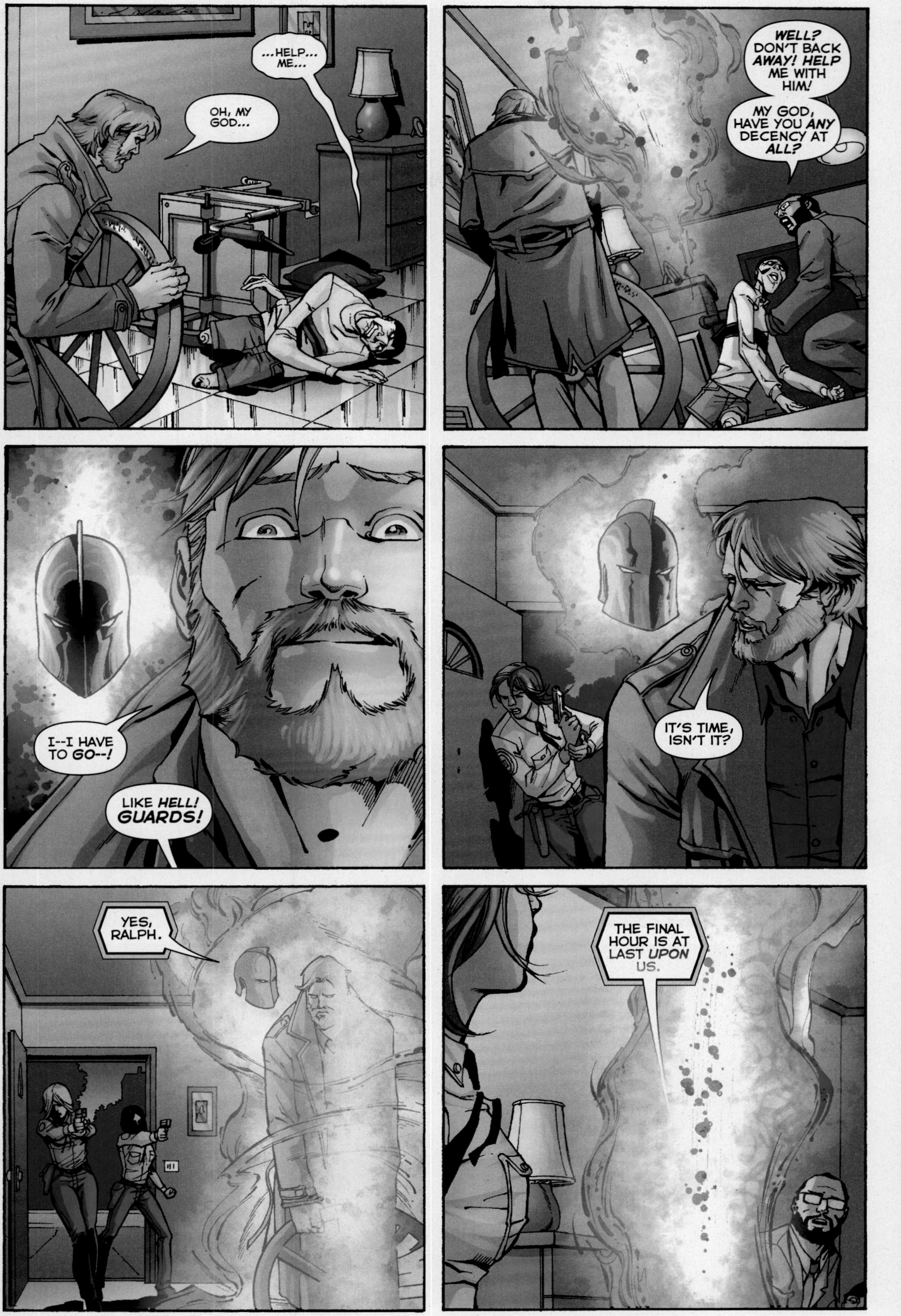
...HELP... ME...
OH, MY GOD...
WELL? DON'T BACK AWAY! HELP ME WITH HIM!
MY GOD, HAVE YOU ANY DECENCY AT ALL?
I--I HAVE TO GO--!
LIKE HELL! GUARDS!
IT'S TIME, ISN'T IT?
YES, RALPH.
THE FINAL HOUR IS AT LAST UPON US.

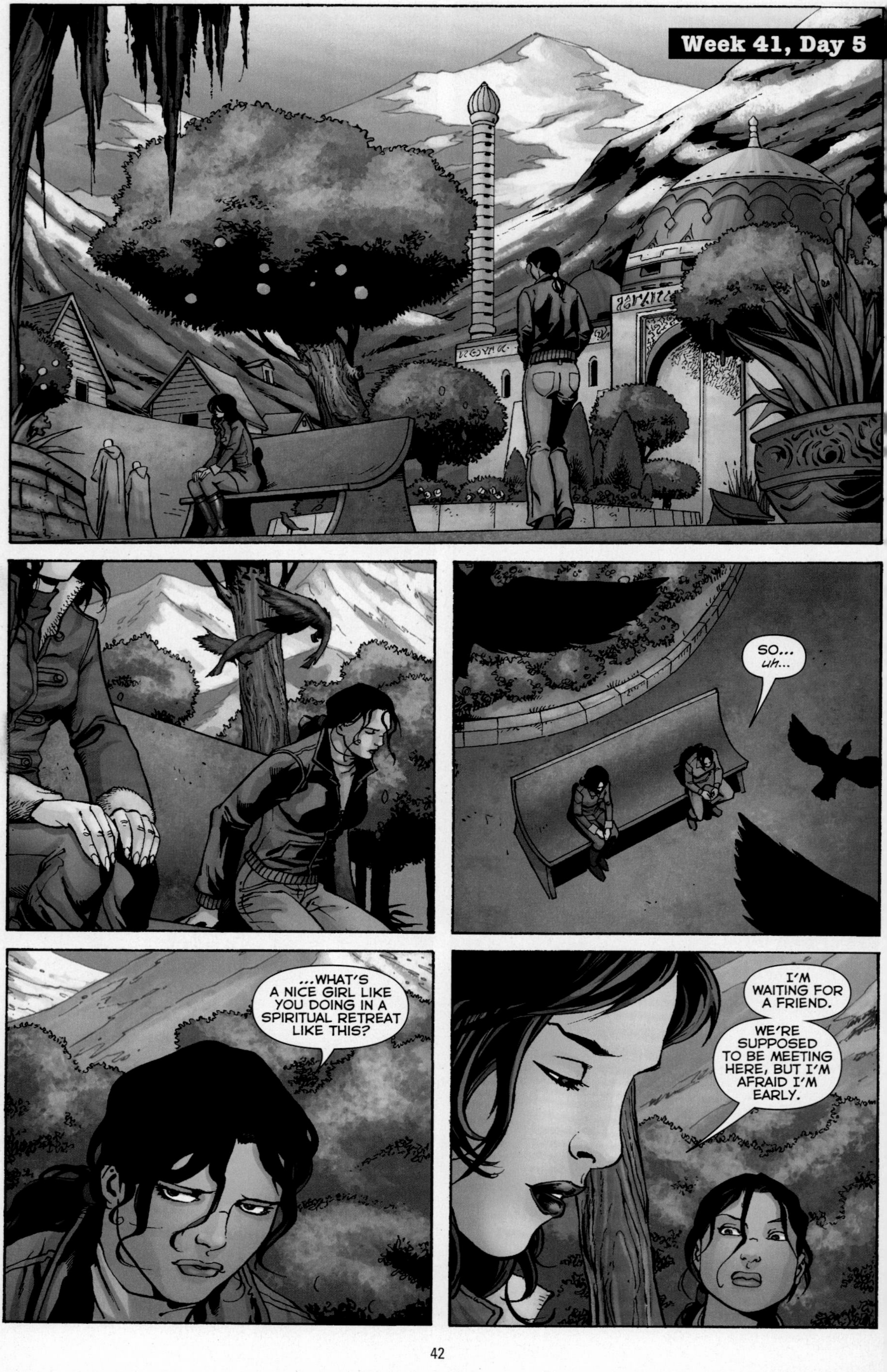

Week 41, Day 5
SO... UH...
...WHAT'S A NICE GIRL LIKE YOU DOING IN A SPIRITUAL RETREAT LIKE THIS?
I'M WAITING FOR A FRIEND.
WE'RE SUPPOSED TO BE MEETING HERE, BUT I'M AFRAID I'M EARLY.

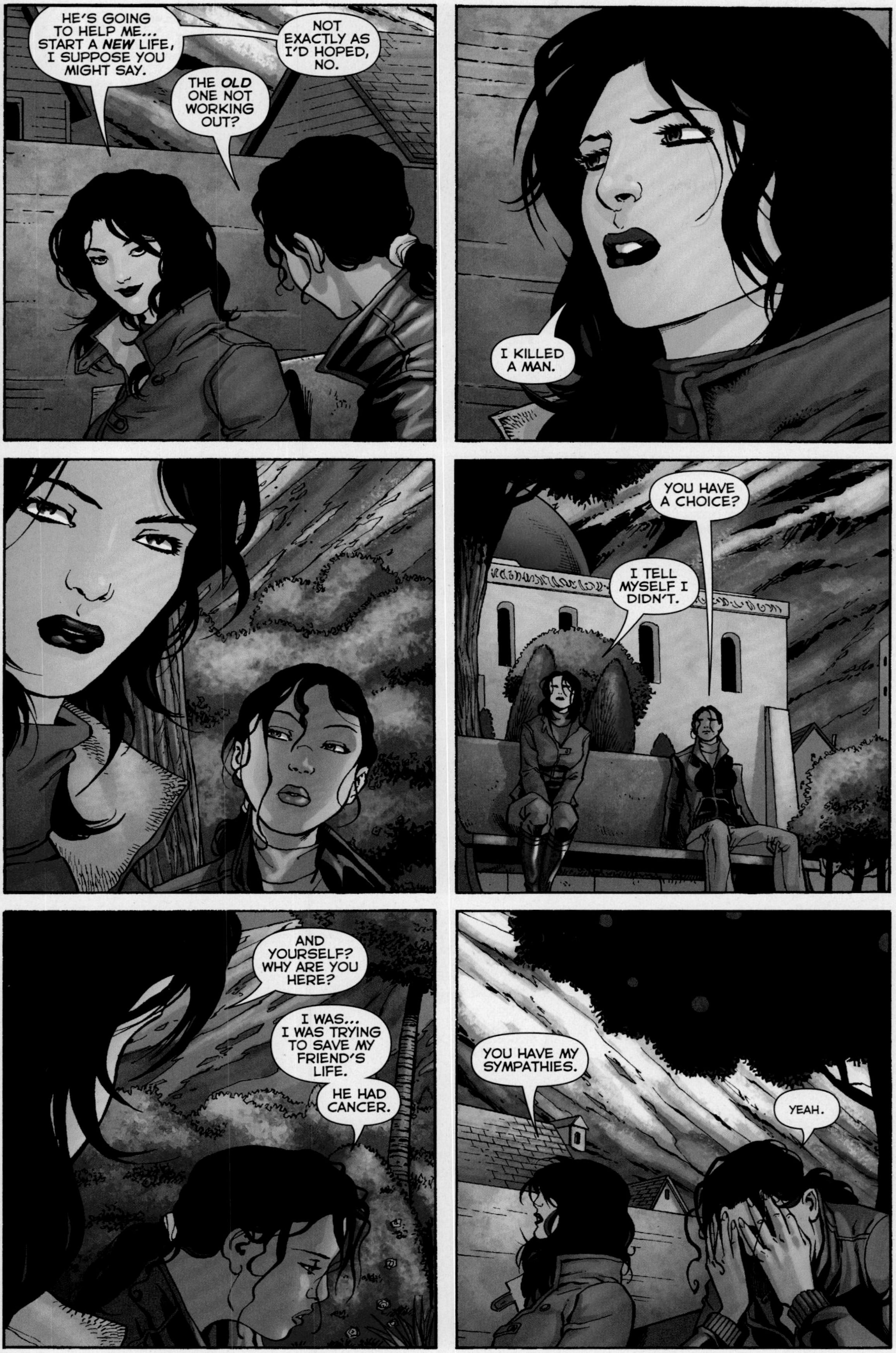
HE'S GOING TO HELP ME... START A *NEW* LIFE, I SUPPOSE YOU MIGHT SAY.
THE *OLD* ONE NOT WORKING OUT?
NOT EXACTLY AS I'D HOPED, NO.
I KILLED A MAN.
YOU HAVE A CHOICE?
I TELL MYSELF I DIDN'T.
AND YOURSELF? WHY ARE YOU HERE?
I WAS... I WAS TRYING TO SAVE MY FRIEND'S LIFE.
HE HAD CANCER.
YOU HAVE MY SYMPATHIES.
YEAH.

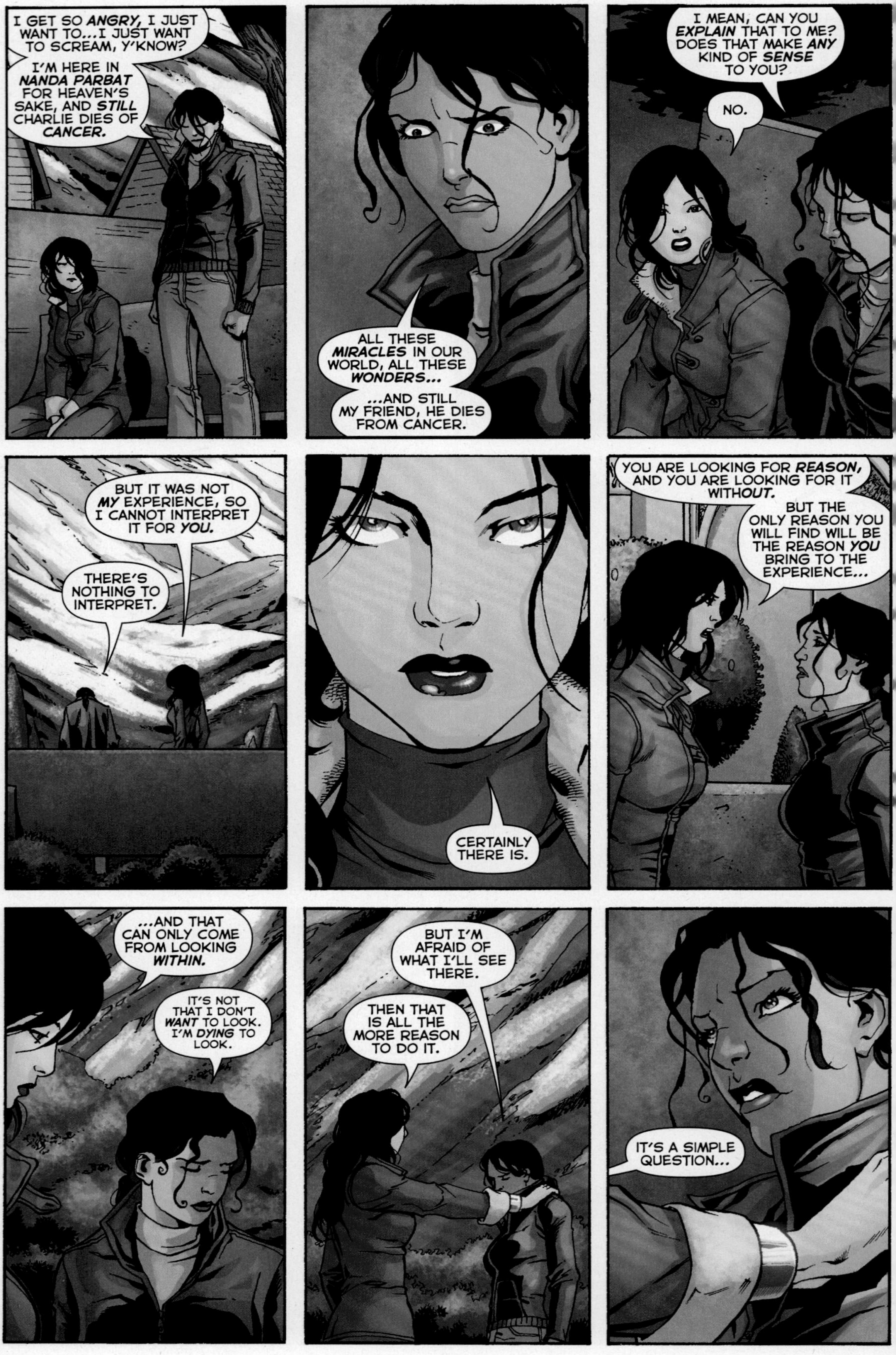
I GET SO ANGRY, I JUST WANT TO...I JUST WANT TO SCREAM, Y'KNOW?
I'M HERE IN NANDA PARBAT FOR HEAVEN'S SAKE, AND STILL CHARLIE DIES OF CANCER.
ALL THESE MIRACLES IN OUR WORLD, ALL THESE WONDERS...
...AND STILL MY FRIEND, HE DIES FROM CANCER.
I MEAN, CAN YOU EXPLAIN THAT TO ME? DOES THAT MAKE ANY KIND OF SENSE TO YOU?
NO.
BUT IT WAS NOT MY EXPERIENCE, SO I CANNOT INTERPRET IT FOR YOU.
THERE'S NOTHING TO INTERPRET.
CERTAINLY THERE IS.
YOU ARE LOOKING FOR REASON, AND YOU ARE LOOKING FOR IT WITHOUT.
BUT THE ONLY REASON YOU WILL FIND WILL BE THE REASON YOU BRING TO THE EXPERIENCE...
...AND THAT CAN ONLY COME FROM LOOKING WITHIN.
IT'S NOT THAT I DON'T WANT TO LOOK. I'M DYING TO LOOK.
BUT I'M AFRAID OF WHAT I'LL SEE THERE.
THEN THAT IS ALL THE MORE REASON TO DO IT.
IT'S A SIMPLE QUESTION...

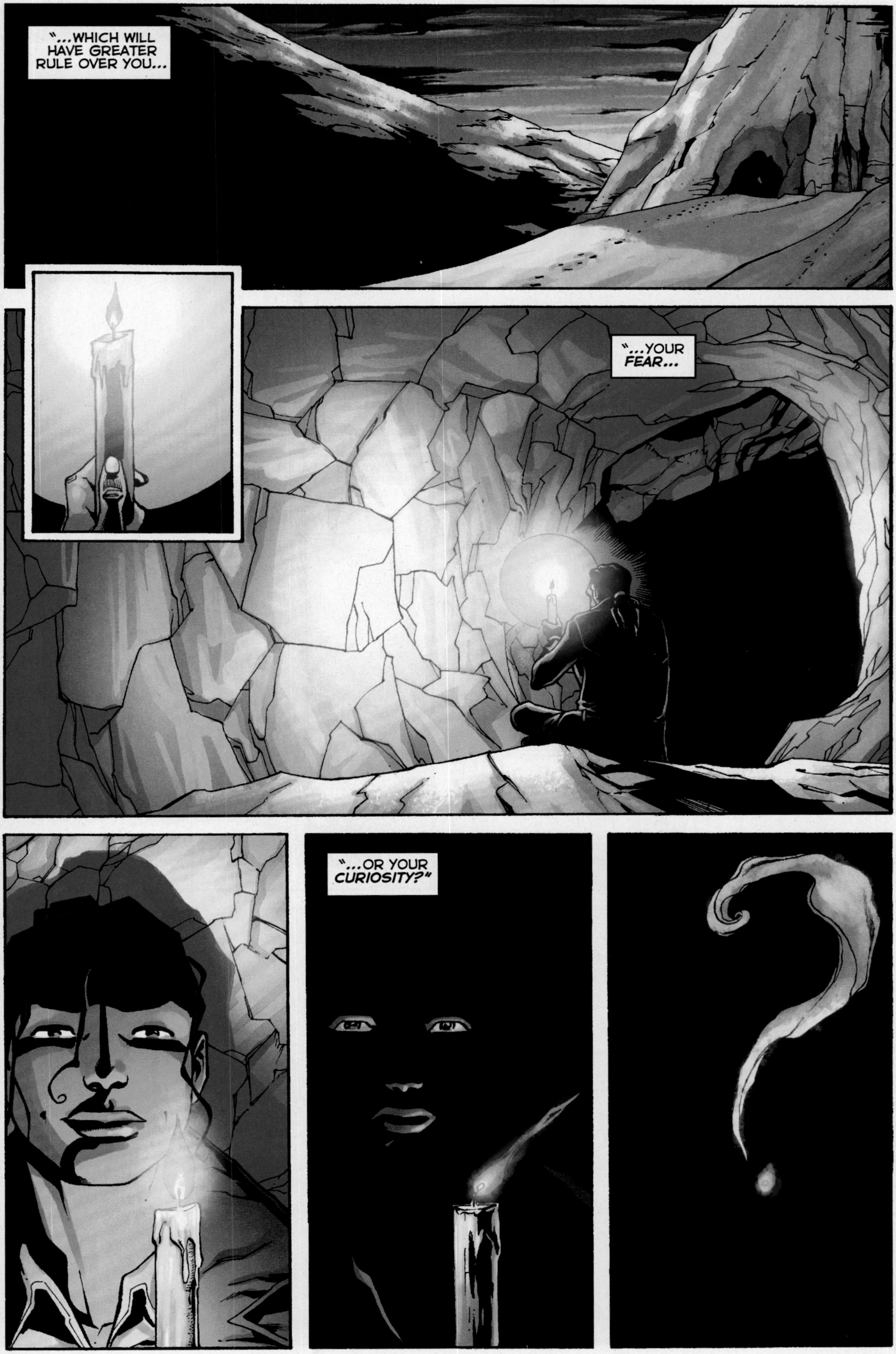
"...WHICH WILL HAVE GREATER RULE OVER YOU...
"...YOUR *FEAR*...
"...OR YOUR *CURIOSITY?*"

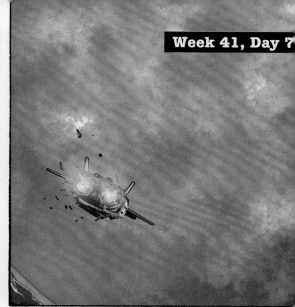

THIS OLD BIRD SAVED OUR *LIVES*... BROUGHT US HALFWAY ACROSS THE GALAXY AGAINST ALL THE ODDS.

NOW SHE'S FALLING APART.

IT WAS *MY* FAULT HE BLEW HIS SHIP UP, PRINCESS, AND IT'S MY FAULT WE'RE ON A *CRIPPLED SHIP* TUMBLING INTO A K-TYPE *SUN.*

I PROMISED I'D GET US ALL *HOME* AND NOW *BUDDY'S* DEAD AND...YOU...

I LET *EVERYONE* DOWN.

GODDAMMIT!

STUPID BLIND MAN!

WHERE ARE THE GREEN LANTERNS?

WE WERE TOLD THERE WOULD BE GREEN LANTERNS.

A-hem.

ON TAMARAN, WE WERE TAUGHT TO MAKE OUR *OWN* DESTINY, ADAM STRANGE.

THE FACT THAT I'M LEAKING *VITAL LIFE ESSENCE* ISN'T BOTHERING *ME* IN THE SLIGHTEST AT THE MOMENT AND IT CERTAINLY *SHOULDN'T* BOTHER *YOU!*

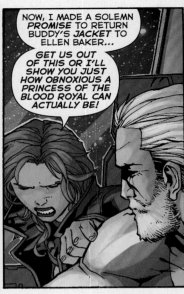

NOW, I MADE A SOLEMN *PROMISE* TO RETURN BUDDY'S *JACKET* TO ELLEN BAKER...

GET US OUT OF THIS OR I'LL SHOW YOU JUST HOW OBNOXIOUS A PRINCESS OF THE BLOOD ROYAL CAN ACTUALLY BE!

YOUR WIFE AND BABY ARE *WAITING* FOR YOU ON THE *OTHER SIDE* OF ALL THIS UNPLEASANTNESS.

SO *PLEASE.*

NO, YOU'RE *RIGHT.*

IT SEEMS SO LONG SINCE I LAST SAW THEM.

YOU KNOW, THERE WAS THIS TIME, NOT LONG AFTER WE *MET,* WHEN I FOUND A WAY TO BRING ALANNA BACK WITH ME, TO *EARTH,* FROM RANN.

I THOUGHT WE COULD *LIVE* TOGETHER, AND SEE ONE ANOTHER MORE *OFTEN,* INSTEAD OF ME HAVING TO TRAVEL *FOUR LIGHT YEARS...*

...VIA *ZETA BEAM.*

BUT ON EARTH, I...I WAS JUST A *MAN,* JUST AN *ARCHAEOLOGIST* WITH AN ADVENTUROUS STREAK.

SURE, NEXT TO THE WEAK, INFERTILE GUYS ON *RANN,* I WAS A *MONSTER-HUNTER,* A GODLIKE PHYSICAL SPECIMEN...

BACK ON EARTH, I WAS JUST LIKE *EVERYONE ELSE.* WE WERE JUST A *MAN* AND *WOMAN* LIVING IN AN APARTMENT ON AVENUE B.

I GOT SCARED SHE'D LEAVE ME FOR A *REAL HERO...*

I BLAMED *ALIEN INTERVENTION* AND SENT HER *BACK* TO RANN, AND WE SAW EACH OTHER *ONCE A MONTH* FOR A LONG TIME AFTER THAT.

IN MY HEAD, I WAS ONLY A HERO AMONG *WEAKLINGS.*

AS A RESULT I'VE BECOME WHAT YOU MIGHT WANT TO CALL AN *OVER-ACHIEVER.*

WE'RE FALLING TOWARDS A *SUN* IN A DISINTEGRATING VESSEL WITH *ZERO POWER,* EXCEPT WHAT'S FEEDING LIFE SUPPORT.

SURE.

I CAN GET US OUT OF THAT...

WE HAVE *NTH METAL* SHIELDING AROUND THE ENGINE CORES, RIGHT?

THAT'S... THAT'S THE SPIRIT...

TOLD YOU SOMETHING WOULD TURN UP...

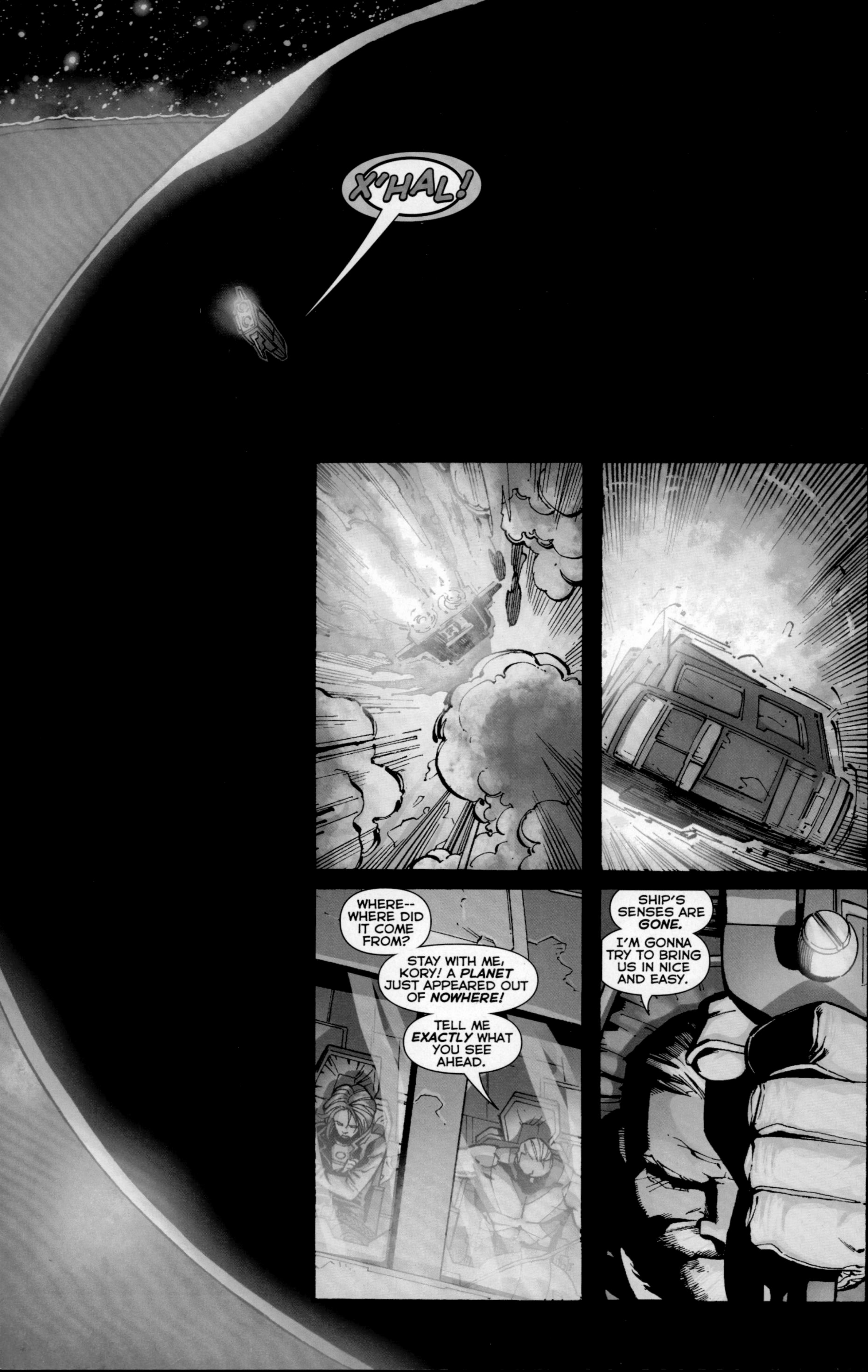
X'HAL!
WHERE-- WHERE DID IT COME FROM?
STAY WITH ME, KORY! A PLANET JUST APPEARED OUT OF NOWHERE!
TELL ME EXACTLY WHAT YOU SEE AHEAD.
SHIP'S SENSES ARE GONE.
I'M GONNA TRY TO BRING US IN NICE AND EASY.

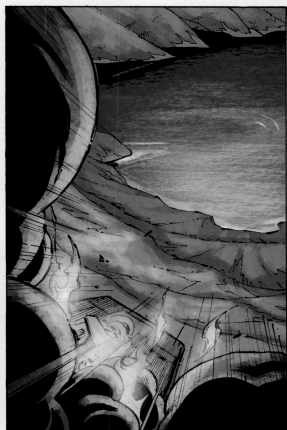

WE GOT 'EM.

STRANGE. IF MOLEK'S TRANSPORT HADN'T *SUICIDED* WHEN IT DID, WE'D HAVE *MISSED* THE RADIATION FLARE THAT BROUGHT US HERE.

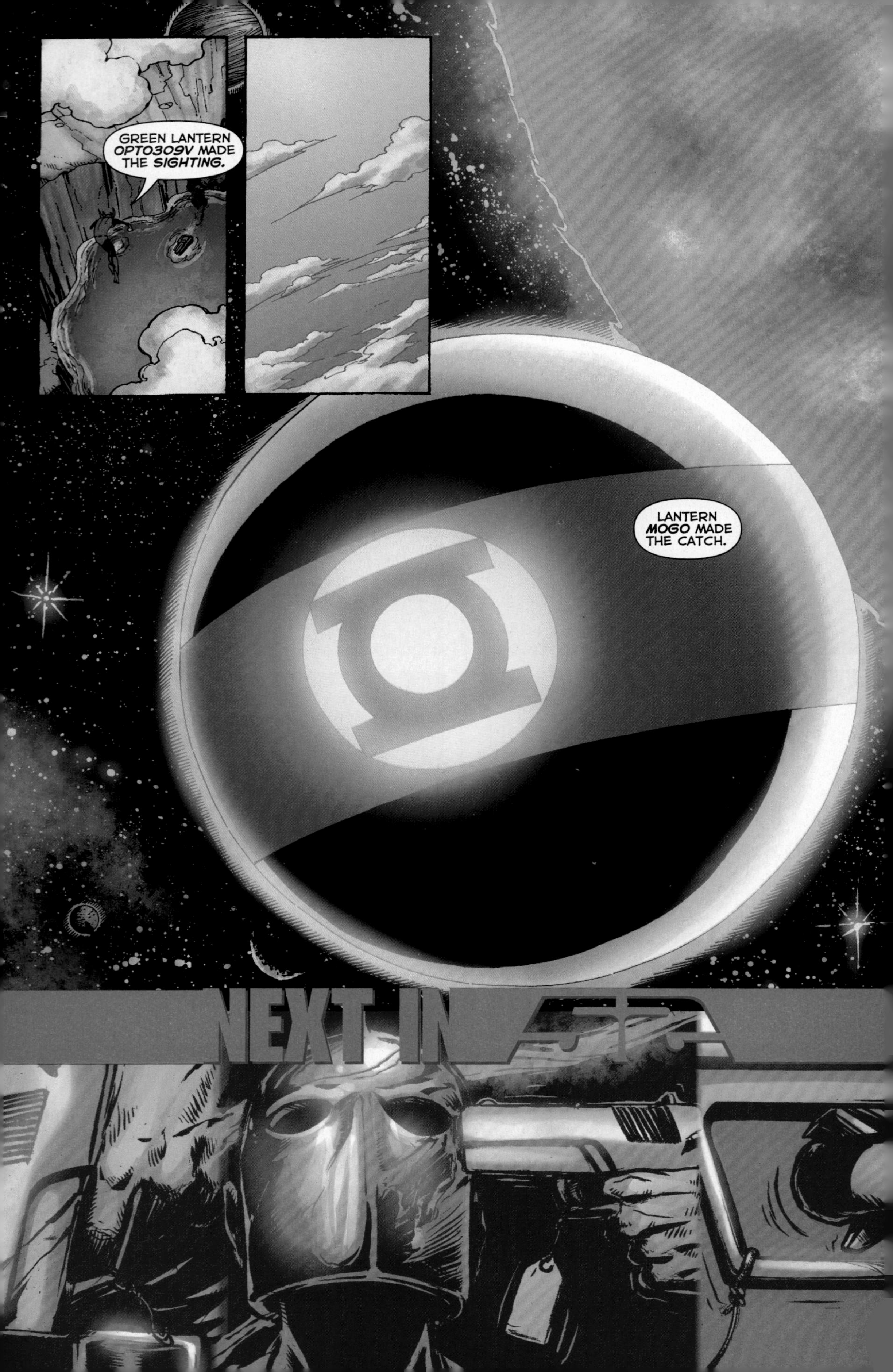
GREEN LANTERN OPTO309V MADE THE SIGHTING.
LANTERN MOGO MADE THE CATCH.
NEXT IN

GREG RUCKA

The Renee stuff this issue came very specifically out of a series of phone calls with the Mighty Mark Waid. We were all seeing the light at the end of the tunnel at this point, and instead of feeling relief, all of us (well, except Grant, I suspect), were beginning to experience a sense of rising panic, as much as a tangible sense of brutal fatigue. We'd still have the weekly phone calls or whatnot, but there wasn't a day passing at this point where I wouldn't have multiple calls with Siglain, Geoff, Mark, or Keith, and most days, it was multiple calls with most of them.

The problem, as I've stated time and again, wasn't that we didn't know our endings; we knew them, we'd known them from the start. The problem was a twofold one: we were running out of time, and we were running out of space. Story beats that had been set for the late 40s had to be moved up to make room for other beats that had also been set for the late 40s-early 50s that needed more space. This led to rewriting of those beats, because the way they'd been paced had initially been contingent on where *other* beats would fall, and once those changed, all bets were off.

I still have my hand-scribbled notes from the conversation where Mark saved my bacon, though, if I remember correctly, it was Geoff who had suggested using the visual of the cave and the multiple reflections. I have, scrawled quickly on the back of an envelope, the words, "faces," "internal v. external," and "Diana shows the way." I'm somewhat embarrassed that Mark had to spell out that last one for me; I like to think I write a good Wonder Woman, and that I know what she's about, but the irony of having her appear in Nanda Parbat, waiting for Bruce Wayne, struggling with her own guilt about having killed Max Lord, and still having her be the final "push" to get Renee to confront her demons, that had never occurred to me. So, once again, thank you, Mark.

Speaking of, I love the panel where Ralph's looking at the file and at the same time offering the flask to Dewhurst. Loved it all the more when I read Week 42.

MIKE SIGLAIN

Ralph, Ralph, Ralph. How low will you go?

Finding leftover mad scientists from the DCU that Grant hadn't already pilfered for Oolong Island was a chore, but I located the right evil genius in Professor Milo — a Batman villain who first appeared in a doublet of stories in the 1950s, didn't resurface again until the 1970s Len Wein/Neal Adams classic "Moon of the Wolf," and hasn't really been too over-booked since. Saying that Milo tended to mix "a little science with his magic" is a tiny bit of a stretch, but not totally out of character. And if he shows up again anytime soon with full mobility, let's not chalk it up to a continuity error; let's just say he built some goblin legs for himself or something. THAT would be in character.

(CONTINUED)

WEEK FORTY-ONE NOTES

(CONTINUED)

The Silver Wheel of Nyorlath was an artifact from the first Felix Faust story in JUSTICE LEAGUE OF AMERICA #10 (1962). Without spoiling next issue's big Ralph finale, I realized only after I'd put it on the list of "Fitting DCU Magical Artifacts" that it had extra resonance to the story. You'll see.

Greg Rucka did a nice job with the Wonder Woman scene in this issue. Placing Princess Diana somewhere in the narrative of 52 was one of the most difficult tasks we faced; due as much to editorial miscommunication as to anything else, we always knew where Superman and Batman were supposed to be during the year of our story, but nobody at DC could give us a straight answer as to where the Amazing Amazon had sequestered herself. Eventually, after rejecting about a million suggestions from one another ("Ancient Greece?" "No, no...Peace Corps in Zimbabwe?" "Nah. How about working undercover at Taco Whiz?" "REALLY no."), Greg turned Nanda Parbat from a contingency to a reality.

Mogo, the planet-sized Green Lantern, was introduced into the DC mythology by the brilliant writer Alan Moore in the 1980s. Mogo is used here by Grant to great effect. I love it when two of my favorite writers team up.

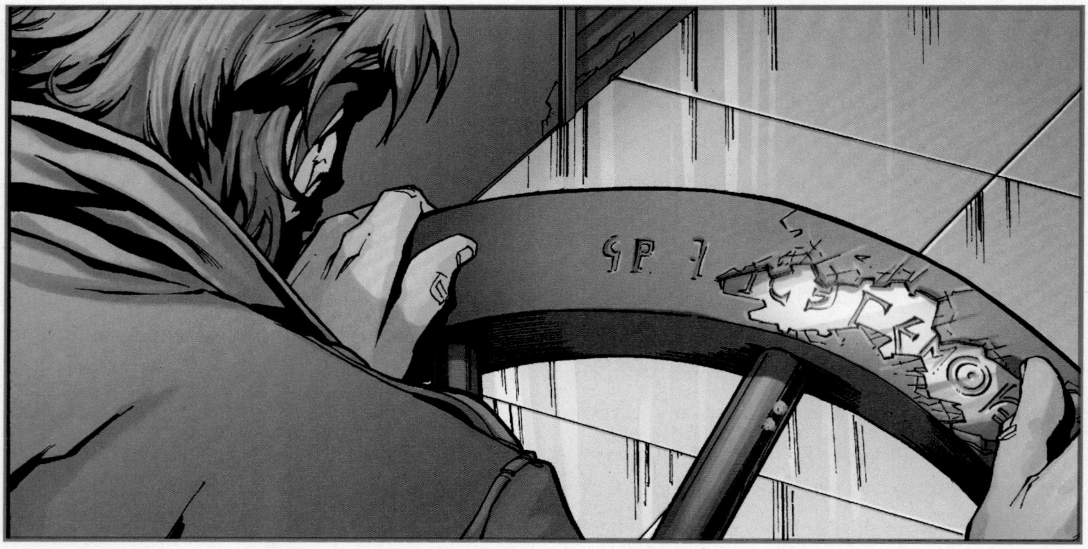

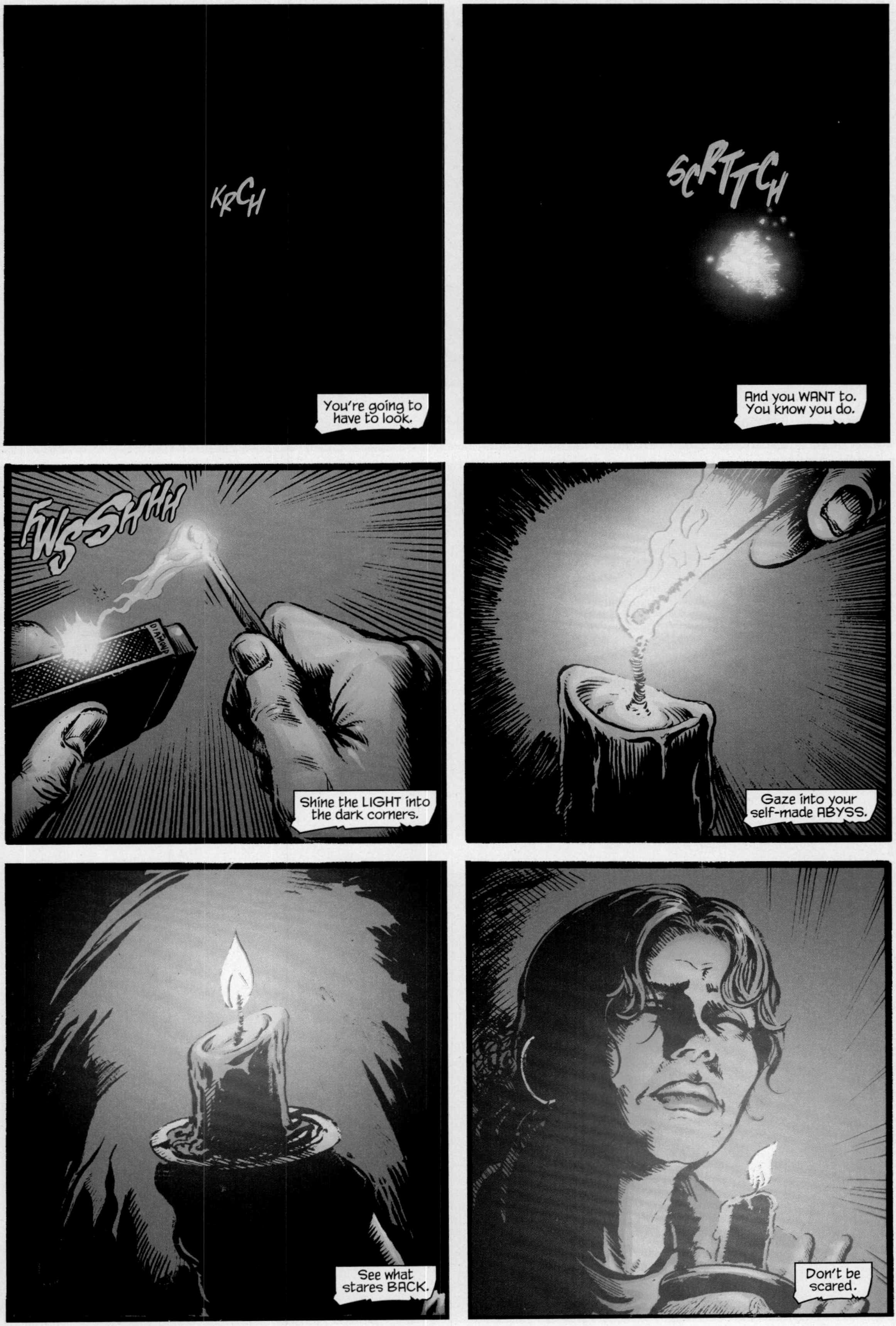
KRCH
You're going to have to look.
SCRTTCH
And you WANT to. You know you do.
FWSSHHH
DIAMOND
Shine the LIGHT into the dark corners.
Gaze into your self-made ABYSS.
See what stares BACK.
Don't be scared.

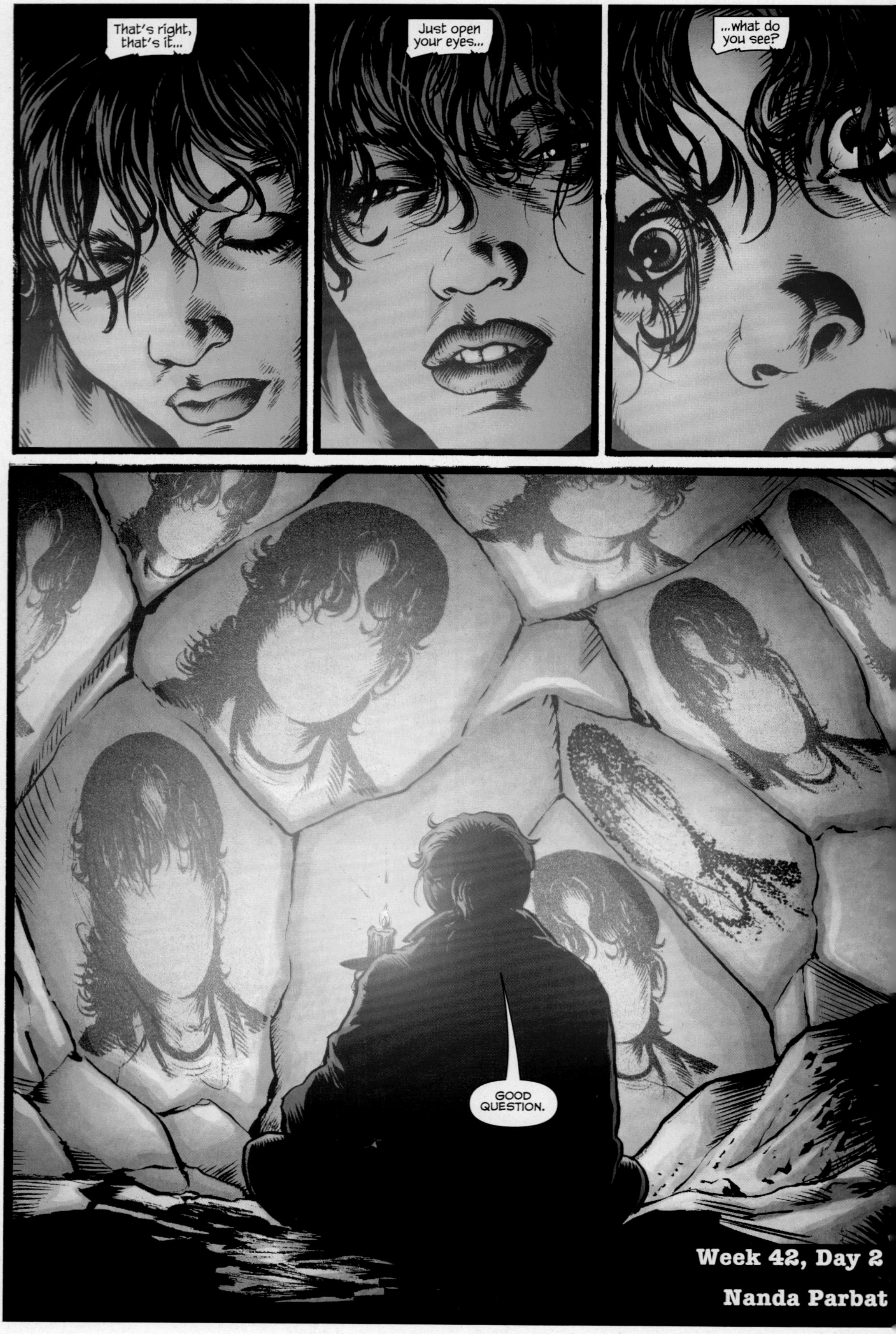
That's right, that's it...
Just open your eyes...
...what do you see?
GOOD QUESTION.
Week 42, Day 2
Nanda Parbat

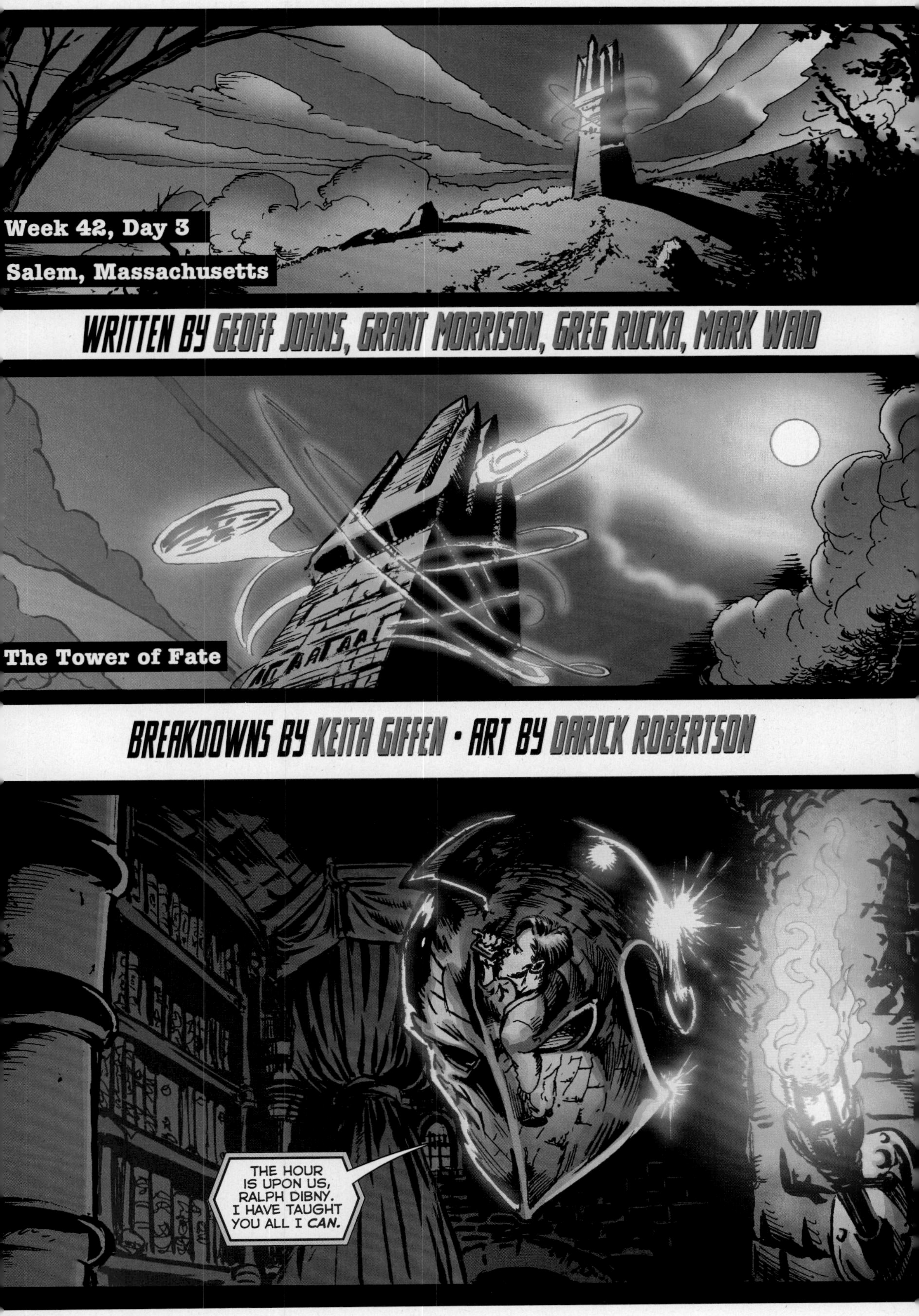
Week 42, Day 3
Salem, Massachusetts
WRITTEN BY GEOFF JOHNS, GRANT MORRISON, GREG RUCKA, MARK WAID
The Tower of Fate
BREAKDOWNS BY KEITH GIFFEN • ART BY DARICK ROBERTSON
THE HOUR IS UPON US, RALPH DIBNY. I HAVE TAUGHT YOU ALL I *CAN.*

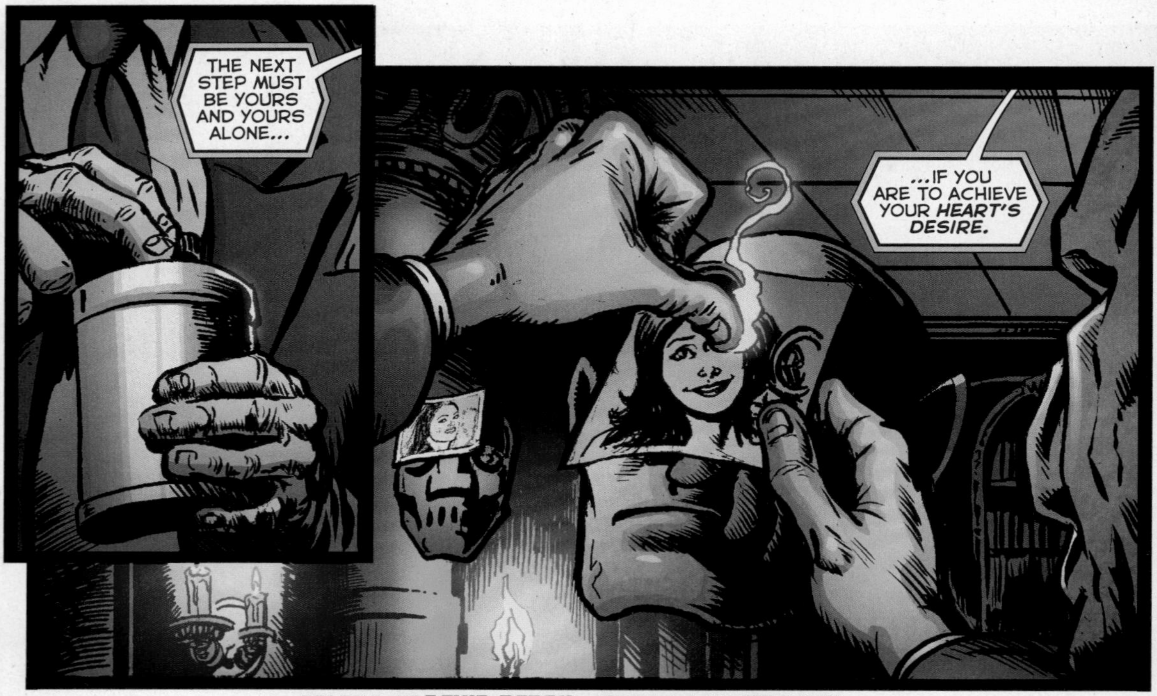
THE NEXT STEP MUST BE YOURS AND YOURS ALONE...
...IF YOU ARE TO ACHIEVE YOUR HEART'S DESIRE.

COLORS BY DAVID BARON • LETTERS BY ROB LEIGH
ASSISTANT EDITOR HARVEY RICHARDS • ASSOCIATE EDITOR JEANINE SCHAEFER
EDITOR MICHAEL SIGLAIN • COVER BY J.G. JONES & ALEX SINCLAIR

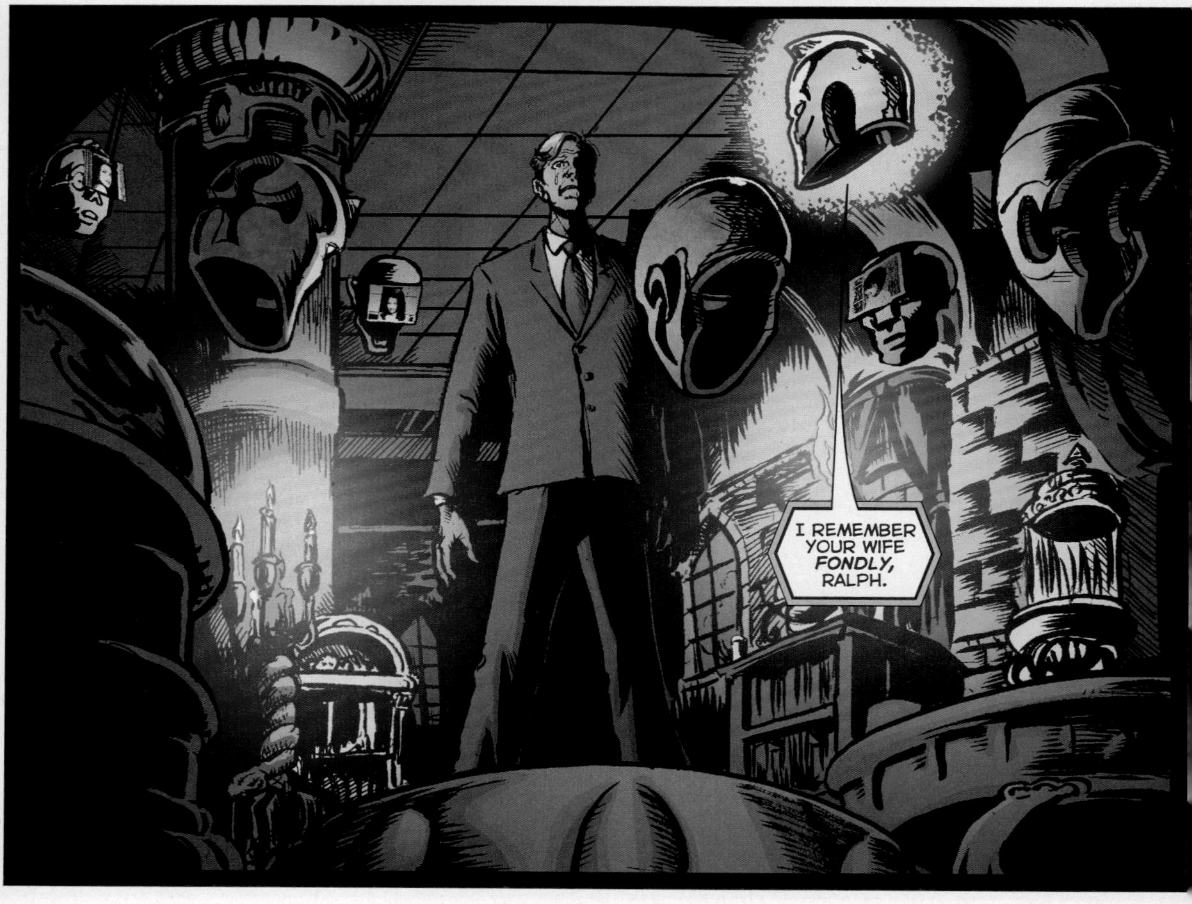
I REMEMBER YOUR WIFE FONDLY, RALPH.

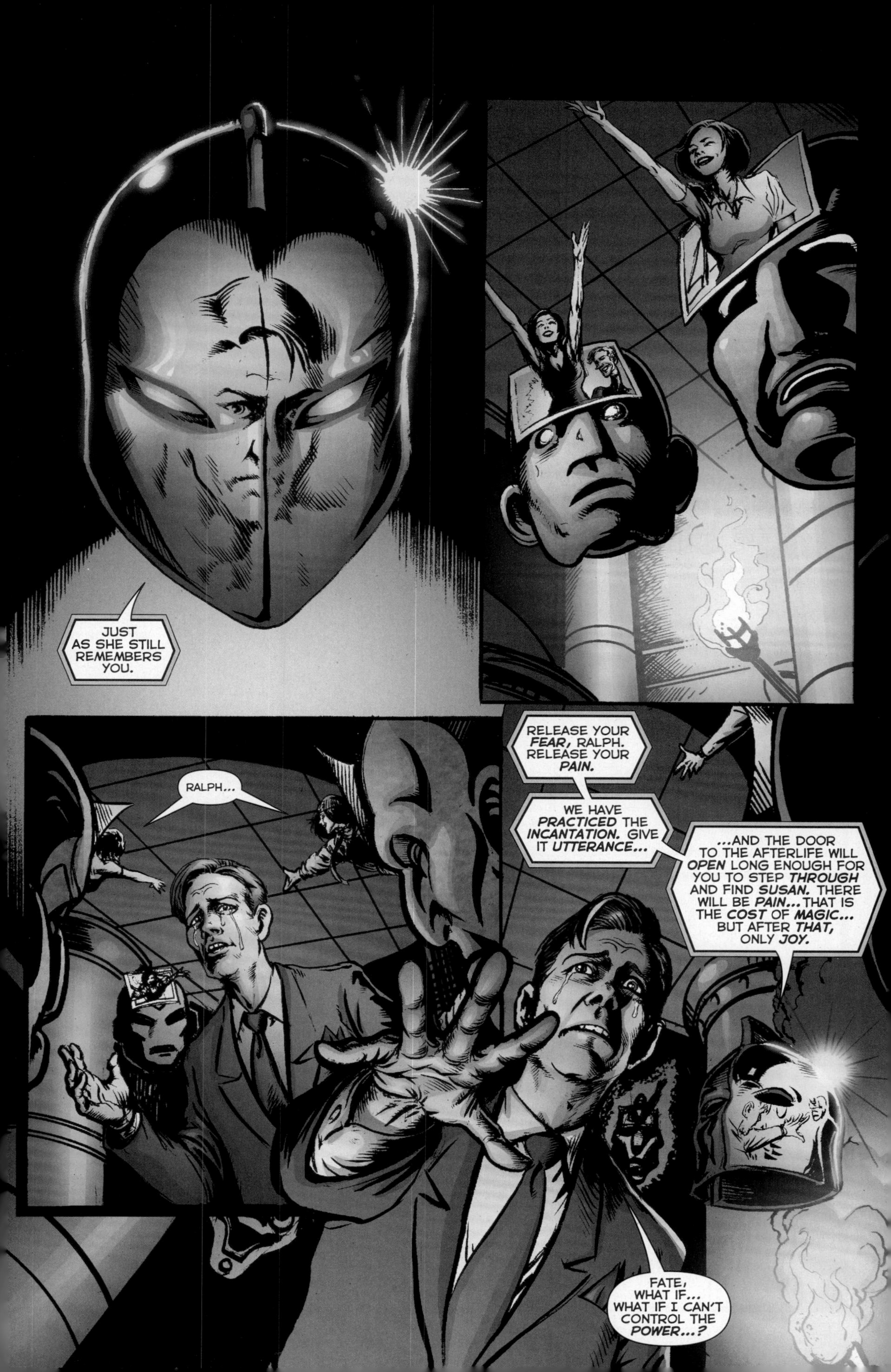
JUST AS SHE STILL REMEMBERS YOU.
RALPH...
RELEASE YOUR FEAR, RALPH. RELEASE YOUR PAIN.
WE HAVE PRACTICED THE INCANTATION. GIVE IT UTTERANCE...
...AND THE DOOR TO THE AFTERLIFE WILL OPEN LONG ENOUGH FOR YOU TO STEP THROUGH AND FIND SUSAN. THERE WILL BE PAIN... THAT IS THE COST OF MAGIC... BUT AFTER THAT, ONLY JOY.
FATE, WHAT IF... WHAT IF I CAN'T CONTROL THE POWER...?

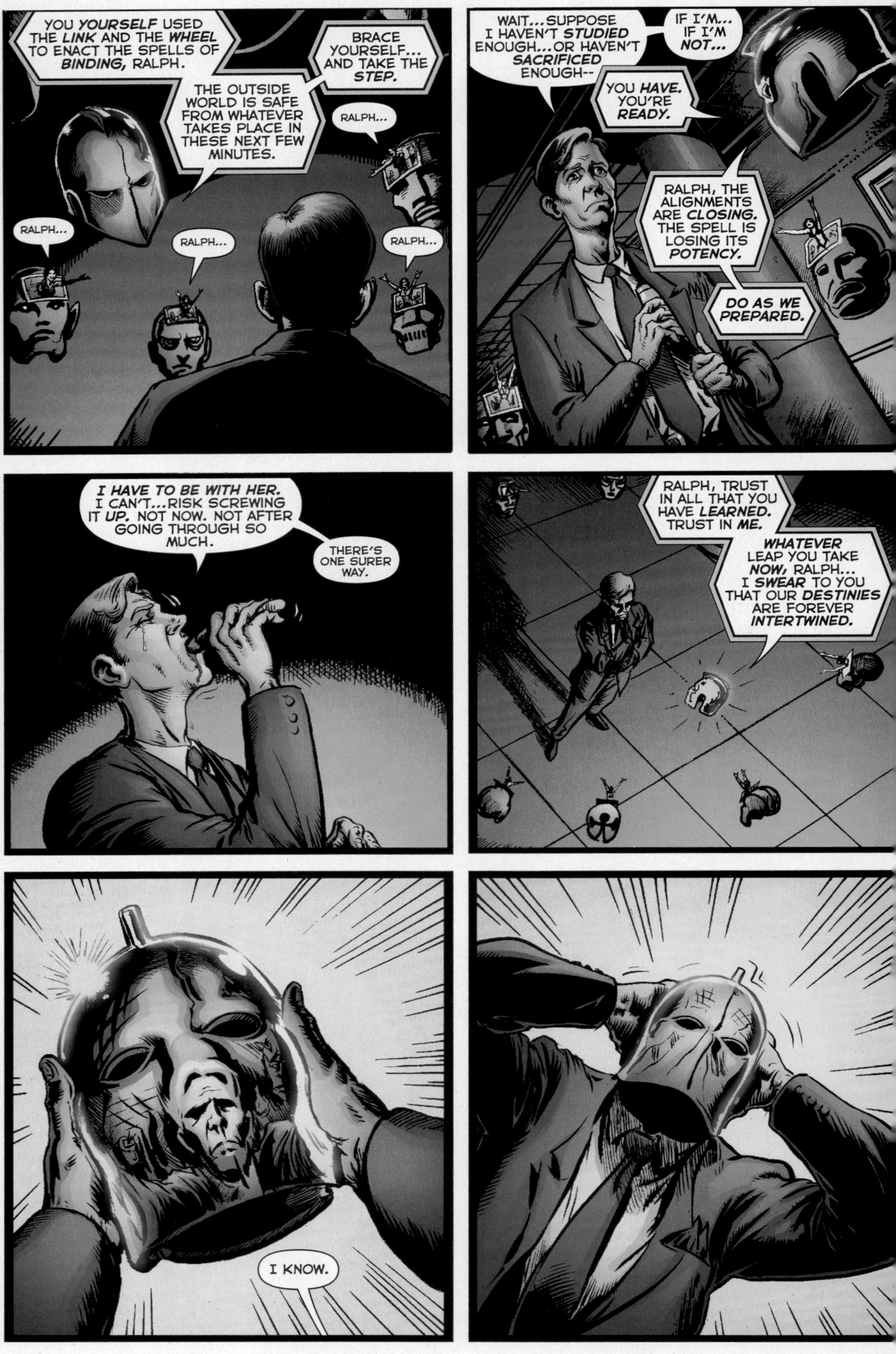
YOU YOURSELF USED THE LINK AND THE WHEEL TO ENACT THE SPELLS OF BINDING, RALPH.
THE OUTSIDE WORLD IS SAFE FROM WHATEVER TAKES PLACE IN THESE NEXT FEW MINUTES.
BRACE YOURSELF... AND TAKE THE STEP.
RALPH...
RALPH...
RALPH...
RALPH...
WAIT... SUPPOSE I HAVEN'T STUDIED ENOUGH... OR HAVEN'T SACRIFICED ENOUGH--
IF I'M... IF I'M NOT...
YOU HAVE. YOU'RE READY.
RALPH, THE ALIGNMENTS ARE CLOSING. THE SPELL IS LOSING ITS POTENCY.
DO AS WE PREPARED.
I HAVE TO BE WITH HER. I CAN'T... RISK SCREWING IT UP. NOT NOW. NOT AFTER GOING THROUGH SO MUCH.
THERE'S ONE SURER WAY.
RALPH, TRUST IN ALL THAT YOU HAVE LEARNED. TRUST IN ME.
WHATEVER LEAP YOU TAKE NOW, RALPH... I SWEAR TO YOU THAT OUR DESTINIES ARE FOREVER INTERTWINED.
I KNOW.

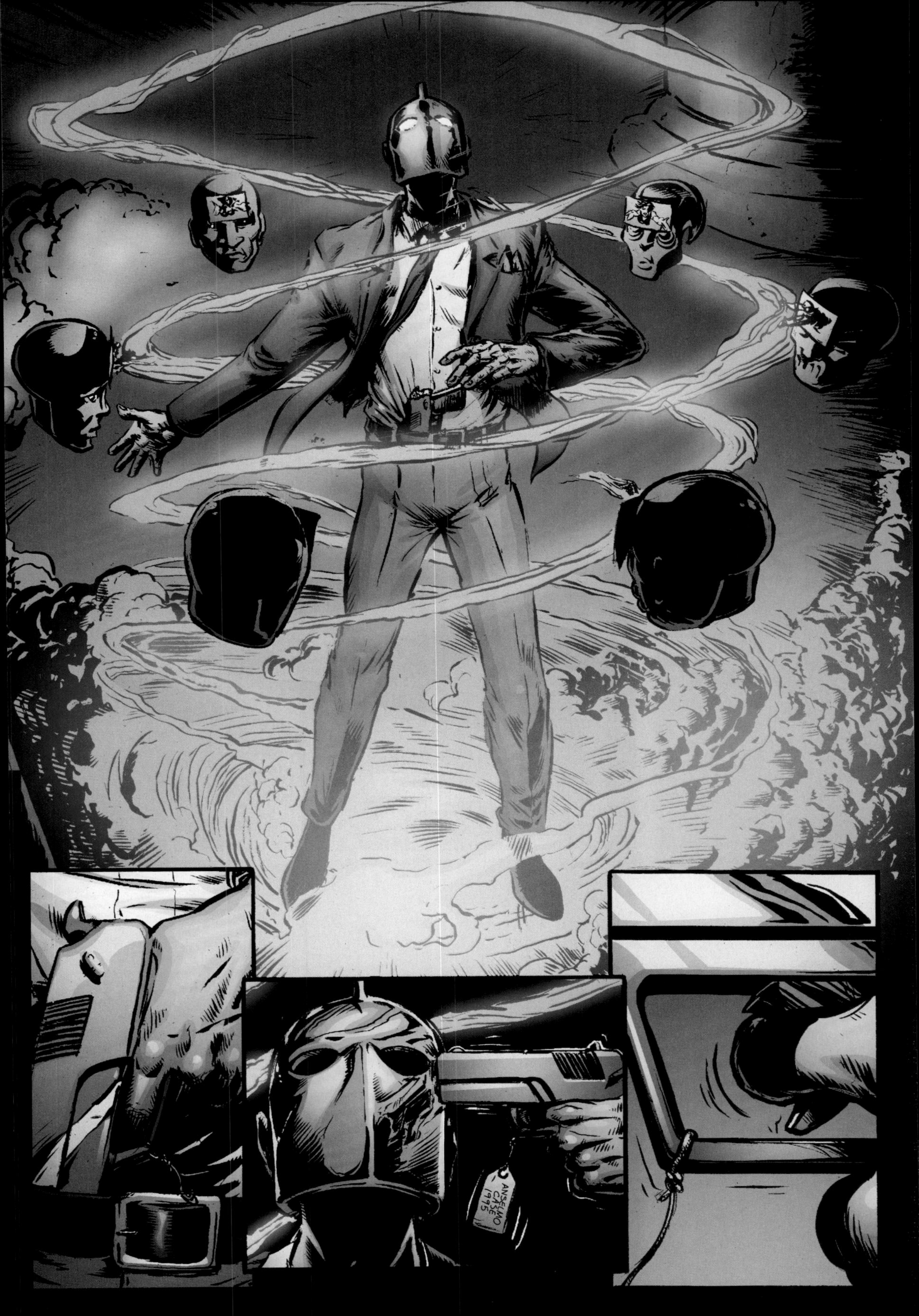
ANSELMO
CASE
1995

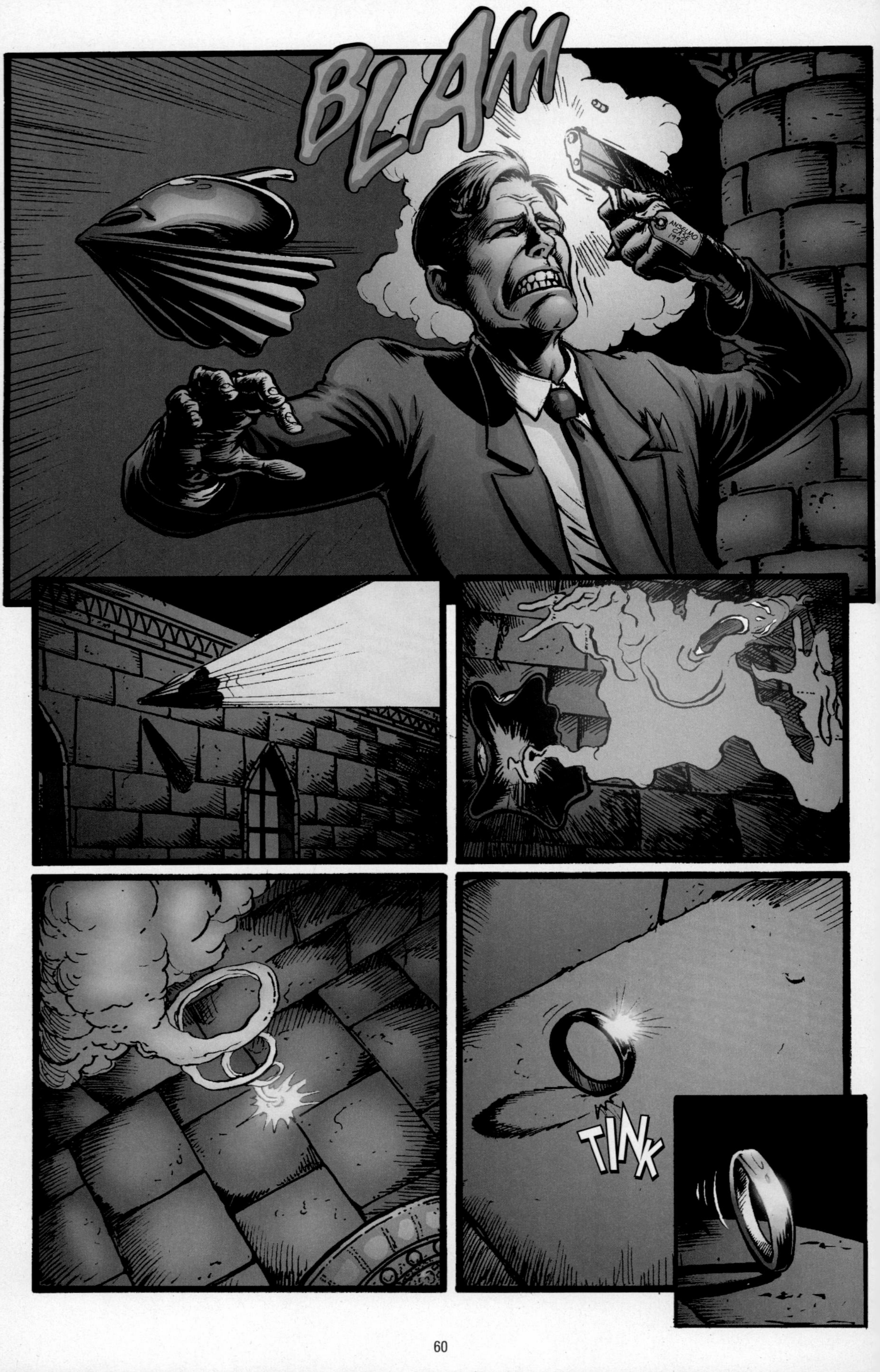
BLAM
ANSELMO CASE 1995
TINK

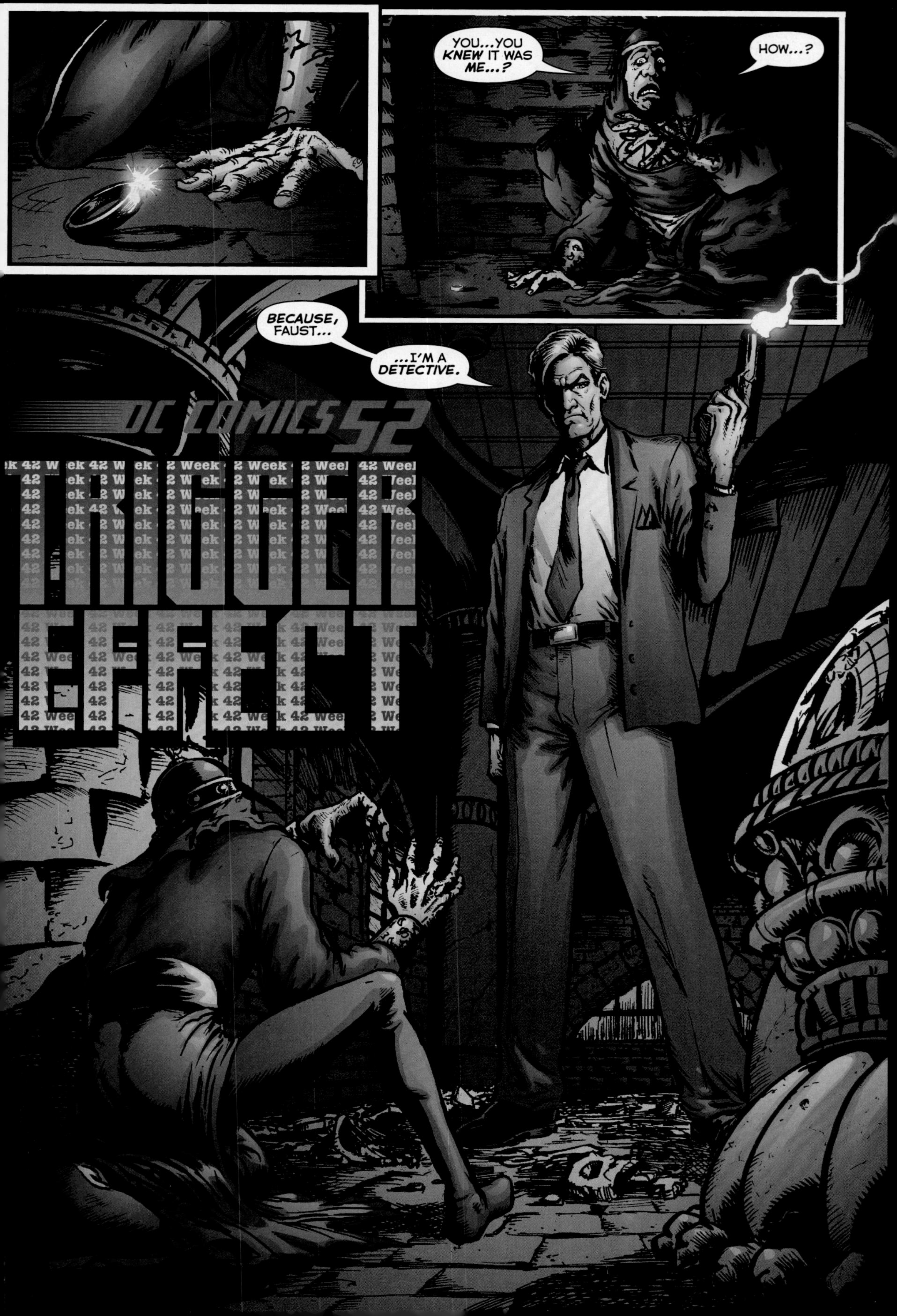
YOU...YOU KNEW IT WAS ME...?
HOW...?
BECAUSE, FAUST...
...I'M A DETECTIVE.
DC COMICS 52
TRIGGER EFFECT
42 Week

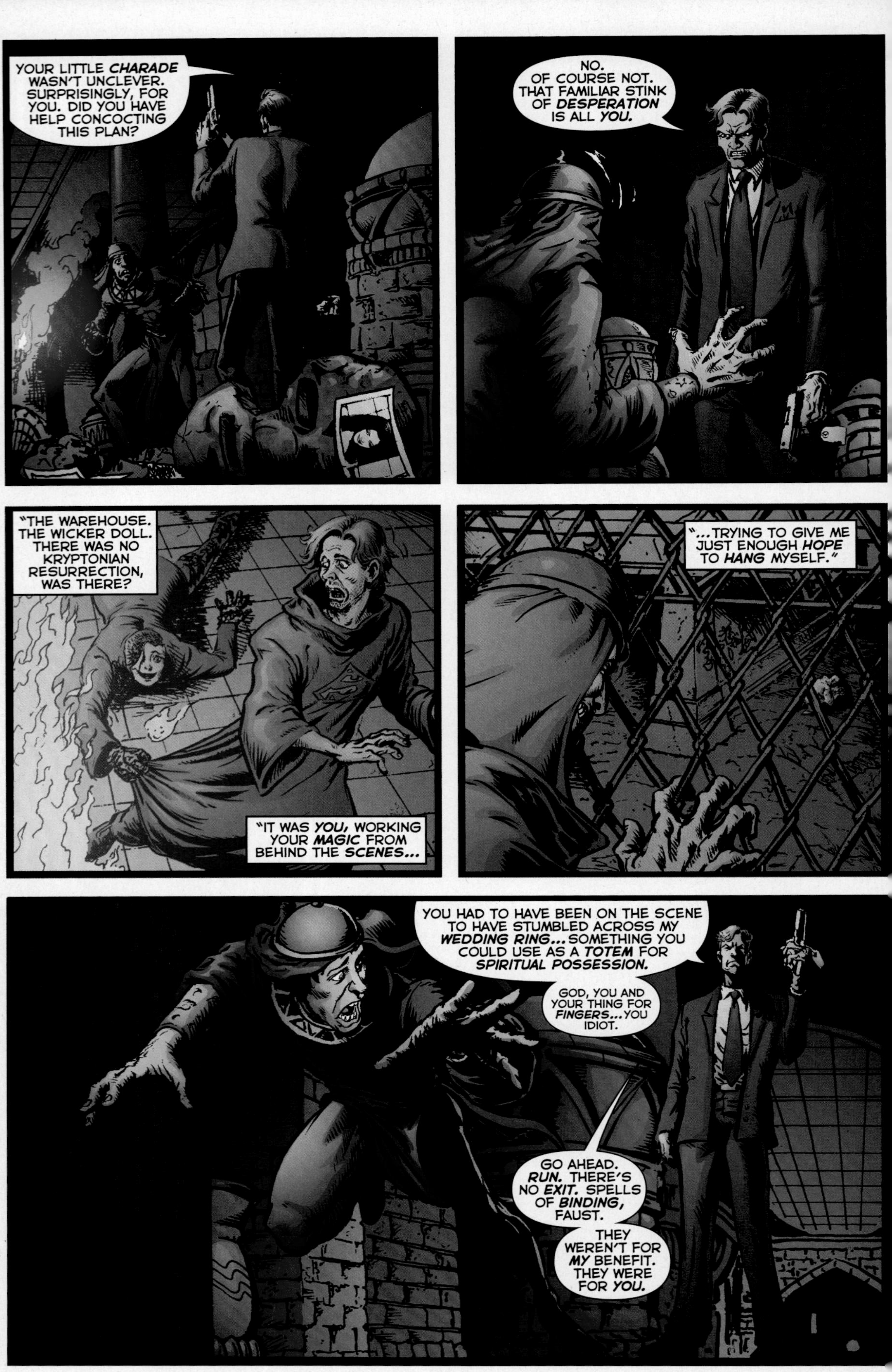
YOUR LITTLE CHARADE WASN'T UNCLEVER. SURPRISINGLY, FOR YOU. DID YOU HAVE HELP CONCOCTING THIS PLAN?
NO. OF COURSE NOT. THAT FAMILIAR STINK OF DESPERATION IS ALL YOU.
"THE WAREHOUSE. THE WICKER DOLL. THERE WAS NO KRYPTONIAN RESURRECTION, WAS THERE?
"IT WAS YOU, WORKING YOUR MAGIC FROM BEHIND THE SCENES...
"...TRYING TO GIVE ME JUST ENOUGH HOPE TO HANG MYSELF."
YOU HAD TO HAVE BEEN ON THE SCENE TO HAVE STUMBLED ACROSS MY WEDDING RING... SOMETHING YOU COULD USE AS A TOTEM FOR SPIRITUAL POSSESSION.
GOD, YOU AND YOUR THING FOR FINGERS... YOU IDIOT.
GO AHEAD. RUN. THERE'S NO EXIT. SPELLS OF BINDING, FAUST.
THEY WEREN'T FOR MY BENEFIT. THEY WERE FOR YOU.

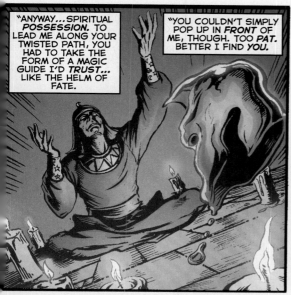

"ANYWAY...SPIRITUAL *POSSESSION.* TO LEAD ME ALONG YOUR TWISTED PATH, YOU HAD TO TAKE THE FORM OF A MAGIC GUIDE I'D *TRUST*... LIKE THE HELM OF FATE.

"YOU COULDN'T SIMPLY POP UP IN *FRONT* OF ME, THOUGH. TOO *PAT.* BETTER I FIND *YOU.*

"SO YOU PLAYED THE *CROATOANS.* THEY PULLED ME IN BECAUSE THEY FOUND TIM TRENCH *DEAD*...

"...AND *YOU* TOLD ME IT WAS BECAUSE HE'D TRIED TO ASSUME YOUR *POWER* WITHOUT *PRECAUTION.*"

THAT WAS THE FIRST OF THE MANY, *MANY* CAUTIONARY TALES WITH WHICH YOU ASSUMED YOU'D EARNED MY *CONFIDENCE.*

AND, TO YOUR *CREDIT,* GIVEN HOW EMOTIONALLY *DAMAGED* I WAS, YOU MIGHT *HAVE.*

EXCEPT.

I CONCLUDED *VERY* EARLY ON THAT, WHOEVER YOU WERE, YOU WERE *LYING* TO ME ABOUT HOW TRENCH *DIED*...AND, THEREFORE, PROBABLY MUCH MORE.

OH, I WAS *GUARDED* FROM THE *START.* AGAIN, YOUR *OFFER* COINCIDED WITH MY *NEED* AWFULLY *CONVENIENTLY,* FAUST.

BUT *MISGIVING* WASN'T *EVIDENCE.* IT WASN'T THE ONE CLUE I *REQUIRED* TO CLINCH MY SUSPICIONS.

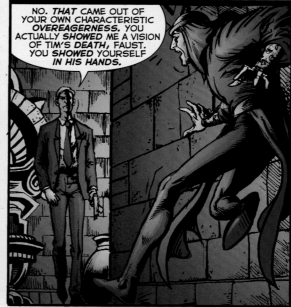

NO. *THAT* CAME OUT OF YOUR OWN CHARACTERISTIC *OVEREAGERNESS.* YOU ACTUALLY *SHOWED* ME A VISION OF TIM'S *DEATH,* FAUST. YOU *SHOWED* YOURSELF IN HIS HANDS.

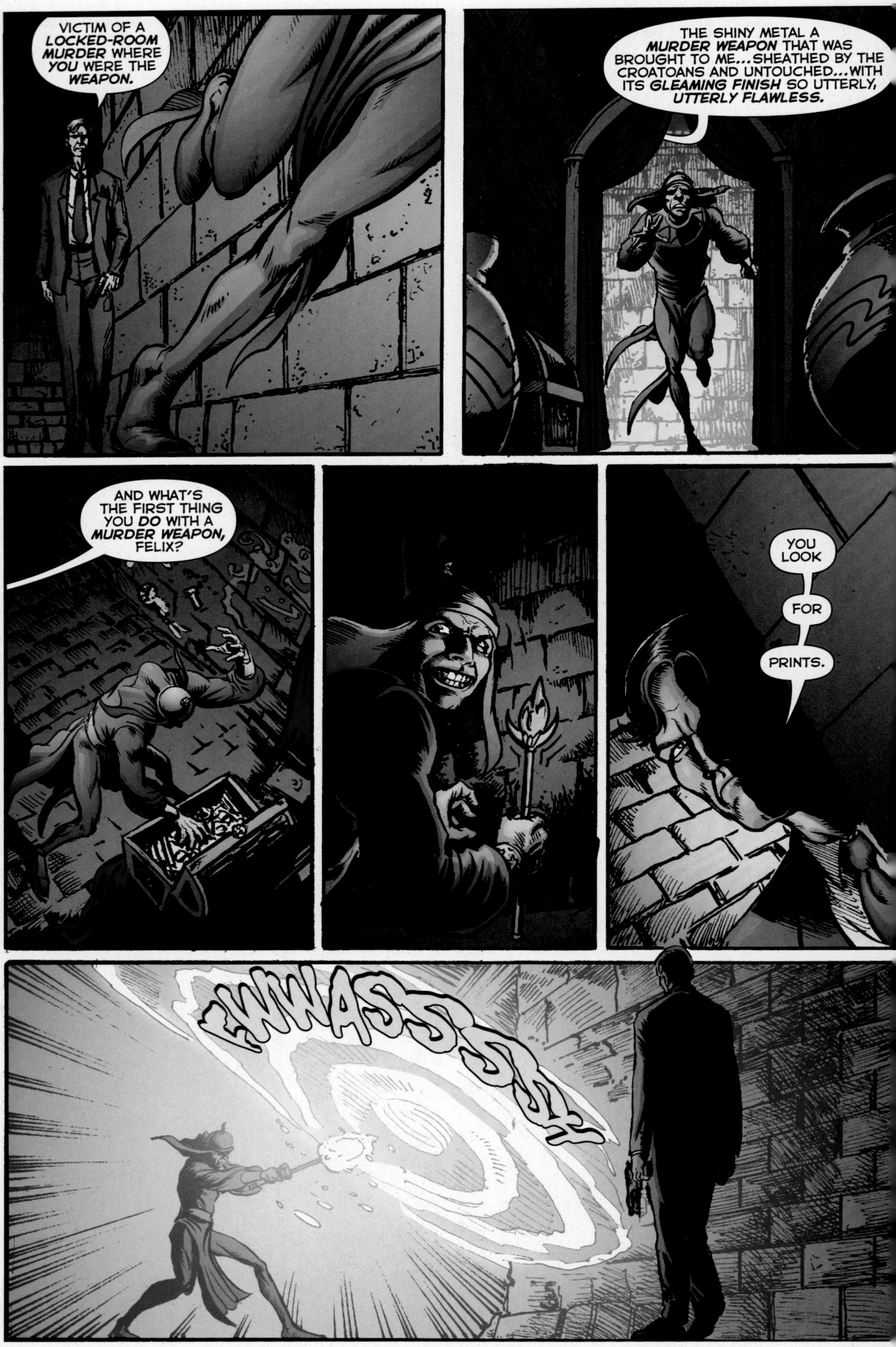
VICTIM OF A LOCKED-ROOM MURDER WHERE YOU WERE THE WEAPON.
THE SHINY METAL A MURDER WEAPON THAT WAS BROUGHT TO ME...SHEATHED BY THE CROATOANS AND UNTOUCHED...WITH ITS GLEAMING FINISH SO UTTERLY, UTTERLY FLAWLESS.
AND WHAT'S THE FIRST THING YOU DO WITH A MURDER WEAPON, FELIX?
YOU LOOK
FOR
PRINTS.
FWWASSSSH

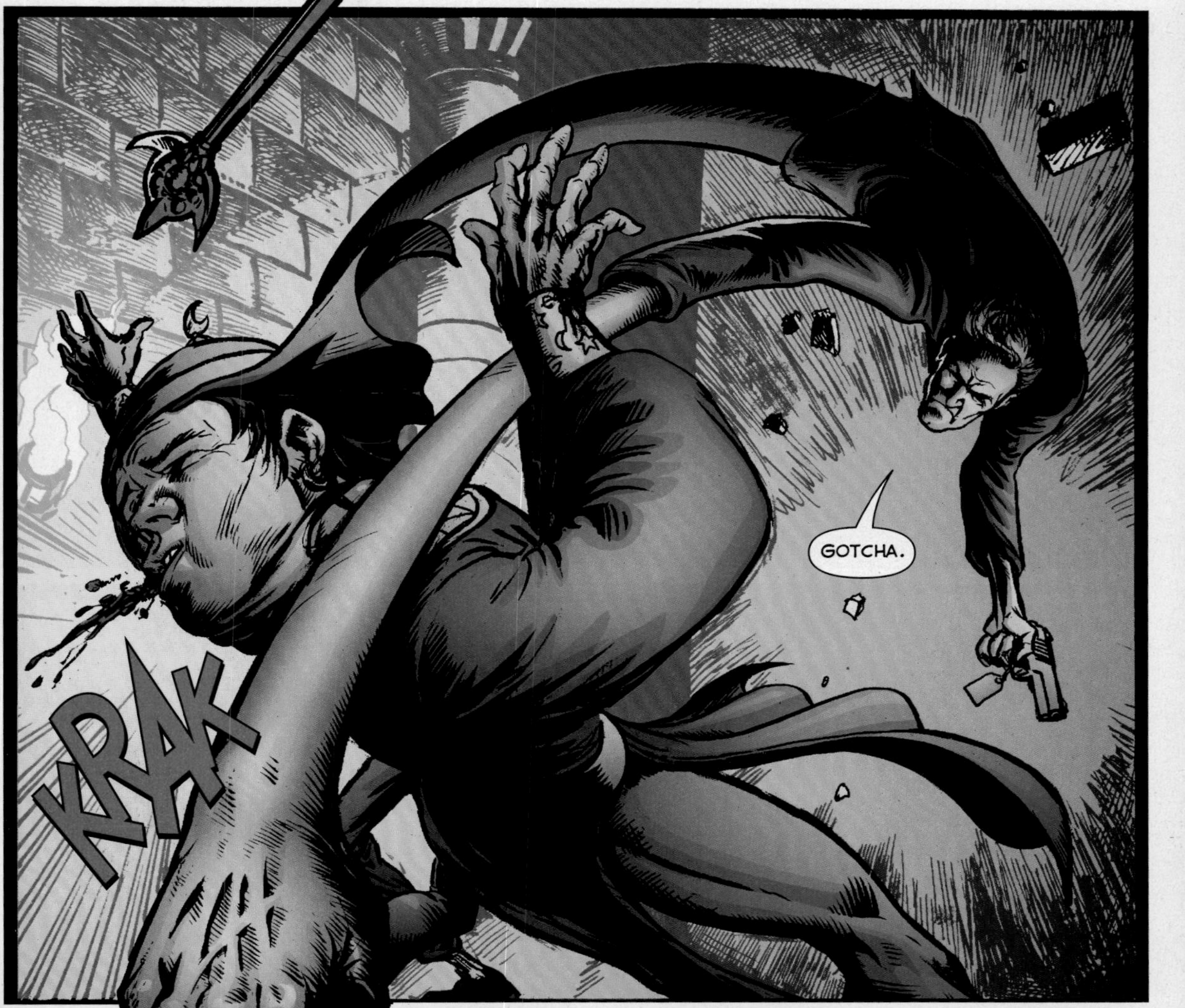
GOTCHA.
KRAK

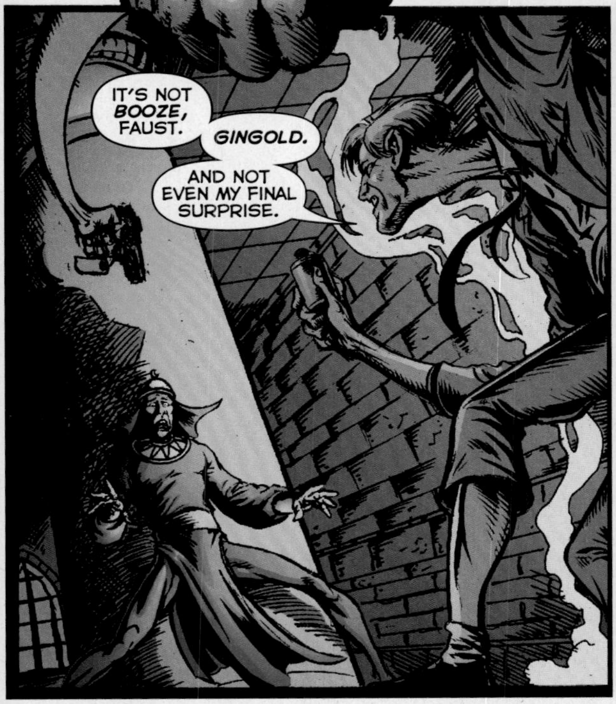
IT'S NOT *BOOZE*, FAUST.
GINGOLD.
AND NOT EVEN MY FINAL SURPRISE.

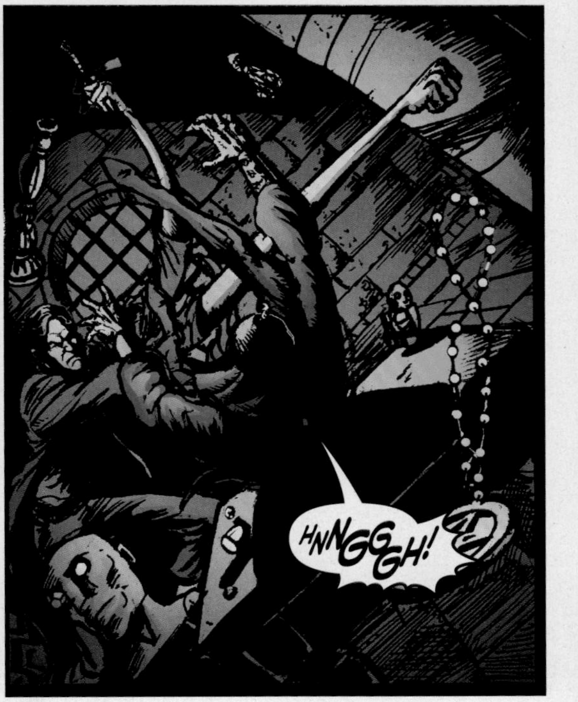
HNNGGGH!

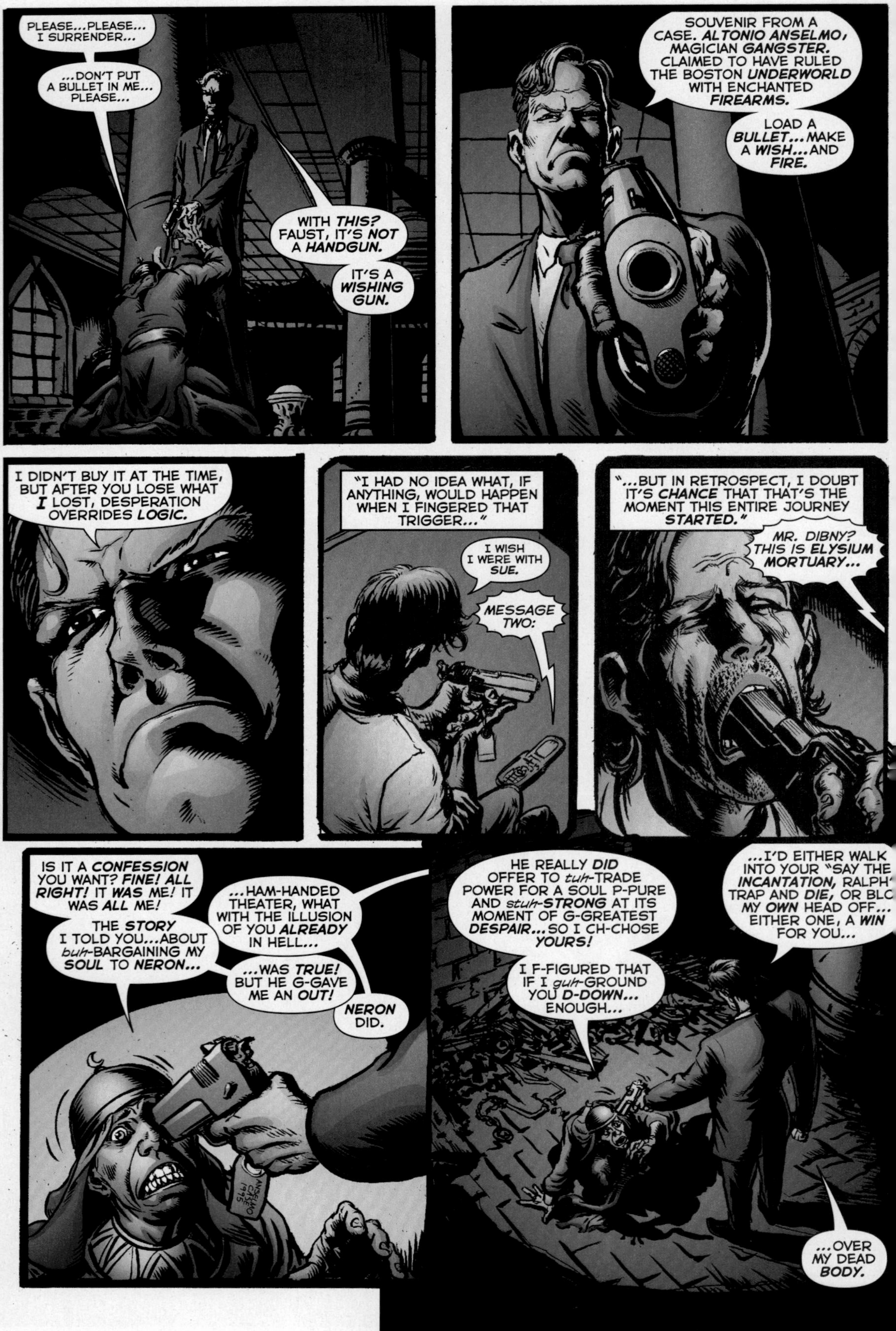
PLEASE...PLEASE... I SURRENDER...
...DON'T PUT A BULLET IN ME... PLEASE...
WITH THIS? FAUST, IT'S NOT A HANDGUN.
IT'S A WISHING GUN.
SOUVENIR FROM A CASE. ALTONIO ANSELMO, MAGICIAN GANGSTER. CLAIMED TO HAVE RULED THE BOSTON UNDERWORLD WITH ENCHANTED FIREARMS.
LOAD A BULLET...MAKE A WISH...AND FIRE.
I DIDN'T BUY IT AT THE TIME, BUT AFTER YOU LOSE WHAT I LOST, DESPERATION OVERRIDES LOGIC.
"I HAD NO IDEA WHAT, IF ANYTHING, WOULD HAPPEN WHEN I FINGERED THAT TRIGGER..."
I WISH I WERE WITH SUE.
MESSAGE TWO:
"...BUT IN RETROSPECT, I DOUBT IT'S CHANCE THAT THAT'S THE MOMENT THIS ENTIRE JOURNEY STARTED."
MR. DIBNY? THIS IS ELYSIUM MORTUARY...
IS IT A CONFESSION YOU WANT? FINE! ALL RIGHT! IT WAS ME! IT WAS ALL ME!
THE STORY I TOLD YOU...ABOUT buh-BARGAINING MY SOUL TO NERON...
...HAM-HANDED THEATER, WHAT WITH THE ILLUSION OF YOU ALREADY IN HELL...
...WAS TRUE! BUT HE G-GAVE ME AN OUT!
NERON DID.
ANSELMO CASE 1995
HE REALLY DID OFFER TO tuh-TRADE POWER FOR A SOUL P-PURE AND stuh-STRONG AT ITS MOMENT OF G-GREATEST DESPAIR...SO I CH-CHOSE YOURS!
I F-FIGURED THAT IF I guh-GROUND YOU D-DOWN... ENOUGH...
...I'D EITHER WALK INTO YOUR "SAY THE INCANTATION, RALPH" TRAP AND DIE, OR BLO MY OWN HEAD OFF... EITHER ONE, A WIN FOR YOU...
...OVER MY DEAD BODY.

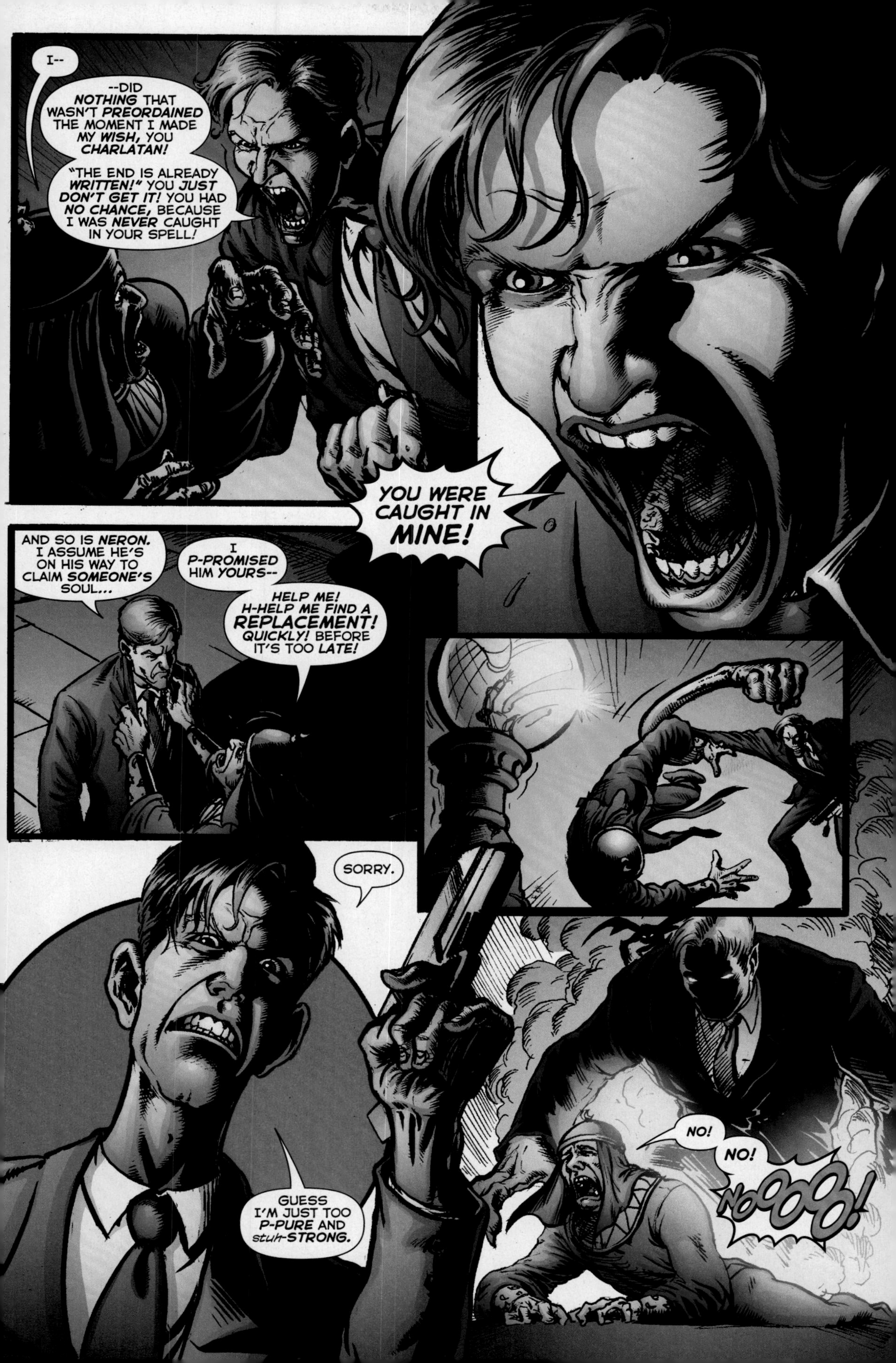
I--
--DID NOTHING THAT WASN'T PREORDAINED THE MOMENT I MADE MY WISH, YOU CHARLATAN!
"THE END IS ALREADY WRITTEN!" YOU JUST DON'T GET IT! YOU HAD NO CHANCE, BECAUSE I WAS NEVER CAUGHT IN YOUR SPELL!
YOU WERE CAUGHT IN MINE!
AND SO IS NERON. I ASSUME HE'S ON HIS WAY TO CLAIM SOMEONE'S SOUL...
I P-PROMISED HIM YOURS--
HELP ME! H-HELP ME FIND A REPLACEMENT! QUICKLY! BEFORE IT'S TOO LATE!
SORRY.
GUESS I'M JUST TOO P-PURE AND stuh-STRONG.
NO!
NO!
NOOOO!

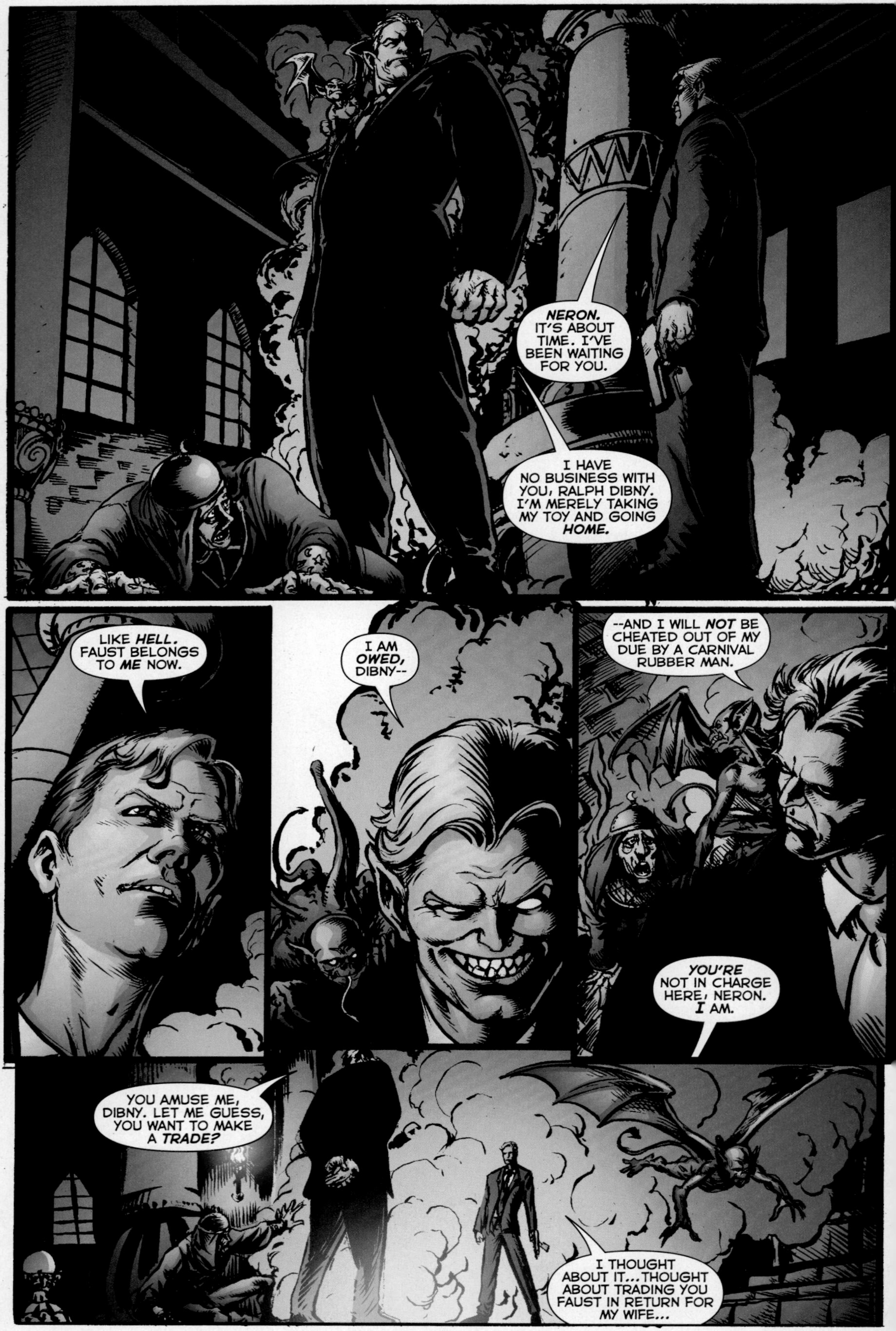
NERON. IT'S ABOUT TIME. I'VE BEEN WAITING FOR YOU.
I HAVE NO BUSINESS WITH YOU, RALPH DIBNY. I'M MERELY TAKING MY TOY AND GOING HOME.
LIKE HELL. FAUST BELONGS TO ME NOW.
I AM OWED, DIBNY--
--AND I WILL NOT BE CHEATED OUT OF MY DUE BY A CARNIVAL RUBBER MAN.
YOU'RE NOT IN CHARGE HERE, NERON. I AM.
YOU AMUSE ME, DIBNY. LET ME GUESS, YOU WANT TO MAKE A TRADE?
I THOUGHT ABOUT IT... THOUGHT ABOUT TRADING YOU FAUST IN RETURN FOR MY WIFE...

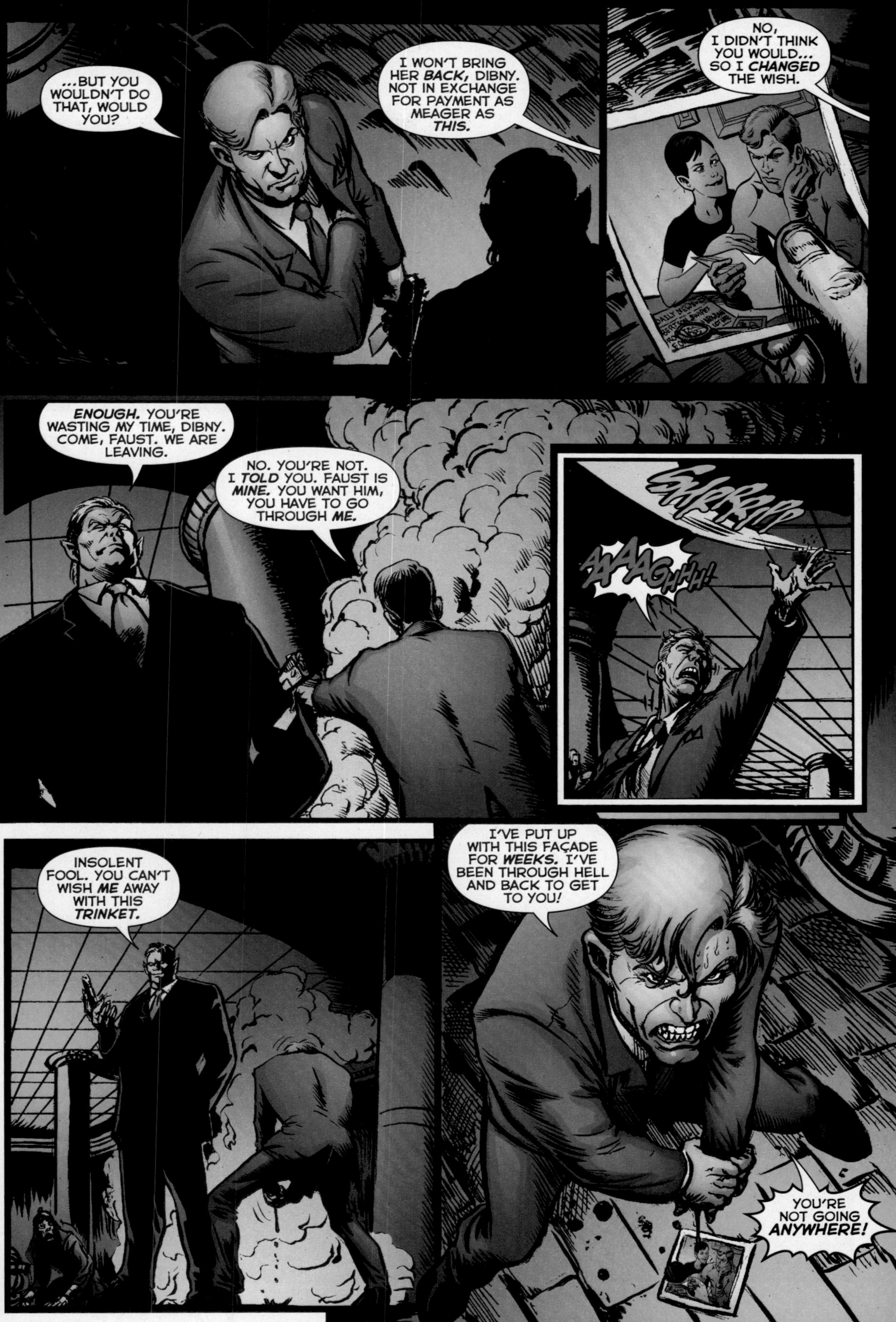
...BUT YOU WOULDN'T DO THAT, WOULD YOU?
I WON'T BRING HER *BACK,* DIBNY. NOT IN EXCHANGE FOR PAYMENT AS MEAGER AS *THIS.*
NO, I DIDN'T THINK YOU WOULD... SO I *CHANGED* THE WISH.
ENOUGH. YOU'RE WASTING MY TIME, DIBNY. COME, FAUST. WE ARE LEAVING.
NO. YOU'RE NOT. I *TOLD* YOU. FAUST IS *MINE.* YOU WANT HIM, YOU HAVE TO GO THROUGH *ME.*
INSOLENT FOOL. YOU CAN'T WISH *ME* AWAY WITH THIS *TRINKET.*
I'VE PUT UP WITH THIS FAÇADE FOR *WEEKS.* I'VE BEEN THROUGH HELL AND BACK TO GET TO YOU!
YOU'RE NOT GOING *ANYWHERE!*

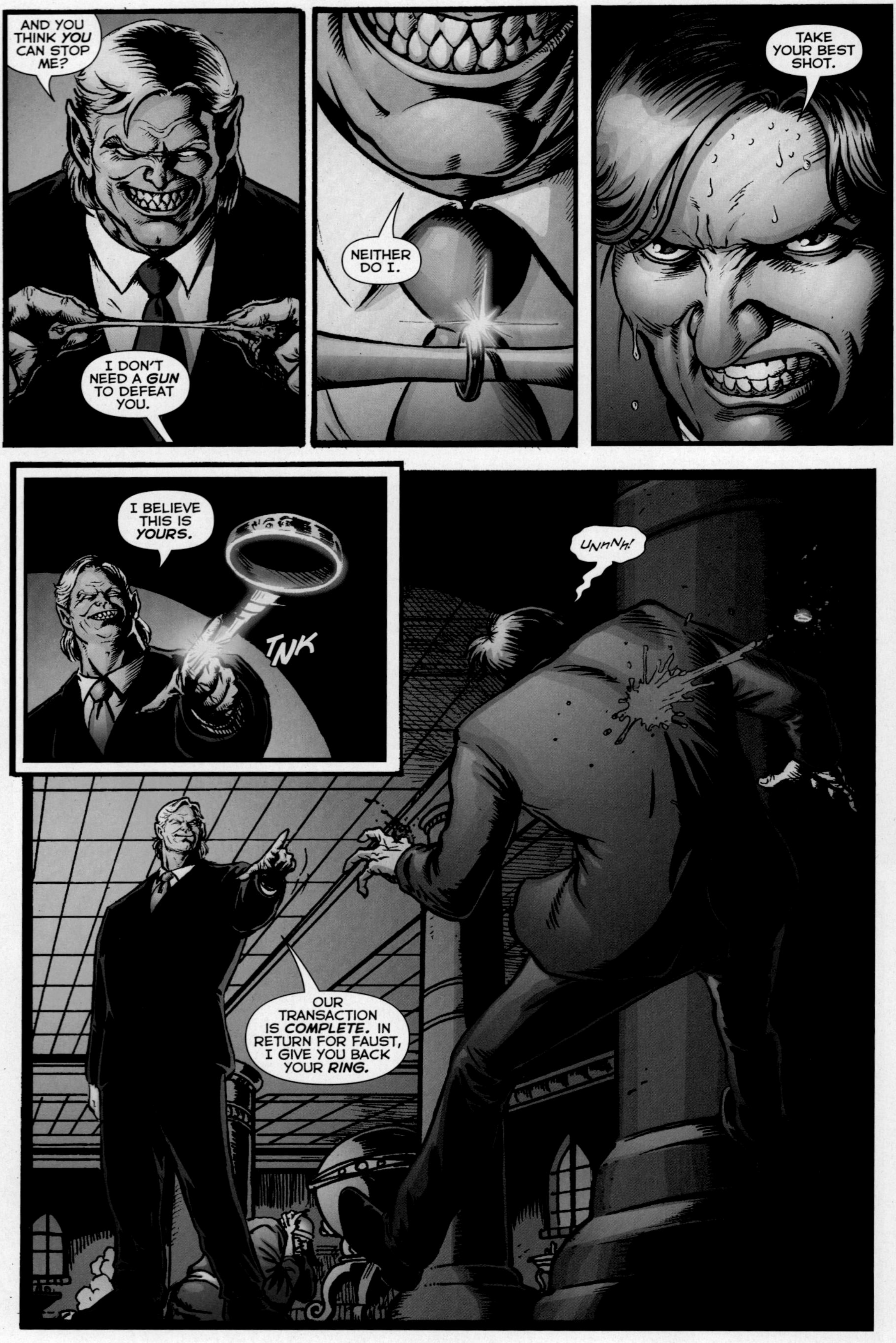
AND YOU THINK YOU CAN STOP ME?
I DON'T NEED A GUN TO DEFEAT YOU.
NEITHER DO I.
TAKE YOUR BEST SHOT.
I BELIEVE THIS IS YOURS.
TNK
UNHNH!
OUR TRANSACTION IS COMPLETE. IN RETURN FOR FAUST, I GIVE YOU BACK YOUR RING.

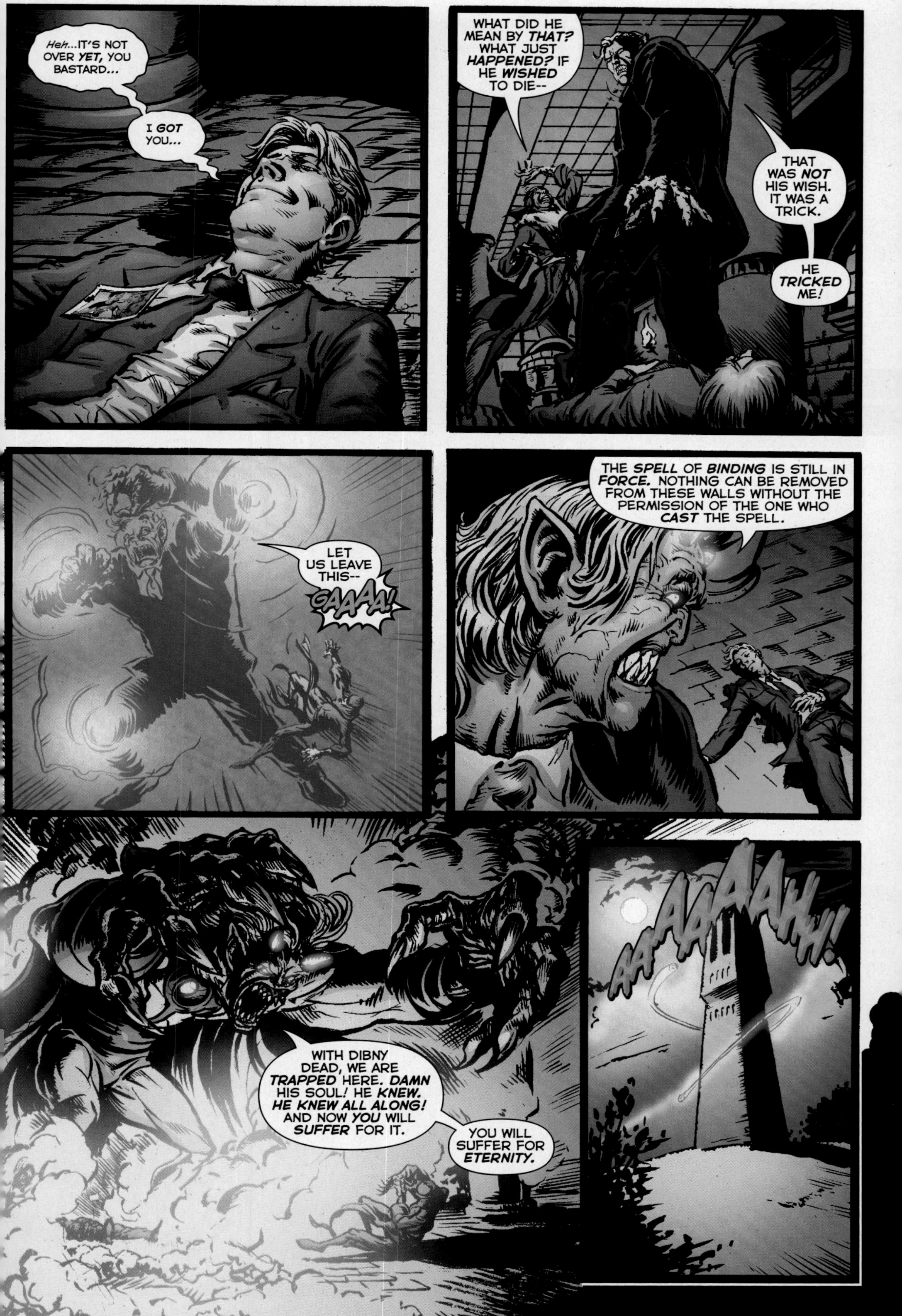
Heh...IT'S NOT OVER YET, YOU BASTARD...
I GOT YOU...
WHAT DID HE MEAN BY THAT? WHAT JUST HAPPENED? IF HE WISHED TO DIE--
THAT WAS NOT HIS WISH. IT WAS A TRICK.
HE TRICKED ME!
LET US LEAVE THIS--
GAAAA!
THE SPELL OF BINDING IS STILL IN FORCE. NOTHING CAN BE REMOVED FROM THESE WALLS WITHOUT THE PERMISSION OF THE ONE WHO CAST THE SPELL.
WITH DIBNY DEAD, WE ARE TRAPPED HERE. DAMN HIS SOUL! HE KNEW. HE KNEW ALL ALONG! AND NOW YOU WILL SUFFER FOR IT.
YOU WILL SUFFER FOR ETERNITY.
AAAAAAAHH!

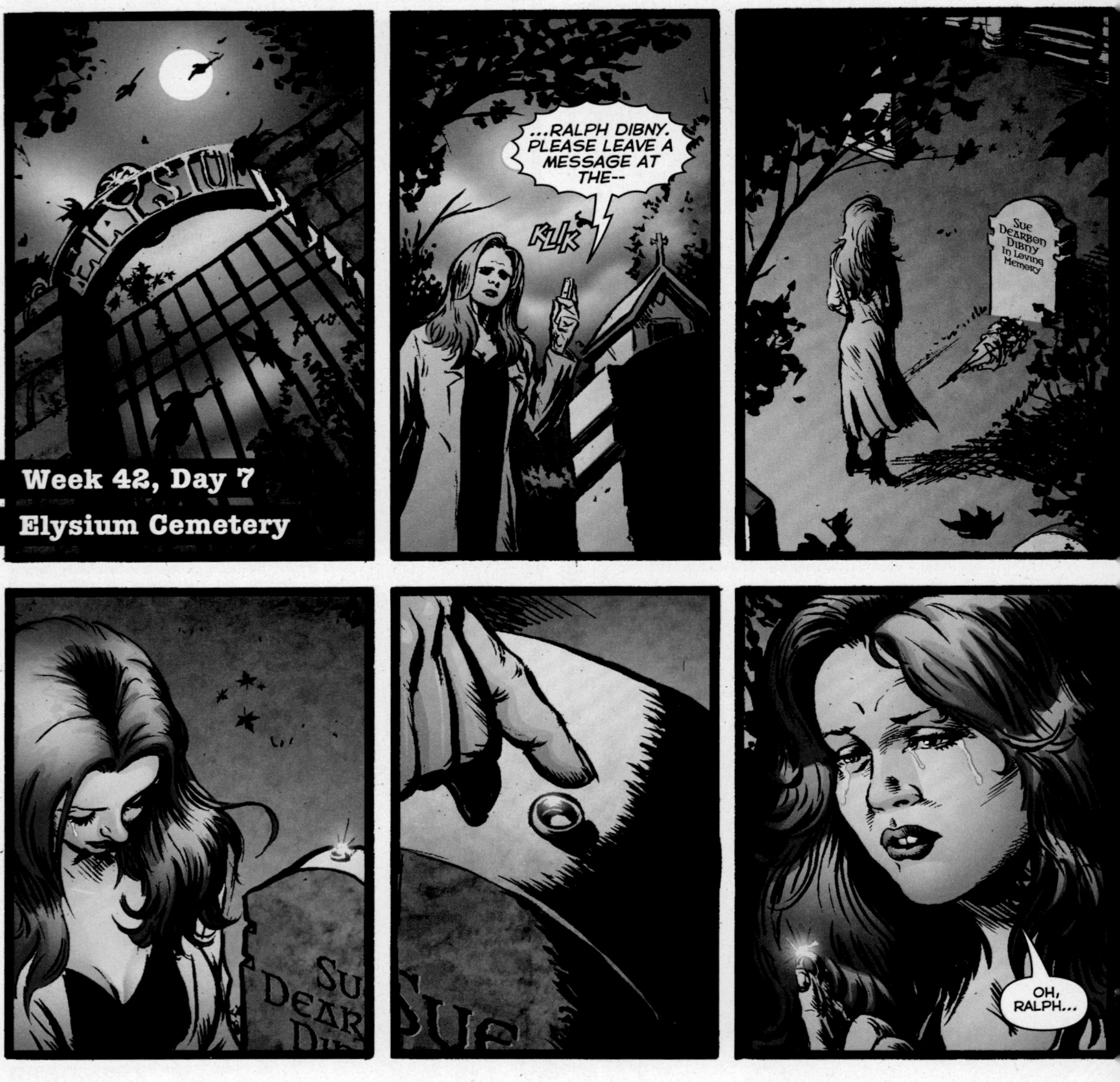
Week 42, Day 7
Elysium Cemetery
...RALPH DIBNY. PLEASE LEAVE A MESSAGE AT THE--
KLIK
Sue Dearbon Dibny In Loving Memory
OH, RALPH...

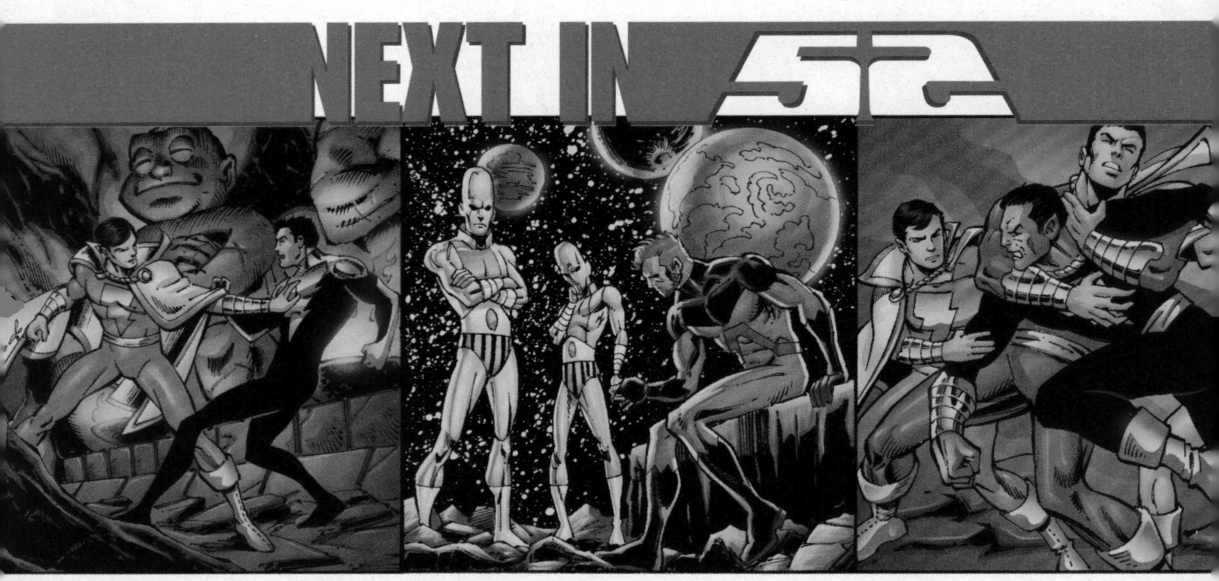
NEXT IN 52

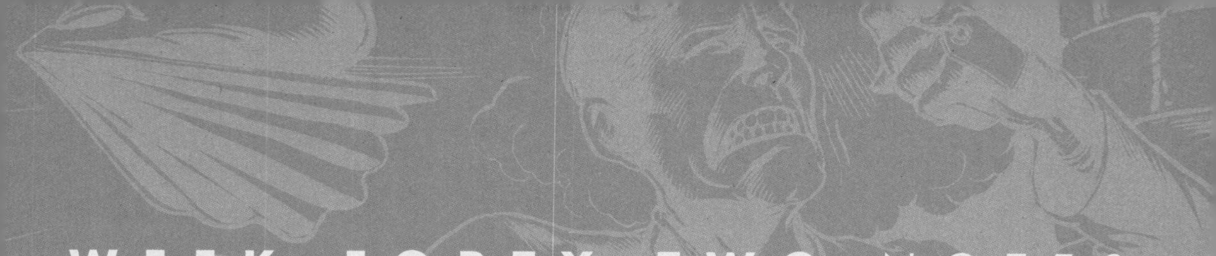

WEEK FORTY-TWO NOTES

DAN DIDIO

Ralph Dibny was always going to die — that was the plan from the moment he was introduced to the series. But *how* he was going to die was a topic that wasn't addressed, as far as I know, until later on.

In one of my earlier commentaries I stated that my greatest contribution to the process of producing this series was staying out of the process of producing this series. That was the way it pretty much worked until we hit this issue.

For me, the death of Ralph and his role as a hero became the focus of several (and sometimes heated) discussions. In my mind, many things needed to be accomplished with this scene. Up until this point Ralph had been led down a long and painful road, he had been beaten, manipulated and thought to have found his wife, only to lose her again. This series was not kind to our once stretchable sleuth. So here, at the end, it was essential for him to meet a hero's death while also obtaining his life's ambition, to be reunited with his lost love, Sue. If not, he was not the hero we all had rooted for and loved for these long years.

This was an emotional moment for everyone, the scene was written and rewritten, and then rewritten again. Faust was revealed as the source of so much of Ralph's pain, and then Neron was revealed to be the demon pulling everyone's strings. With so much being introduced late in the story, and with a main villain not seen or even mentioned until now, it was important that everything didn't feel like it came from out of nowhere. Given the intricacies of the series, that would have felt like a cheat — so while the readers were finding this all out for the first time, Ralph, always a detective first, was way ahead of us.

He had to go out the hero and the husband. The hero beating the unbeatable foe, trapping Neron and Faust, and the husband, who would meet death head on so that he could be reunited with his wife. To achieve these goals and say goodbye to a dear friend in Ralph leads to one of the more frustrating moments in the production of this series. At my request Keith Giffen stepped in and reworked and reboarded the scene of Ralph's death with the complete knowledge of the writing staff. It was a bit of a tense moment, but since everyone involved was uncomfortable with how the story was playing out, the change needed to be made.

Right or wrong, I believe Ralph went out the hero he was meant to be, smarter and better than the devil himself — and as the final issue will prove, his valiant sacrifice will not go unrewarded.

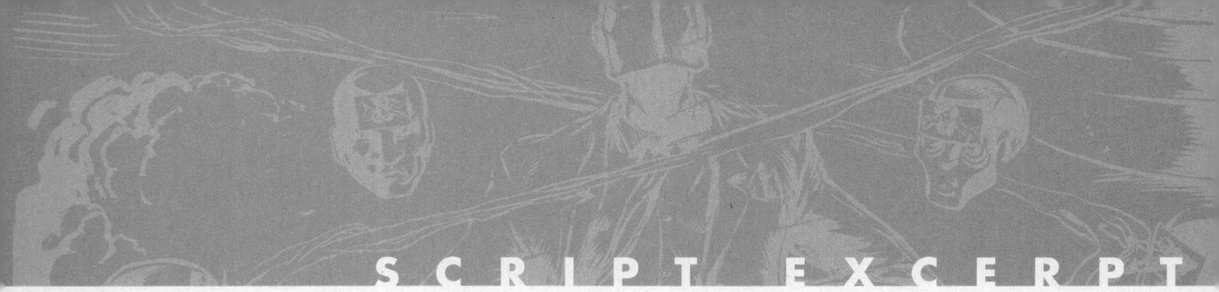
SCRIPT EXCERPT

(COMPARE WITH PAGES 55-56 OF THIS COLLECTION)

52 WEEK FORTY-TWO – PAGE THREE

PANEL ONE
Night. Eastablishing shot, Dr. Fate's Tower. There are two objects circling it at great speed in opposite directions and opposing angles, leaving bright contrails like comets – one gold, one silver.

DATESTAMP: Week 42, Day 3. Salem, Massachusetts

PANEL TWO
Closer, so we can see the actual objects that are in flight – the silver wheel of Nyorlath from last issue and the giant golden chain-link from the Atlantis sequence.

DATESTAMP: The Tower of Fate.

PANEL THREE
Interior, Fate's Tower. Dark, shadowy, torchlit – the usual. We're close on the floating Fate helmet, and in its reflection, we can see (not crystal-clearly, but clearly enough) an image of Ralph swigging high from his flask.

FATE: The hour is upon us, Ralph Dibny. I have taught you all I CAN.

52 WEEK FORTY-TWO – PAGE FOUR

PANEL ONE
Tight on Ralph's trembling hands as he caps the flask.

FATE (off-panel): The next step must be yours and yours alone...

PANEL TWO
Angle on three or four mystic artifacts which hang at about chest-level in mid-air – arcane amulets, magic tomes and scrolls and gems, whatever says "arcane" to you. Ralph's trembling hands enter the shot. One hand holds a snapshot of Sue, and the other has the ball of its thumb pressing the top of the photo to one of the artifacts, like you'd apply a thumbtack. There's a slight glow of magic energy under that thumb, and all the other visible artifacts likewise have snapshots already attached with "magic thumbtacks," if you will.

FATE (off-panel): ...if you are to achieve your HEART'S DESIRE.

PANEL THREE
Big establishing interior. Ralph – clean-shaven and in clean street clothes, as we first saw him (because who wants to meet his wife in the afterlife without looking his best?) – stands upon a large mystic sigil on the stone floor. Tears stream down his face, but he's otherwise rather stoic. Around him, in a circle, hover seven mystic artifacts in total, snapshots attached to all. Most are just of Sue, but at least one must be of Sue and Ralph, happy, laughing, in their prime. The Fate helmet hovers next to him. Important color note: as we did early on with Ralph, we need to keep him in tasteful shades of purple or lavender and maybe white. Nothing garish, just a nod to his classic look.

FATE: I remember your wife FONDLY, Ralph.

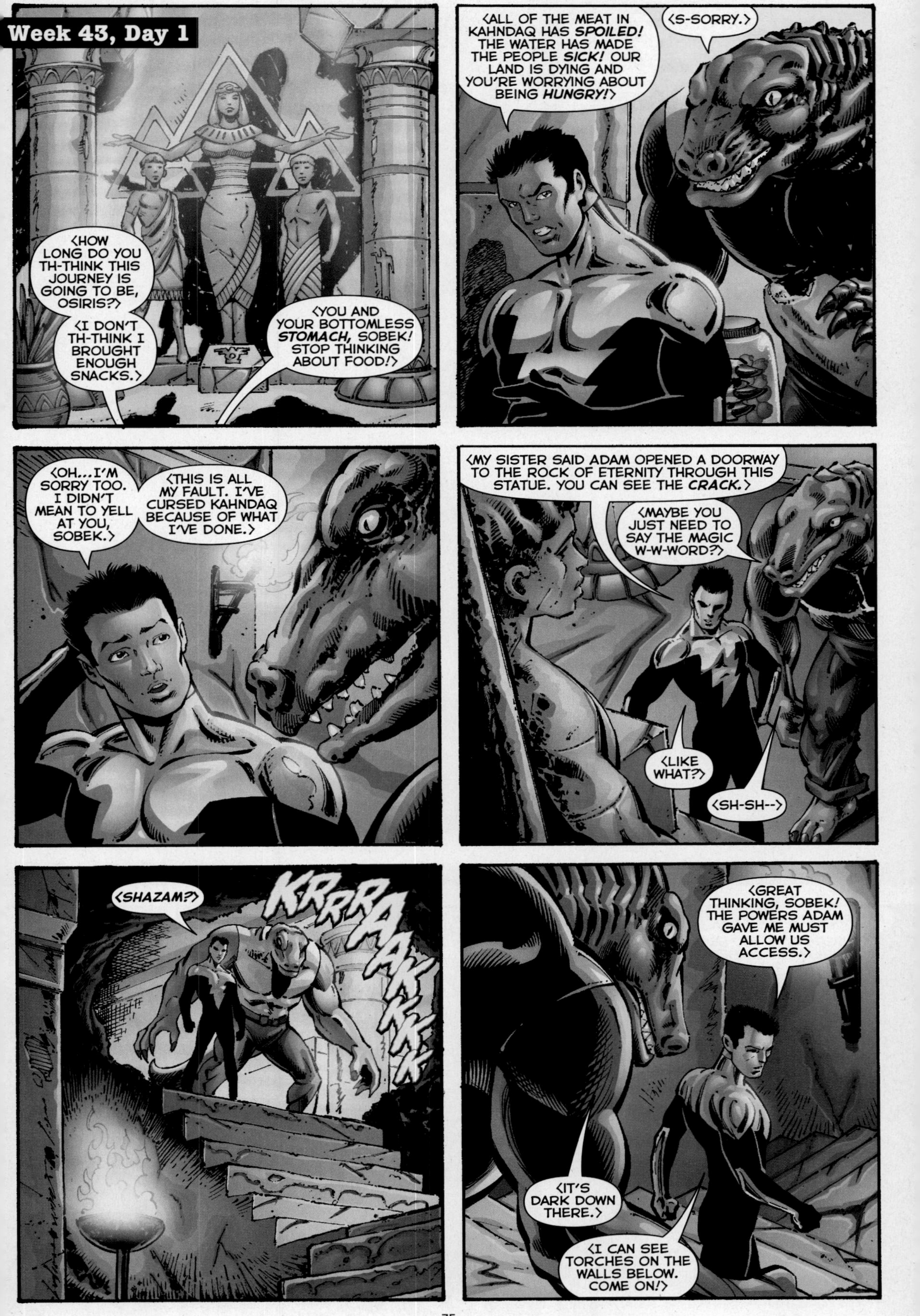
Week 43, Day 1
<HOW LONG DO YOU TH-THINK THIS JOURNEY IS GOING TO BE, OSIRIS?>
<I DON'T TH-THINK I BROUGHT ENOUGH SNACKS.>
<YOU AND YOUR BOTTOMLESS STOMACH, SOBEK! STOP THINKING ABOUT FOOD!>
<ALL OF THE MEAT IN KAHNDAQ HAS SPOILED! THE WATER HAS MADE THE PEOPLE SICK! OUR LAND IS DYING AND YOU'RE WORRYING ABOUT BEING HUNGRY!>
<S-SORRY.>
<OH...I'M SORRY TOO. I DIDN'T MEAN TO YELL AT YOU, SOBEK.>
<THIS IS ALL MY FAULT. I'VE CURSED KAHNDAQ BECAUSE OF WHAT I'VE DONE.>
<MY SISTER SAID ADAM OPENED A DOORWAY TO THE ROCK OF ETERNITY THROUGH THIS STATUE. YOU CAN SEE THE CRACK.>
<MAYBE YOU JUST NEED TO SAY THE MAGIC W-W-WORD?>
<LIKE WHAT?>
<SH-SH-->
<SHAZAM?>
KRRRAAKKKK
<GREAT THINKING, SOBEK! THE POWERS ADAM GAVE ME MUST ALLOW US ACCESS.>
<IT'S DARK DOWN THERE.>
<I CAN SEE TORCHES ON THE WALLS BELOW. COME ON!>

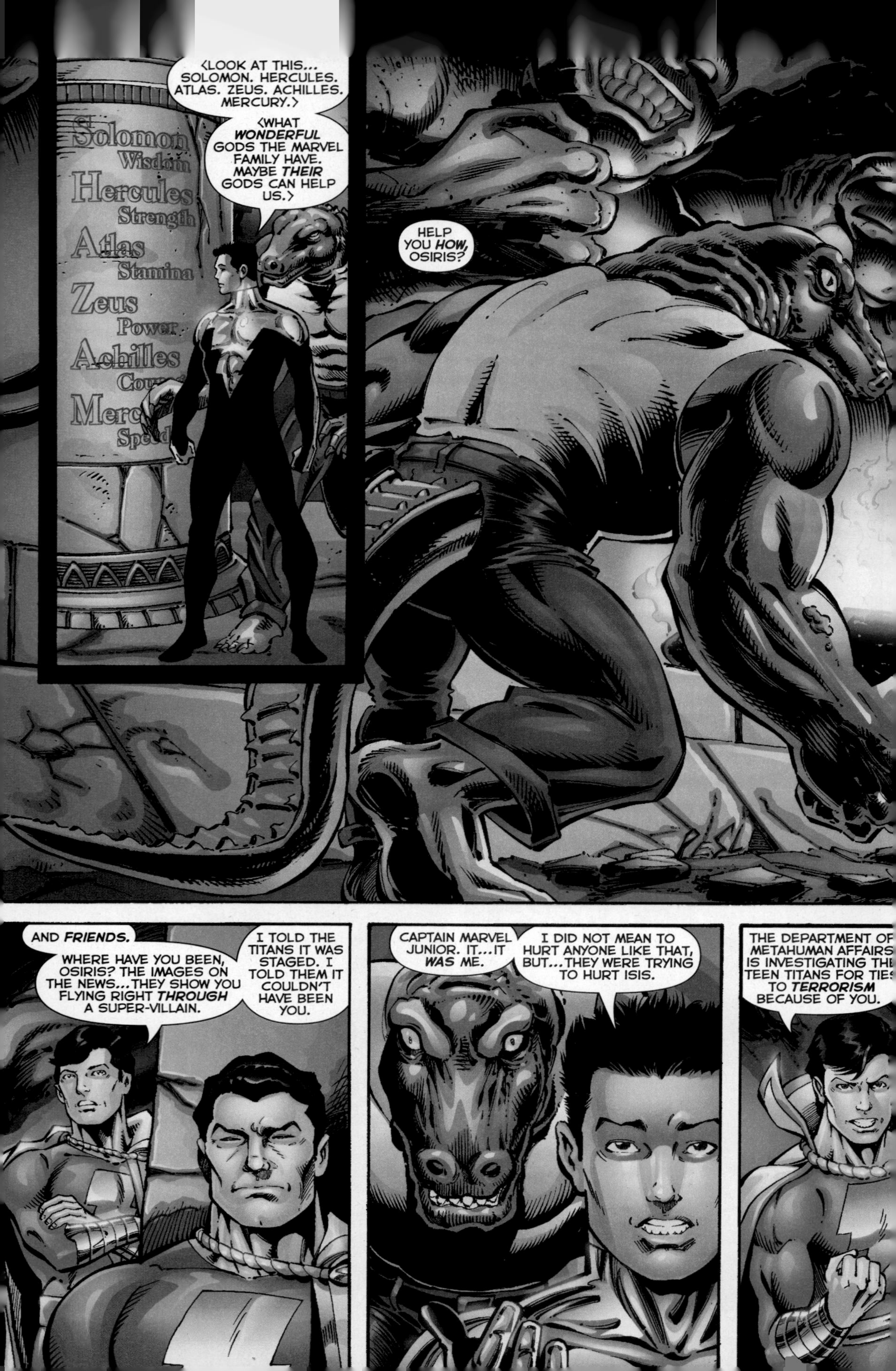
<LOOK AT THIS... SOLOMON. HERCULES. ATLAS. ZEUS. ACHILLES. MERCURY.>
<WHAT WONDERFUL GODS THE MARVEL FAMILY HAVE. MAYBE THEIR GODS CAN HELP US.>
Solomon Wisdom
Hercules Strength
Atlas Stamina
Zeus Power
Achilles
HELP YOU HOW, OSIRIS?
AND FRIENDS.
WHERE HAVE YOU BEEN, OSIRIS? THE IMAGES ON THE NEWS...THEY SHOW YOU FLYING RIGHT THROUGH A SUPER-VILLAIN.
I TOLD THE TITANS IT WAS STAGED. I TOLD THEM IT COULDN'T HAVE BEEN YOU.
CAPTAIN MARVEL JUNIOR. IT...IT WAS ME.
I DID NOT MEAN TO HURT ANYONE LIKE THAT, BUT...THEY WERE TRYING TO HURT ISIS.
THE DEPARTMENT OF METAHUMAN AFFAIRS IS INVESTIGATING THE TEEN TITANS FOR TIES TO TERRORISM BECAUSE OF YOU.

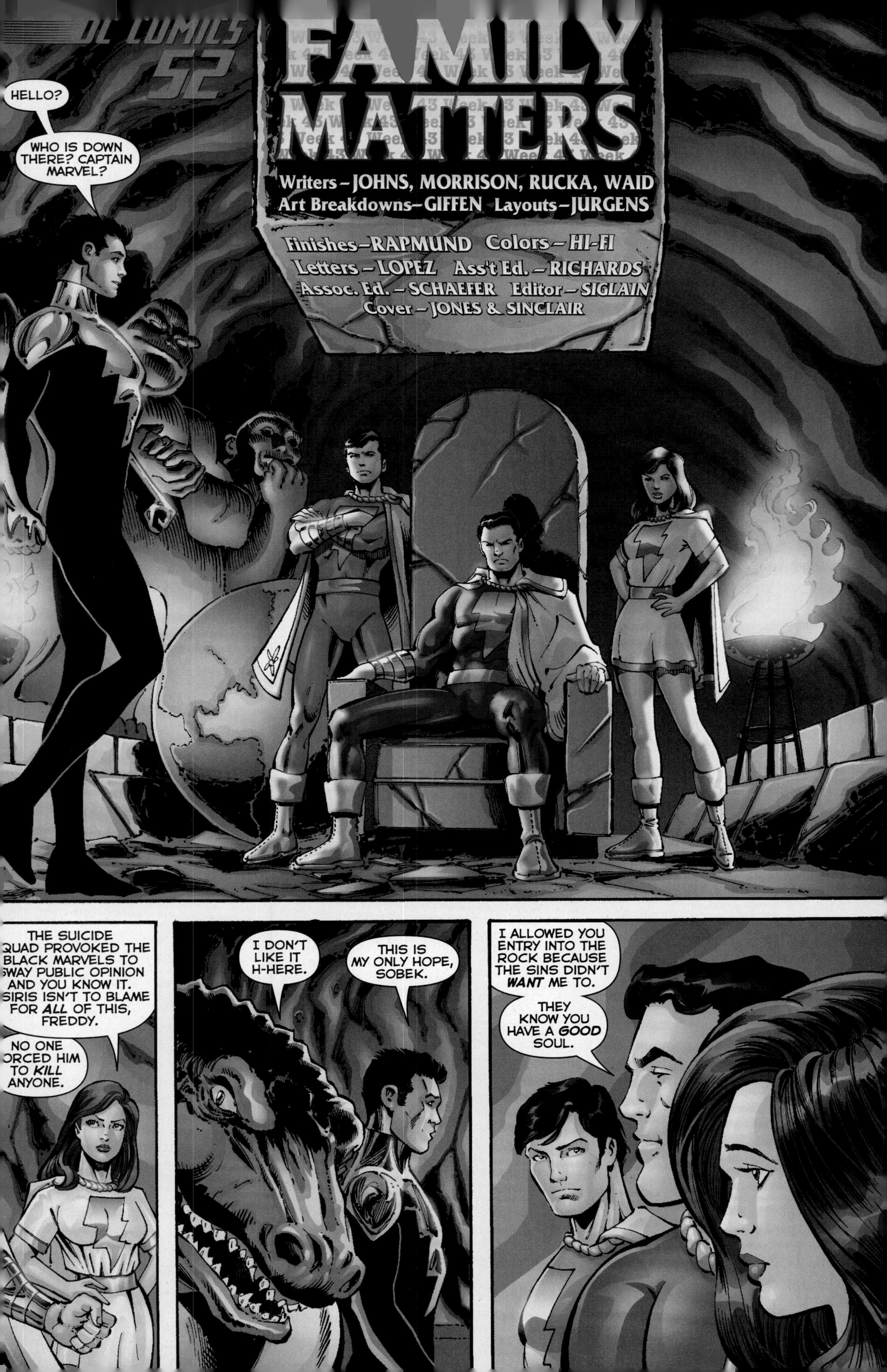
DC COMICS 52
FAMILY MATTERS
Week 43
Writers–JOHNS, MORRISON, RUCKA, WAID
Art Breakdowns–GIFFEN Layouts–JURGENS
Finishes–RAPMUND Colors–HI-FI
Letters–LOPEZ Ass't Ed.–RICHARDS
Assoc. Ed.–SCHAEFER Editor–SIGLAIN
Cover–JONES & SINCLAIR
HELLO?
WHO IS DOWN THERE? CAPTAIN MARVEL?
THE SUICIDE QUAD PROVOKED THE BLACK MARVELS TO SWAY PUBLIC OPINION AND YOU KNOW IT. SIRIS ISN'T TO BLAME FOR ALL OF THIS, FREDDY.
NO ONE ORCED HIM TO KILL ANYONE.
I DON'T LIKE IT H-HERE.
THIS IS MY ONLY HOPE, SOBEK.
I ALLOWED YOU ENTRY INTO THE ROCK BECAUSE THE SINS DIDN'T WANT ME TO.
THEY KNOW YOU HAVE A GOOD SOUL.

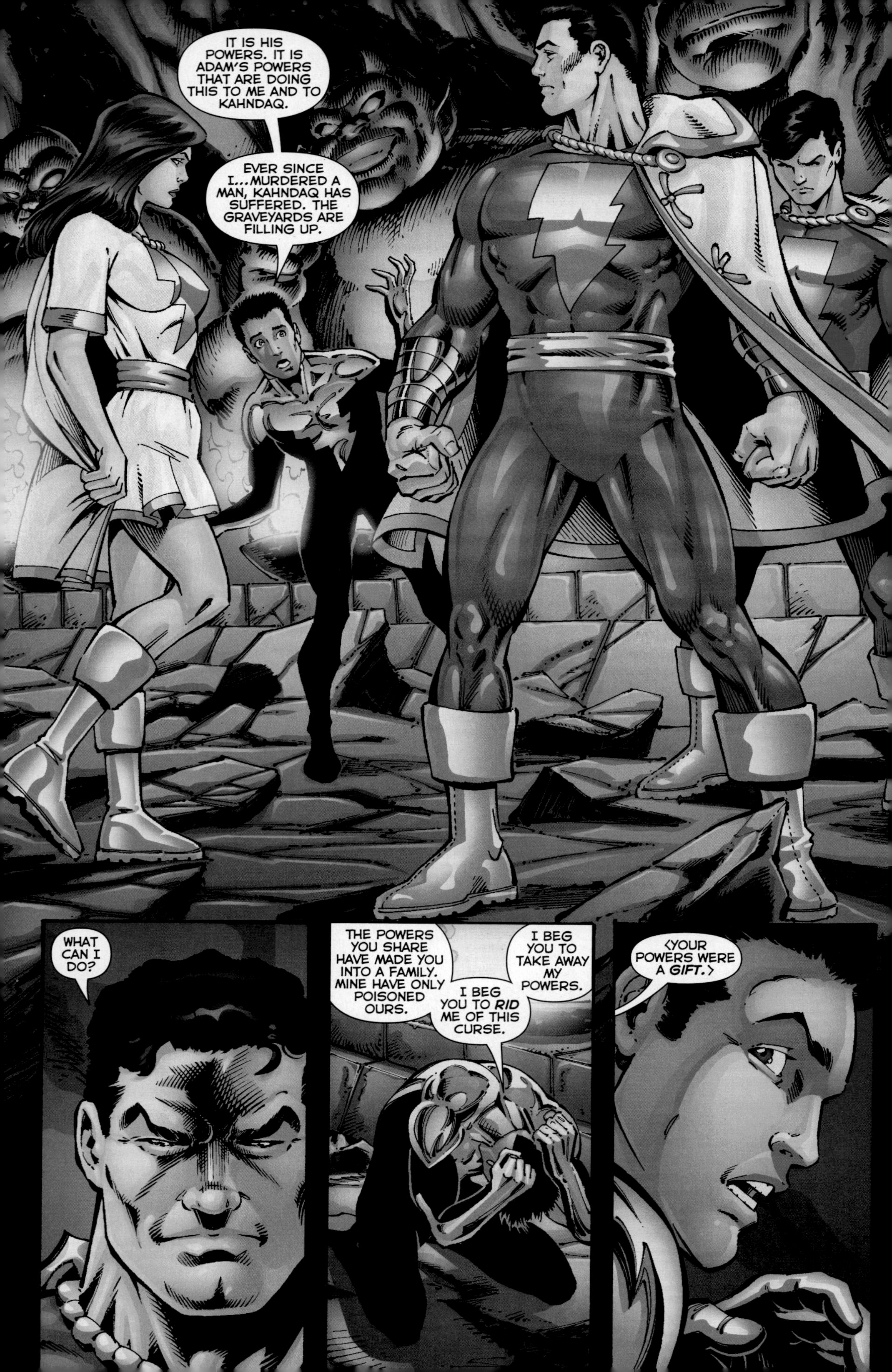
IT IS HIS POWERS. IT IS ADAM'S POWERS THAT ARE DOING THIS TO ME AND TO KAHNDAQ.
EVER SINCE I...MURDERED A MAN, KAHNDAQ HAS SUFFERED. THE GRAVEYARDS ARE FILLING UP.
WHAT CAN I DO?
THE POWERS YOU SHARE HAVE MADE YOU INTO A FAMILY. MINE HAVE ONLY POISONED OURS.
I BEG YOU TO TAKE AWAY MY POWERS.
I BEG YOU TO RID ME OF THIS CURSE.
<YOUR POWERS WERE A GIFT.>

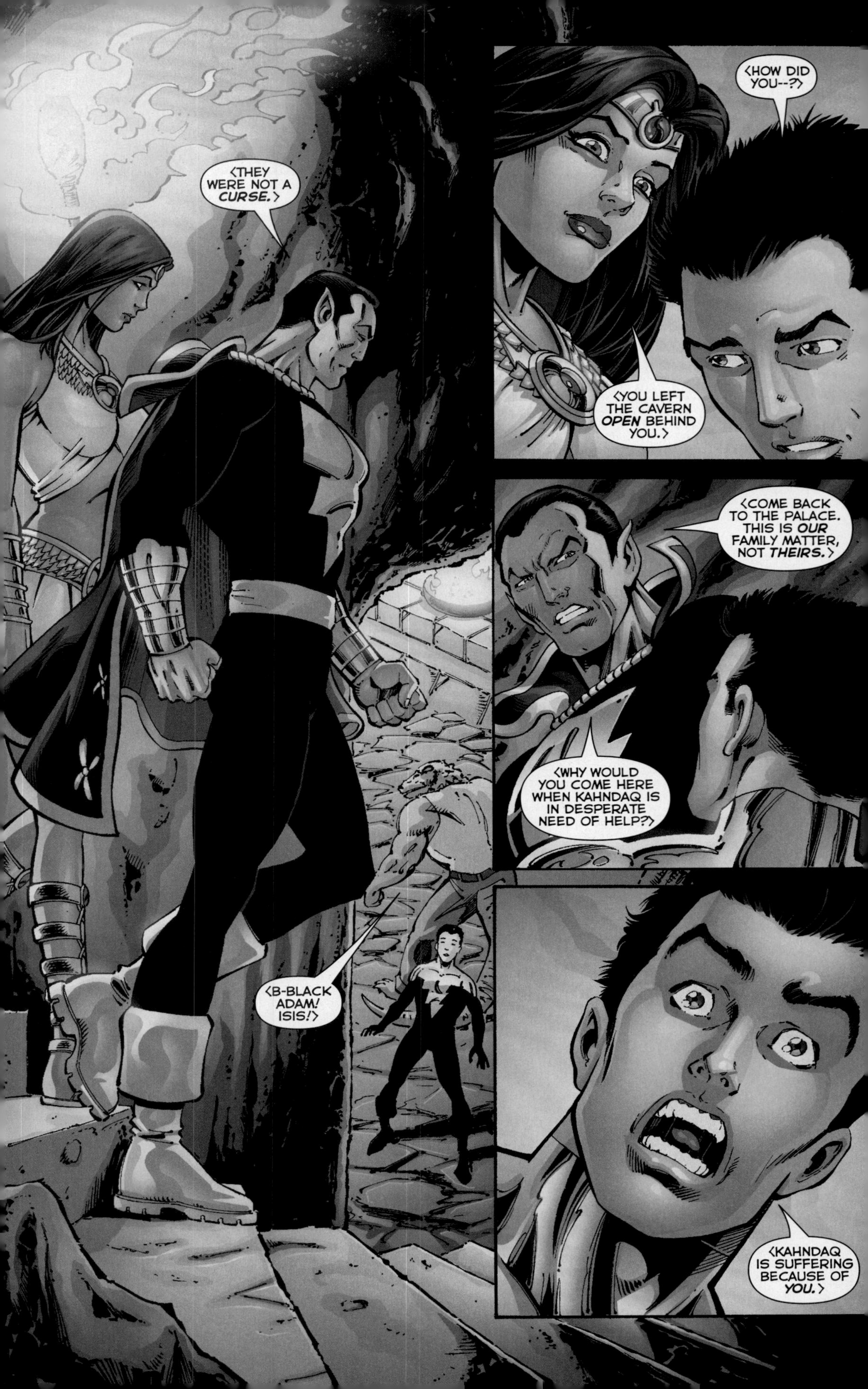

‹THEY WERE NOT A *CURSE.*›
‹B-BLACK ADAM! ISIS!›
‹HOW DID YOU--?›
‹YOU LEFT THE CAVERN *OPEN* BEHIND YOU.›
‹COME BACK TO THE PALACE. THIS IS *OUR* FAMILY MATTER, NOT *THEIRS.*›
‹WHY WOULD YOU COME HERE WHEN KAHNDAQ IS IN DESPERATE NEED OF HELP?›
‹KAHNDAQ IS SUFFERING BECAUSE OF *YOU.*›

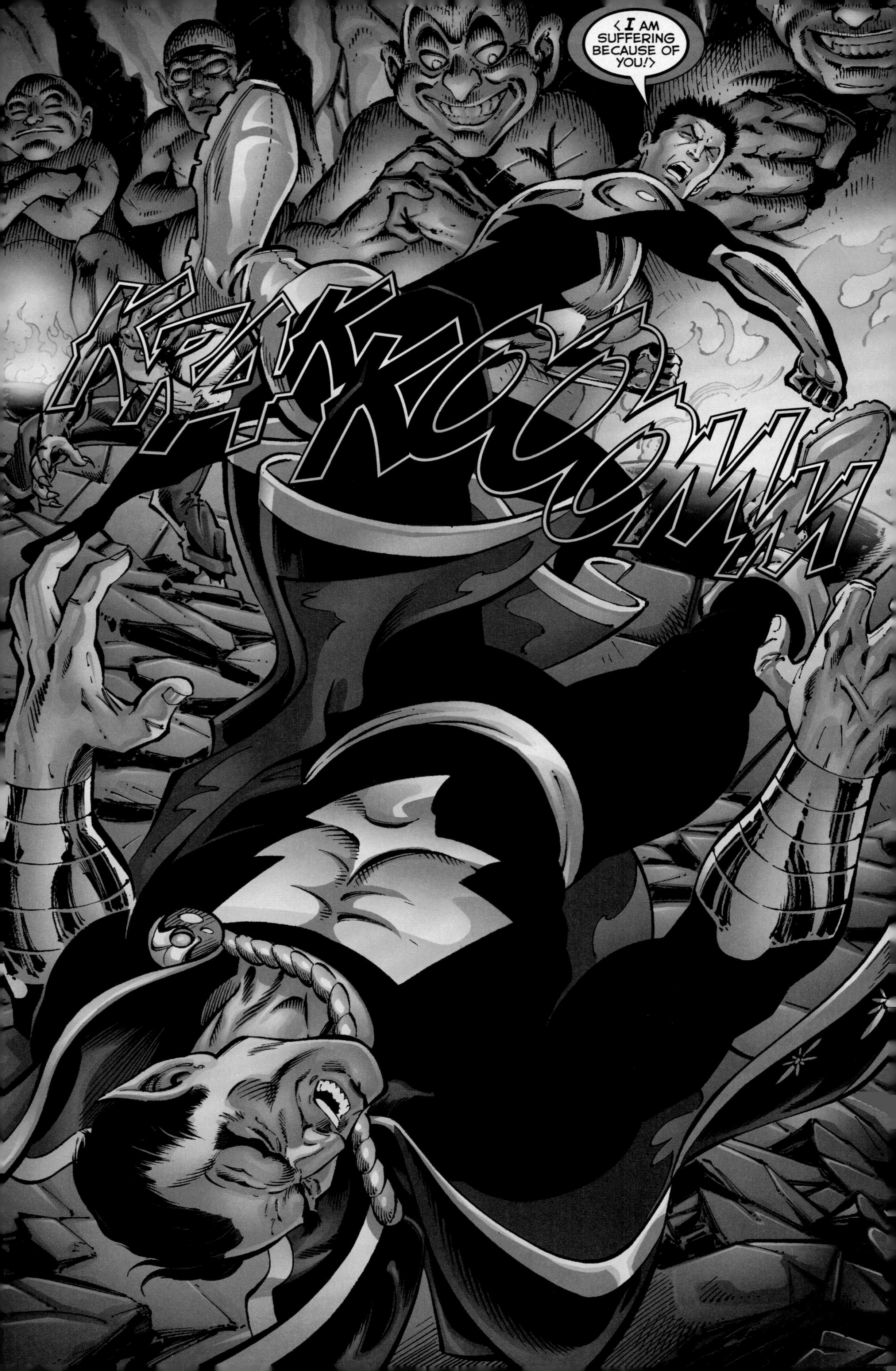
<I AM SUFFERING BECAUSE OF YOU!>

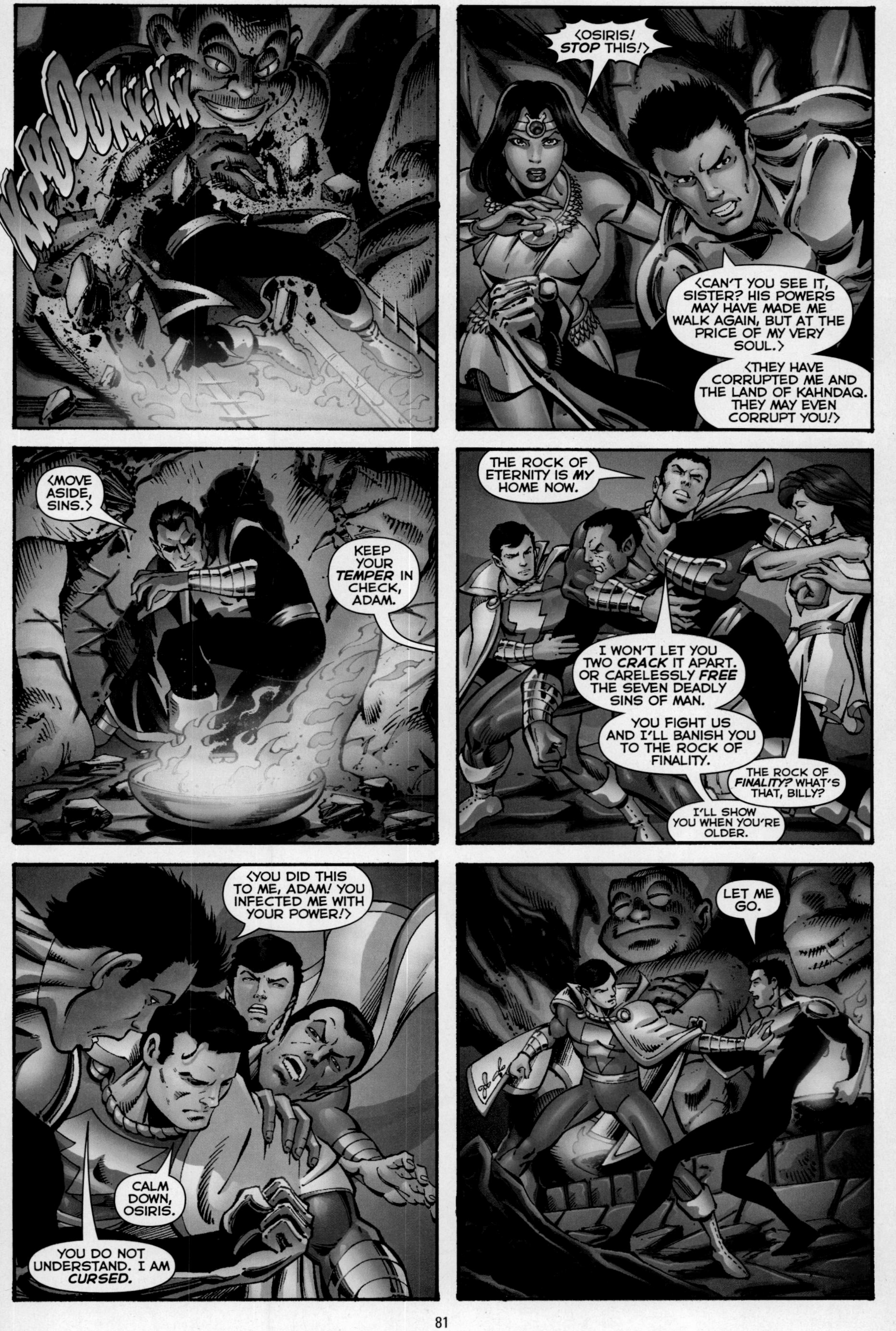
KRROOOKK-KK
‹OSIRIS! STOP THIS!›
‹CAN'T YOU SEE IT, SISTER? HIS POWERS MAY HAVE MADE ME WALK AGAIN, BUT AT THE PRICE OF MY VERY SOUL.›
‹THEY HAVE CORRUPTED ME AND THE LAND OF KAHNDAQ. THEY MAY EVEN CORRUPT YOU!›
‹MOVE ASIDE, SINS.›
KEEP YOUR TEMPER IN CHECK, ADAM.
THE ROCK OF ETERNITY IS MY HOME NOW.
I WON'T LET YOU TWO CRACK IT APART. OR CARELESSLY FREE THE SEVEN DEADLY SINS OF MAN.
YOU FIGHT US AND I'LL BANISH YOU TO THE ROCK OF FINALITY.
THE ROCK OF FINALITY? WHAT'S THAT, BILLY?
I'LL SHOW YOU WHEN YOU'RE OLDER.
‹YOU DID THIS TO ME, ADAM! YOU INFECTED ME WITH YOUR POWER!›
CALM DOWN, OSIRIS.
YOU DO NOT UNDERSTAND. I AM CURSED.
LET ME GO.

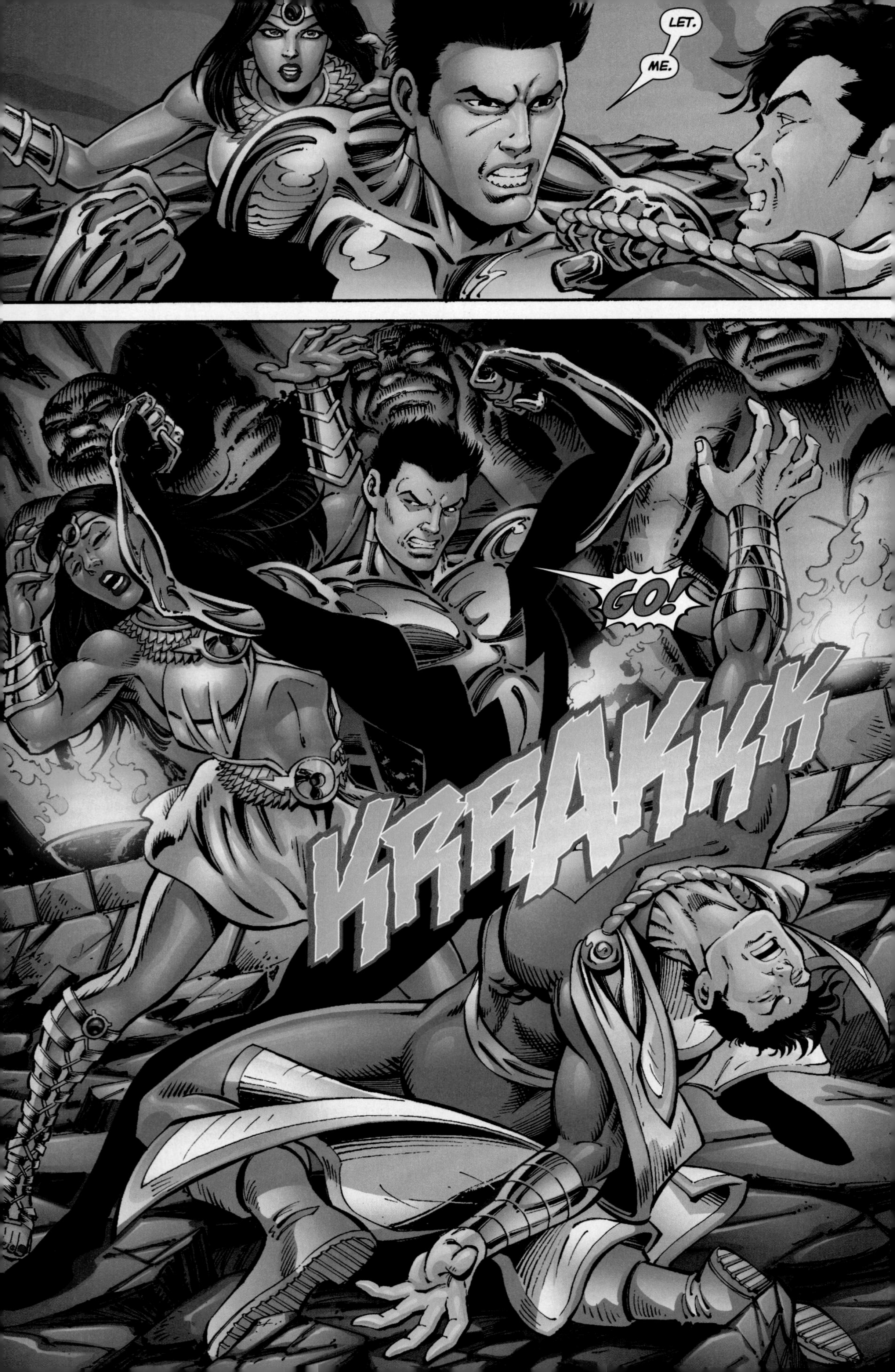
LET.
ME.
GO!
KRRAKKK

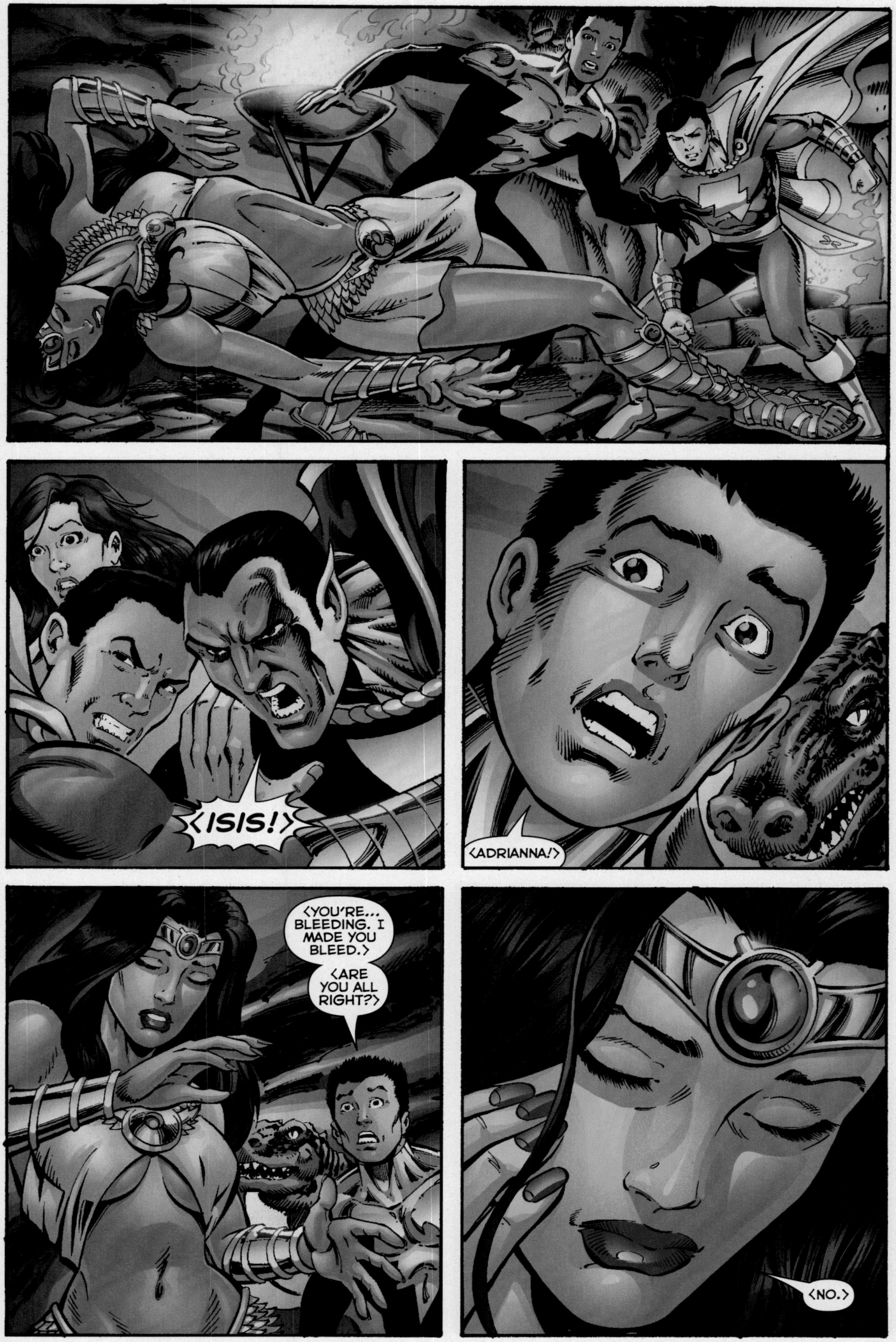
<ISIS!>
<ADRIANNA!>
<YOU'RE... BLEEDING. I MADE YOU BLEED.>
<ARE YOU ALL RIGHT?>
<NO.>

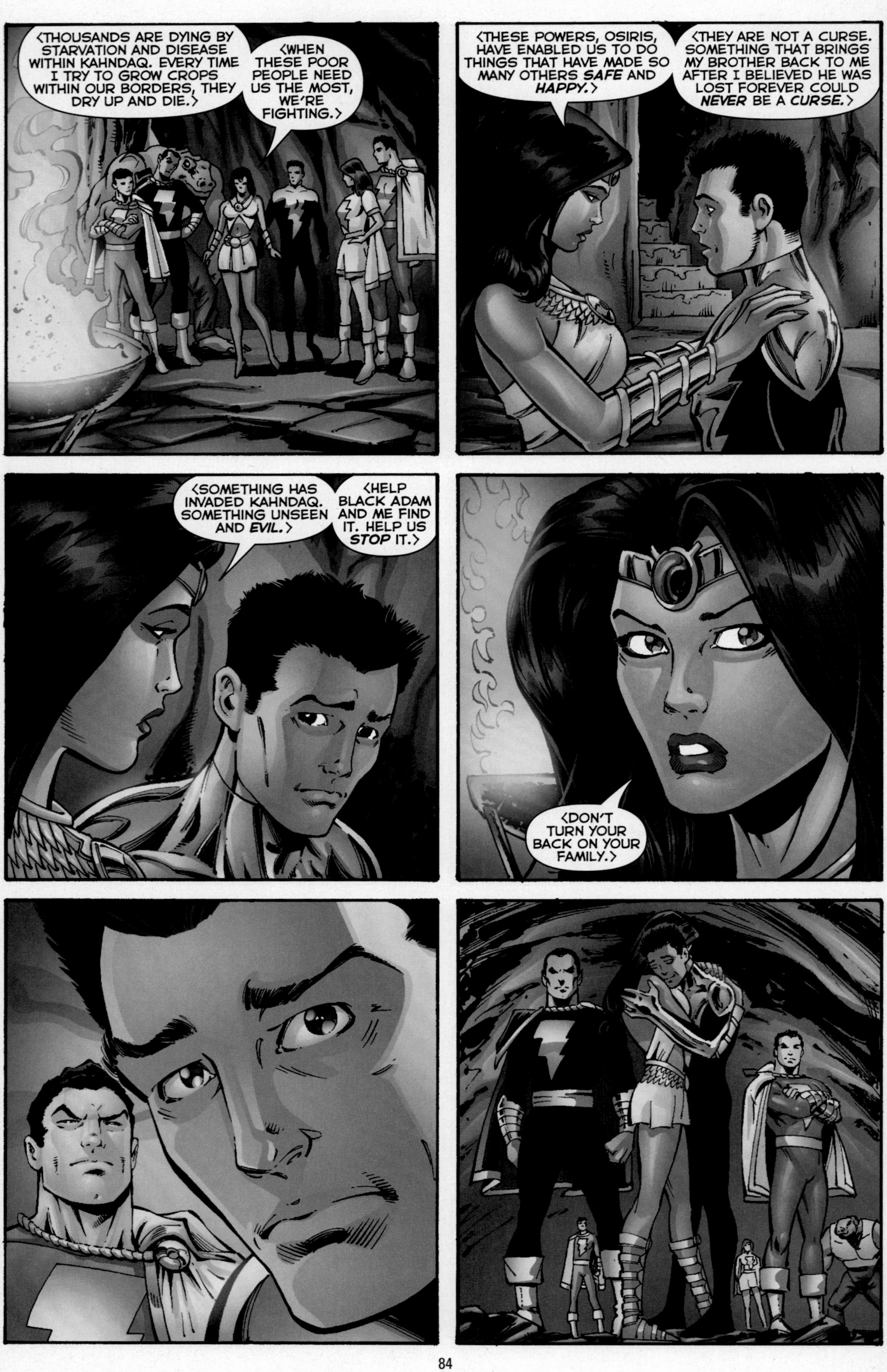

<THOUSANDS ARE DYING BY STARVATION AND DISEASE WITHIN KAHNDAQ. EVERY TIME I TRY TO GROW CROPS WITHIN OUR BORDERS, THEY DRY UP AND DIE.>
<WHEN THESE POOR PEOPLE NEED US THE MOST, WE'RE FIGHTING.>
<THESE POWERS, OSIRIS, HAVE ENABLED US TO DO THINGS THAT HAVE MADE SO MANY OTHERS SAFE AND HAPPY.>
<THEY ARE NOT A CURSE. SOMETHING THAT BRINGS MY BROTHER BACK TO ME AFTER I BELIEVED HE WAS LOST FOREVER COULD NEVER BE A CURSE.>
<SOMETHING HAS INVADED KAHNDAQ. SOMETHING UNSEEN AND EVIL.>
<HELP BLACK ADAM AND ME FIND IT. HELP US STOP IT.>
<DON'T TURN YOUR BACK ON YOUR FAMILY.>

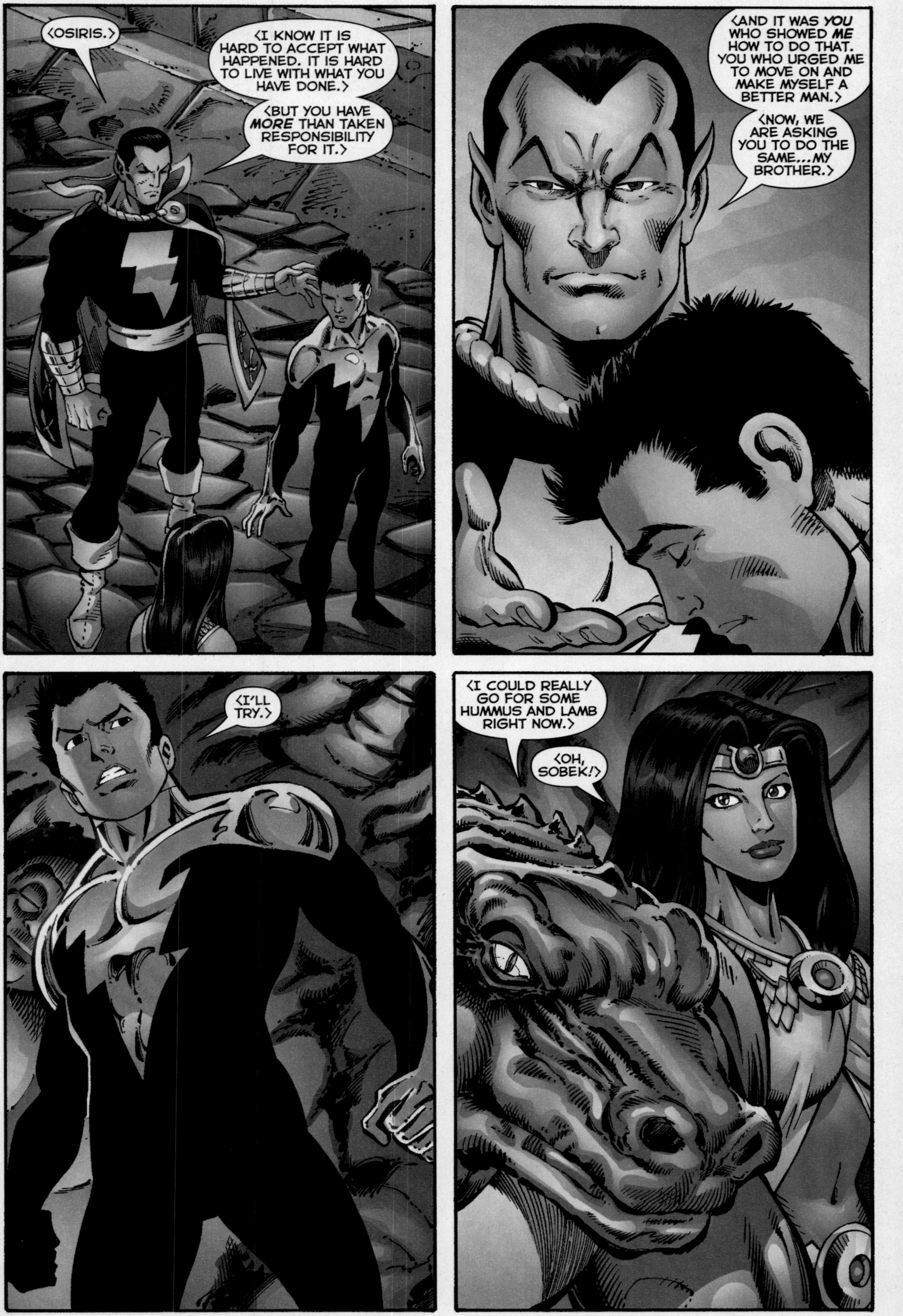
<OSIRIS.>
<I KNOW IT IS HARD TO ACCEPT WHAT HAPPENED. IT IS HARD TO LIVE WITH WHAT YOU HAVE DONE.>
<BUT YOU HAVE *MORE* THAN TAKEN RESPONSIBILITY FOR IT.>
<AND IT WAS *YOU* WHO SHOWED *ME* HOW TO DO THAT. YOU WHO URGED ME TO MOVE ON AND MAKE MYSELF A BETTER MAN.>
<NOW, WE ARE ASKING YOU TO DO THE SAME... MY BROTHER.>
<I'LL TRY.>
<I COULD REALLY GO FOR SOME HUMMUS AND LAMB RIGHT NOW.>
<OH, SOBEK!>

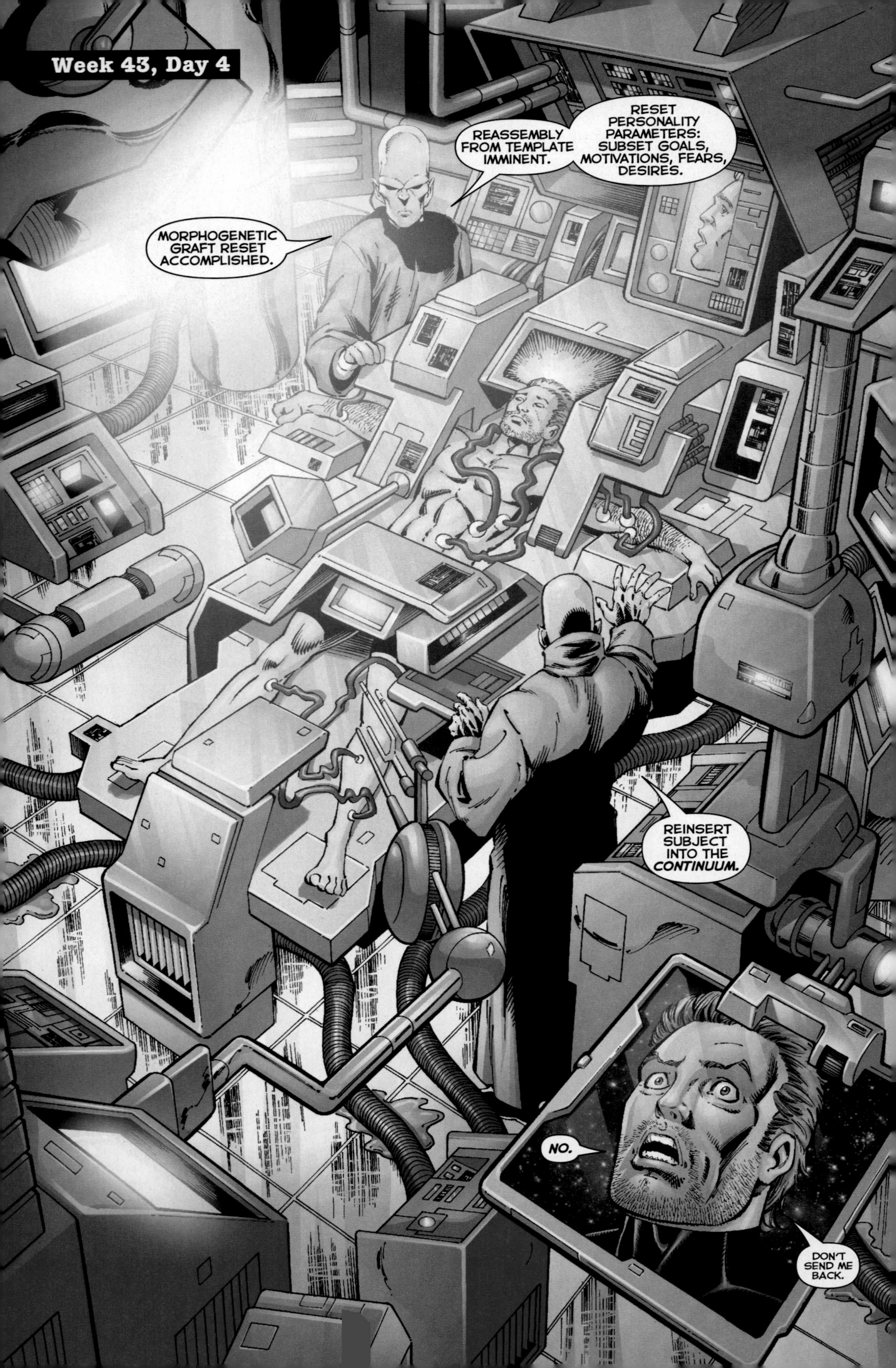
Week 43, Day 4
MORPHOGENETIC GRAFT RESET ACCOMPLISHED.
REASSEMBLY FROM TEMPLATE IMMINENT.
RESET PERSONALITY PARAMETERS: SUBSET GOALS, MOTIVATIONS, FEARS, DESIRES.
REINSERT SUBJECT INTO THE CONTINUUM.
NO.
DON'T SEND ME BACK.

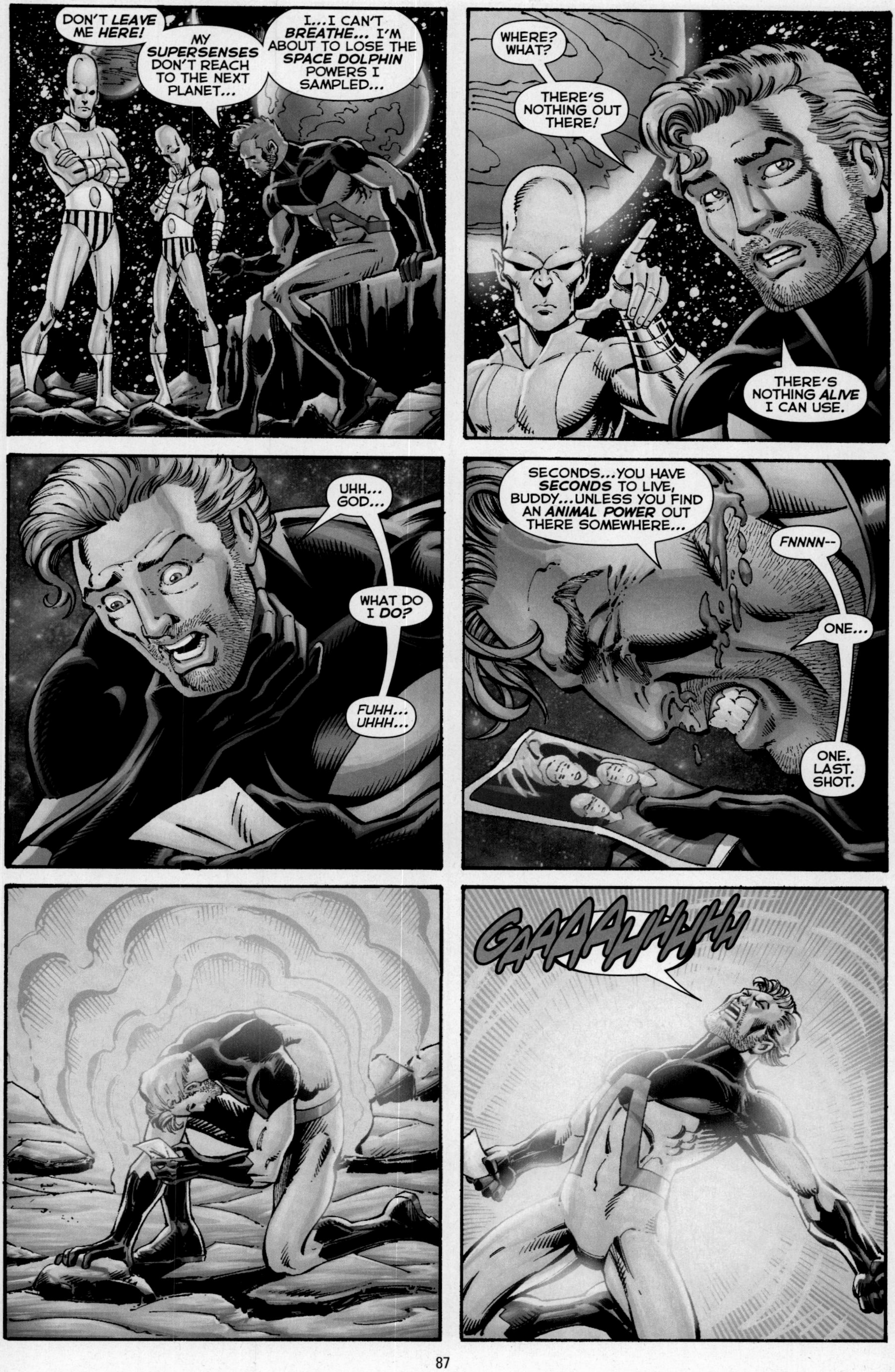

DON'T LEAVE ME HERE!
MY SUPERSENSES DON'T REACH TO THE NEXT PLANET...
I...I CAN'T BREATHE... I'M ABOUT TO LOSE THE SPACE DOLPHIN POWERS I SAMPLED...
WHERE? WHAT?
THERE'S NOTHING OUT THERE!
THERE'S NOTHING ALIVE I CAN USE.
UHH... GOD...
WHAT DO I DO?
FUHH... UHHH...
SECONDS...YOU HAVE SECONDS TO LIVE, BUDDY...UNLESS YOU FIND AN ANIMAL POWER OUT THERE SOMEWHERE...
FNNNN--
ONE...
ONE. LAST. SHOT.
GAAAAHHHH

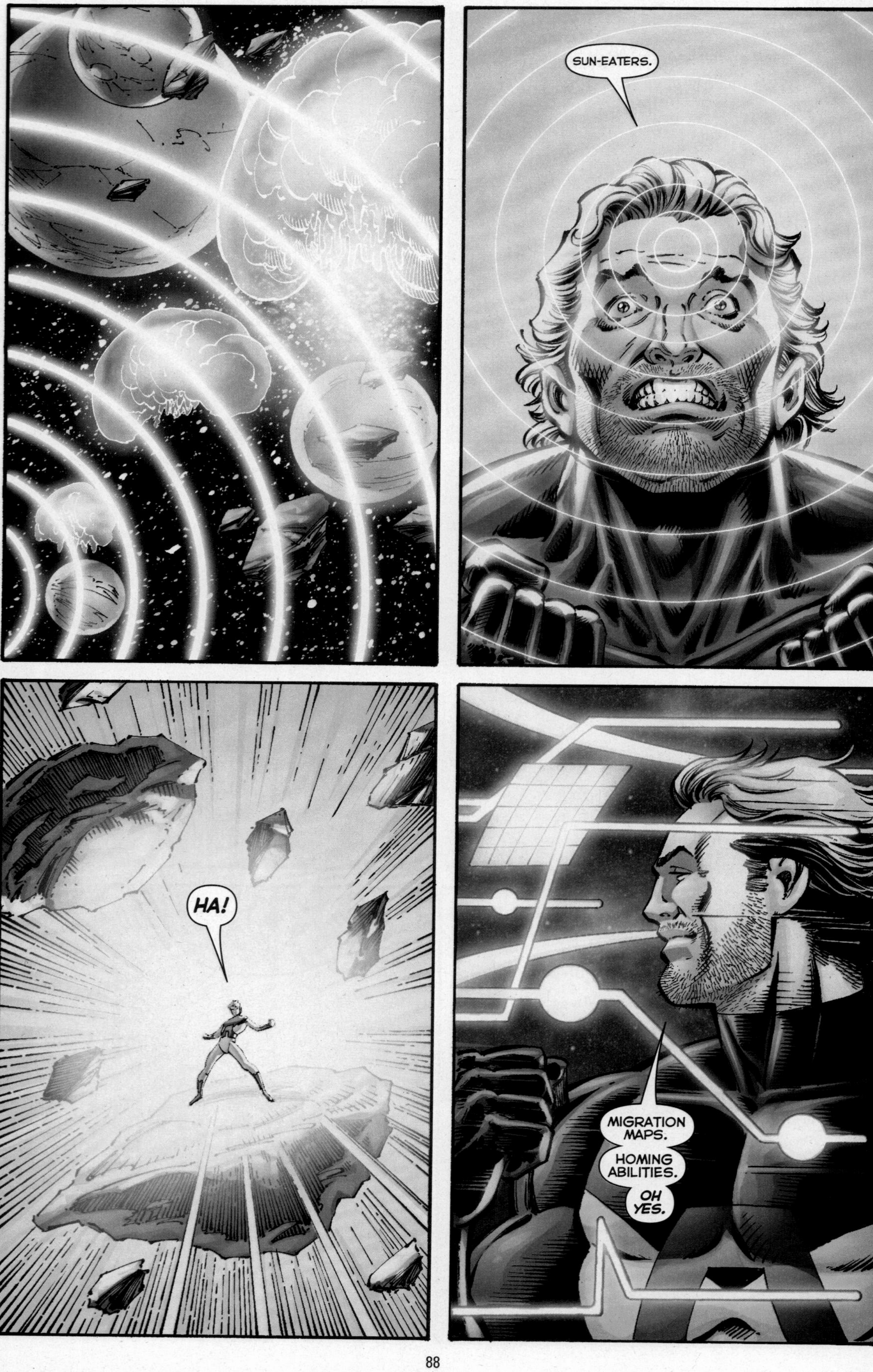
SUN-EATERS.
HA!
MIGRATION MAPS.
HOMING ABILITIES.
OH YES.

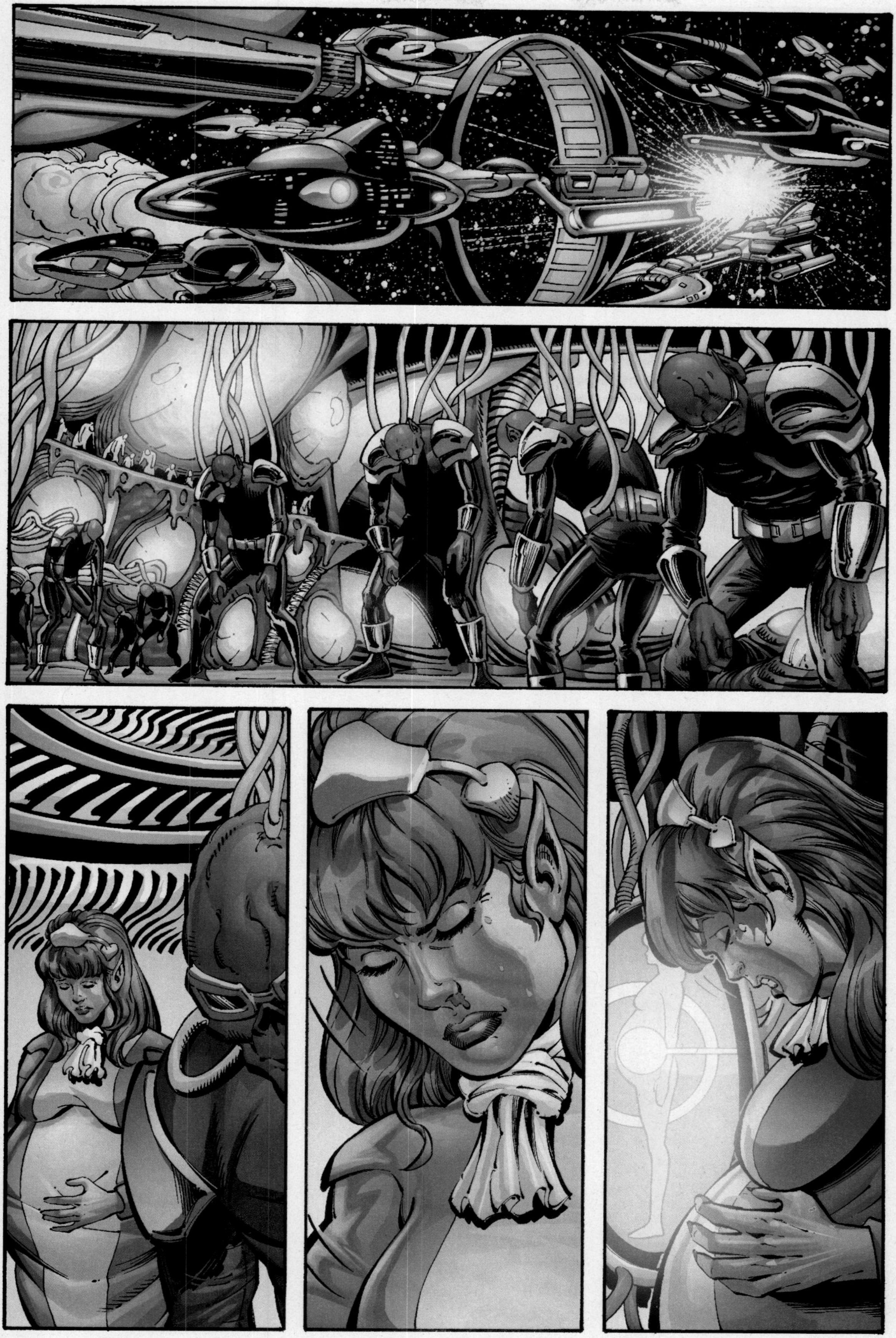

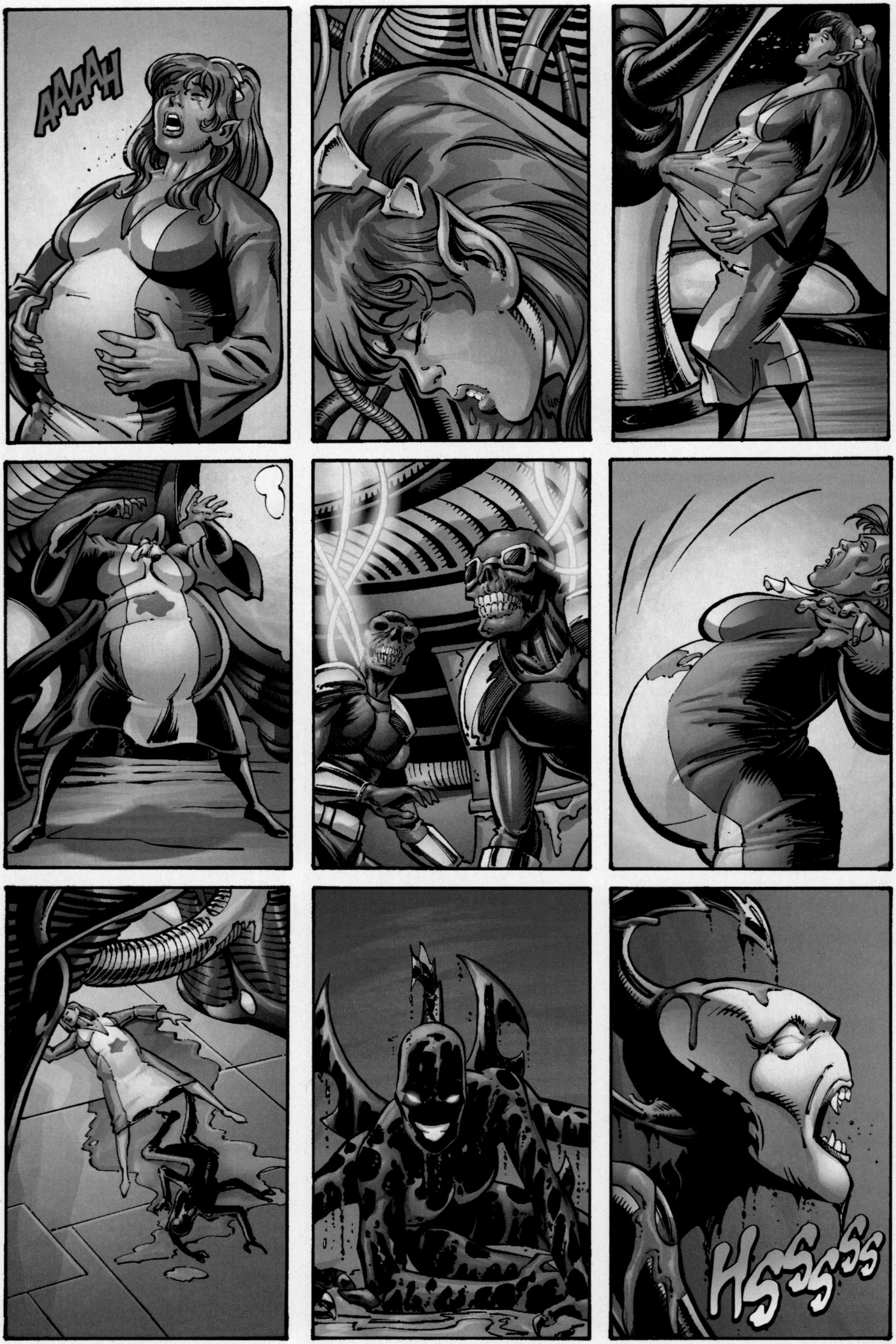
AAAAH
HSSSSS

<OSIRIS?>

Week 43, Day 5

Kahndaq

<WHAT ARE YOU DOING UP HERE? I TH-THOUGHT YOU WERE MEETING BLACK ADAM AND ISIS.>

<THEY'RE GOING TO DIG A NEW R-R-RIVER THROUGH TOWN. THEY KEEP DRYING UP, BUT...>

<I'M NOT GOING. I'M LEAVING KAHNDAQ.>

<W-W-WHAT? WHAT ABOUT WHAT YOU SAID? AT THE ROCK OF ETERNITY?>

<I SAID WHAT THEY WANTED TO HEAR. THAT'S ALL.>

<ADAM MAY BE ABLE TO LIVE WITH WHAT HE DID BUT I CAN'T. AS LONG AS I HAVE THESE POWERS I NEED TO BE FAR AWAY FROM ANYONE--->

<B-BUT THAT'S IT, OSIRIS!>

<YOU CAN RID YOURSELF OF YOUR POWERS. YOU CAN SPEAK BLACK ADAM'S NAME AND RID YOURSELF OF THE CURSE.>

<BUT THEN... OH, OSIRIS...YOU WILL NOT BE ABLE TO WALK.>

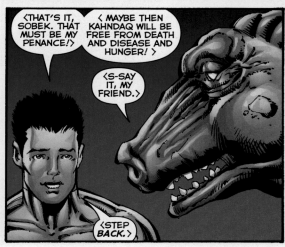

<THAT'S IT, SOBEK. THAT MUST BE MY PENANCE!>

<MAYBE THEN KAHNDAQ WILL BE FREE FROM DEATH AND DISEASE AND HUNGER!>

<S-SAY IT, MY FRIEND.>

<STEP BACK.>

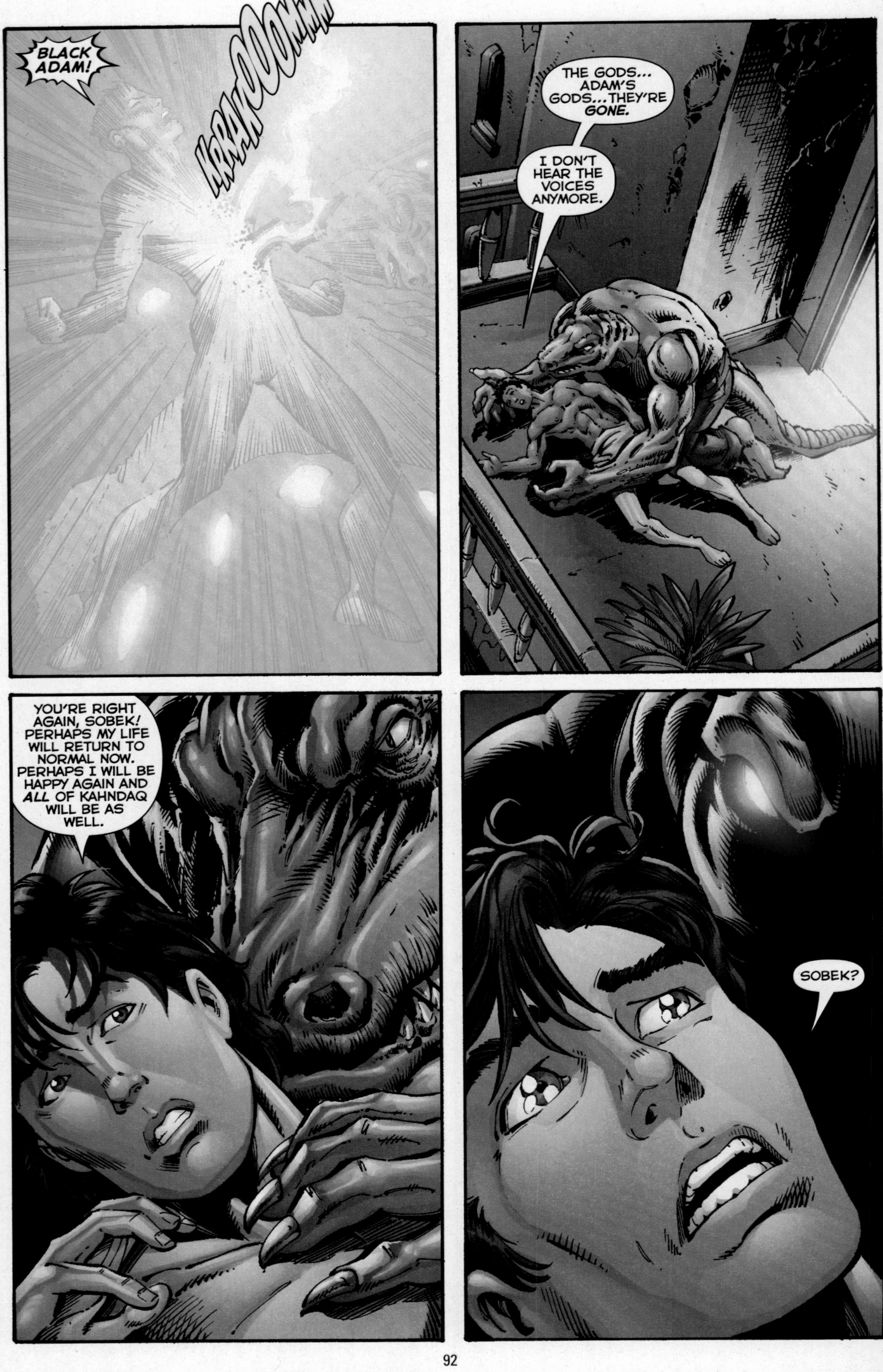
BLACK ADAM!
KRRAKOOOOMMM
THE GODS... ADAM'S GODS... THEY'RE GONE.
I DON'T HEAR THE VOICES ANYMORE.
YOU'RE RIGHT AGAIN, SOBEK! PERHAPS MY LIFE WILL RETURN TO NORMAL NOW. PERHAPS I WILL BE HAPPY AGAIN AND ALL OF KAHNDAQ WILL BE AS WELL.
SOBEK?

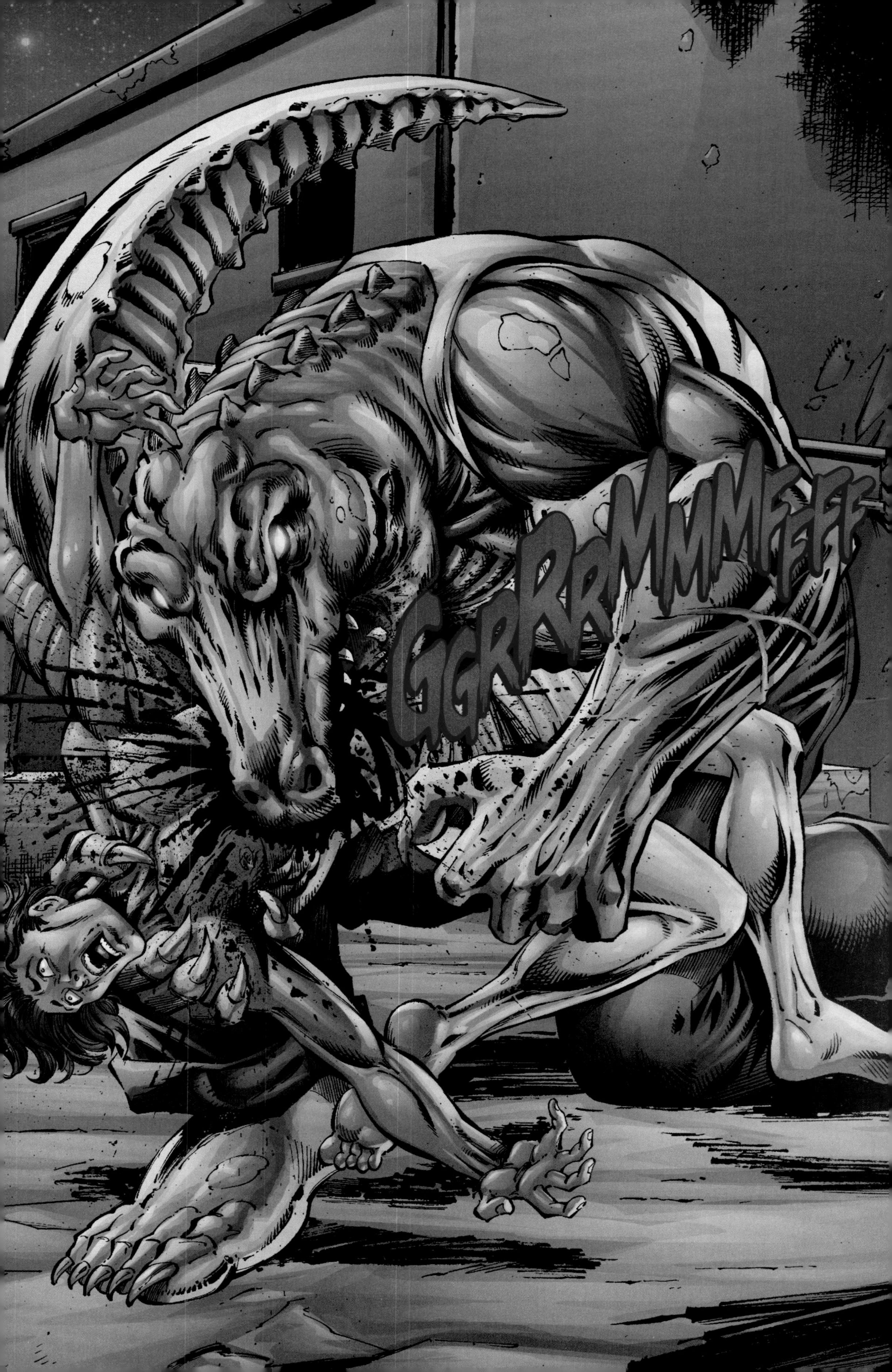
GGRRRMMMFFFF

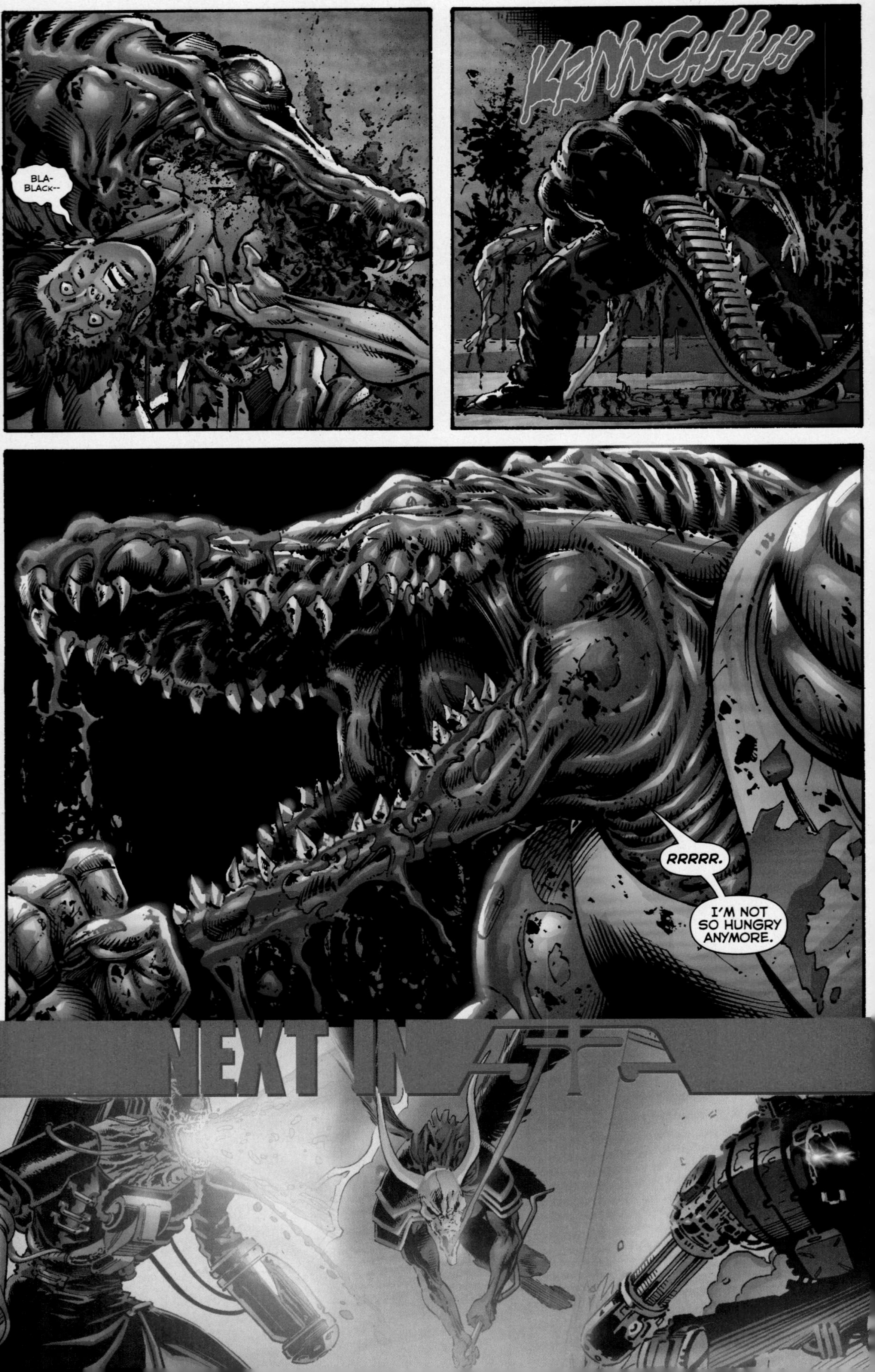
BLA-
BLACK--
KRNNCHHHH
RRRRR.
I'M NOT SO HUNGRY ANYMORE.
NEXT IN JSA

WEEK FORTY-THREE NOTES

GEOFF JOHNS

When we first broke the story of Black Adam we went through several established characters we believed he might find romance with. We threw out some names, from Power Girl to Hippolyta (yeah, we know those are bad ideas, which is why we didn't use them!), but it was clear that Black Adam would be better served by surrounding him with his own new supporting cast. We hit upon a new Isis in one of the very first story meetings. The rest of the Black Marvel Family, however, didn't develop until a little later in the process. Getting married and finding a wife was one thing, but gaining an entirely new family over the course of his journey added a whole lot more. A brother-in-law in Osiris and a "mascot" of sorts with Sobek the Talking Crocodile (or obvious darker version of Tawky Tawny, the talking tiger).

Now Sobek, at first glance, might seem like you'd find him in Scooby-Doo before the world of Black Adam — talking about how he was hungry all the time, stuttering, making jokes. In fact, Keith Giffen couldn't stand the "goofiness" of the character. But therein lies the twist and what many call the most shocking last page in 52's weekly series — the revelation that Sobek was not a friend, but an enemy. And an extremely ruthless one at that.

The graphic nature was controversial — some condemned it and some were floored by it.

Keith Giffen decided to turn the one-page sequence into two, turning it into something even more horrific, but the impact on the readers was undeniable. Love it or hate it, it was a moment to remember.

And, quite honestly, one I wouldn't change.

Breakdowns by **Keith Giffen**

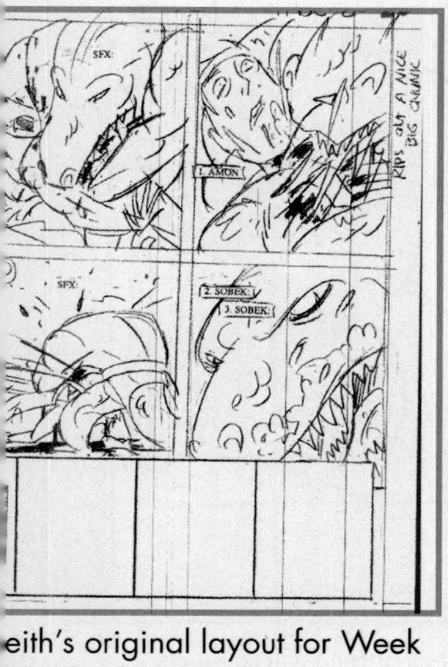
SFX:
1. AMON
RIPS OUT A NICE BIG CHUNK
SFX:
2. SOBEK:
3. SOBEK:

eith's original layout for Week 3's shocking ending.

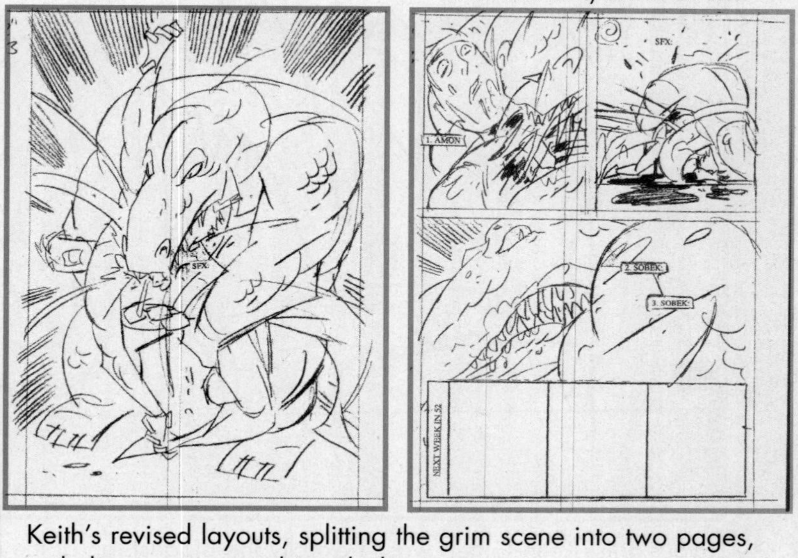
SFX:
SFX:
1. AMON
2. SOBEK:
3. SOBEK:
NEXT WEEK IN 52

Keith's revised layouts, splitting the grim scene into two pages, including a very graphic splash page.

BREAKDOWNS

BY **KEITH GIFFEN**

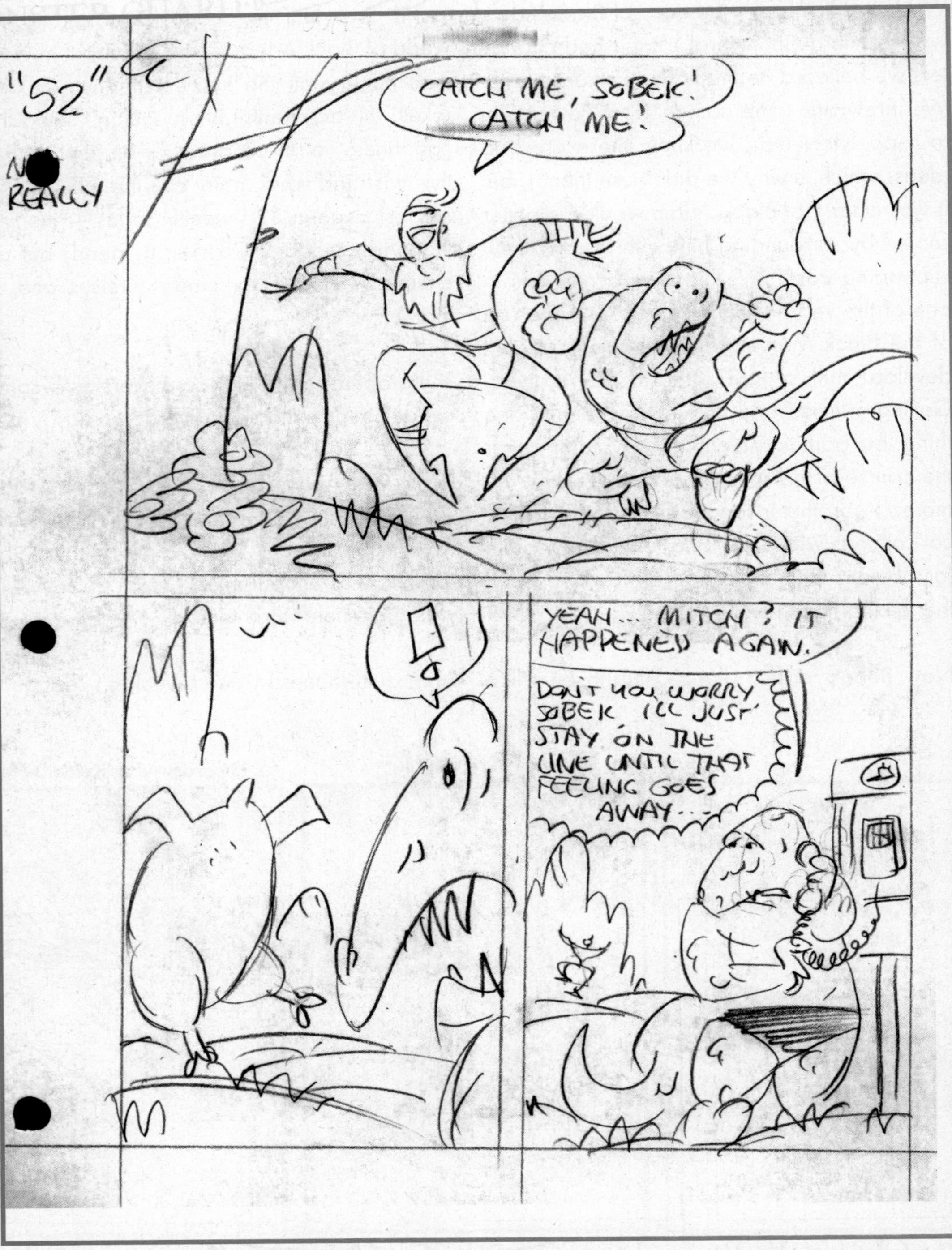
"52"
REALLY
CATCH ME, SOBEK! CATCH ME!
YEAH... MITCH? IT HAPPENED AGAIN.
DON'T YOU WORRY SOBEK I'LL JUST STAY ON THE LINE UNTIL THAT FEELING GOES AWAY...

Layout artist Keith Giffen wasn't exactly the biggest fan of the character Osiris — as evidenced in the above sketch, done before he knew Osiris's actual fate.

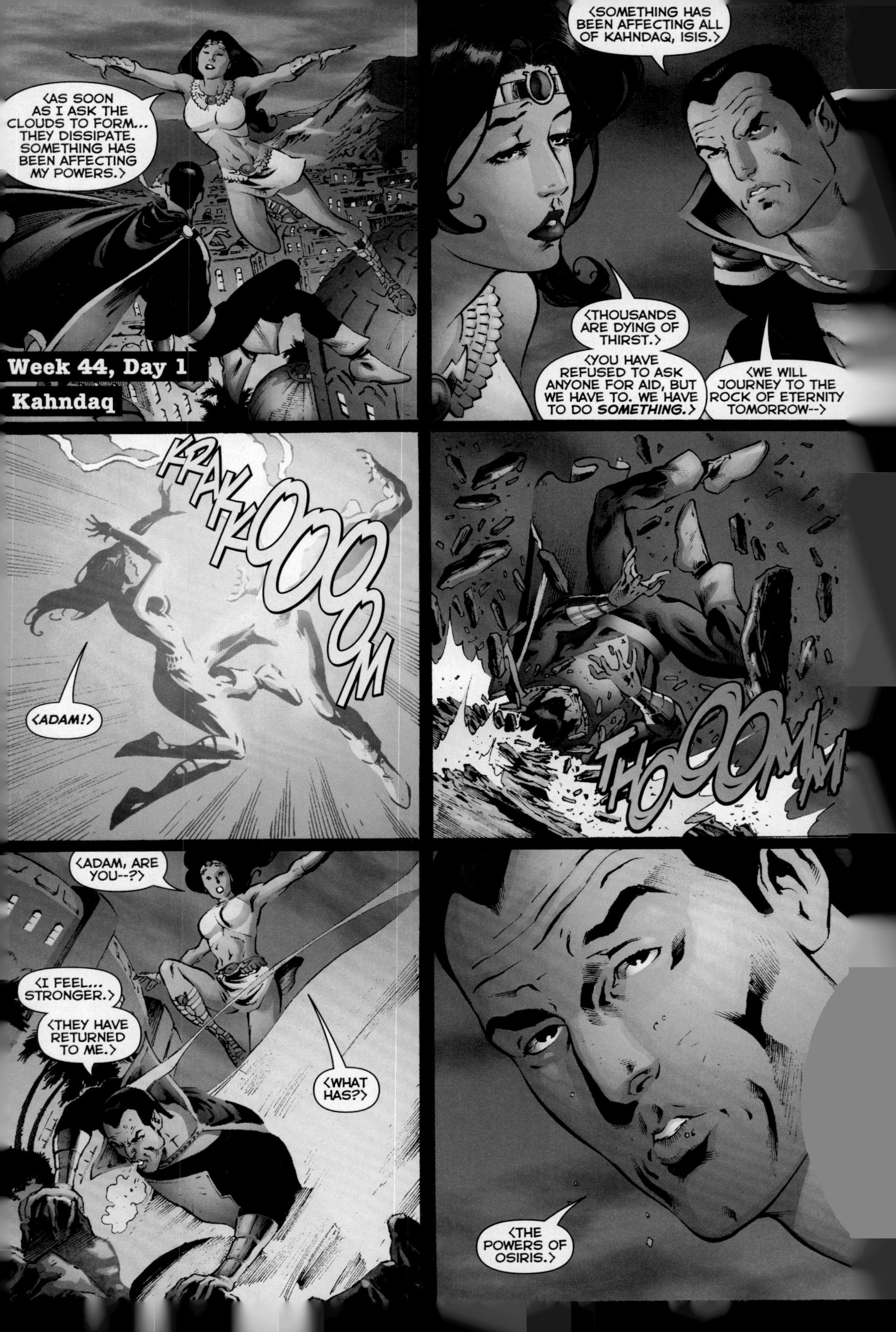

Week 44, Day 1
Kahndaq
‹AS SOON AS I ASK THE CLOUDS TO FORM... THEY DISSIPATE. SOMETHING HAS BEEN AFFECTING MY POWERS.›
‹SOMETHING HAS BEEN AFFECTING ALL OF KAHNDAQ, ISIS.›
‹THOUSANDS ARE DYING OF THIRST.›
‹YOU HAVE REFUSED TO ASK ANYONE FOR AID, BUT WE HAVE TO. WE HAVE TO DO SOMETHING.›
‹WE WILL JOURNEY TO THE ROCK OF ETERNITY TOMORROW--›
KRAKOOOOOM
‹ADAM!›
THOOOMM
‹ADAM, ARE YOU--?›
‹I FEEL... STRONGER.›
‹THEY HAVE RETURNED TO ME.›
‹WHAT HAS?›
‹THE POWERS OF OSIRIS.›

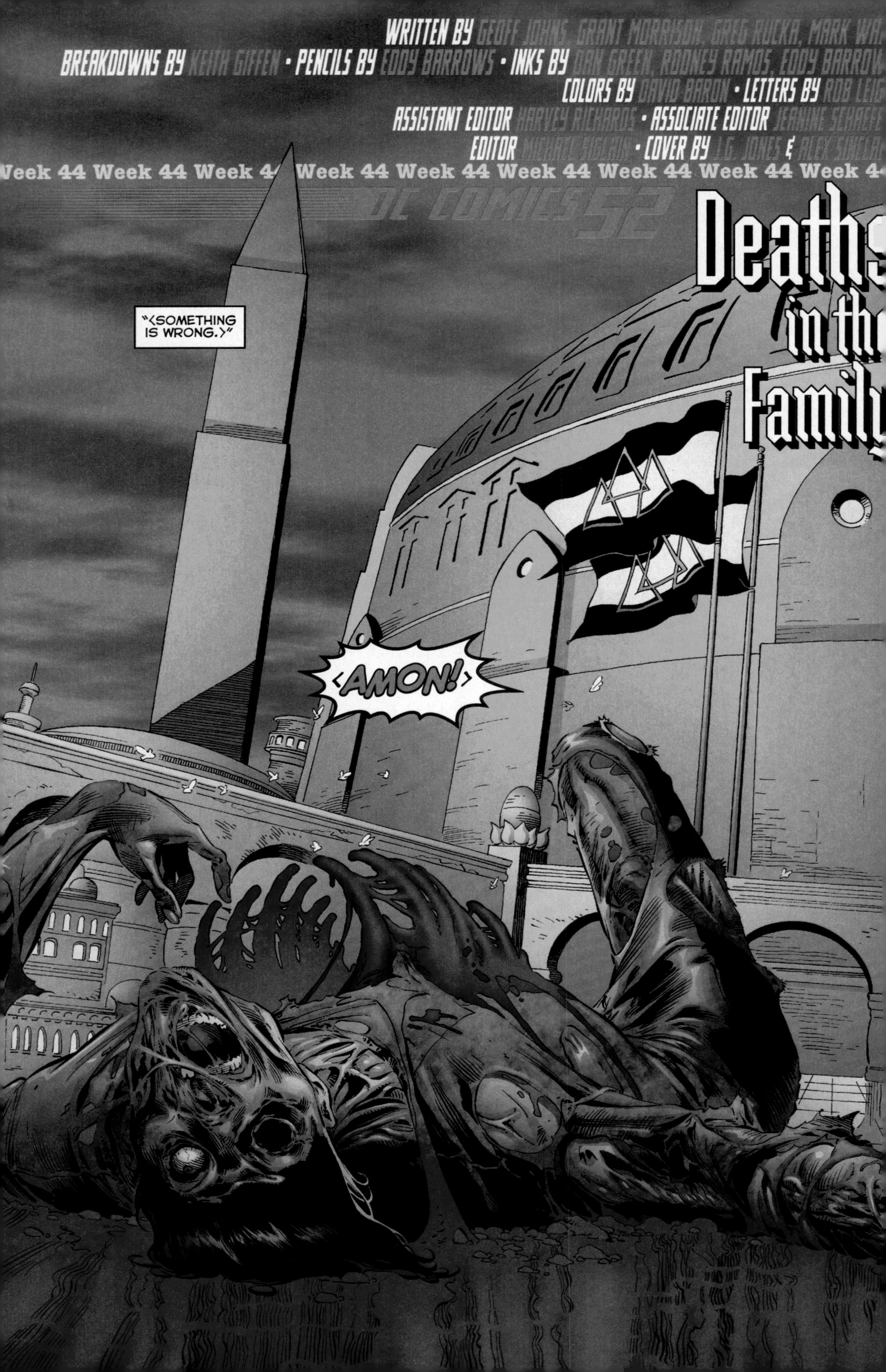
WRITTEN BY GEOFF JOHNS, GRANT MORRISON, GREG RUCKA, MARK WA
BREAKDOWNS BY KEITH GIFFEN • PENCILS BY EDDY BARROWS • INKS BY DAN GREEN, RODNEY RAMOS, EDDY BARROW
COLORS BY DAVID BARON • LETTERS BY ROB LEIG
ASSISTANT EDITOR HARVEY RICHARDS • ASSOCIATE EDITOR JEANINE SCHAEFE
EDITOR MICHAEL SIGLAIN • COVER BY J.G. JONES & ALEX SINCLA
Week 44 Week 44 Week 44 Week 44 Week 44 Week 44 Week 44 Week 44 Week 4
DC COMICS 52
Deaths in the Family
"‹SOMETHING IS WRONG.›"
‹AMON!›

<NO!>

<DO SOMETHING, ADAM!!>

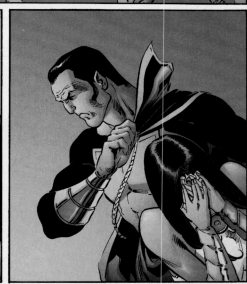

<WHY DID HE CHANGE?>

<WHY DID HE CHANGE BACK?!>

<OSIRIS BELIEVED HIS POWERS WERE THE CAUSE OF KAHNDAQ'S MISERY.>

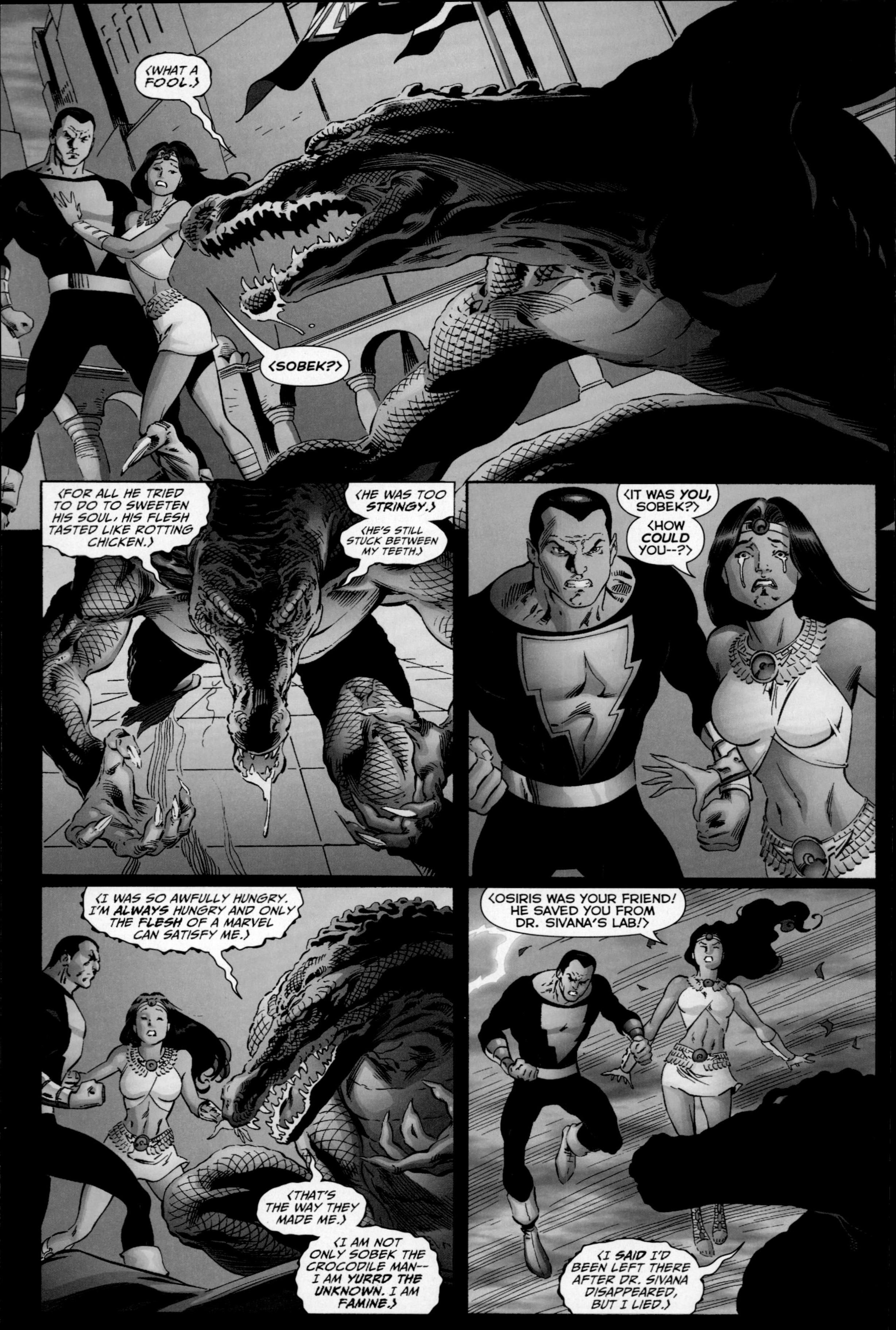

‹WHAT A FOOL.›
‹SOBEK?›
‹FOR ALL HE TRIED TO DO TO SWEETEN HIS SOUL, HIS FLESH TASTED LIKE ROTTING CHICKEN.›
‹HE WAS TOO STRINGY.›
‹HE'S STILL STUCK BETWEEN MY TEETH.›
‹IT WAS YOU, SOBEK?›
‹HOW COULD YOU--?›
‹I WAS SO AWFULLY HUNGRY. I'M ALWAYS HUNGRY AND ONLY THE FLESH OF A MARVEL CAN SATISFY ME.›
‹THAT'S THE WAY THEY MADE ME.›
‹I AM NOT ONLY SOBEK THE CROCODILE MAN-- I AM YURRD THE UNKNOWN. I AM FAMINE.›
‹OSIRIS WAS YOUR FRIEND! HE SAVED YOU FROM DR. SIVANA'S LAB!›
‹I SAID I'D BEEN LEFT THERE AFTER DR. SIVANA DISAPPEARED, BUT I LIED.›

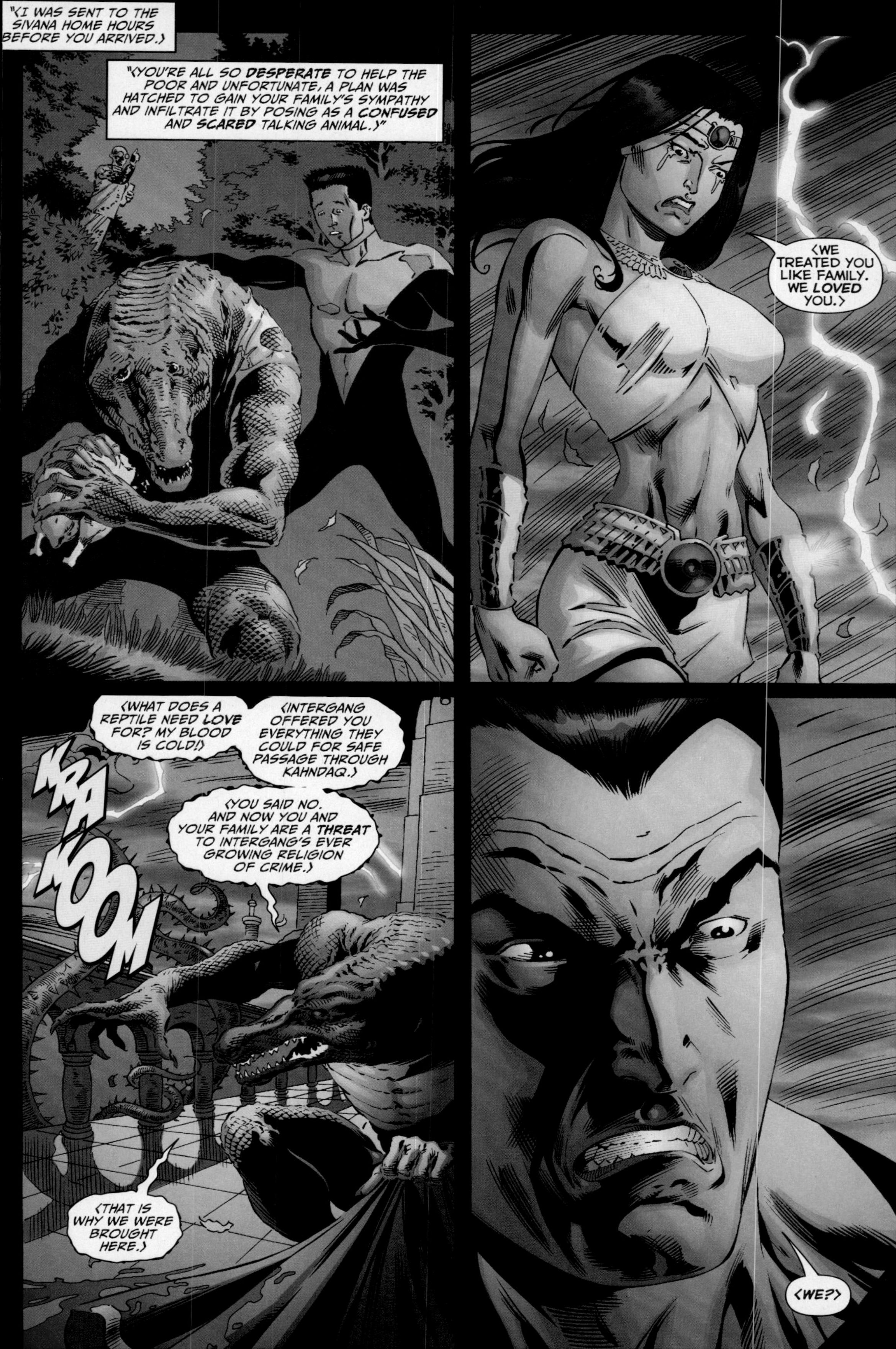

"‹I WAS SENT TO THE SIVANA HOME HOURS BEFORE YOU ARRIVED.›
"‹YOU'RE ALL SO DESPERATE TO HELP THE POOR AND UNFORTUNATE, A PLAN WAS HATCHED TO GAIN YOUR FAMILY'S SYMPATHY AND INFILTRATE IT BY POSING AS A CONFUSED AND SCARED TALKING ANIMAL.›"
‹WE TREATED YOU LIKE FAMILY. WE LOVED YOU.›
‹WHAT DOES A REPTILE NEED LOVE FOR? MY BLOOD IS COLD!›
‹INTERGANG OFFERED YOU EVERYTHING THEY COULD FOR SAFE PASSAGE THROUGH KAHNDAQ.›
‹YOU SAID NO. AND NOW YOU AND YOUR FAMILY ARE A THREAT TO INTERGANG'S EVER GROWING RELIGION OF CRIME.›
KRA-KOOM
‹THAT IS WHY WE WERE BROUGHT HERE.›
‹WE?›

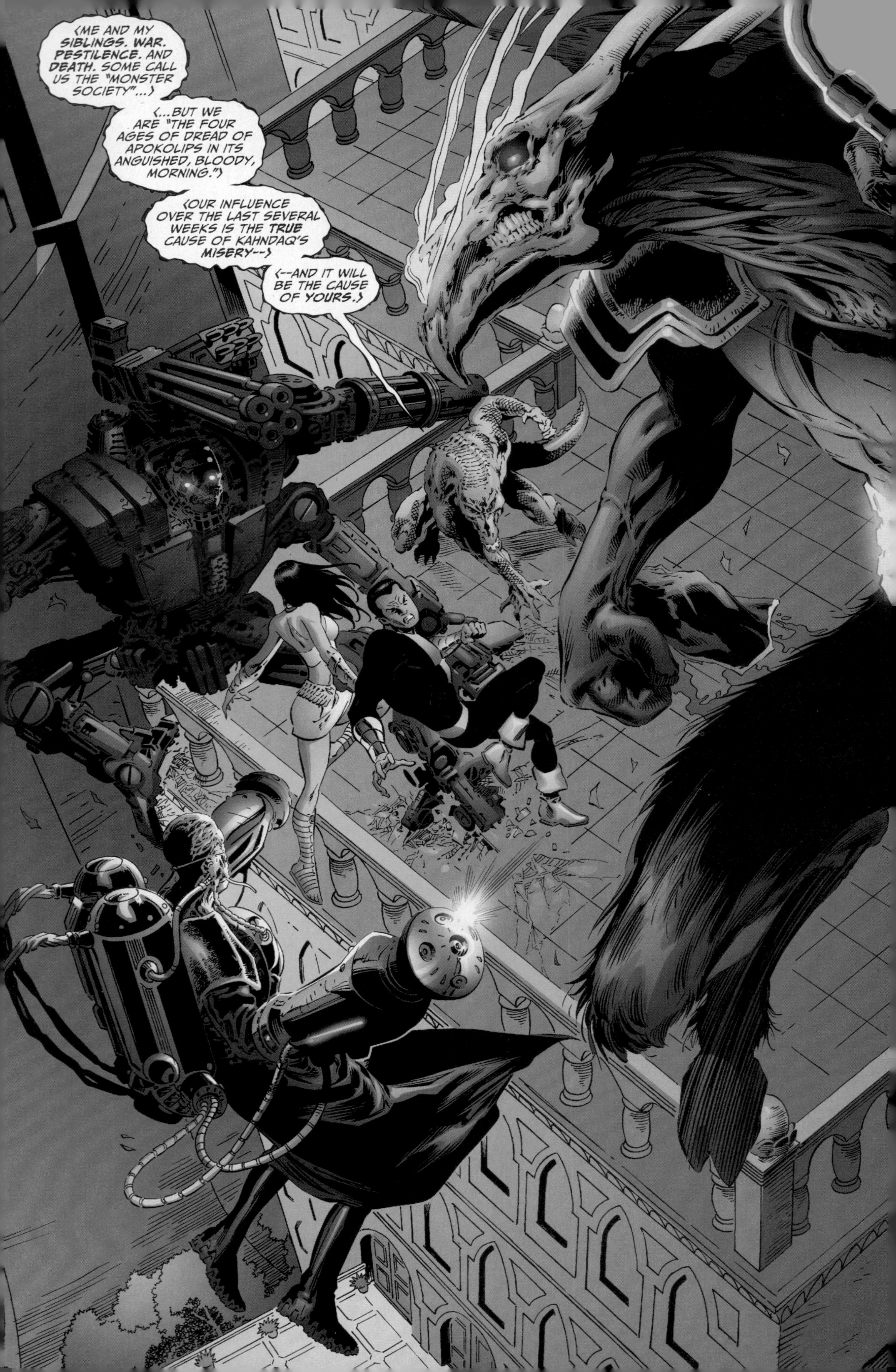
‹ME AND MY SIBLINGS. WAR. PESTILENCE. AND DEATH. SOME CALL US THE "MONSTER SOCIETY"...›
‹...BUT WE ARE "THE FOUR AGES OF DREAD OF APOKOLIPS IN ITS ANGUISHED, BLOODY, MORNING."›
‹OUR INFLUENCE OVER THE LAST SEVERAL WEEKS IS THE TRUE CAUSE OF KAHNDAQ'S MISERY--›
‹--AND IT WILL BE THE CAUSE OF YOURS.›

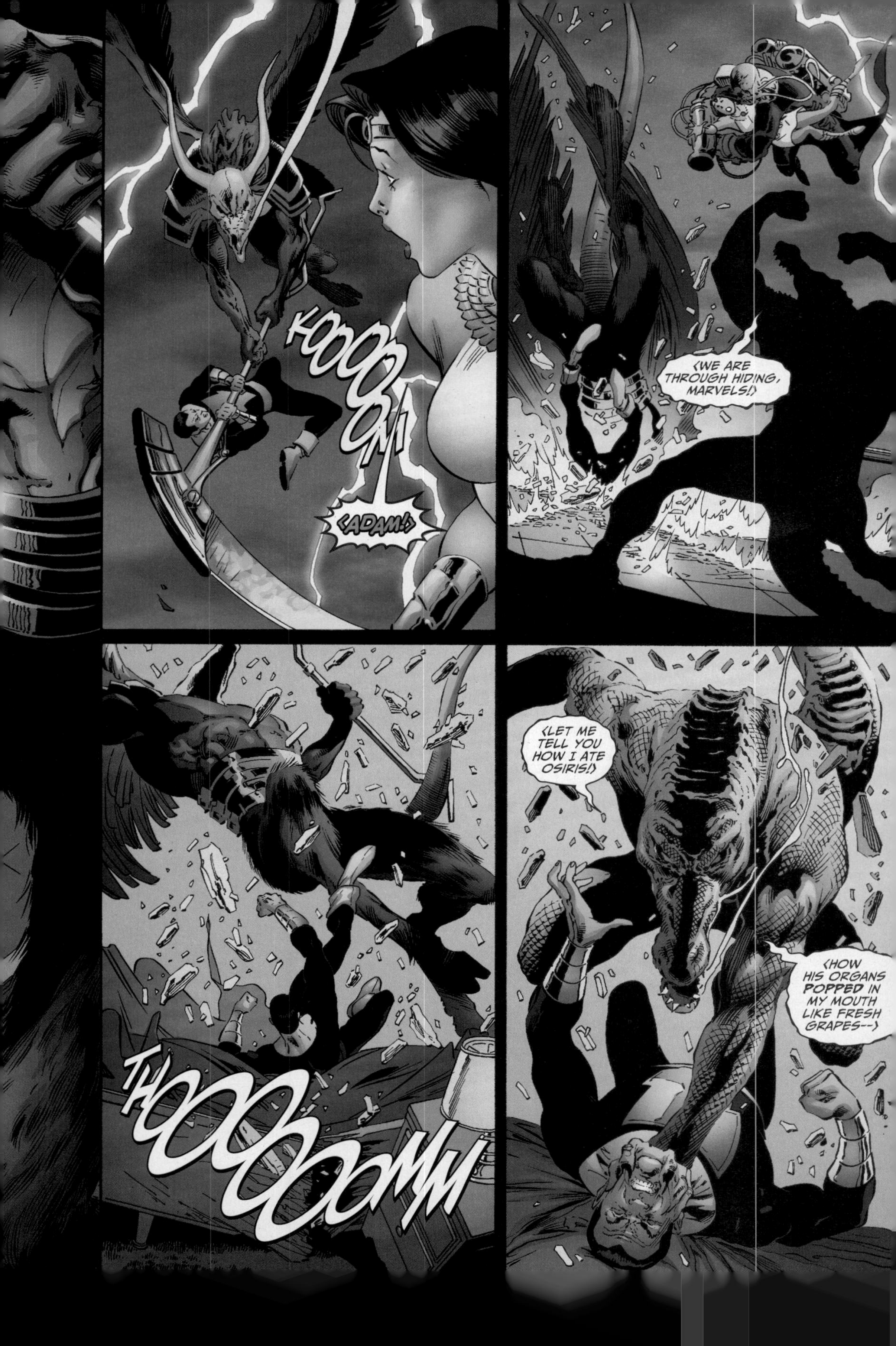
KOOOOOOOM!
<ADAM!>
<WE ARE THROUGH HIDING, MARVELS!>
THOOOOOOOMM
<LET ME TELL YOU HOW I ATE OSIRIS!>
<HOW HIS ORGANS **POPPED** IN MY MOUTH LIKE FRESH GRAPES-->

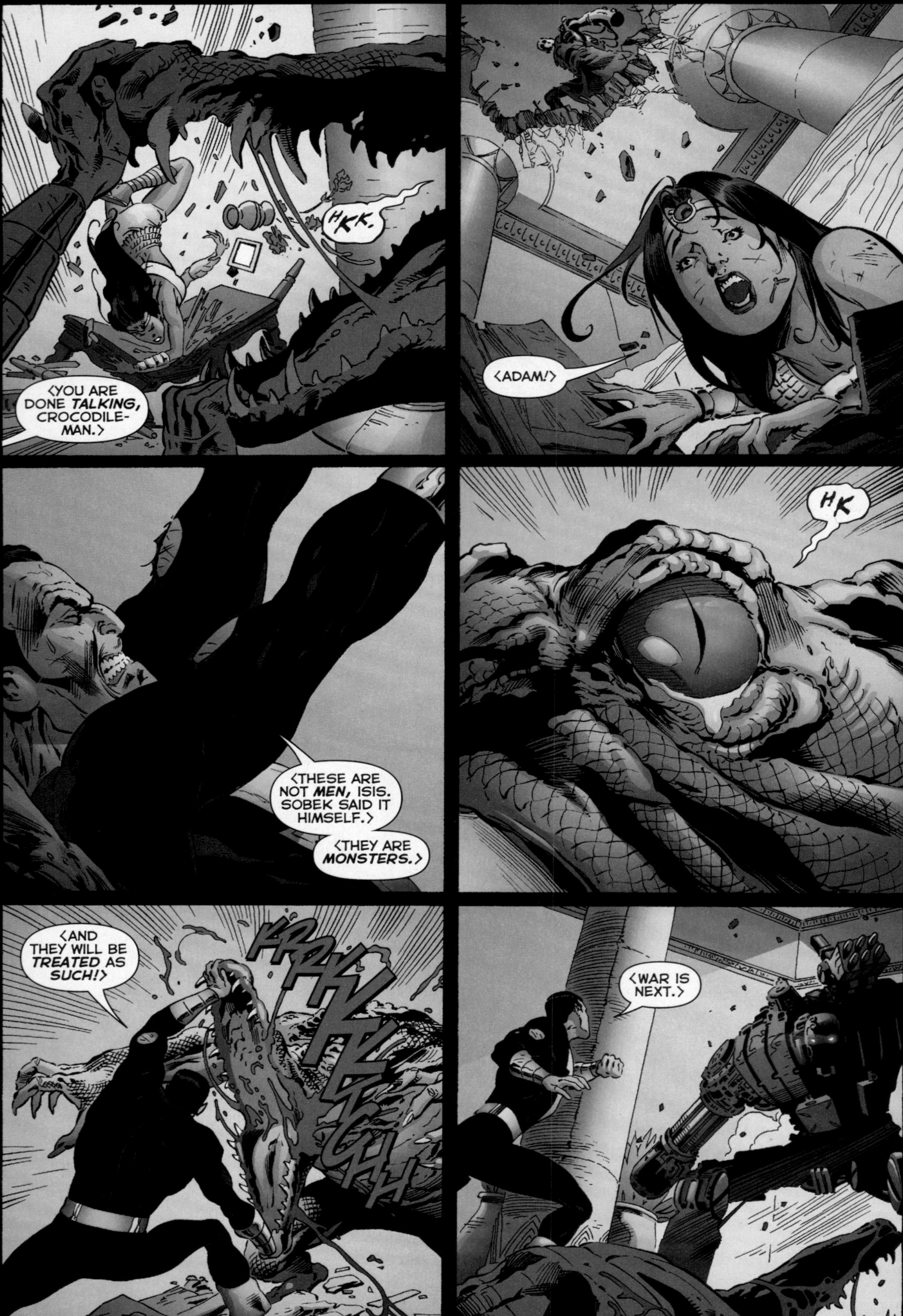
HKK.
<YOU ARE DONE TALKING, CROCODILE-MAN.>
<ADAM!>
HK
<THESE ARE NOT MEN, ISIS. SOBEK SAID IT HIMSELF.>
<THEY ARE MONSTERS.>
<AND THEY WILL BE TREATED AS SUCH!>
<WAR IS NEXT.>

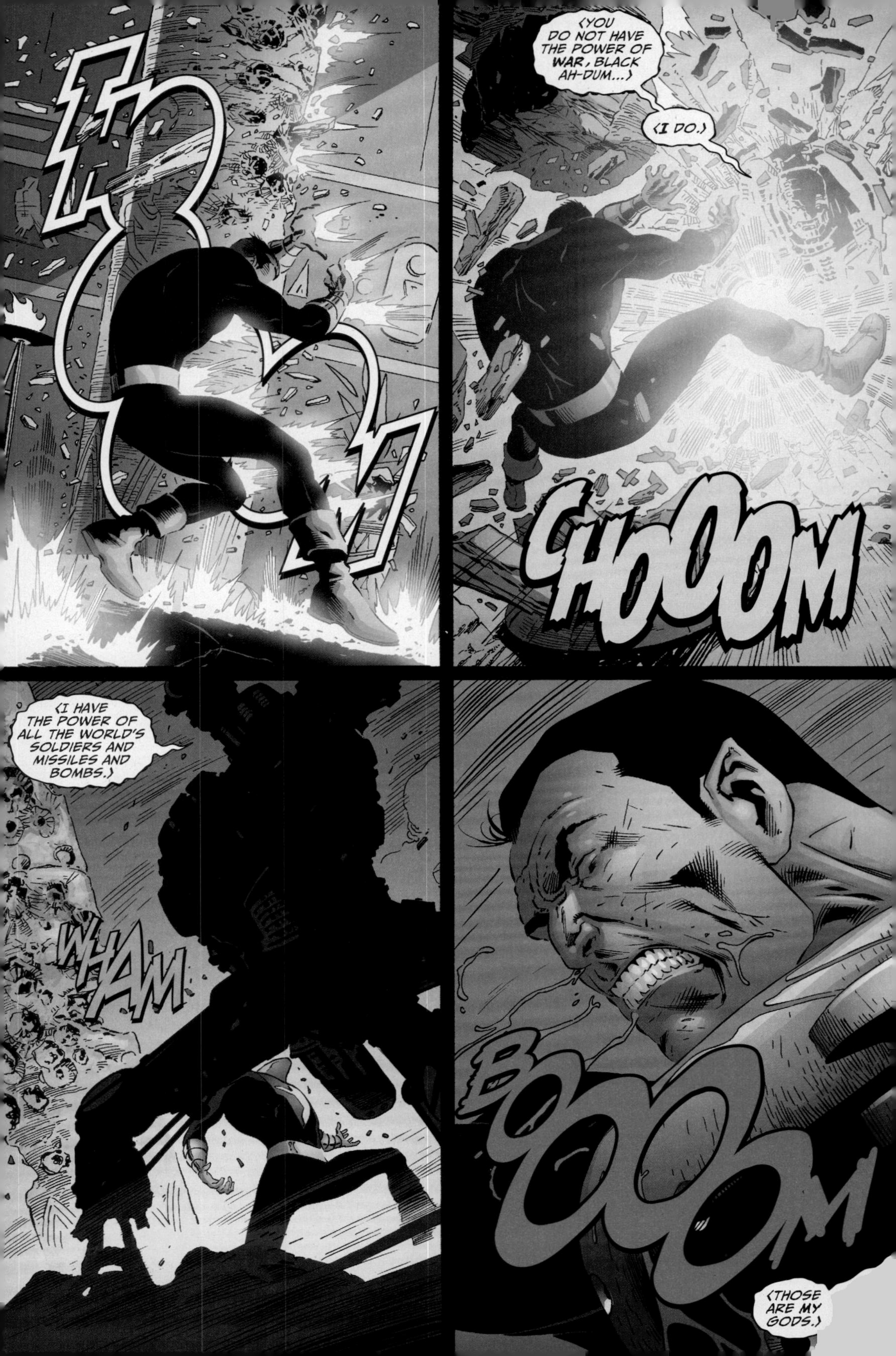

FOOM
‹YOU DO NOT HAVE THE POWER OF WAR, BLACK AH-DUM...›
‹I DO.›
CHOOOM
‹I HAVE THE POWER OF ALL THE WORLD'S SOLDIERS AND MISSILES AND BOMBS.›
WHAM
BOOOOM
‹THOSE ARE MY GODS.›

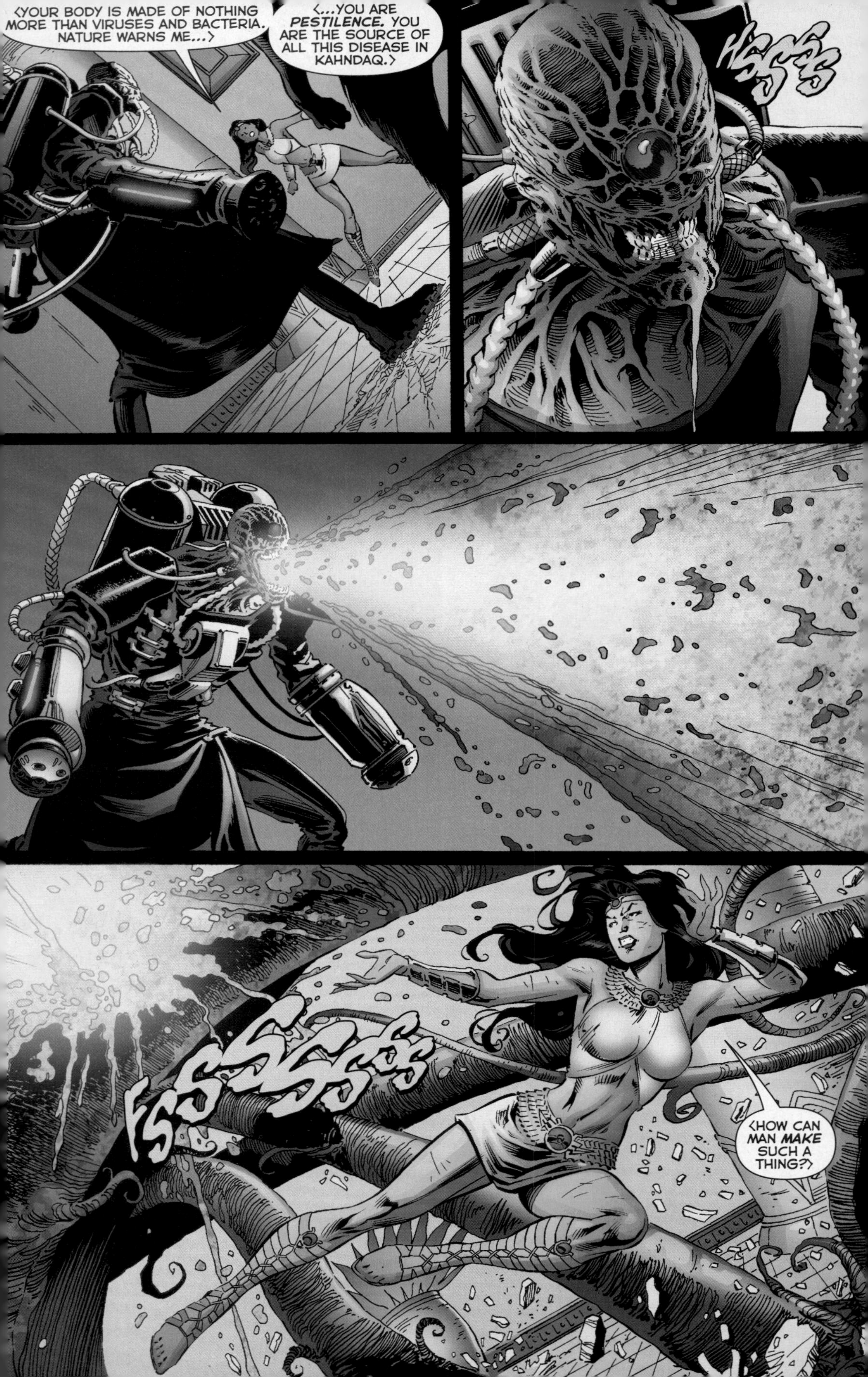

<YOUR BODY IS MADE OF NOTHING MORE THAN VIRUSES AND BACTERIA. NATURE WARNS ME...>
<...YOU ARE PESTILENCE. YOU ARE THE SOURCE OF ALL THIS DISEASE IN KAHNDAQ.>
HSSSSS
FSSSSSS
<HOW CAN MAN MAKE SUCH A THING?>

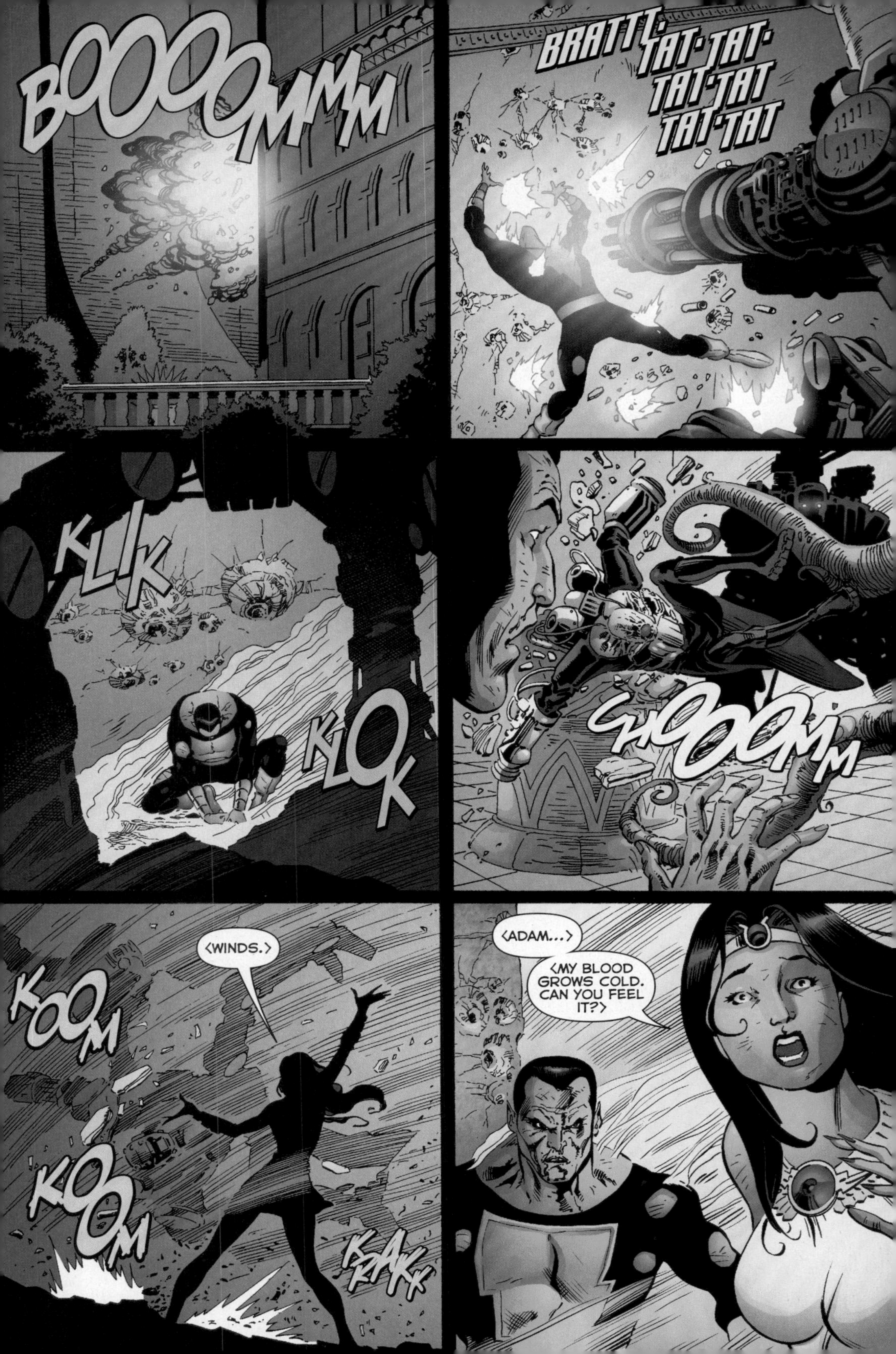
BOOOOMMMM
BRATTT-TAT-TAT-TAT-TAT TAT-TAT
KLIK
KLOK
SHOOOMMM
KOOM
<WINDS.>
KOOM
KRAKK
<ADAM...>
<MY BLOOD GROWS COLD. CAN YOU FEEL IT?>

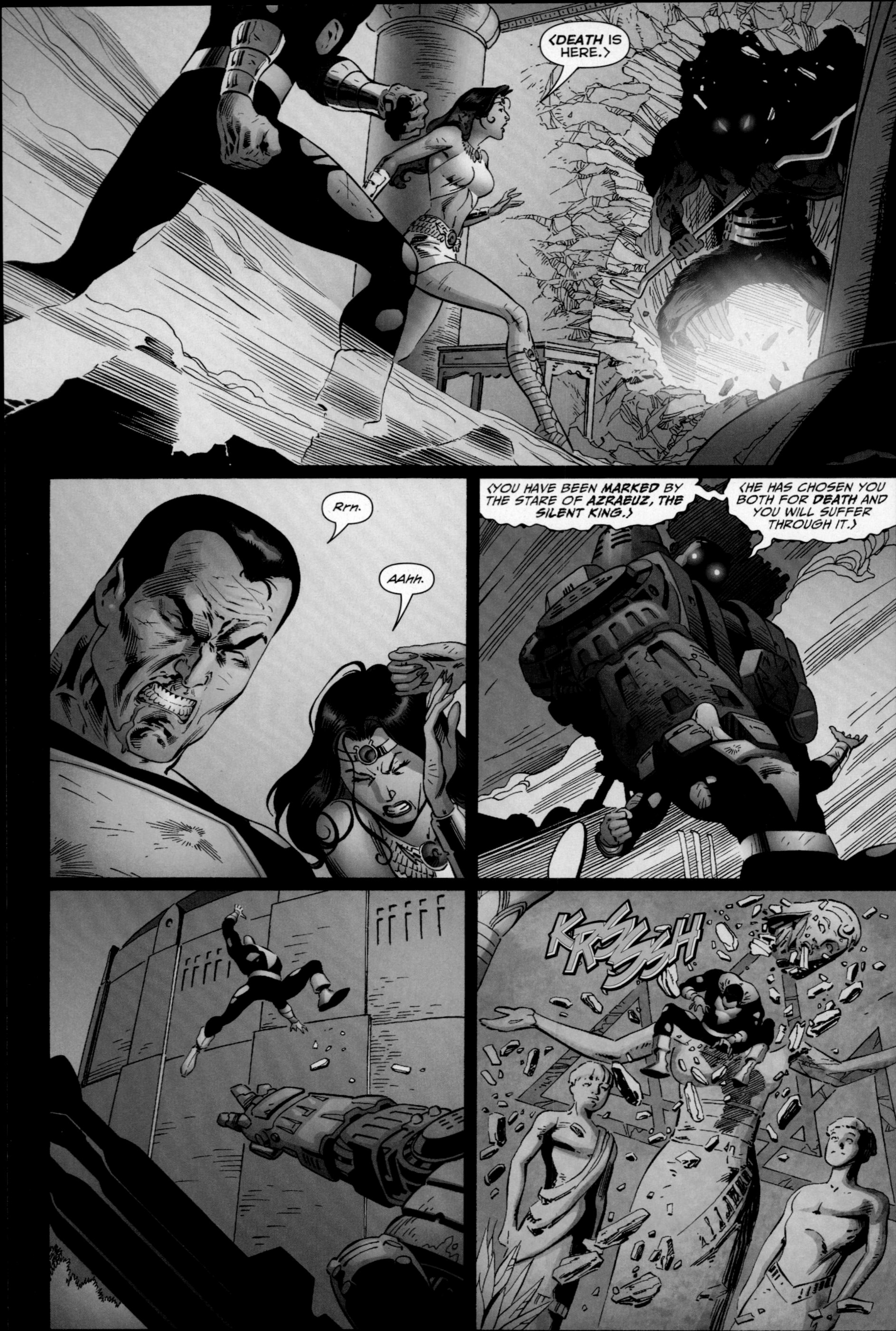

<DEATH IS HERE.>
Rrn.
AAhh.
<YOU HAVE BEEN MARKED BY THE STARE OF AZRAEUZ, THE SILENT KING.>
<HE HAS CHOSEN YOU BOTH FOR DEATH AND YOU WILL SUFFER THROUGH IT.>
KRSSCH

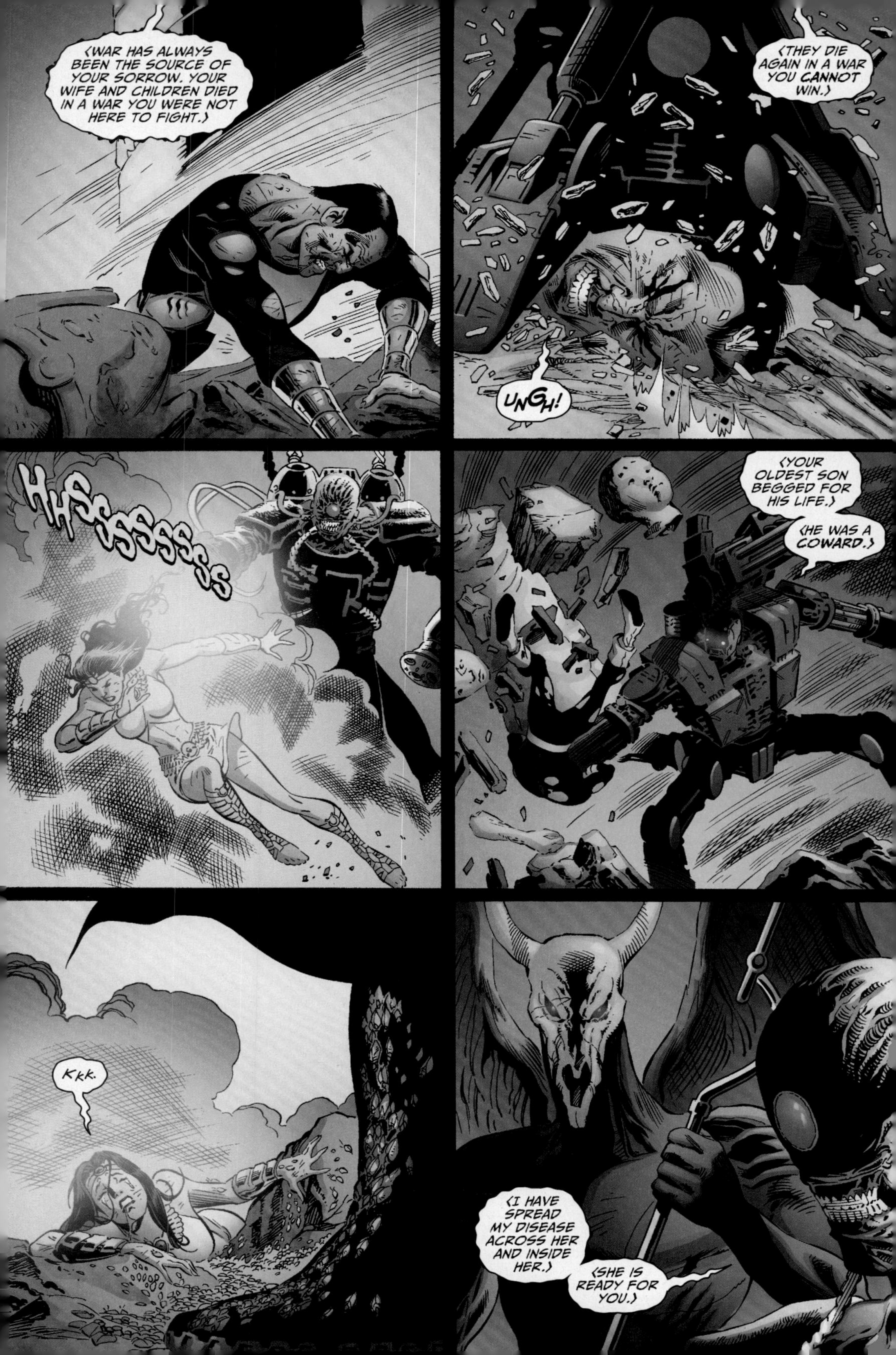

‹WAR HAS ALWAYS BEEN THE SOURCE OF YOUR SORROW. YOUR WIFE AND CHILDREN DIED IN A WAR YOU WERE NOT HERE TO FIGHT.›
‹THEY DIE AGAIN IN A WAR YOU CANNOT WIN.›
UNGH!
HHSSSSSSSS
‹YOUR OLDEST SON BEGGED FOR HIS LIFE.›
‹HE WAS A COWARD.›
Kkk.
‹I HAVE SPREAD MY DISEASE ACROSS HER AND INSIDE HER.›
‹SHE IS READY FOR YOU.›

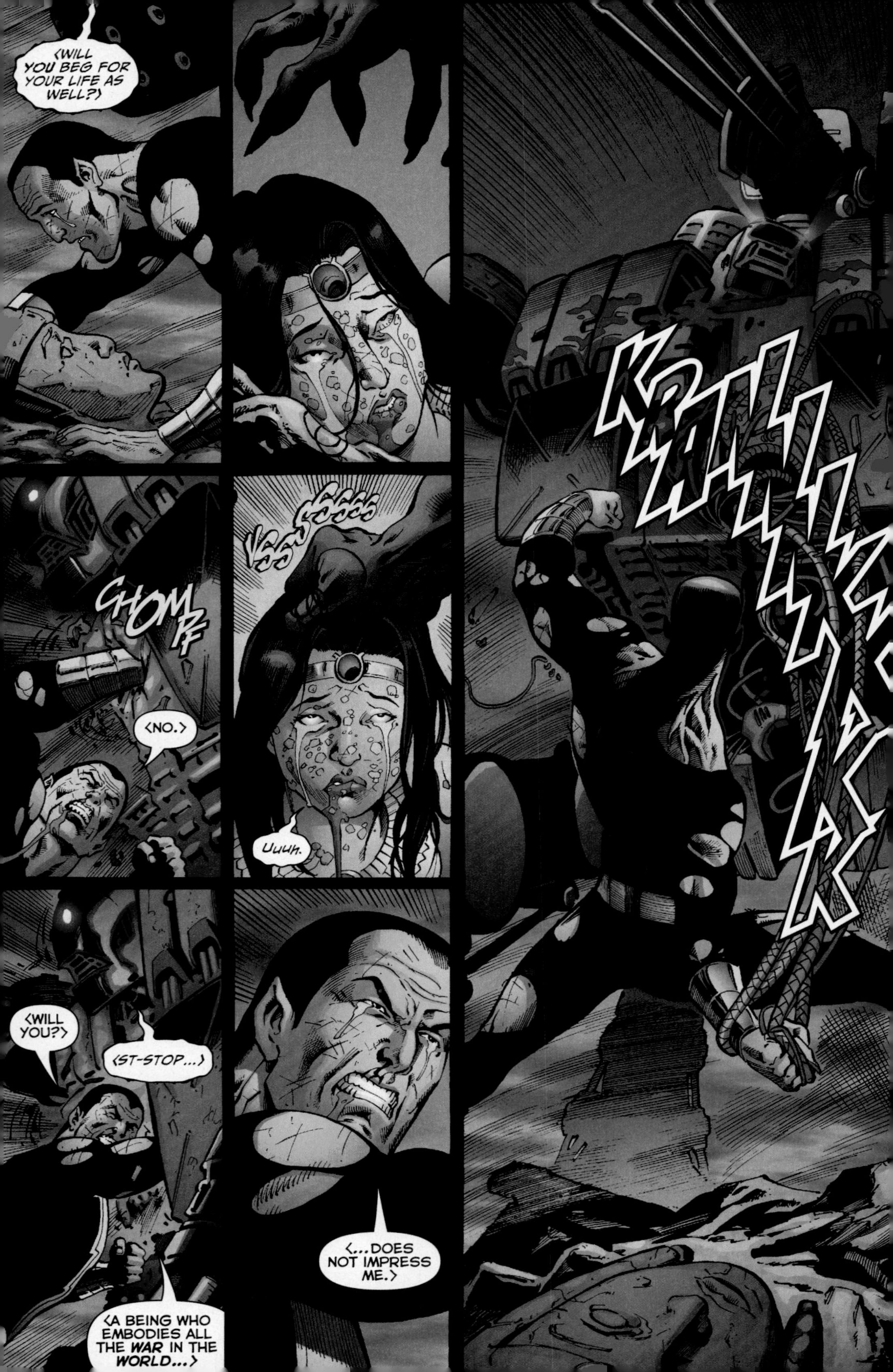
<WILL YOU BEG FOR YOUR LIFE AS WELL?>
<NO.>
Uuuh.
<WILL YOU?>
<ST-STOP...>
<A BEING WHO EMBODIES ALL THE WAR IN THE WORLD...>
<...DOES NOT IMPRESS ME.>

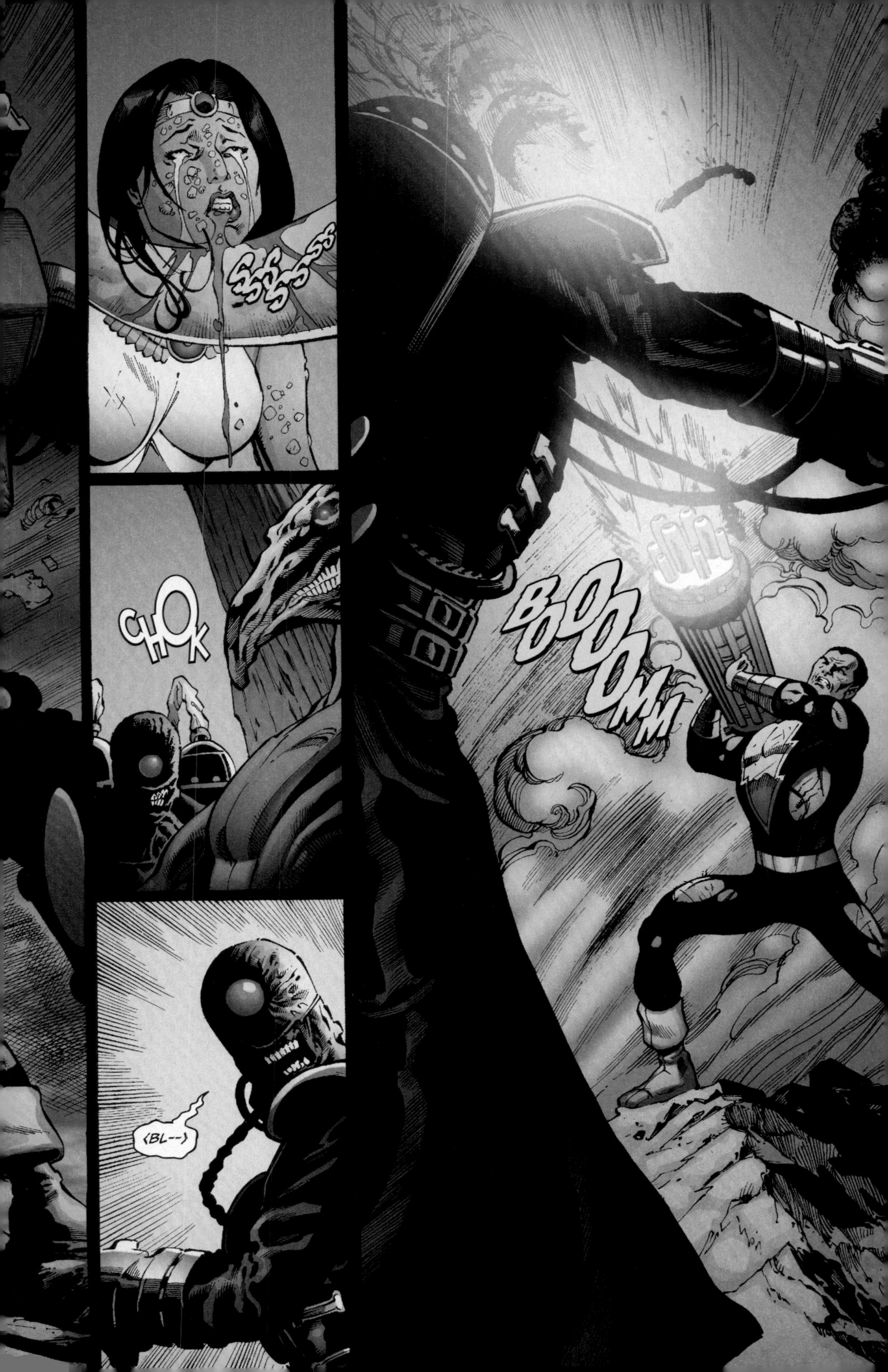

SSSSSSSSS
CHOK
BOOOOMM
<BL-->

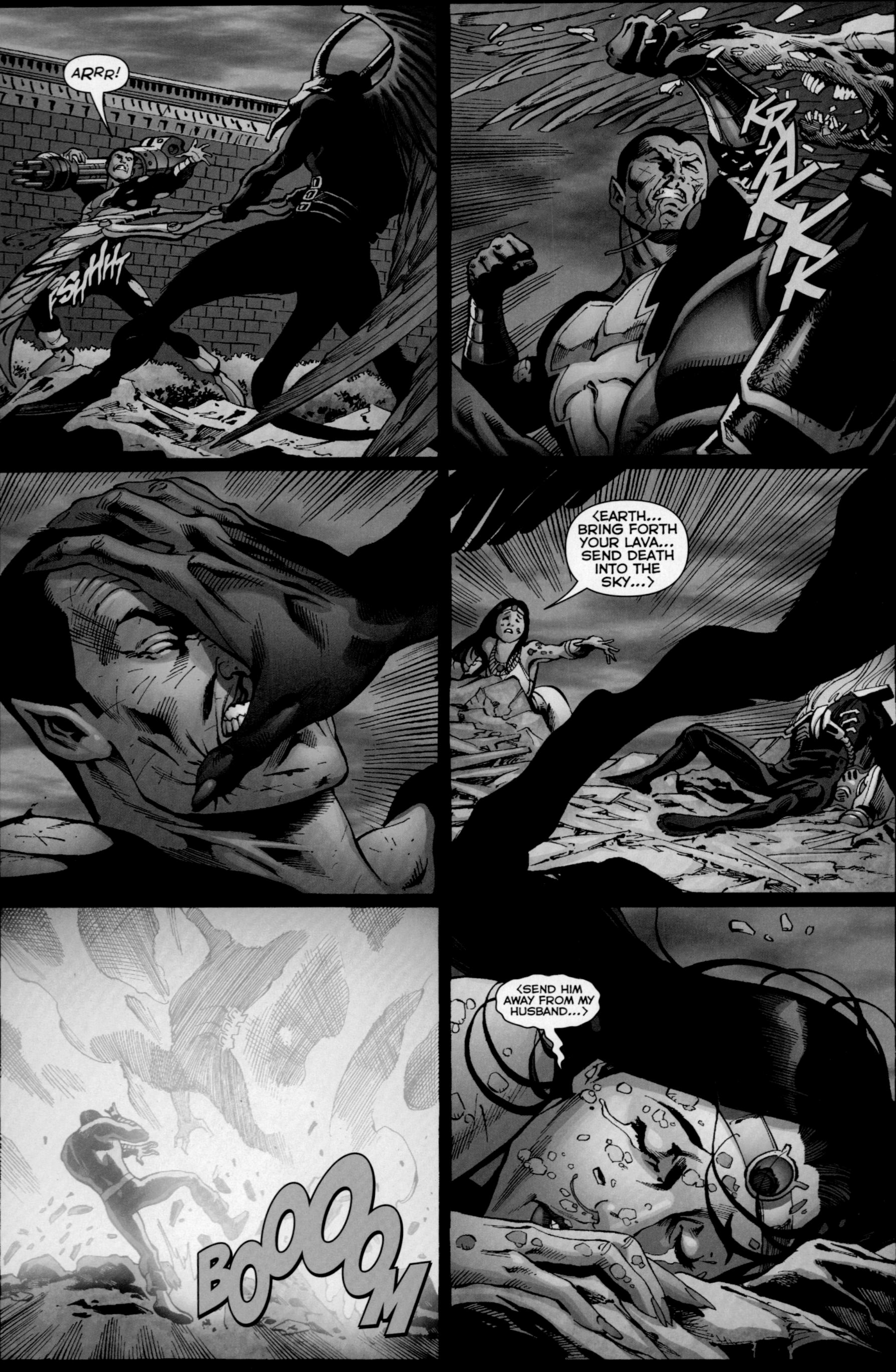
ARRR!
PSHHH
KRAKKKK
<EARTH... BRING FORTH YOUR LAVA... SEND DEATH INTO THE SKY...>
BOOOOOM
<SEND HIM AWAY FROM MY HUSBAND...>

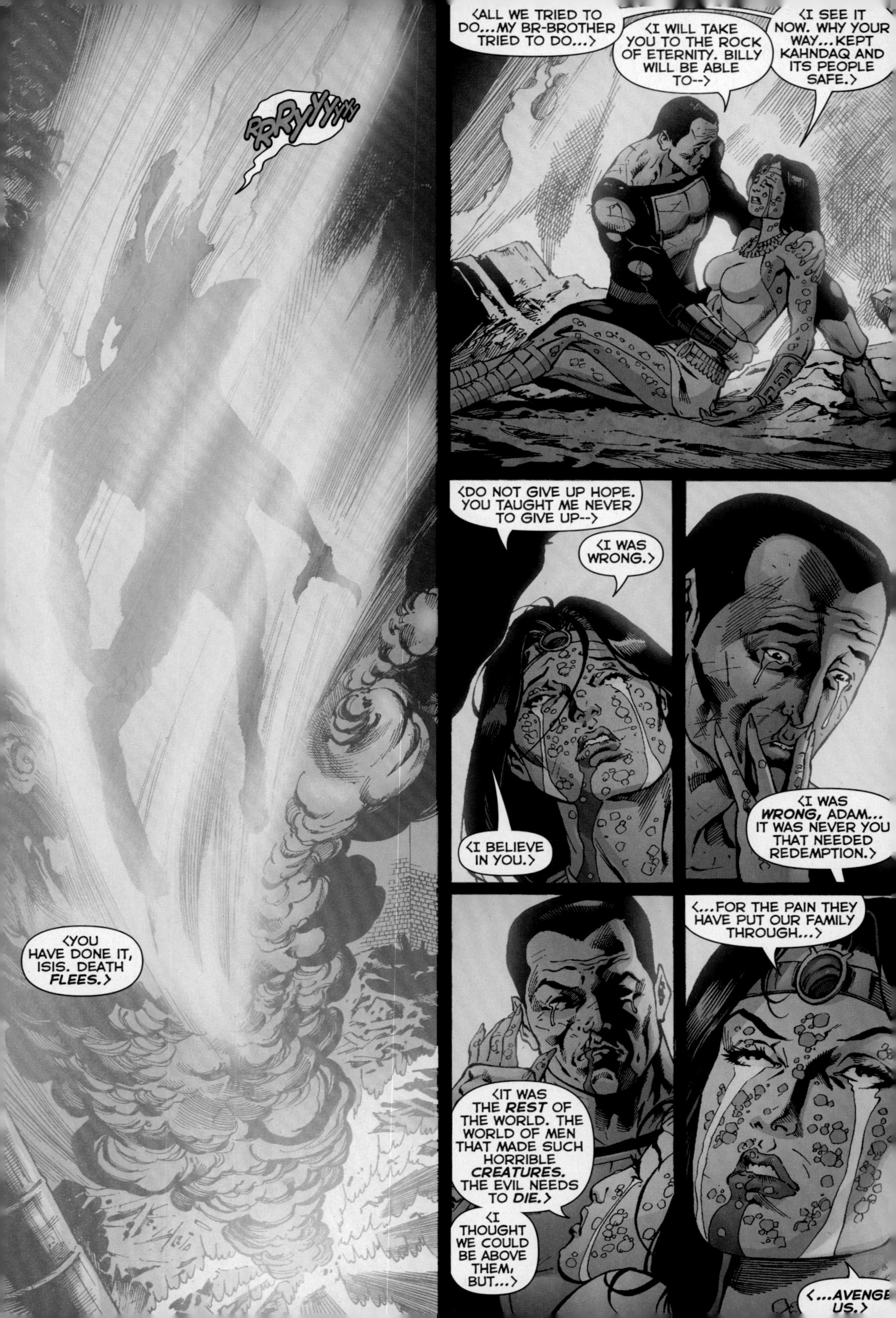
RRRYYYYYH
<YOU HAVE DONE IT, ISIS. DEATH FLEES.>
<ALL WE TRIED TO DO...MY BR-BROTHER TRIED TO DO...>
<I WILL TAKE YOU TO THE ROCK OF ETERNITY. BILLY WILL BE ABLE TO-->
<I SEE IT NOW. WHY YOUR WAY...KEPT KAHNDAQ AND ITS PEOPLE SAFE.>
<DO NOT GIVE UP HOPE. YOU TAUGHT ME NEVER TO GIVE UP-->
<I WAS WRONG.>
<I BELIEVE IN YOU.>
<I WAS WRONG, ADAM... IT WAS NEVER YOU THAT NEEDED REDEMPTION.>
<IT WAS THE REST OF THE WORLD. THE WORLD OF MEN THAT MADE SUCH HORRIBLE CREATURES. THE EVIL NEEDS TO DIE.>
<I THOUGHT WE COULD BE ABOVE THEM, BUT...>
<...FOR THE PAIN THEY HAVE PUT OUR FAMILY THROUGH...>
<...AVENGE US.>

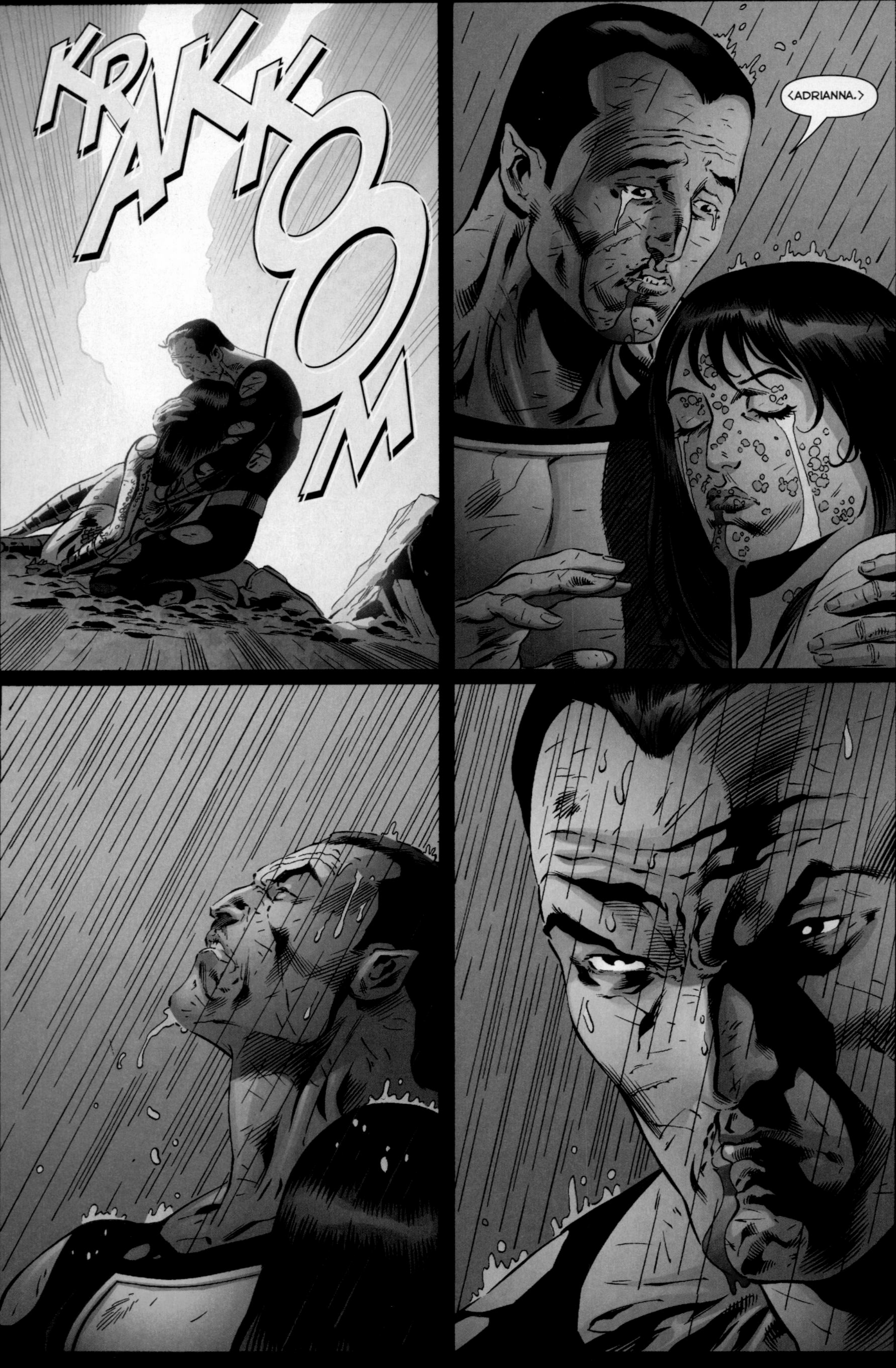
KRAKKA-THOOM
<ADRIANNA.>

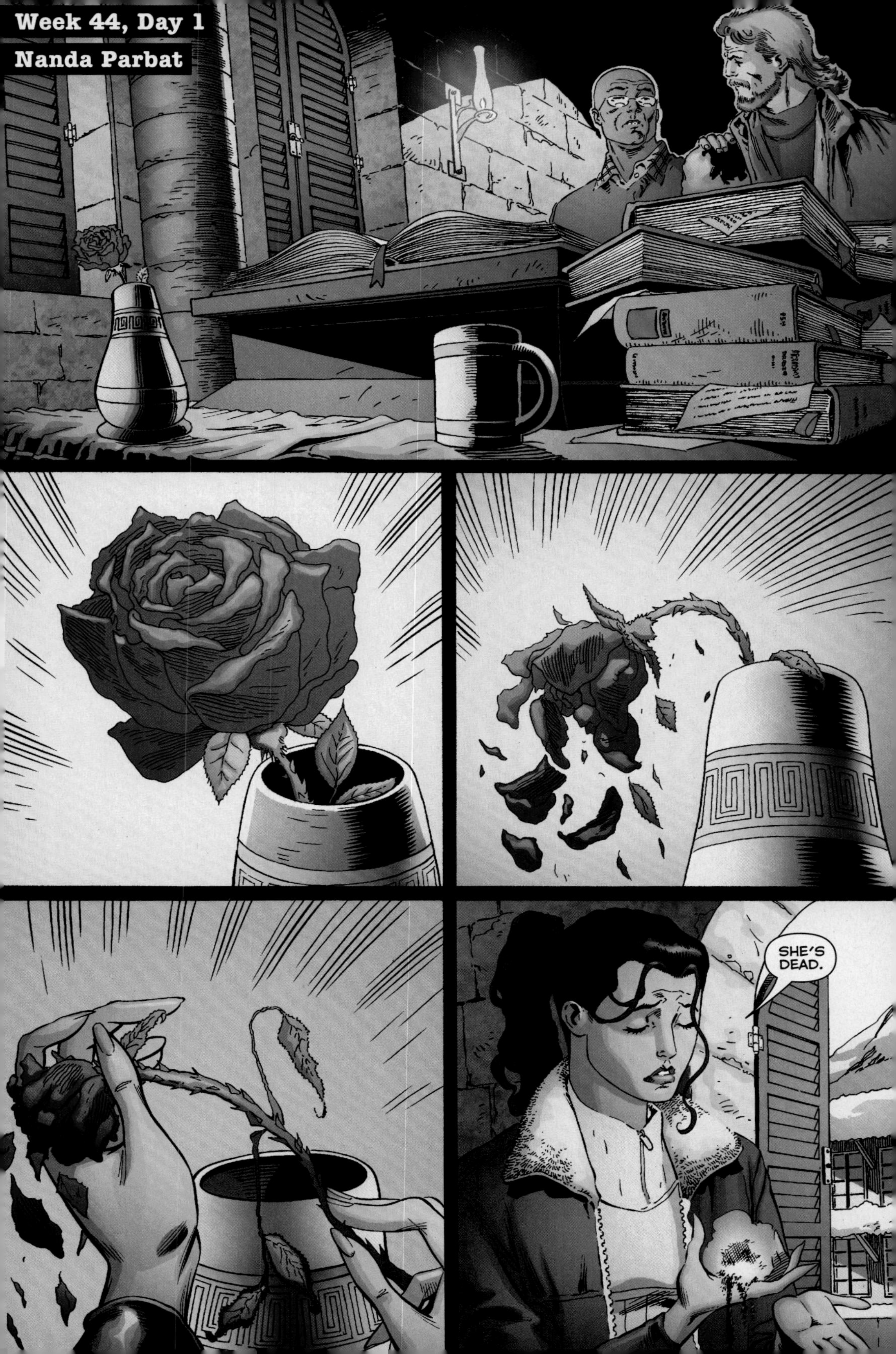
Week 44, Day 1
Nanda Parbat
SHE'S DEAD.

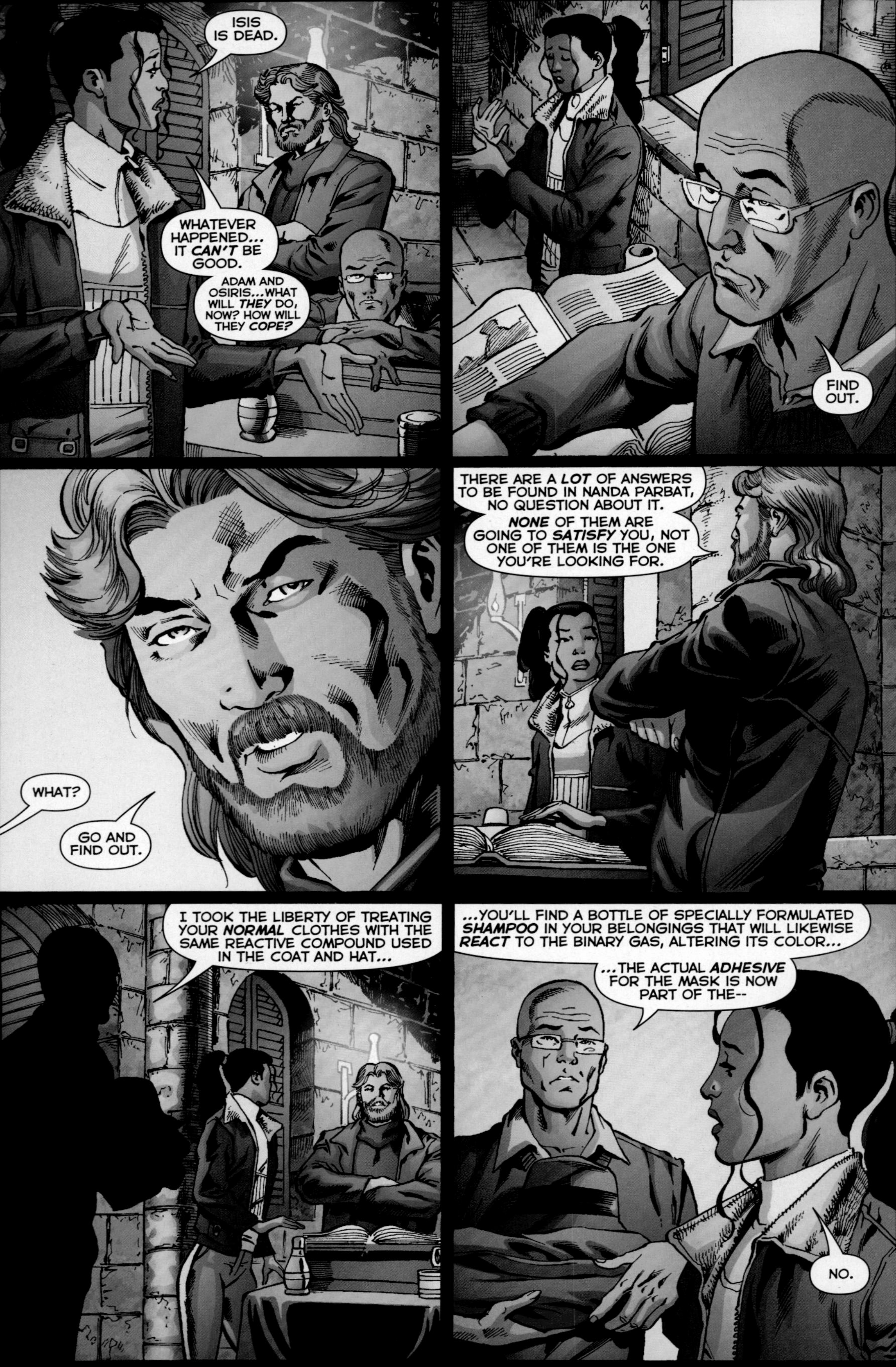
ISIS IS DEAD.
WHATEVER HAPPENED... IT CAN'T BE GOOD.
ADAM AND OSIRIS...WHAT WILL THEY DO, NOW? HOW WILL THEY COPE?
FIND OUT.
WHAT?
GO AND FIND OUT.
THERE ARE A LOT OF ANSWERS TO BE FOUND IN NANDA PARBAT, NO QUESTION ABOUT IT.
NONE OF THEM ARE GOING TO SATISFY YOU, NOT ONE OF THEM IS THE ONE YOU'RE LOOKING FOR.
I TOOK THE LIBERTY OF TREATING YOUR NORMAL CLOTHES WITH THE SAME REACTIVE COMPOUND USED IN THE COAT AND HAT...
...YOU'LL FIND A BOTTLE OF SPECIALLY FORMULATED SHAMPOO IN YOUR BELONGINGS THAT WILL LIKEWISE REACT TO THE BINARY GAS, ALTERING ITS COLOR...
...THE ACTUAL ADHESIVE FOR THE MASK IS NOW PART OF THE--
NO.

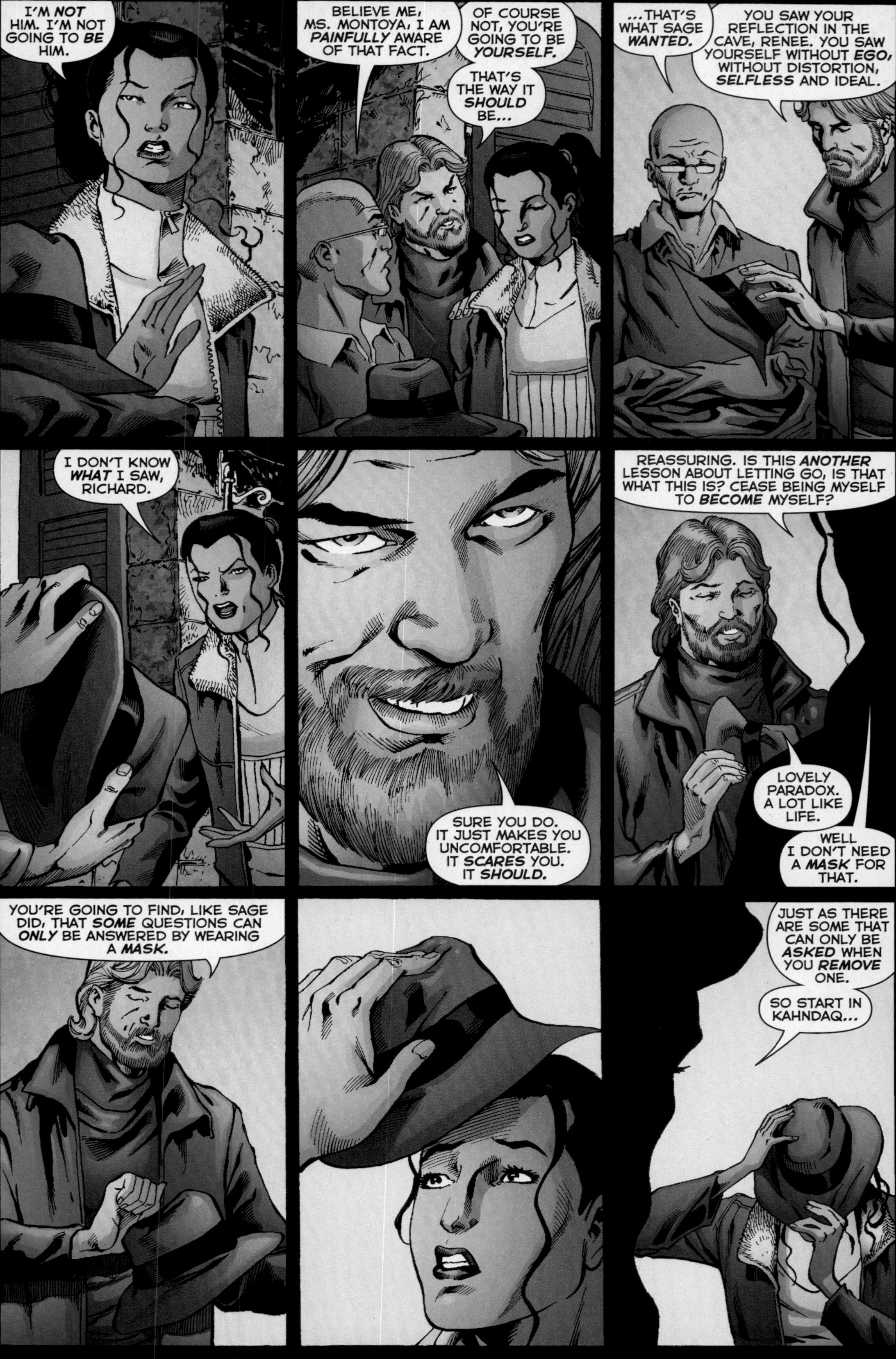
I'M *NOT* HIM. I'M NOT GOING TO *BE* HIM.
BELIEVE ME, MS. MONTOYA, I AM *PAINFULLY* AWARE OF THAT FACT.
OF COURSE NOT, YOU'RE GOING TO BE *YOURSELF.*
THAT'S THE WAY IT *SHOULD* BE...
...THAT'S WHAT SAGE *WANTED.*
YOU SAW YOUR REFLECTION IN THE CAVE, RENEE. YOU SAW YOURSELF WITHOUT *EGO,* WITHOUT DISTORTION, *SELFLESS* AND IDEAL.
I DON'T KNOW *WHAT* I SAW, RICHARD.
SURE YOU DO. IT JUST MAKES YOU UNCOMFORTABLE. IT *SCARES* YOU. IT *SHOULD.*
REASSURING. IS THIS *ANOTHER* LESSON ABOUT LETTING GO, IS THAT WHAT THIS IS? CEASE BEING MYSELF TO *BECOME* MYSELF?
LOVELY PARADOX. A LOT LIKE LIFE.
WELL I DON'T NEED A *MASK* FOR THAT.
YOU'RE GOING TO FIND, LIKE SAGE DID, THAT *SOME* QUESTIONS CAN *ONLY* BE ANSWERED BY WEARING A *MASK.*
JUST AS THERE ARE SOME THAT CAN ONLY BE *ASKED* WHEN YOU *REMOVE* ONE.
SO START IN KAHNDAQ...

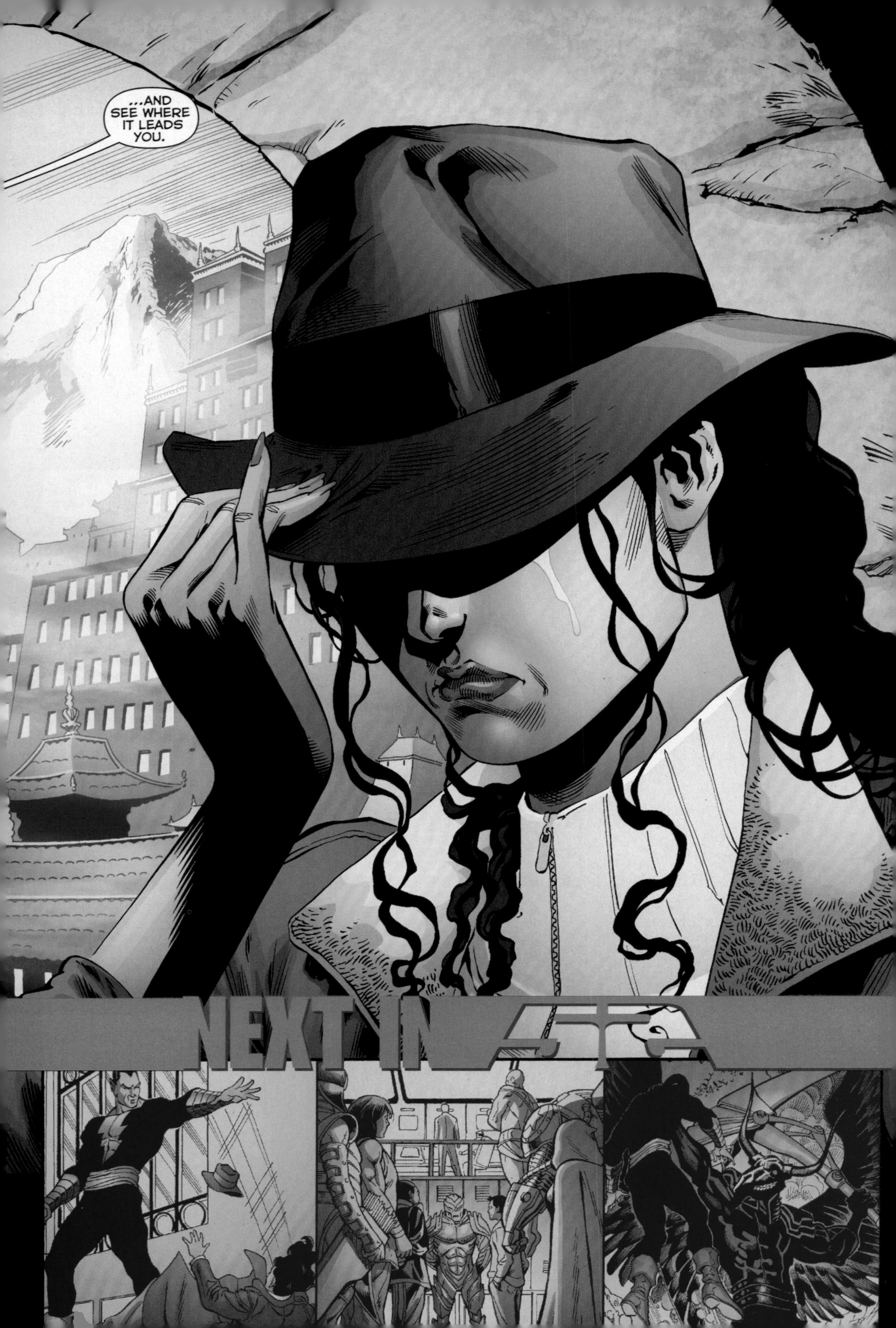
...AND SEE WHERE IT LEADS YOU.
NEXT IN 52

WEEK FORTY-FOUR NOTES

GREG RUCKA

Game, as they say, on.

If you look at the pacing of the fight between Adam and the Four Horsemen, you can see how he's systematically stripped of *every single acquisition* he's made over the course of the year, both literally — Adrianna, his cape — and emotionally, culminating, of course, with Isis recanting her wishes for a "kinder, gentler" Black Adam. Worse, still, is her assertion that she was wrong and that he was right, that his way is the *right* way. It is the kind of deathbed cliché-inversion that Geoff Johns lives for, and it's devastatingly effective, here. The greatest tragedy of the Black Adam storyline, to me, is that Isis is utterly and entirely broken at its end. The advocate of hope becomes the advocate of hopelessness, and after that, what else can Adam do but revert to form a thousand-times more savage than before?

There's another one of our more intentional thematic/symbolic riffs, here. The death of Isis's flower in Nanda Parbat served both as a plot device — it relays to Renee that Isis has died — and as a symbolic trigger; its death leads very directly to the first steps of Renee's "rebirth," literally cuing Tot and Richard to push her into action, because, still, Renee's dragging her feet. And while she receives the trappings here of what she is to become, she still hasn't managed to accept it.

I hated hated hated the single tear-track on the last page, and I fought against it, and I lost. I still think it's far too heavy-handed.

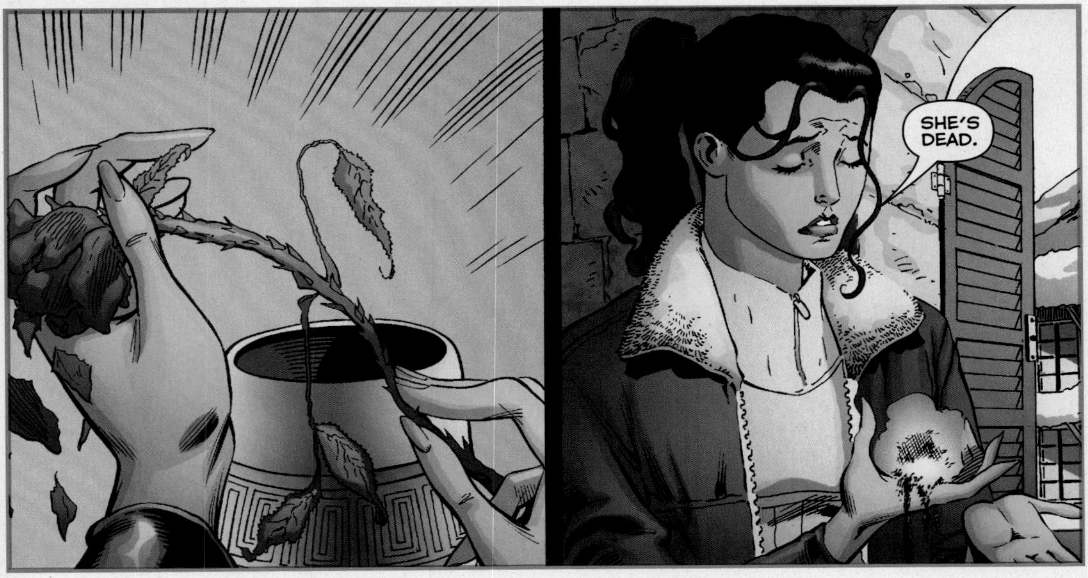
SHE'S DEAD.

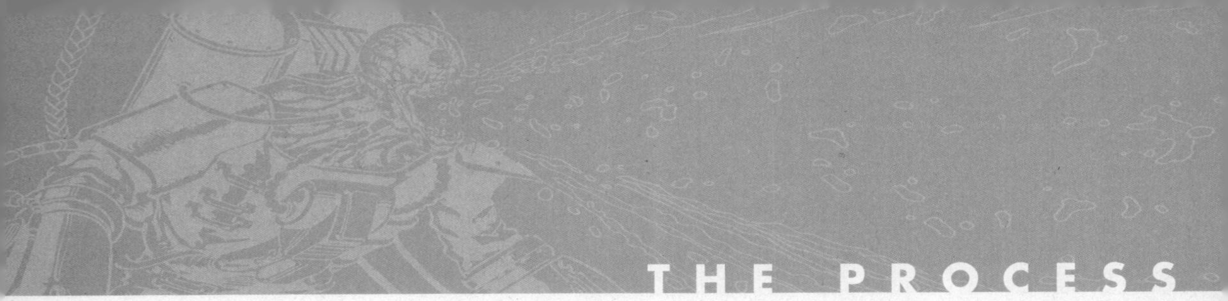

THE PROCESS

(COMPARE WITH PAGE 102 OF THIS COLLECTION)

Original Script

52 WEEK FORTY-FOUR — PAGE SIX

SPLASH PAGE

A huge shot of the other three Horsemen joining Sobek — Death, War and Pestilence. They are all attacking in unison — rushing Black Adam and Isis. [SEE WEEK 38]

SOBEK: <Me and my SIBLINGS. Some call us the "Monster Society"...>

SOBEK: <...but we are "The Four Ages of dread of Apokolips in its anguished bloody, morning.">

SOBEK: <Our influence over the last several weeks is the TRUE cause of Kahndaq's MISERY -- >

SOBEK: < -- and it will be the cause of YOURS.>

Breakdown by Keith Giffen

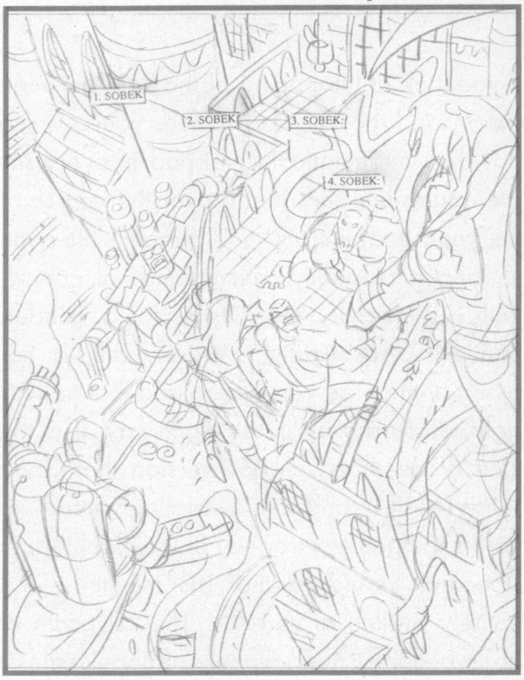
1. SOBEK
2. SOBEK
3. SOBEK:
4. SOBEK:

Pencils by Eddy Barrows

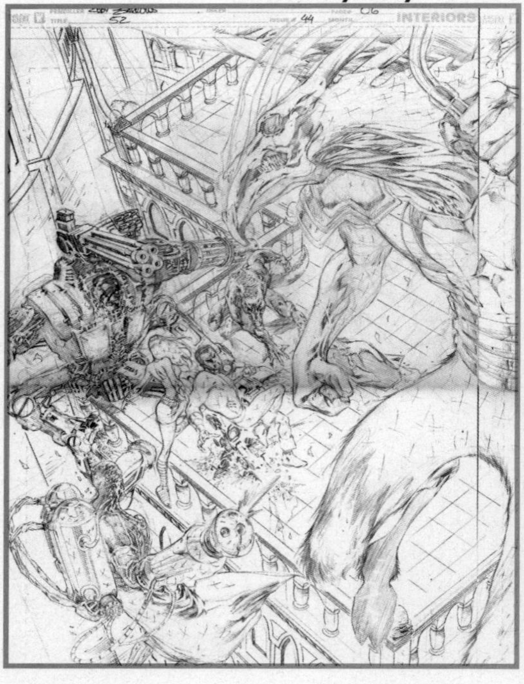
INTERIORS

Final Page

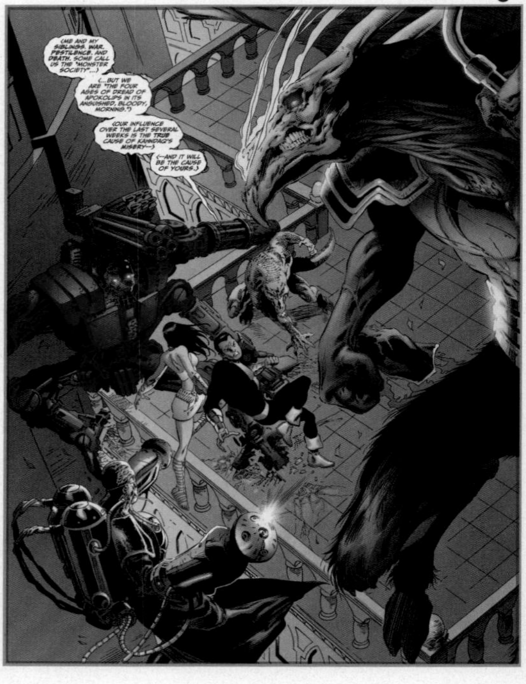
<ME AND MY SIBLINGS. WAR. PESTILENCE. AND DEATH. SOME CALL US THE "MONSTER SOCIETY"...>
<...BUT WE ARE "THE FOUR AGES OF DREAD OF APOKOLIPS IN ITS ANGUISHED, BLOODY, MORNING.">
<OUR INFLUENCE OVER THE LAST SEVERAL WEEKS IS THE TRUE CAUSE OF KAHNDAQ'S MISERY-->
<--AND IT WILL BE THE CAUSE OF YOURS.>

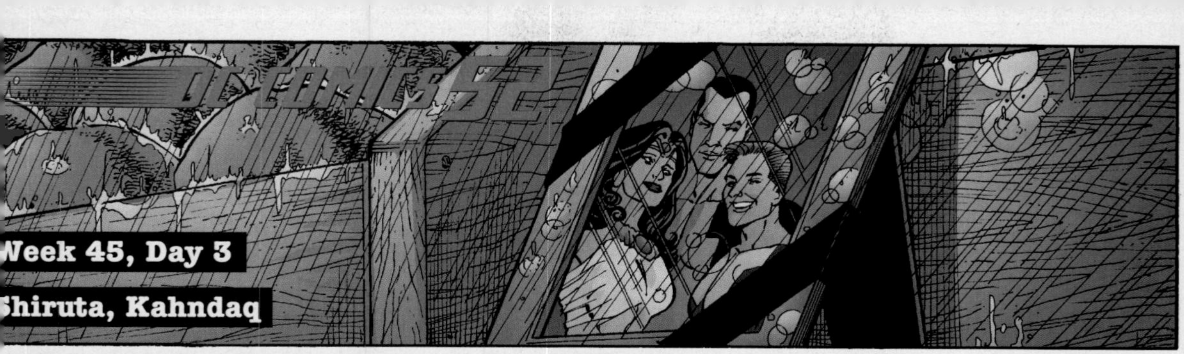
Week 45, Day 3
Shiruta, Kahndaq

WRITTEN BY GEOFF JOHNS, GRANT MORRISON, GREG RUCKA, MARK WAID

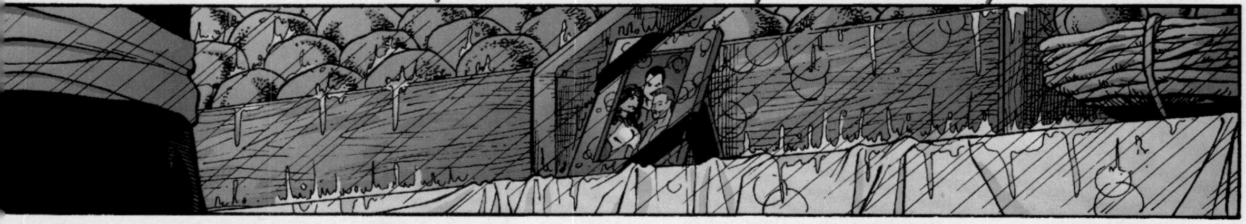

ART BREAKDOWNS BY KEITH GIFFEN • PENCILS BY CHRIS BATISTA AND JAMAL IGLE

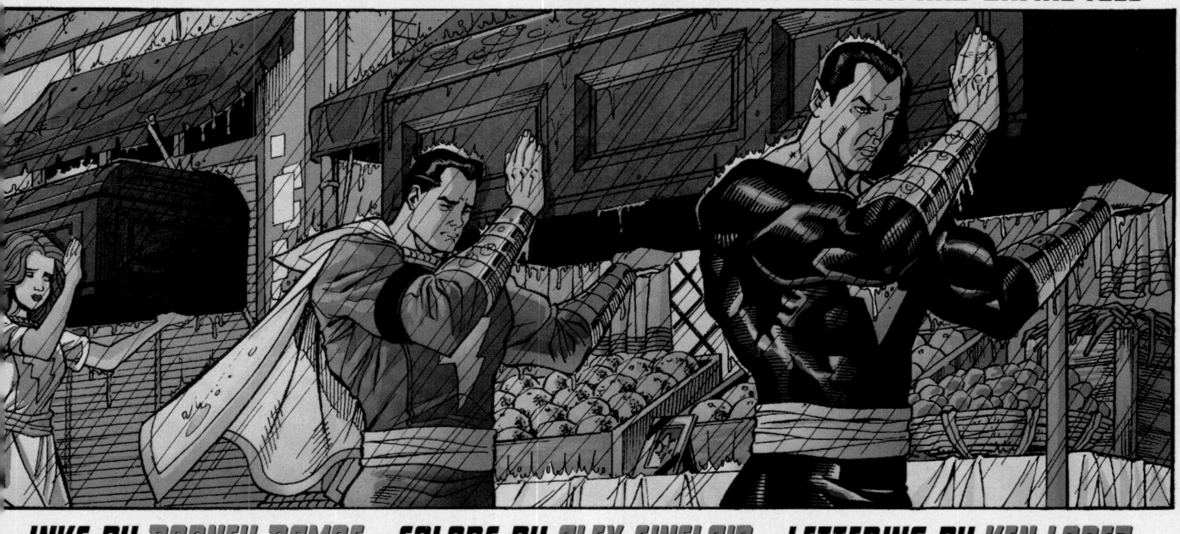

INKS BY RODNEY RAMOS • COLORS BY ALEX SINCLAIR • LETTERING BY KEN LOPEZ

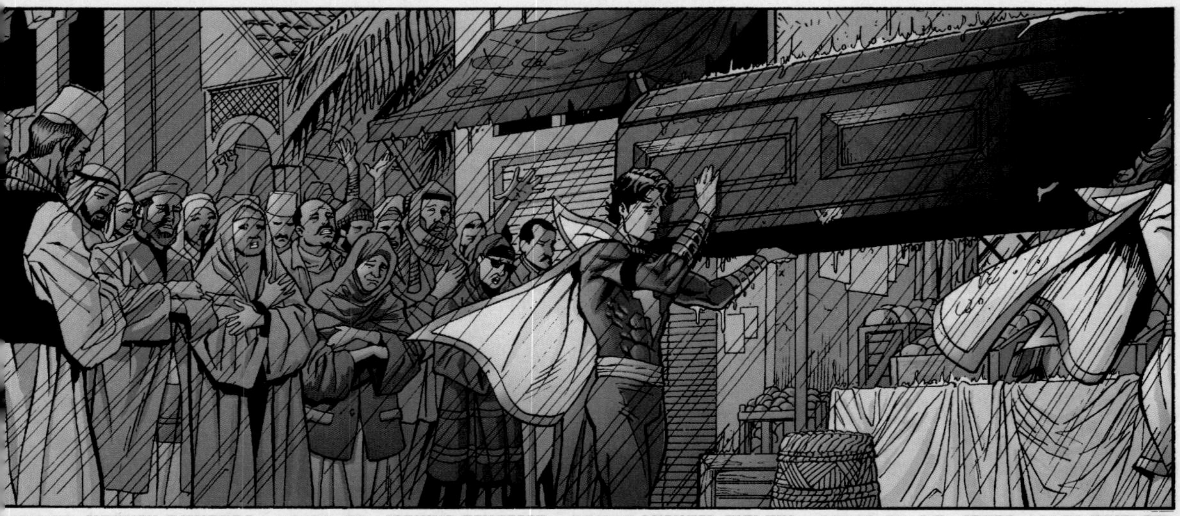

SS'T ED. HARVEY RICHARDS • ASSOC. ED. JEANINE SCHAEFER • EDITOR MICHAEL SIGLAIN • COVER BY J.G. JONES & ALEX SINCLAIR

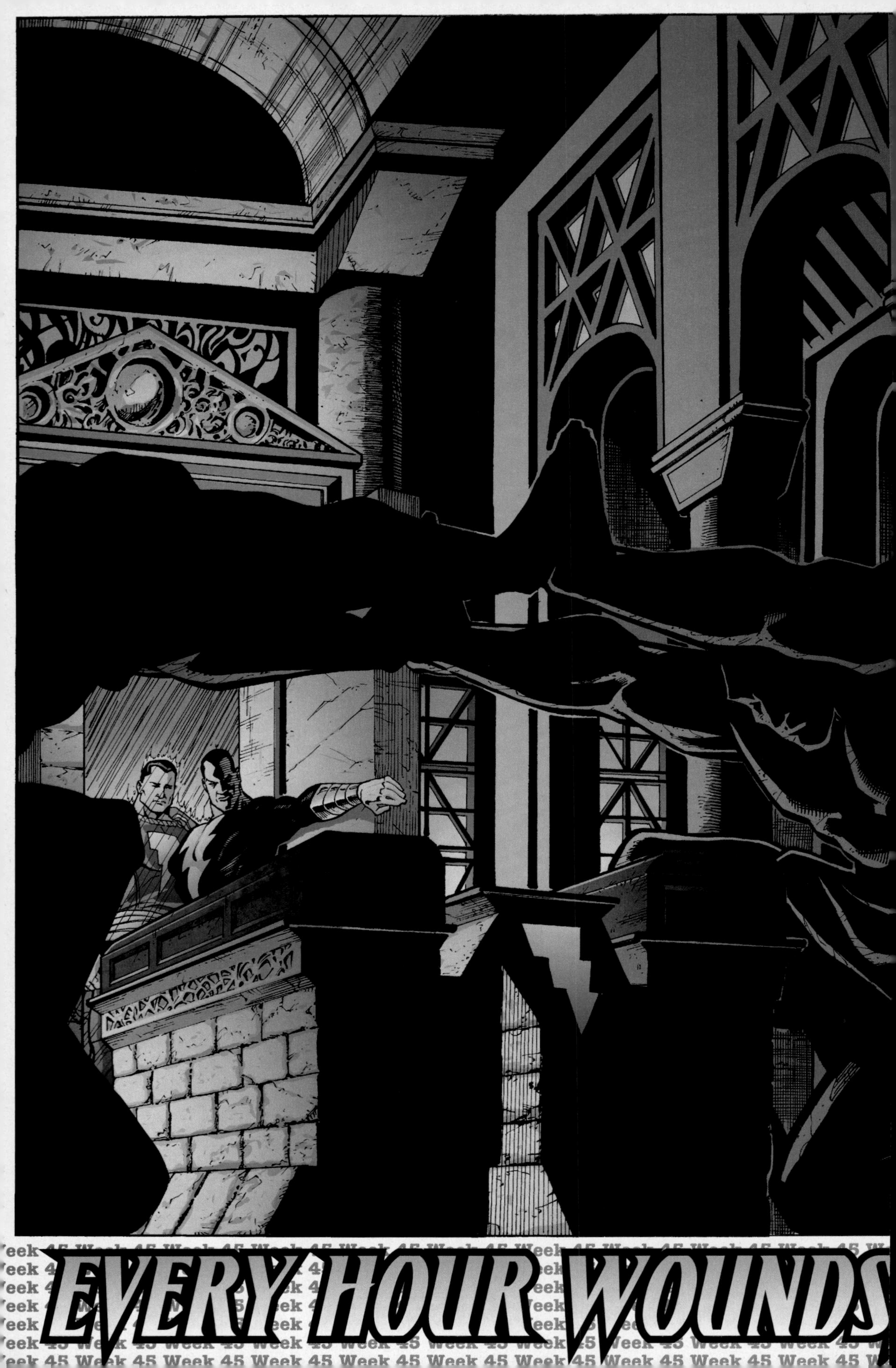
Week 45
EVERY HOUR WOUNDS

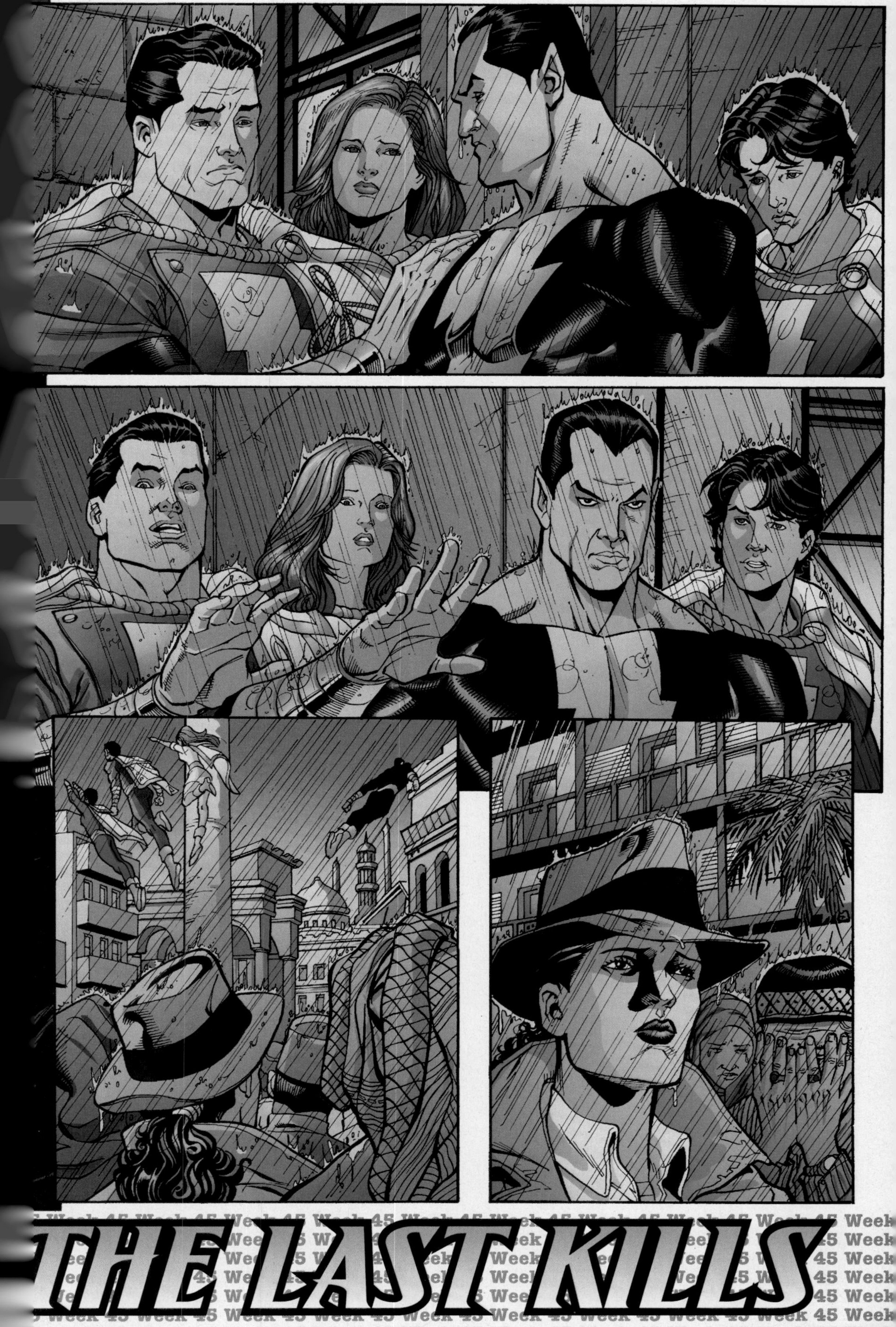

Week 45

THE LAST KILLS

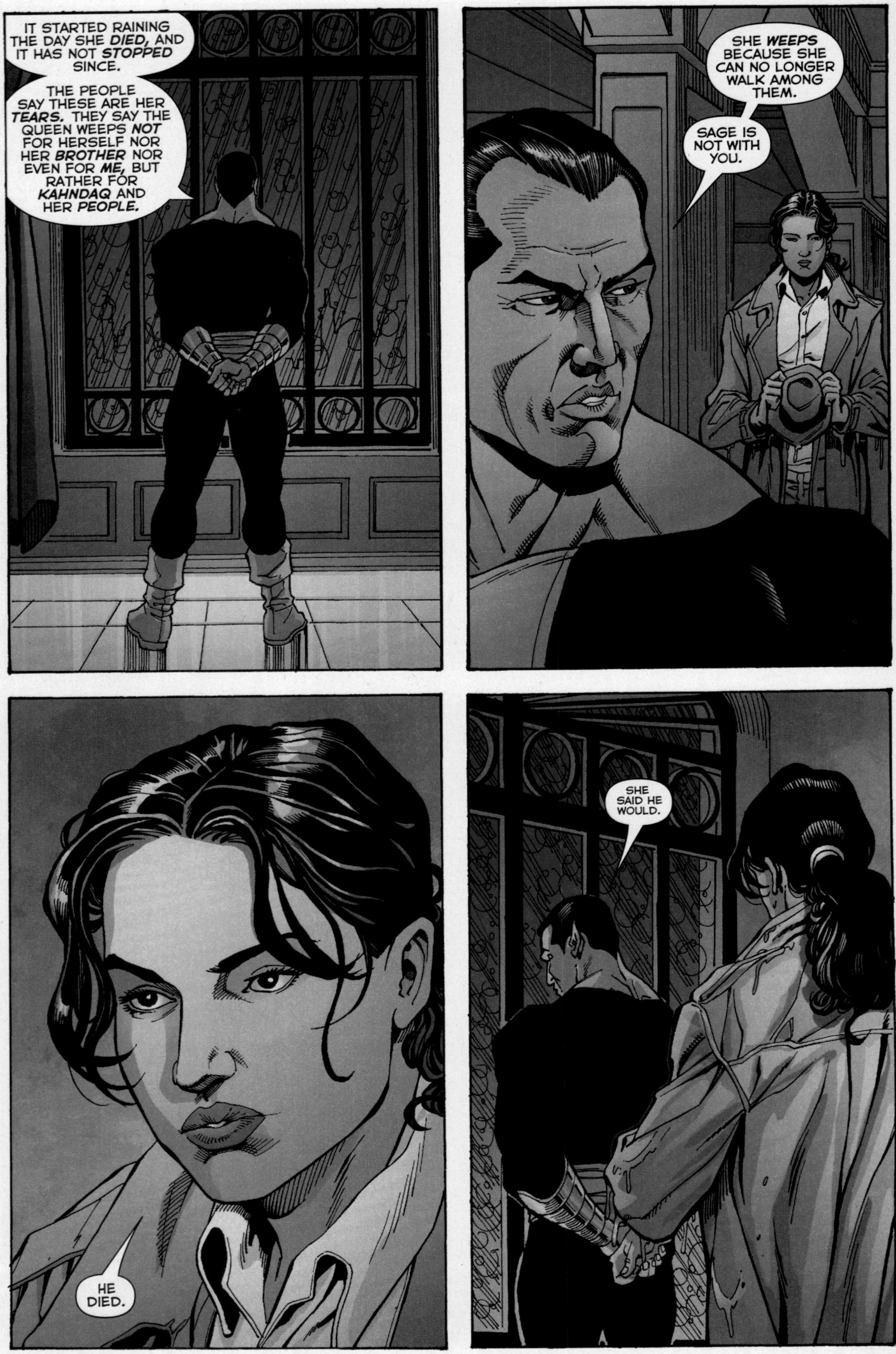
IT STARTED RAINING THE DAY SHE DIED, AND IT HAS NOT STOPPED SINCE.
THE PEOPLE SAY THESE ARE HER TEARS. THEY SAY THE QUEEN WEEPS NOT FOR HERSELF NOR HER BROTHER NOR EVEN FOR ME, BUT RATHER FOR KAHNDAQ AND HER PEOPLE.
SHE WEEPS BECAUSE SHE CAN NO LONGER WALK AMONG THEM.
SAGE IS NOT WITH YOU.
HE DIED.
SHE SAID HE WOULD.

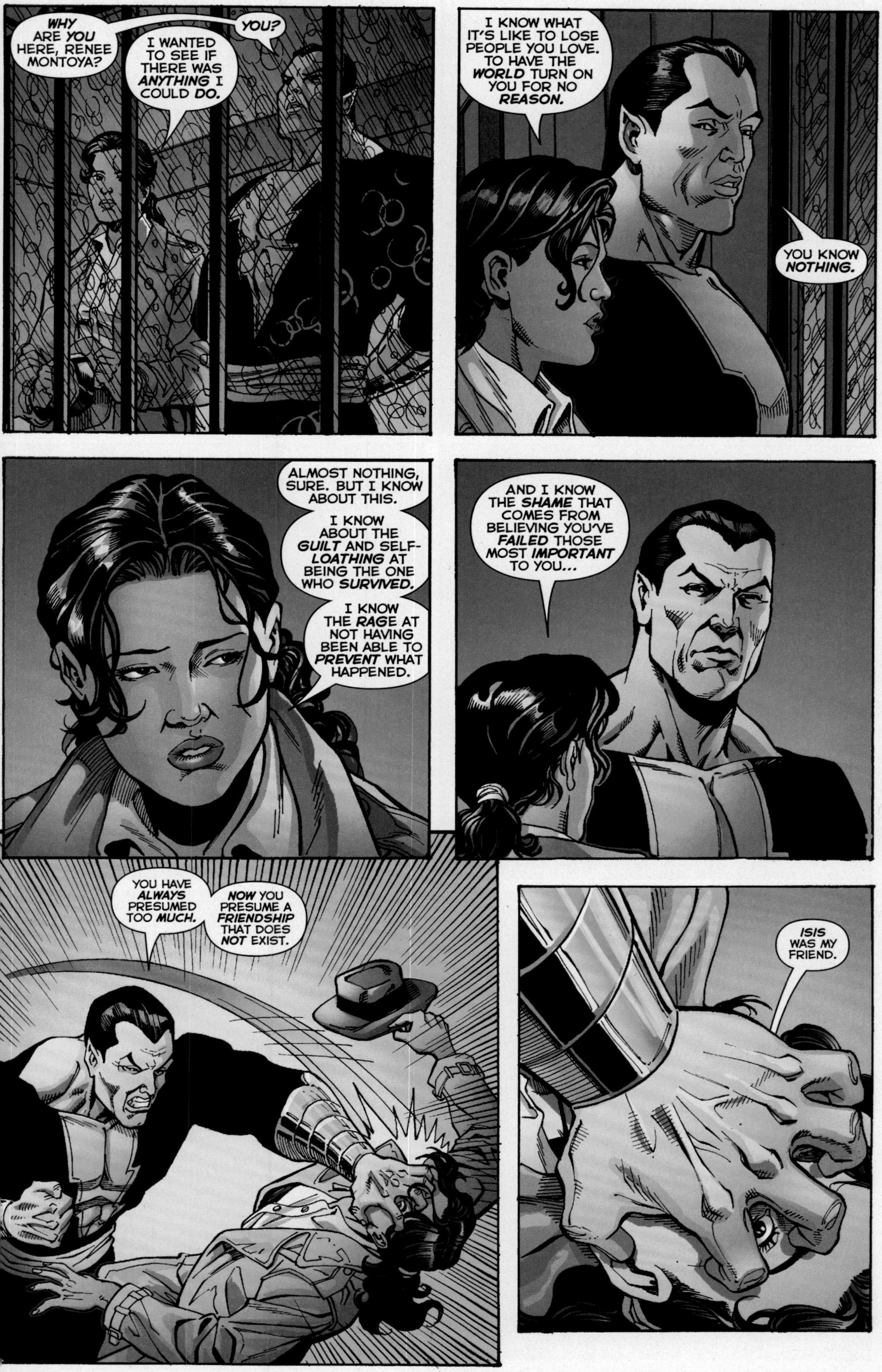
WHY ARE YOU HERE, RENEE MONTOYA?
I WANTED TO SEE IF THERE WAS ANYTHING I COULD DO.
YOU?
I KNOW WHAT IT'S LIKE TO LOSE PEOPLE YOU LOVE. TO HAVE THE WORLD TURN ON YOU FOR NO REASON.
YOU KNOW NOTHING.
ALMOST NOTHING, SURE. BUT I KNOW ABOUT THIS.
I KNOW ABOUT THE GUILT AND SELF-LOATHING AT BEING THE ONE WHO SURVIVED.
I KNOW THE RAGE AT NOT HAVING BEEN ABLE TO PREVENT WHAT HAPPENED.
AND I KNOW THE SHAME THAT COMES FROM BELIEVING YOU'VE FAILED THOSE MOST IMPORTANT TO YOU...
YOU HAVE ALWAYS PRESUMED TOO MUCH.
NOW YOU PRESUME A FRIENDSHIP THAT DOES NOT EXIST.
ISIS WAS MY FRIEND.

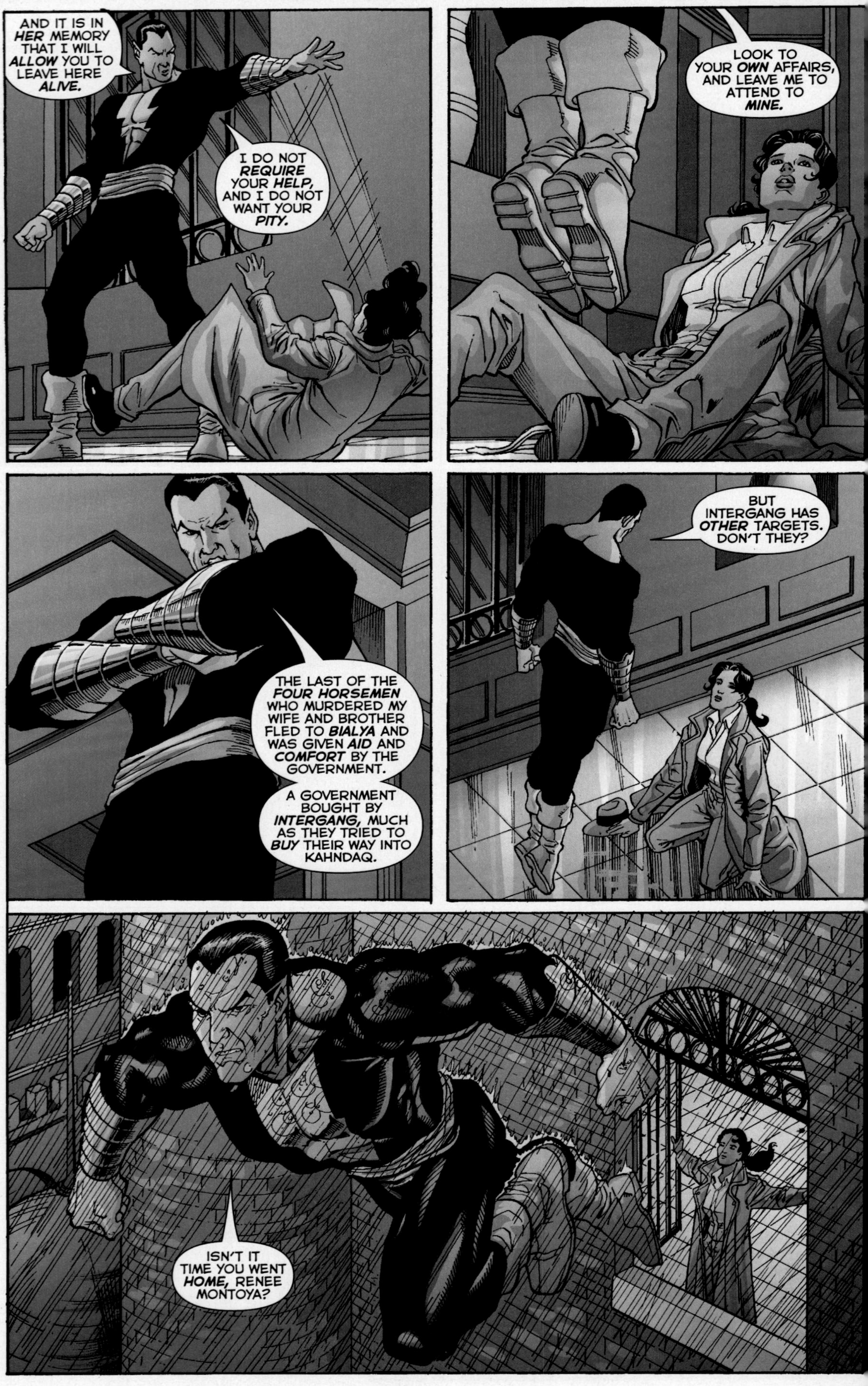

AND IT IS IN HER MEMORY THAT I WILL ALLOW YOU TO LEAVE HERE ALIVE.
I DO NOT REQUIRE YOUR HELP, AND I DO NOT WANT YOUR PITY.
LOOK TO YOUR OWN AFFAIRS, AND LEAVE ME TO ATTEND TO MINE.
THE LAST OF THE FOUR HORSEMEN WHO MURDERED MY WIFE AND BROTHER FLED TO BIALYA AND WAS GIVEN AID AND COMFORT BY THE GOVERNMENT.
A GOVERNMENT BOUGHT BY INTERGANG, MUCH AS THEY TRIED TO BUY THEIR WAY INTO KAHNDAQ.
BUT INTERGANG HAS OTHER TARGETS. DON'T THEY?
ISN'T IT TIME YOU WENT HOME, RENEE MONTOYA?

THIS IS A *BETRAYAL*, MISTER MANNHEIM!

I'D CHOOSE YOUR WORDS *CAREFULLY*, MR. PRESIDENT.

OUR WHOLE *NATION* EMBRACED YOUR WAY OF *CRIME*, YOUR NEW WORLD *ORDER!* YOU SAID IT WAS *PROPHECY*--

--AND THAT BIALYA'S SUPPORT OF YOUR *FOUR HORSEMEN* WOULD REMAIN *SECRET!*

WHY HAS *DEATH* ARRIVED AT OUR DOOR, MISTER MANNHEIM? WHY DOES HE HOVER OVER US IN *SILENCE?*

IS THIS PART OF YOUR *PROPHECY*, TOO?

PROPHESY'S A *FUNNY* THING, MR. PRESIDENT. YOU TRIED CONTACTING CHUNG TZU?

THE OOLONG COMPLEX IS *REFUSING* ALL INCOMING COMMUNICATIONS. THEY APPEAR TO BE IN *LOCKDOWN!*

THEN IT LOOKS LIKE WE'VE BOTH GOT *PROBLEMS* TO DEAL WITH.

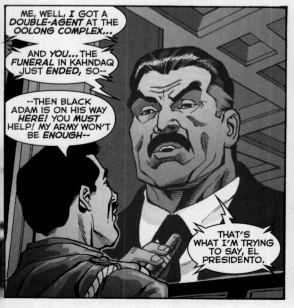

ME, WELL, *I* GOT A *DOUBLE-AGENT* AT THE *OOLONG COMPLEX*...

AND *YOU*... THE *FUNERAL* IN KAHNDAQ JUST *ENDED*, SO--

--THEN BLACK ADAM IS ON HIS WAY *HERE!* YOU *MUST* HELP! MY ARMY WON'T BE *ENOUGH*--

THAT'S WHAT I'M TRYING TO SAY, EL PRESIDENTO.

NICE KNOWIN' YA.

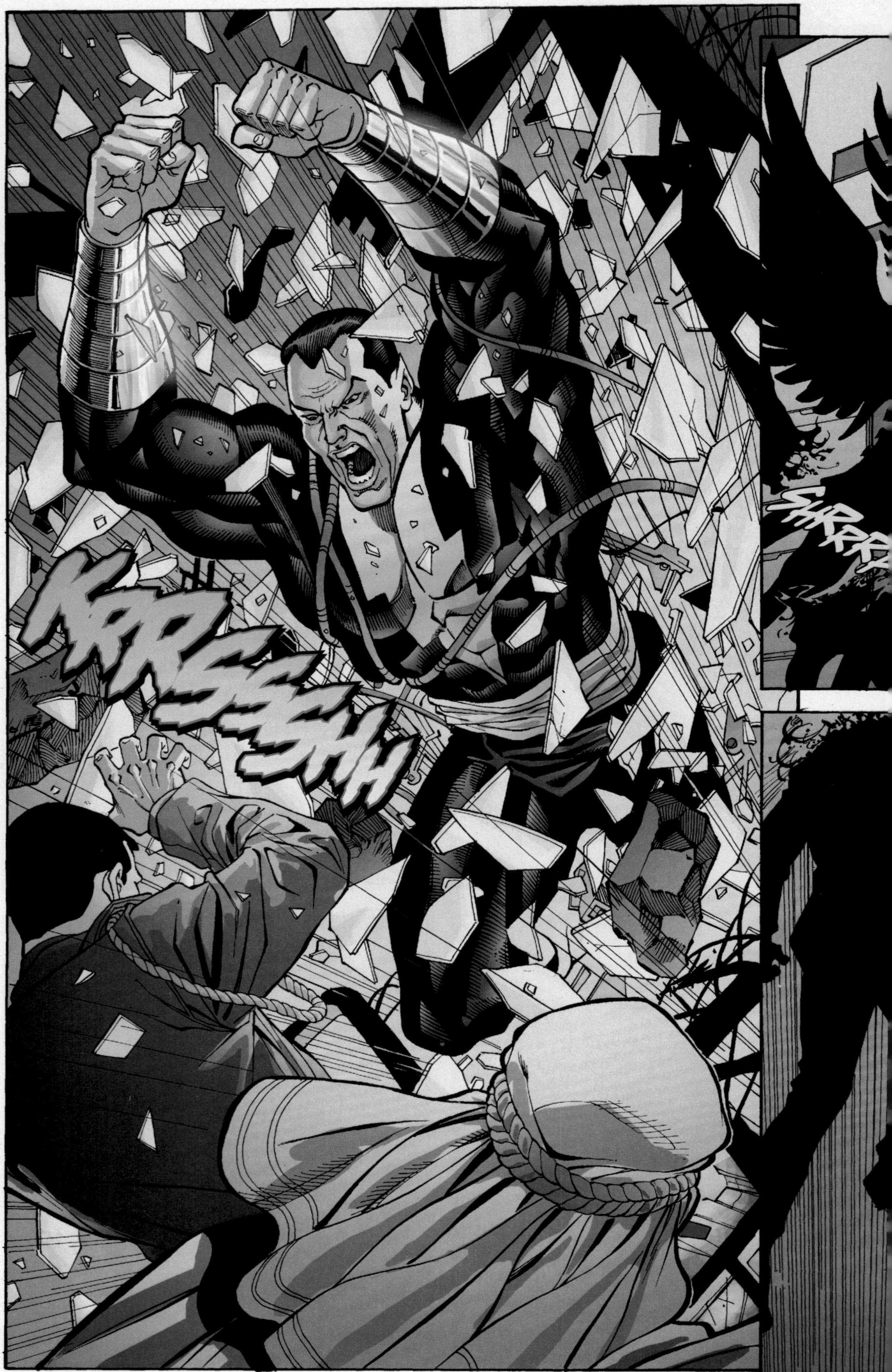
KRRSSSHH

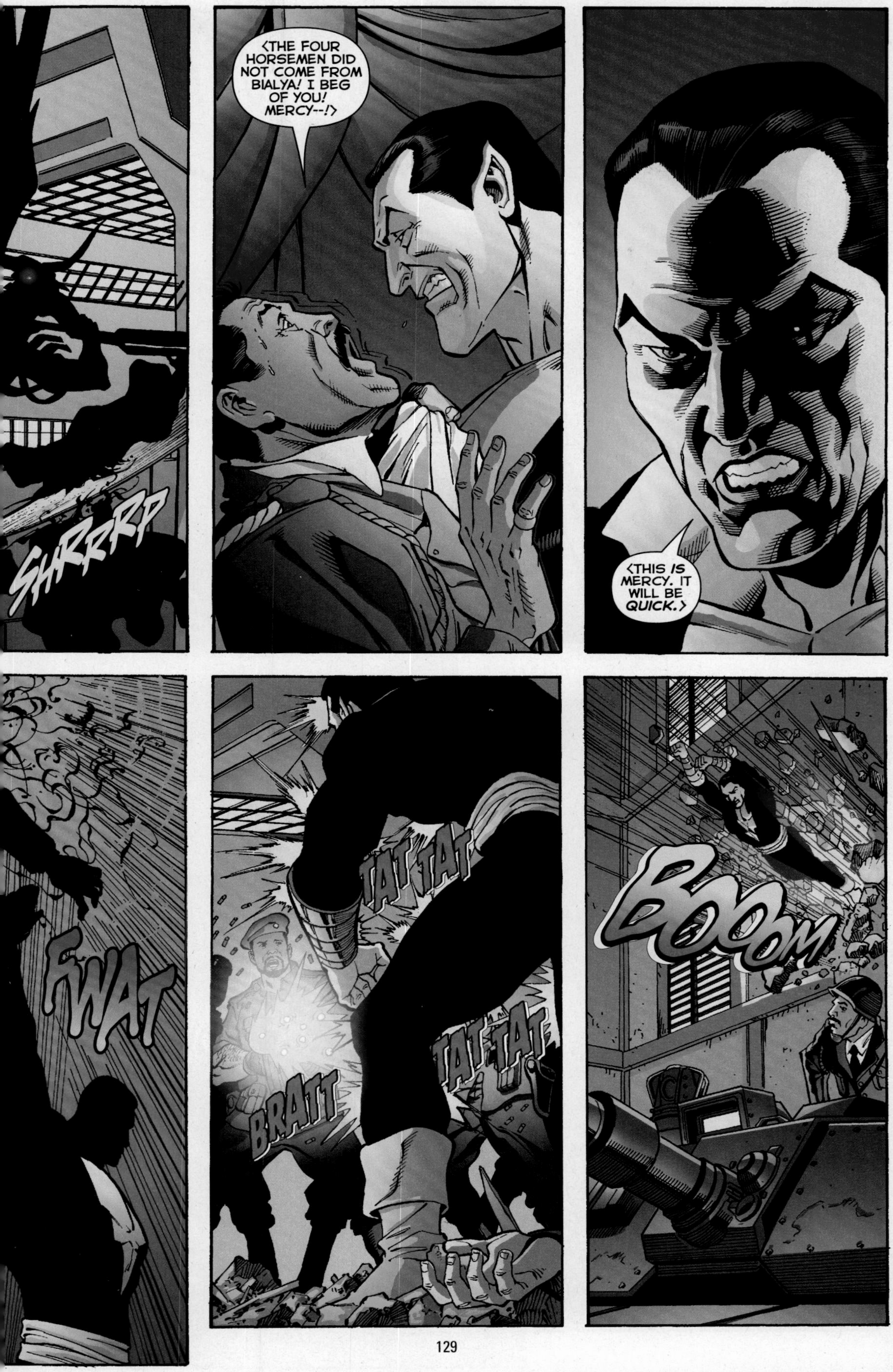
SHRRRP
<THE FOUR HORSEMEN DID NOT COME FROM BIALYA! I BEG OF YOU! MERCY--!>
<THIS IS MERCY. IT WILL BE QUICK.>
FWAT
TAT TAT
BRATT
TAT TAT
BOOOM

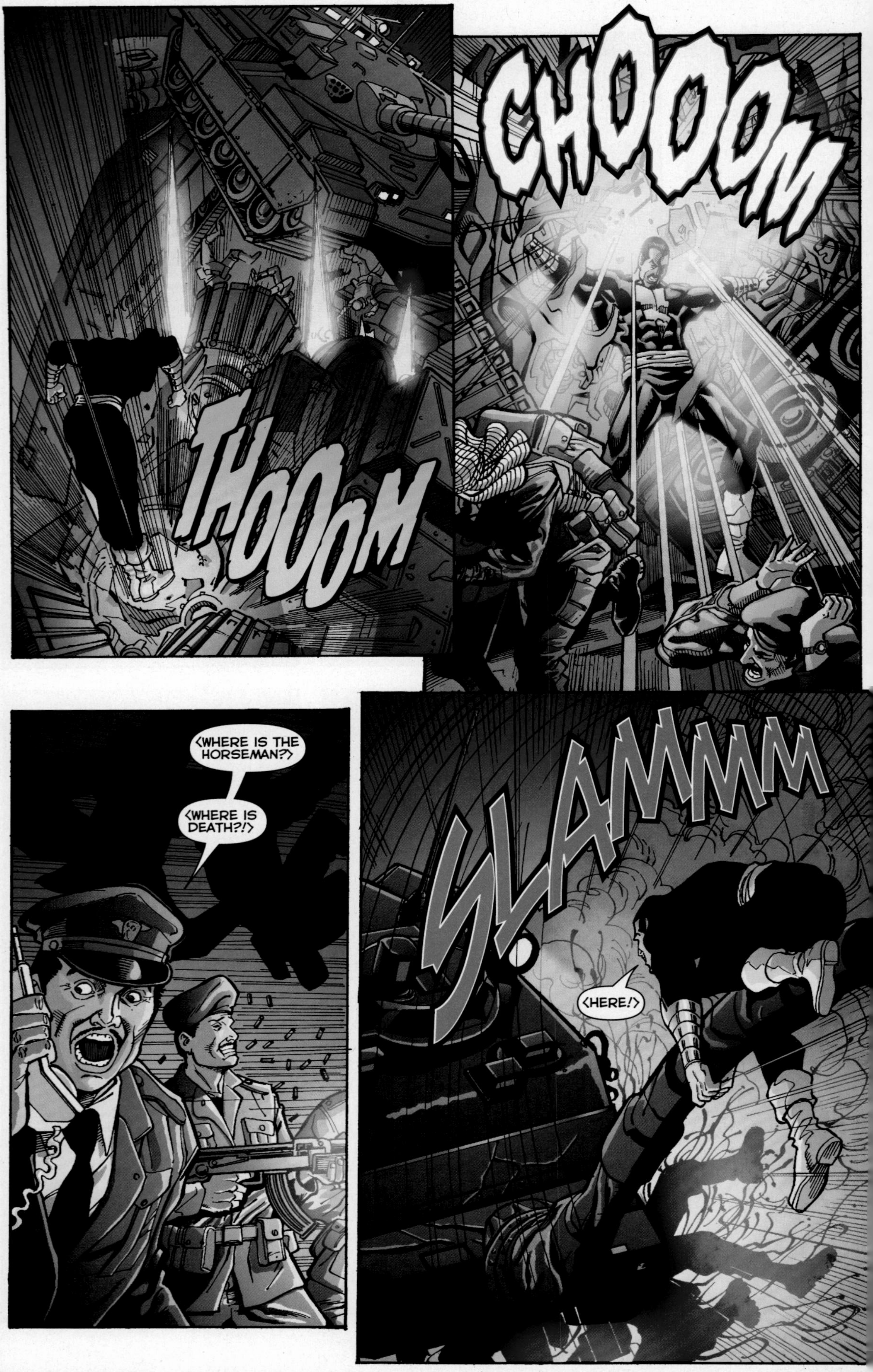
THOOOM
CHOOOM
<WHERE IS THE HORSEMAN?>
<WHERE IS DEATH?!>
SLAMMMM
<HERE!>

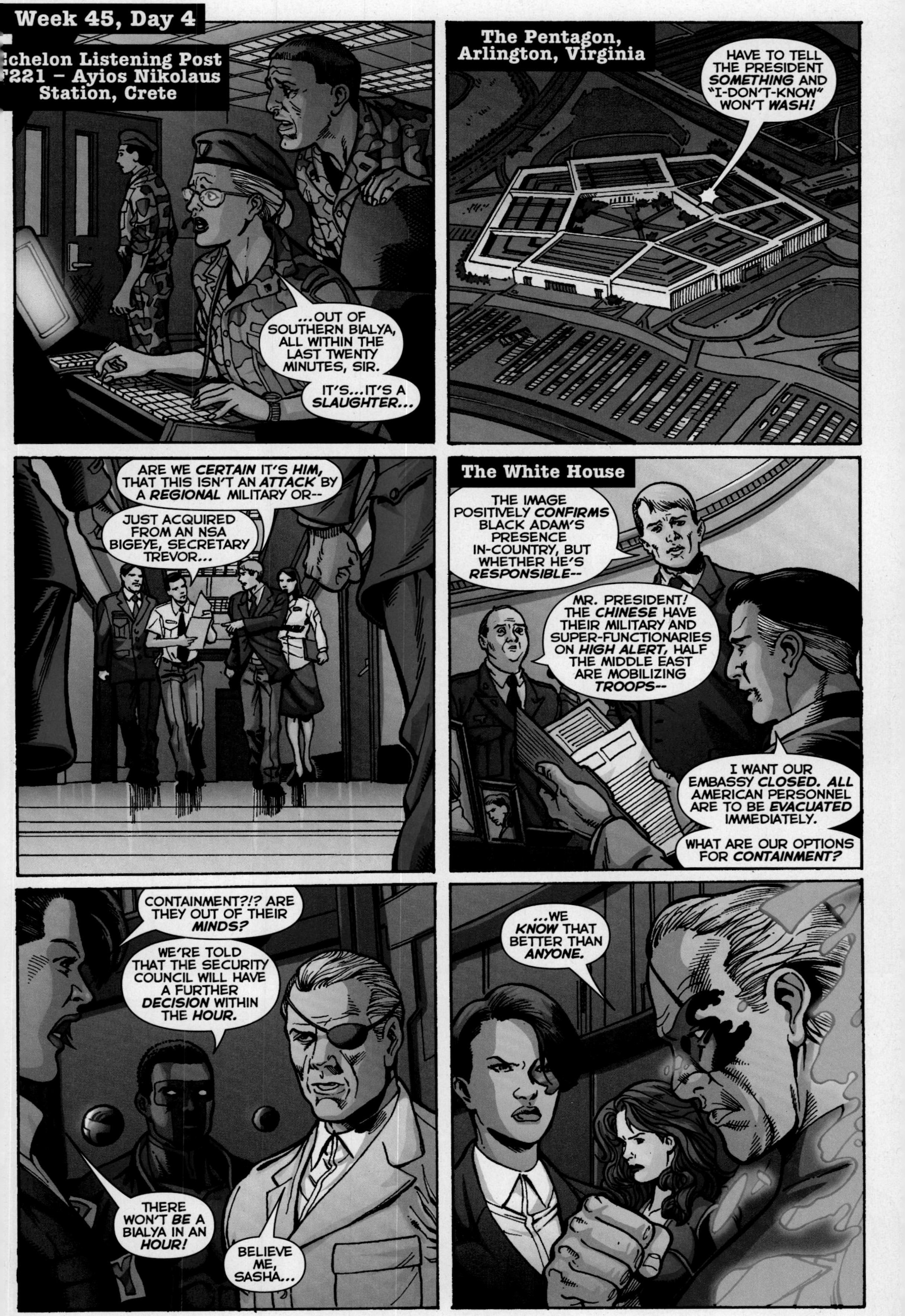
Week 45, Day 4
Echelon Listening Post #221 – Ayios Nikolaus Station, Crete
...OUT OF SOUTHERN BIALYA, ALL WITHIN THE LAST TWENTY MINUTES, SIR.
IT'S...IT'S A SLAUGHTER...
The Pentagon, Arlington, Virginia
HAVE TO TELL THE PRESIDENT SOMETHING AND "I-DON'T-KNOW" WON'T WASH!
ARE WE CERTAIN IT'S HIM, THAT THIS ISN'T AN ATTACK BY A REGIONAL MILITARY OR--
JUST ACQUIRED FROM AN NSA BIGEYE, SECRETARY TREVOR...
The White House
THE IMAGE POSITIVELY CONFIRMS BLACK ADAM'S PRESENCE IN-COUNTRY, BUT WHETHER HE'S RESPONSIBLE--
MR. PRESIDENT! THE CHINESE HAVE THEIR MILITARY AND SUPER-FUNCTIONARIES ON HIGH ALERT, HALF THE MIDDLE EAST ARE MOBILIZING TROOPS--
I WANT OUR EMBASSY CLOSED. ALL AMERICAN PERSONNEL ARE TO BE EVACUATED IMMEDIATELY.
WHAT ARE OUR OPTIONS FOR CONTAINMENT?
CONTAINMENT?!? ARE THEY OUT OF THEIR MINDS?
WE'RE TOLD THAT THE SECURITY COUNCIL WILL HAVE A FURTHER DECISION WITHIN THE HOUR.
THERE WON'T BE A BIALYA IN AN HOUR!
BELIEVE ME, SASHA...
...WE KNOW THAT BETTER THAN ANYONE.

CAPTAIN BOOMERANG | KILLER CROC | SHADOW THIEF | PARASITE | TIGRESS
GIGANTA | DR. PSYCHO | ICICLE | MIRROR MASTER | METALLO
CAPTAIN COLD | BRONZE TIGER | PLASTIQUE | BLACK MANTA | THE TATTOOED MAN
COUNT VERTIGO | DOCTOR LIGHT | | CLAYFACE | CHEETAH

THIS NEW SUICIDE SQUAD NEEDS TO BE *ONE HUNDRED* STRONG IF THEY HAVE ANY HOPE AGAINST BLACK ADAM.

YOU CAN COUNT ME *OUT*, WALLER.

YOU'RE STILL THE *KEY* HERE, ATOM SMASHER. YOU CAN TALK TO HIM--

YOU MEAN *DISTRACT* HIM? THIS IS ANOTHER SETUP. BLACK ADAM WOULDN'T ATTACK BIALYA LIKE THIS--

WE HAVE VISUAL CONFIRMATION--

YOU MEAN LIKE THE DOCTORED FOOTAGE OF WHAT OSIRIS DID TO THE PERSUADER?

YOU SPLICED IN REACTION SHOTS FROM HIS TIME WITH THE TITANS TO MAKE IT LOOK LIKE OSIRIS *ENJOYED* KILLING HIM.

I'LL GO AFTER BLACK ADAM, BUT NOT WITH YOU.

YOU CAN'T JUST *LEAVE.* YOU'RE STILL AN *INMATE* OF BELLE REVE!

YOU'RE GOING TO GIVE ME THAT PARDON YOU GAVE BOOMERANG--

--OR I'M GOING TO LET ALAN SCOTT AND CHECKMATE IN ON YOUR "NEW" SUICIDE SQUAD.

YOU IDIOT! YOU CAN'T POSSIBLY DO THIS ALONE!

I'M NOT GOING TO.

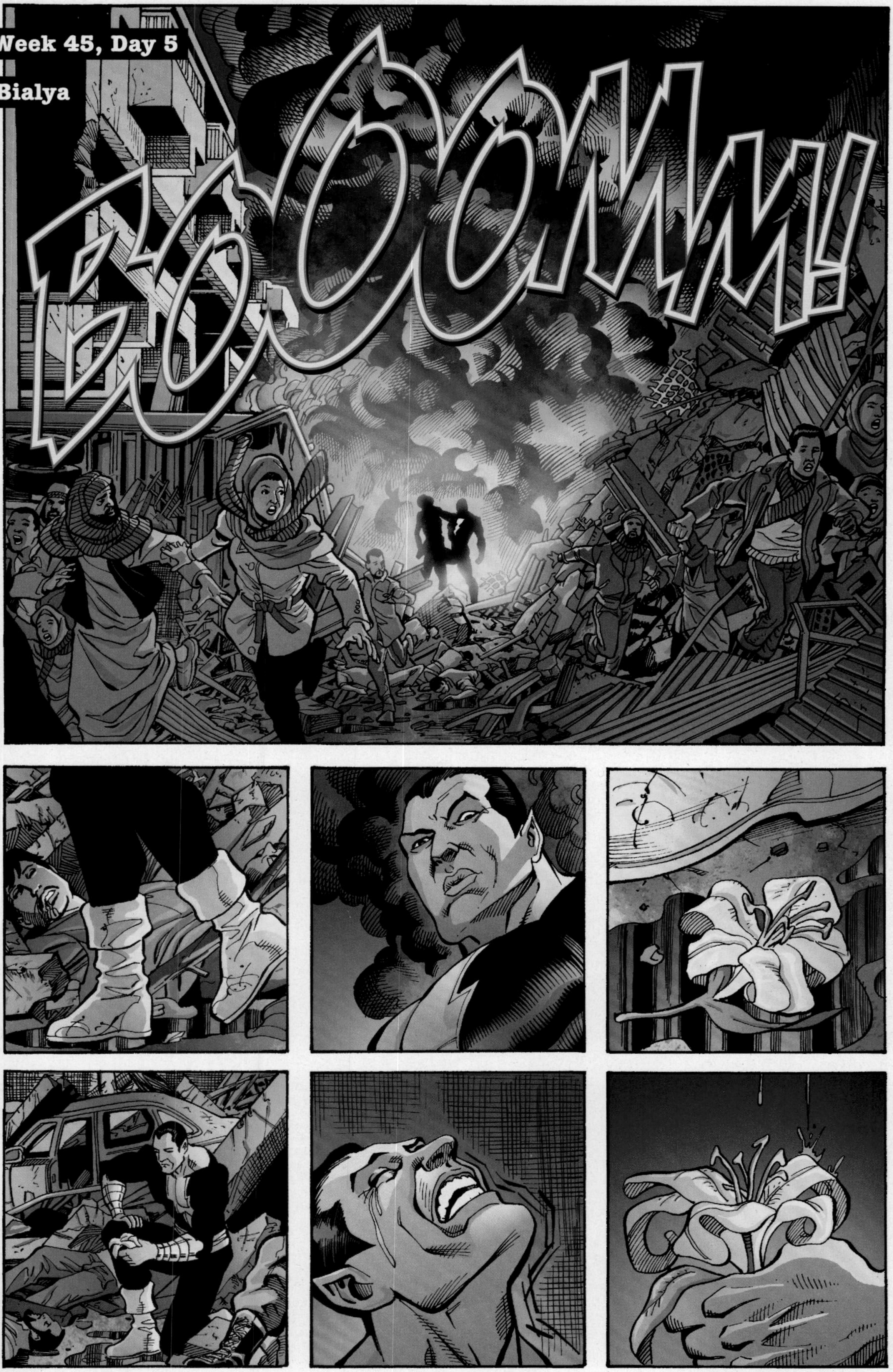

Week 45, Day 5
Bialya
BOOOMM!

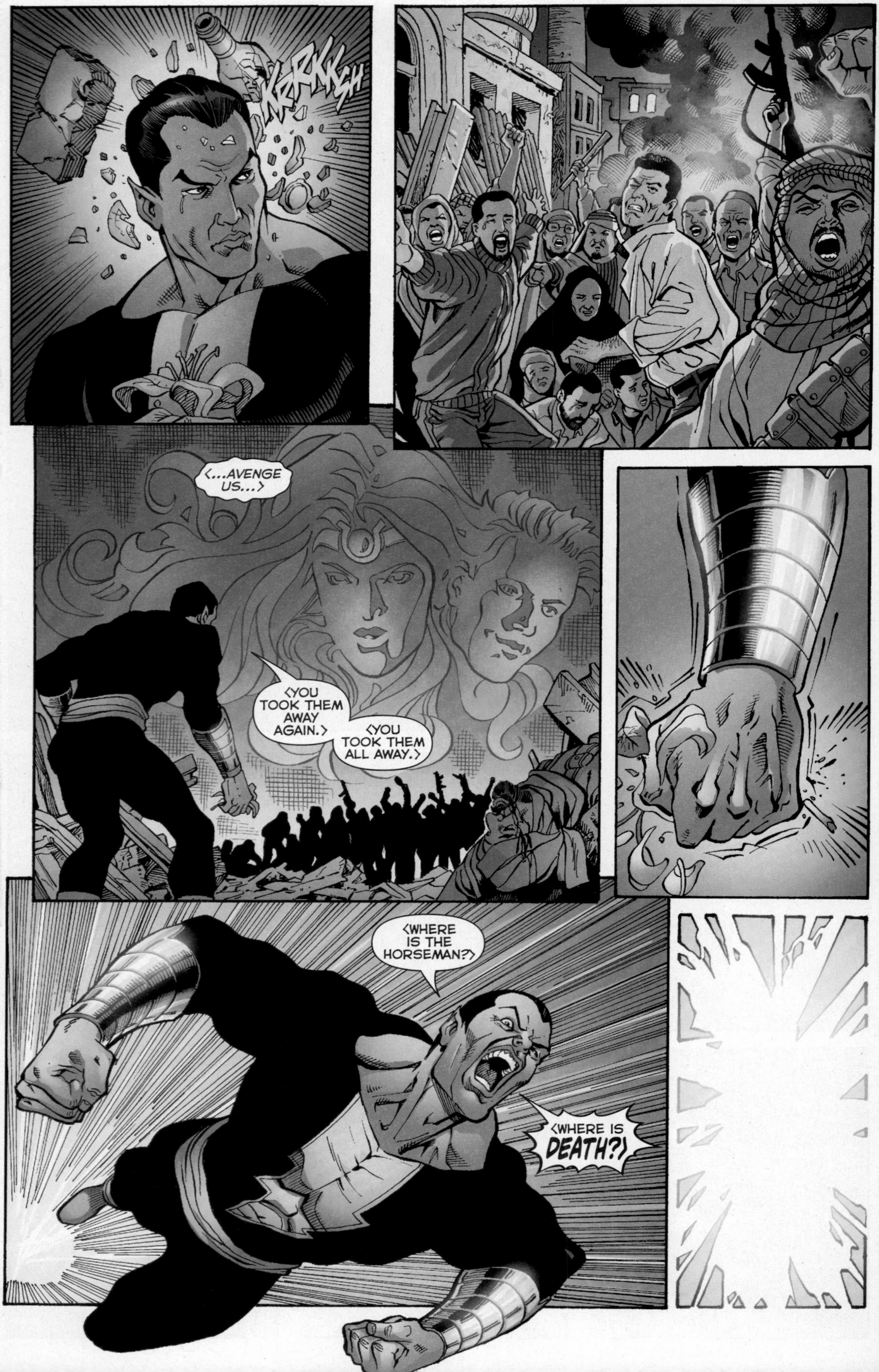
KRRKKSH
<...AVENGE US...>
<YOU TOOK THEM AWAY AGAIN.>
<YOU TOOK THEM ALL AWAY.>
<WHERE IS THE HORSEMAN?>
<WHERE IS DEATH?!>

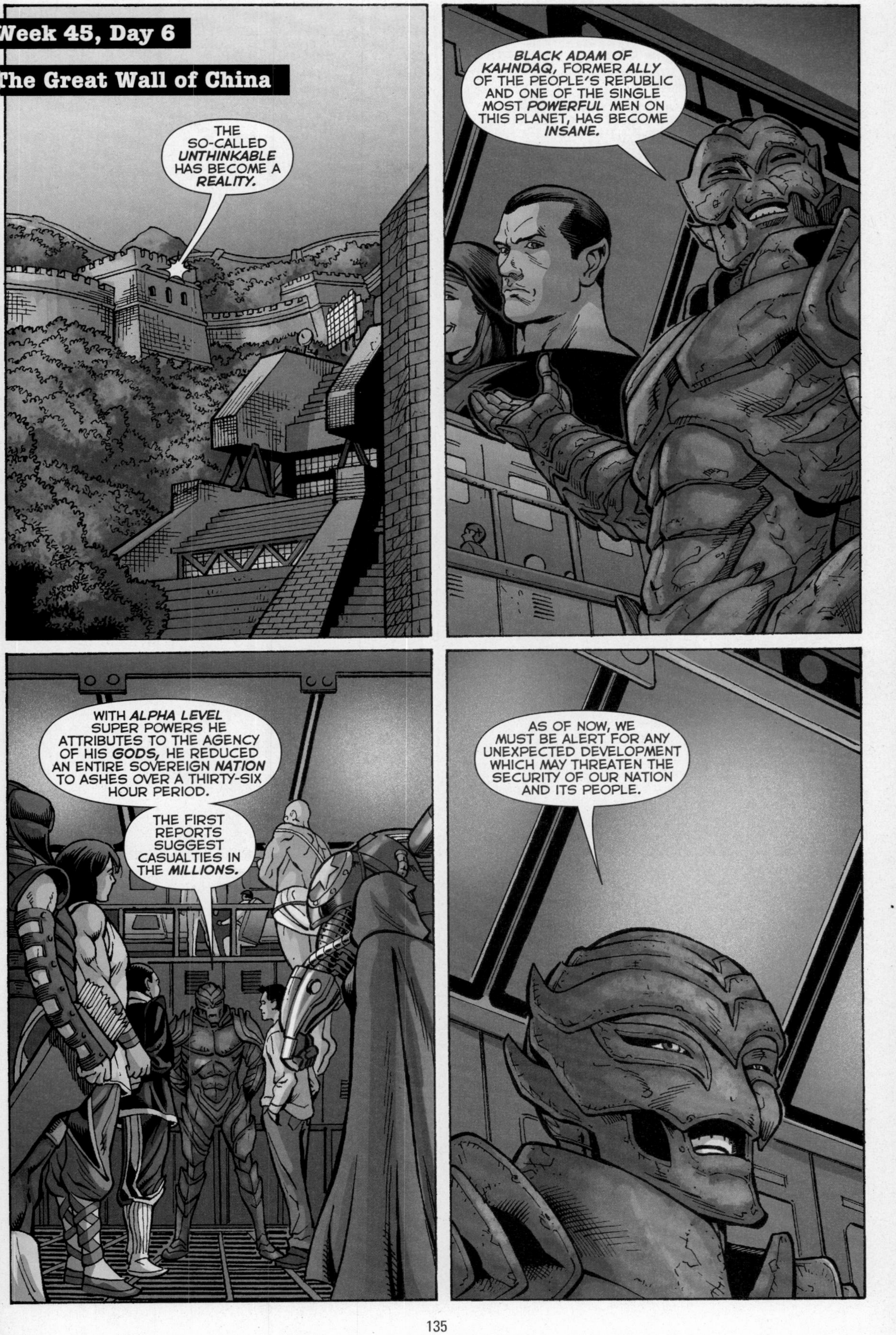
Week 45, Day 6
The Great Wall of China
THE SO-CALLED UNTHINKABLE HAS BECOME A REALITY.
BLACK ADAM OF KAHNDAQ, FORMER ALLY OF THE PEOPLE'S REPUBLIC AND ONE OF THE SINGLE MOST POWERFUL MEN ON THIS PLANET, HAS BECOME INSANE.
WITH ALPHA LEVEL SUPER POWERS HE ATTRIBUTES TO THE AGENCY OF HIS GODS, HE REDUCED AN ENTIRE SOVEREIGN NATION TO ASHES OVER A THIRTY-SIX HOUR PERIOD.
THE FIRST REPORTS SUGGEST CASUALTIES IN THE MILLIONS.
AS OF NOW, WE MUST BE ALERT FOR ANY UNEXPECTED DEVELOPMENT WHICH MAY THREATEN THE SECURITY OF OUR NATION AND ITS PEOPLE.

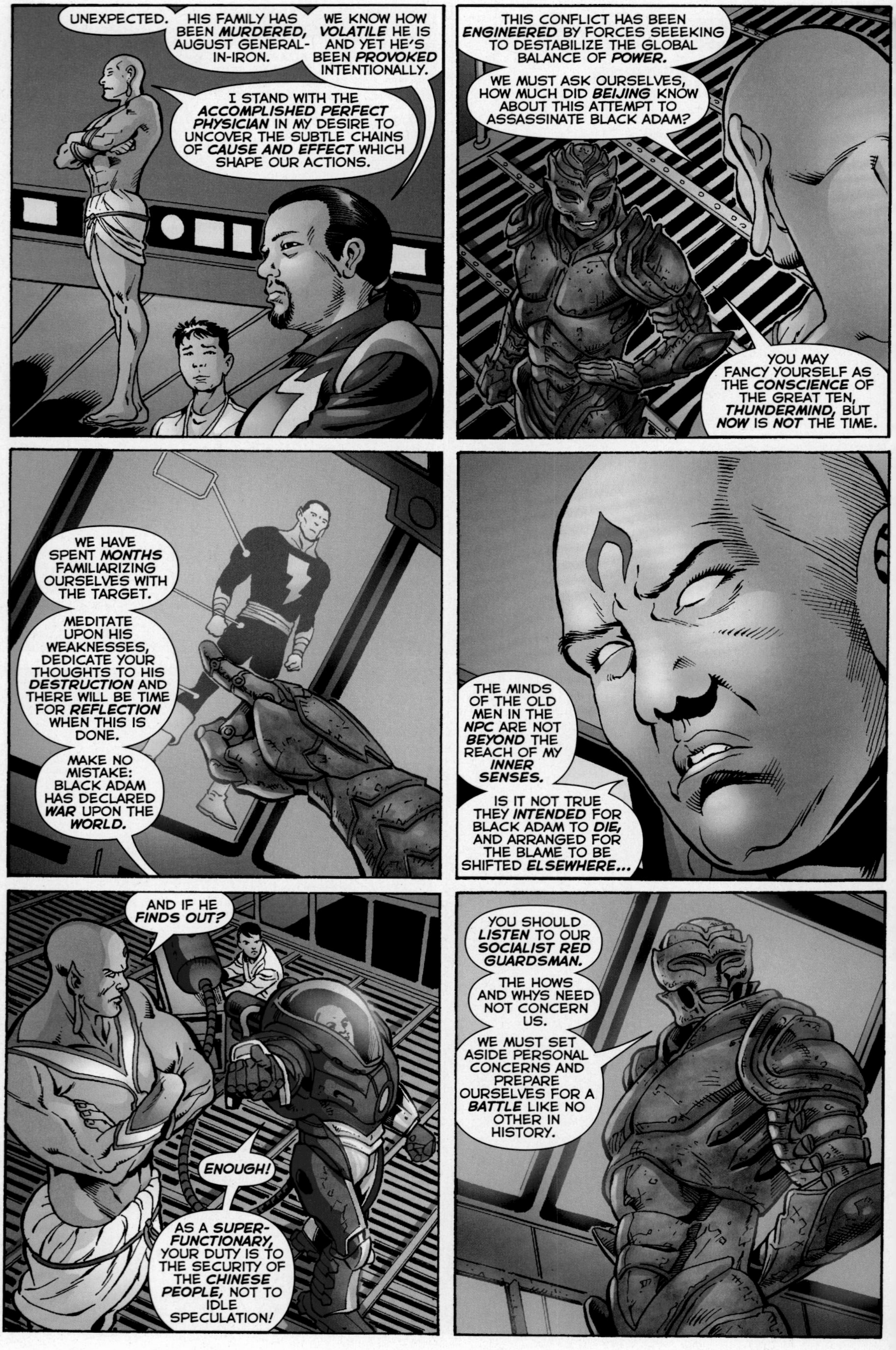

UNEXPECTED.
HIS FAMILY HAS BEEN MURDERED, AUGUST GENERAL-IN-IRON.
WE KNOW HOW VOLATILE HE IS AND YET HE'S BEEN PROVOKED INTENTIONALLY.
I STAND WITH THE ACCOMPLISHED PERFECT PHYSICIAN IN MY DESIRE TO UNCOVER THE SUBTLE CHAINS OF CAUSE AND EFFECT WHICH SHAPE OUR ACTIONS.
THIS CONFLICT HAS BEEN ENGINEERED BY FORCES SEEEKING TO DESTABILIZE THE GLOBAL BALANCE OF POWER.
WE MUST ASK OURSELVES, HOW MUCH DID BEIJING KNOW ABOUT THIS ATTEMPT TO ASSASSINATE BLACK ADAM?
YOU MAY FANCY YOURSELF AS THE CONSCIENCE OF THE GREAT TEN, THUNDERMIND, BUT NOW IS NOT THE TIME.
WE HAVE SPENT MONTHS FAMILIARIZING OURSELVES WITH THE TARGET.
MEDITATE UPON HIS WEAKNESSES, DEDICATE YOUR THOUGHTS TO HIS DESTRUCTION AND THERE WILL BE TIME FOR REFLECTION WHEN THIS IS DONE.
MAKE NO MISTAKE: BLACK ADAM HAS DECLARED WAR UPON THE WORLD.
THE MINDS OF THE OLD MEN IN THE NPC ARE NOT BEYOND THE REACH OF MY INNER SENSES.
IS IT NOT TRUE THEY INTENDED FOR BLACK ADAM TO DIE, AND ARRANGED FOR THE BLAME TO BE SHIFTED ELSEWHERE...
AND IF HE FINDS OUT?
ENOUGH!
AS A SUPER-FUNCTIONARY, YOUR DUTY IS TO THE SECURITY OF THE CHINESE PEOPLE, NOT TO IDLE SPECULATION!
YOU SHOULD LISTEN TO OUR SOCIALIST RED GUARDSMAN.
THE HOWS AND WHYS NEED NOT CONCERN US.
WE MUST SET ASIDE PERSONAL CONCERNS AND PREPARE OURSELVES FOR A BATTLE LIKE NO OTHER IN HISTORY.

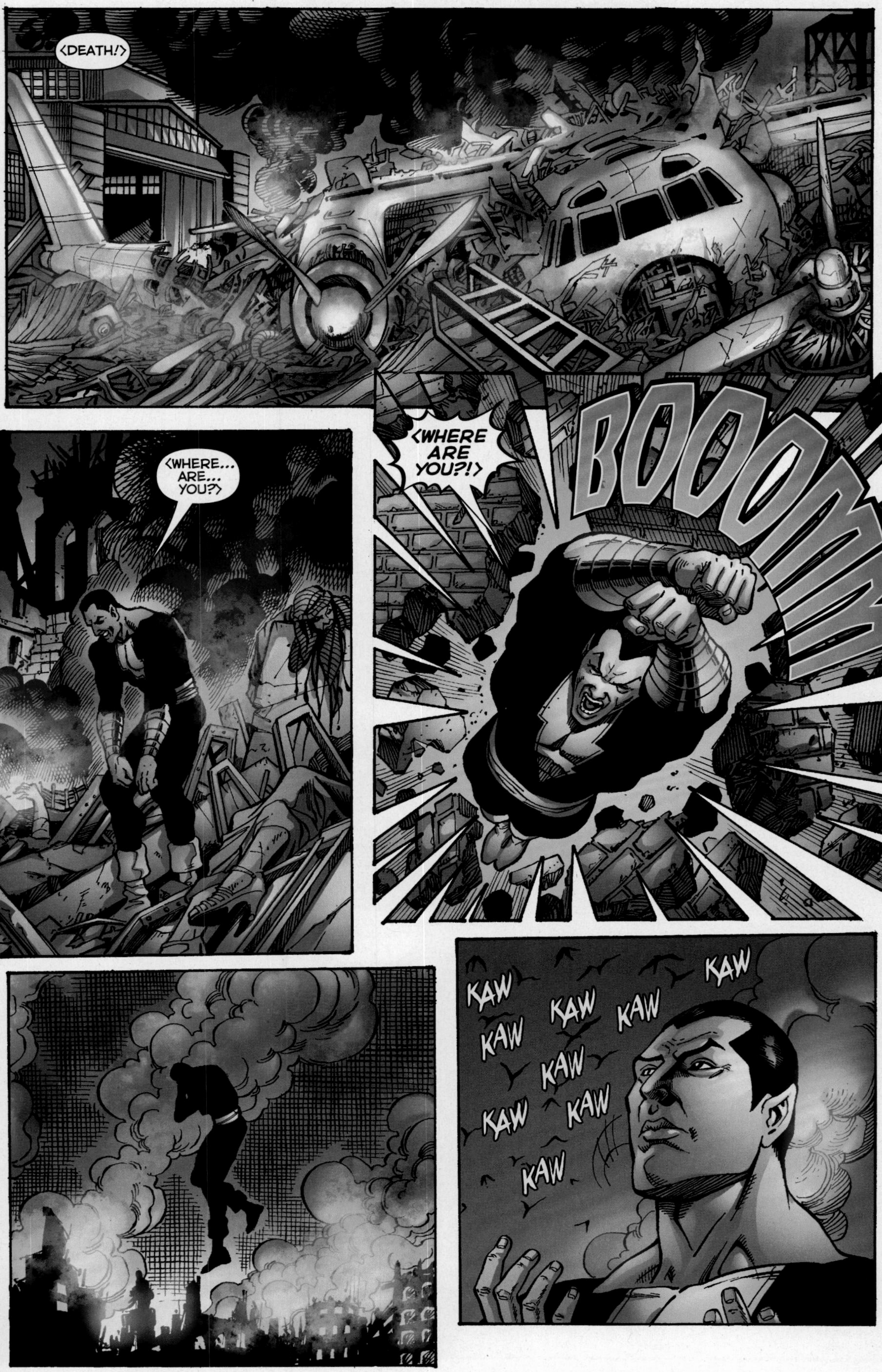
<DEATH!>
<WHERE... ARE... YOU?>
<WHERE ARE YOU?!>
BOOOMMM!
KAW
KAW
KAW
KAW
KAW
KAW
KAW
KAW
KAW

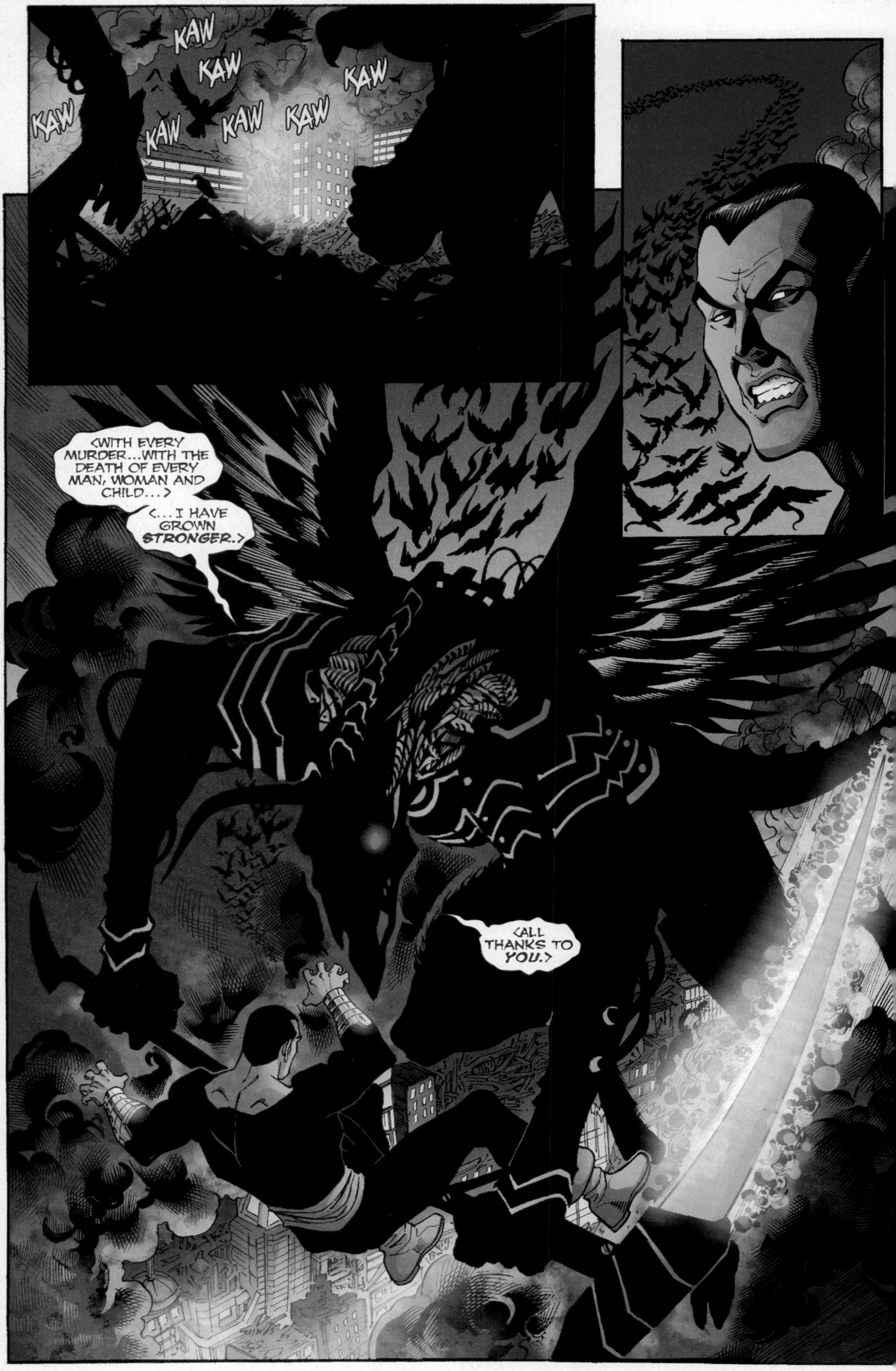
KAW
KAW
KAW
KAW
KAW
KAW
KAW
<WITH EVERY MURDER...WITH THE DEATH OF EVERY MAN, WOMAN AND CHILD...>
<...I HAVE GROWN STRONGER.>
<ALL THANKS TO YOU.>

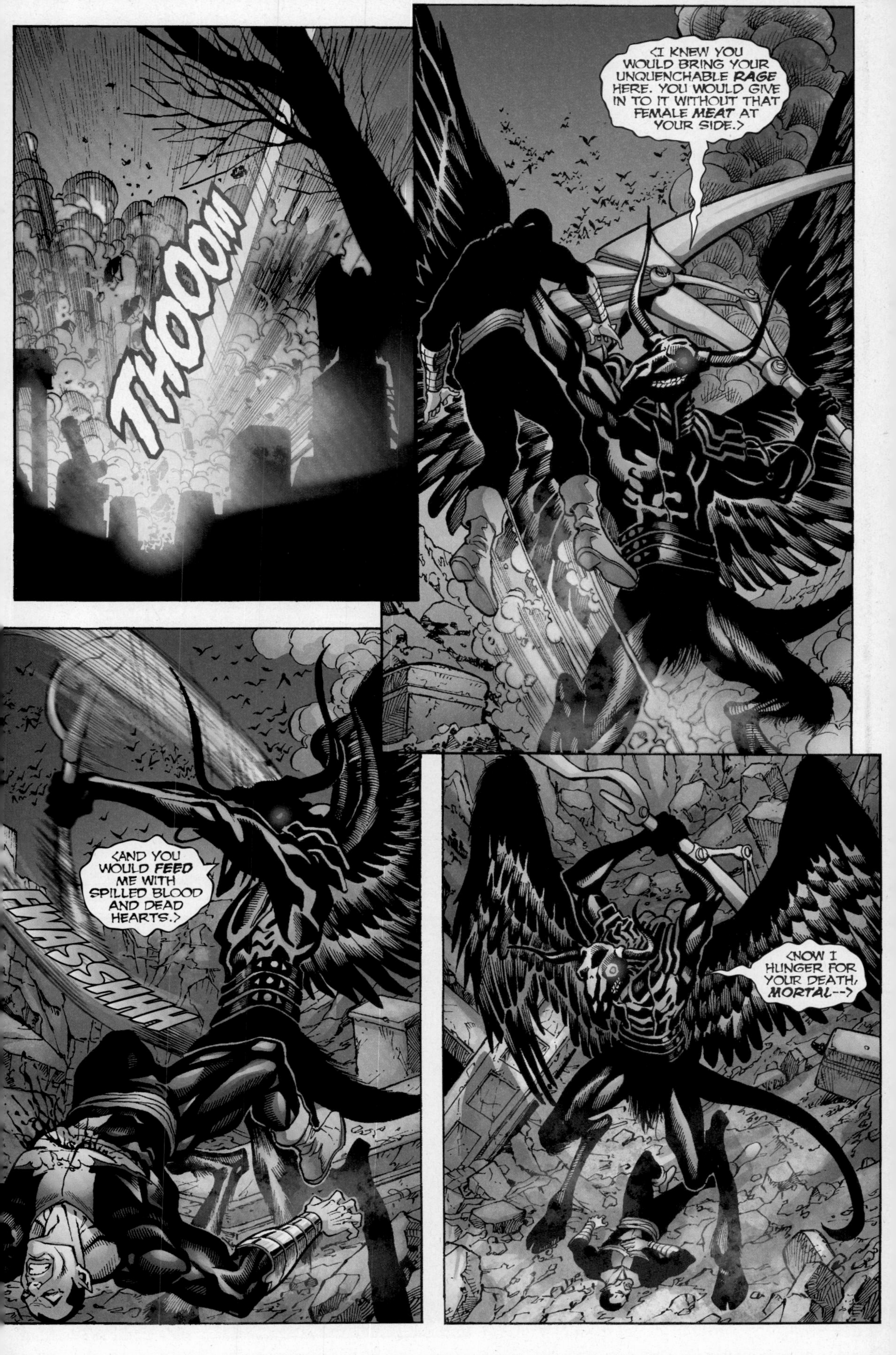
THOOM
<I KNEW YOU WOULD BRING YOUR UNQUENCHABLE RAGE HERE. YOU WOULD GIVE IN TO IT WITHOUT THAT FEMALE MEAT AT YOUR SIDE.>
<AND YOU WOULD FEED ME WITH SPILLED BLOOD AND DEAD HEARTS.>
FWASSHHH
<NOW I HUNGER FOR YOUR DEATH, MORTAL-->

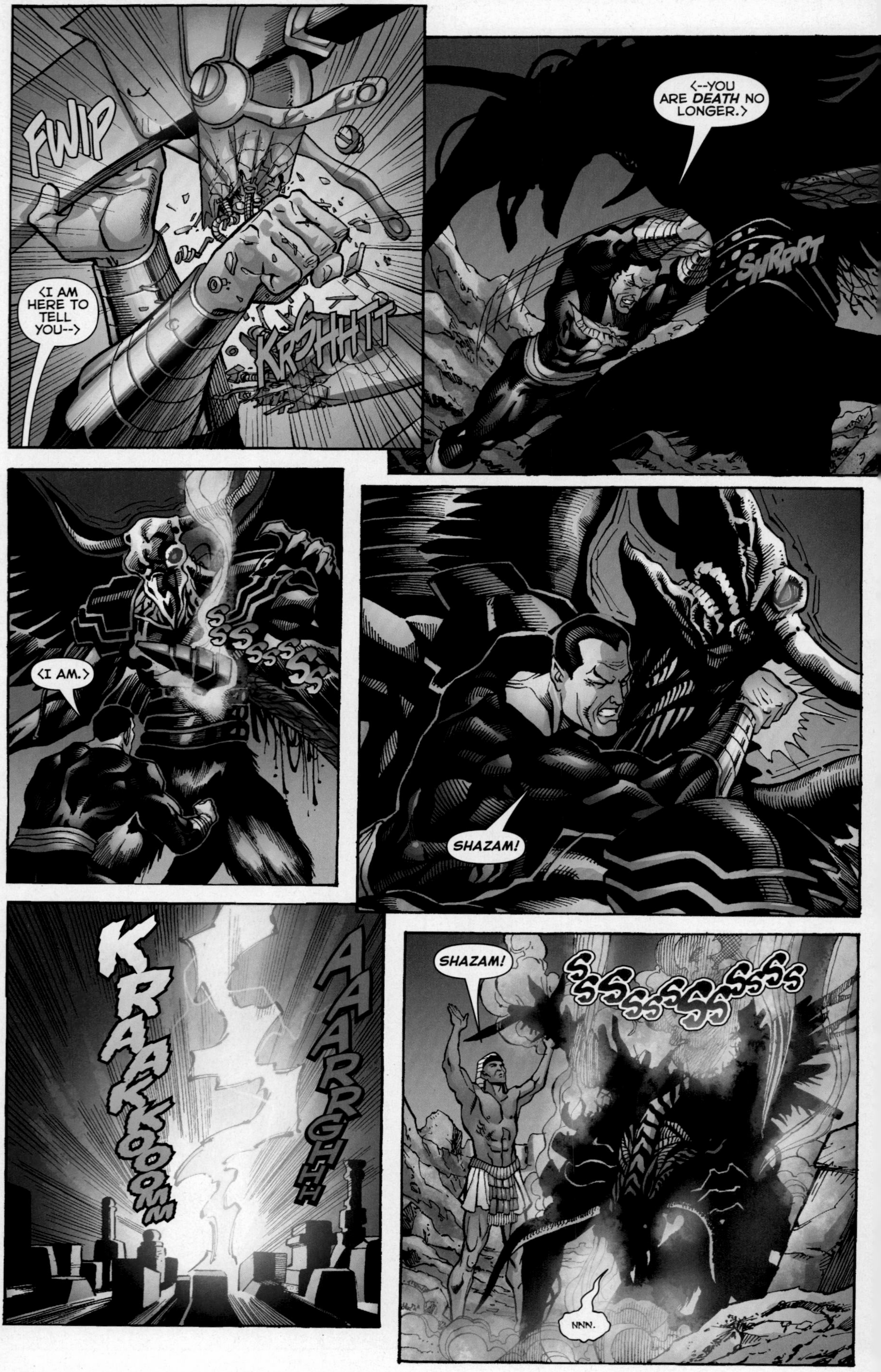
FWIP
<I AM HERE TO TELL YOU-->
KRSHHTT
<--YOU ARE DEATH NO LONGER.>
SHRRRT
SSSSSSSS
<I AM.>
SHAZAM!
KRAAKOOOMM
AAARRRGHHH
SHAZAM!
SSSSSSSSSSSSS
NNN.

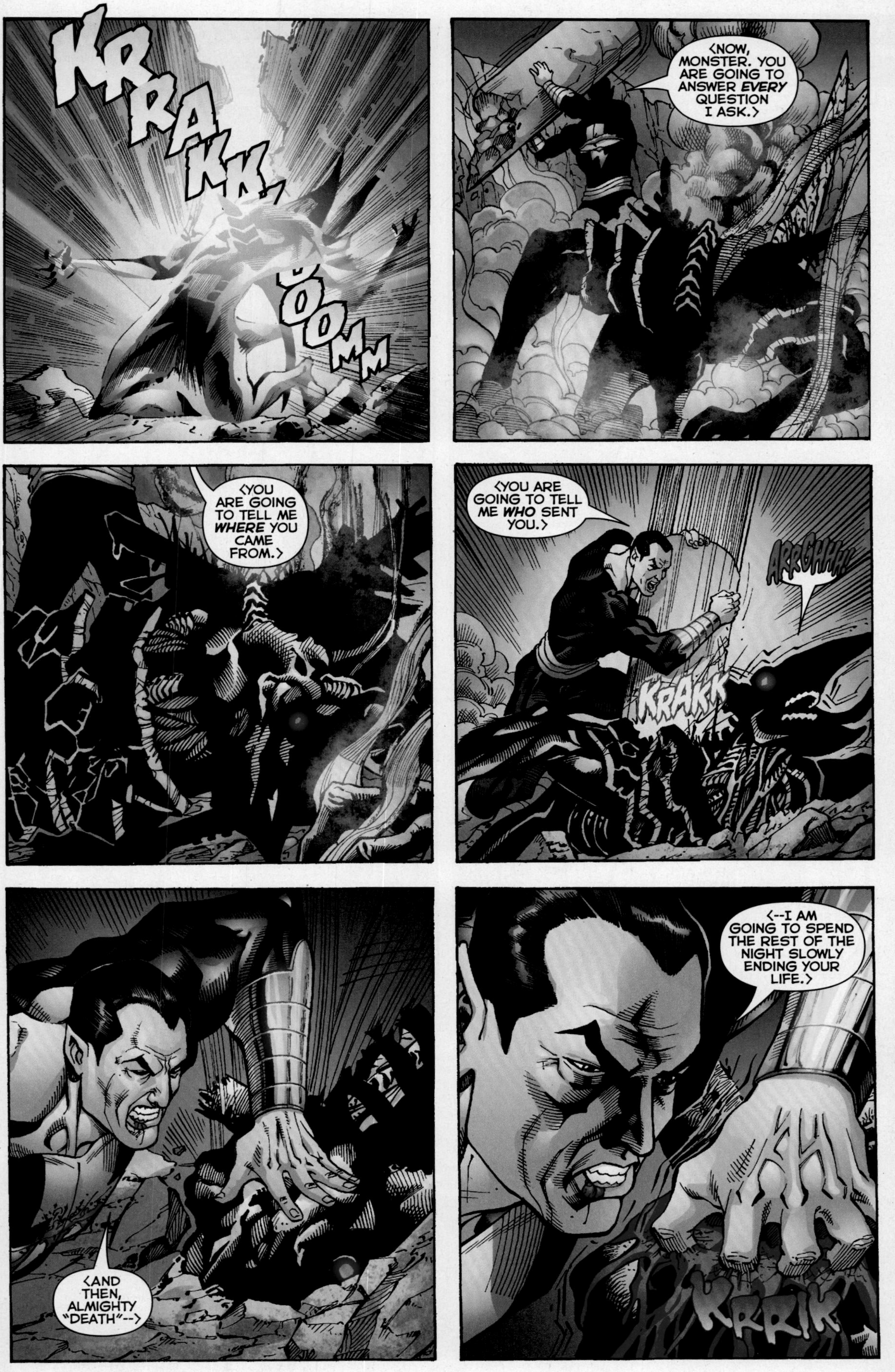
KRRAKK
DOOMM
<NOW, MONSTER. YOU ARE GOING TO ANSWER EVERY QUESTION I ASK.>
<YOU ARE GOING TO TELL ME WHERE YOU CAME FROM.>
<YOU ARE GOING TO TELL ME WHO SENT YOU.>
ARRGHHH
KRAKK
<AND THEN, ALMIGHTY "DEATH"-->
<--I AM GOING TO SPEND THE REST OF THE NIGHT SLOWLY ENDING YOUR LIFE.>
KRRIK

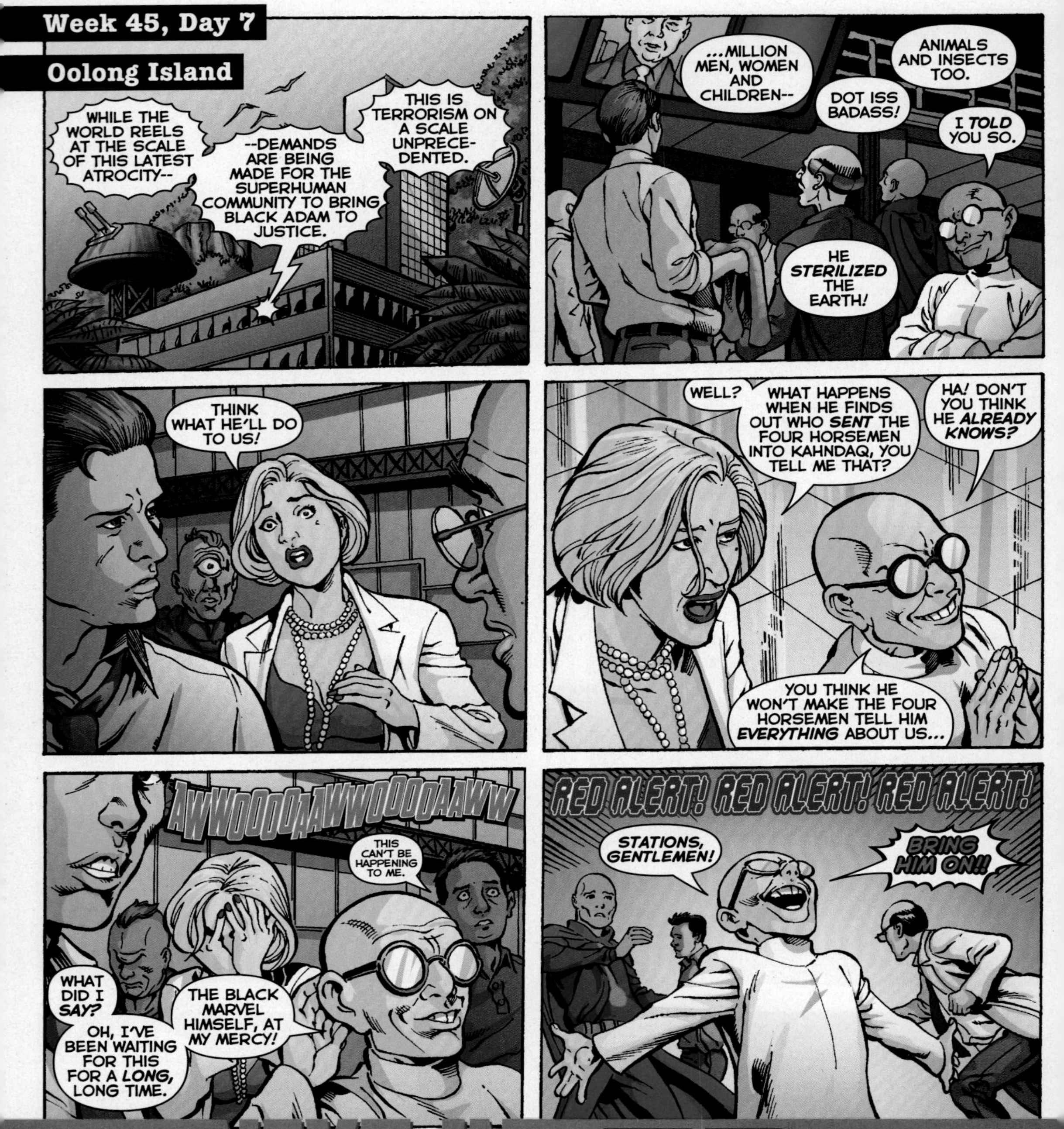
Week 45, Day 7
Oolong Island
WHILE THE WORLD REELS AT THE SCALE OF THIS LATEST ATROCITY--
--DEMANDS ARE BEING MADE FOR THE SUPERHUMAN COMMUNITY TO BRING BLACK ADAM TO JUSTICE.
THIS IS TERRORISM ON A SCALE UNPRECEDENTED.
...MILLION MEN, WOMEN AND CHILDREN--
ANIMALS AND INSECTS TOO.
DOT ISS BADASS!
I TOLD YOU SO.
HE STERILIZED THE EARTH!
THINK WHAT HE'LL DO TO US!
WELL?
WHAT HAPPENS WHEN HE FINDS OUT WHO SENT THE FOUR HORSEMEN INTO KAHNDAQ, YOU TELL ME THAT?
HA! DON'T YOU THINK HE ALREADY KNOWS?
YOU THINK HE WON'T MAKE THE FOUR HORSEMEN TELL HIM EVERYTHING ABOUT US...
AWWOOOOAAWWOOOOAAWW
THIS CAN'T BE HAPPENING TO ME.
WHAT DID I SAY?
OH, I'VE BEEN WAITING FOR THIS FOR A LONG, LONG TIME.
THE BLACK MARVEL HIMSELF, AT MY MERCY!
RED ALERT! RED ALERT! RED ALERT!
STATIONS, GENTLEMEN!
BRING HIM ON!!

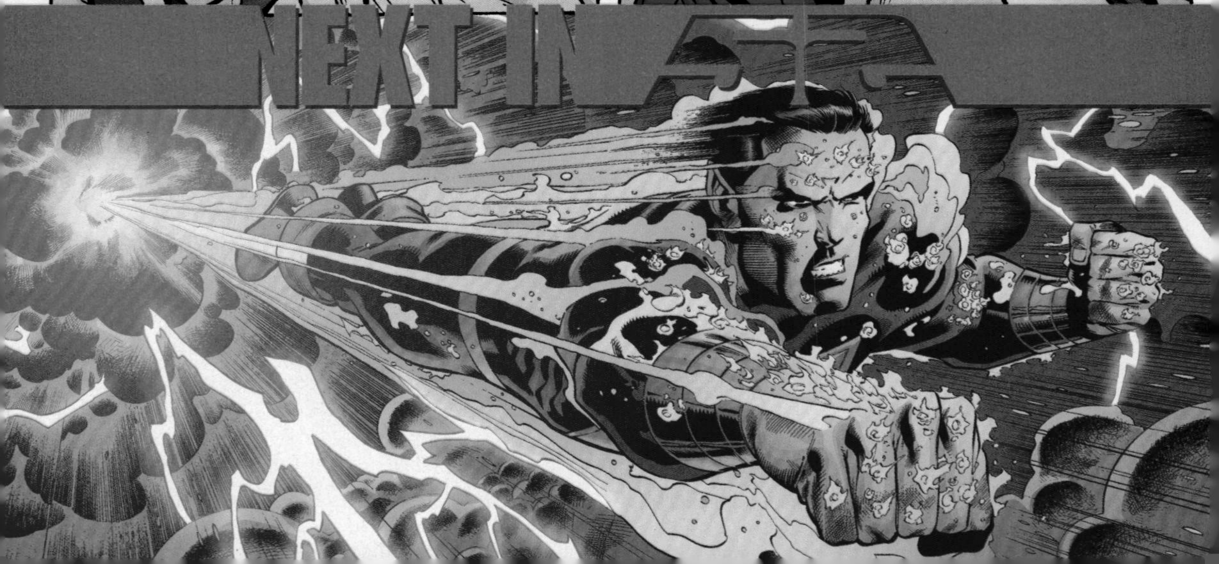
NEXT IN

KEITH GIFFEN

Black Adam devastates Bialya. I knew it was coming but had no idea how the Big Four were going to pull it off without having it devolve into a bad Herschell Gordon Lewis splatterfest (not that there's anything wrong with that).

I was coming off one of the more satisfying sequences in the series, the death of that annoying little twit Osiris (I HATED that kid!) and was up for more mayhem. I got what I wanted. Black Adam's rampage played out equal parts savage and tragic, no mean feat, that. The really amazing thing, to me, was that the slaughter didn't absorb the entire issue. Black Adam's rampage was contained within a series of quick-cut vignettes that played out amid tense worldwide reaction (or inaction, as the case may be). As genocides go... not too shabby.

Bialya, as it turns out, was another one of my questionable additions to Justice League lore way back when "Bwah-Ha-Ha" ruled the world (Andy Helfer, my editor at the time, came up with the name). I remember laying out this issue thinking that, once again, the Big Four had made me an accessory to the destruction of a JLI concept. The thought had, and still does to this day, a perverse appeal. Guess it's the way I'm wired. Just ask Rucka.

I may be wrong, but I think the cover was another one of those images we knew we'd be building toward. If I remember correctly, J.G. flashed the image at one of the first "52" meetings and it met with unanimous acclaim. Whatever. As mood pieces go, you don't get much better.

Speaking of mood, note that the entire funeral opening to the book plays out without a word of dialogue. I wish I could take credit for this but it was spelled out panel by panel in the script. Life is made so much easier for those of us pushing pencils when writers think visually.

Oh, and nice to see that Jamal Igle shook himself free long enough to contribute some art to the issue. Batista and Igle; the issue was in good hands.

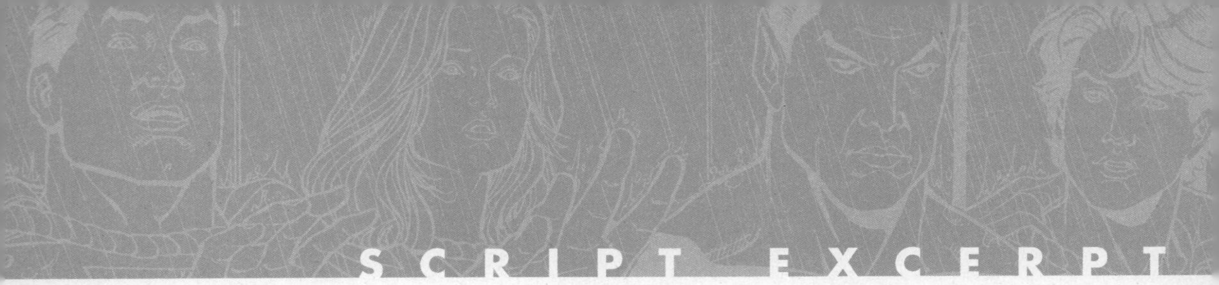

SCRIPT EXCERPT

(COMPARE WITH PAGES 133-134 OF THIS COLLECTION)

52 WEEK FORTY-FIVE — PAGE THIRTEEN

PANEL ONE
The fight has moved across Bialya now to another small city. A fighter jet crashes on the ground into a military convoy in the heart of a market (there should be a small flower vendor established). The jet explodes with fire. Citizens of all ages run in every direction.

SFX: BOOOMMM!

PANEL TWO
Black Adam walks out of the fire, through the pools of blood around him – the entire military force of Bialya is dead.

PANEL THREE
Closer on Black Adam, rage halting for a split second. He sees something below...

PANEL FOUR
...in the pools of blood by his boot, a single flower. The petals soaking up the blood.

PANEL FIVE
Black Adam kneels down in the blood and picks up the flower.

PANEL SIX
Close on Black Adam, finally giving in to sorrow.

PANEL SEVEN
And now Black Adam finally sheds a tear. The weight of everything falls on him.

52 WEEK FORTY-FIVE — PAGE FOURTEEN

PANEL ONE
Suddenly, a bottle shatters on the back of Black Adam's head, interrupting his sorrow.

PANEL TWO
Realizing he's being watched, Black Adam gazes behind him. The men, women and children of Bialya are present, some watching him and some running. Some are armed.

PANEL THREE
Close on Black Adam, rage filling him again. Behind him a ghosted image of Isis dying in his arms. Her words echoing in his ears. Beyond that, a smiling image of Osiris.

ISIS: < ...avenge us... >

BLACK ADAM: < You took them away again.> < You took them all away. >

PANEL FOUR
Black Adam crushes the bloody flower in his hand.

PANEL FIVE
Overtaken by rage and grief, Black Adam flies right at the crowd of people.

BLACK ADAM: < Where is the Horseman?> < Where is DEATH? >

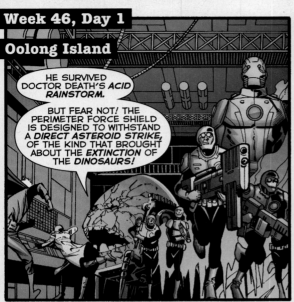

HE SURVIVED DOCTOR DEATH'S *ACID RAINSTORM.*

BUT FEAR NOT! THE PERIMETER FORCE SHIELD IS DESIGNED TO WITHSTAND A *DIRECT ASTEROID STRIKE,* OF THE KIND THAT BROUGHT ABOUT THE *EXTINCTION* OF THE *DINOSAURS!*

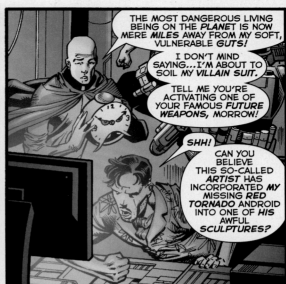

THE MOST DANGEROUS LIVING BEING ON THE *PLANET* IS NOW MERE *MILES* AWAY FROM MY SOFT, VULNERABLE *GUTS!*

I DON'T MIND SAYING...I'M ABOUT TO SOIL MY *VILLAIN SUIT.*

TELL ME YOU'RE ACTIVATING ONE OF YOUR FAMOUS *FUTURE WEAPONS,* MORROW!

SHH!

CAN YOU BELIEVE THIS SO-CALLED *ARTIST* HAS INCORPORATED *MY* MISSING *RED TORNADO* ANDROID INTO ONE OF *HIS* AWFUL *SCULPTURES?*

SCAM ARTIST, MORE LIKE! THE BASTARD'S MAKING ME BID IN A HUMILIATING *ONLINE AUCTION!*

LITTLE DOES HE KNOW I'M HACKING HIS BANK ACCOUNT TO *PAY* FOR IT!

HE IS *FIVE HUNDRED* MILES AWAY!

THREE HUNDRED...

ONE HUNDRED...

DOCTOR CALE, ARE YOU ALL RIGHT?

WE'RE ALL GOING TO *DIE,* WILL.

WE *DESERVE* TO DIE.

THE PERIMETER FORCE FIELD JUST *SHATTERED!*

BLACK ADAM IS HERE!

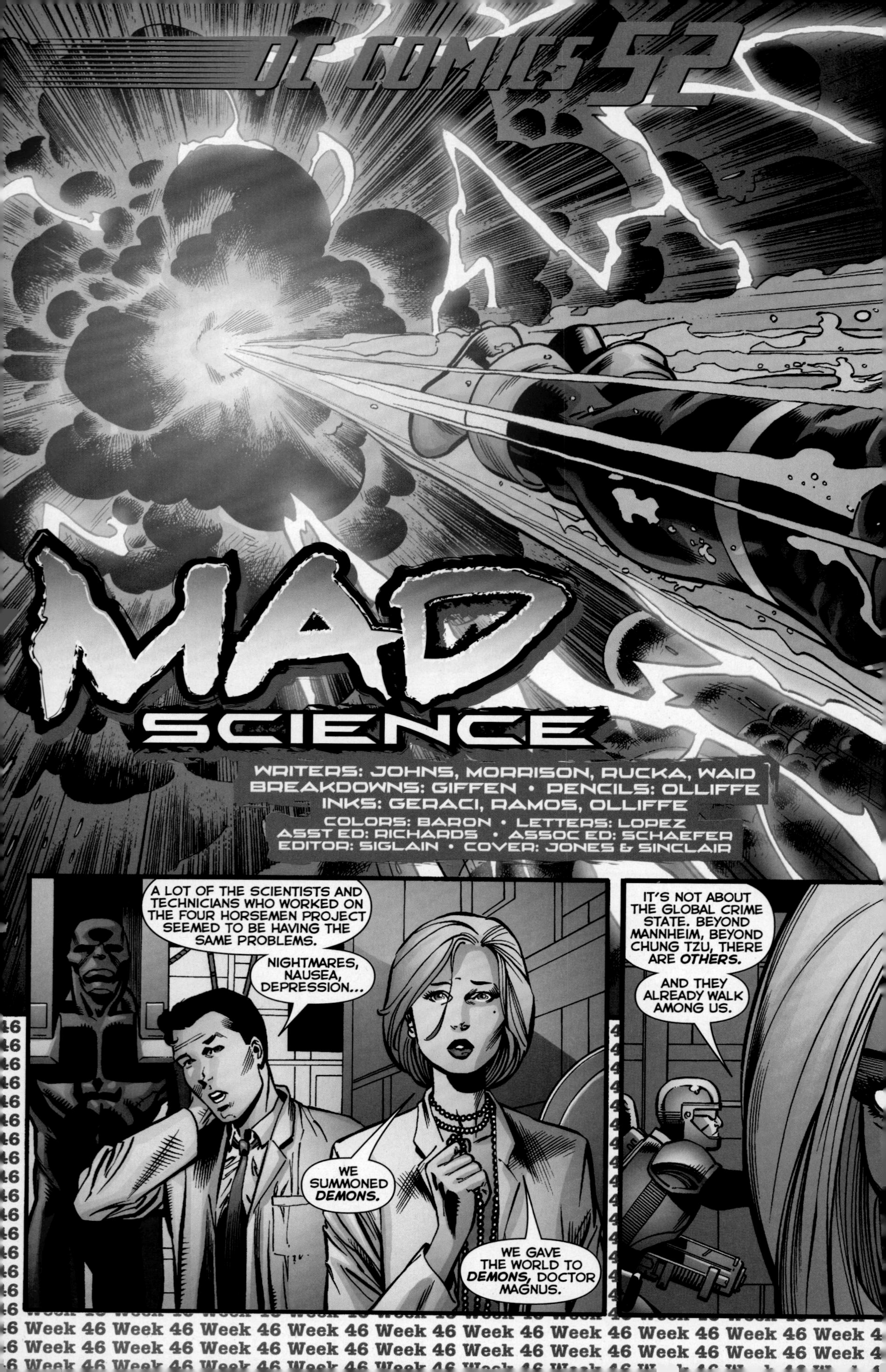
DC COMICS 52
MAD SCIENCE
WRITERS: JOHNS, MORRISON, RUCKA, WAID
BREAKDOWNS: GIFFEN • PENCILS: OLLIFFE
INKS: GERACI, RAMOS, OLLIFFE
COLORS: BARON • LETTERS: LOPEZ
ASST ED: RICHARDS • ASSOC ED: SCHAEFER
EDITOR: SIGLAIN • COVER: JONES & SINCLAIR
A LOT OF THE SCIENTISTS AND TECHNICIANS WHO WORKED ON THE FOUR HORSEMEN PROJECT SEEMED TO BE HAVING THE SAME PROBLEMS.
NIGHTMARES, NAUSEA, DEPRESSION...
WE SUMMONED *DEMONS.*
WE GAVE THE WORLD TO *DEMONS,* DOCTOR MAGNUS.
IT'S NOT ABOUT THE GLOBAL CRIME STATE. BEYOND MANNHEIM, BEYOND CHUNG TZU, THERE ARE *OTHERS.*
AND THEY ALREADY WALK AMONG US.

Week 46 Week 46 Week 46 Week 46 Week 46 Week 46 Week 46 Week 46 Week 46 Week 46

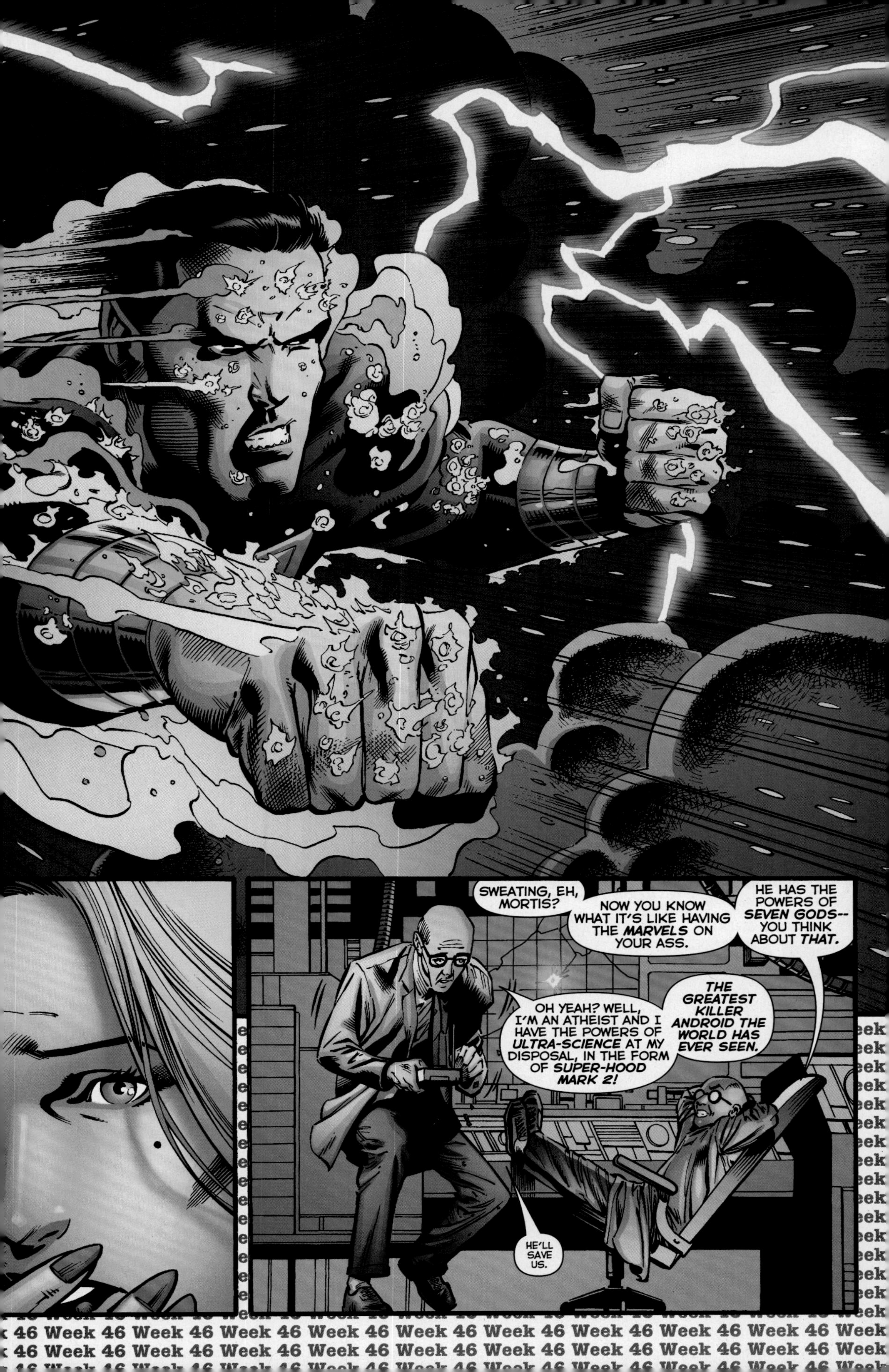
SWEATING, EH, MORTIS?
NOW YOU KNOW WHAT IT'S LIKE HAVING THE *MARVELS* ON YOUR ASS.
HE HAS THE POWERS OF *SEVEN GODS*-- YOU THINK ABOUT *THAT.*
OH YEAH? WELL, I'M AN ATHEIST AND I HAVE THE POWERS OF *ULTRA-SCIENCE* AT MY DISPOSAL, IN THE FORM OF *SUPER-HOOD MARK 2!*
THE GREATEST KILLER ANDROID THE WORLD HAS EVER SEEN.
HE'LL SAVE US.

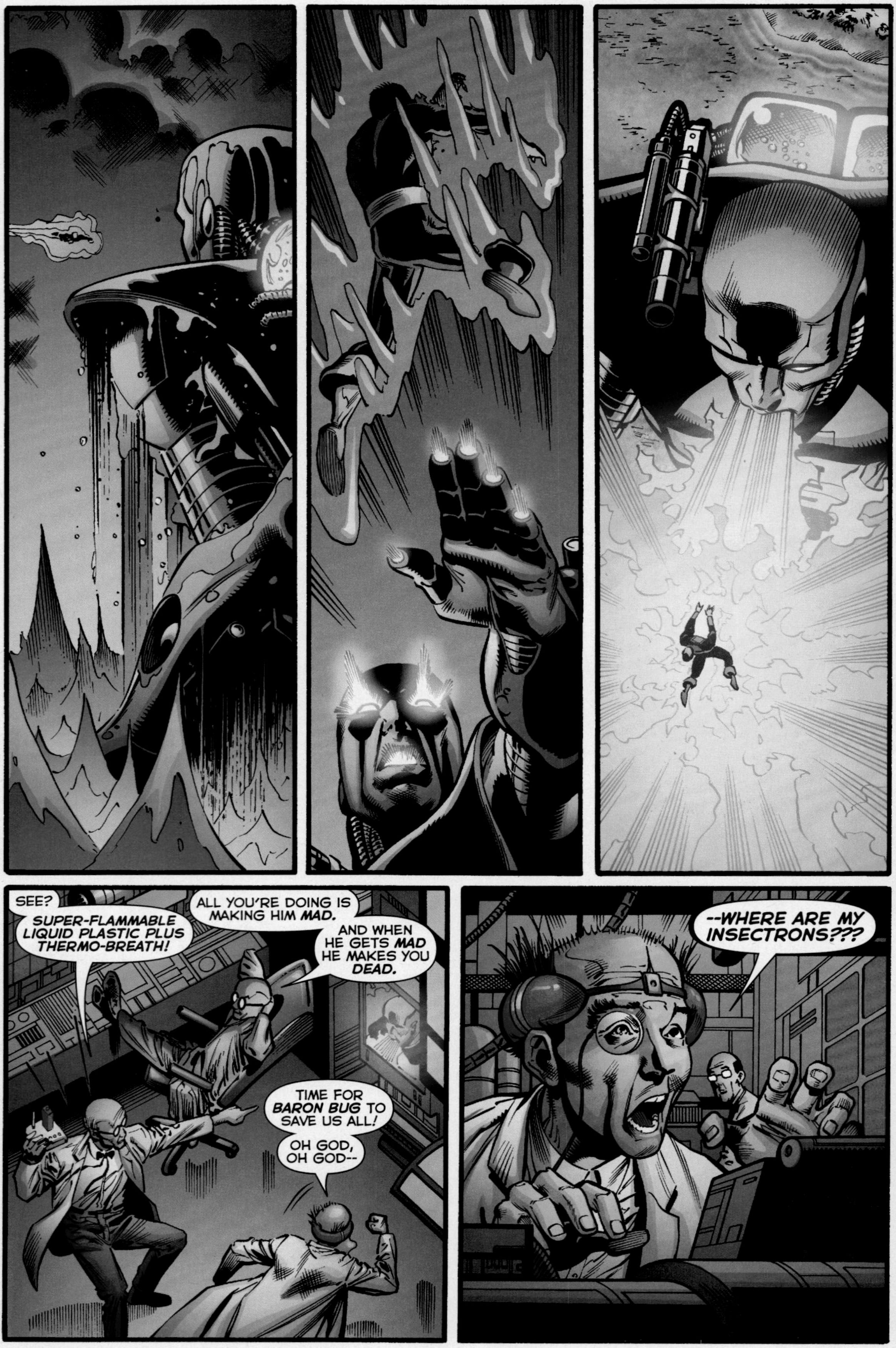
SEE?
SUPER-FLAMMABLE LIQUID PLASTIC PLUS THERMO-BREATH!
ALL YOU'RE DOING IS MAKING HIM MAD.
AND WHEN HE GETS MAD HE MAKES YOU DEAD.
TIME FOR BARON BUG TO SAVE US ALL!
OH GOD, OH GOD--
--WHERE ARE MY INSECTRONS???

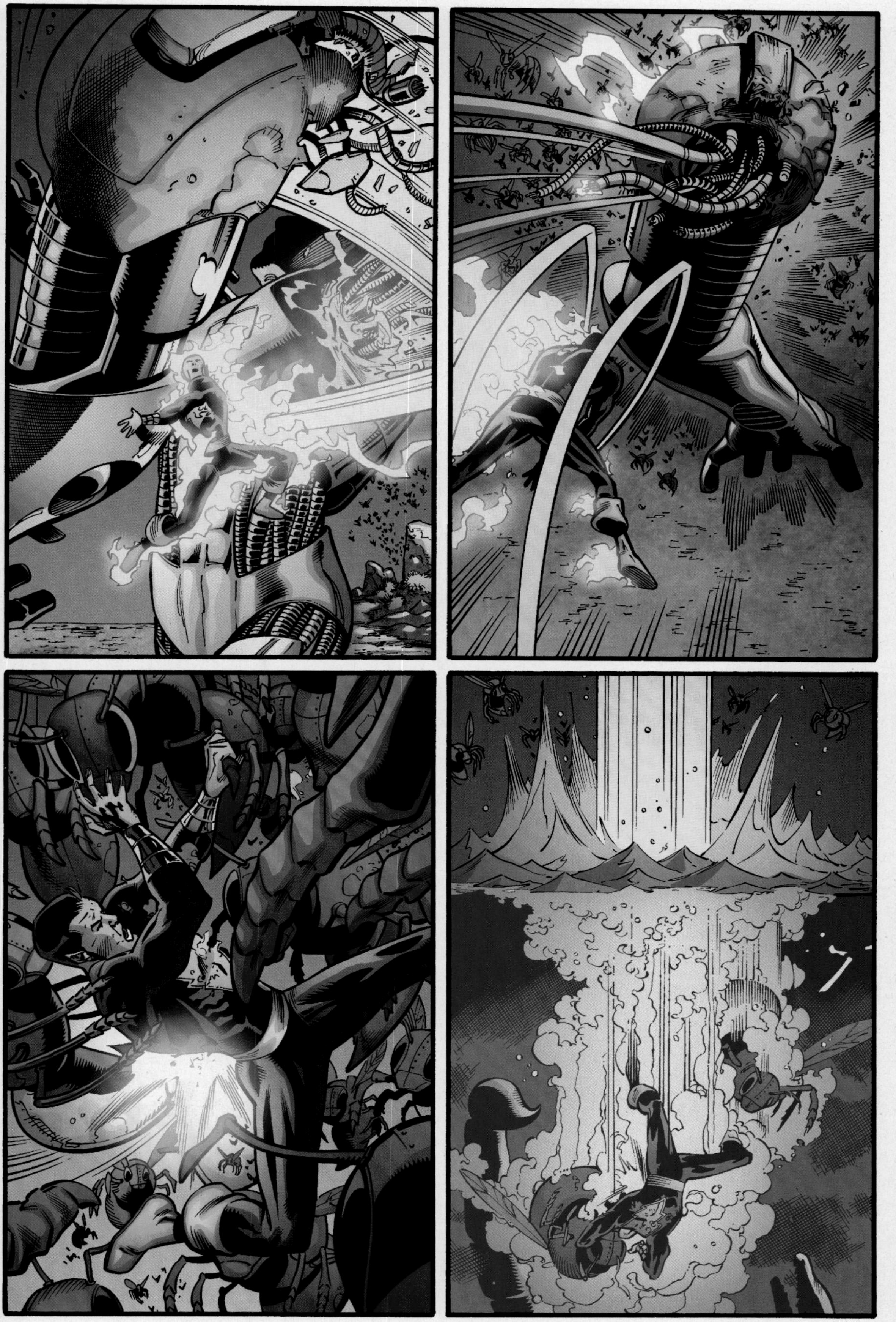

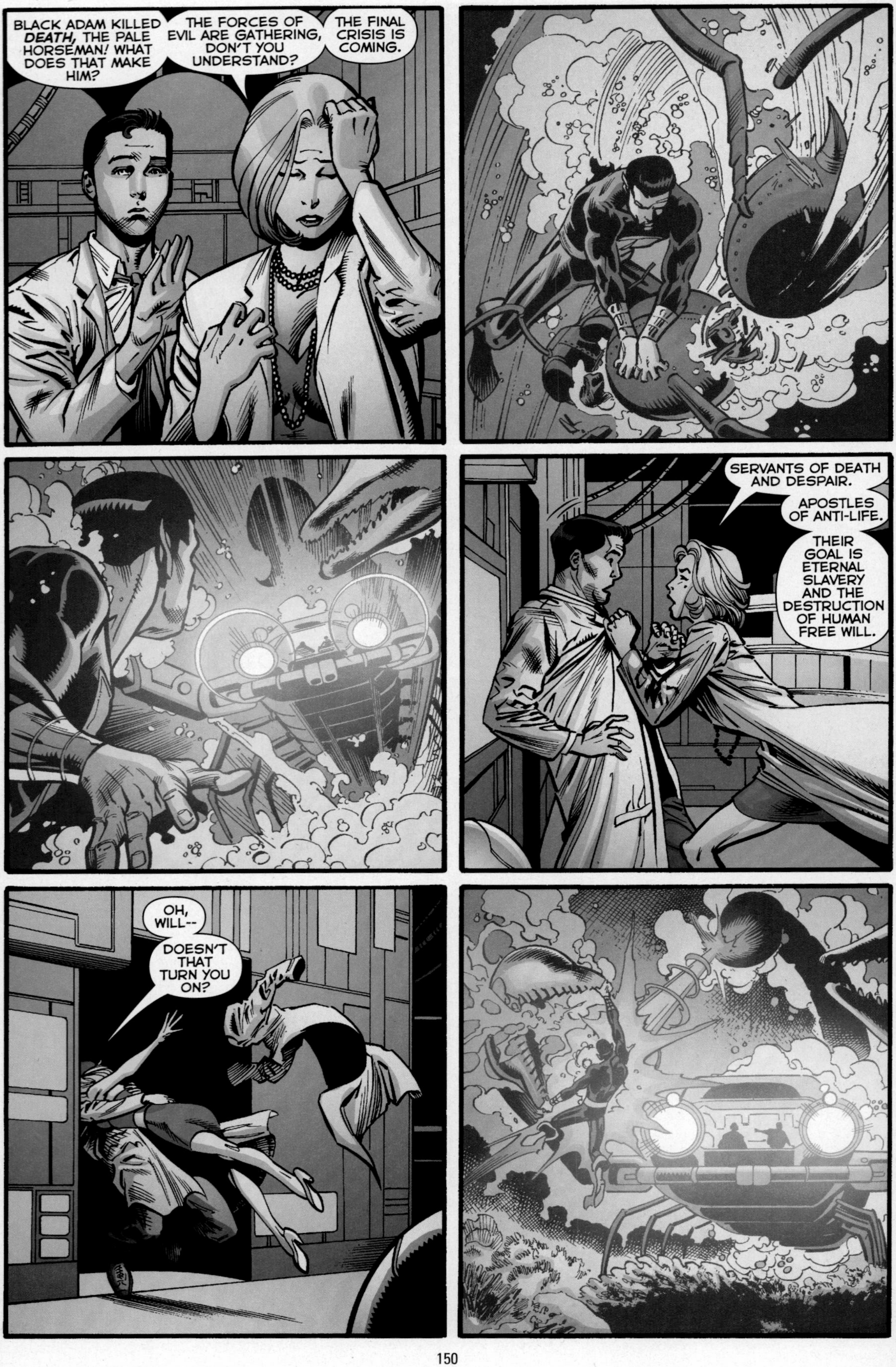
BLACK ADAM KILLED *DEATH,* THE PALE HORSEMAN! WHAT DOES THAT MAKE HIM?
THE FORCES OF EVIL ARE GATHERING, DON'T YOU UNDERSTAND?
THE FINAL CRISIS IS COMING.
SERVANTS OF DEATH AND DESPAIR.
APOSTLES OF ANTI-LIFE.
THEIR GOAL IS ETERNAL SLAVERY AND THE DESTRUCTION OF HUMAN FREE WILL.
OH, WILL--
DOESN'T THAT TURN YOU ON?

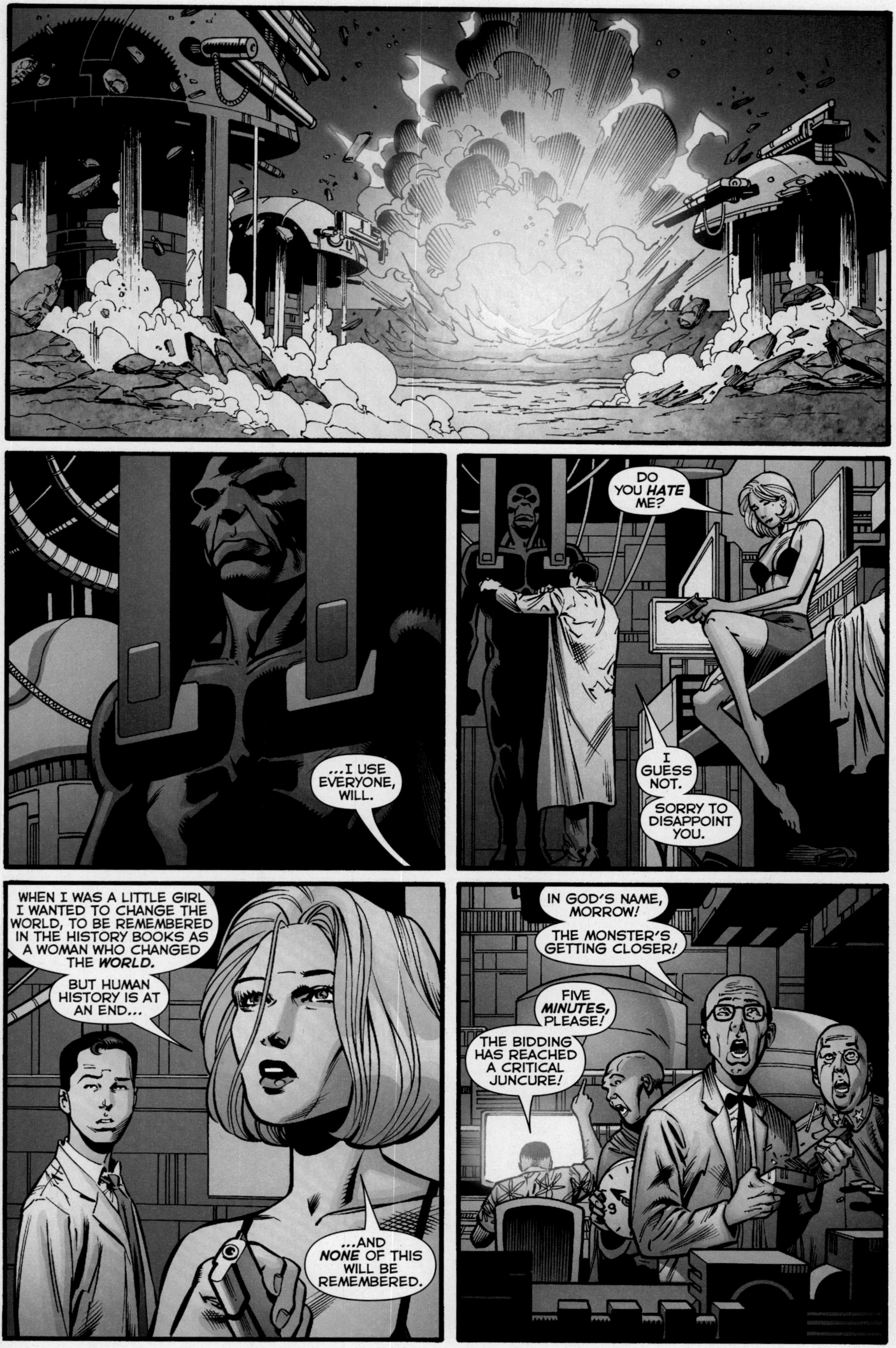
...I USE EVERYONE, WILL.
DO YOU *HATE* ME?
I GUESS NOT.
SORRY TO DISAPPOINT YOU.
WHEN I WAS A LITTLE GIRL I WANTED TO CHANGE THE WORLD, TO BE REMEMBERED IN THE HISTORY BOOKS AS A WOMAN WHO CHANGED THE *WORLD.*
BUT HUMAN HISTORY IS AT AN END...
...AND *NONE* OF THIS WILL BE REMEMBERED.
IN GOD'S NAME, MORROW!
THE MONSTER'S GETTING CLOSER!
FIVE *MINUTES,* PLEASE!
THE BIDDING HAS REACHED A CRITICAL JUNCURE!

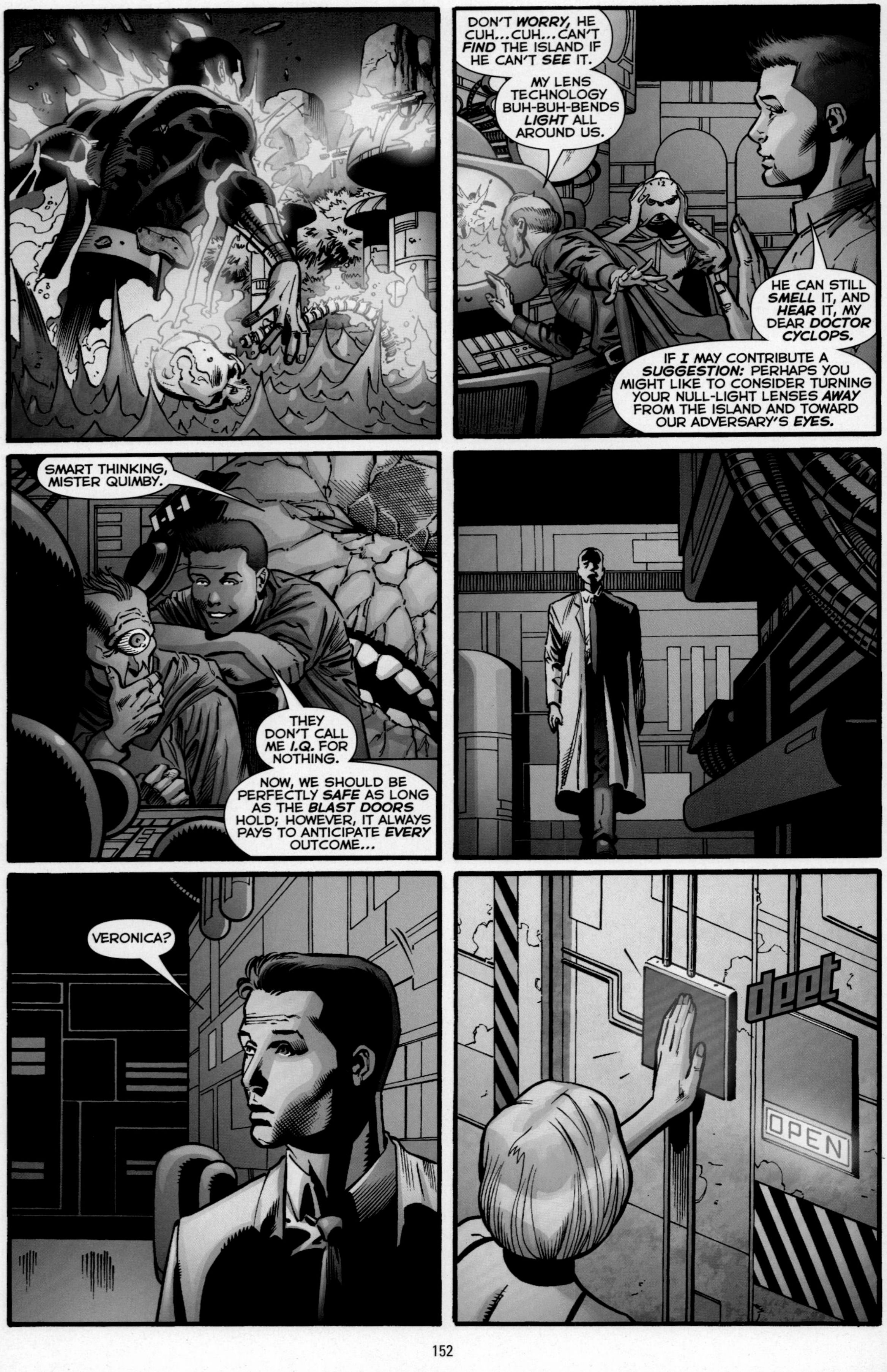
DON'T WORRY, HE CUH...CUH...CAN'T FIND THE ISLAND IF HE CAN'T SEE IT.
MY LENS TECHNOLOGY BUH-BUH-BENDS LIGHT ALL AROUND US.
HE CAN STILL SMELL IT, AND HEAR IT, MY DEAR DOCTOR CYCLOPS.
IF I MAY CONTRIBUTE A SUGGESTION: PERHAPS YOU MIGHT LIKE TO CONSIDER TURNING YOUR NULL-LIGHT LENSES AWAY FROM THE ISLAND AND TOWARD OUR ADVERSARY'S EYES.
SMART THINKING, MISTER QUIMBY.
THEY DON'T CALL ME I.Q. FOR NOTHING.
NOW, WE SHOULD BE PERFECTLY SAFE AS LONG AS THE BLAST DOORS HOLD; HOWEVER, IT ALWAYS PAYS TO ANTICIPATE EVERY OUTCOME...
VERONICA?
deet
OPEN

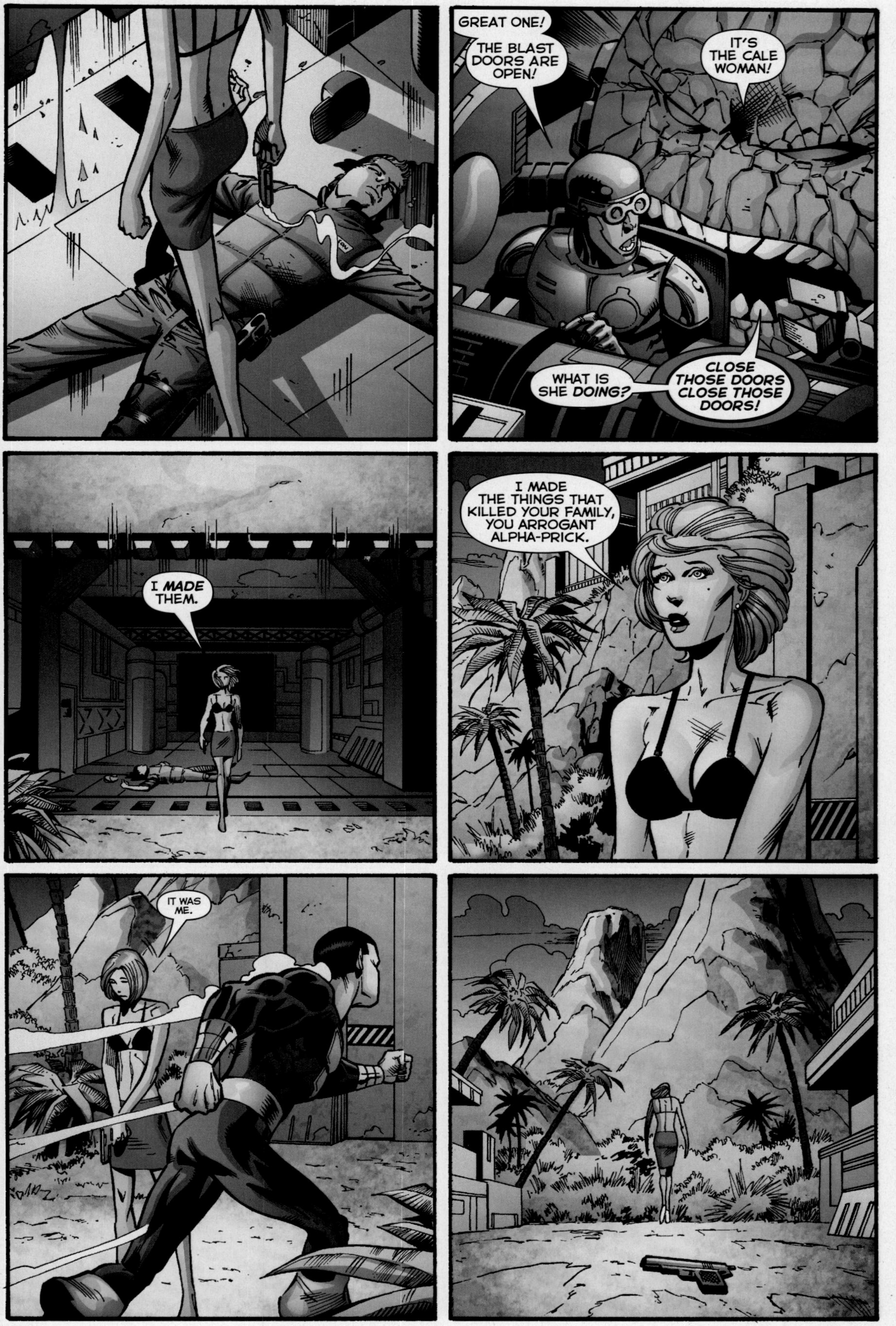
GREAT ONE!
THE BLAST DOORS ARE OPEN!
IT'S THE CALE WOMAN!
WHAT IS SHE *DOING?*
CLOSE THOSE DOORS CLOSE THOSE DOORS!
I *MADE* THEM.
I MADE THE THINGS THAT KILLED YOUR FAMILY, YOU ARROGANT ALPHA-PRICK.
IT WAS ME.

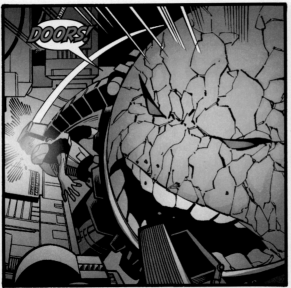

DOORS!

VERONICA! OH GOD--

COME ON, NOW. DON'T BE SCARED, FELLAS!

WE'VE ALL BEEN HERE BEFORE, LET'S FACE IT...

SOME OF YOU BOYS LOOK LIKE YOU'VE BEEN BULLIED ALL YOUR LIVES.

AND NOW THE ULTIMATE BIG, BAD BULLY'S RIGHT OUTSIDE, KNOCKING ON THE DOOR!

DO WE RUN?

DO WE HIDE?

OR DO WE GET EVEN?

THIS TIME WE HAVE THE WEAPONS! THIS TIME WE HAVE THE GANG!

AND THIS TIME, IT'S OUR TURN TO KICK SOME ASS!

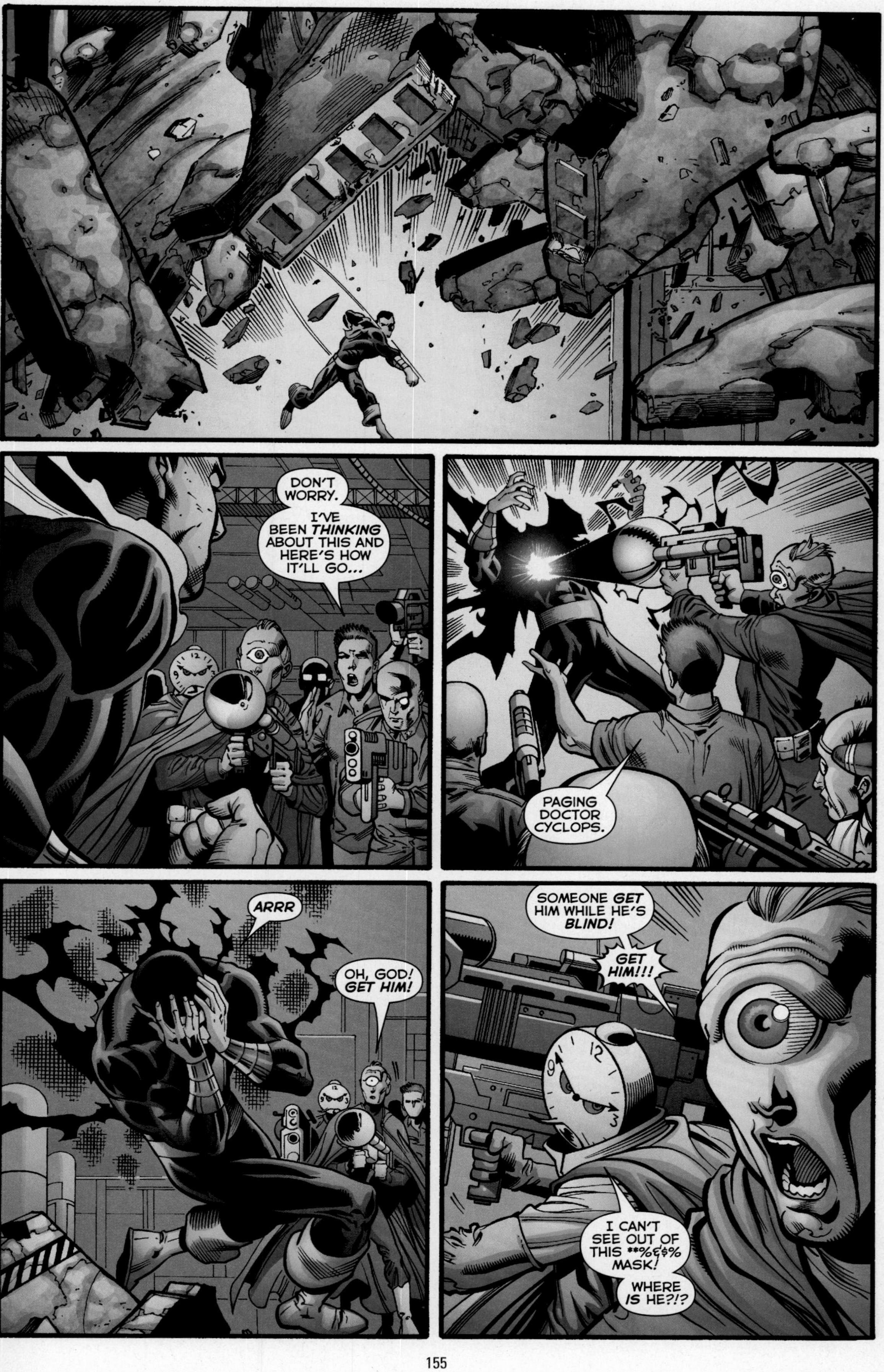
DON'T WORRY.
I'VE BEEN THINKING ABOUT THIS AND HERE'S HOW IT'LL GO...
PAGING DOCTOR CYCLOPS.
ARRR
OH, GOD! GET HIM!
SOMEONE GET HIM WHILE HE'S BLIND!
GET HIM!!!
I CAN'T SEE OUT OF THIS **%&$% MASK!
WHERE IS HE?!?

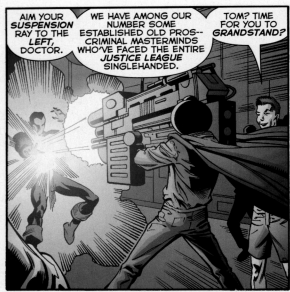

AIM YOUR **SUSPENSION** RAY TO THE **LEFT**, DOCTOR.

WE HAVE AMONG OUR NUMBER SOME ESTABLISHED OLD PROS-- CRIMINAL MASTERMINDS WHO'VE FACED THE ENTIRE **JUSTICE LEAGUE** SINGLEHANDED.

TOM? TIME FOR YOU TO **GRANDSTAND?**

AHEM.

SOMEWHERE AROUND THE 26TH CENTURY, PEOPLE WILL LEARN HOW TO UNFOLD THE **HIDDEN** DIMENSIONS OF SPACE, GENTLEMEN.

TORNADO MAN DREAMING

I INVENTED TESSERACT TECHNOLOGY WHEN I WAS **FIFTEEN.**

WHEN I USE *THIS* DEVICE, AN AREA THE SIZE OF A **FOOTBALL FIELD** WILL ATTEMPT TO OPEN UP *INSIDE* THAT INVULNERABLE BRAIN OF HIS.

IT TAKES A LOT OF POWER FOR A SPLIT SECOND...

clik

BUT THAT'S ALL WE **NEED.**

NOW IF YOU DON'T MIND...

...THE BIDDING'S CLOSING OUT.

TORNADO MAN DREAMING

THAT'S IT, BOYS!

THE SUPER-JOCK'S ON HIS KNEES!

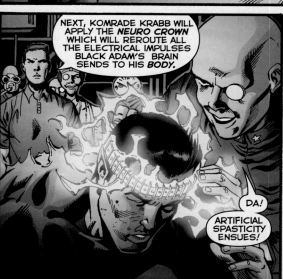

NEXT, KOMRADE KRABB WILL APPLY THE *NEURO CROWN* WHICH WILL REROUTE ALL THE ELECTRICAL IMPULSES BLACK ADAM'S BRAIN SENDS TO HIS *BODY.*

DA! ARTIFICIAL SPASTICITY ENSUES!

INDEED.

EVERYONE WILL FEEL A SENSE OF *ACHIEVEMENT.*

WE'LL HAVE CONQUERED OUR FEARS IN A WAY...

...AND DEAR OLD *THADDEUS* HERE WILL TAKE OVER.

THAT'S HOW I SAW IT ALL WORKING OUT ANYWAY.

I *HATE* YOU.

I WANT YOU ALL TO *KNOW* THAT.

BUT TOGETHER WE'VE DONE SOMETHING I COULD NEVER HAVE ACHIEVED ON MY OWN.

OH, POOR, FOOLISH BLACK ADAM.
YOU SHOULDN'T HAVE COME HERE, SHOULD YOU?
NOT AFTER ALL *YOU'VE* BEEN THROUGH.
BRING HIM TO MY *LABORATORY.*
HEAT UP THE *ACID BATHS.*
I'VE BEEN MAKING *PLANS* FOR THIS MOMENT FOR A VERY, VERY LONG TIME...
YES! *YES!*
WHY ARE YOU ALWAYS SO *SMUG,* MORROW?
OH, I DON'T KNOW...
I BET UNTIL HE *MENTIONED* IT, YOU NEVER THOUGHT OF *ME* GOING UP AGAINST THE WHOLE *JUSTICE LEAGUE* ON MY *OWN* ALL THOSE TIMES, EH?
YOU THINK I'M JUST SOME OLD ROGUE WHO SITS SIPPING COCKTAILS.
TORNADO MAN DREAMING
FDKJL SADFASL
SDFJKL DFKSJ
KDJS KLDS
SKFJSL FAK DS
KS FLKAFJL;FS
FKSJ KDJS KLD
SKFJSL FAK DS
KS FLKAFJL;FS
SKLADSJDSJLA
SLKSL FS LOL
ADFASL SDFJKL
DFKS KLDS JFD
SOLD
WHAT DO *YOU* KNOW?
AND NOW THE SECRETS OF THE COSMOS LOCKED INSIDE THAT ANDROID HEAD ARE *MINE!*
HA! FOR $14,000 DOLLARS PLUS SHIPPING!
I'LL SAY IT IF NO ONE ELSE WILL...
FEEL FREE TO CACKLE HYSTERICALLY, GENTLEMEN!

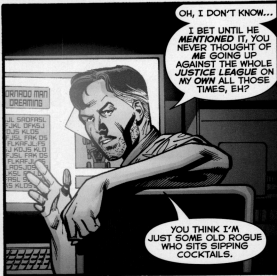

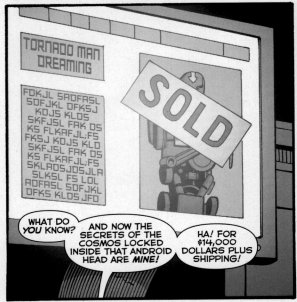

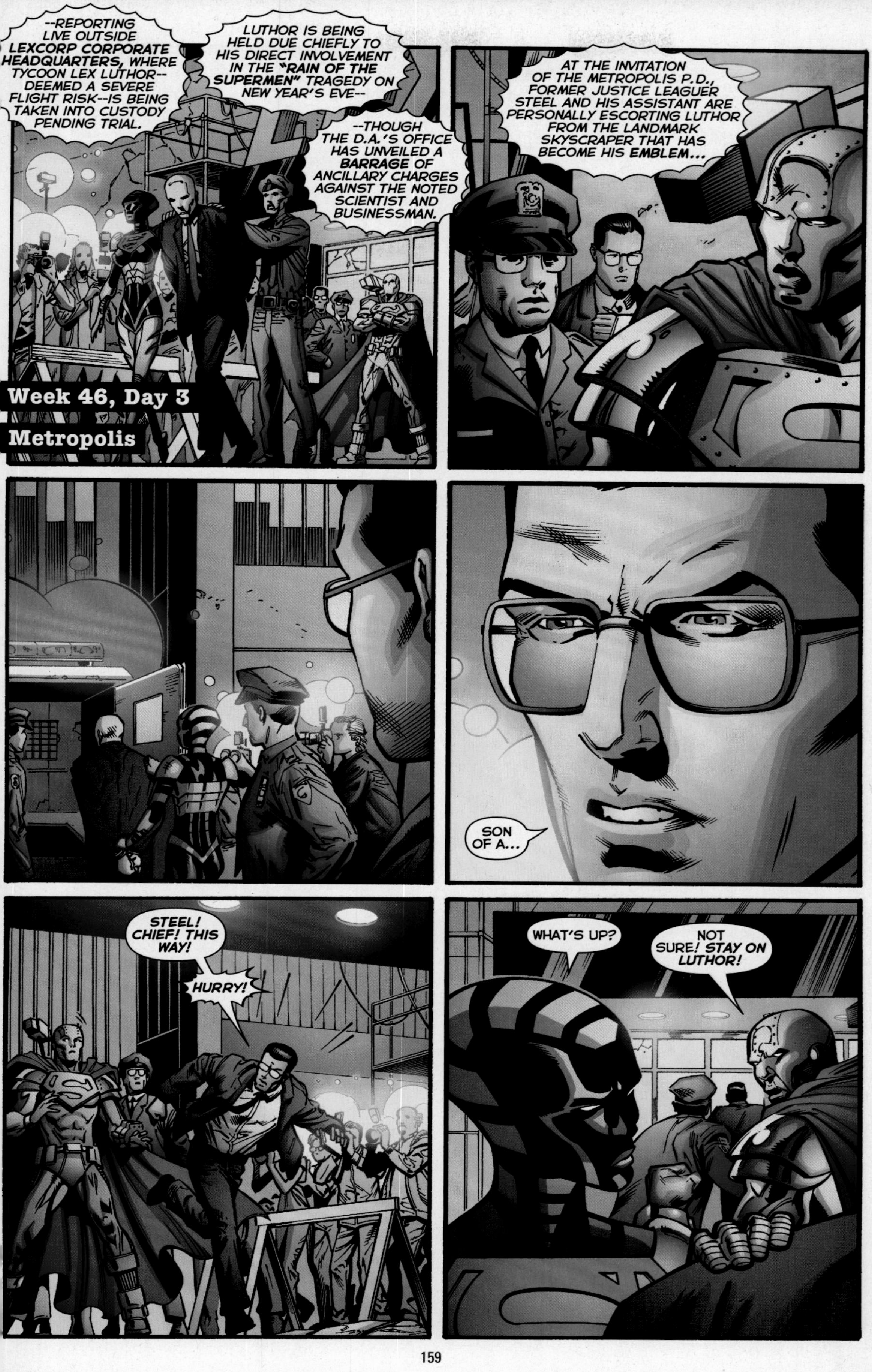
--REPORTING LIVE OUTSIDE LEXCORP CORPORATE HEADQUARTERS, WHERE TYCOON LEX LUTHOR--DEEMED A SEVERE FLIGHT RISK--IS BEING TAKEN INTO CUSTODY PENDING TRIAL.
LUTHOR IS BEING HELD DUE CHIEFLY TO HIS DIRECT INVOLVEMENT IN THE "RAIN OF THE SUPERMEN" TRAGEDY ON NEW YEAR'S EVE--
--THOUGH THE D.A.'S OFFICE HAS UNVEILED A BARRAGE OF ANCILLARY CHARGES AGAINST THE NOTED SCIENTIST AND BUSINESSMAN.
Week 46, Day 3
Metropolis
AT THE INVITATION OF THE METROPOLIS P.D., FORMER JUSTICE LEAGUER STEEL AND HIS ASSISTANT ARE PERSONALLY ESCORTING LUTHOR FROM THE LANDMARK SKYSCRAPER THAT HAS BECOME HIS EMBLEM...
SON OF A...
STEEL! CHIEF! THIS WAY!
HURRY!
WHAT'S UP?
NOT SURE! STAY ON LUTHOR!

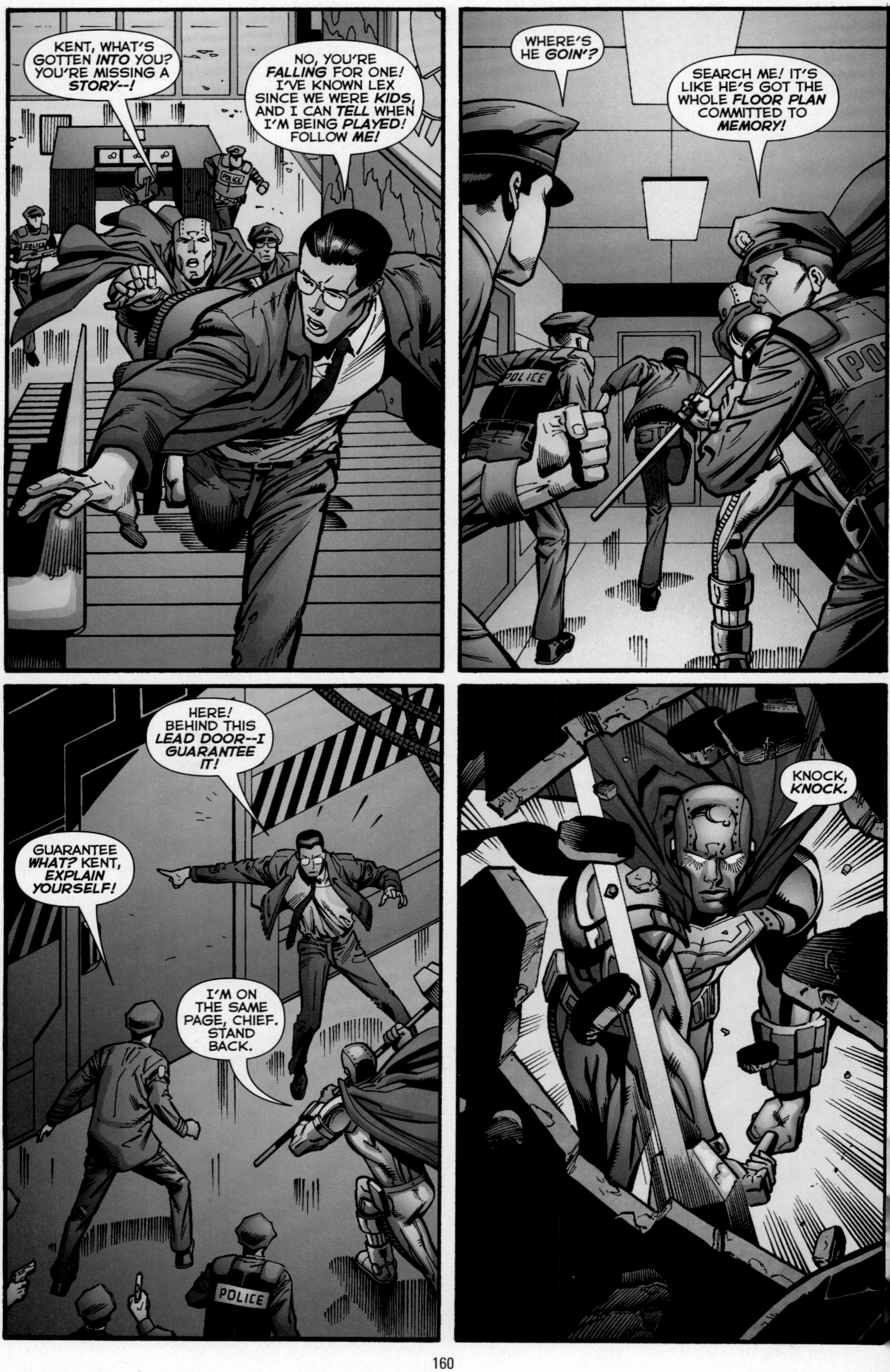
KENT, WHAT'S GOTTEN INTO YOU? YOU'RE MISSING A STORY--!
NO, YOU'RE FALLING FOR ONE! I'VE KNOWN LEX SINCE WE WERE KIDS, AND I CAN TELL WHEN I'M BEING PLAYED! FOLLOW ME!
WHERE'S HE GOIN'?
SEARCH ME! IT'S LIKE HE'S GOT THE WHOLE FLOOR PLAN COMMITTED TO MEMORY!
POLICE
HERE! BEHIND THIS LEAD DOOR--I GUARANTEE IT!
GUARANTEE WHAT? KENT, EXPLAIN YOURSELF!
I'M ON THE SAME PAGE, CHIEF. STAND BACK.
POLICE
KNOCK, KNOCK.

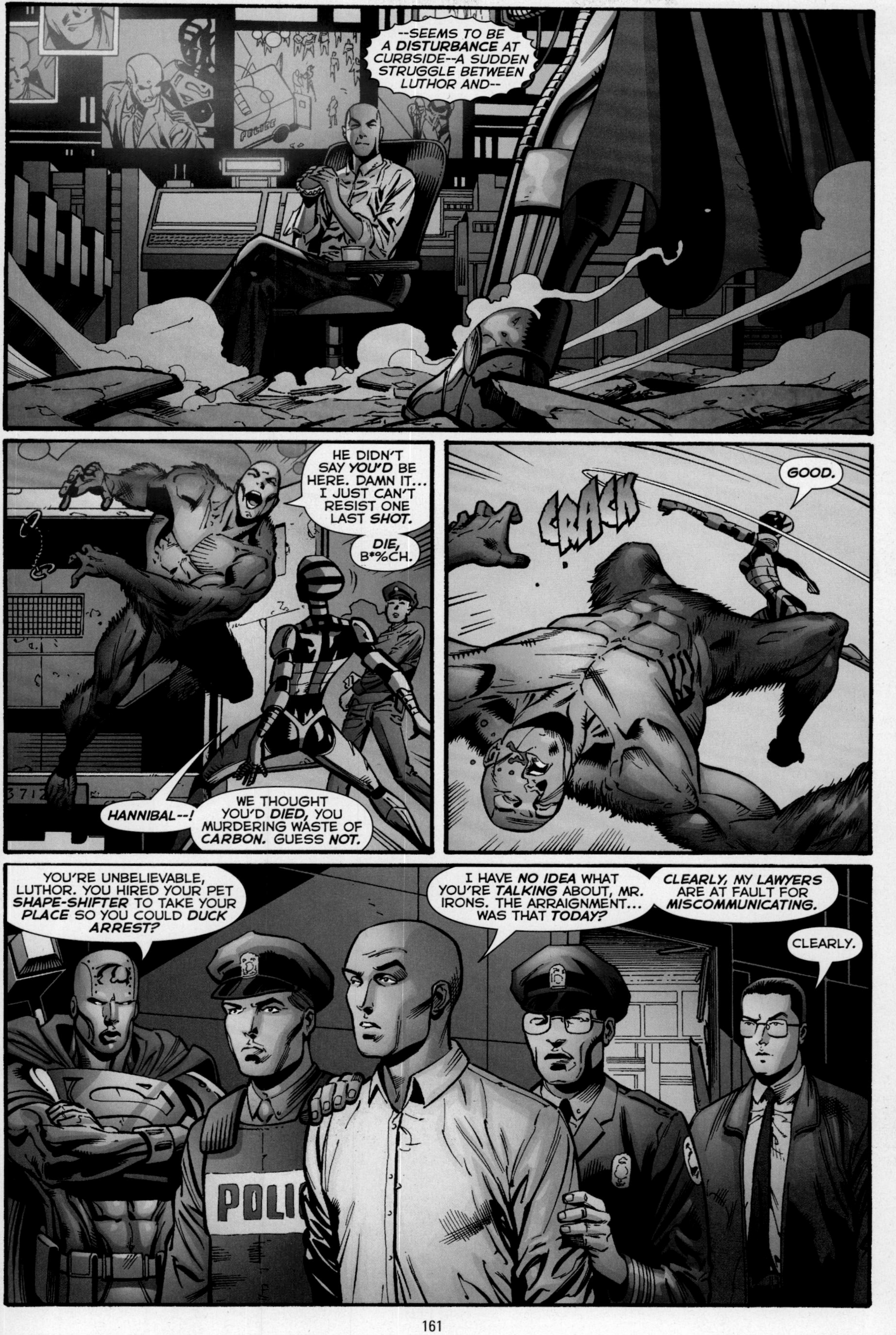
--SEEMS TO BE A DISTURBANCE AT CURBSIDE--A SUDDEN STRUGGLE BETWEEN LUTHOR AND--
HE DIDN'T SAY YOU'D BE HERE. DAMN IT... I JUST CAN'T RESIST ONE LAST SHOT.
DIE, B*%CH.
HANNIBAL--!
WE THOUGHT YOU'D DIED, YOU MURDERING WASTE OF CARBON. GUESS NOT.
CRACK
GOOD.
YOU'RE UNBELIEVABLE, LUTHOR. YOU HIRED YOUR PET SHAPE-SHIFTER TO TAKE YOUR PLACE SO YOU COULD DUCK ARREST?
I HAVE NO IDEA WHAT YOU'RE TALKING ABOUT, MR. IRONS. THE ARRAIGNMENT... WAS THAT TODAY?
CLEARLY, MY LAWYERS ARE AT FAULT FOR MISCOMMUNICATING.
CLEARLY.
POLIC

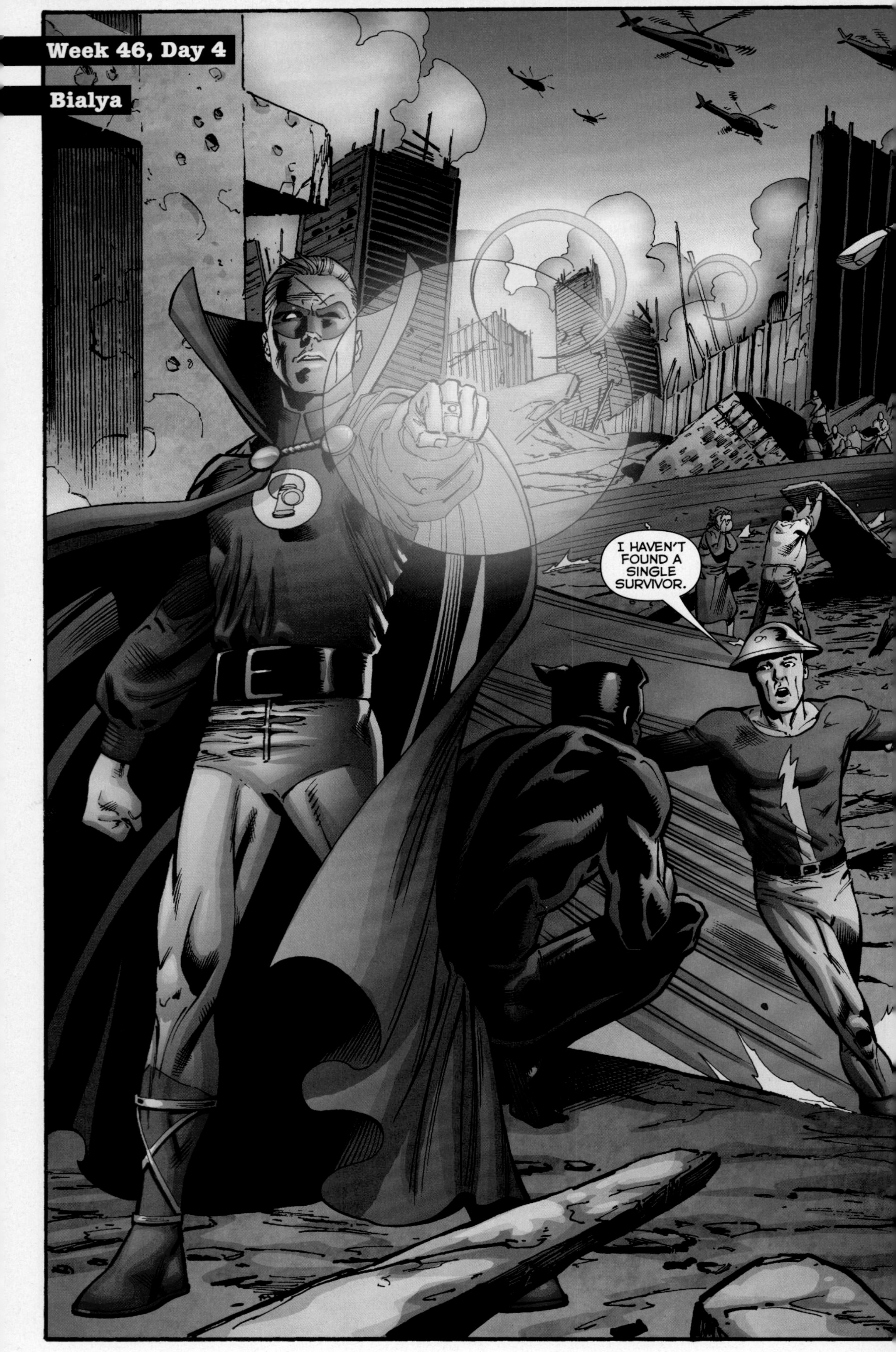
Week 46, Day 4
Bialya
I HAVEN'T FOUND A SINGLE SURVIVOR.

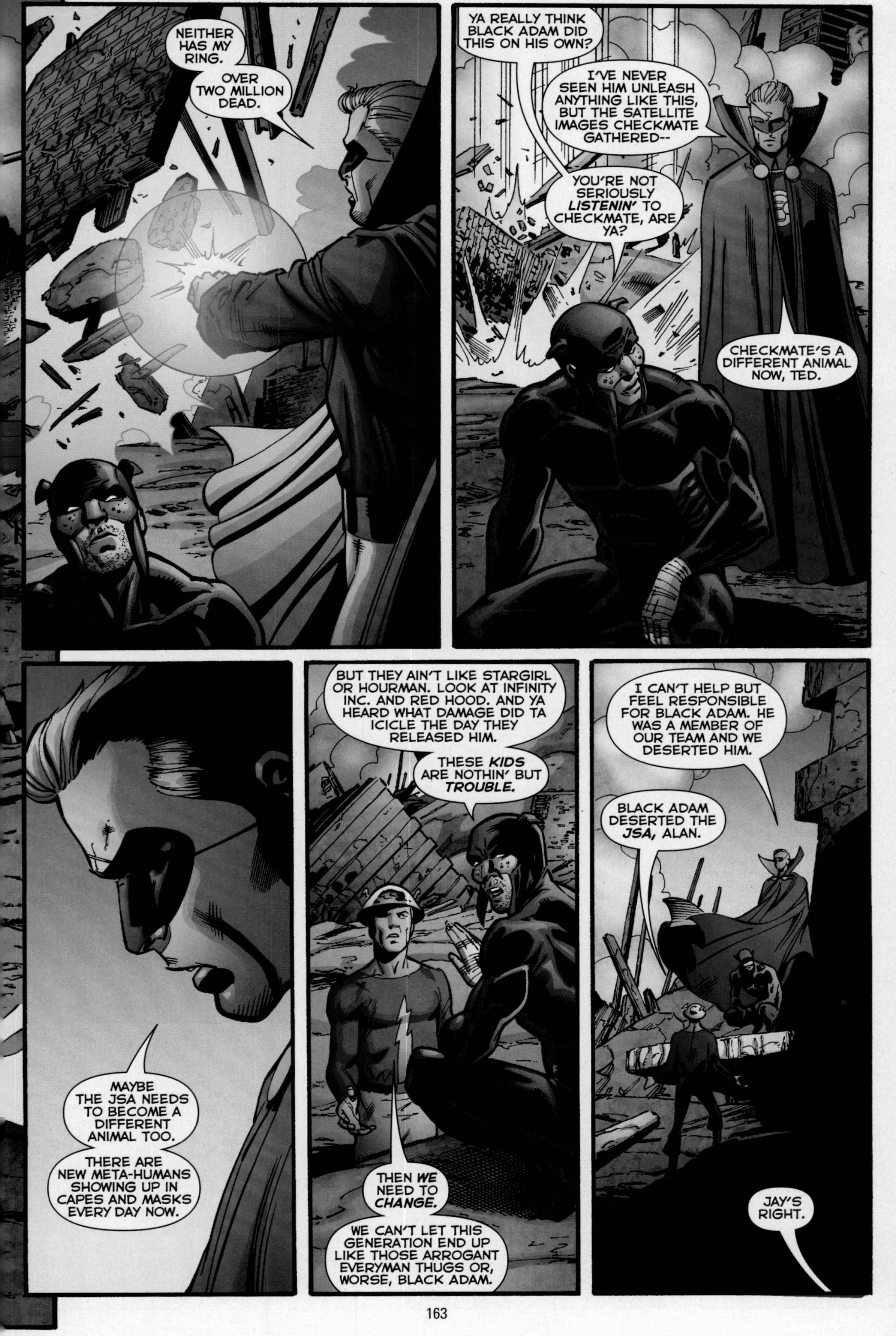
NEITHER HAS MY RING.
OVER TWO MILLION DEAD.
YA REALLY THINK BLACK ADAM DID THIS ON HIS OWN?
I'VE NEVER SEEN HIM UNLEASH ANYTHING LIKE THIS, BUT THE SATELLITE IMAGES CHECKMATE GATHERED--
YOU'RE NOT SERIOUSLY *LISTENIN'* TO CHECKMATE, ARE YA?
CHECKMATE'S A DIFFERENT ANIMAL NOW, TED.
MAYBE THE JSA NEEDS TO BECOME A DIFFERENT ANIMAL TOO.
THERE ARE NEW META-HUMANS SHOWING UP IN CAPES AND MASKS EVERY DAY NOW.
BUT THEY AIN'T LIKE STARGIRL OR HOURMAN. LOOK AT INFINITY INC. AND RED HOOD. AND YA HEARD WHAT DAMAGE DID TA ICICLE THE DAY THEY RELEASED HIM.
THESE *KIDS* ARE NOTHIN' BUT *TROUBLE.*
THEN *WE* NEED TO *CHANGE.*
WE CAN'T LET THIS GENERATION END UP LIKE THOSE ARROGANT EVERYMAN THUGS OR, WORSE, BLACK ADAM.
I CAN'T HELP BUT FEEL RESPONSIBLE FOR BLACK ADAM. HE WAS A MEMBER OF OUR TEAM AND WE DESERTED HIM.
BLACK ADAM DESERTED THE *JSA,* ALAN.
JAY'S RIGHT.

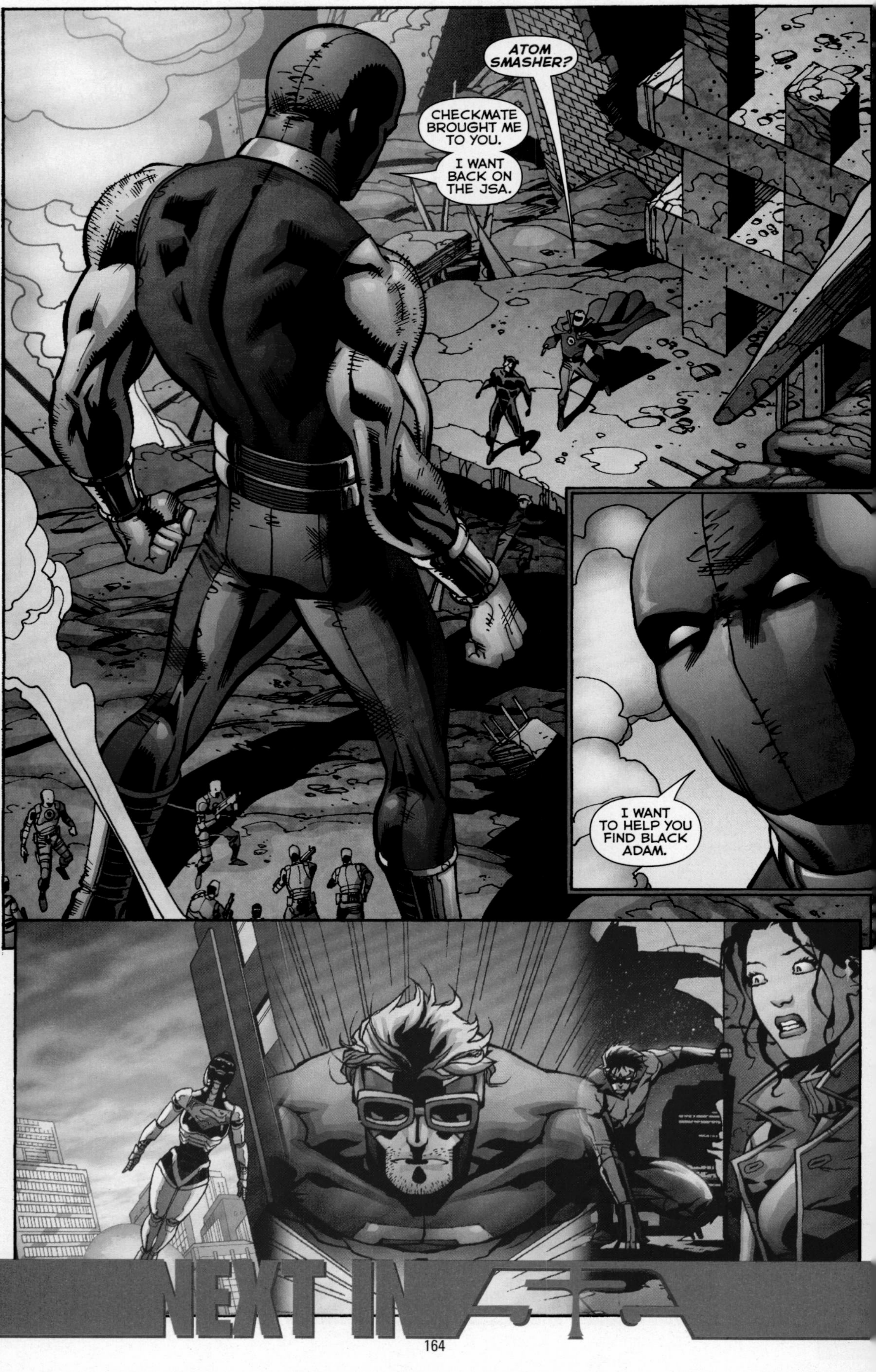
ATOM SMASHER?
CHECKMATE BROUGHT ME TO YOU.
I WANT BACK ON THE JSA.
I WANT TO HELP YOU FIND BLACK ADAM.
NEXT IN JSA

WEEK FORTY-SIX NOTES

KEITH GIFFEN

That Veronica Cale sequence? The one where she loses it and marches out to confront Black Adam? That was pure Rucka. How do I know? Because she was originally slated to die.

If memory serves, her little guilt-driven confrontation originally ended with Black Adam casually snuffing her out. Greg made the case for keeping her alive and suggested the scene as published. In hindsight, a good call. Back then...let's just say that there wasn't a lot of support for the idea and let it go at that.

It took a phone call from Greg (which prompted a quick change of phone number on my part) to convince me that his take on the scene was the better one. I redid the breakdowns and submitted them to Siglain, figuring that having both versions of the scene would make the call easier for him. I think he made the right call.

I'll admit to being kind of partial to the Black Adam/Science Squad showdown as well. It played out with just the right balance of tension and absurdity. I especially like the fact that the mad scientists, geniuses all, used their smarts (as well as an interesting weapon or two) to take down Black Adam. Too often, when it comes to the crunch, a comic book evil genius leaves his/her I.Q. at the door and makes imbecilic mistakes that call his/her genius into question. Not this time. Rallied by I.Q. Quimby, the mad scientists drop Black Adam in his tracks. Revenge of the nerds? I'm thinking that had a lot to do with it.

I hope DC prints the original cover to this issue, if only for JG's sake. That black mass Black Adam is suspended in was originally a hilarious background postcard welcoming one and all to Oolong Island. I guess it was deemed too busy by the powers that be or whatever. Me? I liked the postcard.

Maybe J.G. should have let Rucka plead his case...

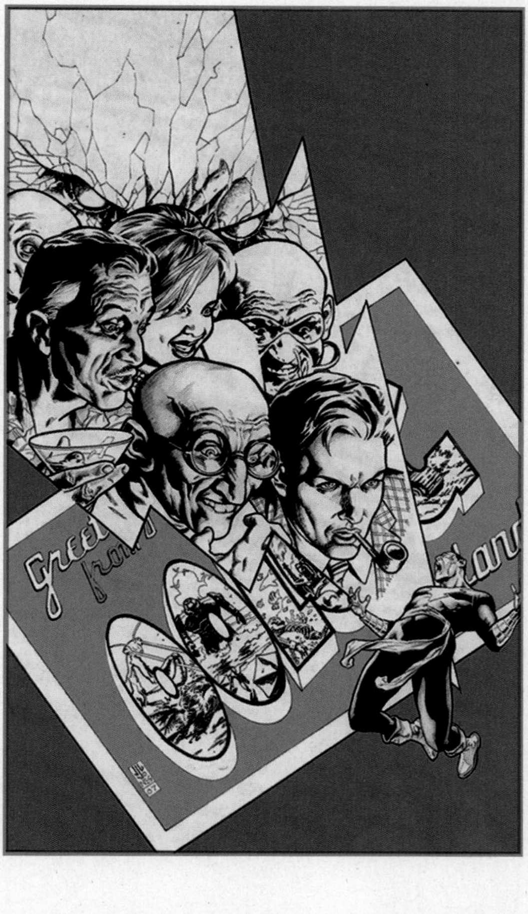

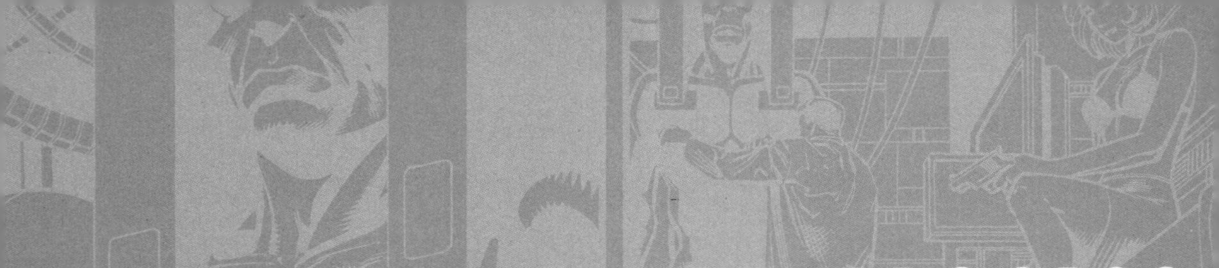

THE PROCESS

(COMPARE WITH PAGE 162 OF THIS COLLECTION)

Original Script

52 WEEK FORTY-SIX – PAGE EIGHTEEN

SPLASH PAGE

Alan Scott, Jay Garrick and Wildcat (all in costume) are among the dozens of volunteer global medical aid units to arrive in Bialya. All over, people are desperately searching for signs of life. This essentially will act as a transition from Week 29 to Week 50 for the JSA.

Jay skids to a halt in front of them.

DATESTAMP: Week 46, Day 4

BANNER: Bialya.

JAY: I haven't found a single survivor.

Breakdown by Keith Giffen

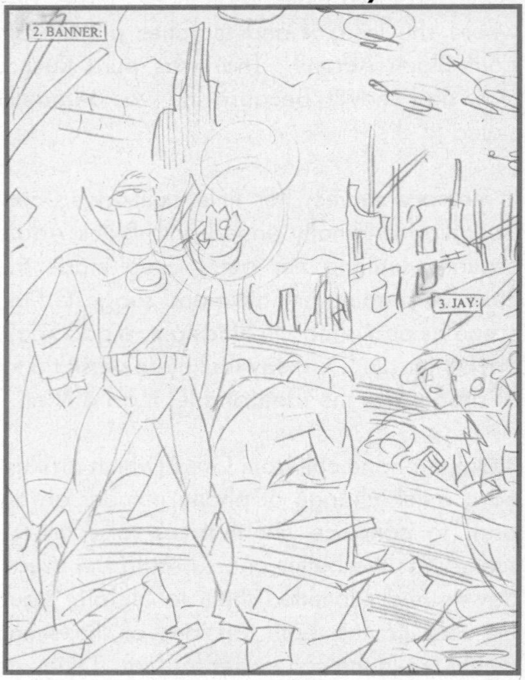
2. BANNER:
3. JAY:

Pencils by Patrick Olliffe

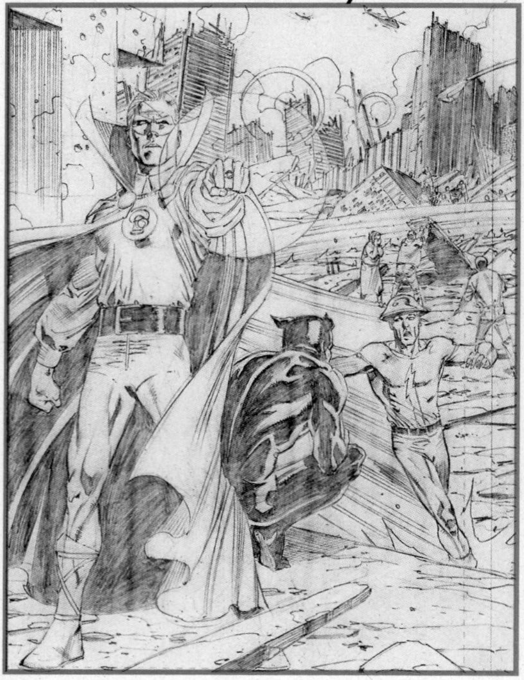

Final Page

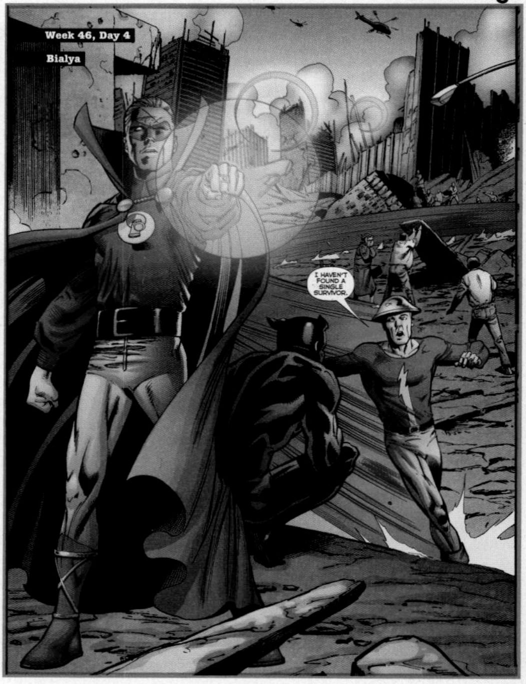
Week 46, Day 4
Bialya
I HAVEN'T FOUND A SINGLE SURVIVOR.

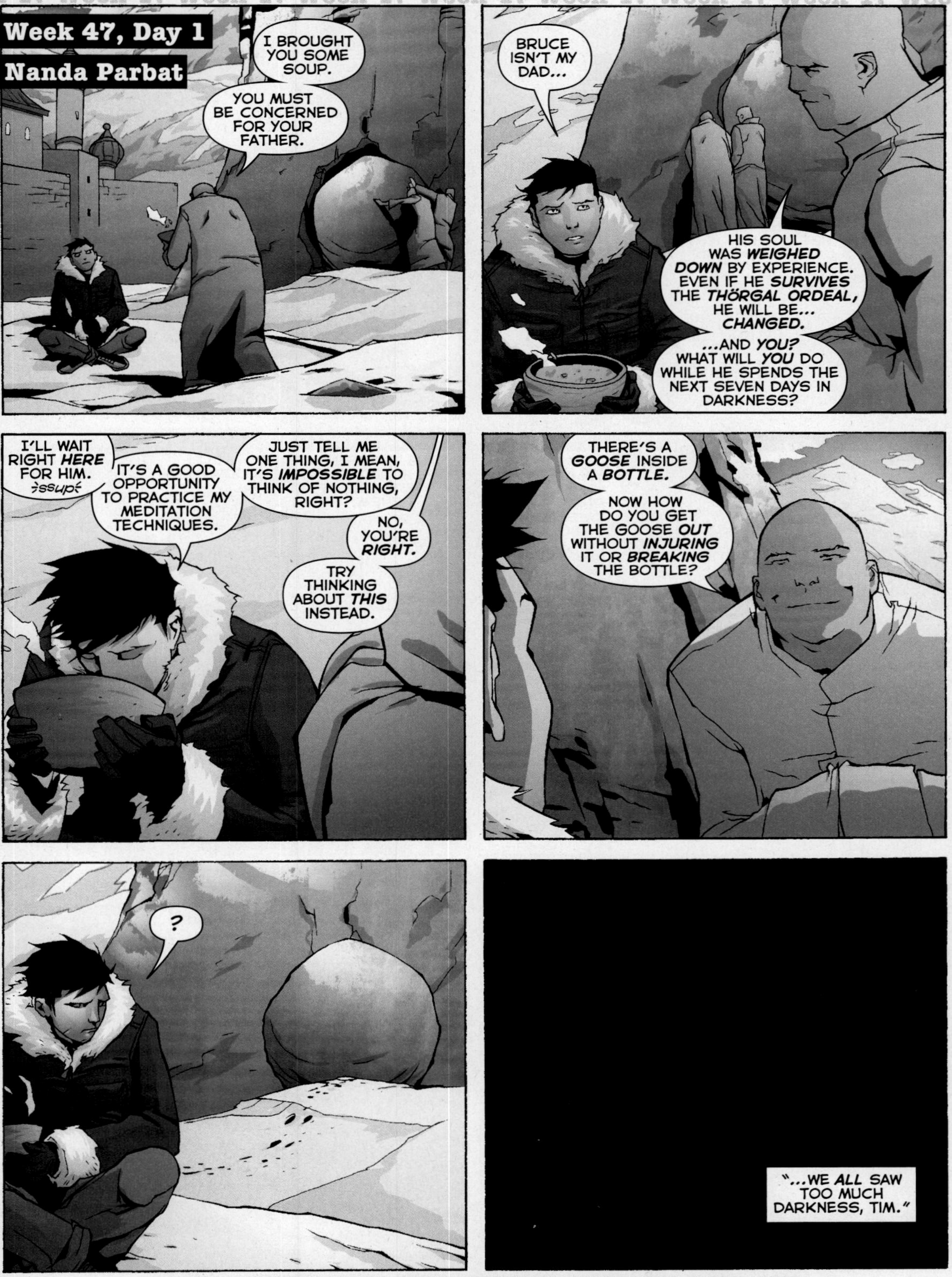
Week 47, Day 1
Nanda Parbat
I BROUGHT YOU SOME SOUP.
YOU MUST BE CONCERNED FOR YOUR FATHER.
BRUCE ISN'T MY DAD...
HIS SOUL WAS WEIGHED DOWN BY EXPERIENCE. EVEN IF HE SURVIVES THE THÖRGAL ORDEAL, HE WILL BE... CHANGED.
...AND YOU? WHAT WILL YOU DO WHILE HE SPENDS THE NEXT SEVEN DAYS IN DARKNESS?
I'LL WAIT RIGHT HERE FOR HIM.
ssup
IT'S A GOOD OPPORTUNITY TO PRACTICE MY MEDITATION TECHNIQUES.
JUST TELL ME ONE THING, I MEAN, IT'S IMPOSSIBLE TO THINK OF NOTHING, RIGHT?
NO, YOU'RE RIGHT.
TRY THINKING ABOUT THIS INSTEAD.
THERE'S A GOOSE INSIDE A BOTTLE.
NOW HOW DO YOU GET THE GOOSE OUT WITHOUT INJURING IT OR BREAKING THE BOTTLE?
?
"...WE ALL SAW TOO MUCH DARKNESS, TIM."

WRITTEN BY GEOFF JOHNS, GRANT MORRISON, GREG RUCKA, MARK WAID
ART BREAKDOWNS BY KEITH GIFFEN • PENCILS BY GIUSEPPE CAMUNCOLI • INKS BY LORENZO RUGGIERO
COLORS BY PETE PANTAZIS • LETTERS BY ROB LEIGH • COVER BY J.G. JONES & ALEX SINCLAIR • SPECIAL THANKS TO STEFANO LANDINI
ASST. EDITOR – HARVEY RICHARDS • ASSOC. EDITOR – JEANINE SCHAEFER • EDITOR – MICHAEL SIGLAIN

REVELATIONS

Week 47, Day 2

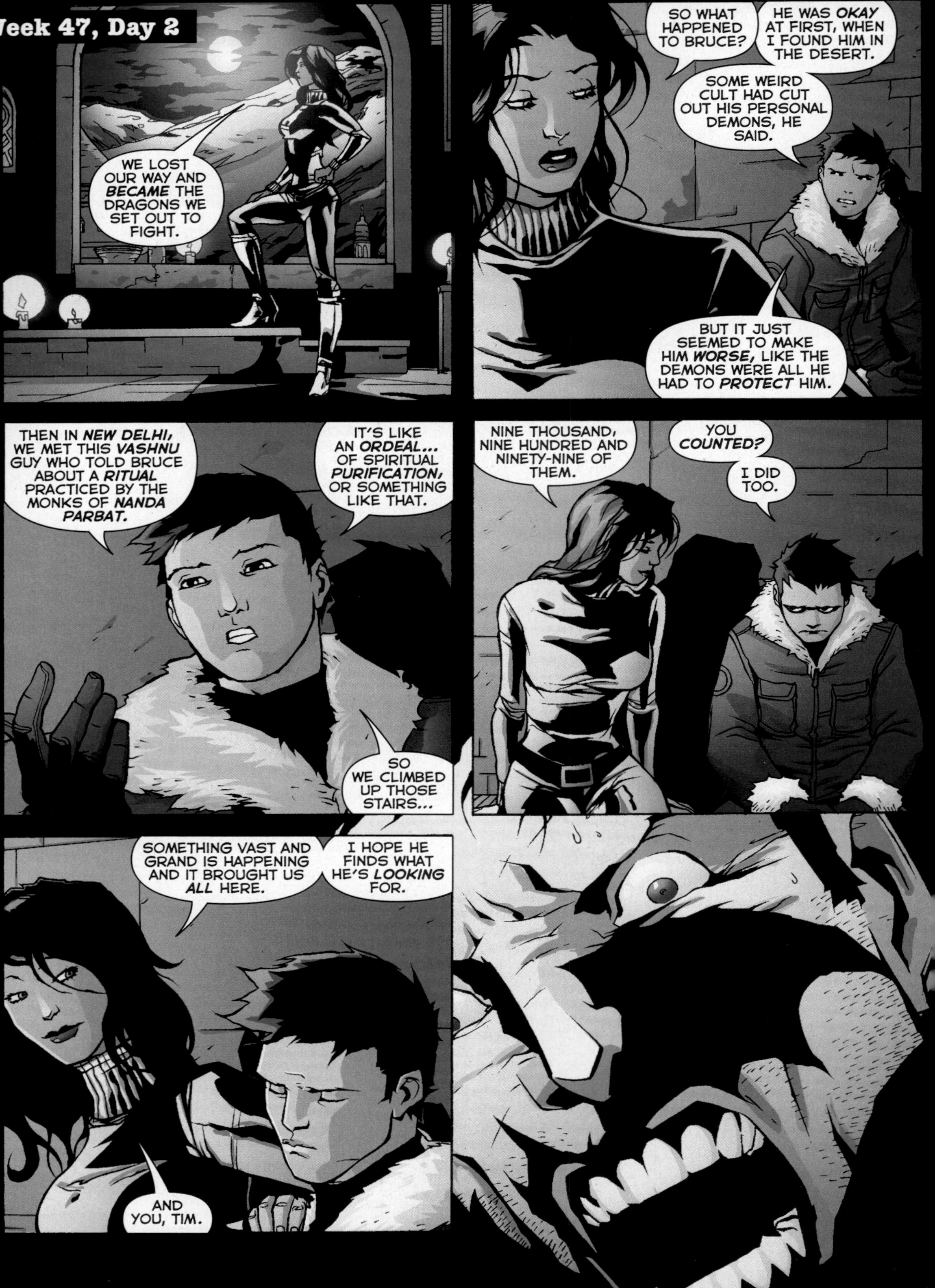
WE LOST OUR WAY AND *BECAME* THE DRAGONS WE SET OUT TO FIGHT.
SO WHAT HAPPENED TO BRUCE?
HE WAS *OKAY* AT FIRST, WHEN I FOUND HIM IN THE DESERT.
SOME WEIRD CULT HAD CUT OUT HIS PERSONAL DEMONS, HE SAID.
BUT IT JUST SEEMED TO MAKE HIM *WORSE,* LIKE THE DEMONS WERE ALL HE HAD TO *PROTECT* HIM.
THEN IN *NEW DELHI,* WE MET THIS *VASHNU* GUY WHO TOLD BRUCE ABOUT A *RITUAL* PRACTICED BY THE MONKS OF *NANDA PARBAT.*
IT'S LIKE AN *ORDEAL...* OF SPIRITUAL *PURIFICATION,* OR SOMETHING LIKE THAT.
SO WE CLIMBED UP THOSE STAIRS...
NINE THOUSAND, NINE HUNDRED AND NINETY-NINE OF THEM.
YOU *COUNTED?*
I DID TOO.
SOMETHING VAST AND GRAND IS HAPPENING AND IT BROUGHT US *ALL* HERE.
I HOPE HE FINDS WHAT HE'S *LOOKING* FOR.
AND YOU, TIM.

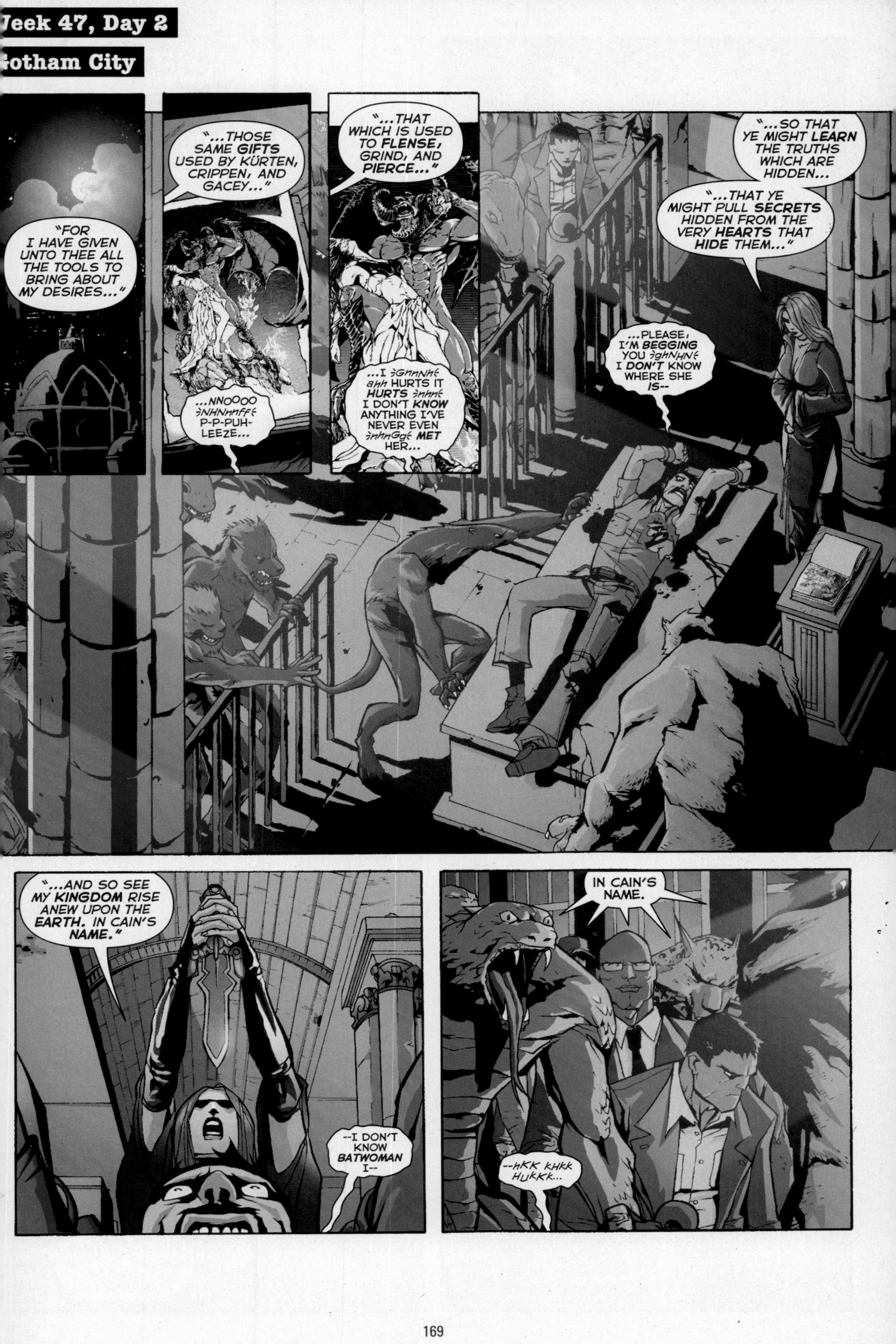
eek 47, Day 2
otham City
"FOR I HAVE GIVEN UNTO THEE ALL THE TOOLS TO BRING ABOUT MY DESIRES..."
"...THOSE SAME GIFTS USED BY KÜRTEN, CRIPPEN, AND GACEY..."
...NNOOOO NHNnnff P-P-PUH-LEEZE...
"...THAT WHICH IS USED TO FLENSE, GRIND, AND PIERCE..."
...I Gnnnh ahh HURTS IT HURTS nhn I DON'T KNOW ANYTHING I'VE NEVER EVEN nhnGg MET HER...
"...SO THAT YE MIGHT LEARN THE TRUTHS WHICH ARE HIDDEN...
"...THAT YE MIGHT PULL SECRETS HIDDEN FROM THE VERY HEARTS THAT HIDE THEM..."
...PLEASE, I'M BEGGING YOU ghNhN I DON'T KNOW WHERE SHE IS--
"...AND SO SEE MY KINGDOM RISE ANEW UPON THE EARTH. IN CAIN'S NAME."
--I DON'T KNOW BATWOMAN I--
IN CAIN'S NAME.
--hKK KHKK HUKKK...

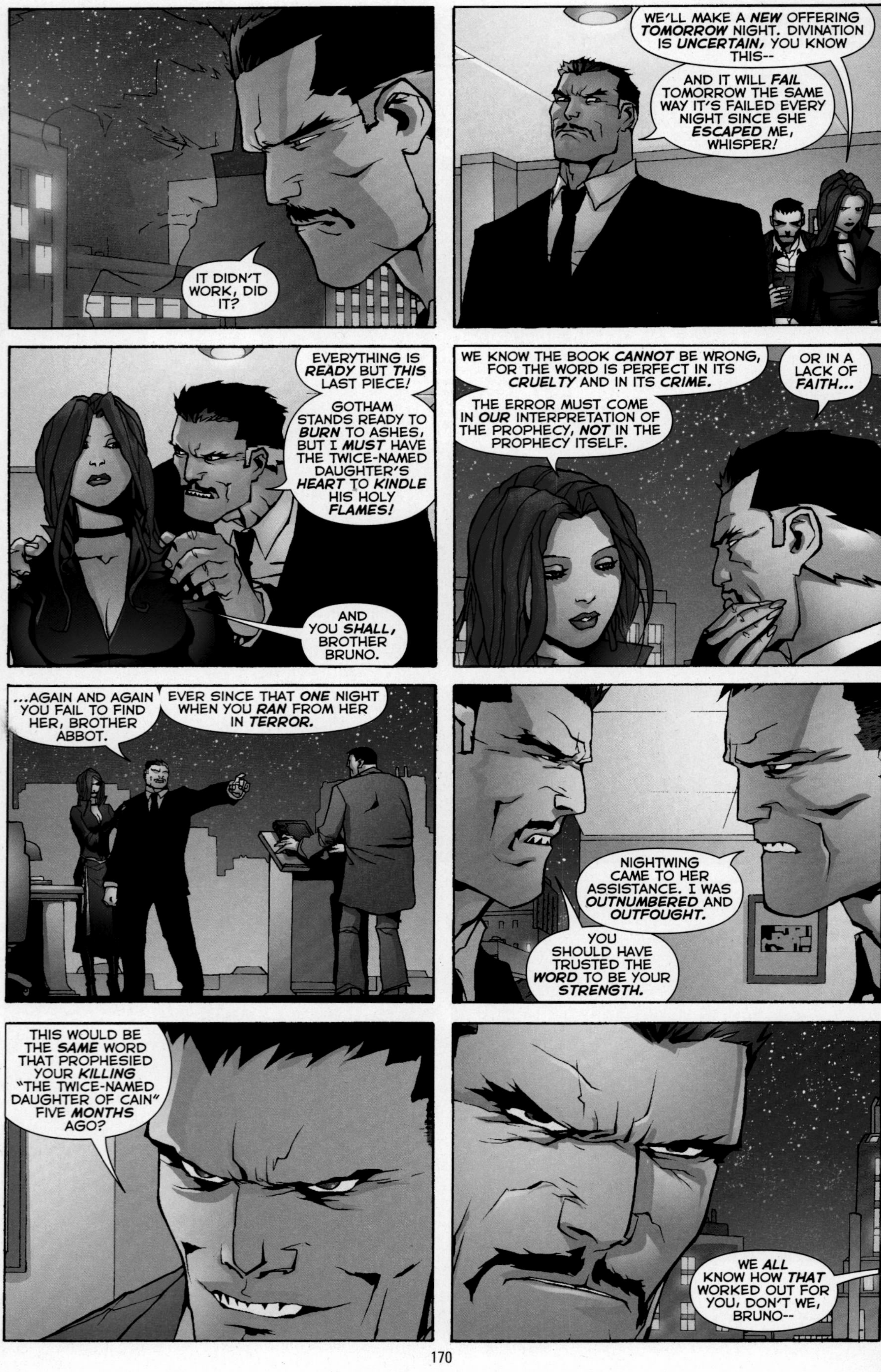
IT DIDN'T WORK, DID IT?
WE'LL MAKE A NEW OFFERING TOMORROW NIGHT. DIVINATION IS UNCERTAIN, YOU KNOW THIS--
AND IT WILL FAIL TOMORROW THE SAME WAY IT'S FAILED EVERY NIGHT SINCE SHE ESCAPED ME, WHISPER!
EVERYTHING IS READY BUT THIS LAST PIECE!
GOTHAM STANDS READY TO BURN TO ASHES, BUT I MUST HAVE THE TWICE-NAMED DAUGHTER'S HEART TO KINDLE HIS HOLY FLAMES!
AND YOU SHALL, BROTHER BRUNO.
WE KNOW THE BOOK CANNOT BE WRONG, FOR THE WORD IS PERFECT IN ITS CRUELTY AND IN ITS CRIME.
THE ERROR MUST COME IN OUR INTERPRETATION OF THE PROPHECY, NOT IN THE PROPHECY ITSELF.
OR IN A LACK OF FAITH...
...AGAIN AND AGAIN YOU FAIL TO FIND HER, BROTHER ABBOT.
EVER SINCE THAT ONE NIGHT WHEN YOU RAN FROM HER IN TERROR.
NIGHTWING CAME TO HER ASSISTANCE. I WAS OUTNUMBERED AND OUTFOUGHT.
YOU SHOULD HAVE TRUSTED THE WORD TO BE YOUR STRENGTH.
THIS WOULD BE THE SAME WORD THAT PROPHESIED YOUR KILLING "THE TWICE-NAMED DAUGHTER OF CAIN" FIVE MONTHS AGO?
WE ALL KNOW HOW THAT WORKED OUT FOR YOU, DON'T WE, BRUNO--

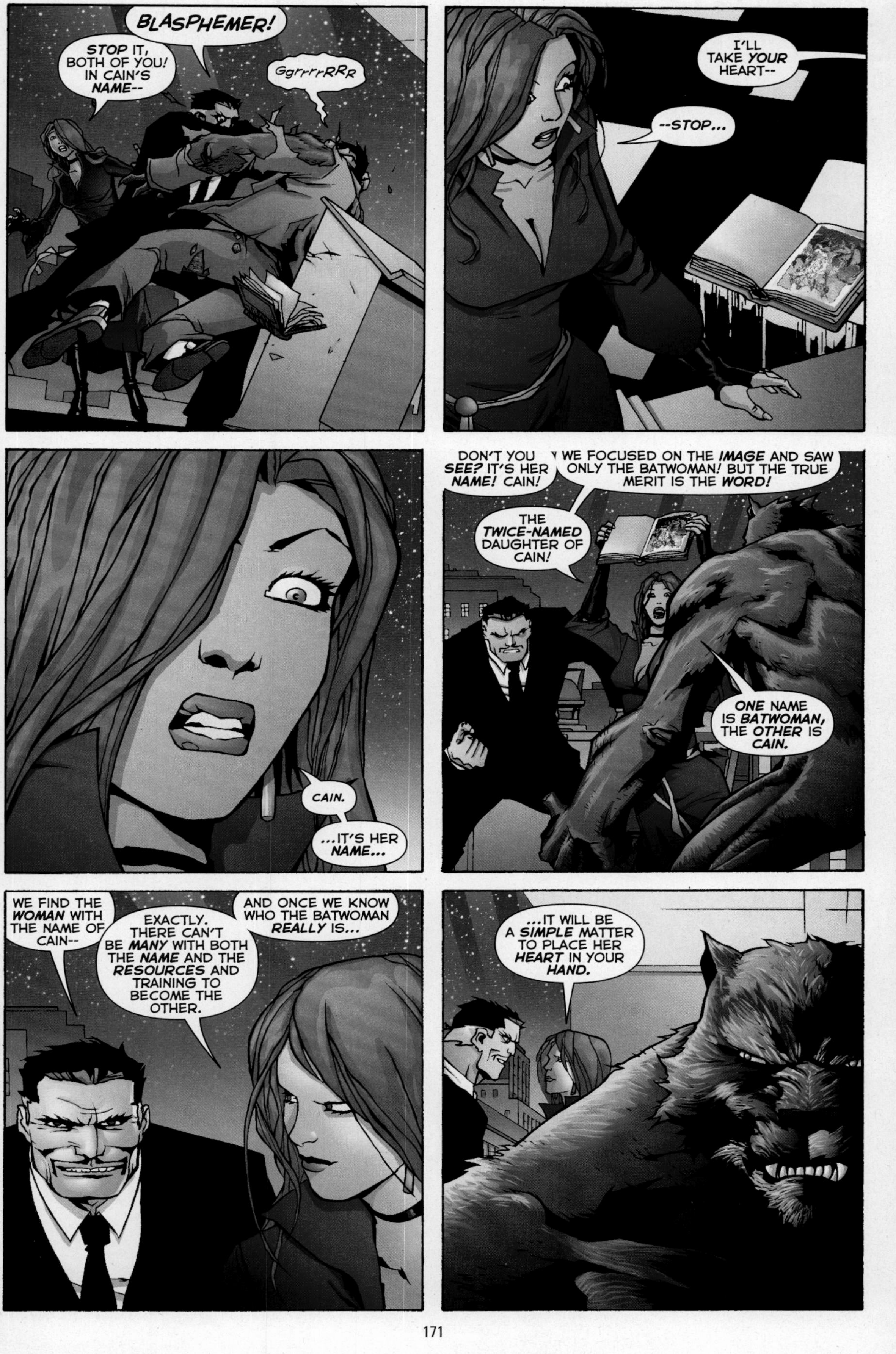
BLASPHEMER!
STOP IT, BOTH OF YOU! IN CAIN'S NAME--
GgrrrrRRR
I'LL TAKE YOUR HEART--
--STOP...
CAIN.
...IT'S HER NAME...
DON'T YOU SEE? IT'S HER NAME! CAIN!
WE FOCUSED ON THE IMAGE AND SAW ONLY THE BATWOMAN! BUT THE TRUE MERIT IS THE WORD!
THE TWICE-NAMED DAUGHTER OF CAIN!
ONE NAME IS BATWOMAN, THE OTHER IS CAIN.
WE FIND THE WOMAN WITH THE NAME OF CAIN--
EXACTLY. THERE CAN'T BE MANY WITH BOTH THE NAME AND THE RESOURCES AND TRAINING TO BECOME THE OTHER.
AND ONCE WE KNOW WHO THE BATWOMAN REALLY IS...
...IT WILL BE A SIMPLE MATTER TO PLACE HER HEART IN YOUR HAND.

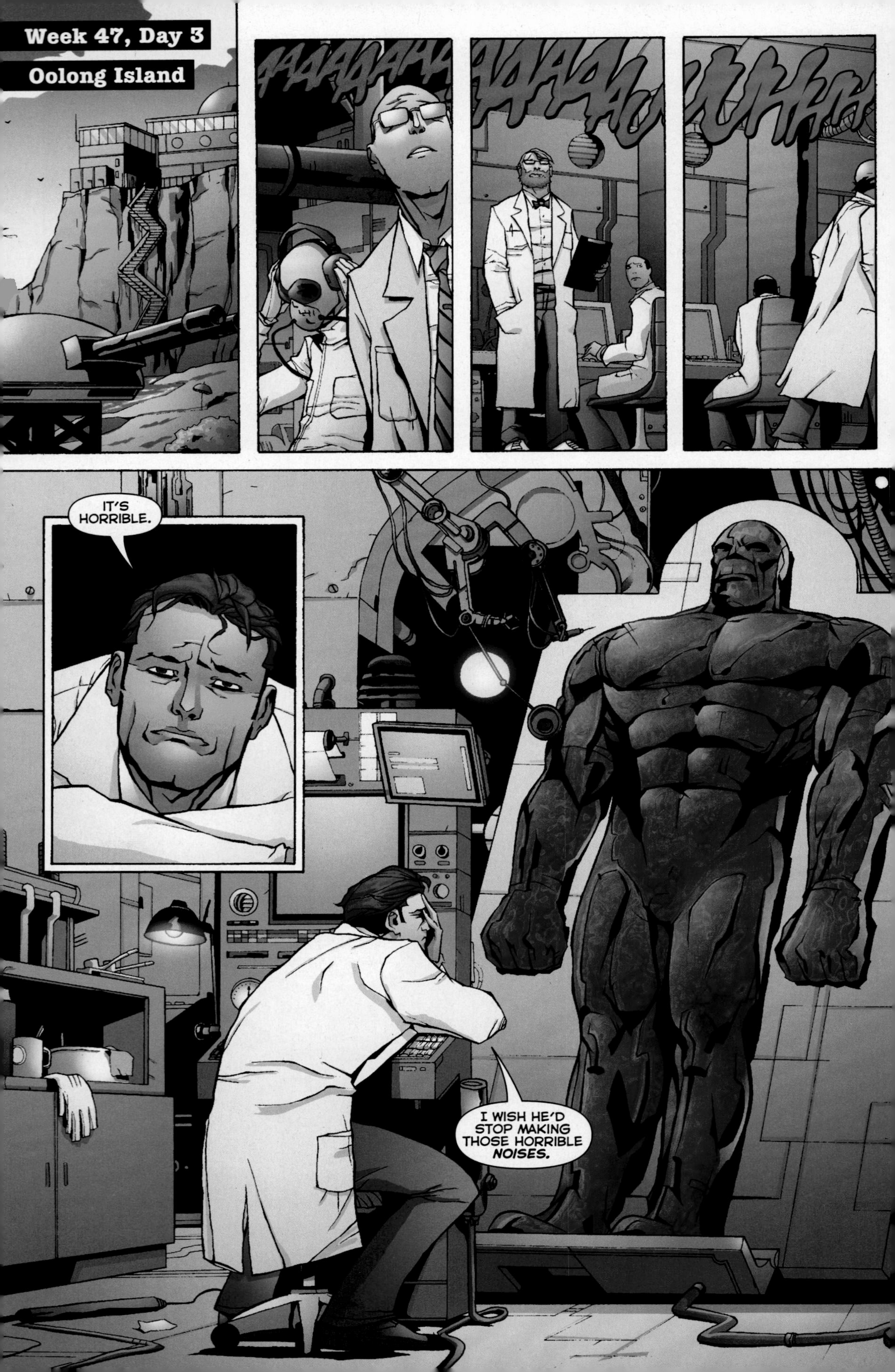

Week 47, Day 3
Oolong Island
AAAAAAAAAAAAAAAAAAAAAAAAAAAAAAAAAAAAAAAAAAAAAAAAAAAAAAAAAAAAAAAAAAAAAAAAAAAAAAAAAA
IT'S HORRIBLE.
I WISH HE'D STOP MAKING THOSE HORRIBLE NOISES.

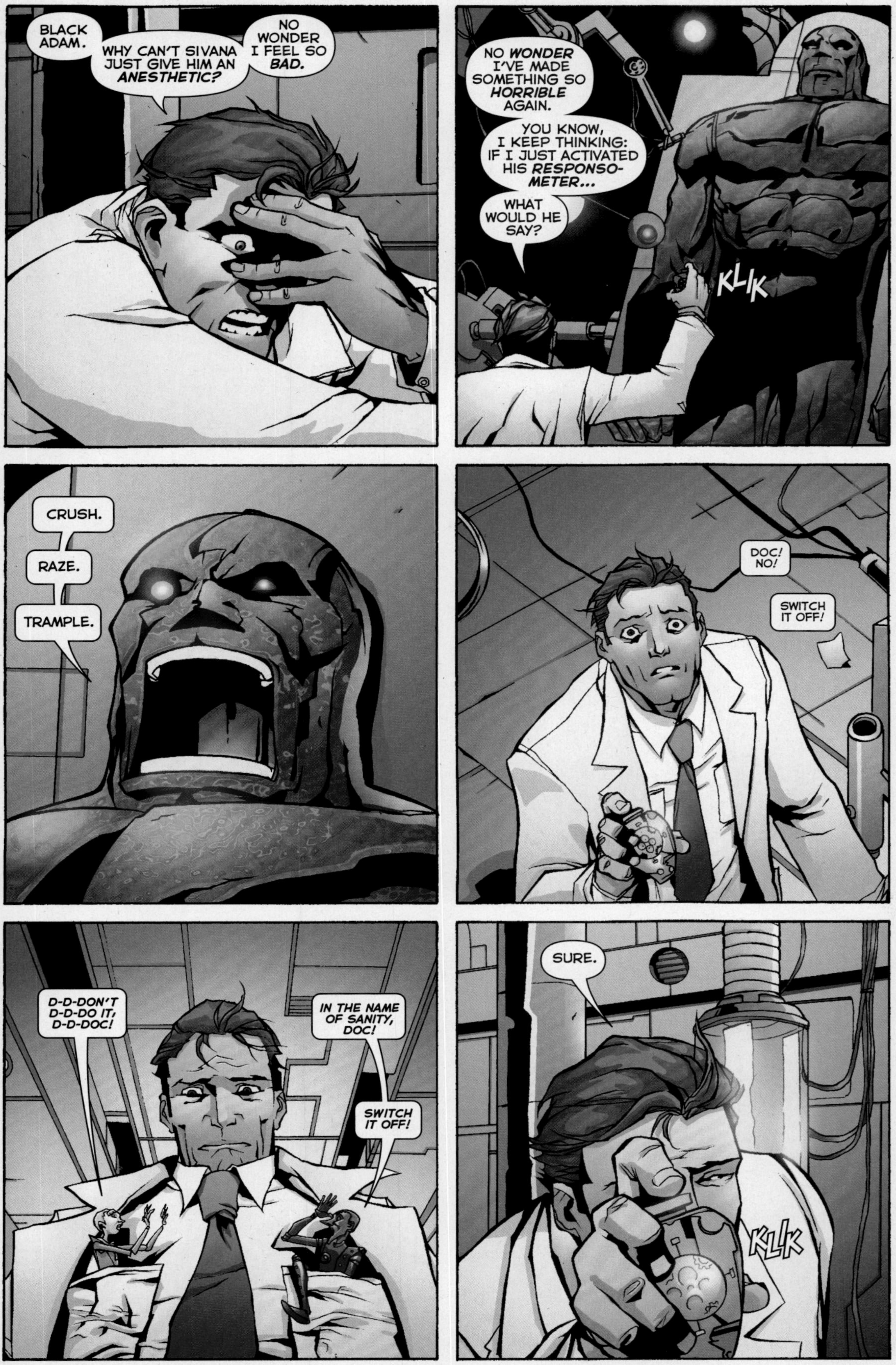
BLACK ADAM.
WHY CAN'T SIVANA JUST GIVE HIM AN ANESTHETIC?
NO WONDER I FEEL SO BAD.
NO WONDER I'VE MADE SOMETHING SO HORRIBLE AGAIN.
YOU KNOW, I KEEP THINKING: IF I JUST ACTIVATED HIS RESPONSO-METER...
WHAT WOULD HE SAY?
KLIK
CRUSH.
RAZE.
TRAMPLE.
DOC! NO!
SWITCH IT OFF!
D-D-DON'T D-D-DO IT, D-D-DOC!
IN THE NAME OF SANITY, DOC!
SWITCH IT OFF!
SURE.
KLIK

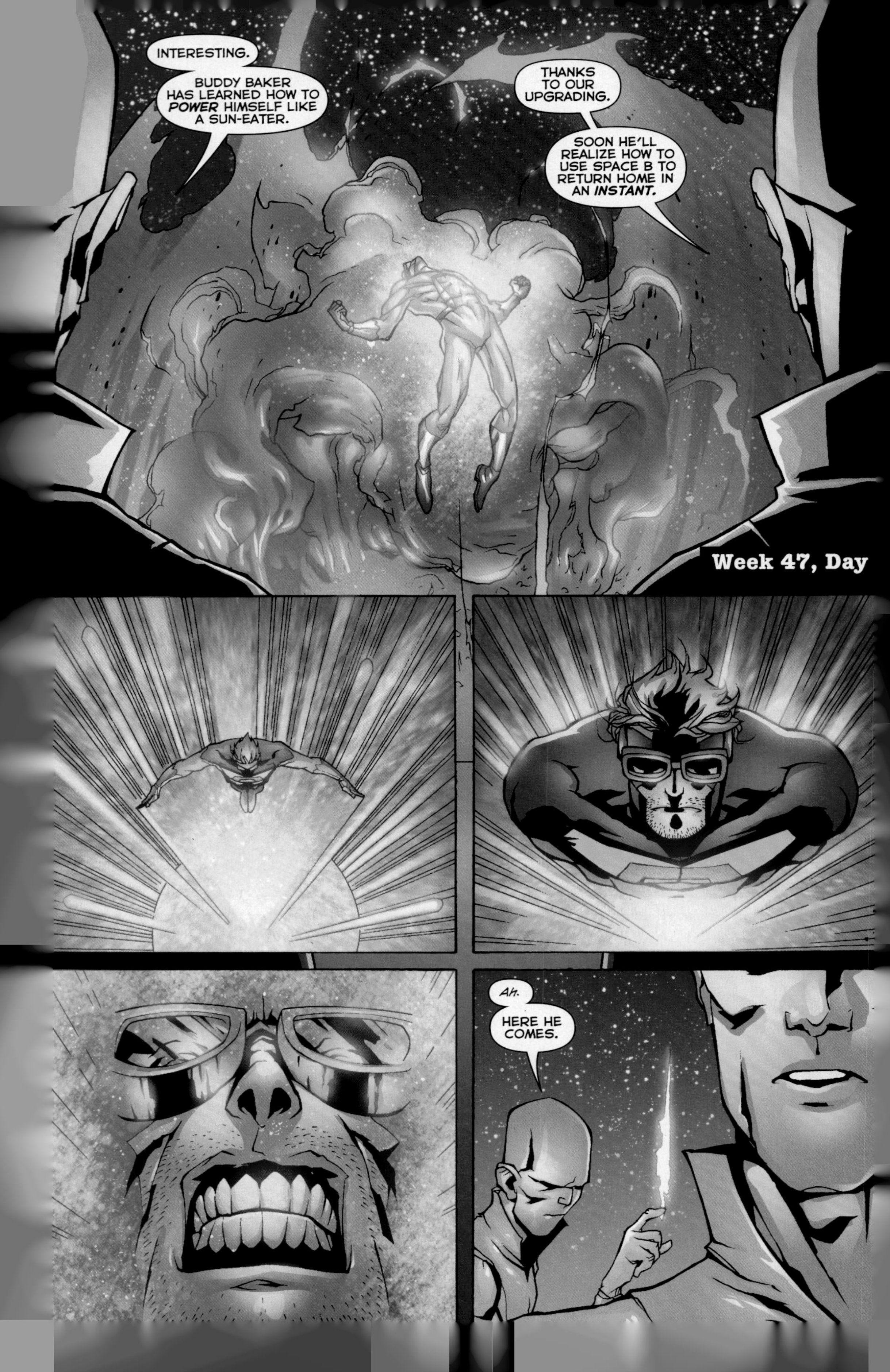
INTERESTING.
BUDDY BAKER HAS LEARNED HOW TO *POWER* HIMSELF LIKE A SUN-EATER.
THANKS TO OUR UPGRADING.
SOON HE'LL REALIZE HOW TO USE SPACE B TO RETURN HOME IN AN *INSTANT.*
Week 47, Day
Ah.
HERE HE COMES.

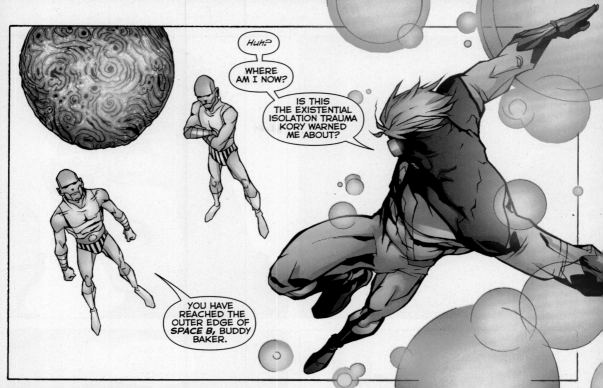

Huh?

WHERE AM I NOW?

IS THIS THE EXISTENTIAL ISOLATION TRAUMA KORY WARNED ME ABOUT?

YOU HAVE REACHED THE OUTER EDGE OF *SPACE B,* BUDDY BAKER.

FROM HERE, YOU CAN ACCESS ANY POINT IN SPACE *OR* TIME IN *THIS,* YOUR *UNIVERSE.*

THIS IS HOW THE SUN-EATER SHOALS *TRAVEL* ON THEIR INTERGALACTIC MIGRATIONS.

LOOK, *WHATEVER YOU GUYS ARE--*

--I JUST WANT TO GET BACK TO MY *WIFE* AND FAMILY!

I NEED TO KNOW SHE GOT THROUGH THE *CRISIS* AND EVERYONE'S *OKAY!*

LOOK, I *KNOW* YOU'RE ON MY SIDE!

OUT HERE, THERE ARE NO *SIDES.*

THIS POINT HERE LIES ONE *MONTH* AHEAD IN YOUR PERSONAL TIMELINE.

ELLEN!

THAT'S MY ELLEN!

OH BABY! I'M COMING HOME!

I'M ALMOST THERE!

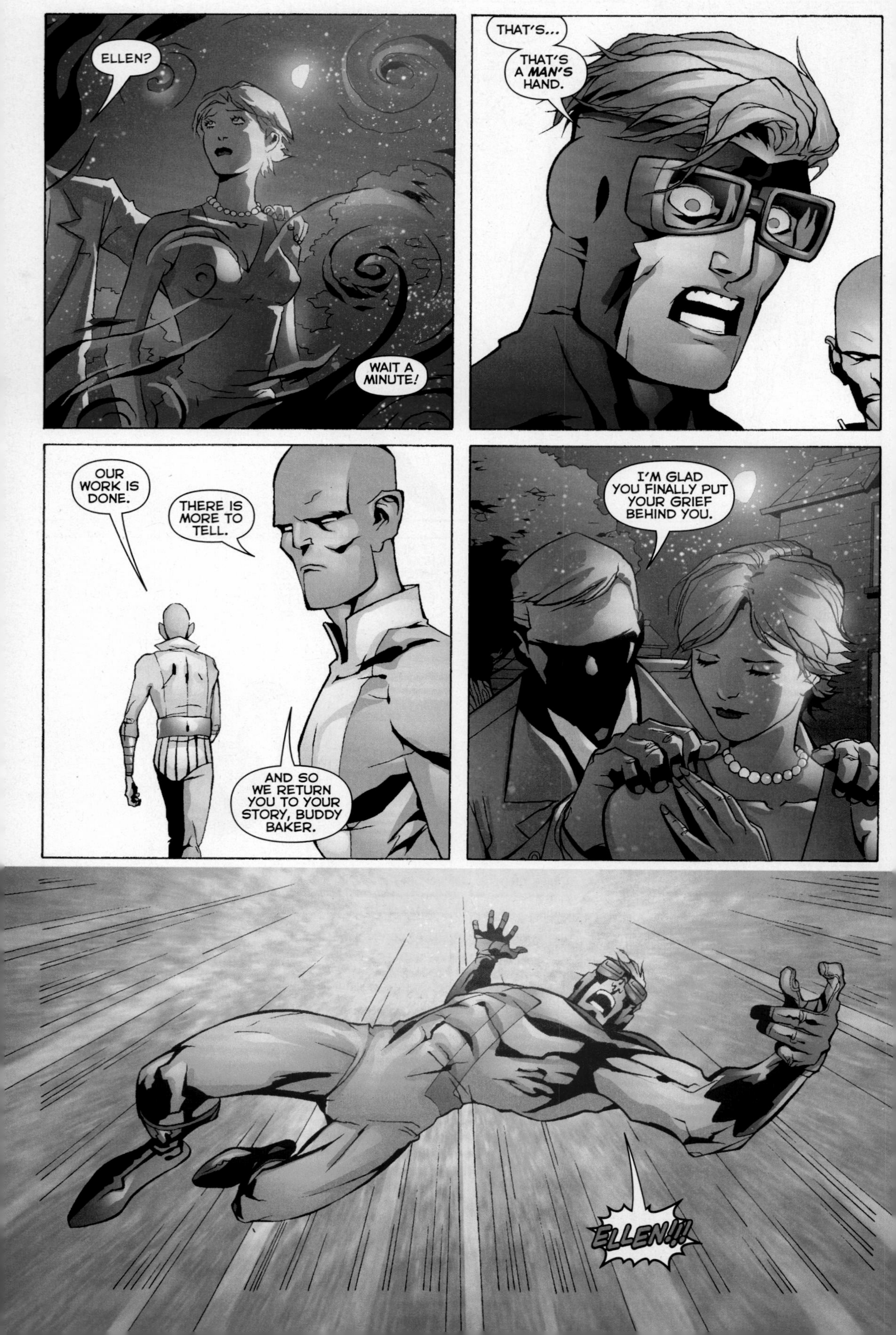
ELLEN?
WAIT A MINUTE!
THAT'S...
THAT'S A *MAN'S* HAND.
OUR WORK IS DONE.
THERE IS MORE TO TELL.
AND SO WE RETURN YOU TO YOUR STORY, BUDDY BAKER.
I'M GLAD YOU FINALLY PUT YOUR GRIEF BEHIND YOU.
ELLEN!!!

I CAN'T BELIEVE WHAT I'M *HEARING*.

I CAN SAY IT *AGAIN*, IF YOU LIKE, GAR...

...I'M NOT *READY* TO BE A TEEN TITAN.

DON'T YOU THINK MAYBE I MIGHT BE A *BETTER* JUDGE OF *THAT*, NATASHA?

SURE. BUT IT DOESN'T CHANGE MY DECISION.

BESIDES, UNCLE JOHN AND I ARE WORKING ON PUTTING TOGETHER A *TEAM* OF OUR *OWN*.

THERE'S STILL A LOT OF EVERYMAN *VICTIMS* OUT THERE WHO COULD USE A HAND.

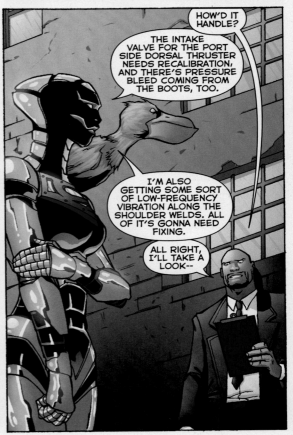

HOW'D IT HANDLE?

THE INTAKE VALVE FOR THE PORT SIDE DORSAL THRUSTER NEEDS RECALIBRATION, AND THERE'S PRESSURE BLEED COMING FROM THE BOOTS, TOO.

I'M ALSO GETTING SOME SORT OF LOW-FREQUENCY VIBRATION ALONG THE SHOULDER WELDS. ALL OF IT'S GONNA NEED FIXING.

ALL RIGHT, I'LL TAKE A LOOK--

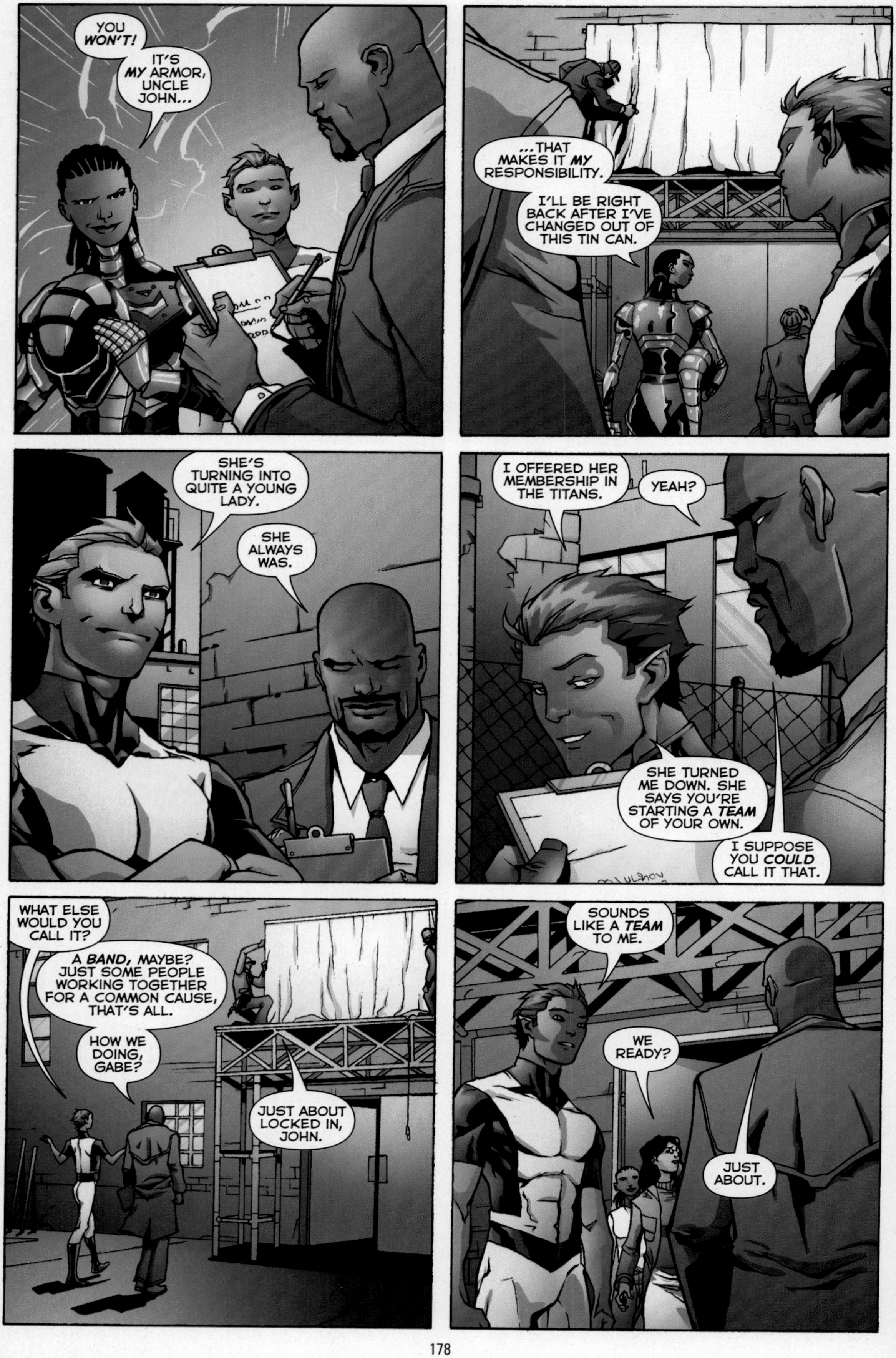
YOU *WON'T!*
IT'S *MY* ARMOR, UNCLE JOHN...
...THAT MAKES IT *MY* RESPONSIBILITY.
I'LL BE RIGHT BACK AFTER I'VE CHANGED OUT OF THIS TIN CAN.
SHE'S TURNING INTO QUITE A YOUNG LADY.
SHE ALWAYS WAS.
I OFFERED HER MEMBERSHIP IN THE TITANS.
YEAH?
SHE TURNED ME DOWN. SHE SAYS YOU'RE STARTING A *TEAM* OF YOUR OWN.
I SUPPOSE YOU *COULD* CALL IT THAT.
WHAT ELSE WOULD YOU CALL IT?
A *BAND,* MAYBE? JUST SOME PEOPLE WORKING TOGETHER FOR A COMMON CAUSE, THAT'S ALL.
HOW WE DOING, GABE?
JUST ABOUT LOCKED IN, JOHN.
SOUNDS LIKE A *TEAM* TO ME.
WE READY?
JUST ABOUT.

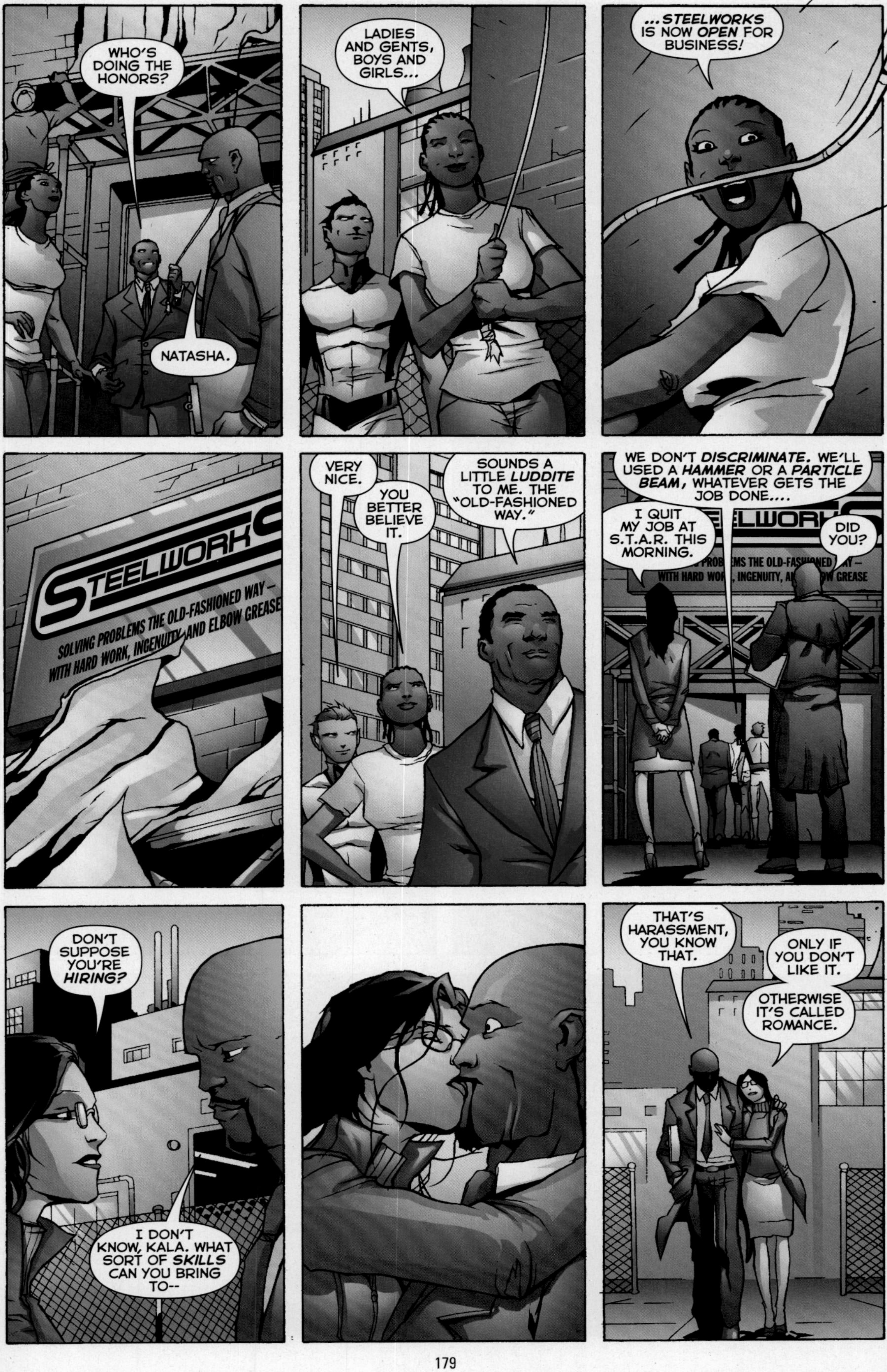
WHO'S DOING THE HONORS?
NATASHA.
LADIES AND GENTS, BOYS AND GIRLS...
...STEELWORKS IS NOW OPEN FOR BUSINESS!
STEELWORKS
SOLVING PROBLEMS THE OLD-FASHIONED WAY — WITH HARD WORK, INGENUITY AND ELBOW GREASE
VERY NICE.
YOU BETTER BELIEVE IT.
SOUNDS A LITTLE LUDDITE TO ME. THE "OLD-FASHIONED WAY."
WE DON'T DISCRIMINATE. WE'LL USED A HAMMER OR A PARTICLE BEAM, WHATEVER GETS THE JOB DONE....
I QUIT MY JOB AT S.T.A.R. THIS MORNING.
DID YOU?
DON'T SUPPOSE YOU'RE HIRING?
I DON'T KNOW, KALA. WHAT SORT OF SKILLS CAN YOU BRING TO--
THAT'S HARASSMENT, YOU KNOW THAT.
ONLY IF YOU DON'T LIKE IT.
OTHERWISE IT'S CALLED ROMANCE.

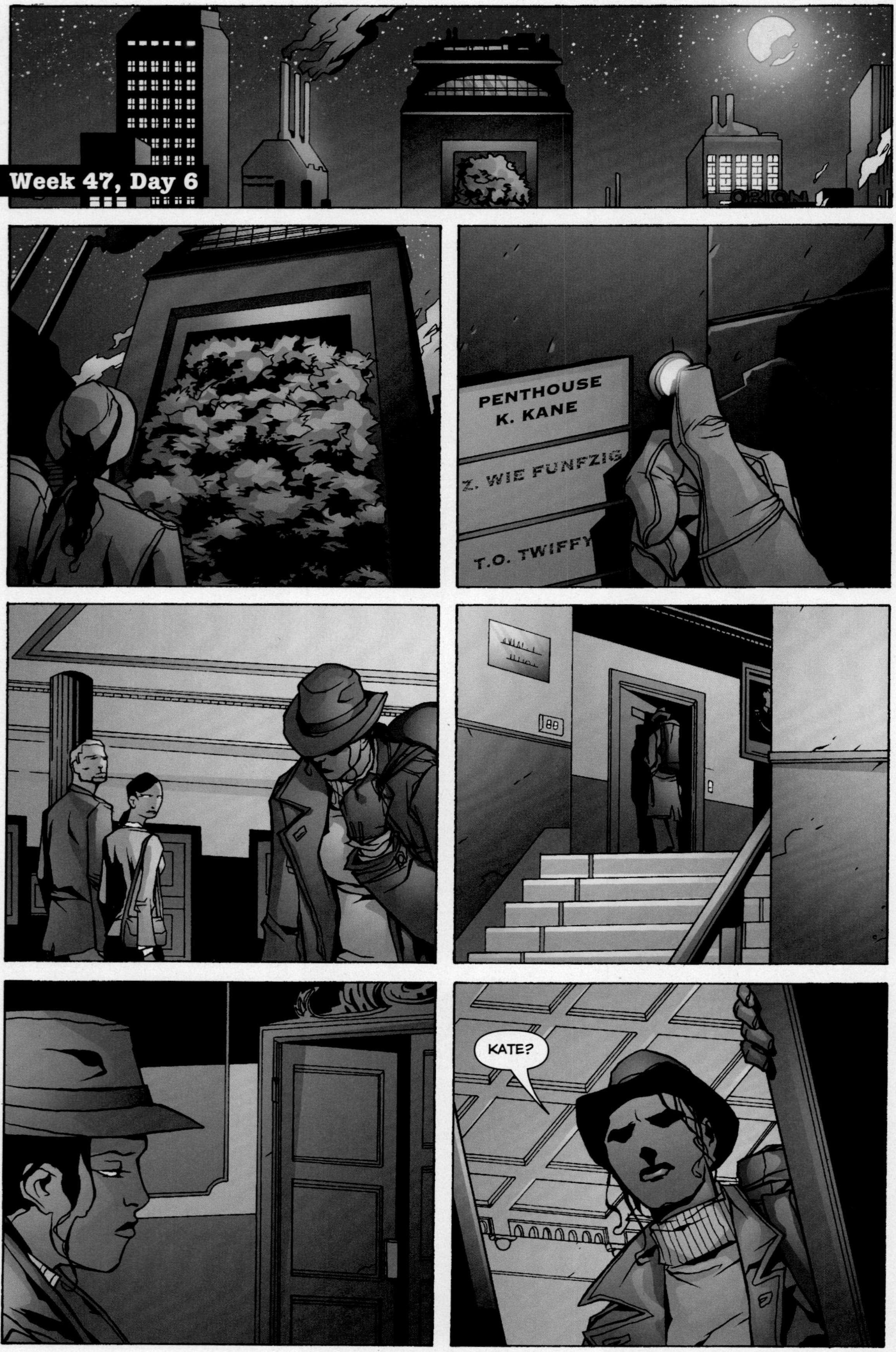

Week 47, Day 6
ORION
PENTHOUSE
K. KANE
Z. WIE FUNFZIG
T.O. TWIFFY
KATE?

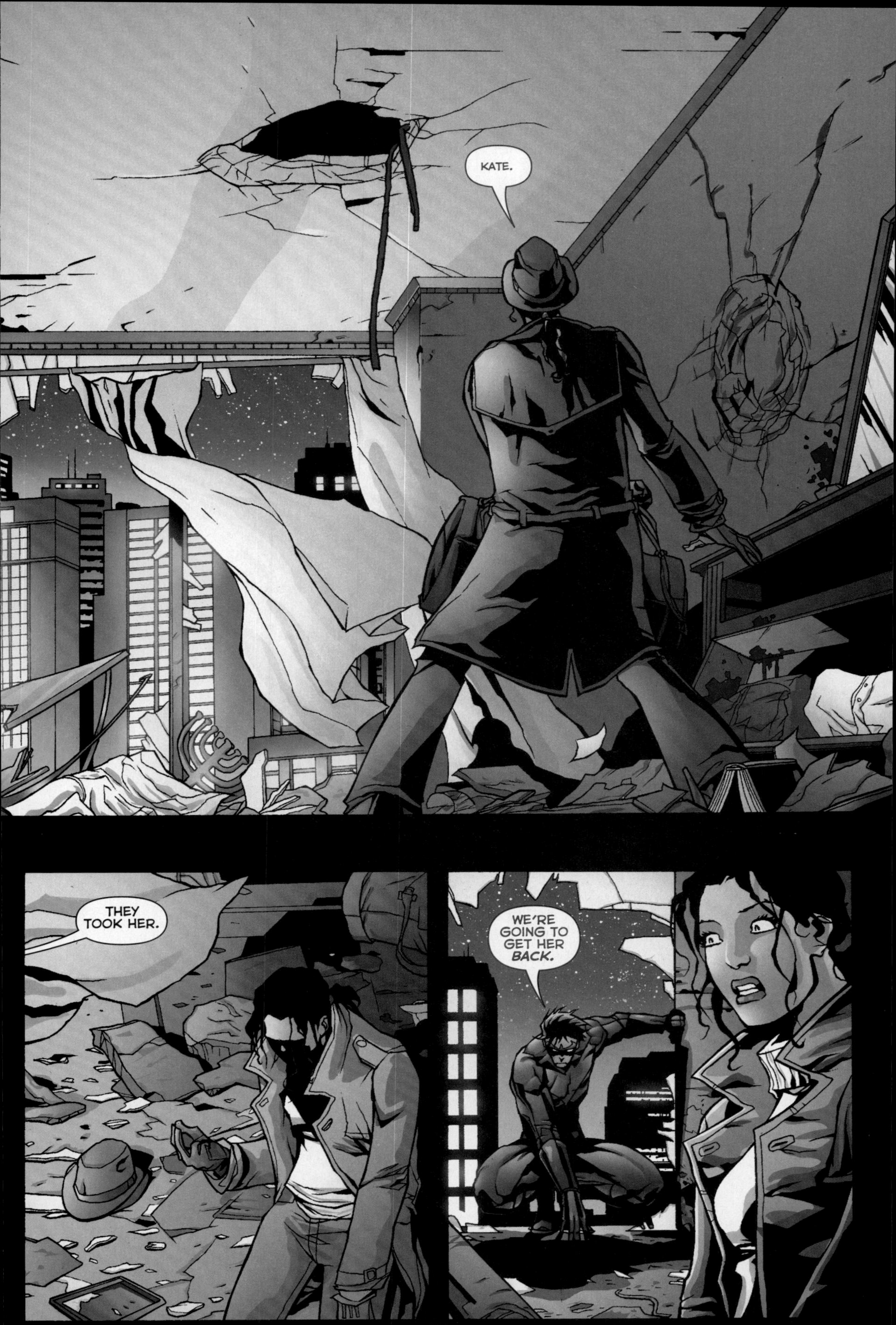
KATE.
THEY TOOK HER.
WE'RE GOING TO GET HER BACK.

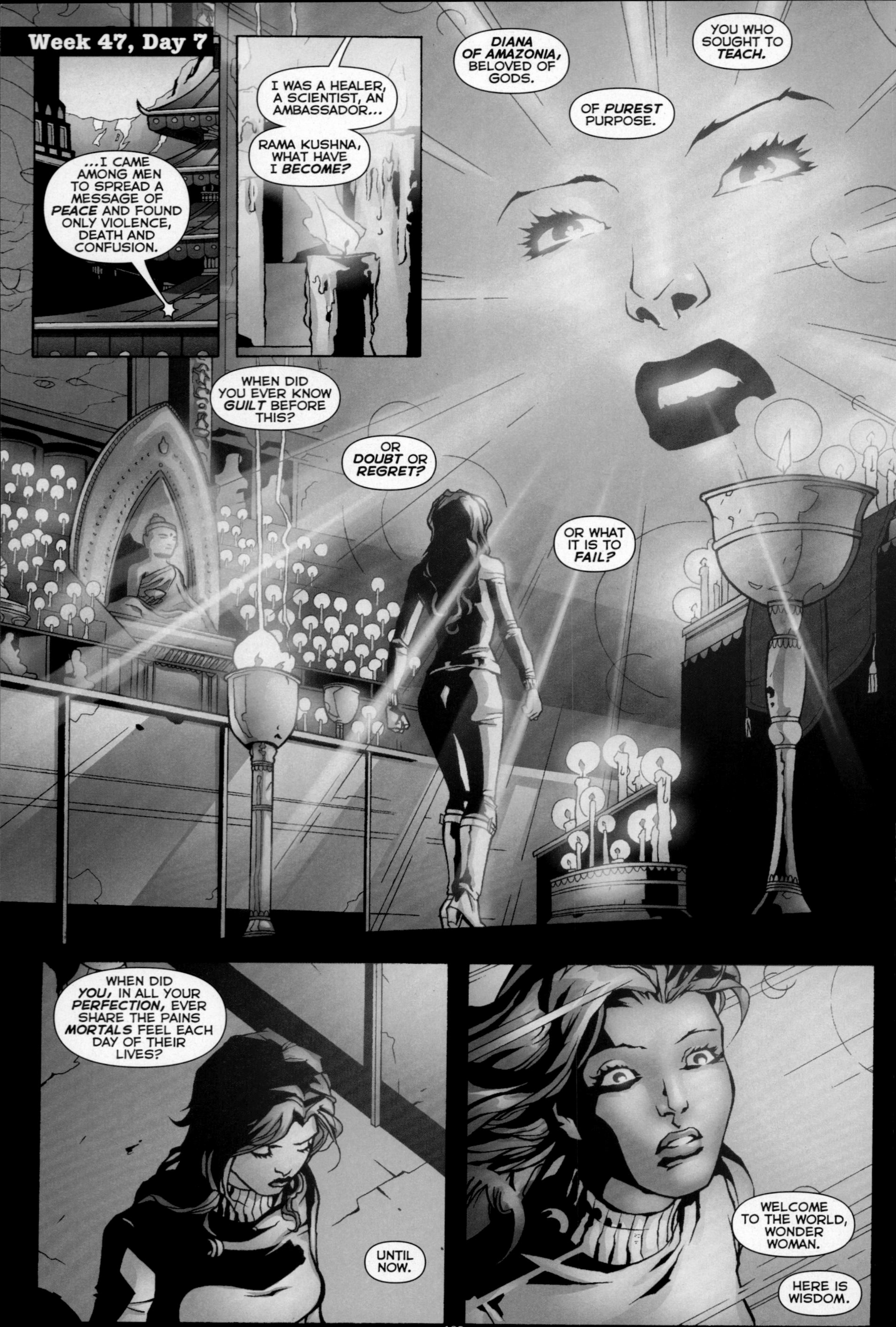
Week 47, Day 7
...I CAME AMONG MEN TO SPREAD A MESSAGE OF PEACE AND FOUND ONLY VIOLENCE, DEATH AND CONFUSION.
I WAS A HEALER, A SCIENTIST, AN AMBASSADOR...
RAMA KUSHNA, WHAT HAVE I BECOME?
DIANA OF AMAZONIA, BELOVED OF GODS.
OF PUREST PURPOSE.
YOU WHO SOUGHT TO TEACH.
WHEN DID YOU EVER KNOW GUILT BEFORE THIS?
OR DOUBT OR REGRET?
OR WHAT IT IS TO FAIL?
WHEN DID YOU, IN ALL YOUR PERFECTION, EVER SHARE THE PAINS MORTALS FEEL EACH DAY OF THEIR LIVES?
UNTIL NOW.
WELCOME TO THE WORLD, WONDER WOMAN.
HERE IS WISDOM.

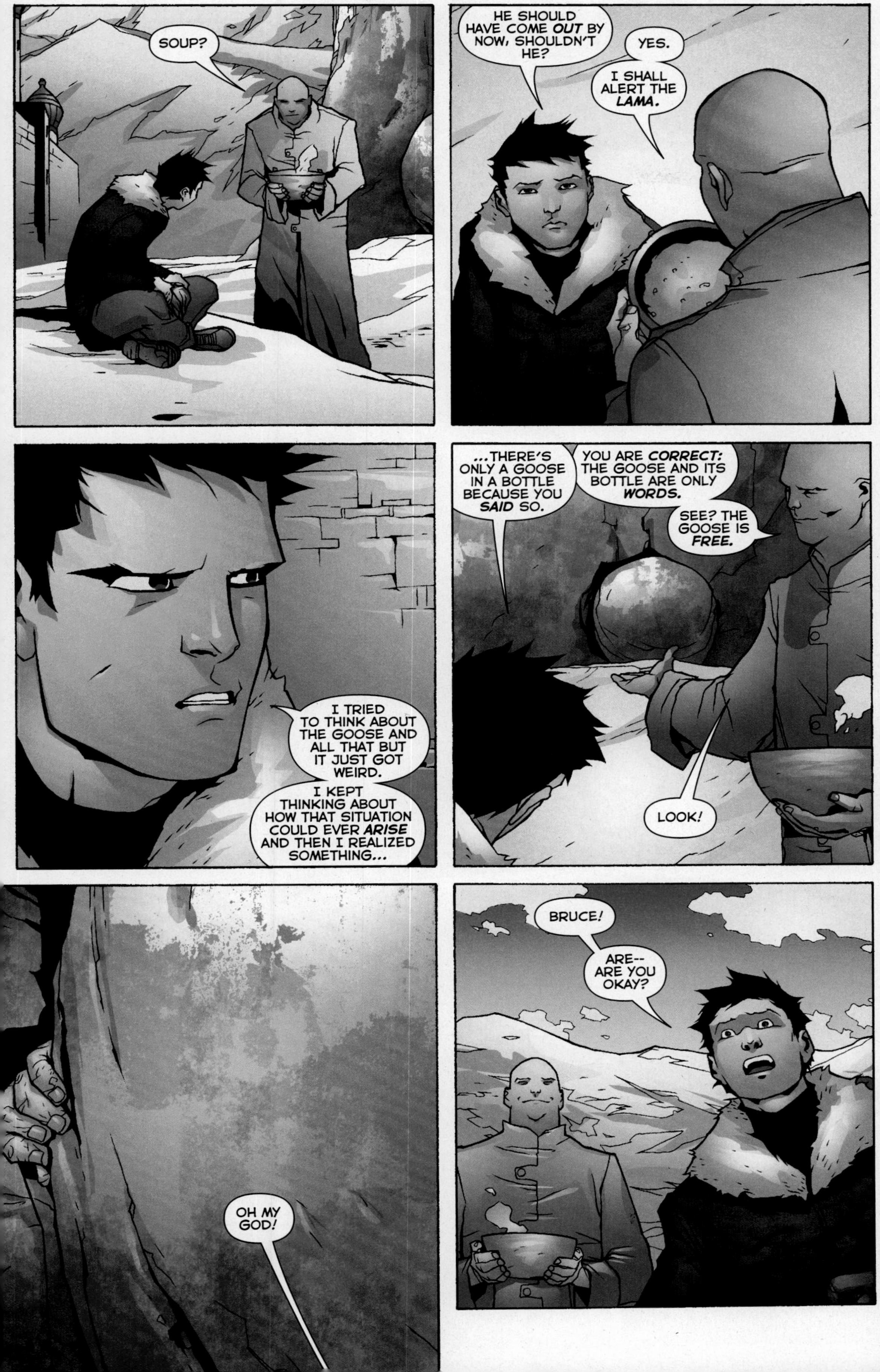
SOUP?
HE SHOULD HAVE COME OUT BY NOW, SHOULDN'T HE?
YES.
I SHALL ALERT THE LAMA.
I TRIED TO THINK ABOUT THE GOOSE AND ALL THAT BUT IT JUST GOT WEIRD.
I KEPT THINKING ABOUT HOW THAT SITUATION COULD EVER ARISE AND THEN I REALIZED SOMETHING...
...THERE'S ONLY A GOOSE IN A BOTTLE BECAUSE YOU SAID SO.
YOU ARE CORRECT: THE GOOSE AND ITS BOTTLE ARE ONLY WORDS.
SEE? THE GOOSE IS FREE.
LOOK!
OH MY GOD!
BRUCE!
ARE-- ARE YOU OKAY?

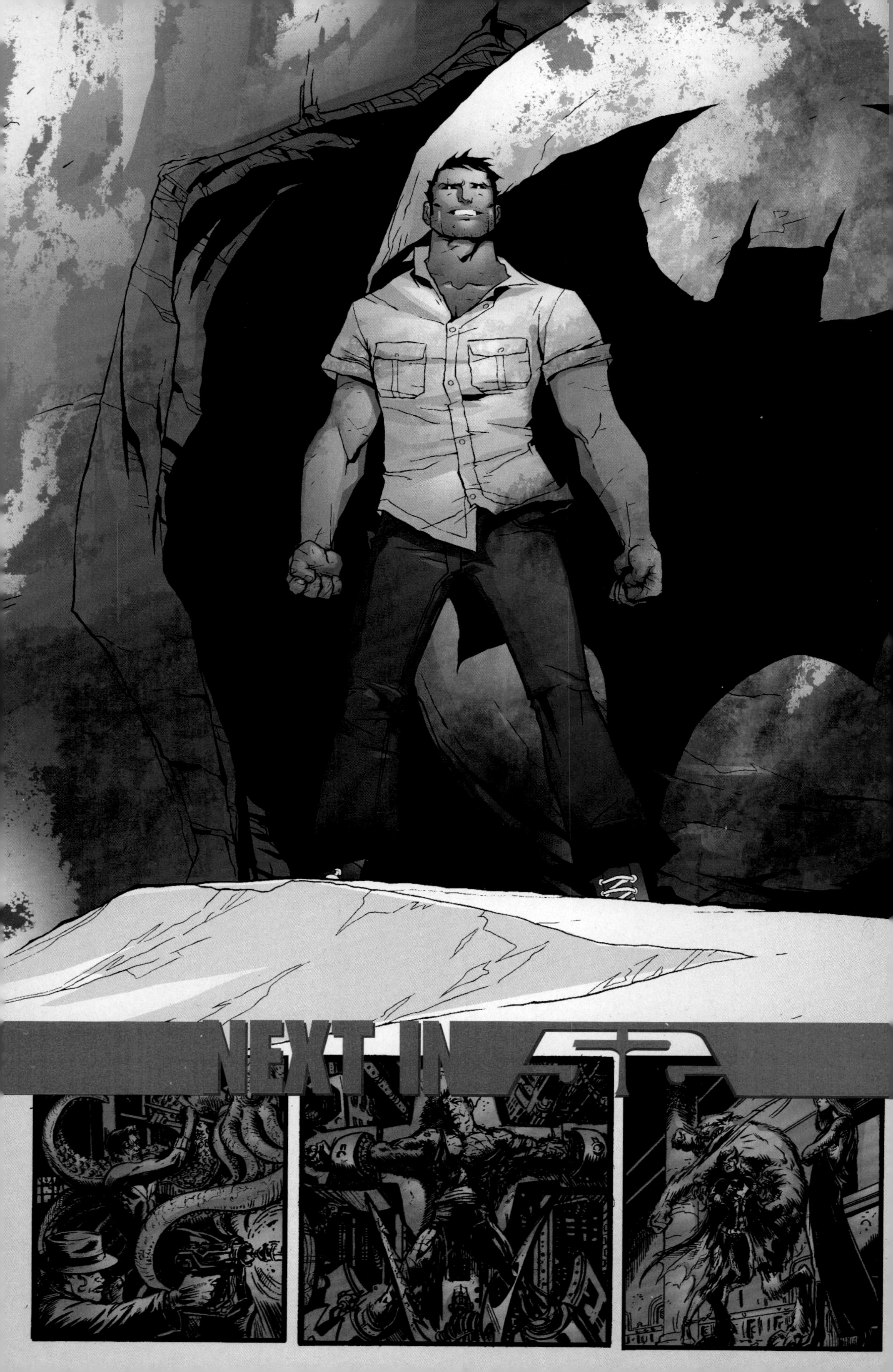
NEXT IN

WEEK FORTY-SEVEN NOTES

GREG RUCKA

The pause before the storm. The last of what we would call our "quiet issues." Relatively light in the way of fisticuffs (and frankly, after Black Adam's bloody swath of the last few weeks, none of us had a problem with that), but pretty heavy on the emotional charge. Another way to look at it might be to say we were positioning our pieces for the final issues, tying off the loose ends where we could, i.e., John Henry and Natasha's story, the Wonder Woman and Batman threads. The Wonder Woman resolve bothered me — I think it was Grant who wrote it specifically — and to this day still doesn't sit right to me. While Bruce got most of the year to both define and then to "solve" his dilemma, Diana was relegated to three appearances in the course of two weeks, and I still think that Rama Kushna telling her that her whole problem is that she's "not human enough" is garbage. It's reductive and it's simplistic, and it was, in my opinion, unworthy of the character. I was, clearly, in a minority, as her entire relaunch was based on this premise.

The prophecy issue is raised again here, as well, the problem with an absolute faith in the face of an uncertain world. The idea that the Religion of Crime is spinning its wheels in Gotham because what the "word" said would happen didn't happen, and yet Mannheim and Whisper both still maintain their fervent devotion. The word cannot be wrong, and therefore, imperfection must lie with them. Only Abbot is willing to even consider that the word is wrong, something that I'd tried to seed back in the 20s, and which will come to a head in the next issue. Yet, even if the book has been somehow discredited in its prophecies, it's still correct about the identity of Batwoman.

SCRIPT EXCERPT

(COMPARE WITH PAGES 180-181 OF THIS COLLECTION)

52 WEEK FORTY SEVEN — PAGE FOURTEEN

PANEL ONE
Exterior establishing shot of the KANE APARTMENT BUILDING — you know, the one with the tree — in GOTHAM CITY. Night. Twinkling lights. The PENTHOUSE is dark.

TIMESTAMP: Week 47, Day 6

PANEL TWO
On MONTOYA, her "new look," her expression thoughtful and serious, as she looks up atthe building. She has a DUFFEL BAG slung over her shoulder. Wearing her Question clothes, but obviously they've not been "activated" yet.

(CONTINUED)

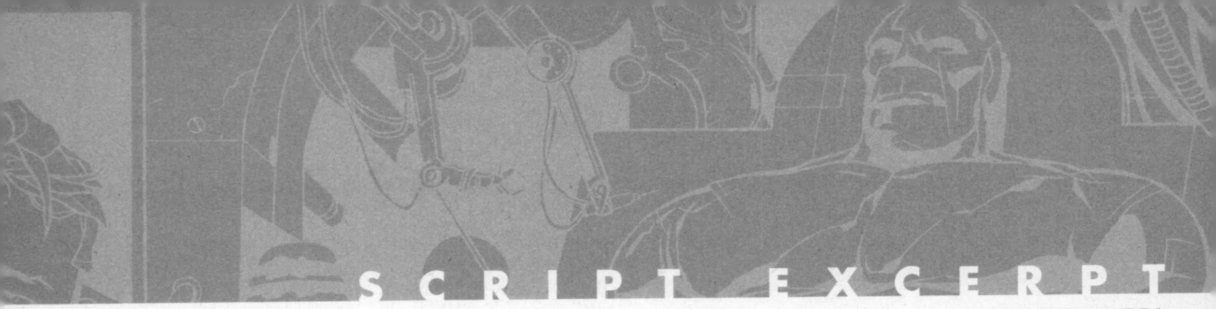

(CONTINUED)

PANEL THREE
CU of the INTERCOM/DIRECTORY for the building, MONTOYA'S THUMB pressing the BUTTON marked "PENTHOUSE — K. KANE."

PANEL FOUR
On MONTOYA, entering the LOBBY at the same time a YOUNG COUPLE is exiting. The couple is looking after MONTOYA in that fashion that says they don't know if they should stop her or not.

PANEL FIVE
Hallway, penthouse level, MONTOYA is exiting the STAIRWELL into the hallway.

PANEL SIX
Past MONTOYA, down the hallway, to the FRONT DOOR of Kate's penthouse apartment. The DOOR is AJAR slightly.

PANEL SEVEN
MONTOYA pushing the DOOR open gently and cautiously.

MONTOYA: Kate?

52 WEEK FORTY SEVEN – PAGE FIFTEEN

PANEL ONE
Big damn panel.

Past MONTOYA, revealing the interior of the penthouse, or at least what we can see of this main entry room.

The PENTHOUSE has been totaled. The fight that took place here was epic. Furniture is shattered. Glass is shattered. Windows are BROKEN out, and the CURTAINS flutter in the breeze this high up. The LIGHTS are OFF, so the only light comes from the outside.

It should look awful. It should look like Mannheim sent 30 monster men to bring him Kate, and that she fought every one of them before they beat her into bloody submission.

BLOOD spatters the WALL in places, and PUDDLES here and there on the floor.

MONTOYA (small): Kate.

PANEL TWO
MONTOYA has knelt to one knee, the DUFFEL now off her shoulder. She's touched the BLOOD on the floor, looking at it on her FINGERS. Her expression is dire concern.

NIGHTWING (off-panel): They took her.

PANEL THREE
Past MONTOYA, to the reveal of NIGHTWING, posed dramatically on the sill of one of the SHATTERED WINDOWS.

NIGHTWING: We're going to get her BACK.

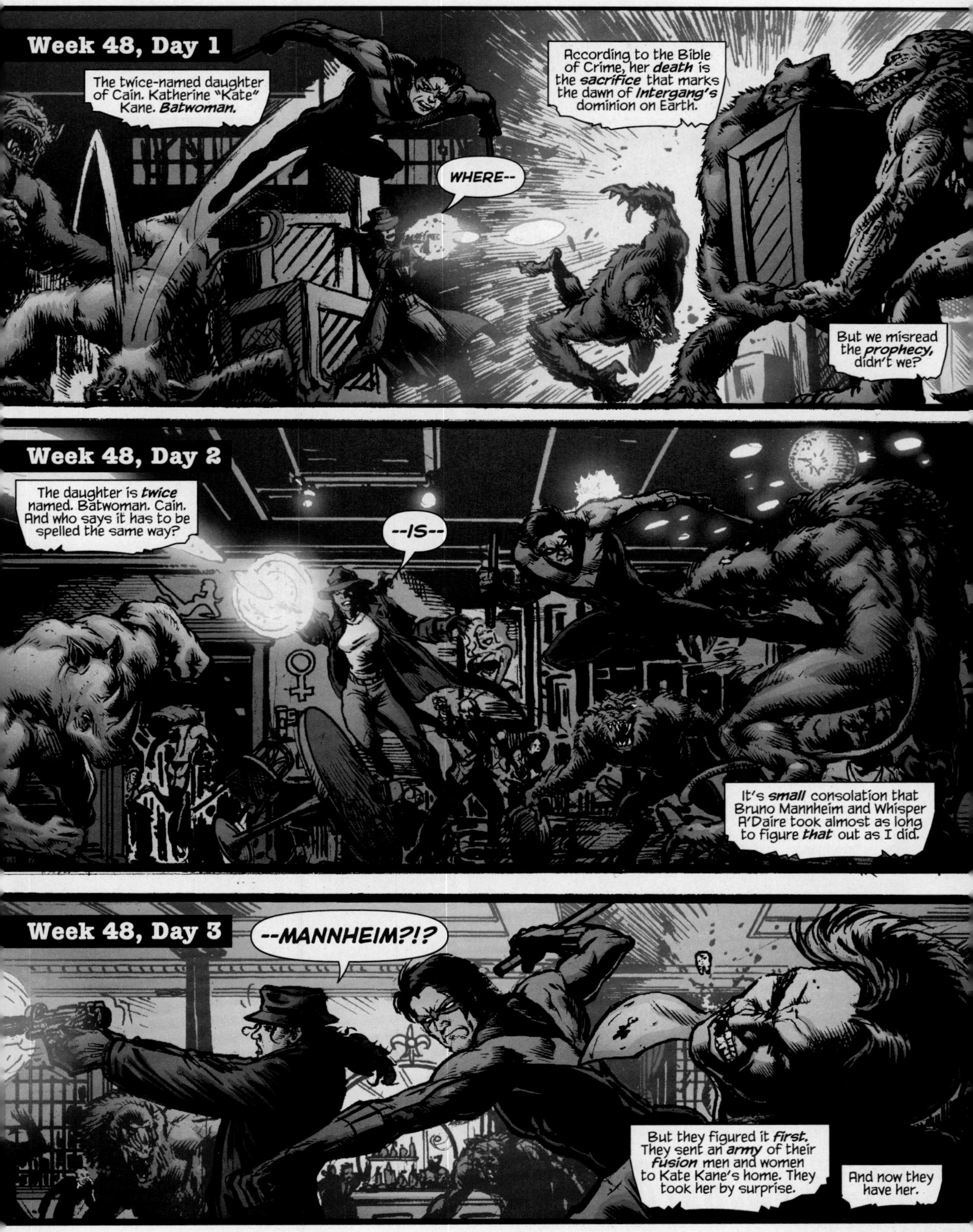
Week 48, Day 1
The twice-named daughter of Cain. Katherine "Kate" Kane. Batwoman.
According to the Bible of Crime, her death is the sacrifice that marks the dawn of Intergang's dominion on Earth.
WHERE--
But we misread the prophecy, didn't we?
Week 48, Day 2
The daughter is twice named. Batwoman. Cain. And who says it has to be spelled the same way?
--IS--
It's small consolation that Bruno Mannheim and Whisper A'Daire took almost as long to figure that out as I did.
Week 48, Day 3
--MANNHEIM?!?
But they figured it first. They sent an army of their fusion men and women to Kate Kane's home. They took her by surprise.
And now they have her.

WRITTEN BY GEOFF JOHNS, GRANT MORRISON, GREG RUCKA, MARK WAID

I don't know if I *believe* in the prophecy.
It doesn't matter.
Does the man dream he's the butterfly, or does the *butterfly* dream he's the *man?*
It's like Charlie would've said, all that matters is that *they* believe it, and they *do.*
They believe it *enough* that-- like all zealots-- they'll do whatever it takes to make it come true, to bring their vision of the world into being.
That world is framed by the Bible of Crime.
It's a world *devoid* of *virtue.*

ART BREAKDOWNS BY KEITH GIFFEN • ART BY DARICK ROBERTSON

COLORS BY DAVID BARON • LETTERING BY JARED K. FLETCHER

ASS'T ED. HARVEY RICHARDS • ASSOC. ED. JEANINE SCHAEFER

EDITOR MICHAEL SIGLAIN • COVER BY J.G. JONES & ALEX SINCLAIR

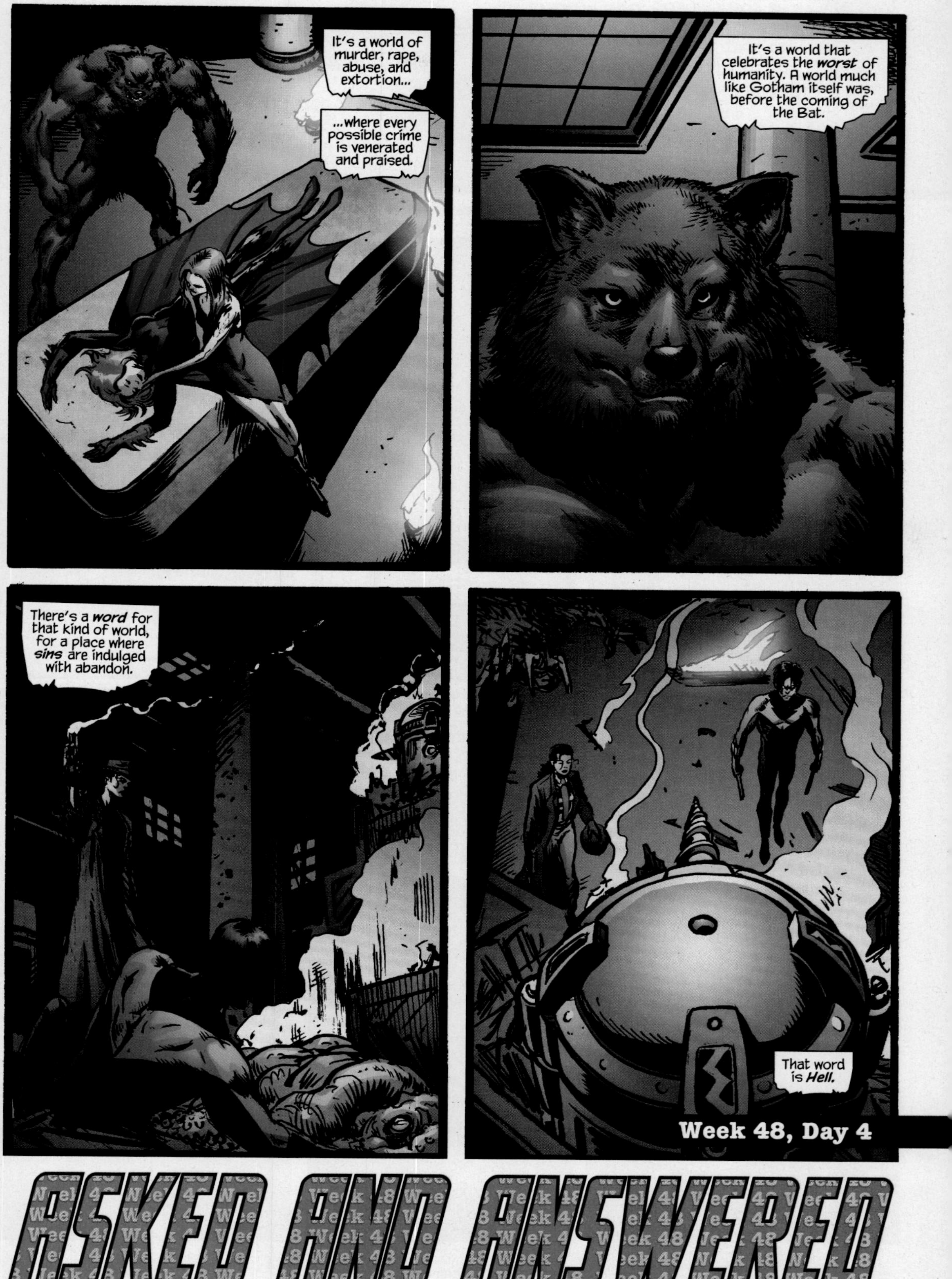

It's a world of murder, rape, abuse, and extortion...
...where every possible crime is venerated and praised.
It's a world that celebrates the *worst* of humanity. A world much like Gotham itself was, before the coming of the Bat.
There's a *word* for that kind of world, for a place where *sins* are indulged with abandon.
That word is *Hell.*
Week 48, Day 4

ASKED AND ANSWERED

EVERY SINGLE *WORD* AS HE *COMMANDED* US, WHISPER! ALL FOR TONIGHT, ALL TO SPILL THE HOLY BLOOD *TONIGHT!*

THIS WASN'T SUPPOSED TO HAPPEN!

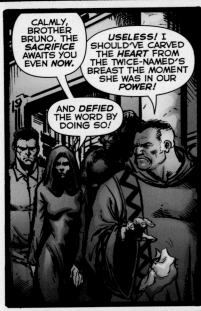

CALMLY, BROTHER BRUNO. THE *SACRIFICE* AWAITS YOU EVEN *NOW.*

USELESS! I SHOULD'VE CARVED THE *HEART* FROM THE TWICE-NAMED'S BREAST THE MOMENT SHE WAS IN OUR *POWER!*

AND *DEFIED* THE WORD BY DOING SO!

WE WERE NOT *READY* TO UNLEASH THE *FIRES,* BROTHER!

THE WORD IS *INFALLIBLE,* IT IS *WE* WHO ARE *FLAWED,* WHO MISREAD AND *MISINTERPRET.*

TONIGHT, YOU ARE DESTINED TO WELCOME THE RULE OF RAGE WITH THE TWICE-NAMED'S *HEART* IN YOUR *HAND.*

AND *HOW* DO I DO THAT WHEN ONE OF THE *KEYS* IS *LOST?*

BROTHER *ABBOT* WILL RECOVER THE *KEY,* YOU'LL SEE...

...THE FLAMES SHALL BE KINDLED AND ALL SHALL COME TO PASS AS *WRITTEN.*

AND IF IT *DOESN'T?* IF, ONCE MORE, THE BOOK IS WRONG?

THE BOOK IS NOT *WRONG!* THE BOOK IS *NEVER* WRONG!

BRUNO--

NO! SEND *OTHERS!* YOUR *DOG'S* TIME IS *DONE* HERE, WHISPER--

--I'LL SEE HIM *CARVED* APART FOR HIS *HERESIES!*

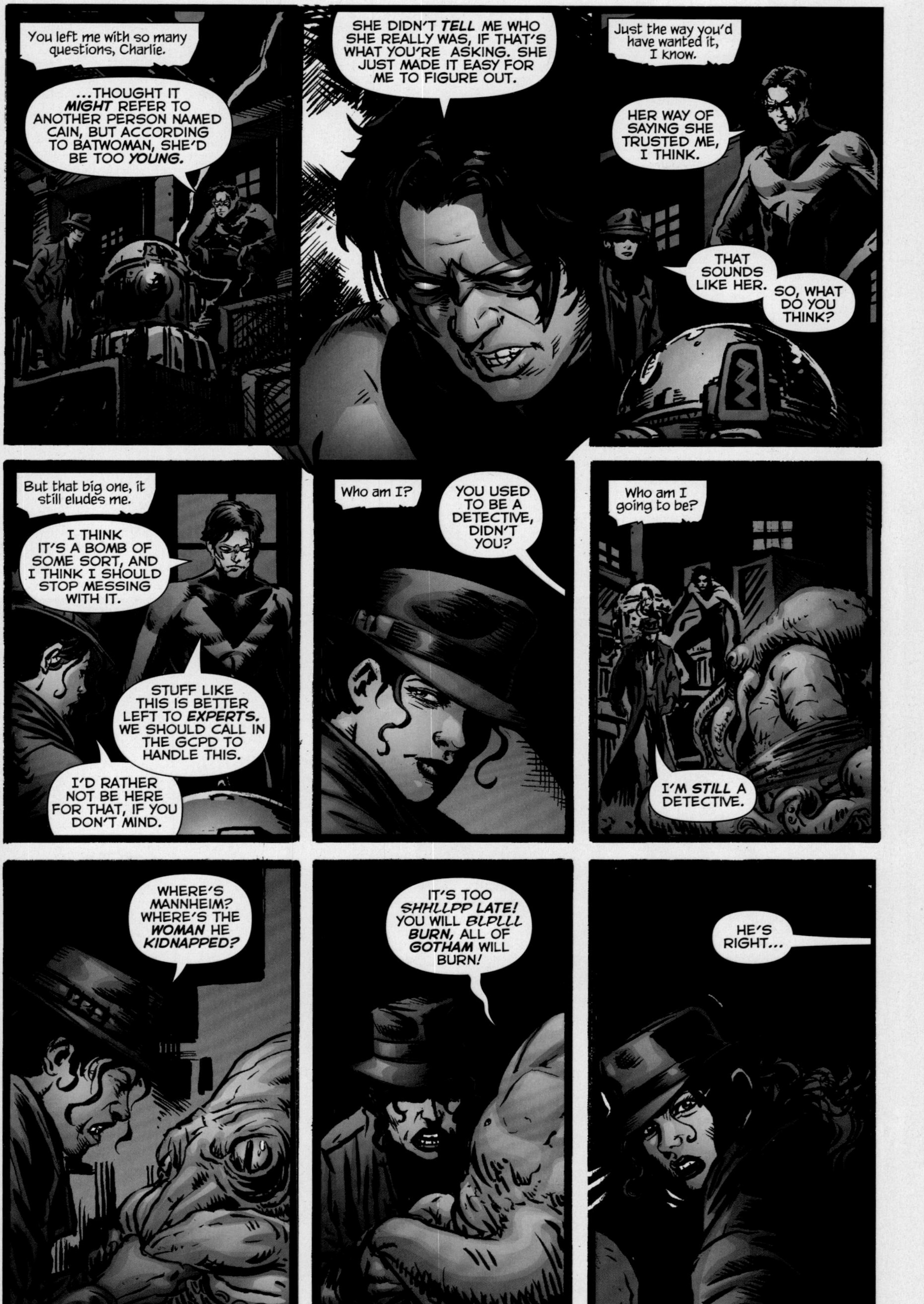

You left me with so many questions, Charlie.
...THOUGHT IT MIGHT REFER TO ANOTHER PERSON NAMED CAIN, BUT ACCORDING TO BATWOMAN, SHE'D BE TOO YOUNG.
SHE DIDN'T TELL ME WHO SHE REALLY WAS, IF THAT'S WHAT YOU'RE ASKING. SHE JUST MADE IT EASY FOR ME TO FIGURE OUT.
Just the way you'd have wanted it, I know.
HER WAY OF SAYING SHE TRUSTED ME, I THINK.
THAT SOUNDS LIKE HER.
SO, WHAT DO YOU THINK?
But that big one, it still eludes me.
I THINK IT'S A BOMB OF SOME SORT, AND I THINK I SHOULD STOP MESSING WITH IT.
STUFF LIKE THIS IS BETTER LEFT TO EXPERTS. WE SHOULD CALL IN THE GCPD TO HANDLE THIS.
I'D RATHER NOT BE HERE FOR THAT, IF YOU DON'T MIND.
Who am I?
YOU USED TO BE A DETECTIVE, DIDN'T YOU?
Who am I going to be?
I'M STILL A DETECTIVE.
WHERE'S MANNHEIM? WHERE'S THE WOMAN HE KIDNAPPED?
IT'S TOO SHHLLPP LATE! YOU WILL BLPLLL BURN, ALL OF GOTHAM WILL BURN!
HE'S RIGHT...

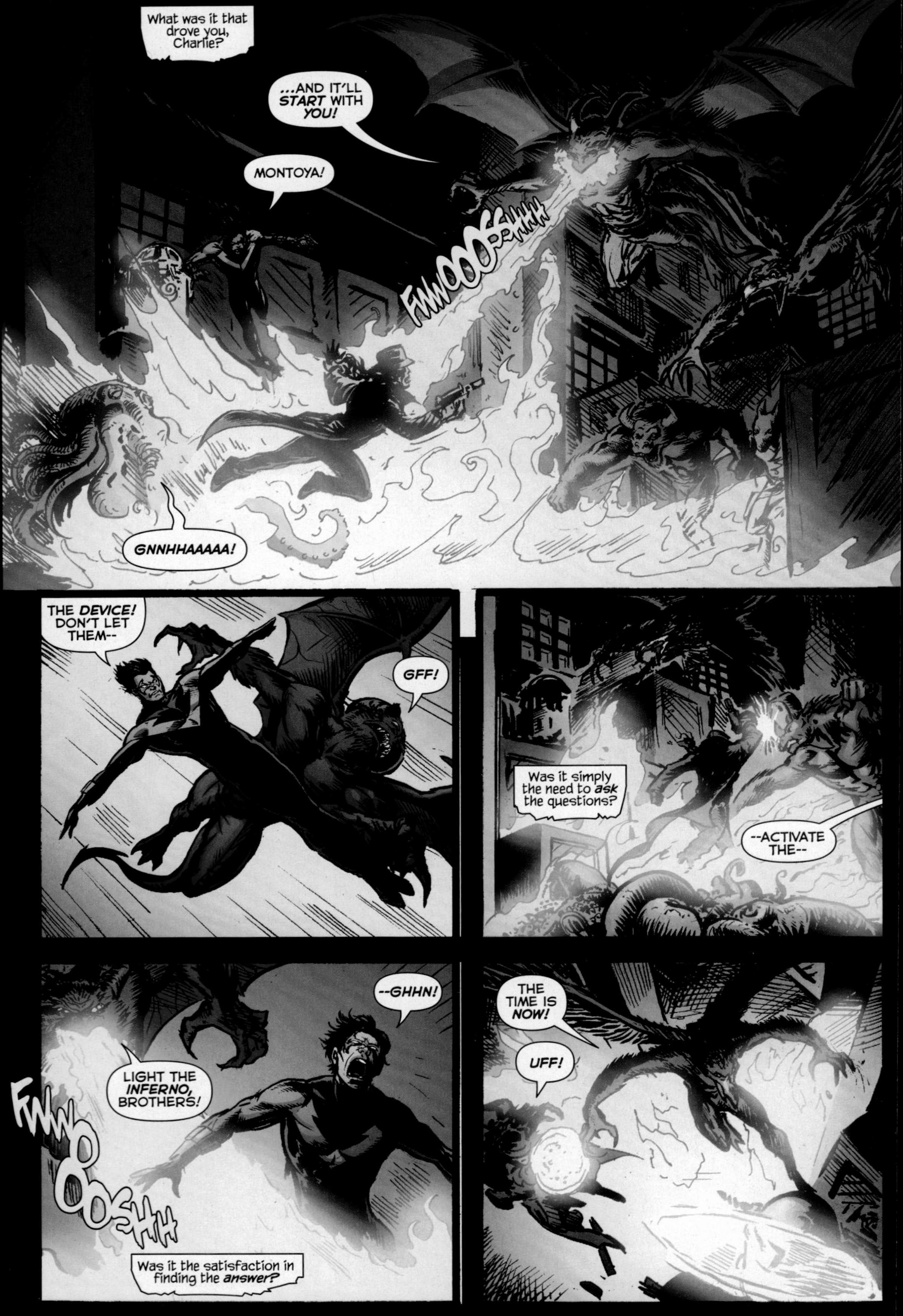
What was it that drove you, Charlie?
...AND IT'LL START WITH YOU!
MONTOYA!
FWOOOSHHH
GNNHHAAAAA!
THE DEVICE! DON'T LET THEM--
GFF!
Was it simply the need to ask the questions?
--ACTIVATE THE--
--GHHN!
LIGHT THE INFERNO, BROTHERS!
FWOOOSHH
Was it the satisfaction in finding the answer?
THE TIME IS NOW!
UFF!

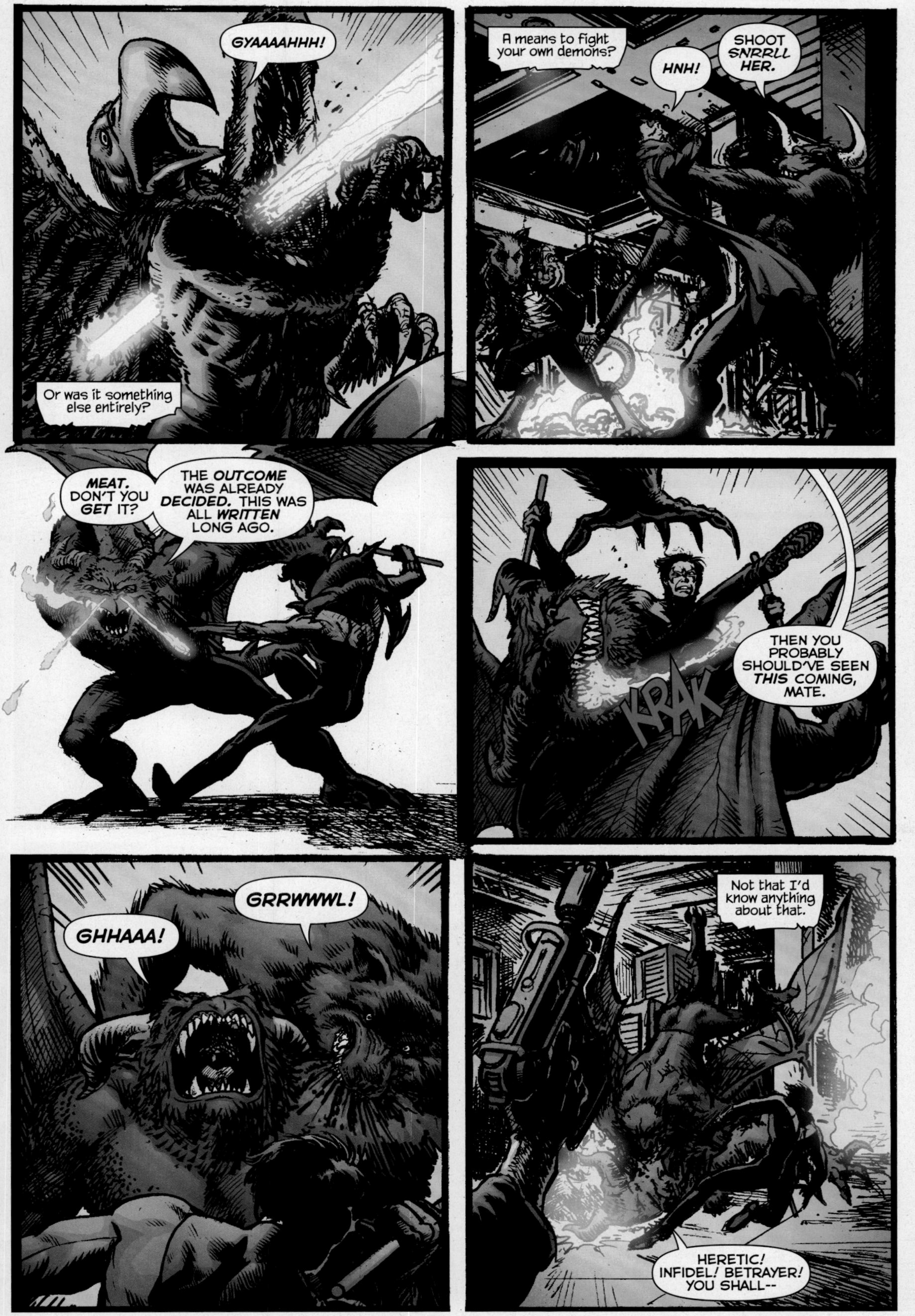
GYAAAAHHH!
Or was it something else entirely?
A means to fight your own demons?
HNH!
SHOOT SNRRLL HER.
MEAT. DON'T YOU GET IT?
THE OUTCOME WAS ALREADY DECIDED. THIS WAS ALL WRITTEN LONG AGO.
THEN YOU PROBABLY SHOULD'VE SEEN THIS COMING, MATE.
KRAK
GHHAAA!
GRRWWWL!
Not that I'd know anything about that.
HERETIC! INFIDEL! BETRAYER! YOU SHALL--

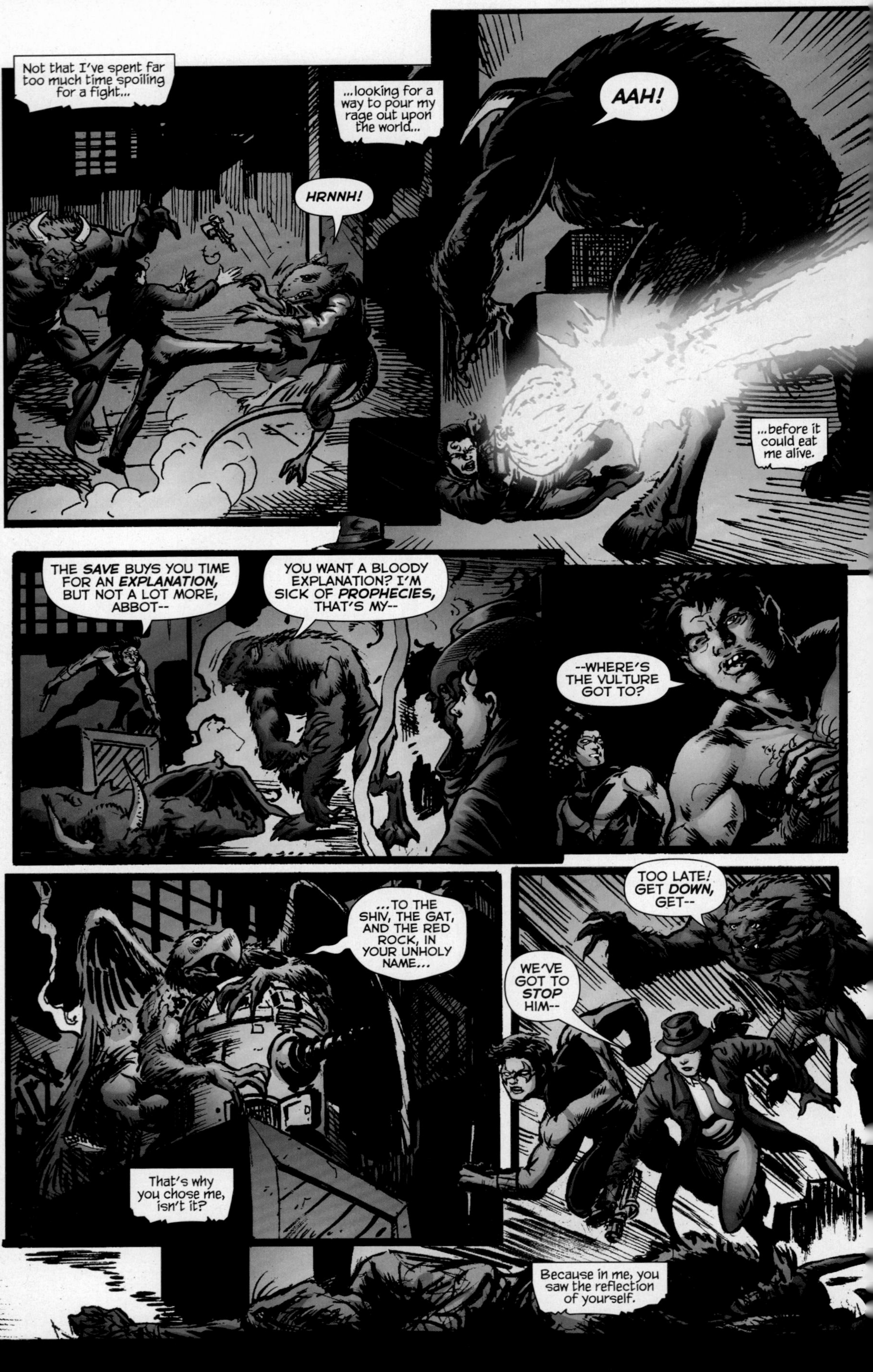
Not that I've spent far too much time spoiling for a fight...
...looking for a way to pour my rage out upon the world...
HRNNH!
AAH!
...before it could eat me alive.
THE SAVE BUYS YOU TIME FOR AN EXPLANATION, BUT NOT A LOT MORE, ABBOT--
YOU WANT A BLOODY EXPLANATION? I'M SICK OF PROPHECIES, THAT'S MY--
--WHERE'S THE VULTURE GOT TO?
...TO THE SHIV, THE GAT, AND THE RED ROCK, IN YOUR UNHOLY NAME...
That's why you chose me, isn't it?
TOO LATE! GET DOWN, GET--
WE'VE GOT TO STOP HIM--
Because in me, you saw the reflection of yourself.

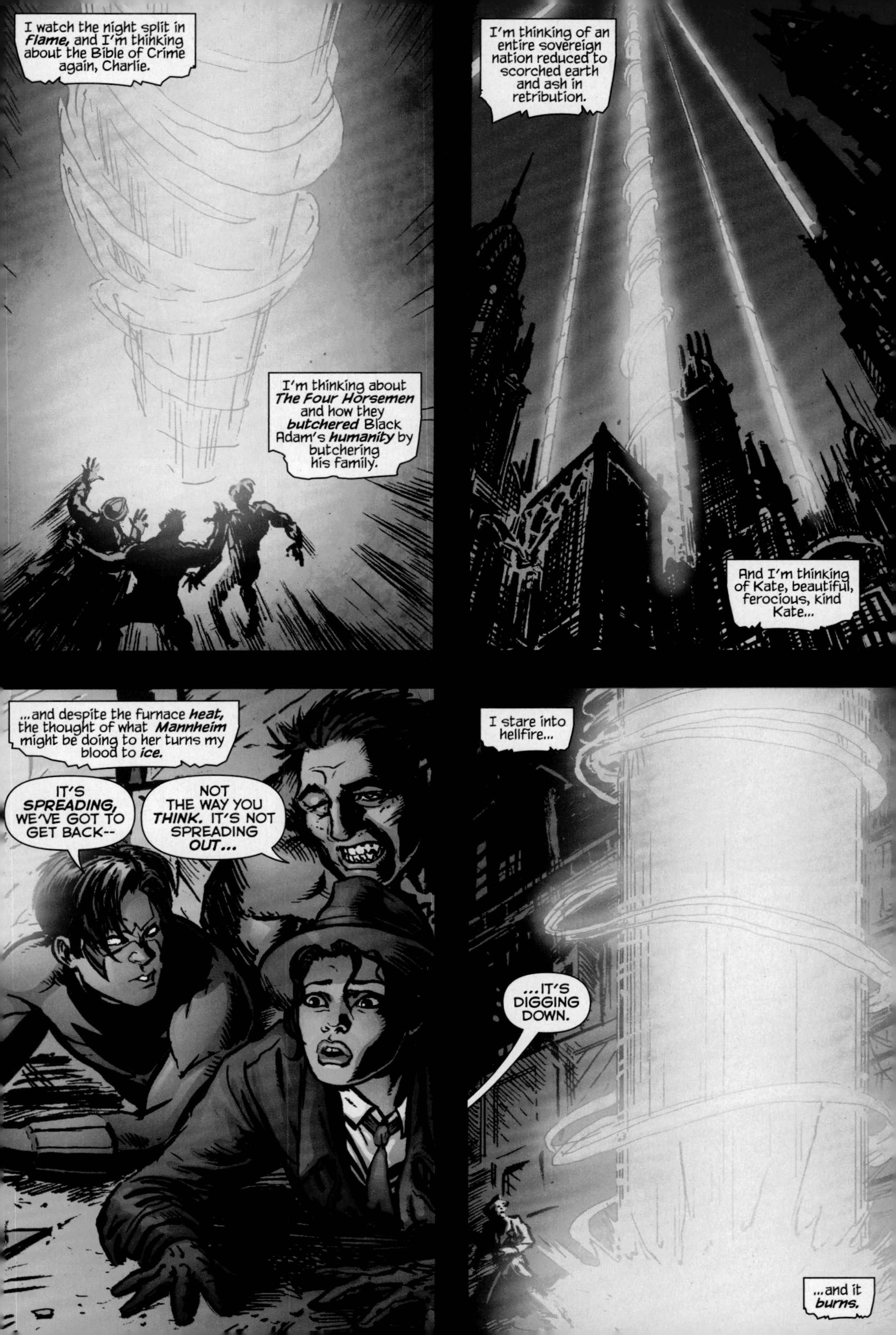
I watch the night split in *Flame,* and I'm thinking about the Bible of Crime again, Charlie.
I'm thinking about *The Four Horsemen* and how they *butchered* Black Adam's *humanity* by butchering his family.
I'm thinking of an entire sovereign nation reduced to scorched earth and ash in retribution.
And I'm thinking of Kate, beautiful, ferocious, kind Kate...
...and despite the furnace *heat,* the thought of what *Mannheim* might be doing to her turns my blood to *ice.*
IT'S *SPREADING,* WE'VE GOT TO GET BACK--
NOT THE WAY YOU *THINK.* IT'S NOT SPREADING *OUT...*
I stare into hellfire...
...IT'S DIGGING DOWN.
...and it *burns.*

Who am I, Charlie?

GOTHAM *BURNS* TONIGHT.

EACH DEVICE TEARS INTO THE FLESH OF THE CITY, IGNITING EVERYTHING IT TOUCHES.

BY DAWN, A *PIT* OF *FIRE* WILL ROAR AT YOUR CITY'S *HEART.*

IT DOESN'T MAKE *SENSE!* IF INTERGANG WANTS GOTHAM, WHY TURN IT INTO A *FIRE PIT?!?*

BECAUSE MANNHEIM BELIEVES *EVERYTHING* IN THE BIBLE OF CRIME IS *TRUE* AND MUST COME TO *PASS.*

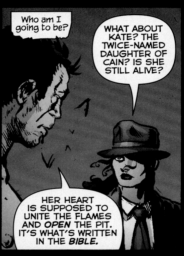

Who am I going to be?

WHAT ABOUT KATE? THE TWICE-NAMED DAUGHTER OF CAIN? IS SHE STILL ALIVE?

HER HEART IS SUPPOSED TO UNITE THE FLAMES AND *OPEN* THE PIT. IT'S WHAT'S WRITTEN IN THE *BIBLE.*

You knew this night would come.

MANNHEIM INTENDS TO SACRIFICE HER AT *DAWN.*

OVER MY DEAD BODY.

But you have to know the question to find the answer.

...IT'S GOT TO BE YOU TWO WHO GO AFTER THE *DEVICES...*

...ABBOT KNOWS HOW TO SHUT THEM *DOWN...*

The binary gas smells like baby powder and cardamom.

Richard's words sing through my head.

EASY ENOUGH FOR HIM TO DO, GIRL!

BLOODY HELL, EVEN IF YOU *COULD* SAVE HER, IT WON'T BE *ENOUGH!*

THEN *STOP* WASTING *TIME* AND TELL US WHAT *WILL* BE!

EACH DEVICE HAS TO BE SHUT DOWN--

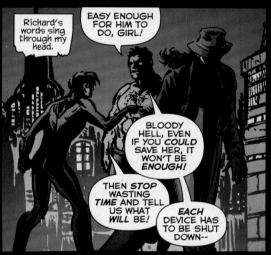

"Some questions can only be answered by wearing a mask."

--OTHERWISE THEY'LL SIMPLY *BURN* WHERE THEY LIE UNTIL NOTHING IS *LEFT!*

WE'LL SPLIT UP. YOU AND MONTOYA GO AFTER THE *DEVICES,* I'LL--

NO...

Who am I?

...AND NIGHTWING IS THE ONLY ONE OF US FAST ENOUGH TO GET AROUND THE CITY IN TIME TO REACH THEM *ALL* BEFORE DAWN...

Who am I going to be?

...I'LL TAKE CARE OF MANNHEIM.

YOU'LL BE GOING TO RESCUE KATE *ALONE.*

WOULD YOU REALLY DIE FOR THIS?

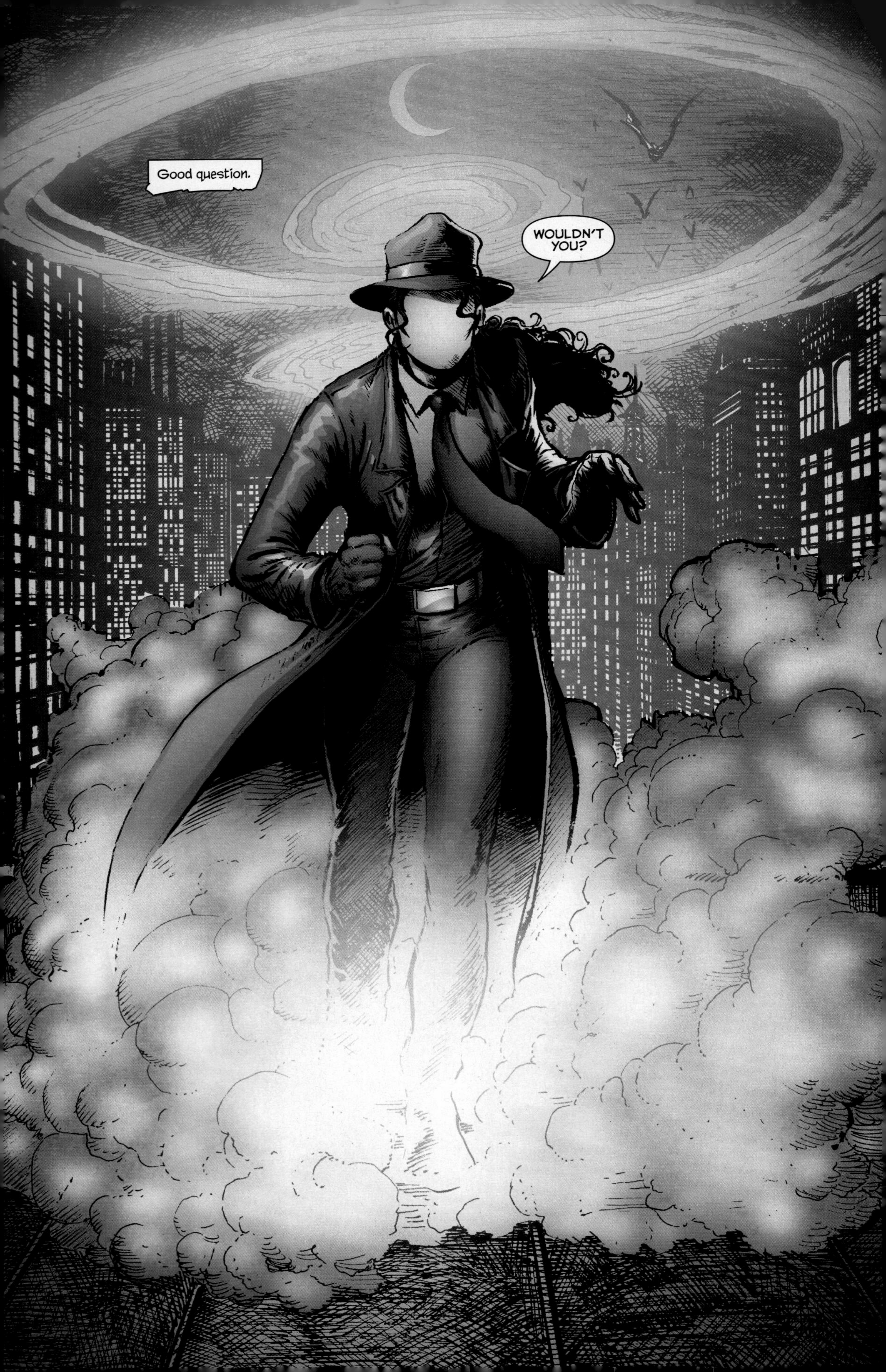
Good question.
WOULDN'T YOU?

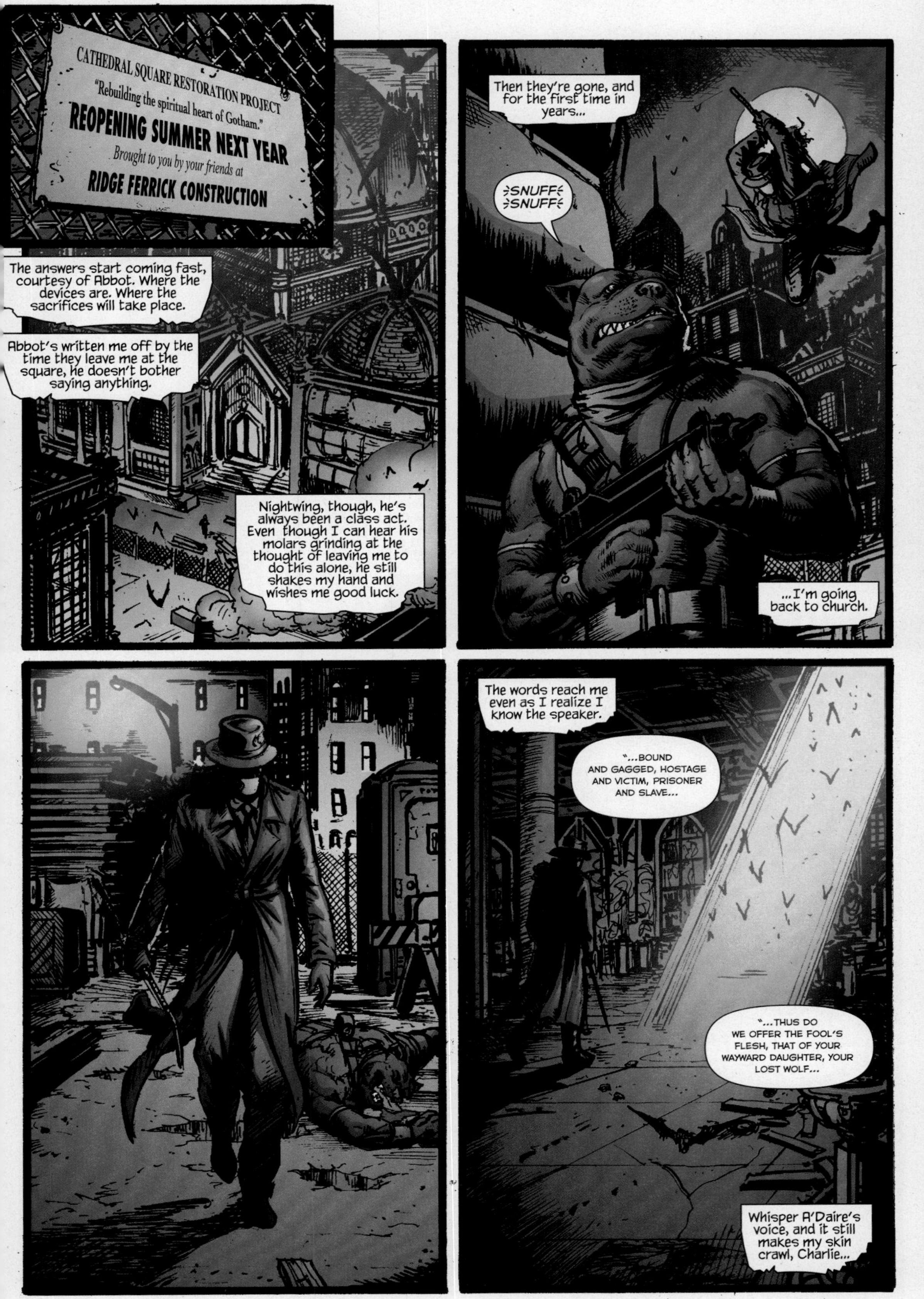
CATHEDRAL SQUARE RESTORATION PROJECT
"Rebuilding the spiritual heart of Gotham."
REOPENING SUMMER NEXT YEAR
Brought to you by your friends at
RIDGE FERRICK CONSTRUCTION
The answers start coming fast, courtesy of Abbot. Where the devices are. Where the sacrifices will take place.
Abbot's written me off by the time they leave me at the square, he doesn't bother saying anything.
Nightwing, though, he's always been a class act. Even though I can hear his molars grinding at the thought of leaving me to do this alone, he still shakes my hand and wishes me good luck.
Then they're gone, and for the first time in years...
SNUFF SNUFF
...I'm going back to church.
The words reach me even as I realize I know the speaker.
"...BOUND AND GAGGED, HOSTAGE AND VICTIM, PRISONER AND SLAVE...
"...THUS DO WE OFFER THE FOOL'S FLESH, THAT OF YOUR WAYWARD DAUGHTER, YOUR LOST WOLF...
Whisper A'Daire's voice, and it still makes my skin crawl, Charlie...

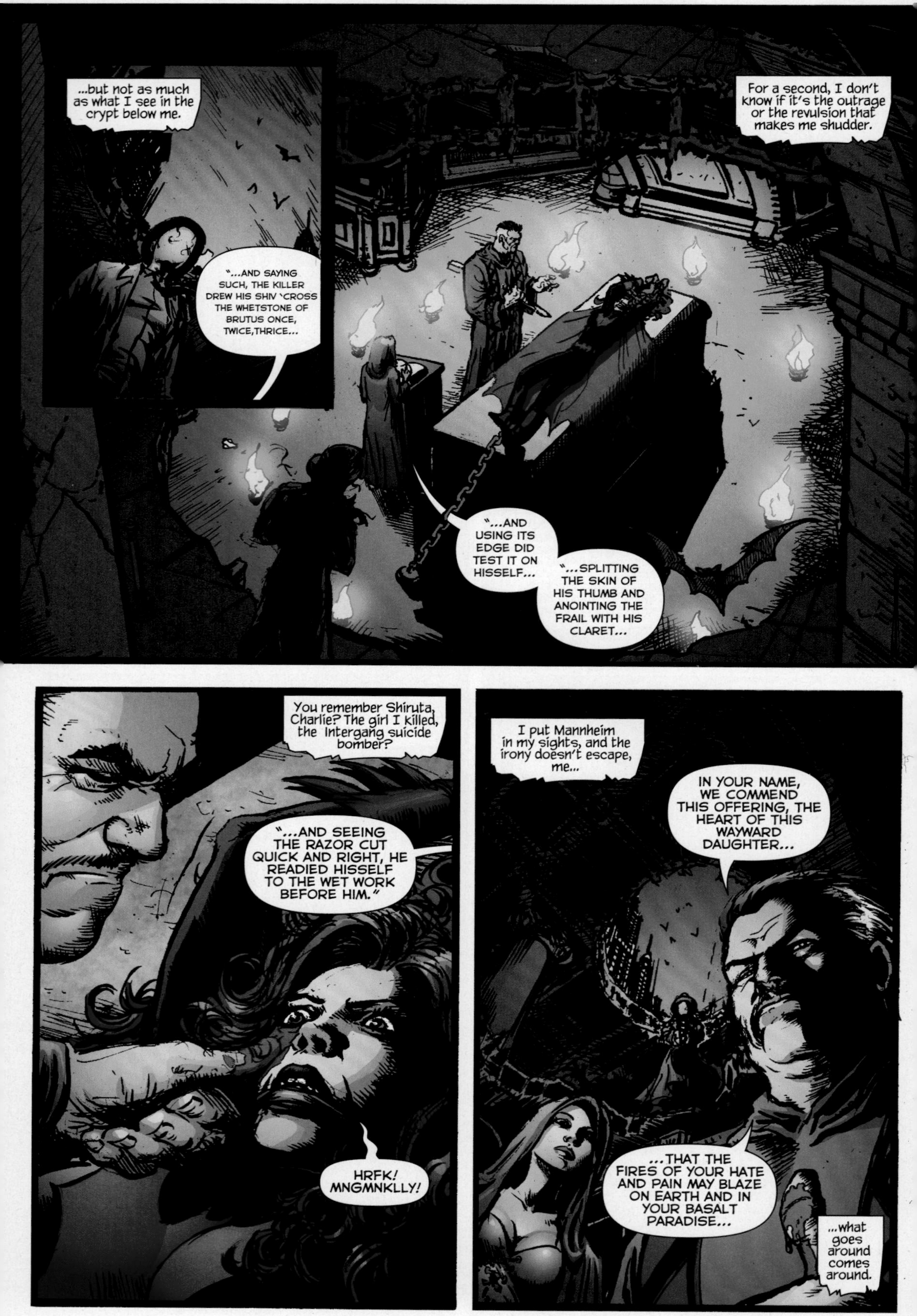
...but not as much as what I see in the crypt below me.
"...AND SAYING SUCH, THE KILLER DREW HIS SHIV 'CROSS THE WHETSTONE OF BRUTUS ONCE, TWICE,THRICE...
For a second, I don't know if it's the outrage or the revulsion that makes me shudder.
"...AND USING ITS EDGE DID TEST IT ON HISSELF...
"...SPLITTING THE SKIN OF HIS THUMB AND ANOINTING THE FRAIL WITH HIS CLARET...
You remember Shiruta, Charlie? The girl I killed, the Intergang suicide bomber?
"...AND SEEING THE RAZOR CUT QUICK AND RIGHT, HE READIED HISSELF TO THE WET WORK BEFORE HIM."
HRFK! MNGMNKLLY!
I put Mannheim in my sights, and the irony doesn't escape, me...
IN YOUR NAME, WE COMMEND THIS OFFERING, THE HEART OF THIS WAYWARD DAUGHTER...
...THAT THE FIRES OF YOUR HATE AND PAIN MAY BLAZE ON EARTH AND IN YOUR BASALT PARADISE...
...what goes around comes around.

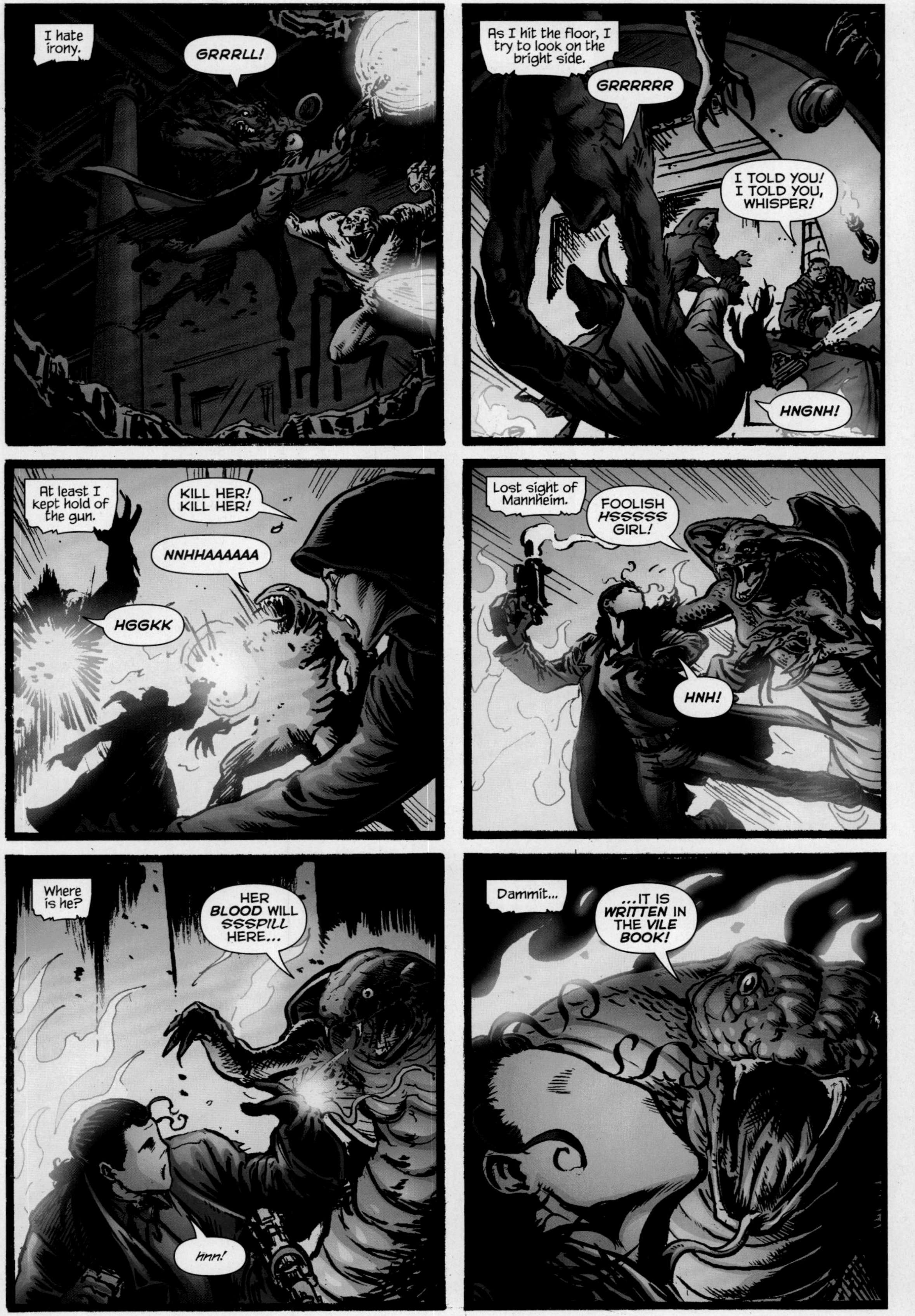
I hate irony.
GRRRLL!
As I hit the floor, I try to look on the bright side.
GRRRRRR
I TOLD YOU! I TOLD YOU, WHISPER!
HNGNH!
At least I kept hold of the gun.
KILL HER! KILL HER!
NNHHAAAAAA
HGGKK
Lost sight of Mannheim.
FOOLISH HSSSSS GIRL!
HNH!
Where is he?
HER BLOOD WILL SSSPILL HERE...
hnn!
Dammit...
...IT IS WRITTEN IN THE VILE BOOK!

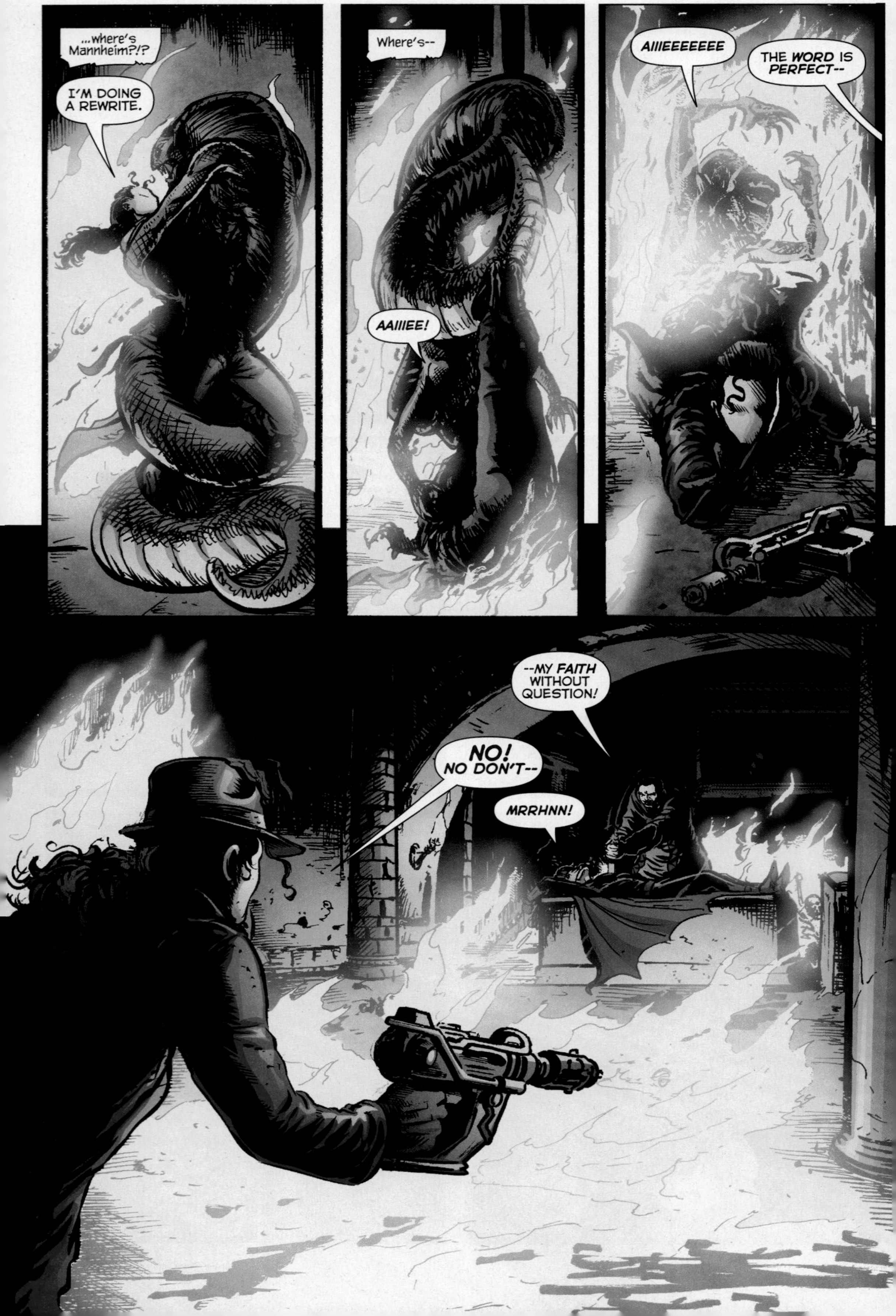
...where's Mannheim?!?
I'M DOING A REWRITE.
Where's--
AAIIIEE!
AIIIEEEEEEE
THE WORD IS PERFECT--
--MY FAITH WITHOUT QUESTION!
NO! NO DON'T--
MRRHNN!

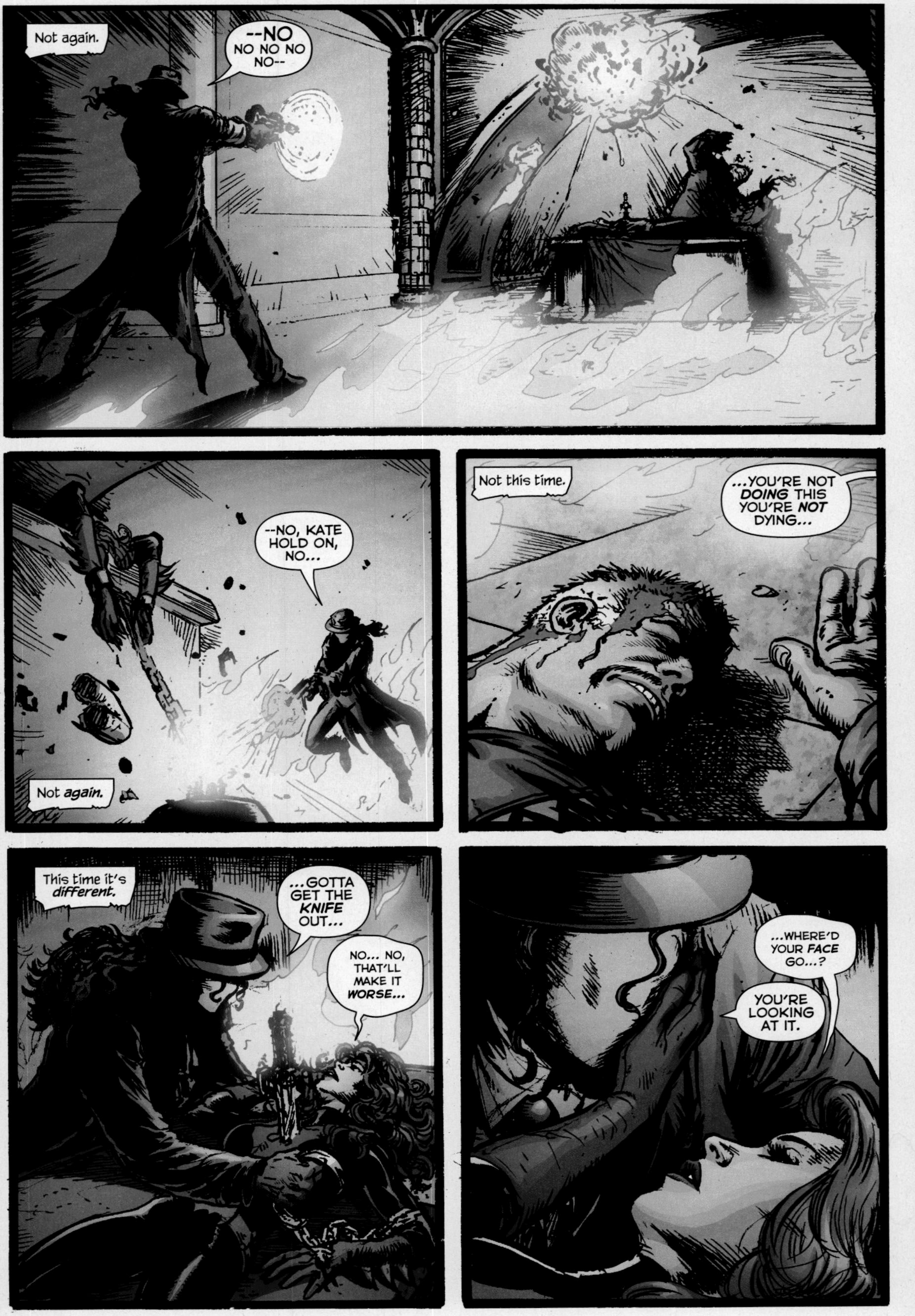
Not again.
--NO NO NO NO NO--
--NO, KATE HOLD ON, NO...
Not again.
Not this time.
...YOU'RE NOT DOING THIS YOU'RE NOT DYING...
This time it's different.
...GOTTA GET THE KNIFE OUT...
NO... NO, THAT'LL MAKE IT WORSE...
...WHERE'D YOUR FACE GO...?
YOU'RE LOOKING AT IT.

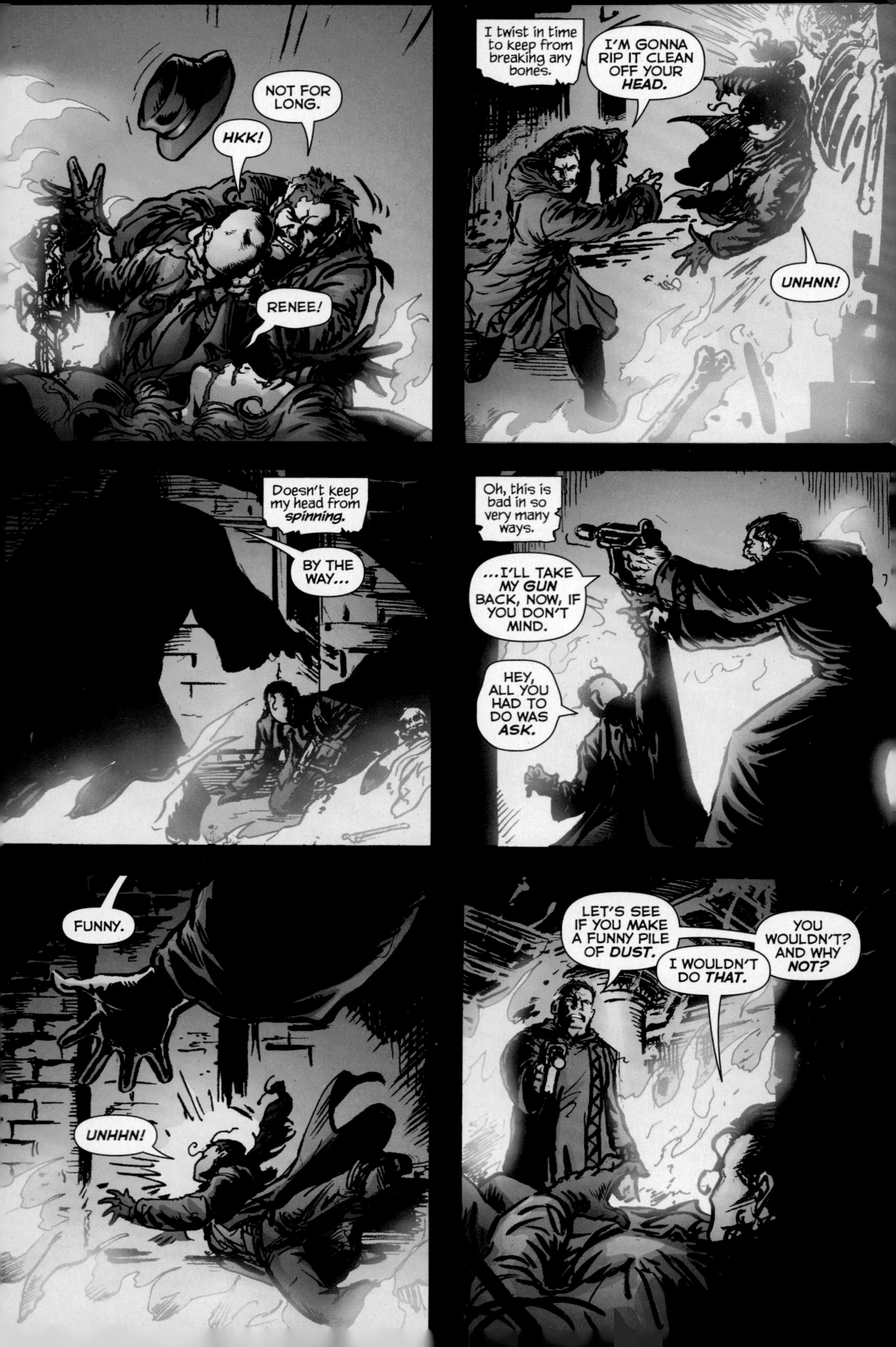
NOT FOR LONG.
HKK!
RENEE!
I twist in time to keep from breaking any bones.
I'M GONNA RIP IT CLEAN OFF YOUR HEAD.
UNHNN!
Doesn't keep my head from spinning.
BY THE WAY...
Oh, this is bad in so very many ways.
...I'LL TAKE MY GUN BACK, NOW, IF YOU DON'T MIND.
HEY, ALL YOU HAD TO DO WAS ASK.
FUNNY.
UNHHN!
LET'S SEE IF YOU MAKE A FUNNY PILE OF DUST.
I WOULDN'T DO THAT.
YOU WOULDN'T? AND WHY NOT?

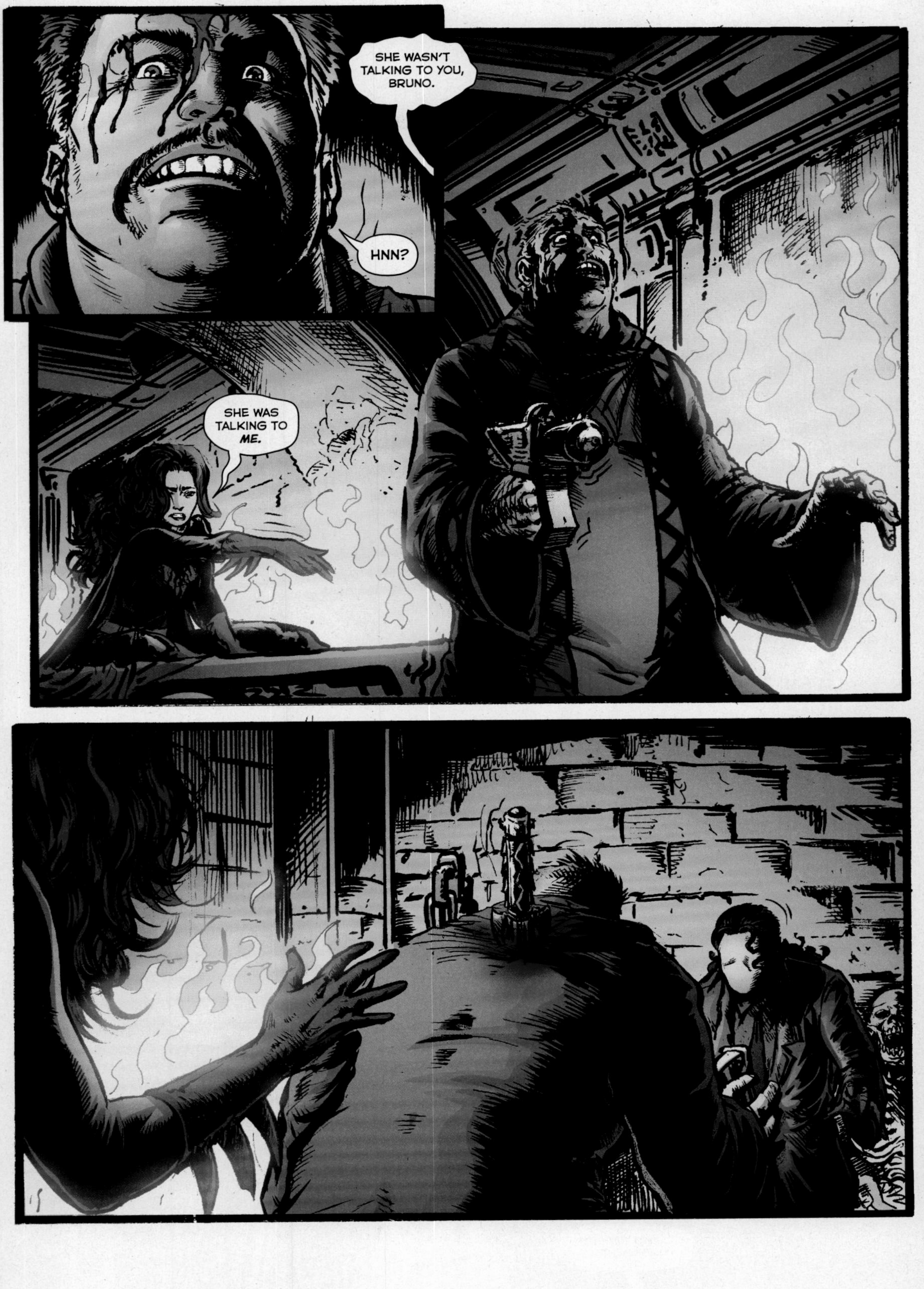
SHE WASN'T TALKING TO YOU, BRUNO.
HNN?
SHE WAS TALKING TO *ME.*

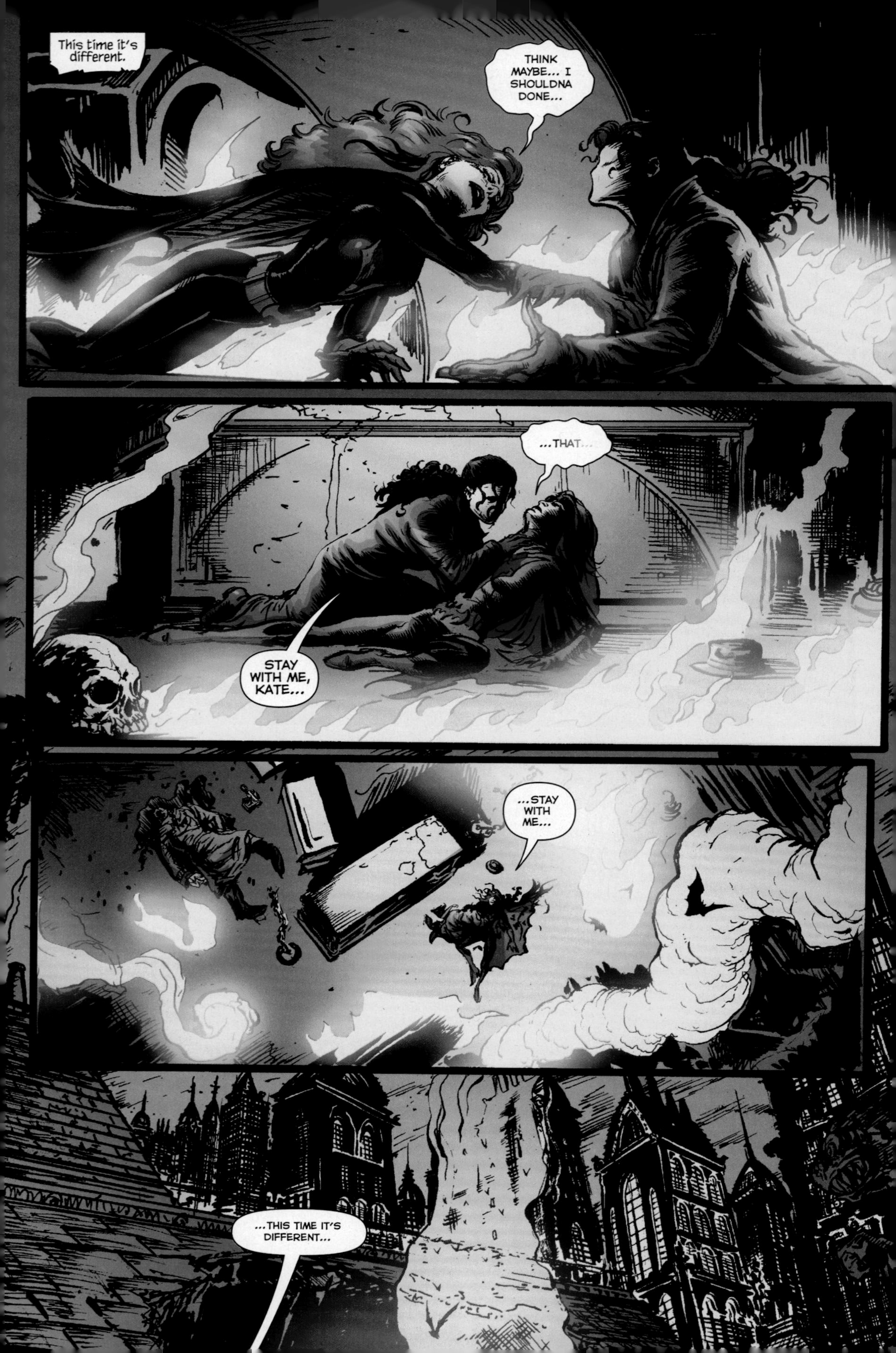
This time it's different.
THINK MAYBE... I SHOULDNA DONE...
...THAT...
STAY WITH ME, KATE...
...STAY WITH ME...
...THIS TIME IT'S DIFFERENT...

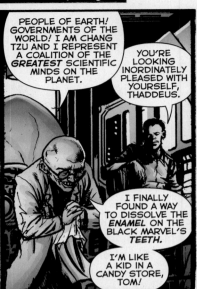

PEOPLE OF EARTH! GOVERNMENTS OF THE WORLD! I AM CHANG TZU AND I REPRESENT A COALITION OF THE *GREATEST* SCIENTIFIC MINDS ON THE PLANET.

YOU'RE LOOKING INORDINATELY PLEASED WITH YOURSELF, THADDEUS.

I FINALLY FOUND A WAY TO DISSOLVE THE *ENAMEL* ON THE BLACK MARVEL'S *TEETH.*

I'M LIKE A KID IN A CANDY STORE, TOM!

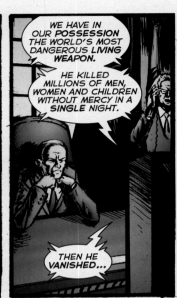

WE HAVE IN OUR POSSESSION THE WORLD'S MOST DANGEROUS *LIVING WEAPON.*

HE KILLED MILLIONS OF MEN, WOMEN AND CHILDREN WITHOUT MERCY IN A SINGLE NIGHT.

THEN HE *VANISHED...*

BUT HE IS HERE! WE HAVE PUBLIC ENEMY NUMBER ONE!

BLACK ADAM BELONGS TO CHANG TZU'S SCIENCE SQUAD!

NOW...

HOW MUCH AM I *BID?*

NEXT IN 52

GREG RUCKA

The cover of this issue is yet another example of J.G.'s brilliance. It's so wonderfully subtle, and at the same time terrifically striking, and conveys so much with such a simple design and composition. I remember seeing some of the preliminaries for it, watching J.G. work out the stencil. It's the posture that sells it for me; you can't tell if she's tipping the hat or adjusting the brim, and thus, inherent in the image itself, is a question.

The Gotham/Batwoman/Renee storyline culminates here, with the final confrontation between Renee and The Question, and then with The Question and the Religion of Crime. The idea of turning Gotham City into a mini-Apokolips by opening multiple fire-pits is one that I cannot claim as my own; I got it from a friend, and I'm not sure where he got it. I'm sure Waid knows, and if he doesn't, Geoff does. Wherever its genesis, it seemed appropriately Apocalyptic, and that was the intention at the time, though now, in rereading, I'm not certain it was the best way to go.

My biggest problem (well, *one* of my biggest problems) as a writer of comics is that, time and again, I don't go big *enough*. My natural inclination is to limit stories, I suppose as some sort of nod to "realism," and, in truth, I'm probably more comfortable writing what I refer to as "human" moments rather than grand "end of all things" scenes. Burning Gotham seemed like a happy medium, but, as always, that's not really what the story is about. It's Renee's story; once again she finds herself facing the death of someone she loves, but for the first time, she can truly do something to prevent it. The question, asked over and over, of "who will she become?" is

yet another trick question, and potentially unanswerable. Even in the DCU, the number of people who truly know their own destinies is few and far between. But the act of donning Charlie's mask is, for the first time, Renee's embracing of both the question and the future. And that marks, for her, the end of one journey and the start of another. It's not coincidence that her sequence ends with another question (will Kate live?), even if it's not a terribly difficult one for those devotees of comics to answer.

As an aside, I discovered, quite by accident, that Renee became much funnier (or at least *tried* to be funnier) once the mask was back on. That came out in the writing, rather than in the planning, but it made such perfect sense; the mask is truly a liberating force, yet another secret that Charlie tried to share with Renee.

MIKE SIGLAIN

We were going back and forth on the cover for this issue, and just when it looked as if we were running out of time, the light bulb once again went off in J.G.'s head. He wanted to go with stencil graffiti, which he described as "guerrilla street art that you find in our hipper urban underbellies." So, early one Saturday morning in December, the stencil image of Montoya as the Question was e-mailed to both Rucka and myself. Needless to say, we loved it. And we weren't the only ones. On Monday, when I got back to the office, I added the image to my giant wall of 52 covers, and it caught everyone's eye. "That's awesome!" "I want to buy that!" "They should make posters of that!" Well, that's the genius of J.G. Jones.

And extra special thank-you goes out to Greg Rucka, who did all of the heavy lifting for this issue. This is the end of our Montoya story line, and Greg pulled out all the stops. Not only do we get the much-anticipated debut of Montoya as the Question, but we get a deeper insight into the Dark Faith, and Batwoman gets stabbed in the heart. Nicely done, Greg. Nicely done.

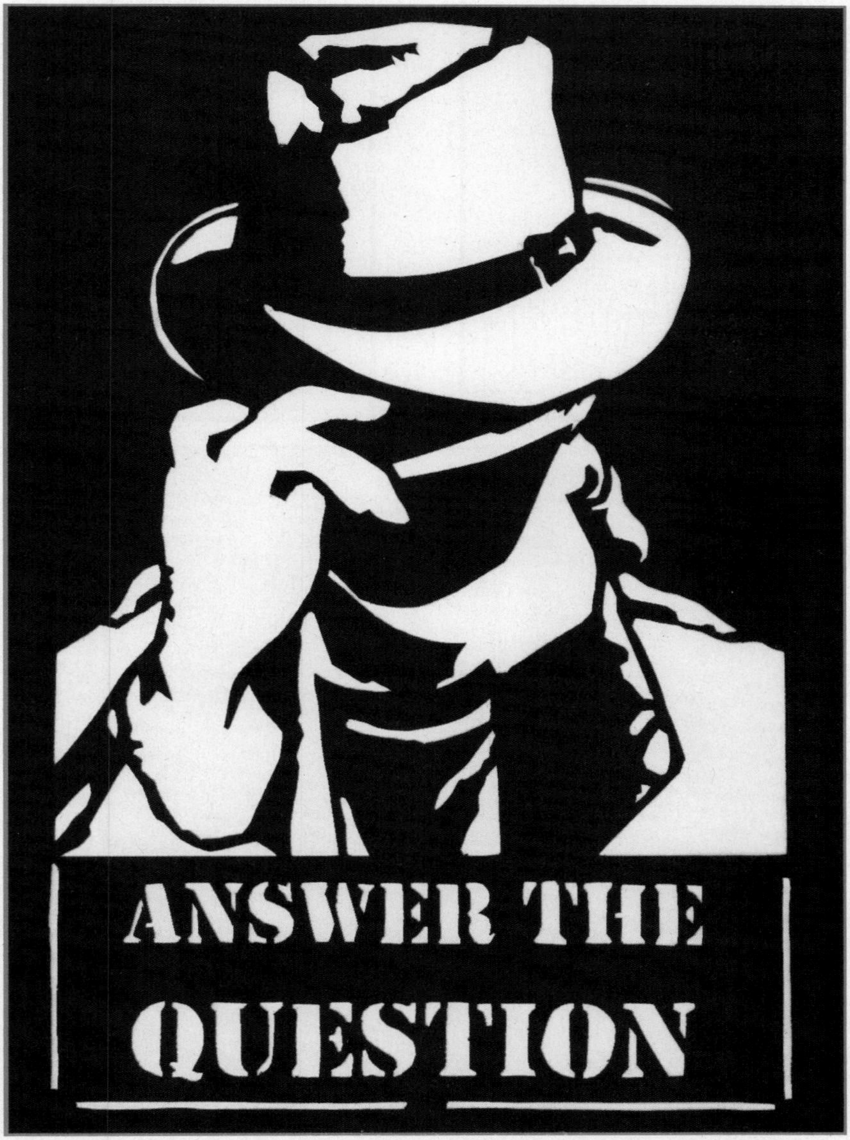
ANSWER THE
QUESTION

J.G. Jones's stencil used for the cover of Week#48

BREAKDOWNS

BY **KEITH GIFFEN**

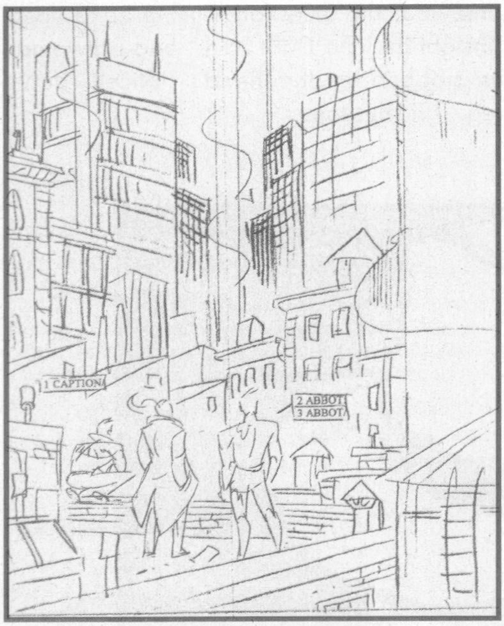
1 CAPTION
2 ABBOT
3 ABBOT

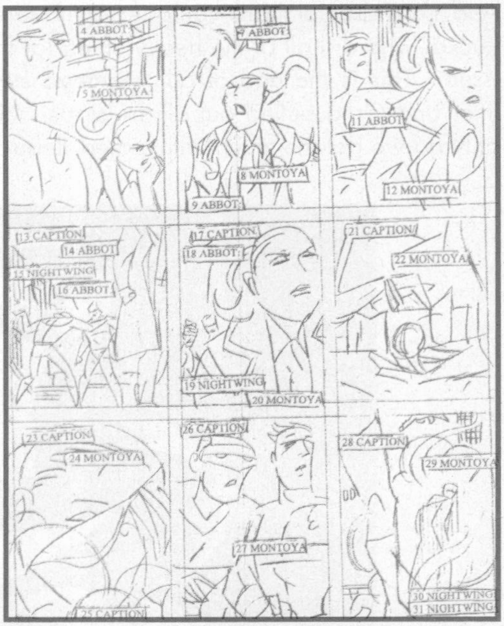
4 ABBOT
5 MONTOYA
7 ABBOT
8 MONTOYA
9 ABBOT
11 ABBOT
12 MONTOYA
13 CAPTION
14 ABBOT
15 NIGHTWING
16 ABBOT
17 CAPTION
18 ABBOT
19 NIGHTWING
20 MONTOYA
21 CAPTION
22 MONTOYA
23 CAPTION
24 MONTOYA
25 CAPTION
26 CAPTION
27 MONTOYA
28 CAPTION
29 MONTOYA
30 NIGHTWING
31 NIGHTWING

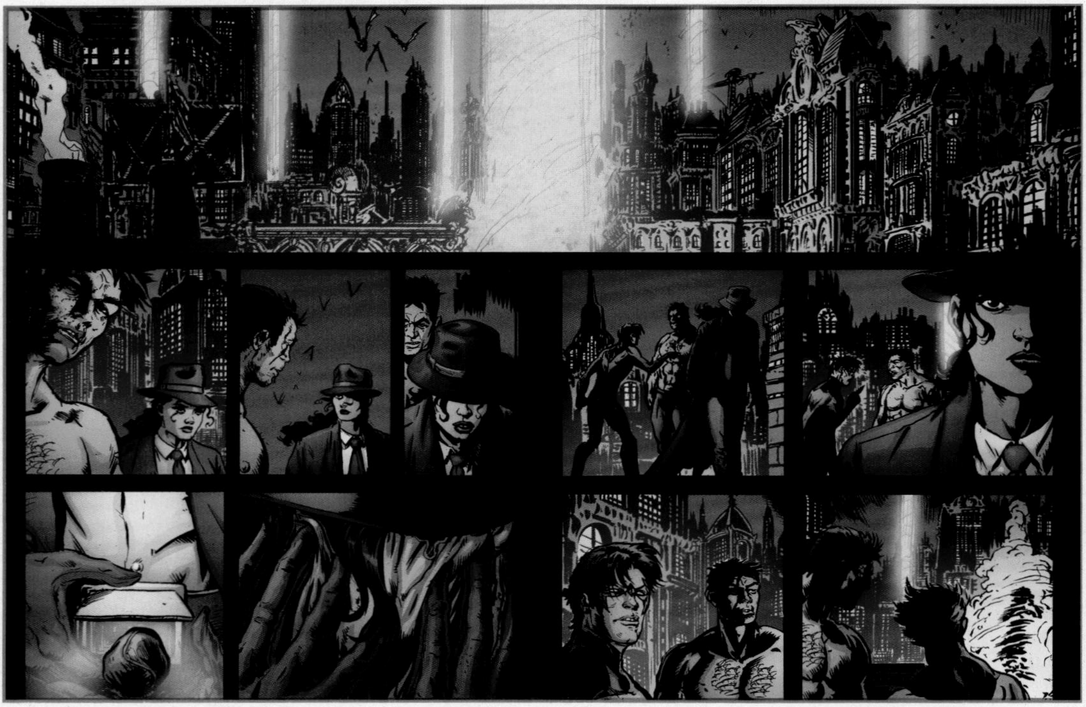

Pages 196 and 197 were originally laid out by breakdown artist Keith Giffen as a single splash page, followed by a 9-panel grid. In the final version, the shot of Gotham City was extended over the top of a 2-page spread, with the nine panels incorporated beneath it.

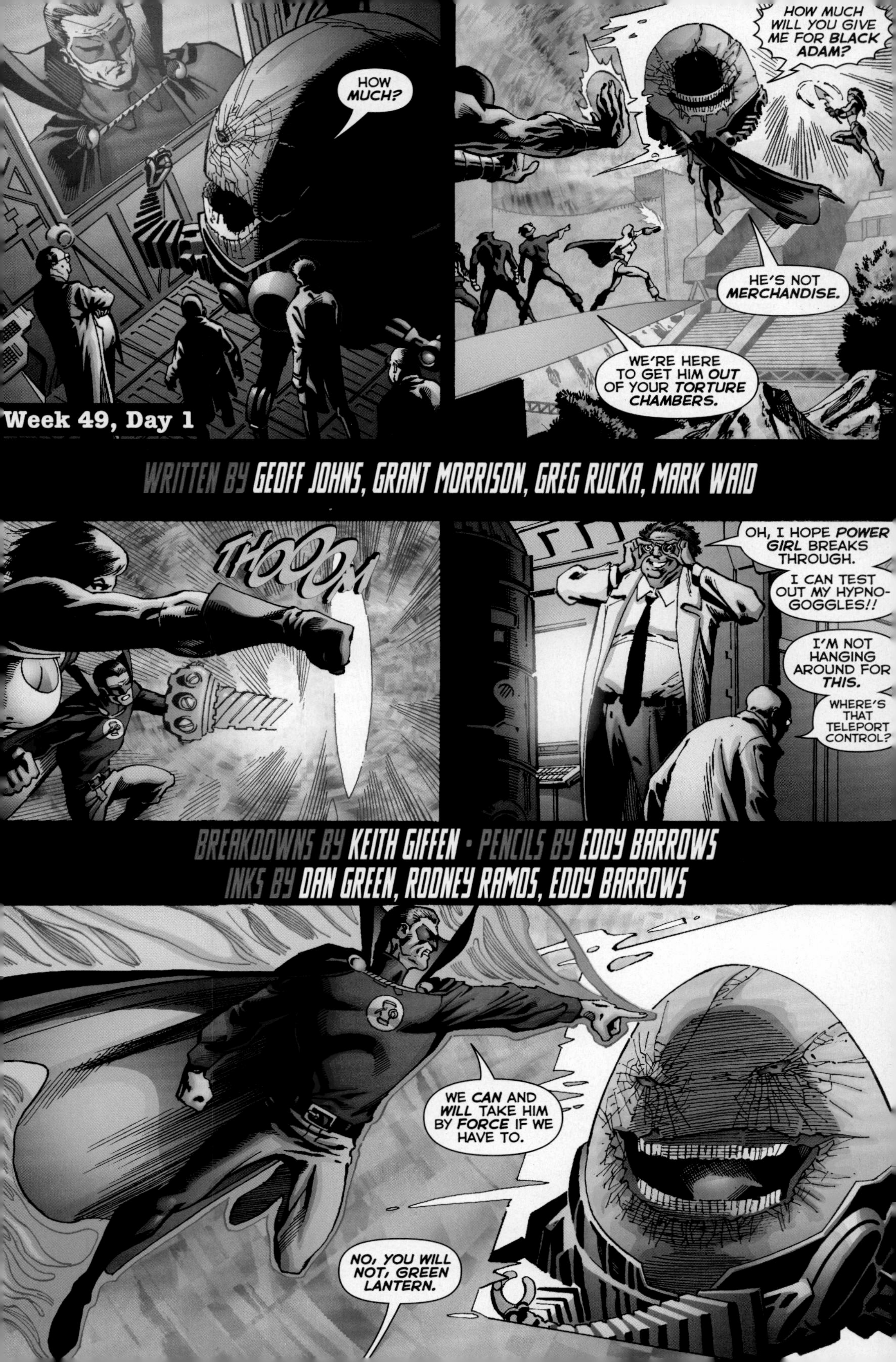
HOW MUCH?
HOW MUCH WILL YOU GIVE ME FOR BLACK ADAM?
HE'S NOT MERCHANDISE.
WE'RE HERE TO GET HIM OUT OF YOUR TORTURE CHAMBERS.
Week 49, Day 1
WRITTEN BY GEOFF JOHNS, GRANT MORRISON, GREG RUCKA, MARK WAID
THOOOM
OH, I HOPE POWER GIRL BREAKS THROUGH.
I CAN TEST OUT MY HYPNO-GOGGLES!!
I'M NOT HANGING AROUND FOR THIS.
WHERE'S THAT TELEPORT CONTROL?
BREAKDOWNS BY KEITH GIFFEN • PENCILS BY EDDY BARROWS
INKS BY DAN GREEN, RODNEY RAMOS, EDDY BARROWS
WE CAN AND WILL TAKE HIM BY FORCE IF WE HAVE TO.
NO, YOU WILL NOT, GREEN LANTERN.

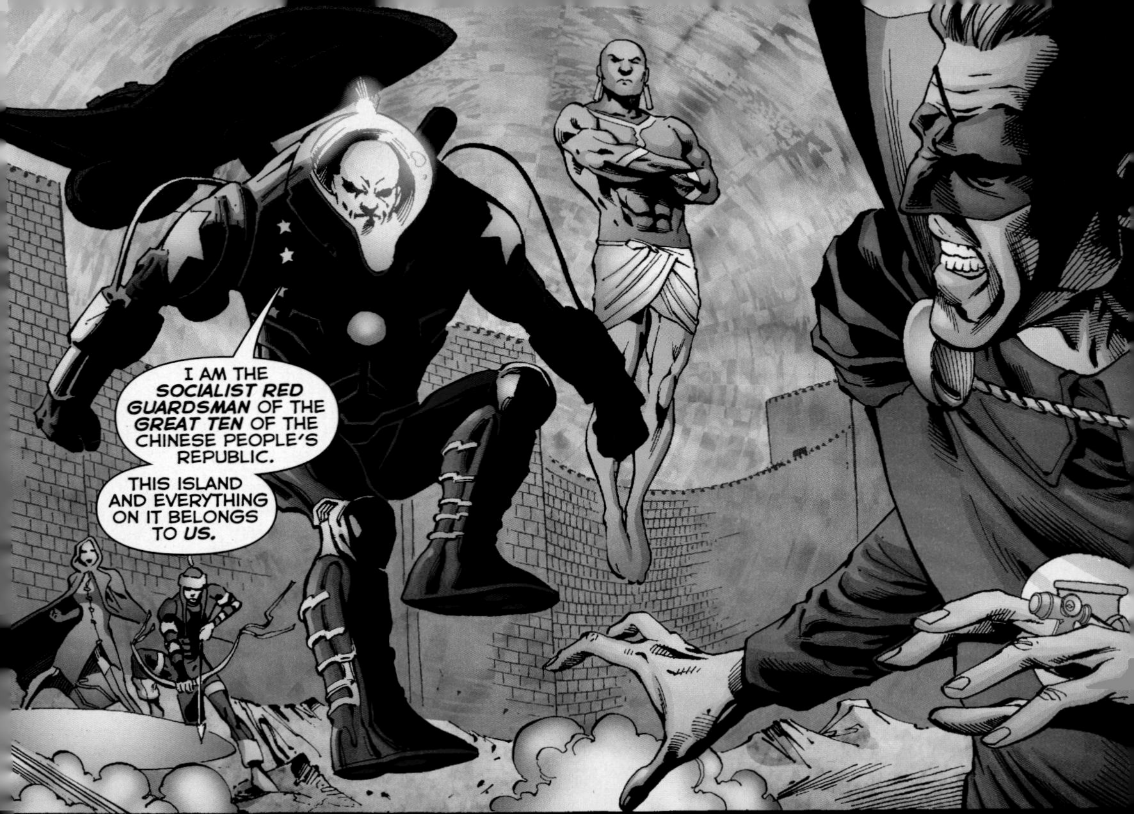
I AM THE SOCIALIST RED GUARDSMAN OF THE GREAT TEN OF THE CHINESE PEOPLE'S REPUBLIC.
THIS ISLAND AND EVERYTHING ON IT BELONGS TO US.

COLORS BY DAVID BARON • LETTERS BY ROB LEIGH • COVER BY J.G. JONES & ALEX SINCLAIR
ASSISTANT EDITOR – HARVEY RICHARDS • ASSOCIATE EDITOR – JEANINE SCHAEFER • EDITOR – MICHAEL SIGLAIN

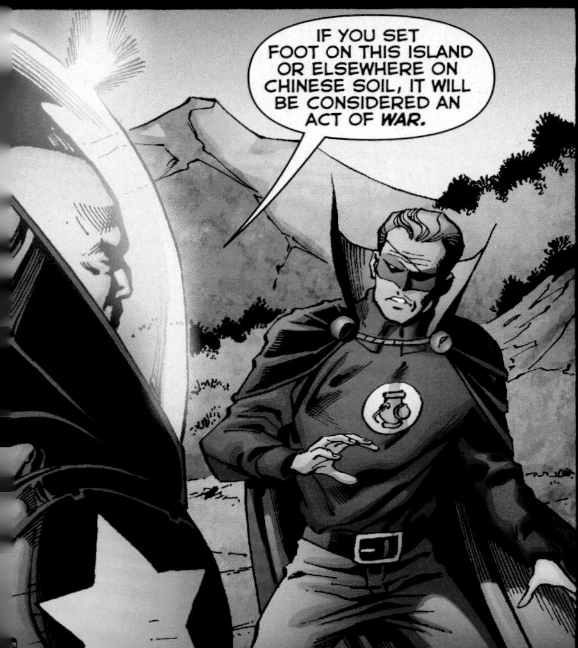
IF YOU SET FOOT ON THIS ISLAND OR ELSEWHERE ON CHINESE SOIL, IT WILL BE CONSIDERED AN ACT OF WAR.

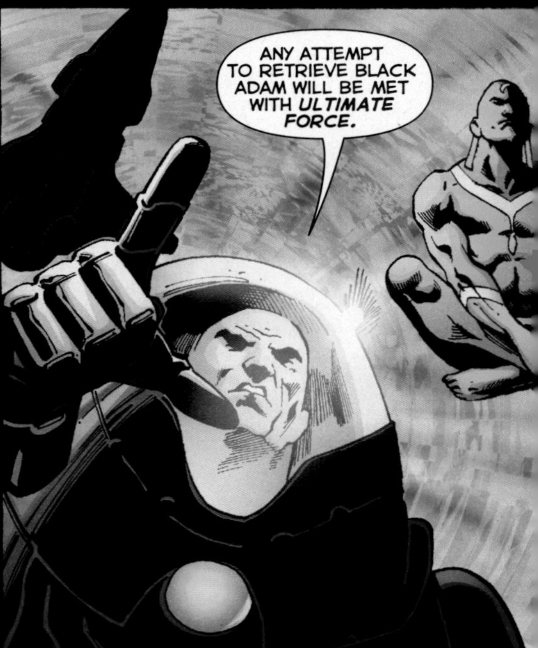
ANY ATTEMPT TO RETRIEVE BLACK ADAM WILL BE MET WITH ULTIMATE FORCE.

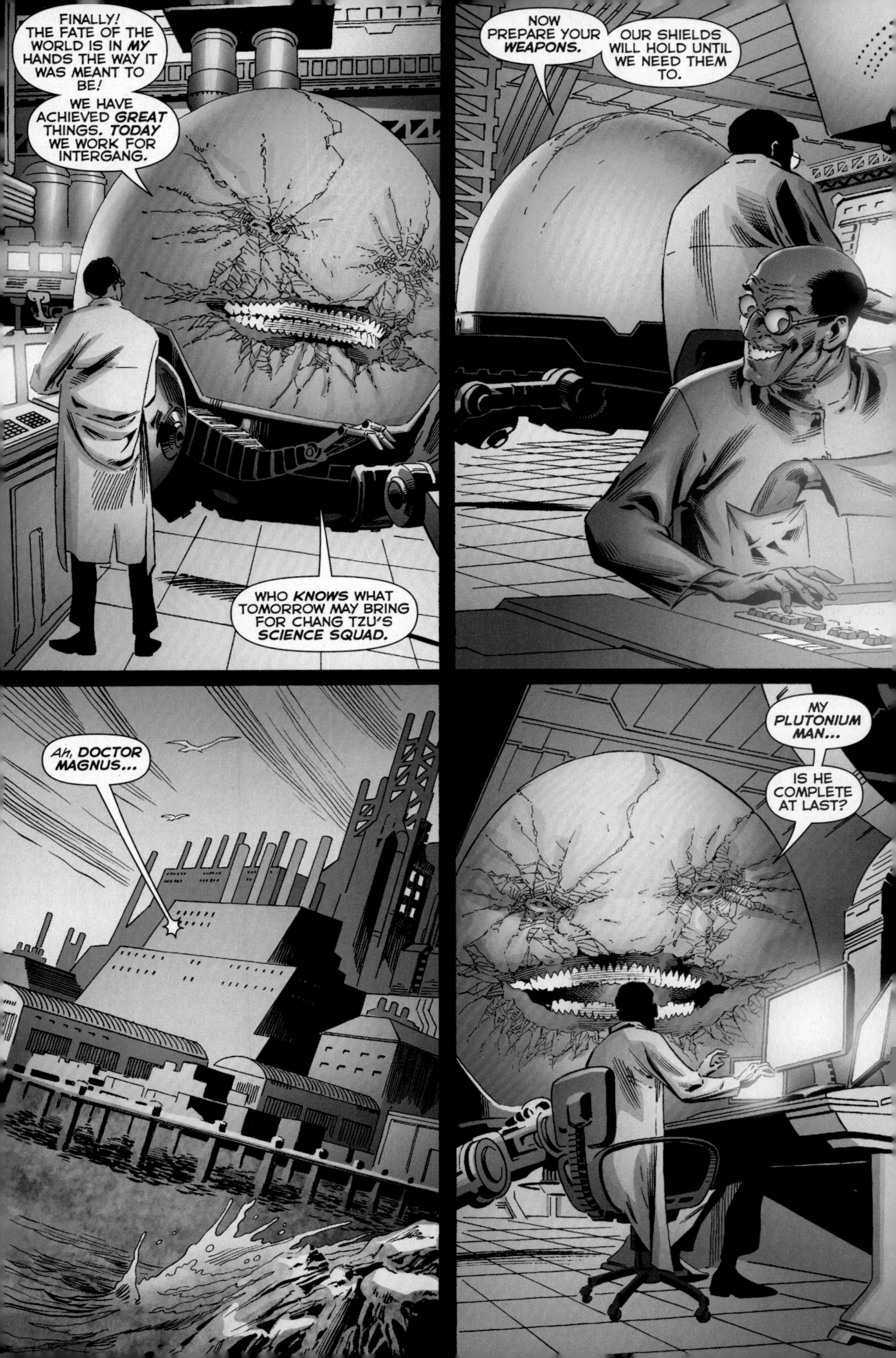
FINALLY! THE FATE OF THE WORLD IS IN MY HANDS THE WAY IT WAS MEANT TO BE!
WE HAVE ACHIEVED GREAT THINGS. TODAY WE WORK FOR INTERGANG.
WHO KNOWS WHAT TOMORROW MAY BRING FOR CHANG TZU'S SCIENCE SQUAD.
NOW PREPARE YOUR WEAPONS.
OUR SHIELDS WILL HOLD UNTIL WE NEED THEM TO.
Ah, DOCTOR MAGNUS...
MY PLUTONIUM MAN...
IS HE COMPLETE AT LAST?

OH, *THIS*... THIS IS WHAT MAKES IT ALL POSSIBLE.

RESPONSOMETER TECHNOLOGY.

DO YOU KNOW *MUCH* ABOUT MY WORK, MISTER CHANG TZU?

ENLIGHTEN ME.

WELL, I THOUGHT THEY WERE ALL LOOKING IN THE *WRONG* DIRECTION FOR ARTIFICIAL INTELLIGENCE BASICALLY.

I FIGURED THINGS WERE *ALREADY* SMART.

I HAD THE IDEA THAT WHAT WE CALL PERSONALITY TRAITS MIGHT ACTUALLY INDICATE THE PRESENCE OF CERTAIN *METALS* IN OUR BODIES.

WE MAY WISH TO *ACTIVATE* HIM AS AN OPPONENT FOR THE AMERICAN SUPERHUMAN *ATOM SMASHER.*

I WONDERED, HOW *IS* IT THAT YOU ENDOW THE METALS WITH *LIFE*?

WE EXPERIENCE THE HARMONIOUS ATOMIC GRID OF *GOLD* AS FEELINGS OF SELFLESSNESS, NOBILITY AND HEROISM: *"RIGHTNESS."*

LEAD IS OUR STUBBORN REFUSAL TO QUIT, *IRON* OUR INFLEXIBLE, INDOMITABLE SELF-DETERMINATION...

I WAS REGARDED AS NO BETTER THAN A MEDIEVAL *ALCHEMIST.*

EASY TO SEE WHY. IT SEEMS LIKE ROMANCE, DOCTOR MAGNUS, NOT SCIENCE.

PROFESSOR MORROW WAS THE ONLY ONE WHO DIDN'T LAUGH AT ME.

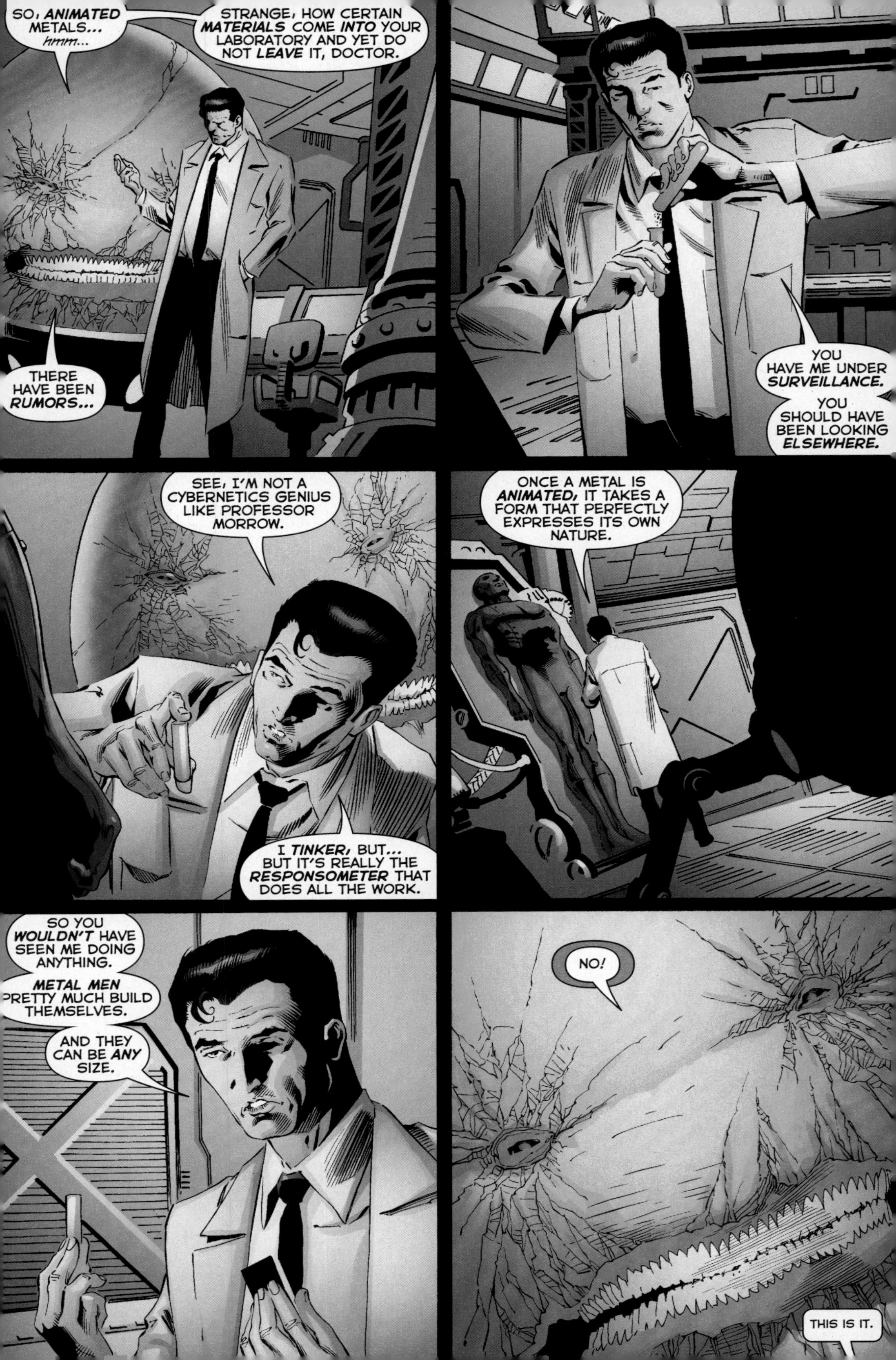

SO, ANIMATED METALS... hmm...
STRANGE, HOW CERTAIN MATERIALS COME INTO YOUR LABORATORY AND YET DO NOT LEAVE IT, DOCTOR.
THERE HAVE BEEN RUMORS...
YOU HAVE ME UNDER SURVEILLANCE.
YOU SHOULD HAVE BEEN LOOKING ELSEWHERE.
SEE, I'M NOT A CYBERNETICS GENIUS LIKE PROFESSOR MORROW.
I TINKER, BUT... BUT IT'S REALLY THE RESPONSOMETER THAT DOES ALL THE WORK.
ONCE A METAL IS ANIMATED, IT TAKES A FORM THAT PERFECTLY EXPRESSES ITS OWN NATURE.
SO YOU WOULDN'T HAVE SEEN ME DOING ANYTHING.
METAL MEN PRETTY MUCH BUILD THEMSELVES.
AND THEY CAN BE ANY SIZE.
NO!
THIS IS IT.

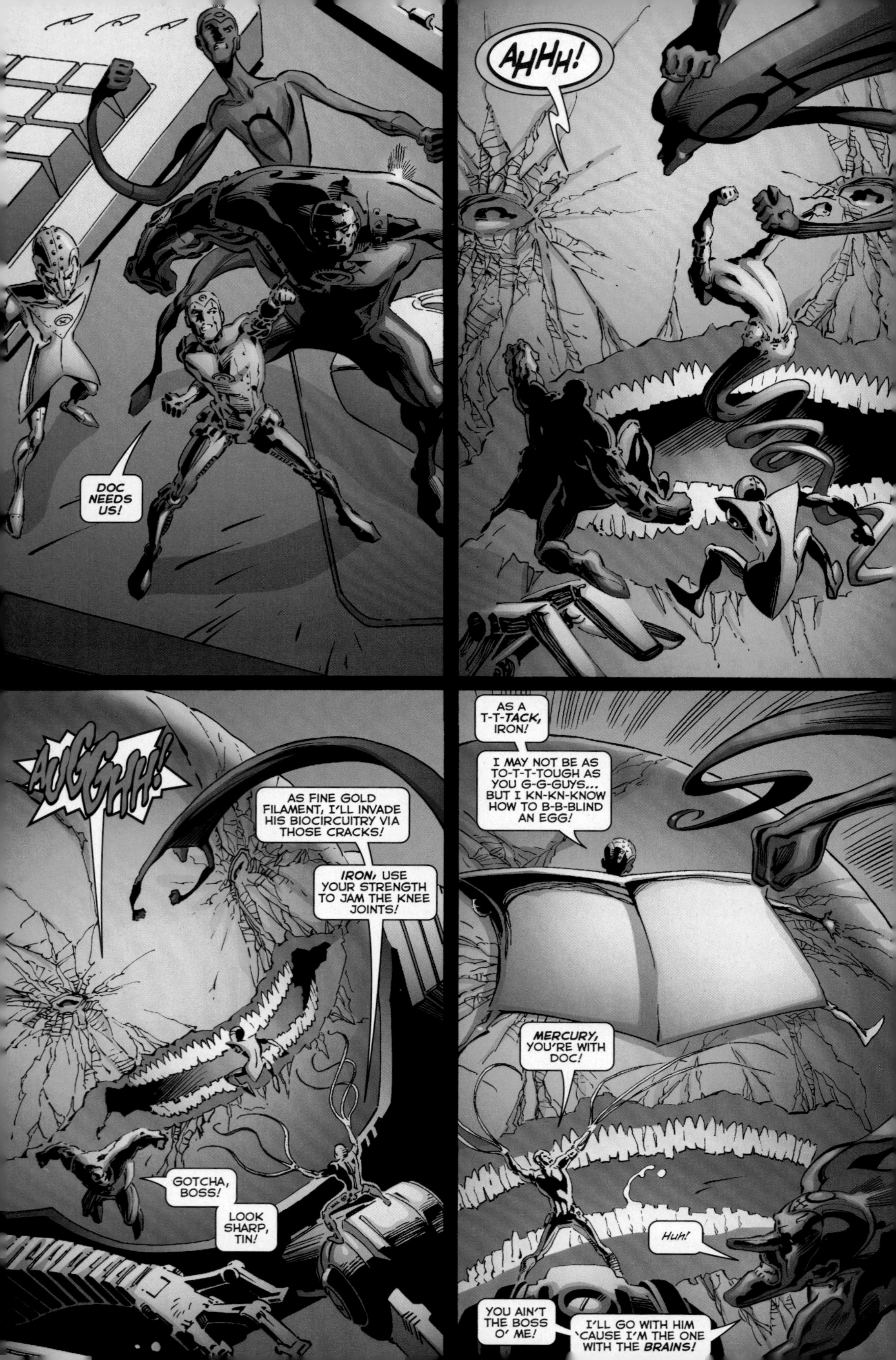
DOC NEEDS US!
AHHH!
AUGGHH!
AS FINE GOLD FILAMENT, I'LL INVADE HIS BIOCIRCUITRY VIA THOSE CRACKS!
IRON, USE YOUR STRENGTH TO JAM THE KNEE JOINTS!
GOTCHA, BOSS!
LOOK SHARP, TIN!
AS A T-T-TACK, IRON!
I MAY NOT BE AS TO-T-T-TOUGH AS YOU G-G-GUYS... BUT I KN-KN-KNOW HOW TO B-B-BLIND AN EGG!
MERCURY, YOU'RE WITH DOC!
Huh!
YOU AIN'T THE BOSS O' ME!
I'LL GO WITH HIM 'CAUSE I'M THE ONE WITH THE BRAINS!

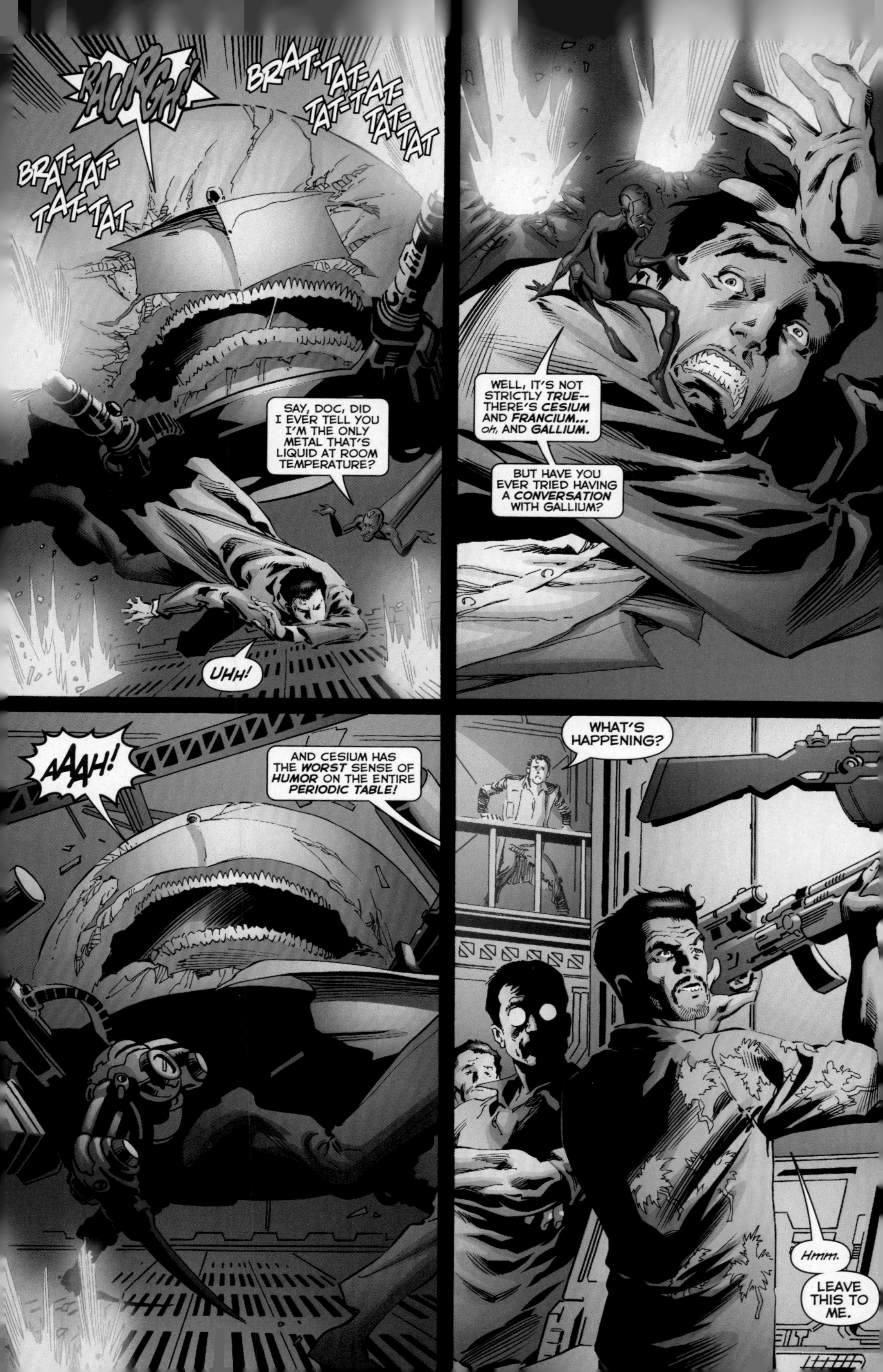
BAURGH!
BRAT-TAT-TAT-TAT-TAT-TAT-TAT
BRAT-TAT-TAT-TAT
SAY, DOC, DID I EVER TELL YOU I'M THE ONLY METAL THAT'S LIQUID AT ROOM TEMPERATURE?
UHH!
WELL, IT'S NOT STRICTLY TRUE-- THERE'S CESIUM AND FRANCIUM... oh, AND GALLIUM.
BUT HAVE YOU EVER TRIED HAVING A CONVERSATION WITH GALLIUM?
AAAH!
AND CESIUM HAS THE WORST SENSE OF HUMOR ON THE ENTIRE PERIODIC TABLE!
WHAT'S HAPPENING?
Hmm.
LEAVE THIS TO ME.

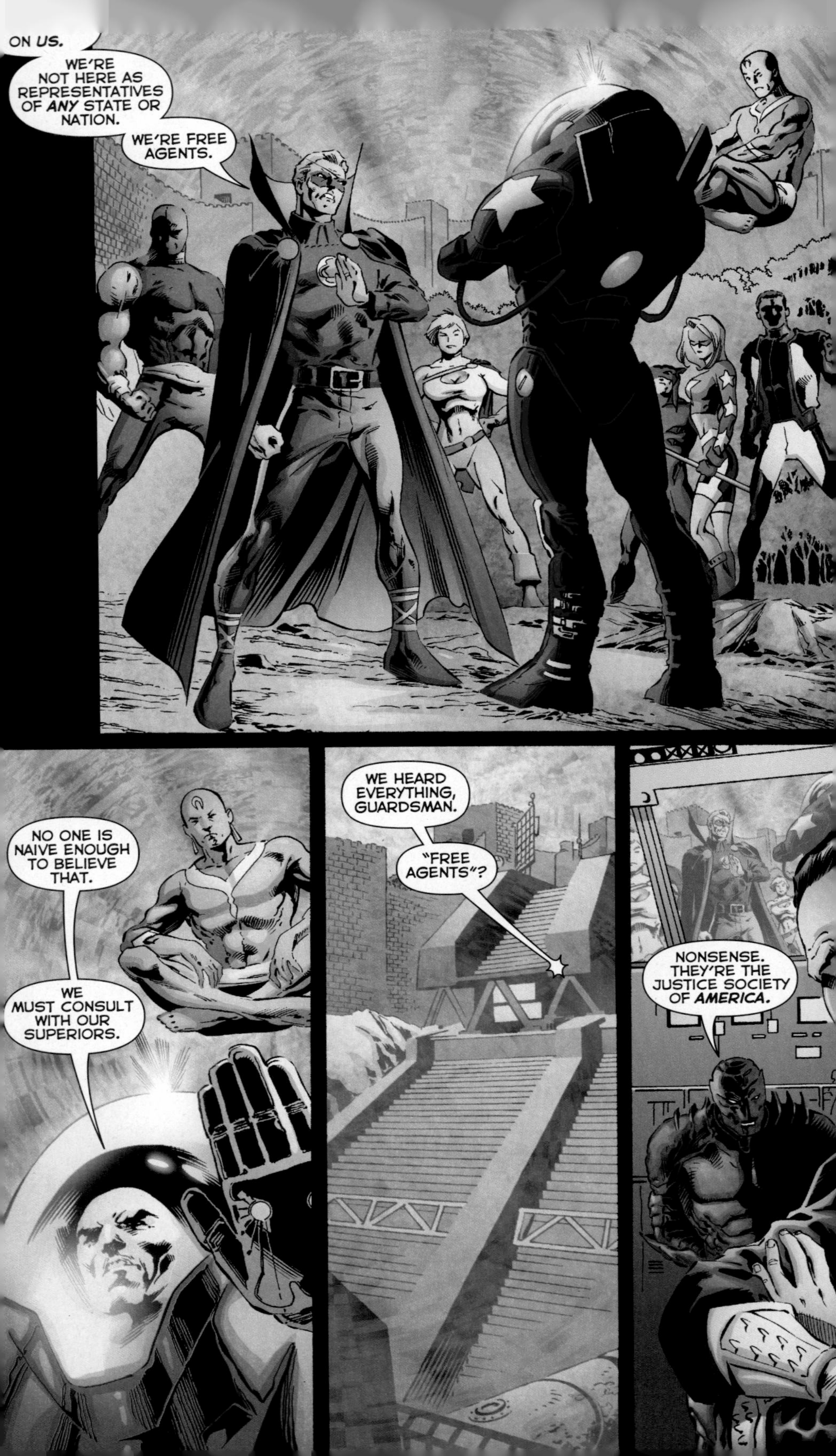

ON US.
WE'RE NOT HERE AS REPRESENTATIVES OF ANY STATE OR NATION.
WE'RE FREE AGENTS.
NO ONE IS NAIVE ENOUGH TO BELIEVE THAT.
WE MUST CONSULT WITH OUR SUPERIORS.
WE HEARD EVERYTHING, GUARDSMAN.
"FREE AGENTS"?
NONSENSE. THEY'RE THE JUSTICE SOCIETY OF AMERICA.

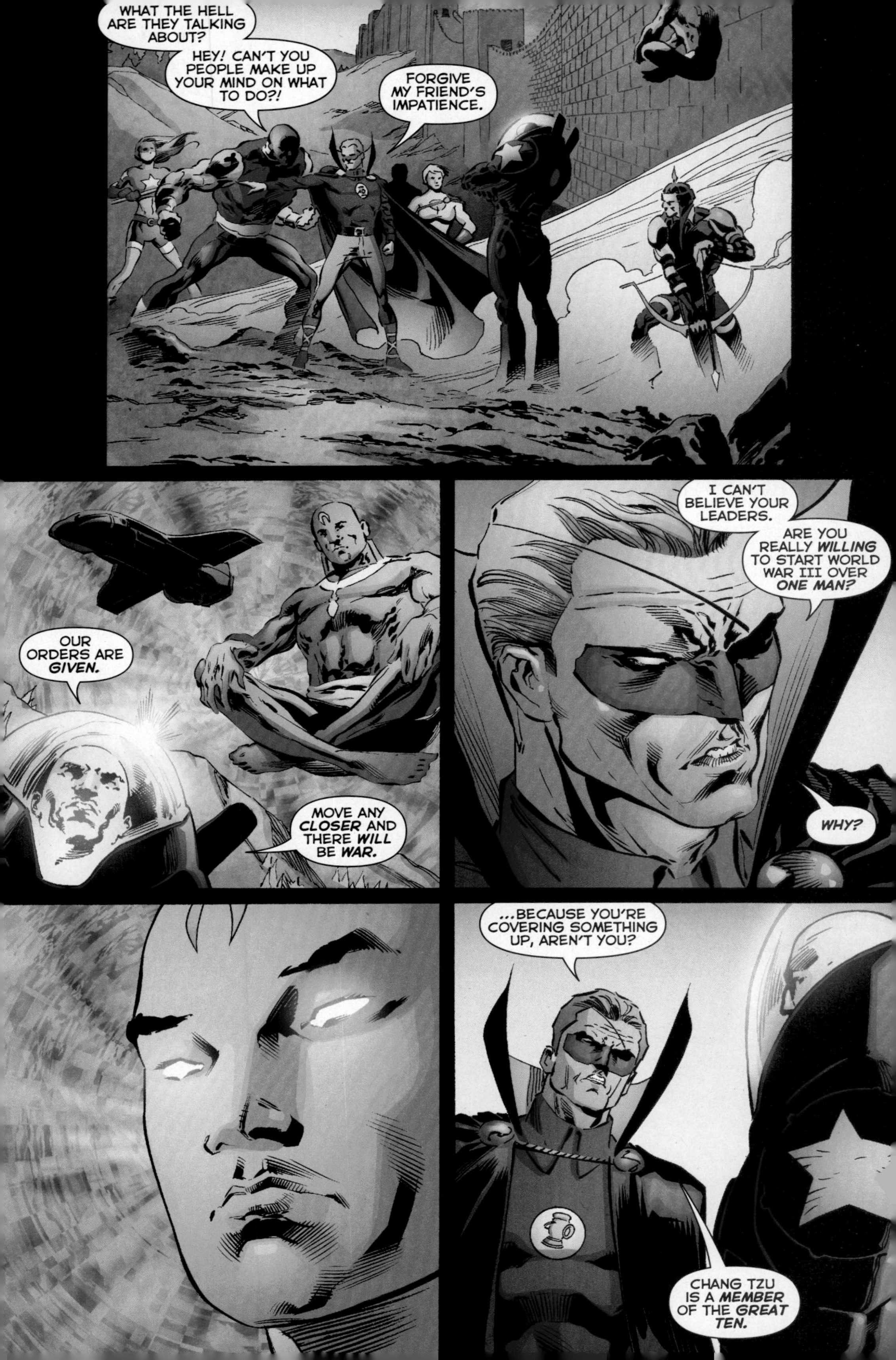
WHAT THE HELL ARE THEY TALKING ABOUT?
HEY! CAN'T YOU PEOPLE MAKE UP YOUR MIND ON WHAT TO DO?!
FORGIVE MY FRIEND'S IMPATIENCE.
OUR ORDERS ARE GIVEN.
MOVE ANY CLOSER AND THERE WILL BE WAR.
I CAN'T BELIEVE YOUR LEADERS.
ARE YOU REALLY WILLING TO START WORLD WAR III OVER ONE MAN?
WHY?
...BECAUSE YOU'RE COVERING SOMETHING UP, AREN'T YOU?
CHANG TZU IS A MEMBER OF THE GREAT TEN.

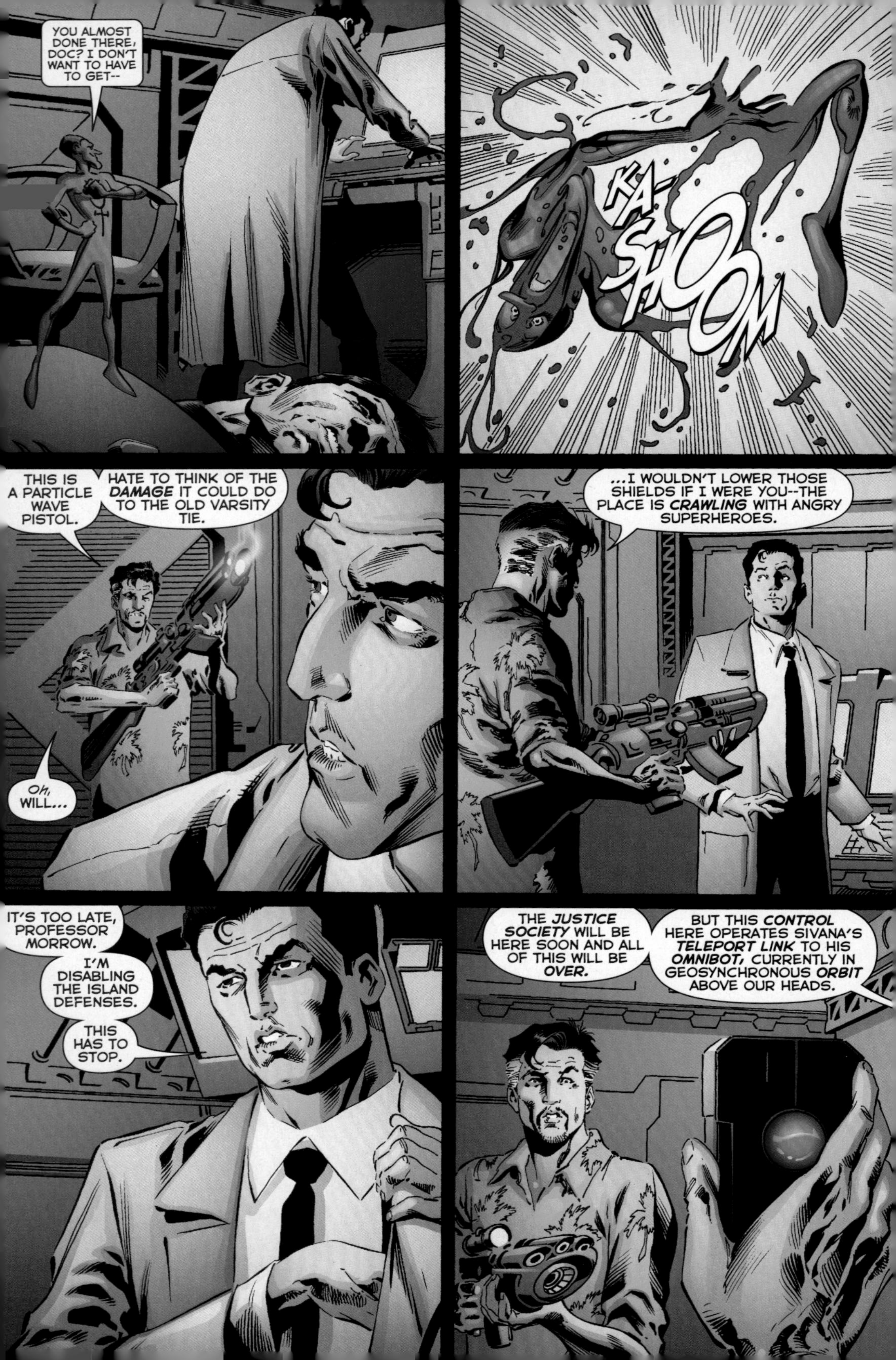
YOU ALMOST DONE THERE, DOC? I DON'T WANT TO HAVE TO GET--
KA-SHOOOM
THIS IS A PARTICLE WAVE PISTOL.
HATE TO THINK OF THE DAMAGE IT COULD DO TO THE OLD VARSITY TIE.
Oh, WILL...
...I WOULDN'T LOWER THOSE SHIELDS IF I WERE YOU--THE PLACE IS CRAWLING WITH ANGRY SUPERHEROES.
IT'S TOO LATE, PROFESSOR MORROW.
I'M DISABLING THE ISLAND DEFENSES.
THIS HAS TO STOP.
THE JUSTICE SOCIETY WILL BE HERE SOON AND ALL OF THIS WILL BE OVER.
BUT THIS CONTROL HERE OPERATES SIVANA'S TELEPORT LINK TO HIS OMNIBOT, CURRENTLY IN GEOSYNCHRONOUS ORBIT ABOVE OUR HEADS.

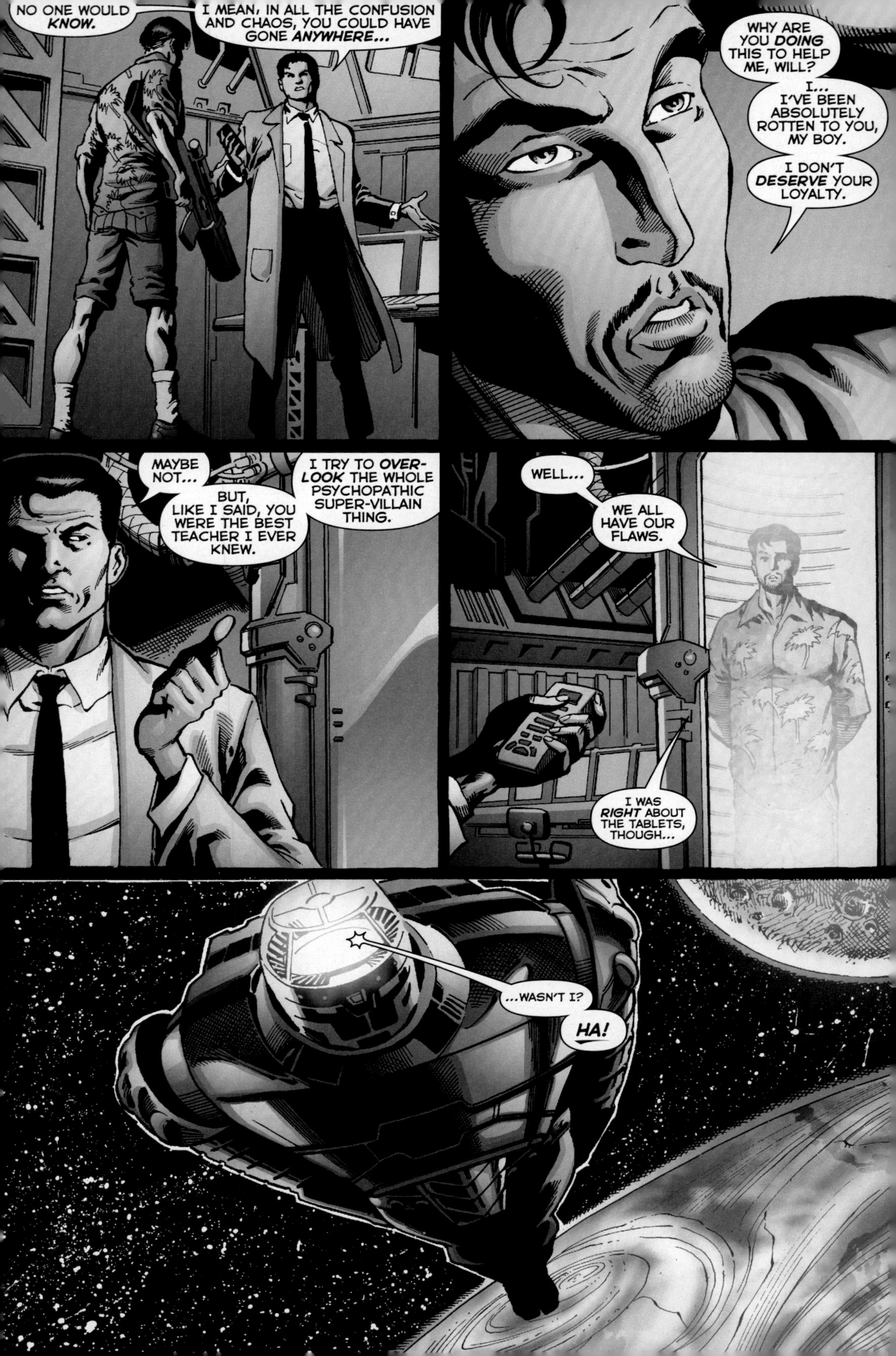
NO ONE WOULD KNOW.
I MEAN, IN ALL THE CONFUSION AND CHAOS, YOU COULD HAVE GONE ANYWHERE...
WHY ARE YOU DOING THIS TO HELP ME, WILL?
I... I'VE BEEN ABSOLUTELY ROTTEN TO YOU, MY BOY.
I DON'T DESERVE YOUR LOYALTY.
MAYBE NOT...
BUT, LIKE I SAID, YOU WERE THE BEST TEACHER I EVER KNEW.
I TRY TO OVERLOOK THE WHOLE PSYCHOPATHIC SUPER-VILLAIN THING.
WELL...
WE ALL HAVE OUR FLAWS.
I WAS RIGHT ABOUT THE TABLETS, THOUGH...
...WASN'T I?
HA!

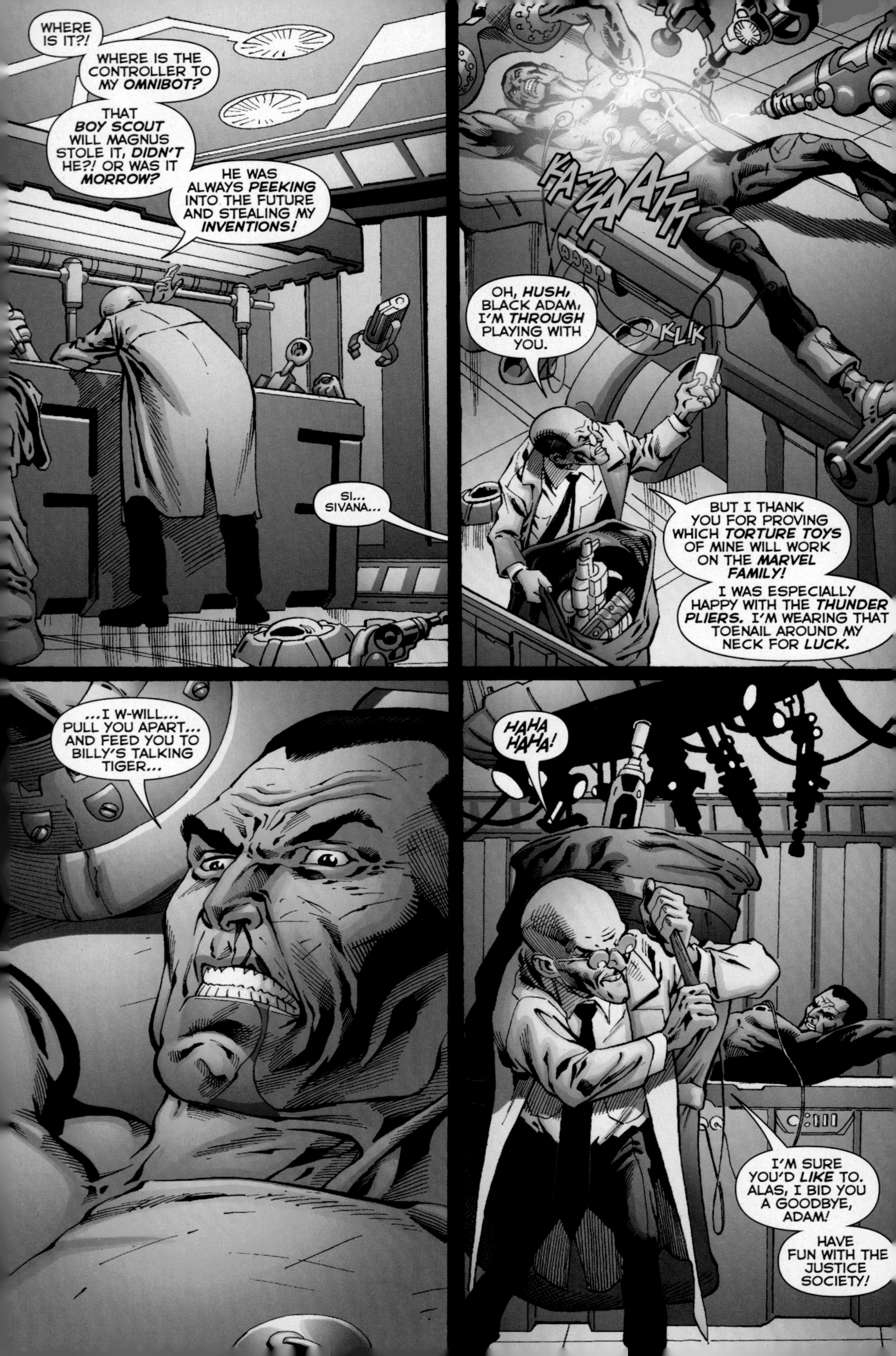
WHERE IS IT?!
WHERE IS THE CONTROLLER TO MY OMNIBOT?
THAT BOY SCOUT WILL MAGNUS STOLE IT, DIDN'T HE?! OR WAS IT MORROW?
HE WAS ALWAYS PEEKING INTO THE FUTURE AND STEALING MY INVENTIONS!
SI... SIVANA...
KA-ZAAATTT
KLIK
OH, HUSH, BLACK ADAM, I'M THROUGH PLAYING WITH YOU.
BUT I THANK YOU FOR PROVING WHICH TORTURE TOYS OF MINE WILL WORK ON THE MARVEL FAMILY!
I WAS ESPECIALLY HAPPY WITH THE THUNDER PLIERS. I'M WEARING THAT TOENAIL AROUND MY NECK FOR LUCK.
...I W-WILL... PULL YOU APART... AND FEED YOU TO BILLY'S TALKING TIGER...
HAHA HAHA!
I'M SURE YOU'D LIKE TO. ALAS, I BID YOU A GOODBYE, ADAM!
HAVE FUN WITH THE JUSTICE SOCIETY!

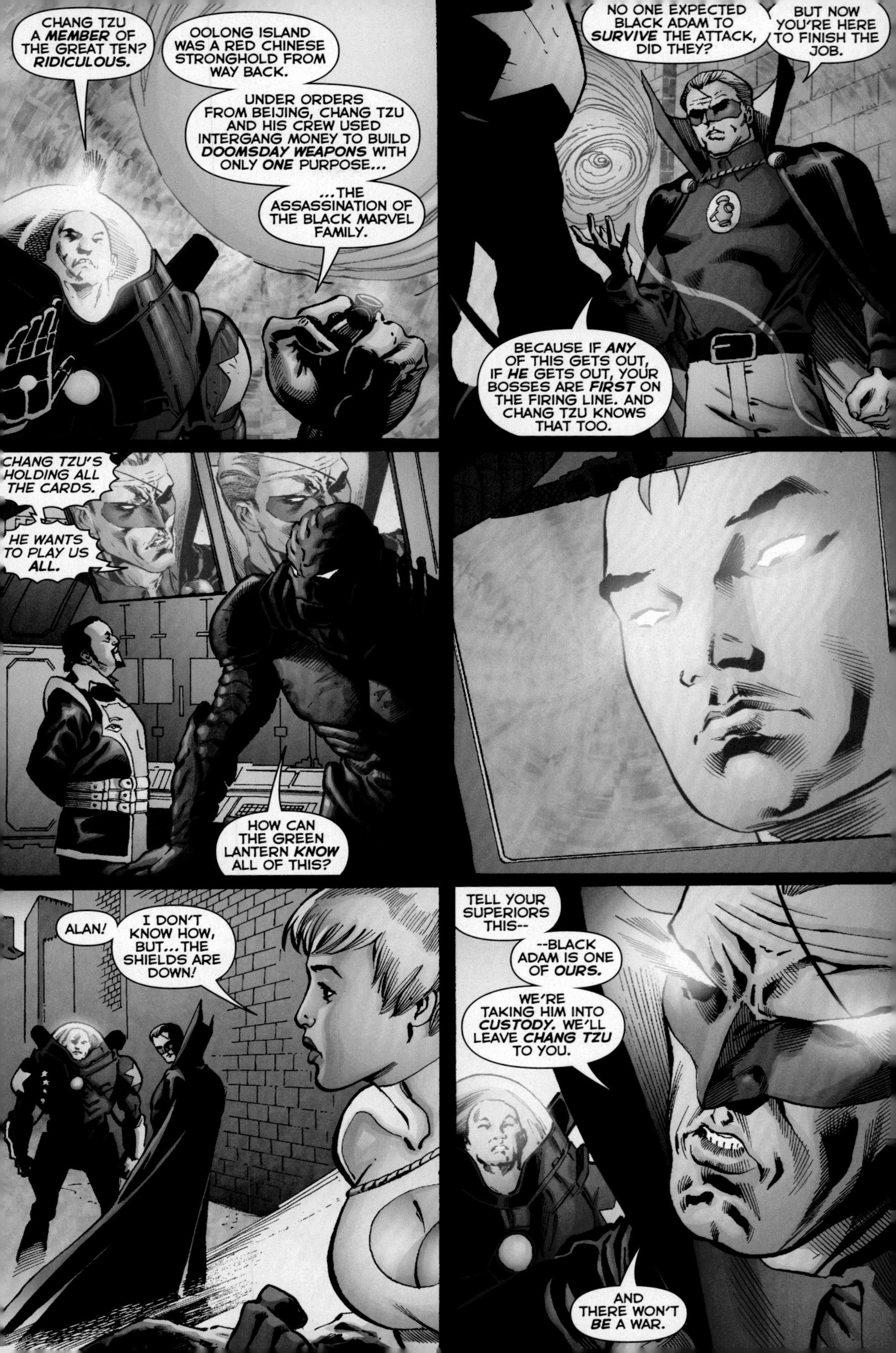

CHANG TZU A *MEMBER* OF THE GREAT TEN? *RIDICULOUS.*
OOLONG ISLAND WAS A RED CHINESE STRONGHOLD FROM WAY BACK.
UNDER ORDERS FROM BEIJING, CHANG TZU AND HIS CREW USED INTERGANG MONEY TO BUILD *DOOMSDAY WEAPONS* WITH ONLY *ONE* PURPOSE...
...THE ASSASSINATION OF THE BLACK MARVEL FAMILY.
NO ONE EXPECTED BLACK ADAM TO *SURVIVE* THE ATTACK, DID THEY?
BUT NOW YOU'RE HERE TO FINISH THE JOB.
BECAUSE IF *ANY* OF THIS GETS OUT, IF *HE* GETS OUT, YOUR BOSSES ARE *FIRST* ON THE FIRING LINE. AND CHANG TZU KNOWS THAT TOO.
CHANG TZU'S HOLDING ALL THE CARDS.
HE WANTS TO PLAY US *ALL.*
HOW CAN THE GREEN LANTERN *KNOW* ALL OF THIS?
ALAN!
I DON'T KNOW HOW, BUT... THE SHIELDS ARE DOWN!
TELL YOUR SUPERIORS THIS--
--BLACK ADAM IS ONE OF *OURS.*
WE'RE TAKING HIM INTO *CUSTODY.* WE'LL LEAVE *CHANG TZU* TO YOU.
AND THERE WON'T *BE* A WAR.

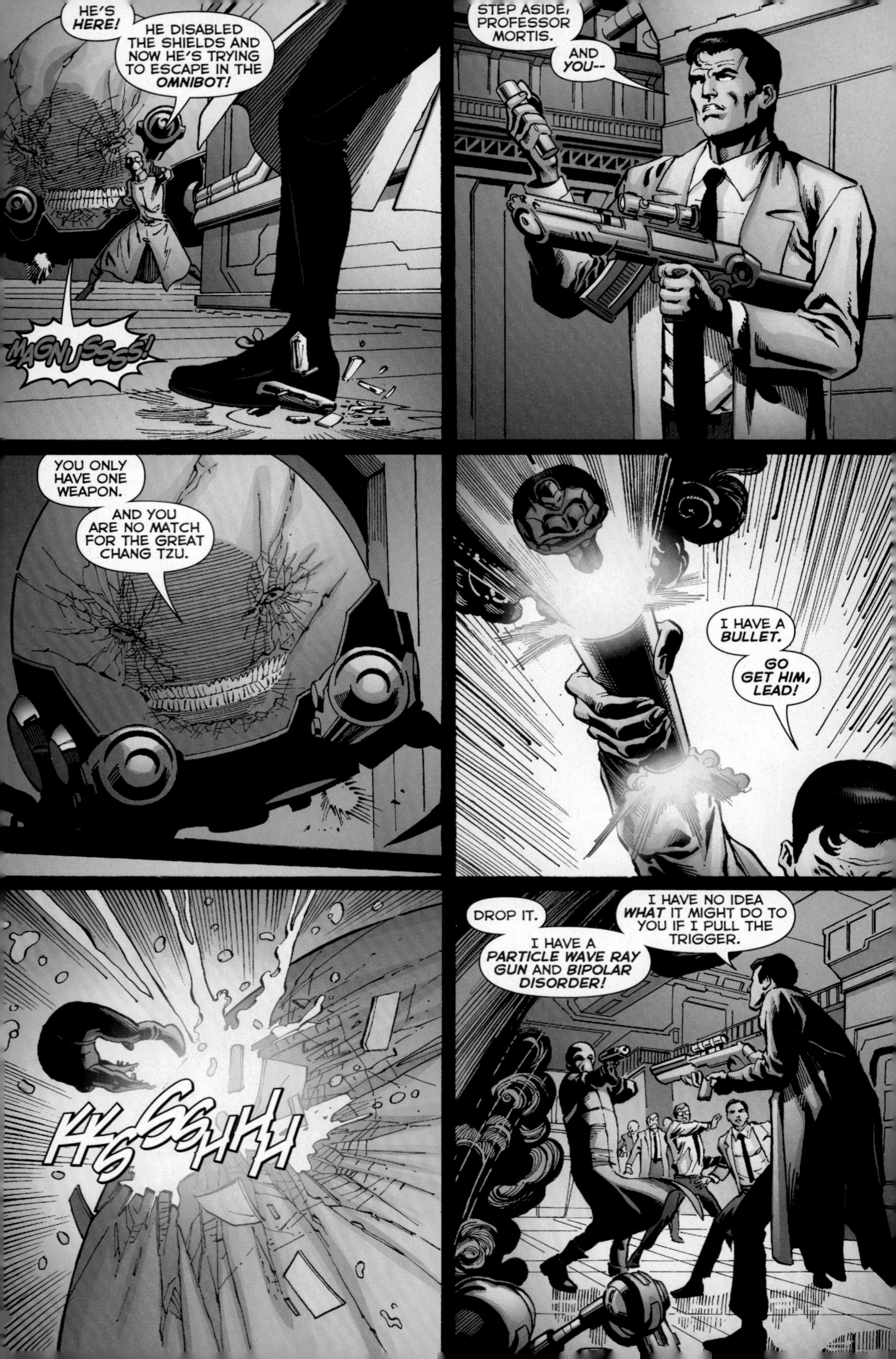
HE'S HERE!
HE DISABLED THE SHIELDS AND NOW HE'S TRYING TO ESCAPE IN THE OMNIBOT!
MAGNUSSSSS!
STEP ASIDE, PROFESSOR MORTIS.
AND YOU--
YOU ONLY HAVE ONE WEAPON.
AND YOU ARE NO MATCH FOR THE GREAT CHANG TZU.
I HAVE A BULLET.
GO GET HIM, LEAD!
KKSSHHH
DROP IT.
I HAVE A PARTICLE WAVE RAY GUN AND BIPOLAR DISORDER!
I HAVE NO IDEA WHAT IT MIGHT DO TO YOU IF I PULL THE TRIGGER.

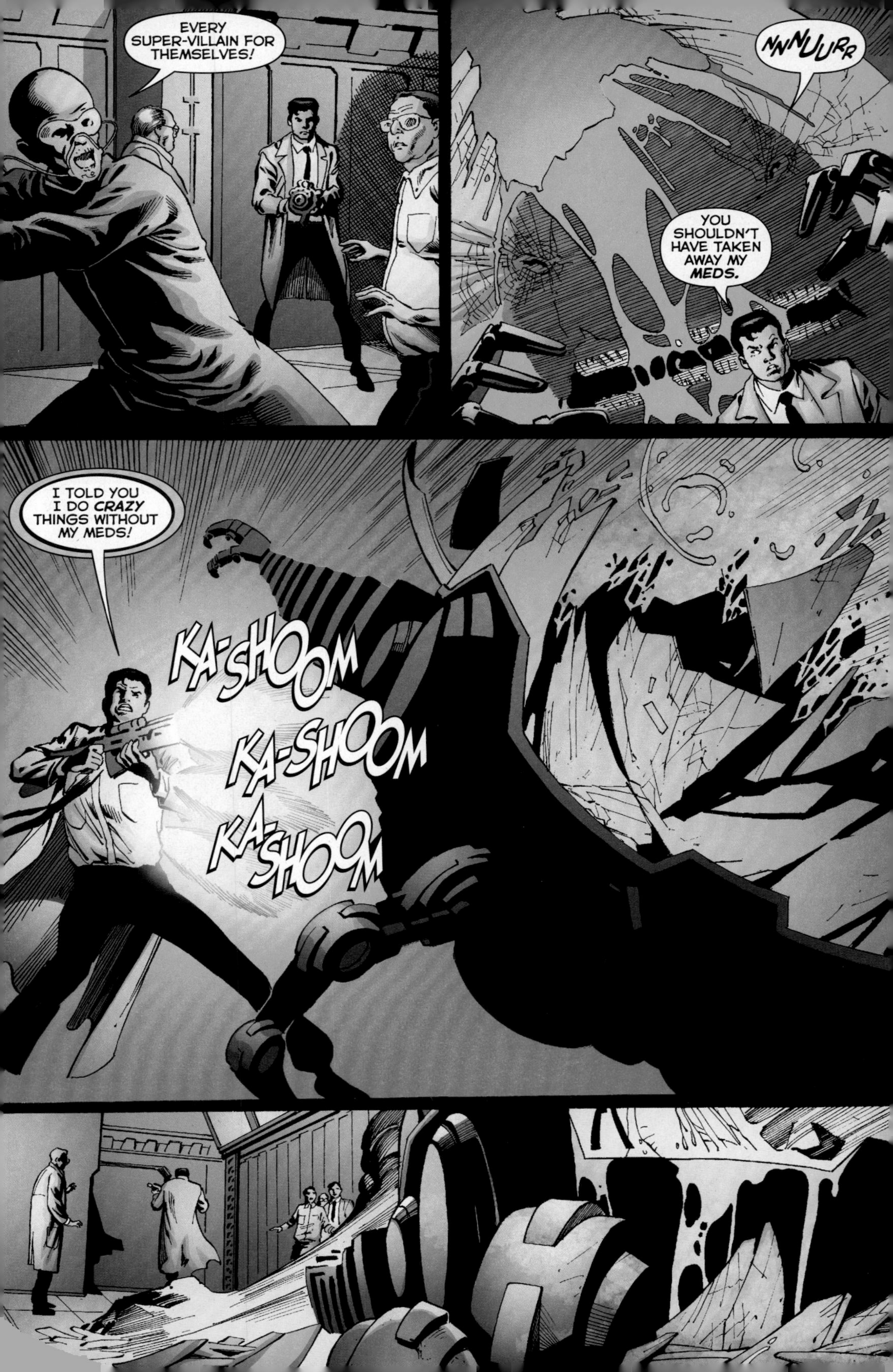
EVERY SUPER-VILLAIN FOR THEMSELVES!
NNNUURR
YOU SHOULDN'T HAVE TAKEN AWAY MY MEDS.
I TOLD YOU I DO CRAZY THINGS WITHOUT MY MEDS!
KA-SHOOM
KA-SHOOM
KA-SHOOM

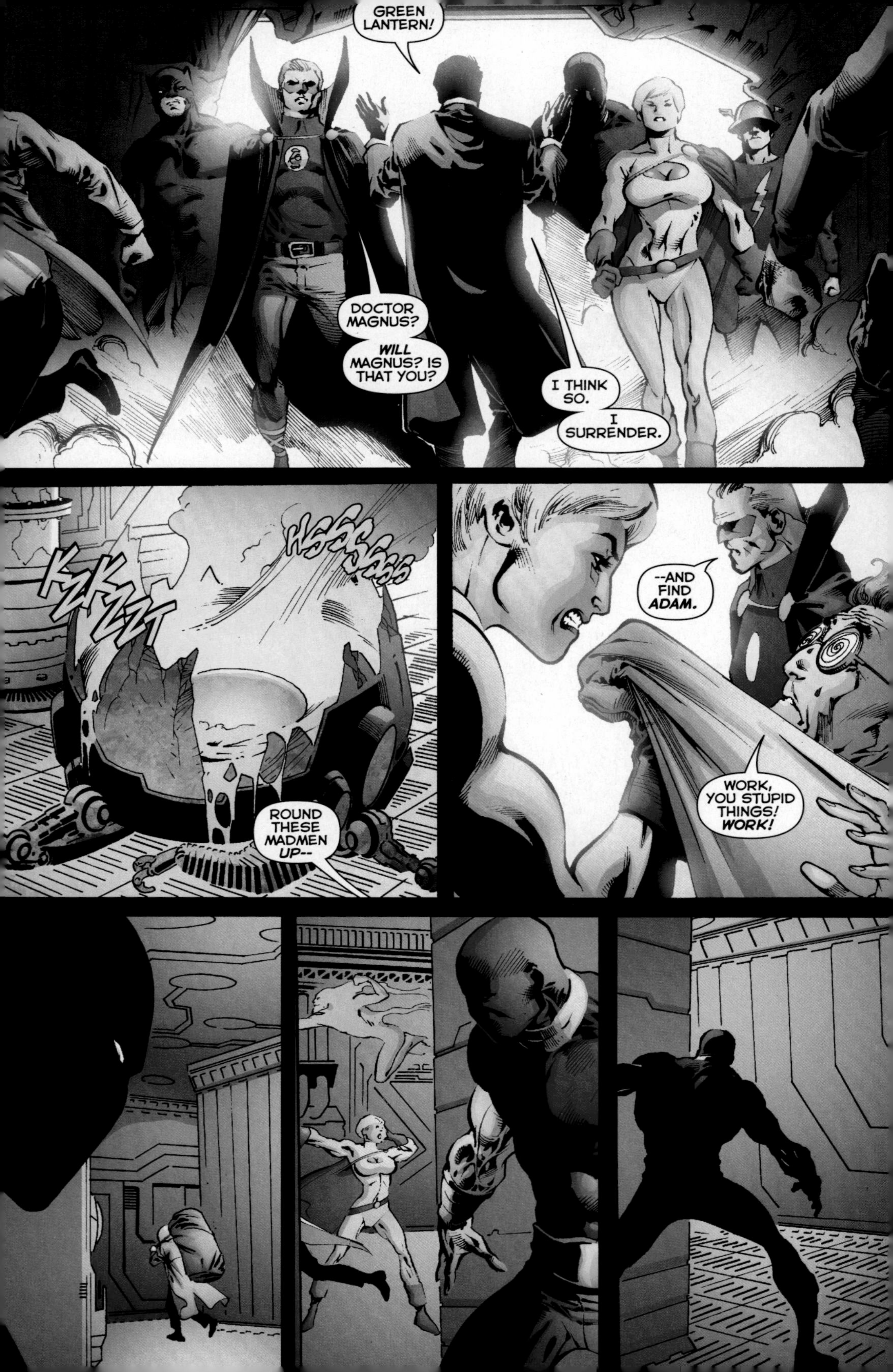
GREEN LANTERN!
DOCTOR MAGNUS?
WILL MAGNUS? IS THAT YOU?
I THINK SO.
I SURRENDER.
KZKZZZT
HSSSSSSS
ROUND THESE MADMEN UP--
--AND FIND ADAM.
WORK, YOU STUPID THINGS! WORK!

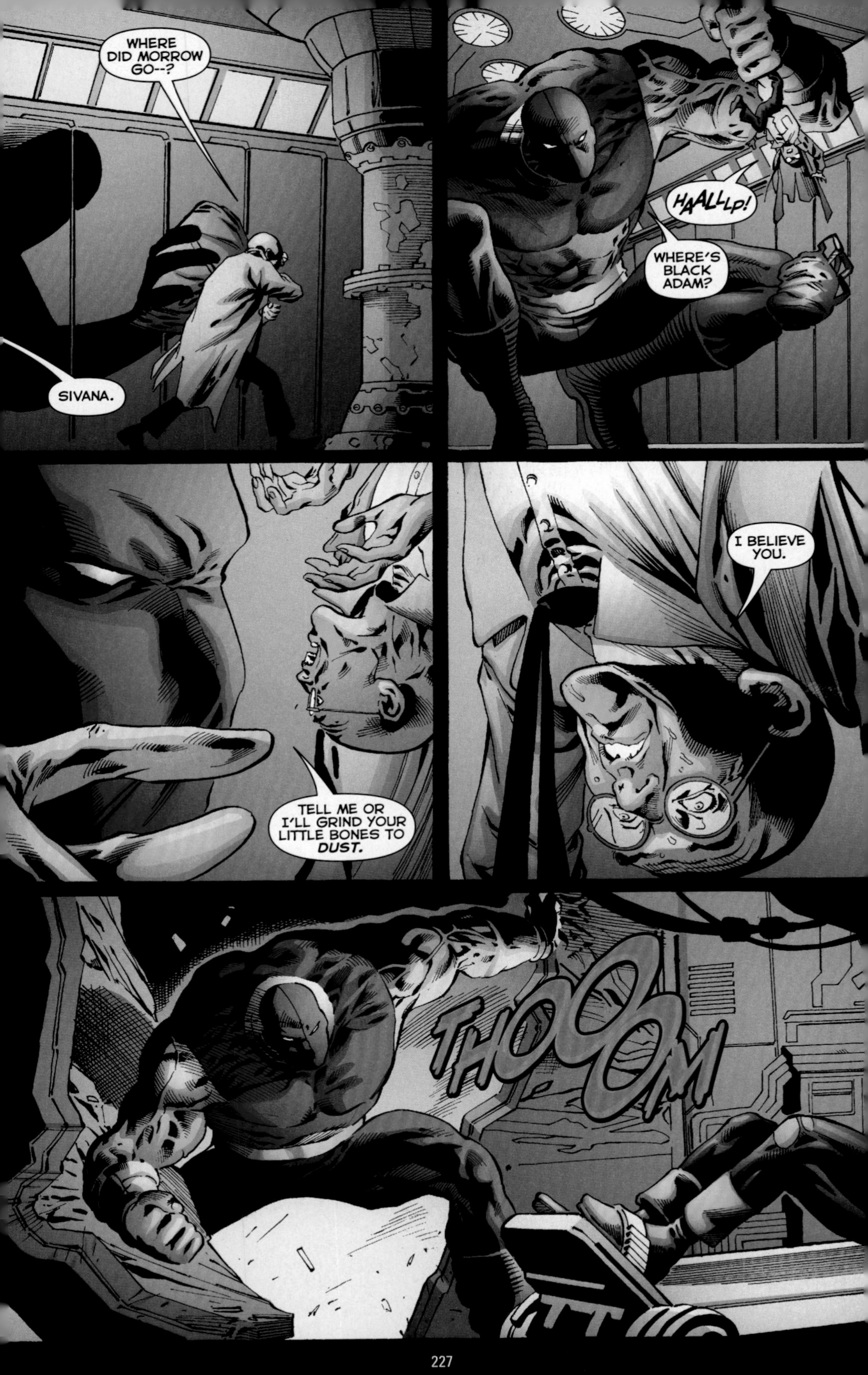
WHERE DID MORROW GO--?
SIVANA.
HAALLLP!
WHERE'S BLACK ADAM?
TELL ME OR I'LL GRIND YOUR LITTLE BONES TO DUST.
I BELIEVE YOU.
THOOOM

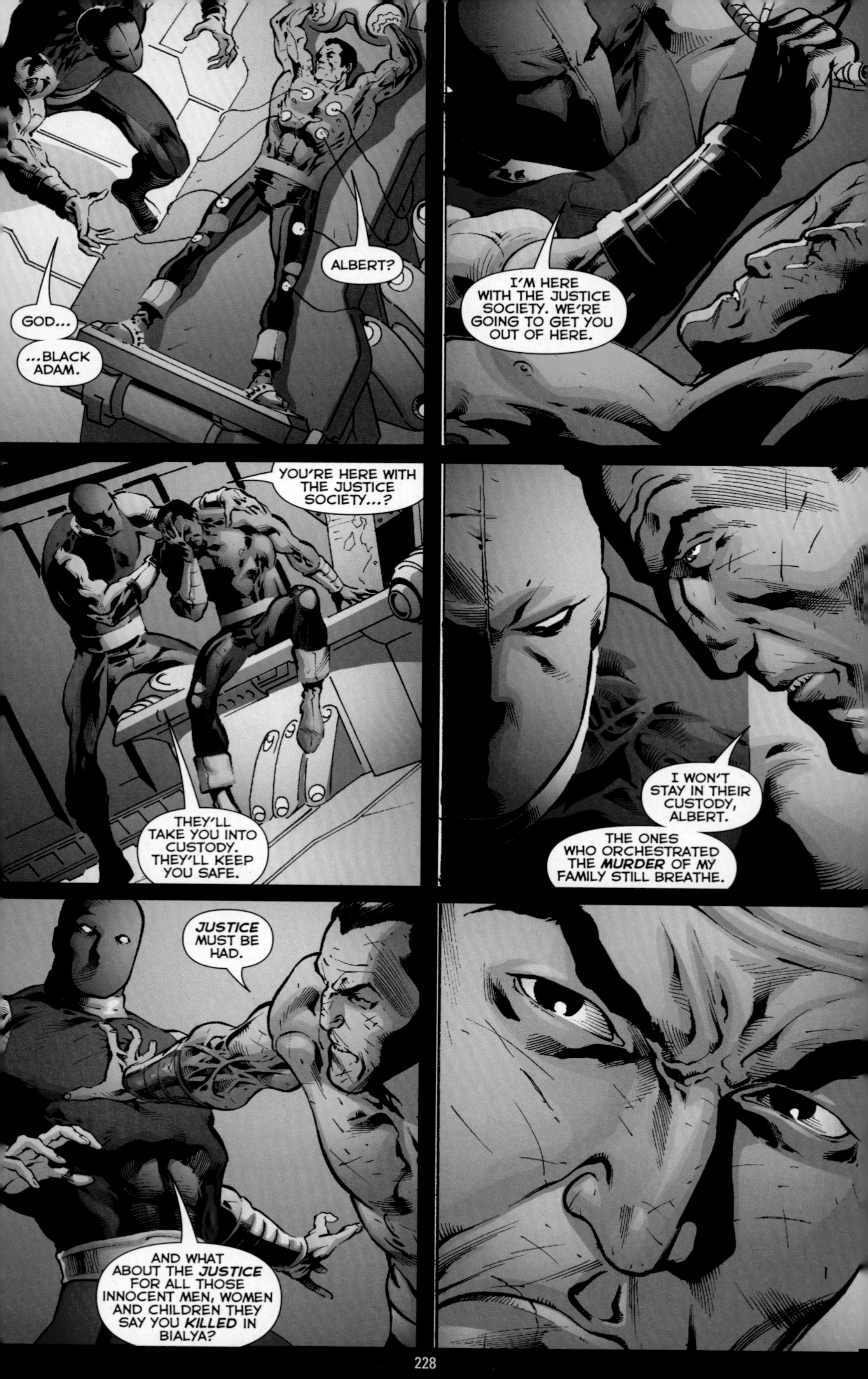

ALBERT?
GOD...
...BLACK ADAM.
I'M HERE WITH THE JUSTICE SOCIETY. WE'RE GOING TO GET YOU OUT OF HERE.
YOU'RE HERE WITH THE JUSTICE SOCIETY...?
THEY'LL TAKE YOU INTO CUSTODY. THEY'LL KEEP YOU SAFE.
I WON'T STAY IN THEIR CUSTODY, ALBERT.
THE ONES WHO ORCHESTRATED THE MURDER OF MY FAMILY STILL BREATHE.
JUSTICE MUST BE HAD.
AND WHAT ABOUT THE JUSTICE FOR ALL THOSE INNOCENT MEN, WOMEN AND CHILDREN THEY SAY YOU KILLED IN BIALYA?

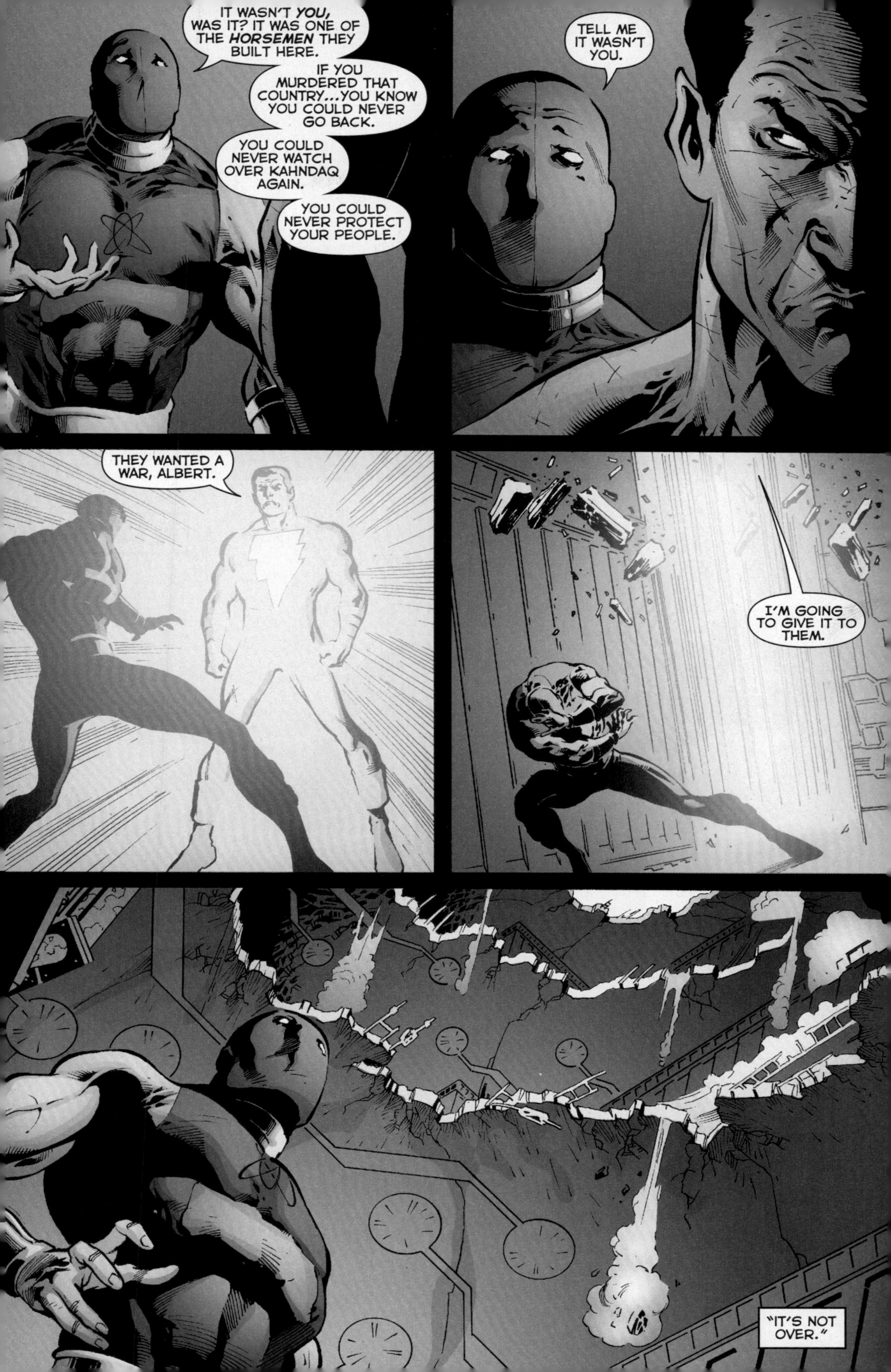
IT WASN'T *YOU*, WAS IT? IT WAS ONE OF THE *HORSEMEN* THEY BUILT HERE.
IF YOU MURDERED THAT COUNTRY...YOU KNOW YOU COULD NEVER GO BACK.
YOU COULD NEVER WATCH OVER KAHNDAQ AGAIN.
YOU COULD NEVER PROTECT YOUR PEOPLE.
TELL ME IT WASN'T YOU.
THEY WANTED A WAR, ALBERT.
I'M GOING TO GIVE IT TO THEM.
"IT'S NOT OVER."

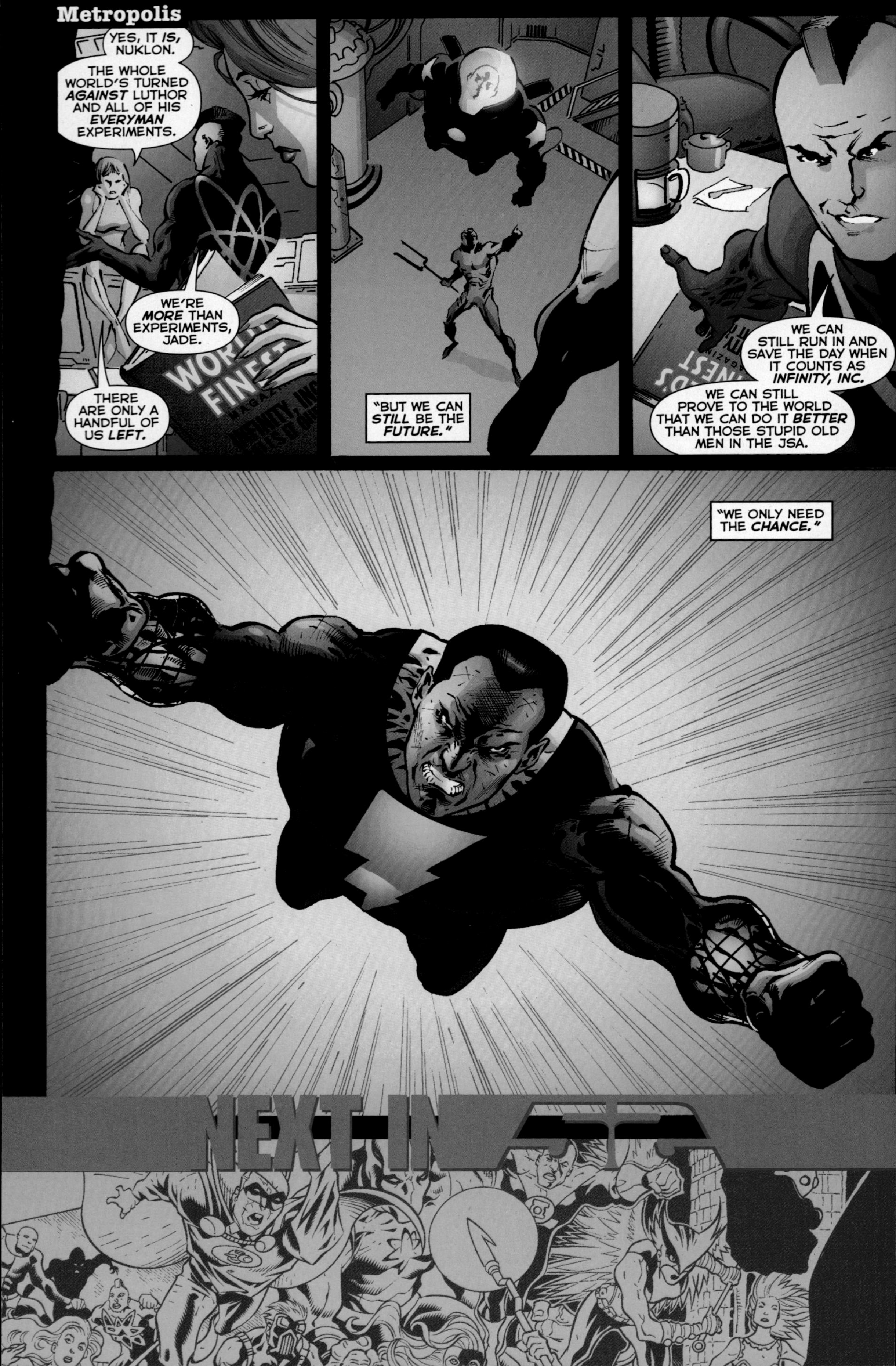
Metropolis
YES, IT *IS*, NUKLON.
THE WHOLE WORLD'S TURNED *AGAINST* LUTHOR AND ALL OF HIS *EVERYMAN* EXPERIMENTS.
WE'RE *MORE* THAN EXPERIMENTS, JADE.
THERE ARE ONLY A HANDFUL OF US *LEFT*.
"BUT WE CAN *STILL* BE THE *FUTURE*."
WE CAN STILL RUN IN AND SAVE THE DAY WHEN IT COUNTS AS *INFINITY, INC.*
WE CAN STILL PROVE TO THE WORLD THAT WE CAN DO IT *BETTER* THAN THOSE STUPID OLD MEN IN THE JSA.
"WE ONLY NEED THE *CHANCE*."
NEXT IN JSA

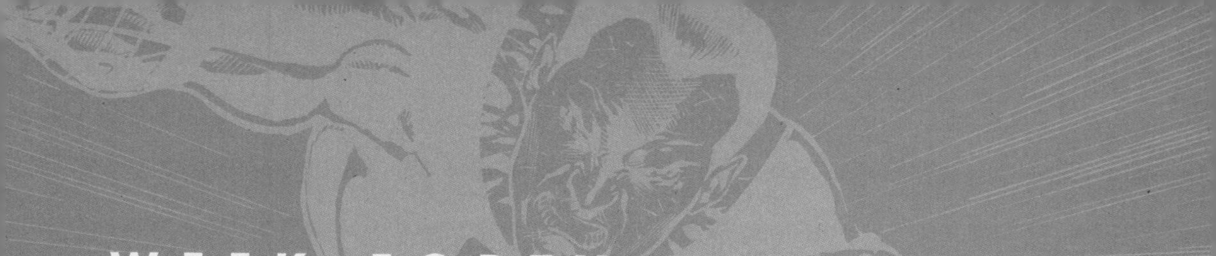

KEITH GIFFEN

The visual gaff that drove me crazy.

If you look, you'll see that the Great Wall of China, the Great Ten's HQ site, keeps cropping up in the background even though everyone's supposed to be on Oolong Island. I want to blame myself for the mixup but I'm pretty sure I broke the scene down with Oolong Island backdrops. The odd thing is...no one commented on it, not to me.

This leads me to believe that I may have tried playing a visual trick or two that didn't play out. I know you're asking yourselves, "why not just check your layouts and find out?" Because I don't have them, that's why. Once finished with an issue, I'd stack up the layouts until the pile became intrusive, then FedEx the lot to DC for scanning and posting on the "52" web site. And before you ask, yes, I am too lazy to call up the site and do a visual check.

I guess I should comment on the return of the (mini) Metal Men, but the characters have never placed very high on my favorite characters list so let's move on to Egg Fu.

Fried, scrambled or poached? As it turned out, fried. I can't help but think that had he still had his prehensile moustache, things would have turned out different.

49 issues in and charging for the finish line. We were going to do it. We were going to produce a weekly comic book, set in real time, and hit all the marks. No delays, no skipped weeks, no sadly inadequate excuses for failing to deliver as promised. That felt soooo good.

Since this is the last you'll be hearing from me in these collected editions, I'd like to thank Geoff, Greg, Grant and Mark for keeping things interesting and fun, J.G. for making us look better than we'd thought possible, the various contributing artists (with special nods to our anchor crew; Bennett, Batista, Barrows and Olliffe) for coming through under grueling conditions, Wacker and Siglain for knowing when to step back and, more important, when to step in, Dan DiDio for...let me get back to you on that one, and anyone else who sweated bullets to make "52" a reality.

It was fun. Root canal fun but hey, you take what you can get.

MIKE SIGLAIN

The Great Wall of China on Oolong Island? Really? Nonsense! Um... These aren't the droids you're looking for. Move along, move along...

Oh, all right. Here's the story behind the gaff: As the readers know by now, the Great Ten are based out of China, and the Great Wall is clearly visible from their headquarters. The readers also know that issue took place on Oolong Island, featuring many members of the Great Ten. But, what the readers didn't know was that when it came time for the artist to draw this issue, he confused the two and mistakenly put the wall on Oolong Island AND in China. Now, the wall is big, but it's not that big, but due to ridiculous time constraints (has anyone mentioned that this book was a weekly?), we did not have the time to correct the pages. At the time, no one seemed to notice. Except, of course, for Keith. Thanks, buddy.

This issue also had my favorite 52 cover of the bunch: Will Magnus in his best James Bond pose, firing mini-Metal Men bullets with the cracked face of Egg Fu in the background. Absolutely beautiful. I had the Bond music going for weeks after that cover came in. In fact, it's still on...

(COMPARE WITH PAGE 224 OF THIS COLLECTION)

52 WEEK FORTY-NINE — PAGE 15

PANEL ONE
Will is in foreground breaking the teleporter control. In background, RIGORO MORTIS (52 issue 23) is pointing at Will's back from the doorway, yelping angrily. Dominating the background behind Mortis is the huge figure of Egg Fu appearing in the frame of the doorway. He's lurching forward, dragging two ruined legs. His guns are smoldering, his cracked face snarling. It's like a nightmare.

   MORTIS: He's HERE! He disabled the shields and now he's trying to escape in the OMNIBOT!

   EGG FU (large): MAGNUSSSS!

PANEL TWO
Calmly, Will lifts his hand up in front of his face with the finger tube. His eyes are steady. He's looking directly at us. His right arm is extended also with the particle ray gun, which he's aiming at Mortis off panel

   WILL: Drop the gun, Professor Mortis. And YOU--

PANEL THREE
Nice shot of Egg Fu lifting his wrist guns, aiming directly at us. He's tilted, unsteady on four legs. Smoke rises from the broken limbs. Egg Fu's eyes blaze red. His face is a mask of hate, scorched and pitted.

   EGG FU: You only have one weapon. And you are no match for the great Chang Tzu.

PANEL FOUR
Will aims the finger tube at us, averting his head from the blast as a bullet-sized version of LEAD of the METAL MEN comes hurtling into closeup foreground like a speeding bullet. Lead's arms at his side, head lowered, shoulders brace for impact.

   WILL: I have a BULLET. GO GET HIM, LEAD!

PANEL FIVE
The little Lead bullet fires from Will's hand, hits Egg Fu above the eyebrow and comes out the other end in an explosion of eggshell and goo and machine parts.

PANEL SIX
Doc calmly walks forward, aiming his ray gun at Mortis' head. Mortis has his own weapon at the ready, but his shoulders are slumping and his knees are giving out as he loses his nerve in the face of true madness. Other mad scientists and guards should start to fill the background as they arrive on the scene

   Doc: Drop it. I have a PARTICLE WAVE RAY GUN and BIPOLAR DISORDER! I have no idea WHAT it might do to you if I pull the trigger.

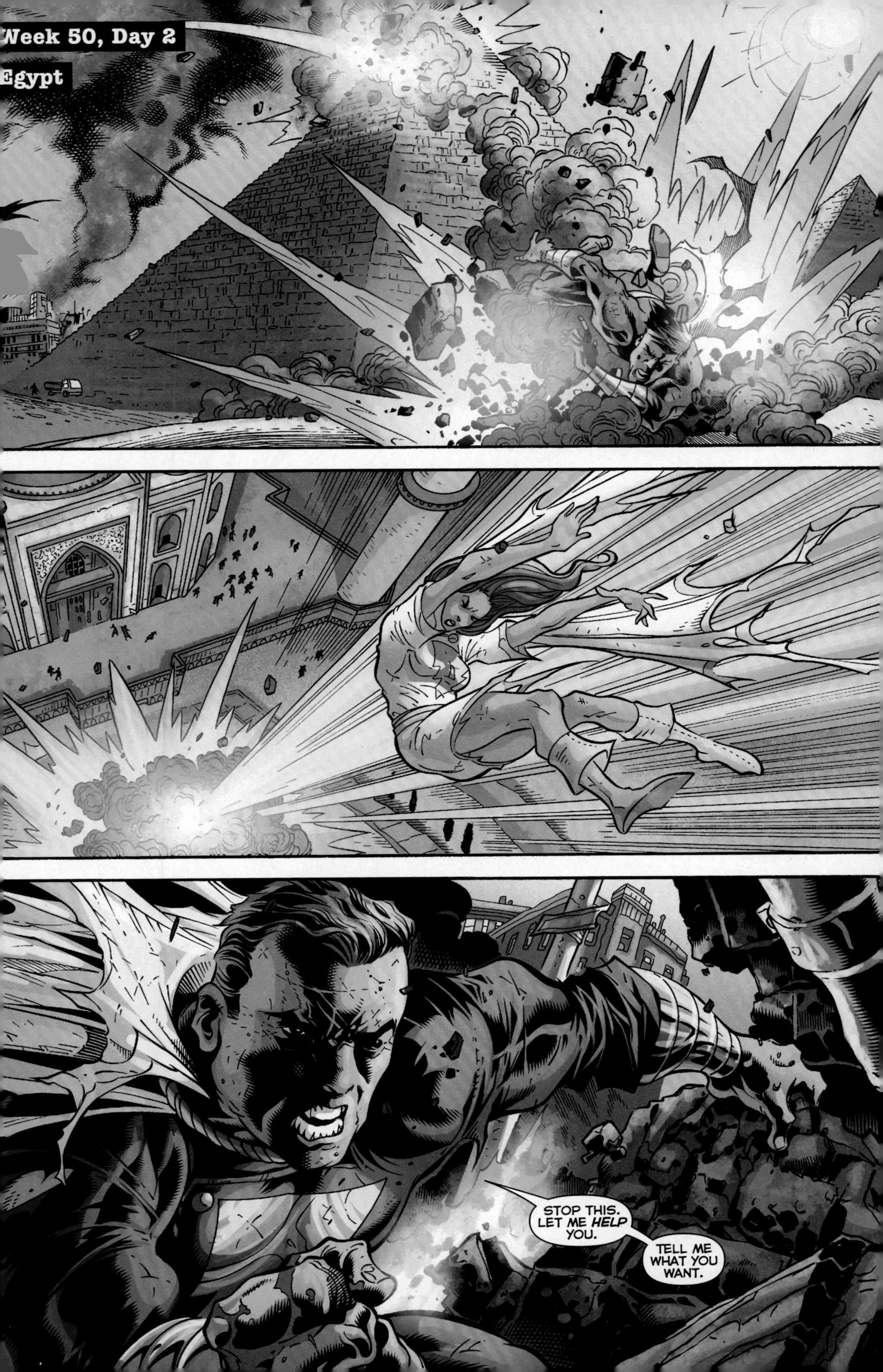
Week 50, Day 2
Egypt
STOP THIS. LET ME HELP YOU.
TELL ME WHAT YOU WANT.

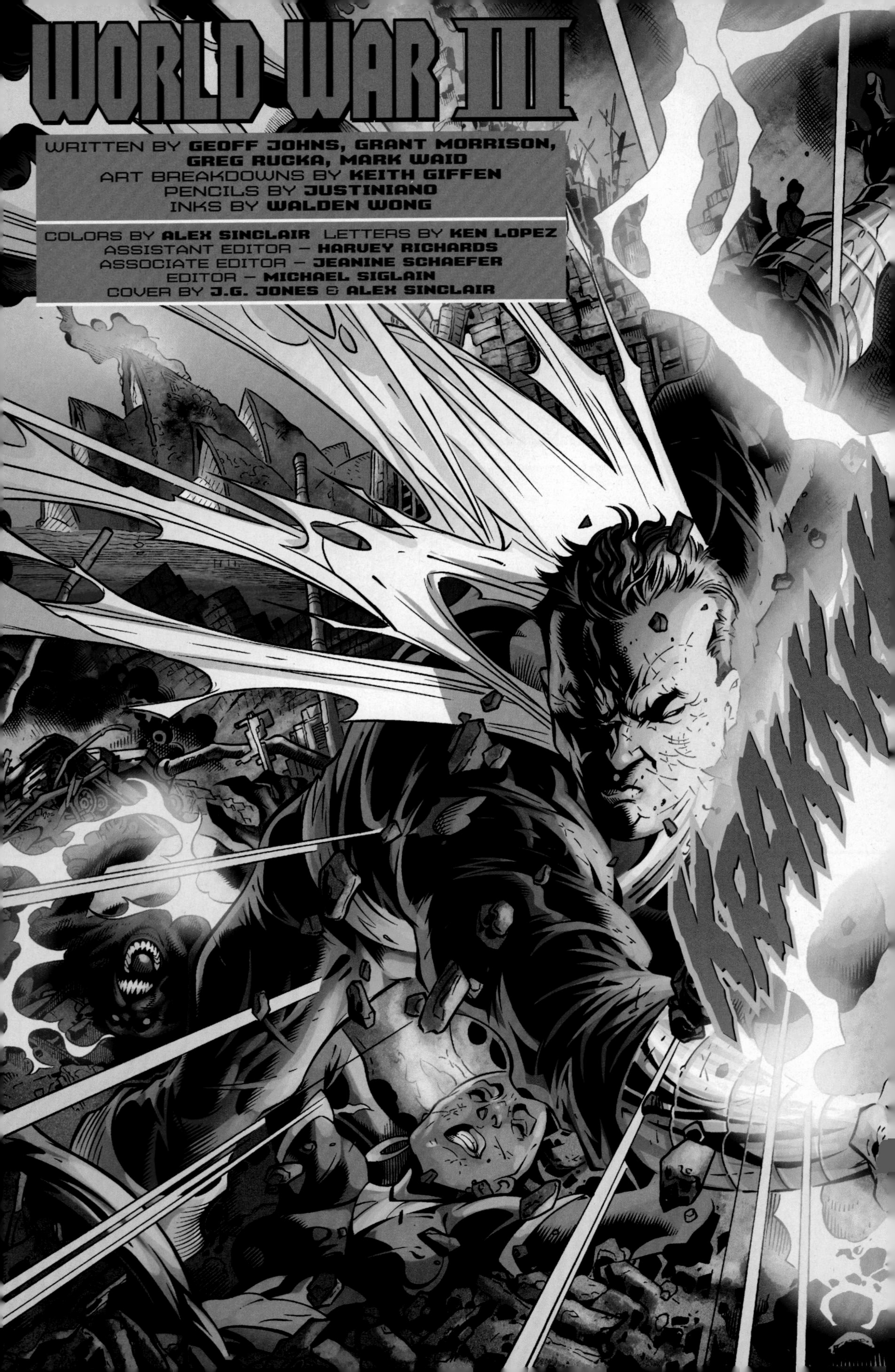
WORLD WAR III
WRITTEN BY GEOFF JOHNS, GRANT MORRISON, GREG RUCKA, MARK WAID
ART BREAKDOWNS BY KEITH GIFFEN
PENCILS BY JUSTINIANO
INKS BY WALDEN WONG
COLORS BY ALEX SINCLAIR LETTERS BY KEN LOPEZ
ASSISTANT EDITOR – HARVEY RICHARDS
ASSOCIATE EDITOR – JEANINE SCHAEFER
EDITOR – MICHAEL SIGLAIN
COVER BY J.G. JONES & ALEX SINCLAIR

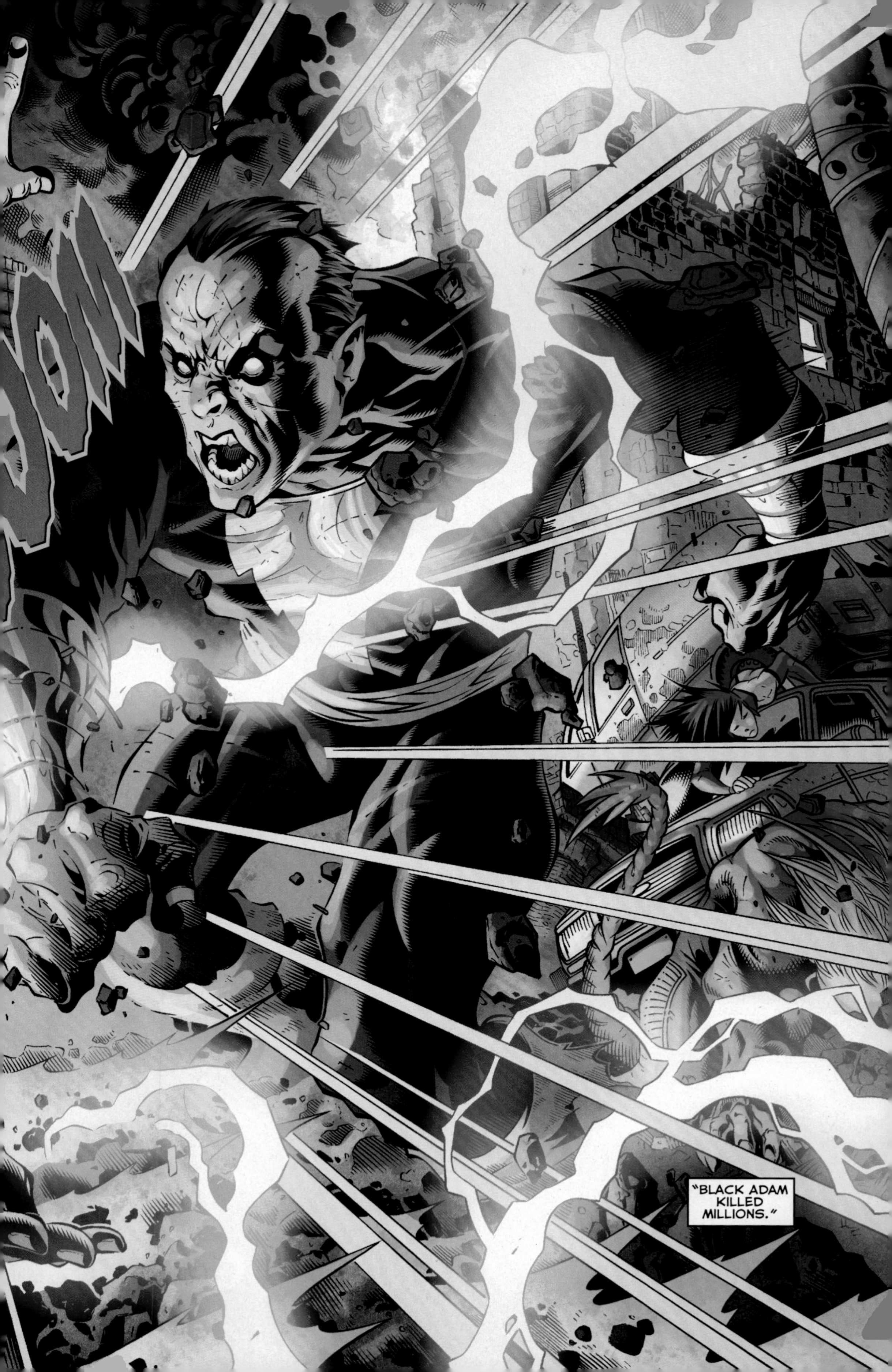
"BLACK ADAM KILLED MILLIONS."

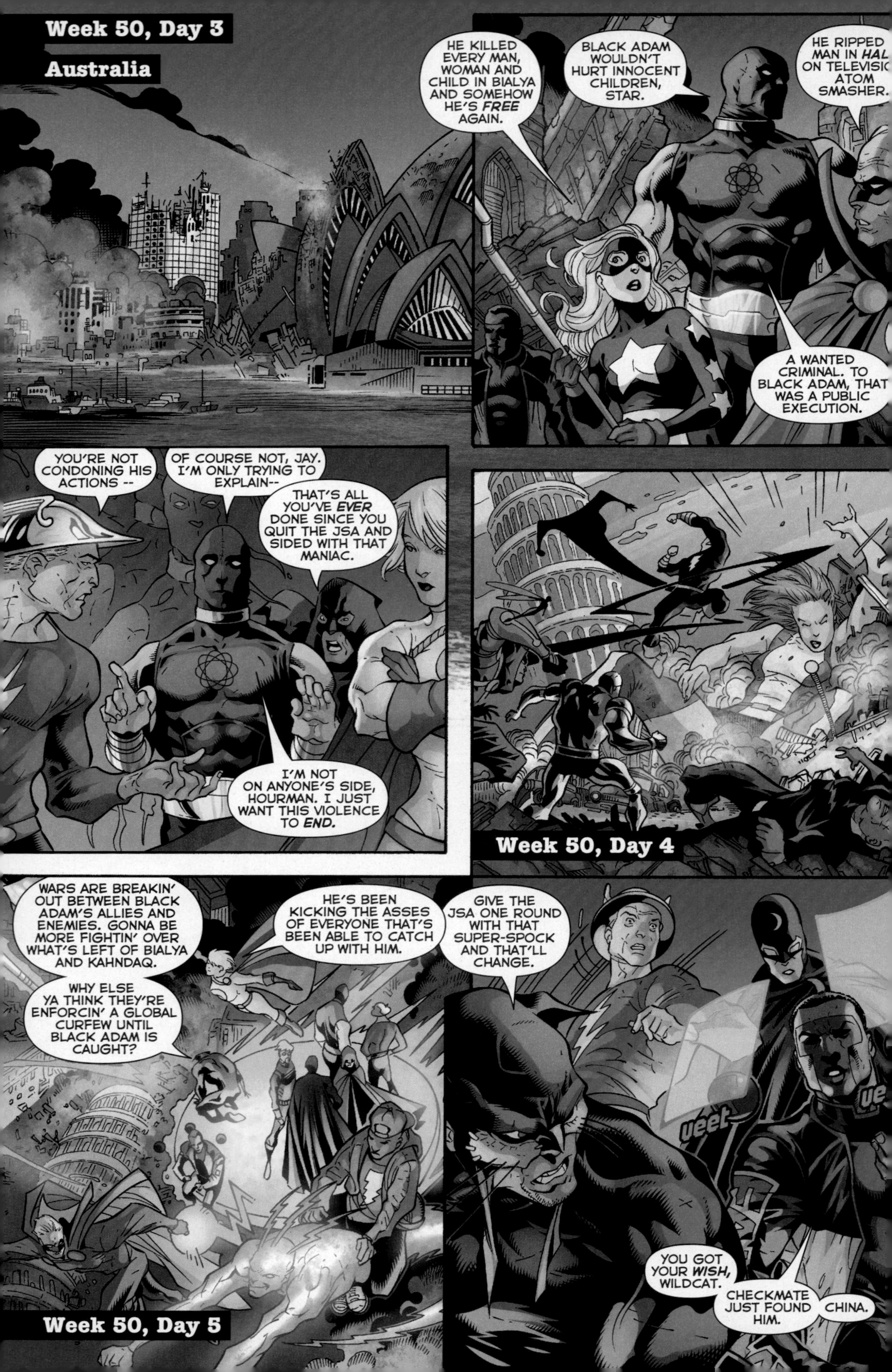

Week 50, Day 3
Australia
HE KILLED EVERY MAN, WOMAN AND CHILD IN BIALYA AND SOMEHOW HE'S *FREE* AGAIN.
BLACK ADAM WOULDN'T HURT INNOCENT CHILDREN, STAR.
HE RIPPED MAN IN *HAL* ON TELEVISIO ATOM SMASHER.
A WANTED CRIMINAL. TO BLACK ADAM, THAT WAS A PUBLIC EXECUTION.
YOU'RE NOT CONDONING HIS ACTIONS --
OF COURSE NOT, JAY. I'M ONLY TRYING TO EXPLAIN--
THAT'S ALL YOU'VE *EVER* DONE SINCE YOU QUIT THE JSA AND SIDED WITH THAT MANIAC.
I'M NOT ON ANYONE'S SIDE, HOURMAN. I JUST WANT THIS VIOLENCE TO *END.*
Week 50, Day 4
WARS ARE BREAKIN' OUT BETWEEN BLACK ADAM'S ALLIES AND ENEMIES. GONNA BE MORE FIGHTIN' OVER WHAT'S LEFT OF BIALYA AND KAHNDAQ.
WHY ELSE YA THINK THEY'RE ENFORCIN' A GLOBAL CURFEW UNTIL BLACK ADAM IS CAUGHT?
HE'S BEEN KICKING THE ASSES OF EVERYONE THAT'S BEEN ABLE TO CATCH UP WITH HIM.
Week 50, Day 5
GIVE THE JSA ONE ROUND WITH THAT SUPER-SPOCK AND THAT'LL CHANGE.
ueet
ueet
YOU GOT YOUR *WISH*, WILDCAT.
CHECKMATE JUST FOUND HIM.
CHINA.

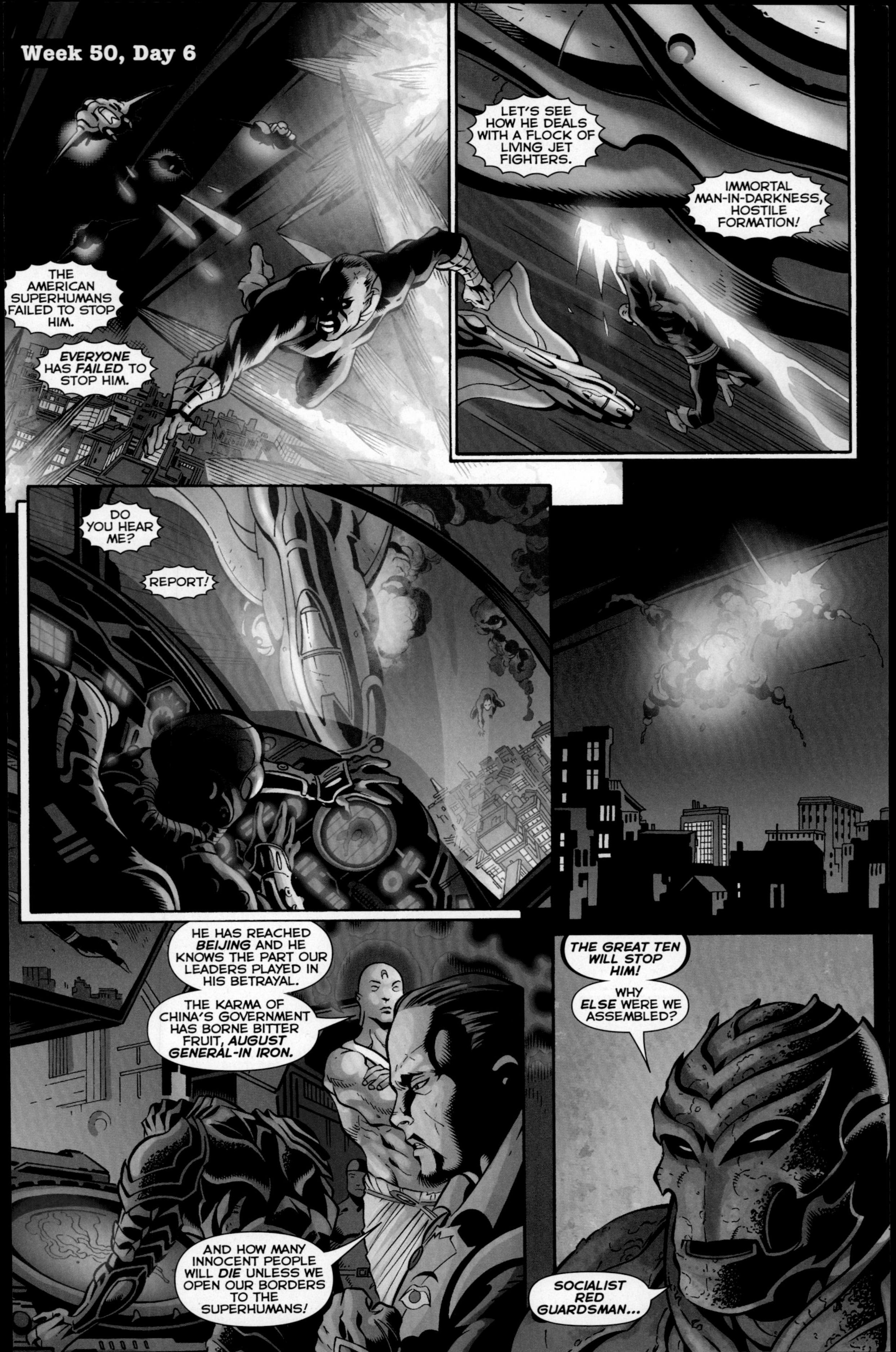
Week 50, Day 6
THE AMERICAN SUPERHUMANS FAILED TO STOP HIM.
EVERYONE HAS FAILED TO STOP HIM.
LET'S SEE HOW HE DEALS WITH A FLOCK OF LIVING JET FIGHTERS.
IMMORTAL MAN-IN-DARKNESS, HOSTILE FORMATION!
DO YOU HEAR ME?
REPORT!
HE HAS REACHED BEIJING AND HE KNOWS THE PART OUR LEADERS PLAYED IN HIS BETRAYAL.
THE KARMA OF CHINA'S GOVERNMENT HAS BORNE BITTER FRUIT, AUGUST GENERAL-IN IRON.
AND HOW MANY INNOCENT PEOPLE WILL DIE UNLESS WE OPEN OUR BORDERS TO THE SUPERHUMANS!
THE GREAT TEN WILL STOP HIM!
WHY ELSE WERE WE ASSEMBLED?
SOCIALIST RED GUARDSMAN...

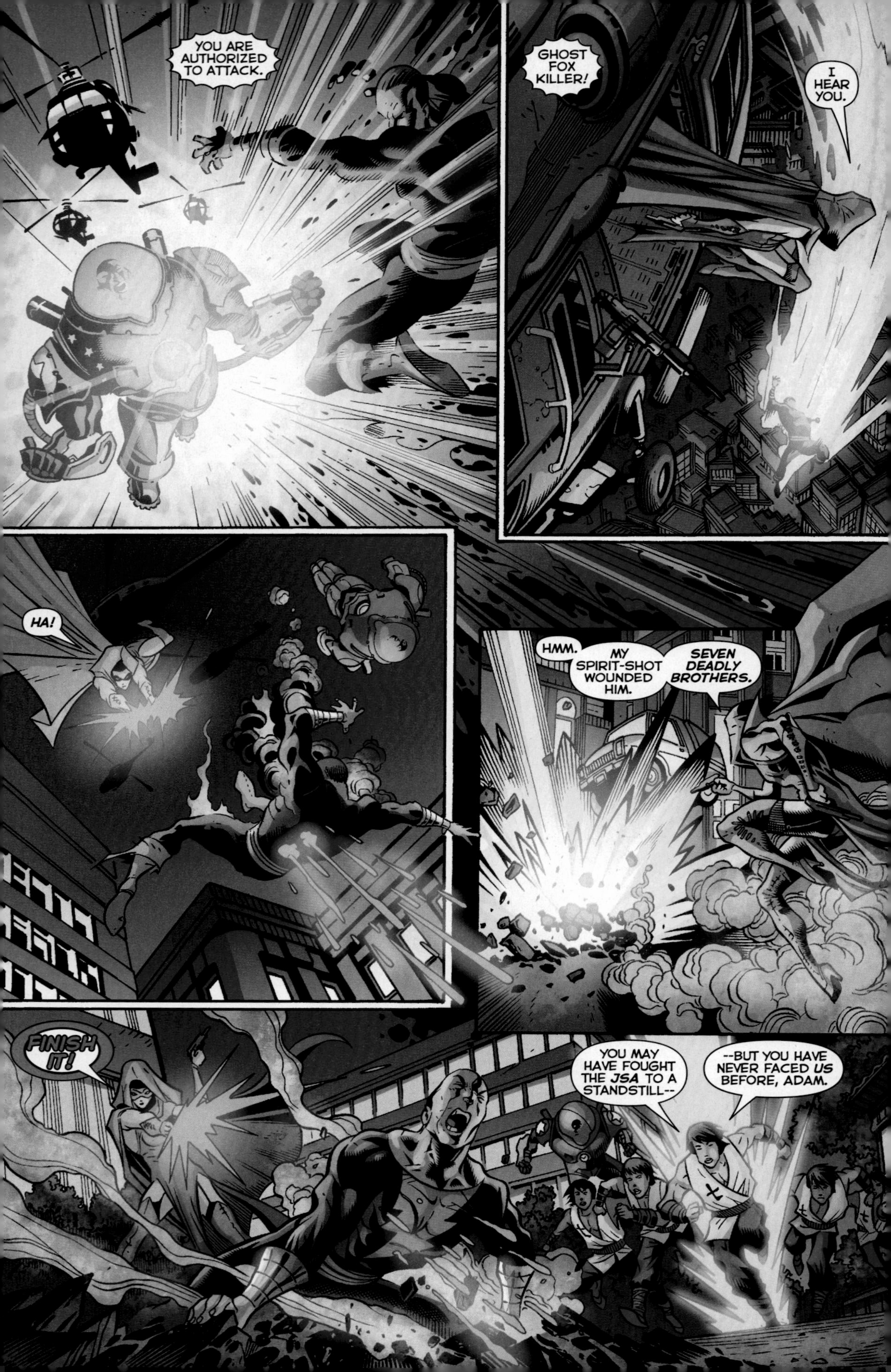

YOU ARE AUTHORIZED TO ATTACK.
GHOST FOX KILLER!
I HEAR YOU.
HA!
HMM.
MY SPIRIT-SHOT WOUNDED HIM.
SEVEN DEADLY BROTHERS.
FINISH IT!
YOU MAY HAVE FOUGHT THE JSA TO A STANDSTILL--
--BUT YOU HAVE NEVER FACED US BEFORE, ADAM.

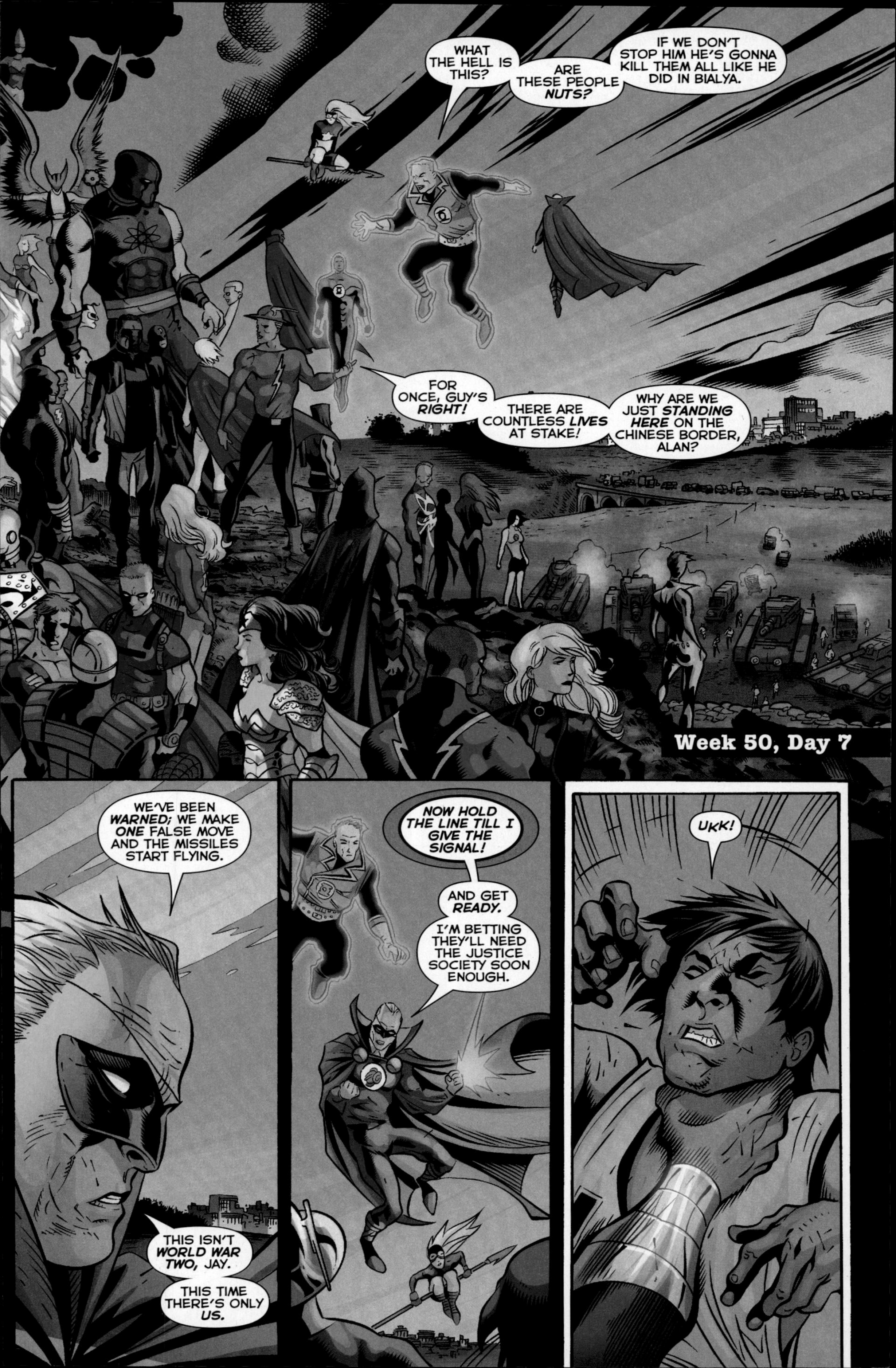

WHAT THE HELL IS THIS?
ARE THESE PEOPLE NUTS?
IF WE DON'T STOP HIM HE'S GONNA KILL THEM ALL LIKE HE DID IN BIALYA.
FOR ONCE, GUY'S RIGHT!
THERE ARE COUNTLESS LIVES AT STAKE!
WHY ARE WE JUST STANDING HERE ON THE CHINESE BORDER, ALAN?
Week 50, Day 7
WE'VE BEEN WARNED; WE MAKE ONE FALSE MOVE AND THE MISSILES START FLYING.
THIS ISN'T WORLD WAR TWO, JAY.
THIS TIME THERE'S ONLY US.
NOW HOLD THE LINE TILL I GIVE THE SIGNAL!
AND GET READY.
I'M BETTING THEY'LL NEED THE JUSTICE SOCIETY SOON ENOUGH.
UKK!

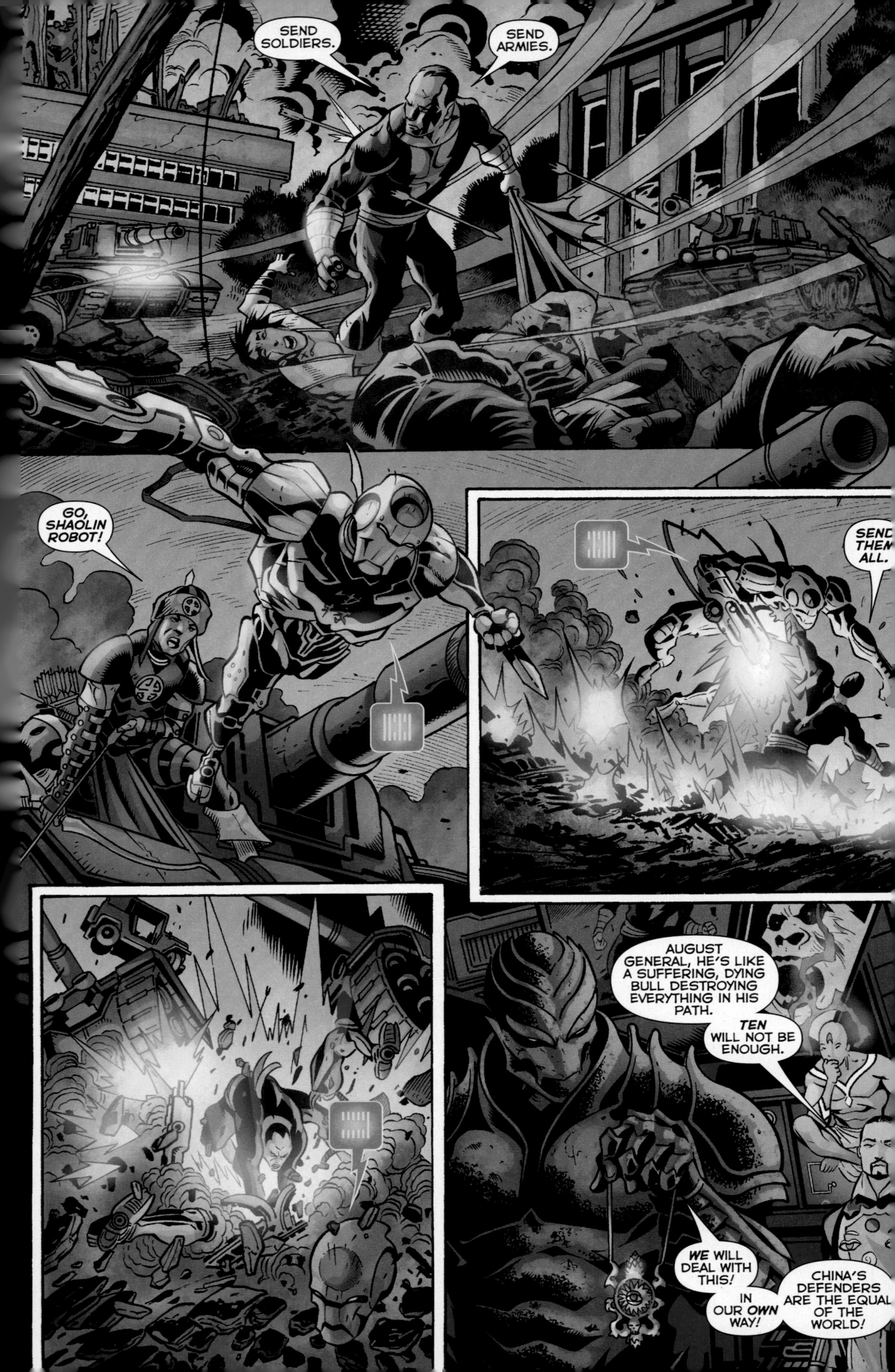
SEND SOLDIERS.
SEND ARMIES.
GO, SHAOLIN ROBOT!
SEND THEM ALL.
AUGUST GENERAL, HE'S LIKE A SUFFERING, DYING BULL DESTROYING EVERYTHING IN HIS PATH.
TEN WILL NOT BE ENOUGH.
WE WILL DEAL WITH THIS!
IN OUR OWN WAY!
CHINA'S DEFENDERS ARE THE EQUAL OF THE WORLD!

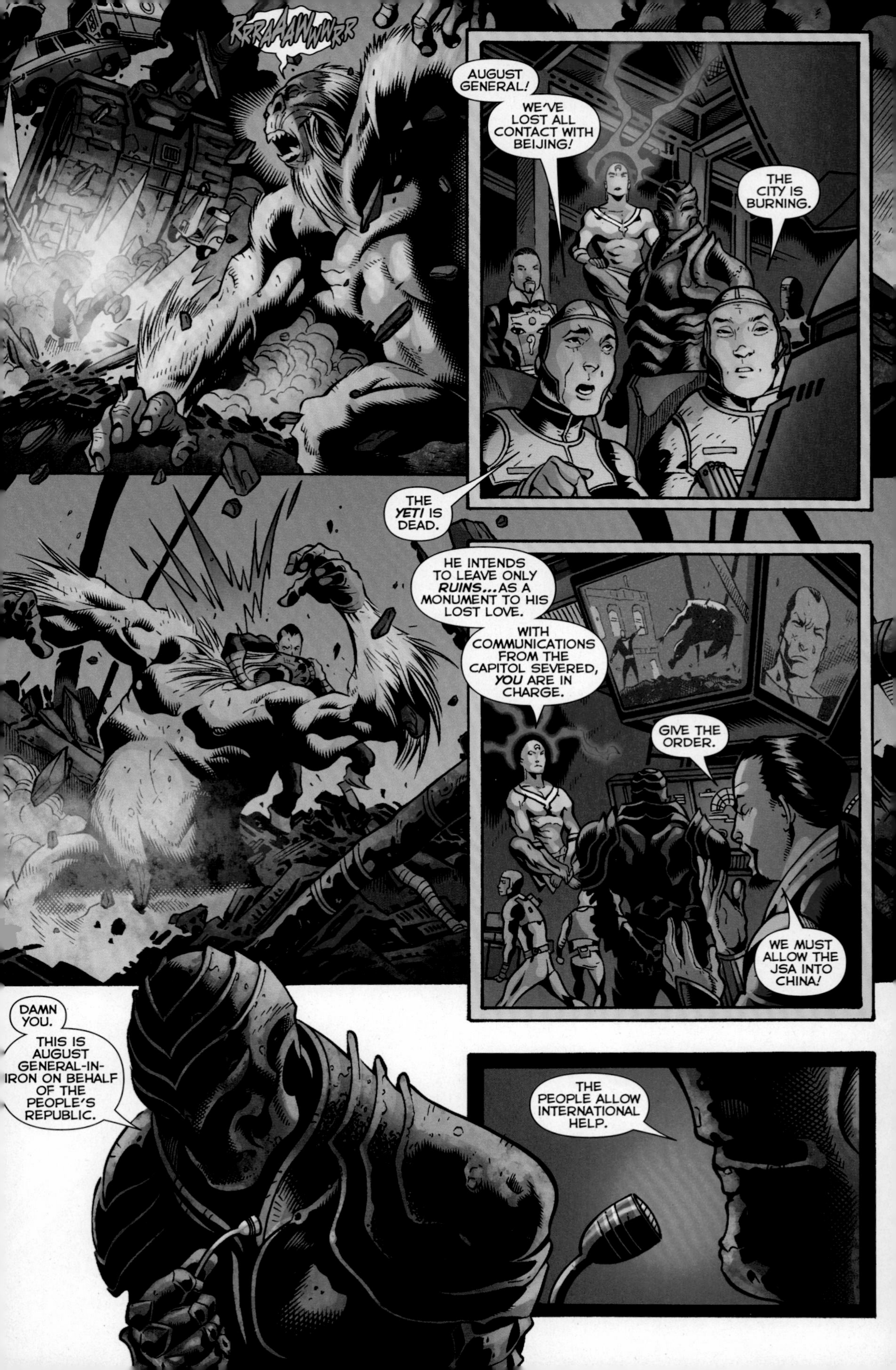
RRRAAAWWWRR
AUGUST GENERAL!
WE'VE LOST ALL CONTACT WITH BEIJING!
THE CITY IS BURNING.
THE YETI IS DEAD.
HE INTENDS TO LEAVE ONLY RUINS...AS A MONUMENT TO HIS LOST LOVE.
WITH COMMUNICATIONS FROM THE CAPITOL SEVERED, YOU ARE IN CHARGE.
GIVE THE ORDER.
WE MUST ALLOW THE JSA INTO CHINA!
DAMN YOU.
THIS IS AUGUST GENERAL-IN-IRON ON BEHALF OF THE PEOPLE'S REPUBLIC.
THE PEOPLE ALLOW INTERNATIONAL HELP.

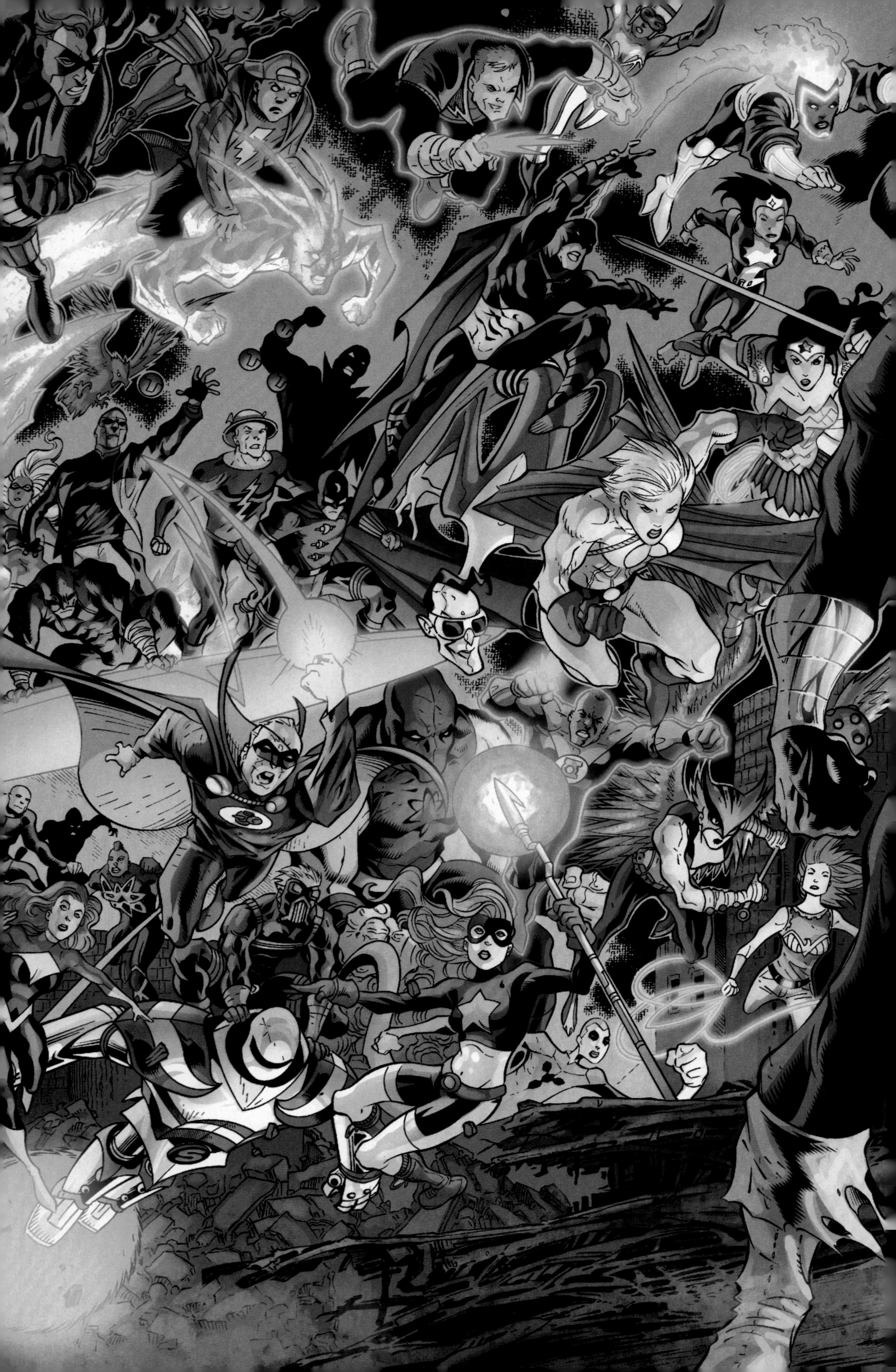

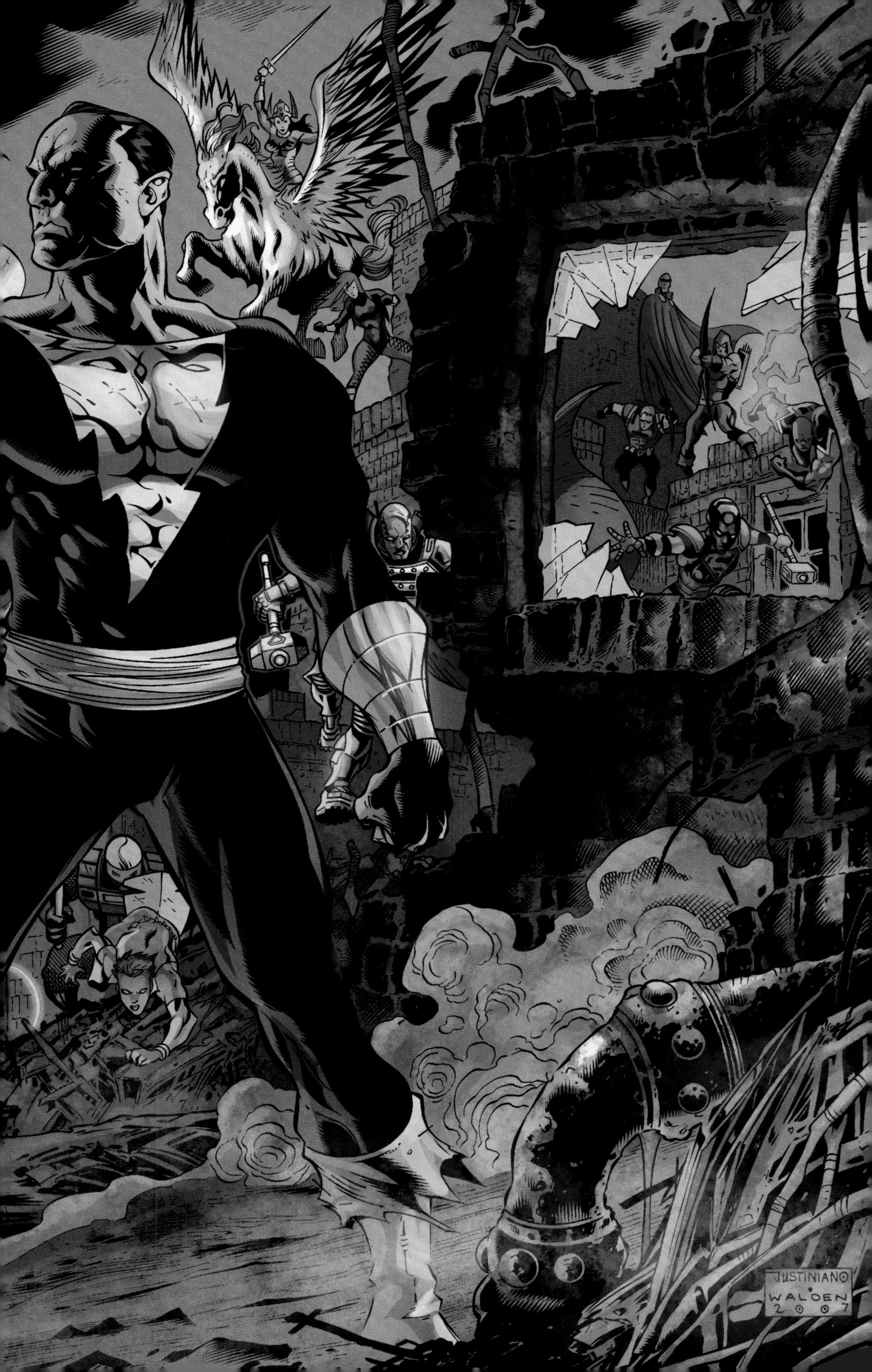
JUSTINIANO
WALDEN
2007

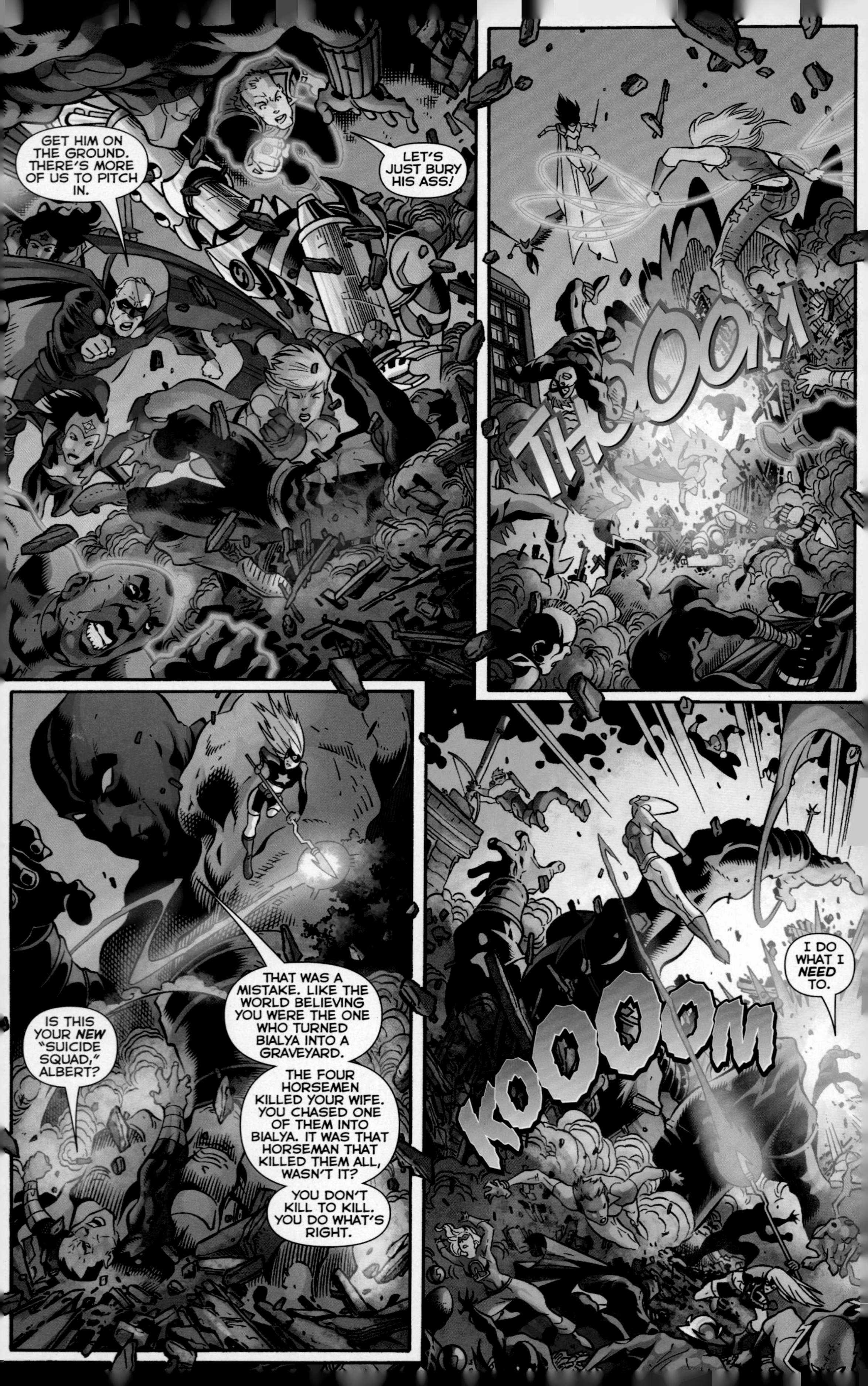
GET HIM ON THE GROUND. THERE'S MORE OF US TO PITCH IN.
LET'S JUST BURY HIS ASS!
THOOOM
IS THIS YOUR *NEW* "SUICIDE SQUAD," ALBERT?
THAT WAS A MISTAKE. LIKE THE WORLD BELIEVING YOU WERE THE ONE WHO TURNED BIALYA INTO A GRAVEYARD.
THE FOUR HORSEMEN KILLED YOUR WIFE. YOU CHASED ONE OF THEM INTO BIALYA. IT WAS THAT HORSEMAN THAT KILLED THEM ALL, WASN'T IT?
YOU DON'T KILL TO KILL. YOU DO WHAT'S RIGHT.
KOOOOOM
I DO WHAT I *NEED* TO.

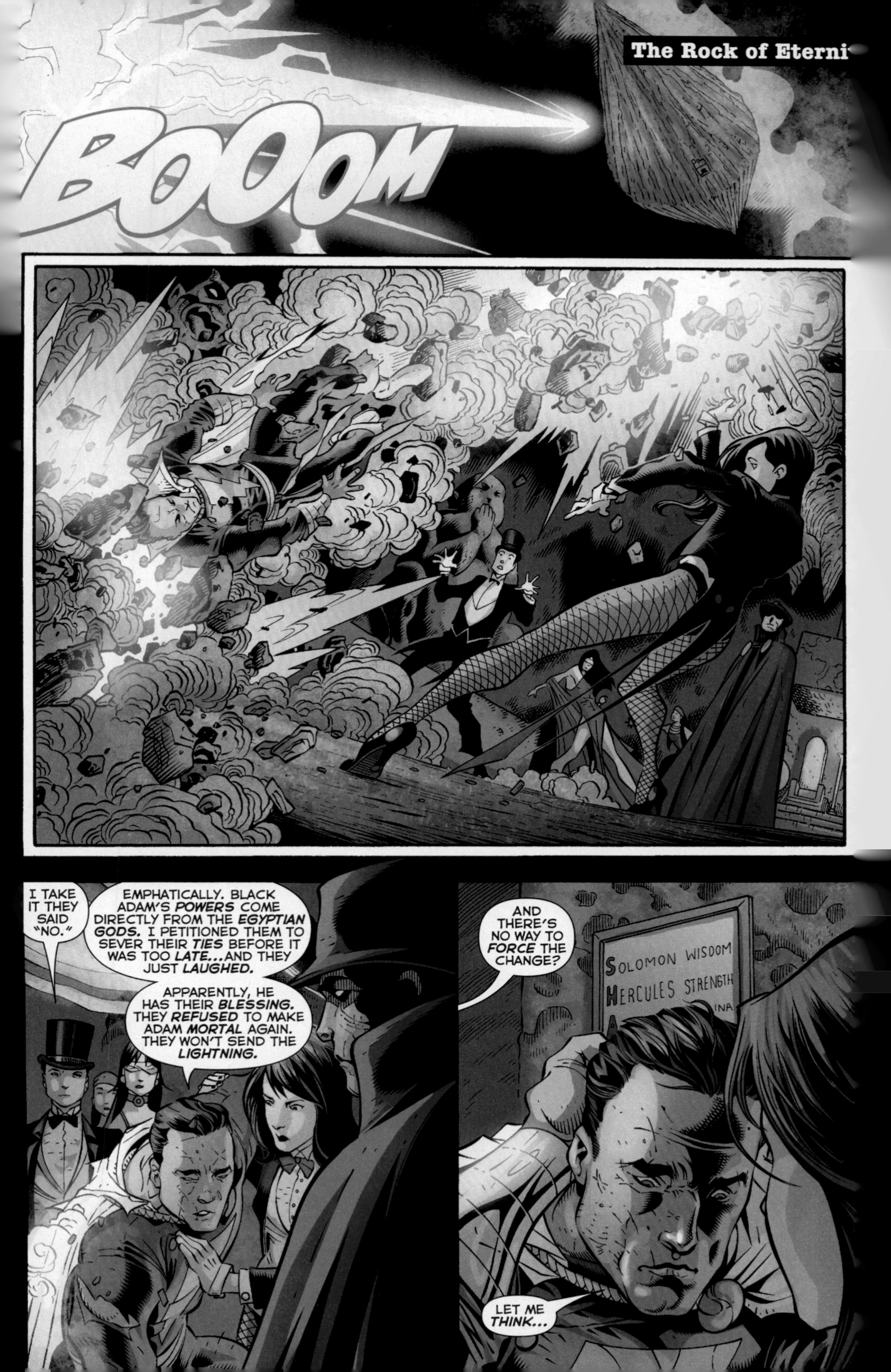
The Rock of Eterni
BOOOM
I TAKE IT THEY SAID "NO."
EMPHATICALLY. BLACK ADAM'S POWERS COME DIRECTLY FROM THE EGYPTIAN GODS. I PETITIONED THEM TO SEVER THEIR TIES BEFORE IT WAS TOO LATE...AND THEY JUST LAUGHED.
APPARENTLY, HE HAS THEIR BLESSING. THEY REFUSED TO MAKE ADAM MORTAL AGAIN. THEY WON'T SEND THE LIGHTNING.
AND THERE'S NO WAY TO FORCE THE CHANGE?
SOLOMON WISDOM
HERCULES STRENGTH
LET ME THINK...

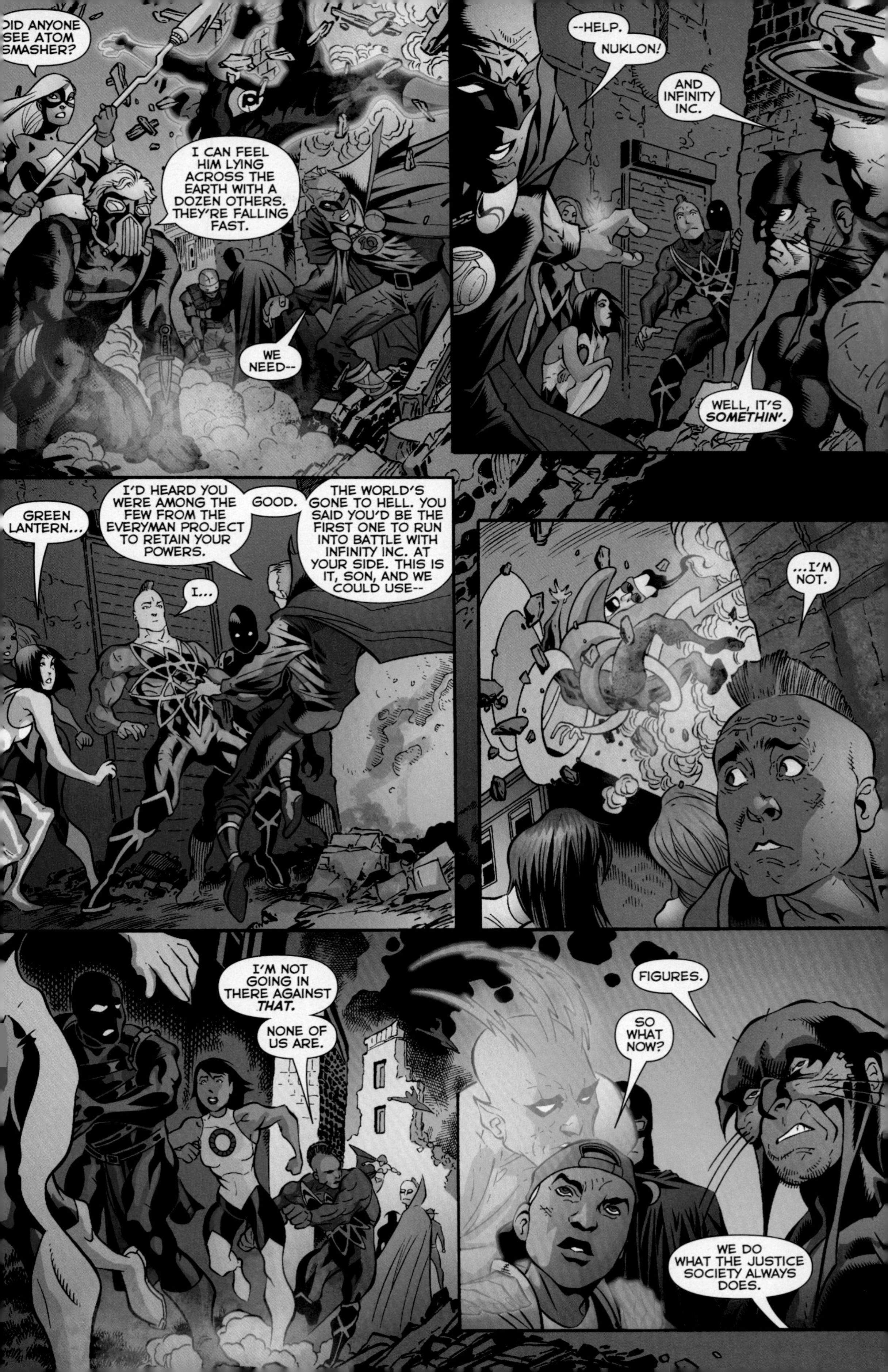
DID ANYONE SEE ATOM SMASHER?
I CAN FEEL HIM LYING ACROSS THE EARTH WITH A DOZEN OTHERS. THEY'RE FALLING FAST.
WE NEED--
--HELP.
NUKLON!
AND INFINITY INC.
WELL, IT'S SOMETHIN'.
GREEN LANTERN...
I'D HEARD YOU WERE AMONG THE FEW FROM THE EVERYMAN PROJECT TO RETAIN YOUR POWERS.
GOOD.
I...
THE WORLD'S GONE TO HELL. YOU SAID YOU'D BE THE FIRST ONE TO RUN INTO BATTLE WITH INFINITY INC. AT YOUR SIDE. THIS IS IT, SON, AND WE COULD USE--
...I'M NOT.
I'M NOT GOING IN THERE AGAINST THAT.
NONE OF US ARE.
FIGURES.
SO WHAT NOW?
WE DO WHAT THE JUSTICE SOCIETY ALWAYS DOES.

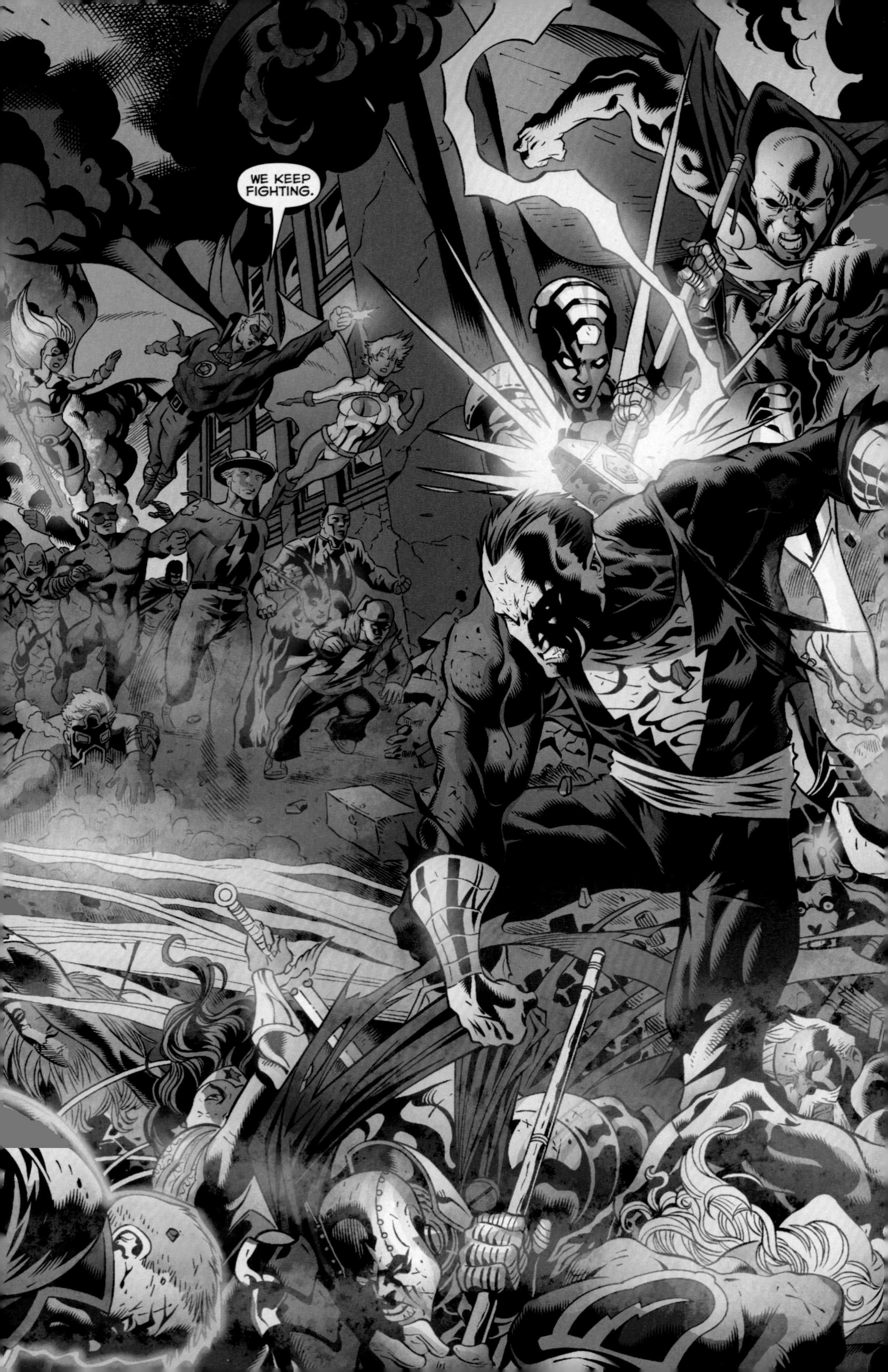
WE KEEP FIGHTING.

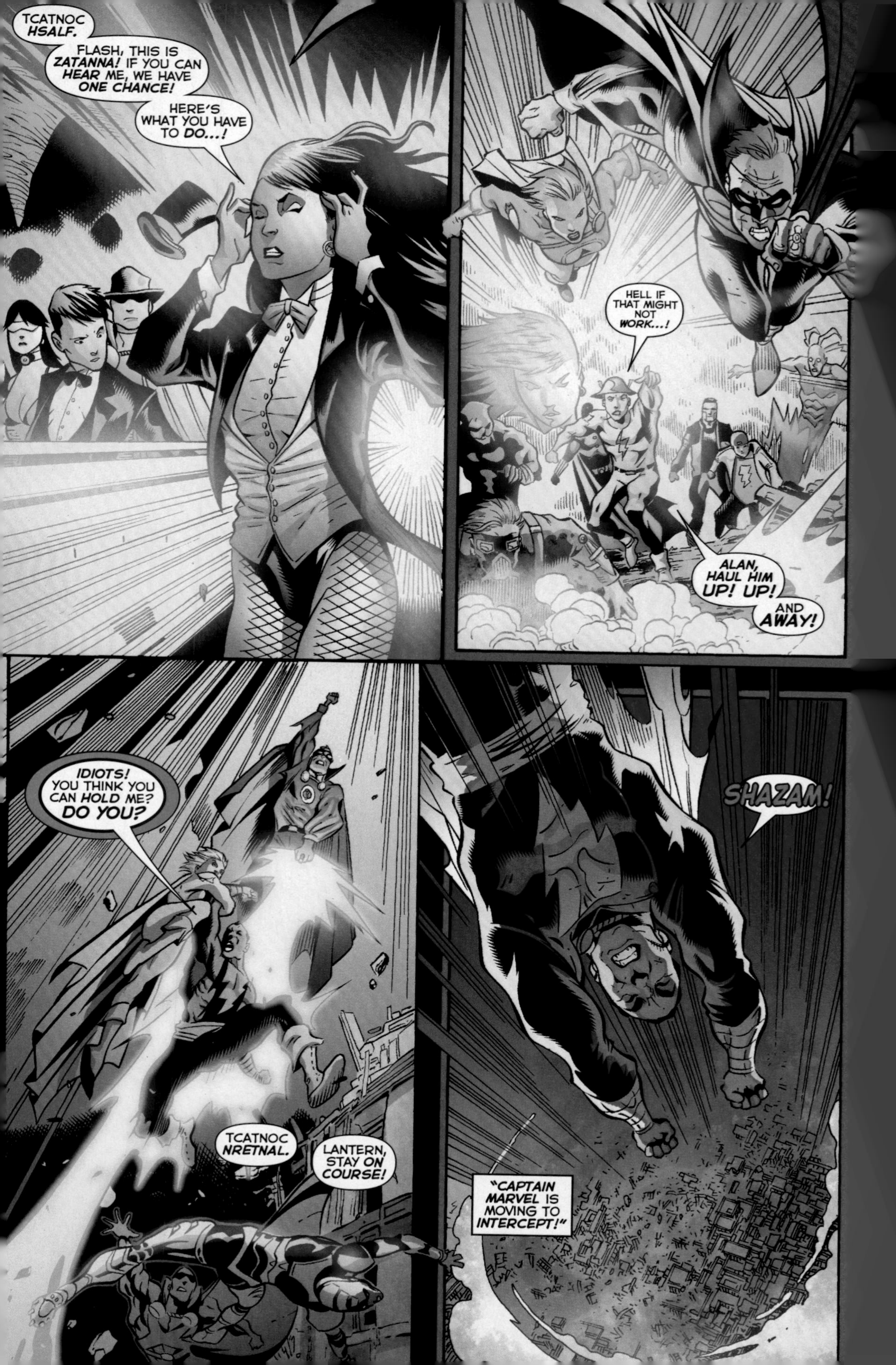

TCATNOC HSALF.
FLASH, THIS IS ZATANNA! IF YOU CAN HEAR ME, WE HAVE ONE CHANCE!
HERE'S WHAT YOU HAVE TO DO...!
HELL IF THAT MIGHT NOT WORK...!
ALAN, HAUL HIM UP! UP!
AND AWAY!
IDIOTS! YOU THINK YOU CAN HOLD ME? DO YOU?
TCATNOC NRETNAL.
LANTERN, STAY ON COURSE!
SHAZAM!
"CAPTAIN MARVEL IS MOVING TO INTERCEPT!"

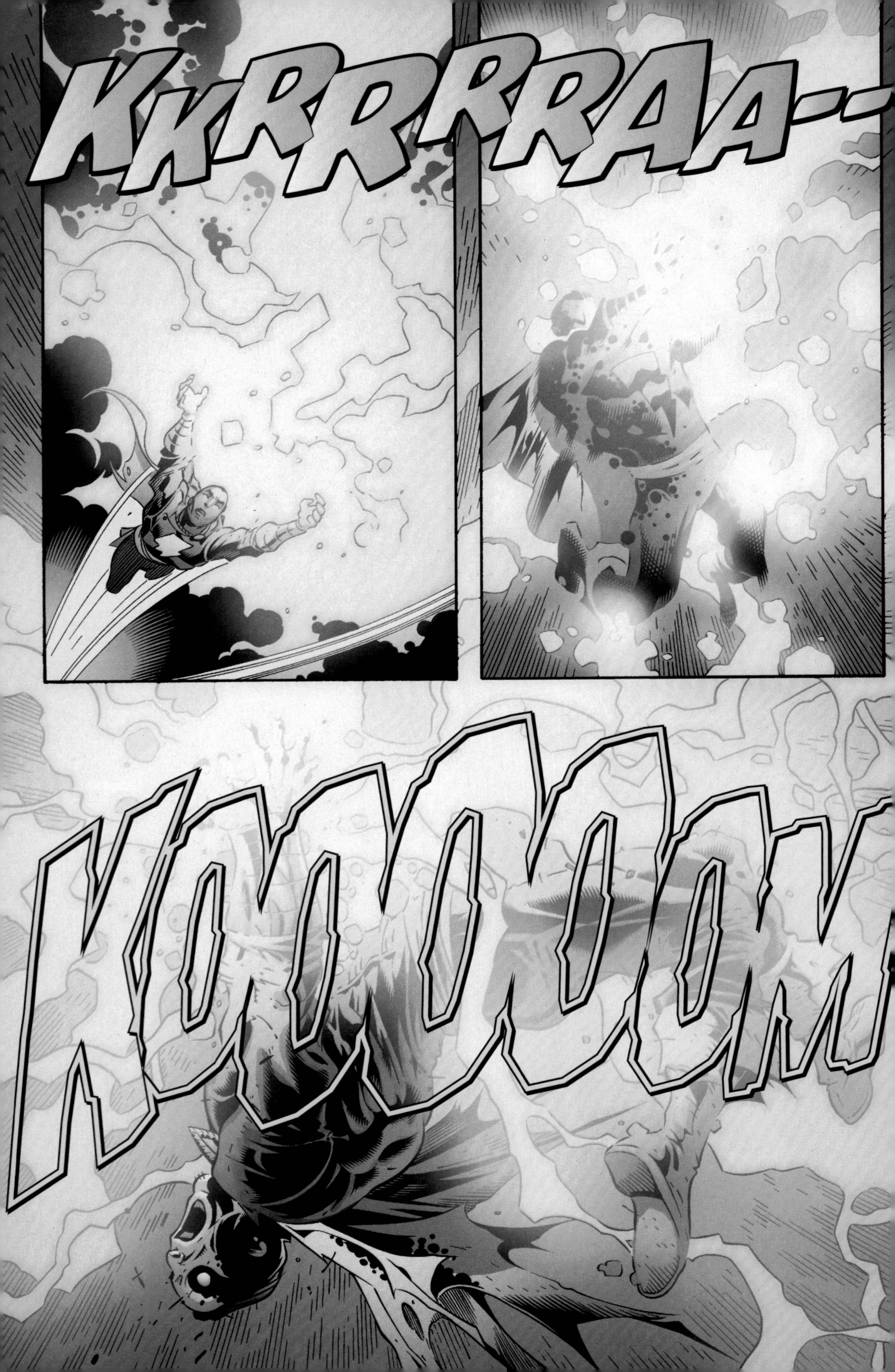
KKRRRRAA--
KOOOOOM

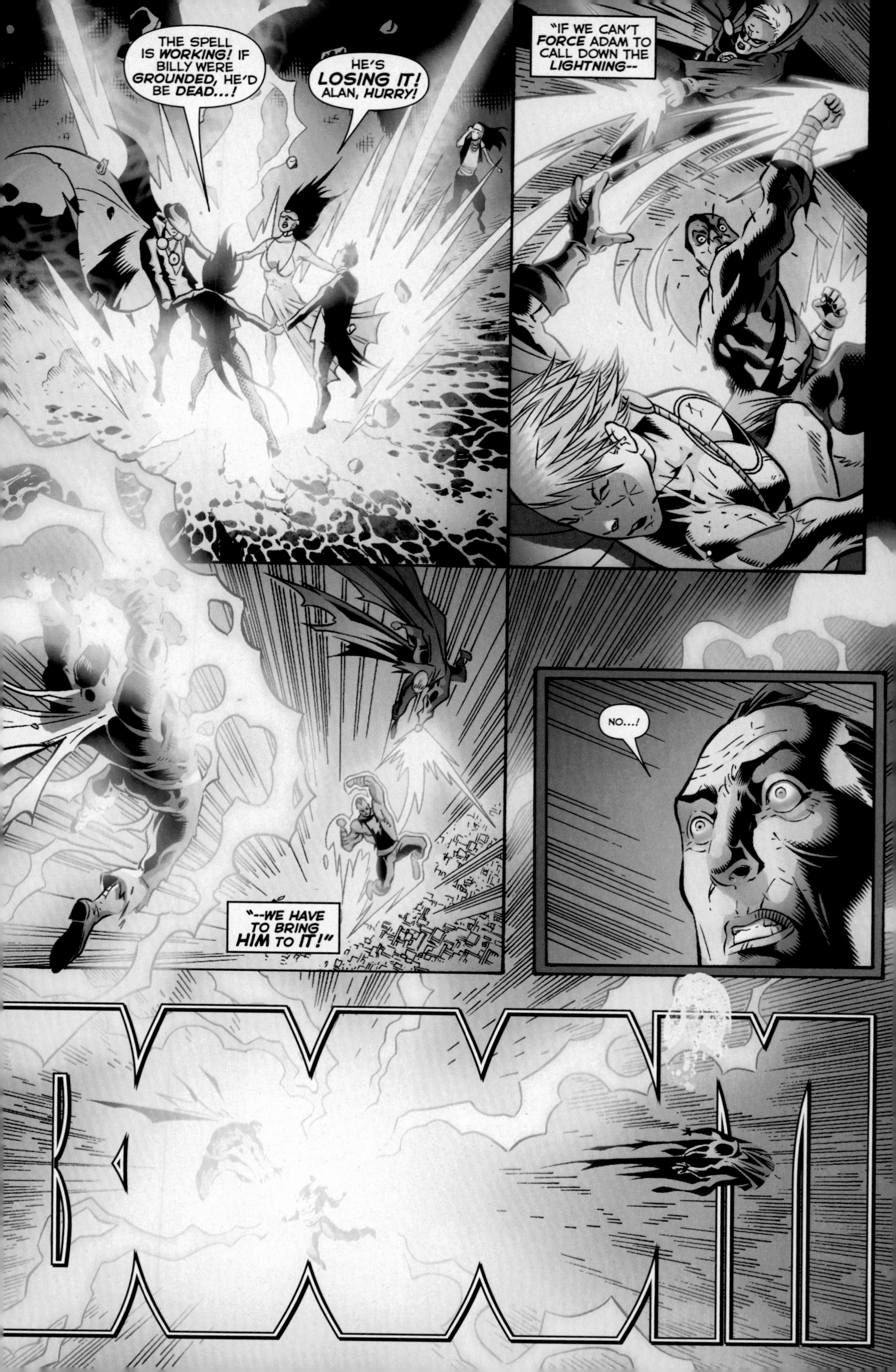
THE SPELL IS WORKING! IF BILLY WERE GROUNDED, HE'D BE DEAD...!
HE'S LOSING IT! ALAN, HURRY!
"IF WE CAN'T FORCE ADAM TO CALL DOWN THE LIGHTNING--
"--WE HAVE TO BRING HIM TO IT!"
NO...!
BWAM

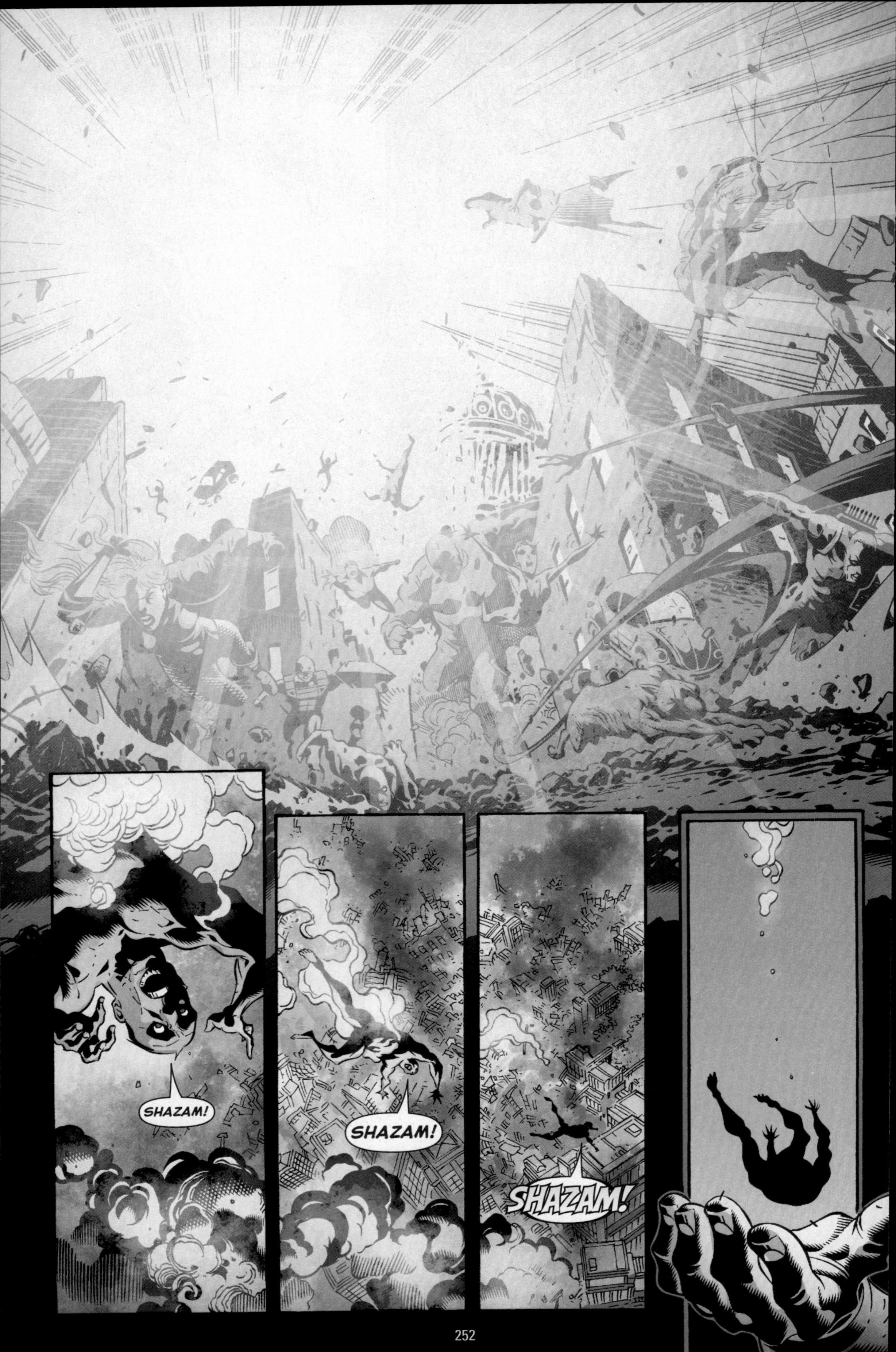
SHAZAM!
SHAZAM!
SHAZAM!

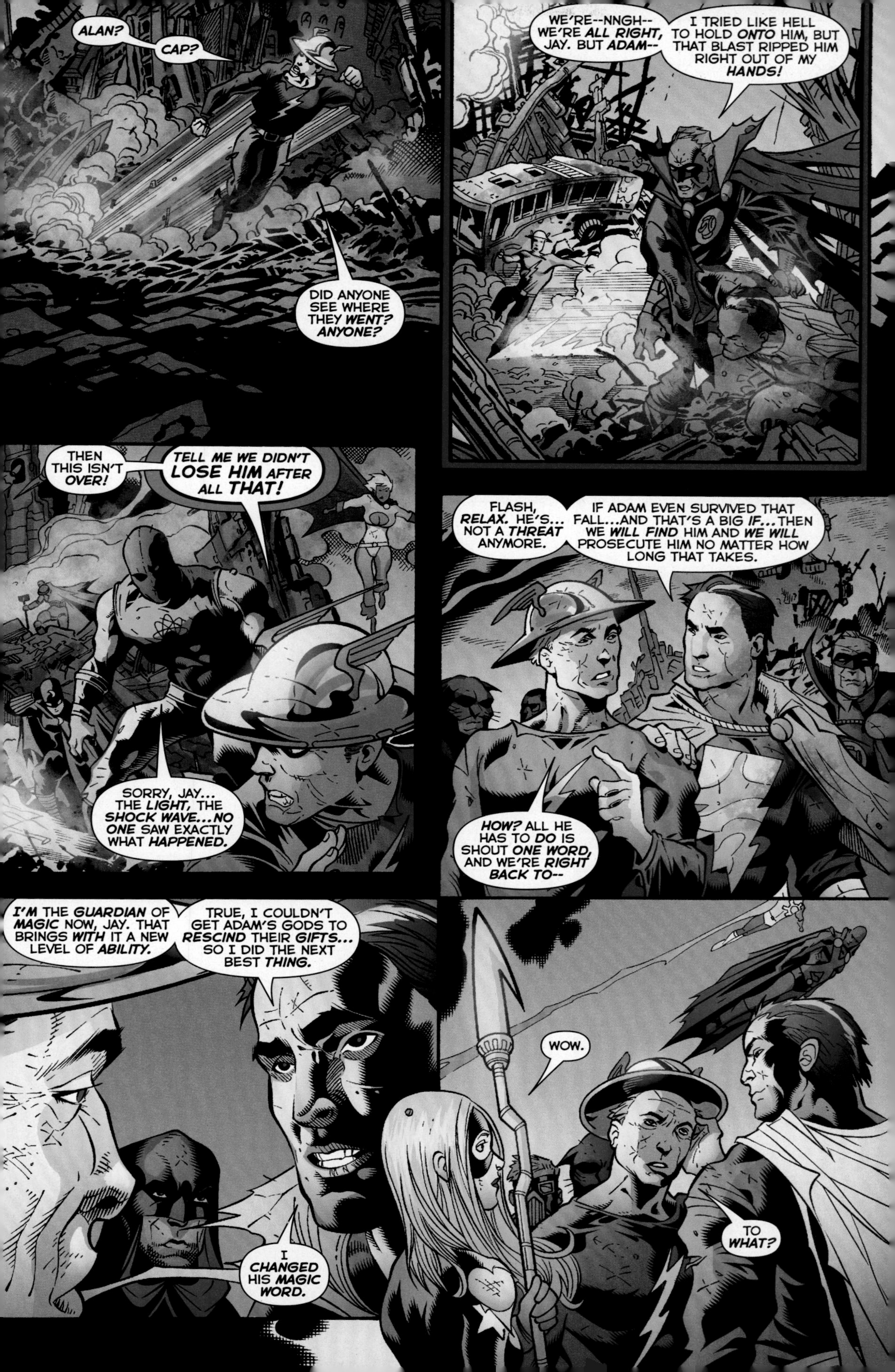
ALAN?
CAP?
DID ANYONE SEE WHERE THEY WENT? ANYONE?
WE'RE--NNGH-- WE'RE ALL RIGHT, JAY. BUT ADAM--
I TRIED LIKE HELL TO HOLD ONTO HIM, BUT THAT BLAST RIPPED HIM RIGHT OUT OF MY HANDS!
THEN THIS ISN'T OVER!
TELL ME WE DIDN'T LOSE HIM AFTER ALL THAT!
SORRY, JAY... THE LIGHT, THE SHOCK WAVE...NO ONE SAW EXACTLY WHAT HAPPENED.
FLASH, RELAX. HE'S... NOT A THREAT ANYMORE.
IF ADAM EVEN SURVIVED THAT FALL...AND THAT'S A BIG IF...THEN WE WILL FIND HIM AND WE WILL PROSECUTE HIM NO MATTER HOW LONG THAT TAKES.
HOW? ALL HE HAS TO DO IS SHOUT ONE WORD, AND WE'RE RIGHT BACK TO--
I'M THE GUARDIAN OF MAGIC NOW, JAY. THAT BRINGS WITH IT A NEW LEVEL OF ABILITY.
TRUE, I COULDN'T GET ADAM'S GODS TO RESCIND THEIR GIFTS... SO I DID THE NEXT BEST THING.
I CHANGED HIS MAGIC WORD.
WOW.
TO WHAT?

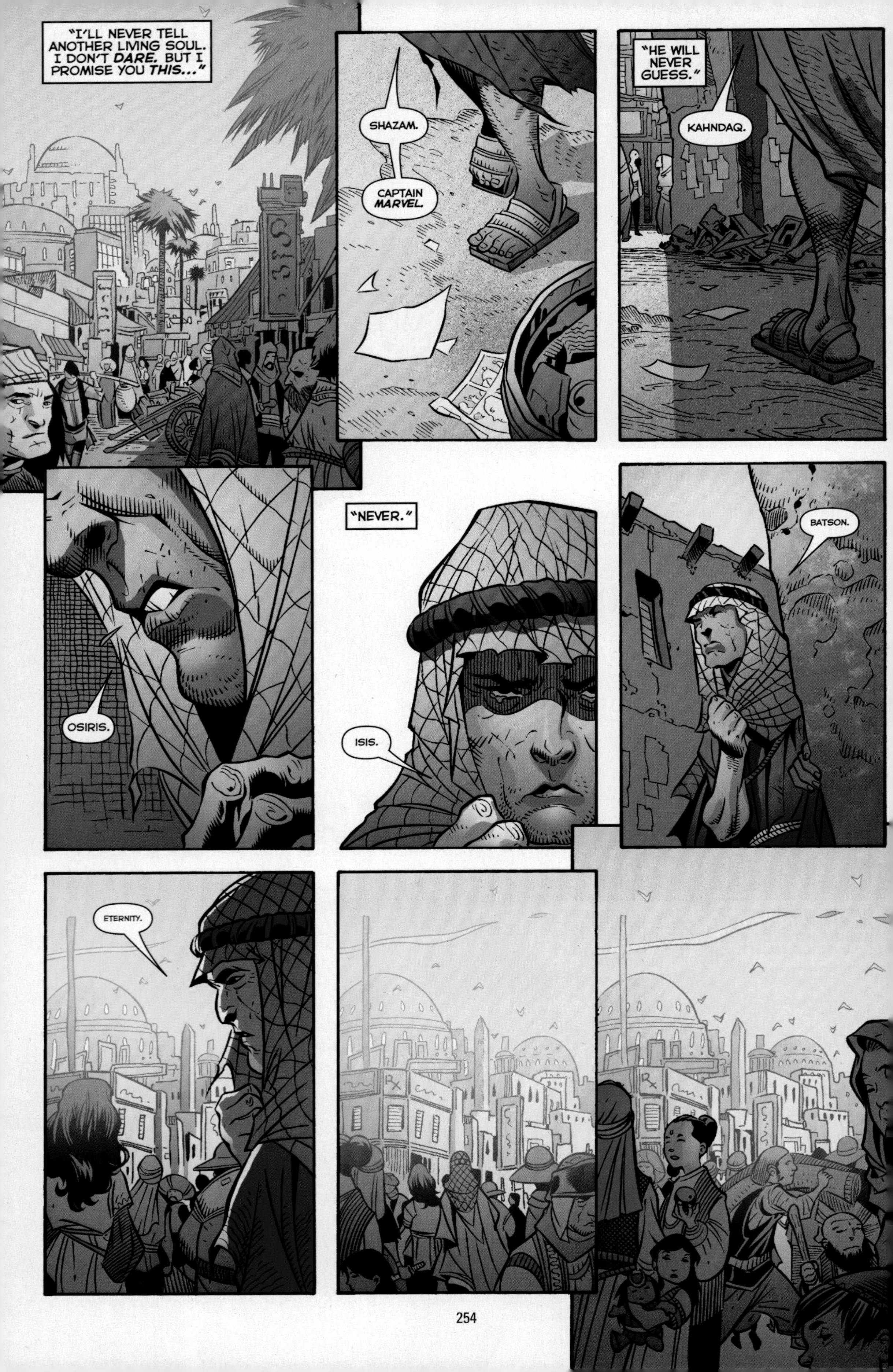
"I'LL NEVER TELL ANOTHER LIVING SOUL. I DON'T DARE. BUT I PROMISE YOU THIS..."
SHAZAM.
CAPTAIN MARVEL.
"HE WILL NEVER GUESS."
KAHNDAQ.
"NEVER."
OSIRIS.
ISIS.
BATSON.
ETERNITY.

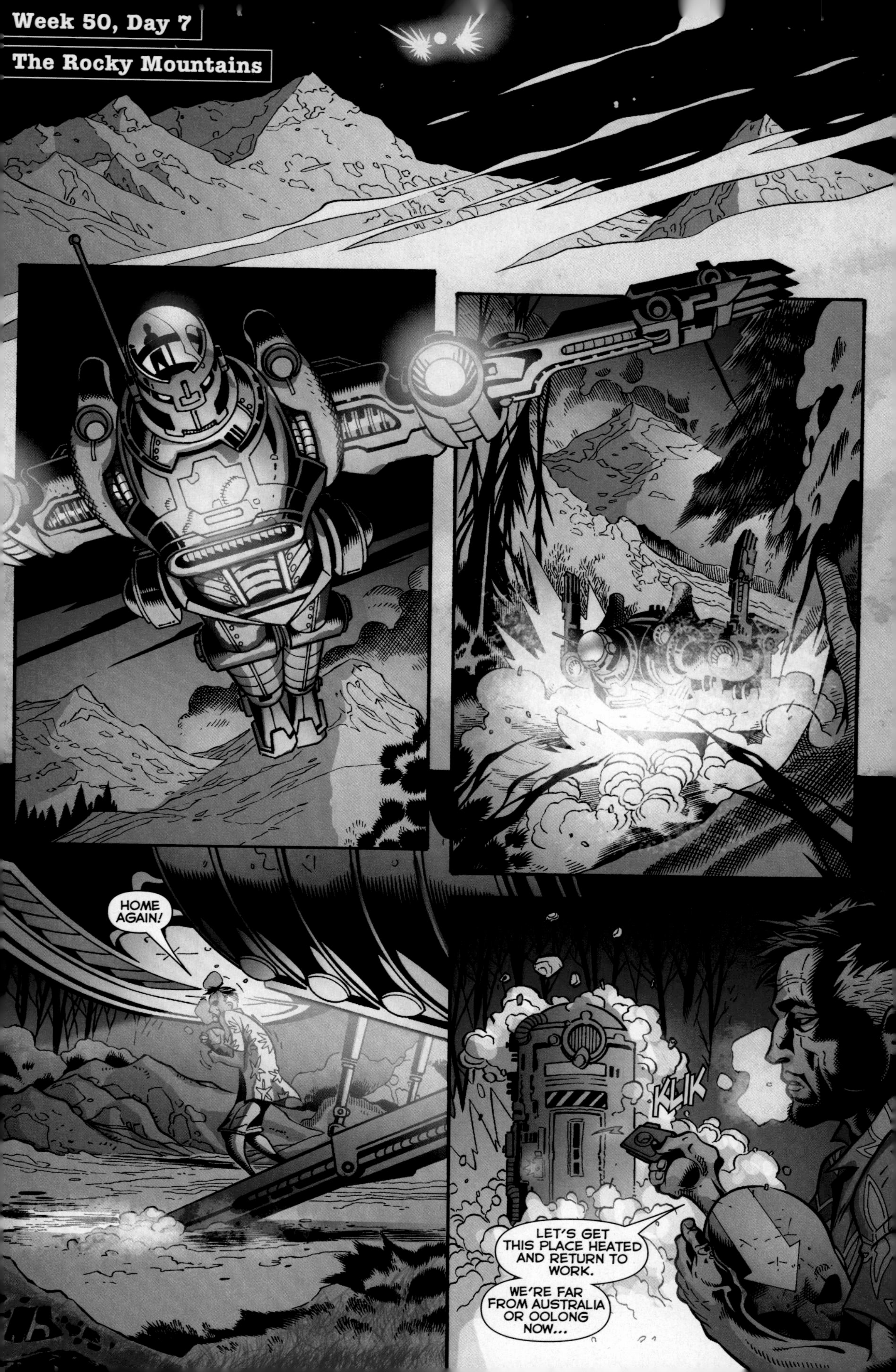

Week 50, Day 7
The Rocky Mountains
HOME AGAIN!
KLIK
LET'S GET THIS PLACE HEATED AND RETURN TO WORK.
WE'RE FAR FROM AUSTRALIA OR OOLONG NOW...

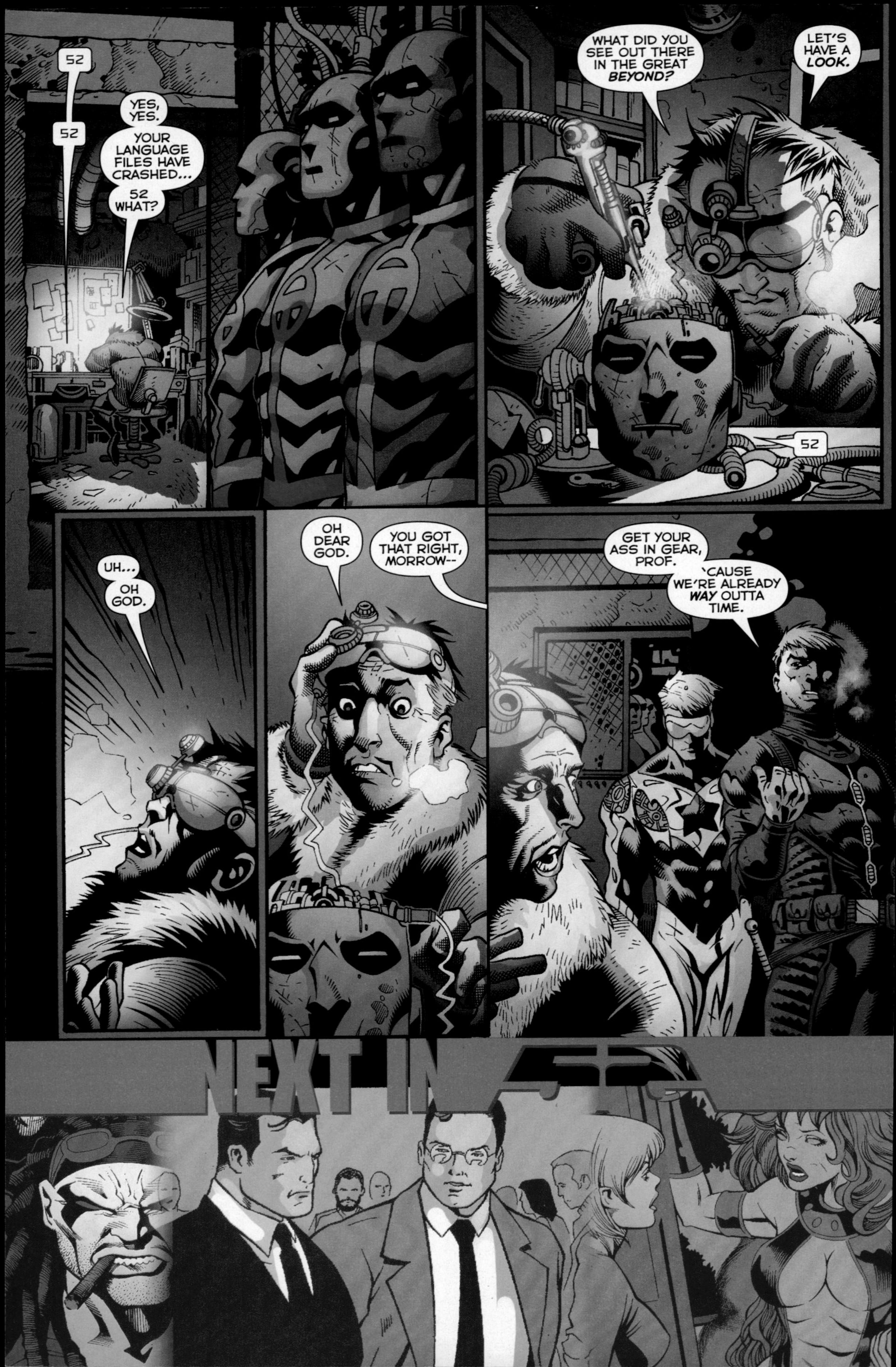
52
52
YES, YES.
YOUR LANGUAGE FILES HAVE CRASHED...
52 WHAT?
WHAT DID YOU SEE OUT THERE IN THE GREAT BEYOND?
LET'S HAVE A LOOK.
52
UH... OH GOD.
OH DEAR GOD.
YOU GOT THAT RIGHT, MORROW--
GET YOUR ASS IN GEAR, PROF.
'CAUSE WE'RE ALREADY WAY OUTTA TIME.
NEXT IN 52

WEEK FIFTY NOTES

MARK WAID

This is the kind of issue that Geoff writes better than any of us. Big, blowout action with half a million super-heroes. My contributions to this particular week were not huge, but I did come up with a couple of little touches of which I'm proud. One was concocting a good, satisfying answer as to where all the super-magicians of the DCU are while the fighting's going on (a perennial quandary when one writes a world-spanning battle in a DC comic, take it from me). The other, which I didn't convey well enough to the artist, apparently, was the notion that Captain Marvel could — this one time, with the extra help of the gods — literally seize the thunderbolt that's to change him into Billy and hold it to reroute against Black Adam. That part's pretty clear; what isn't, alas, is that as he holds it, he's constantly phase-shifting between Cap and Billy in rolling half-and-half waves.

BREAKDOWNS

BY **KEITH GIFFEN**

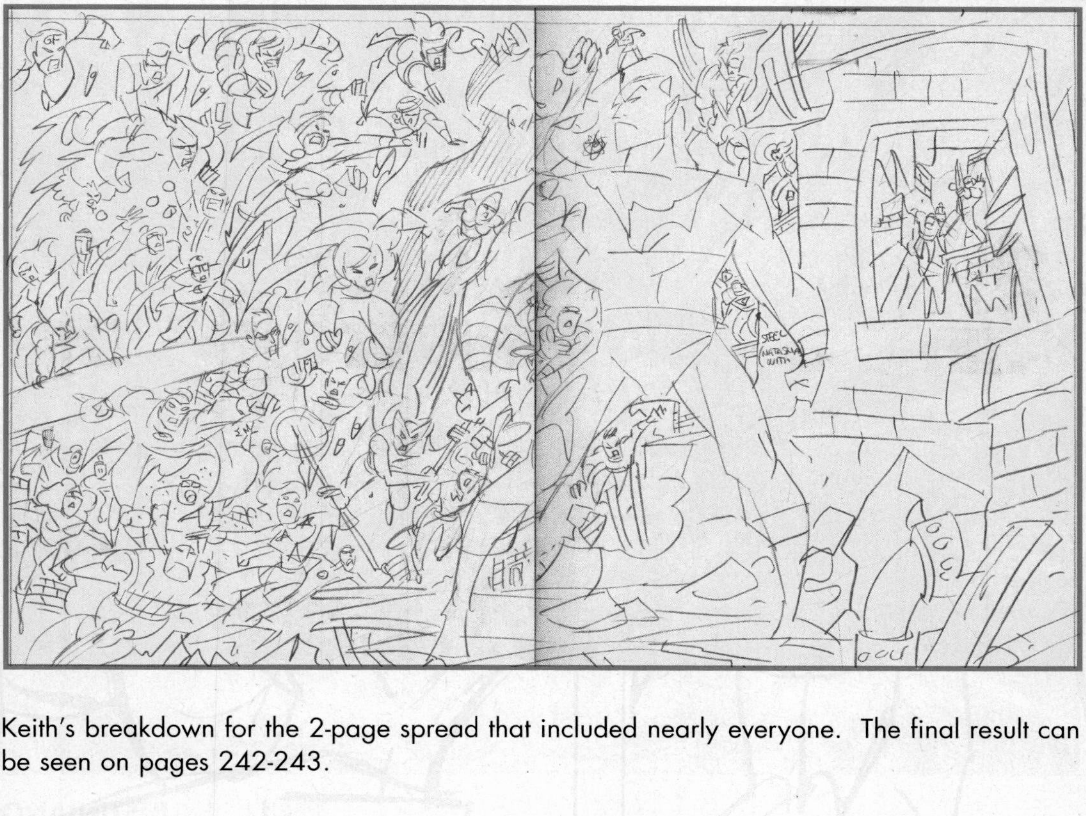

Keith's breakdown for the 2-page spread that included nearly everyone. The final result can be seen on pages 242-243.

SCRIPT EXCERPT

(COMPARE WITH PAGES 234-235 OF THIS COLLECTION)

52 WEEK FIFTY – PAGES TWO AND THREE

A DOUBLE-PAGE SPREAD
Massive figures in the foreground of Black Adam and Captain Marvel.

Black Adam smashes his fist into Captain Marvel, exploding with electrical current.

We reveal that we are in Sydney, Australia where Black Adam has been battling the Marvel Family and their allies for hours. And the city looks like it. The famous Opera House has been clearly damaged. The military force of Australia is in total ruins. Overturned and burning tanks – some with handprints in them from Black Adam, others have their turrets bent.

Other heroes strewn about include the Global Guardians: JET, GLOSS, Australia's own TASMANIAN DEVIL, MANTICORE, FREEDOM BEAST and SANDSTORM.

SFX: KRAAKKOOOMM

CAPTION (STARGIRL): "Black Adam killed millions."

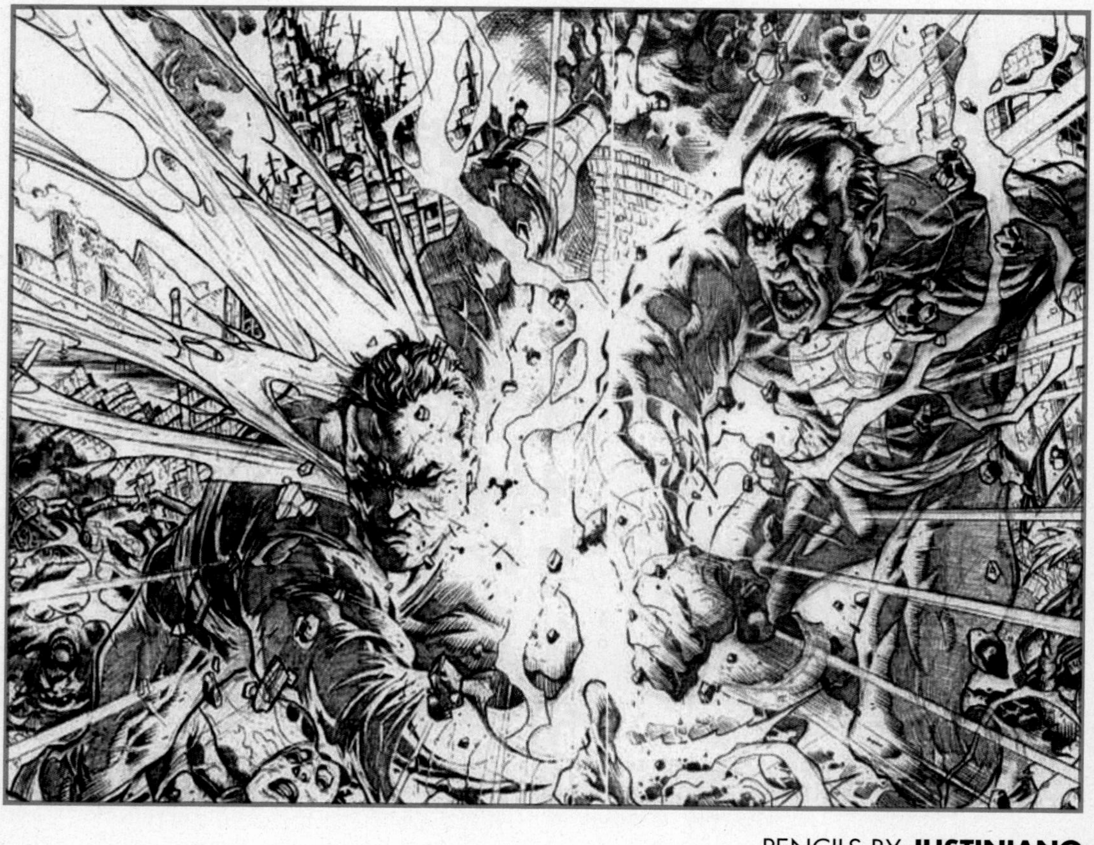

PENCILS BY **JUSTINIANO**

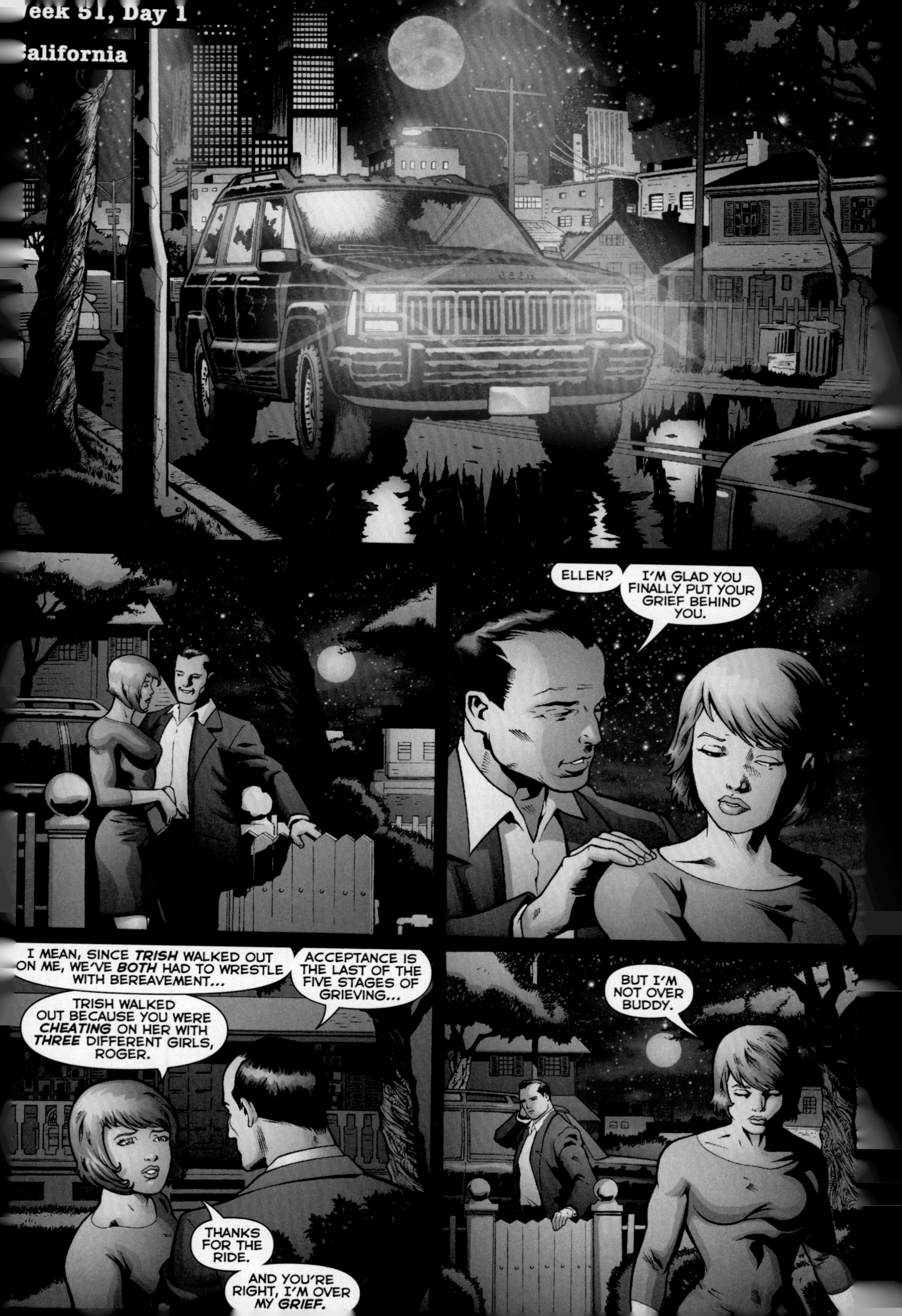

Week 51, Day 1
California
ELLEN?
I'M GLAD YOU FINALLY PUT YOUR GRIEF BEHIND YOU.
I MEAN, SINCE TRISH WALKED OUT ON ME, WE'VE BOTH HAD TO WRESTLE WITH BEREAVEMENT...
ACCEPTANCE IS THE LAST OF THE FIVE STAGES OF GRIEVING...
TRISH WALKED OUT BECAUSE YOU WERE CHEATING ON HER WITH THREE DIFFERENT GIRLS, ROGER.
THANKS FOR THE RIDE.
AND YOU'RE RIGHT, I'M OVER MY GRIEF.
BUT I'M NOT OVER BUDDY.

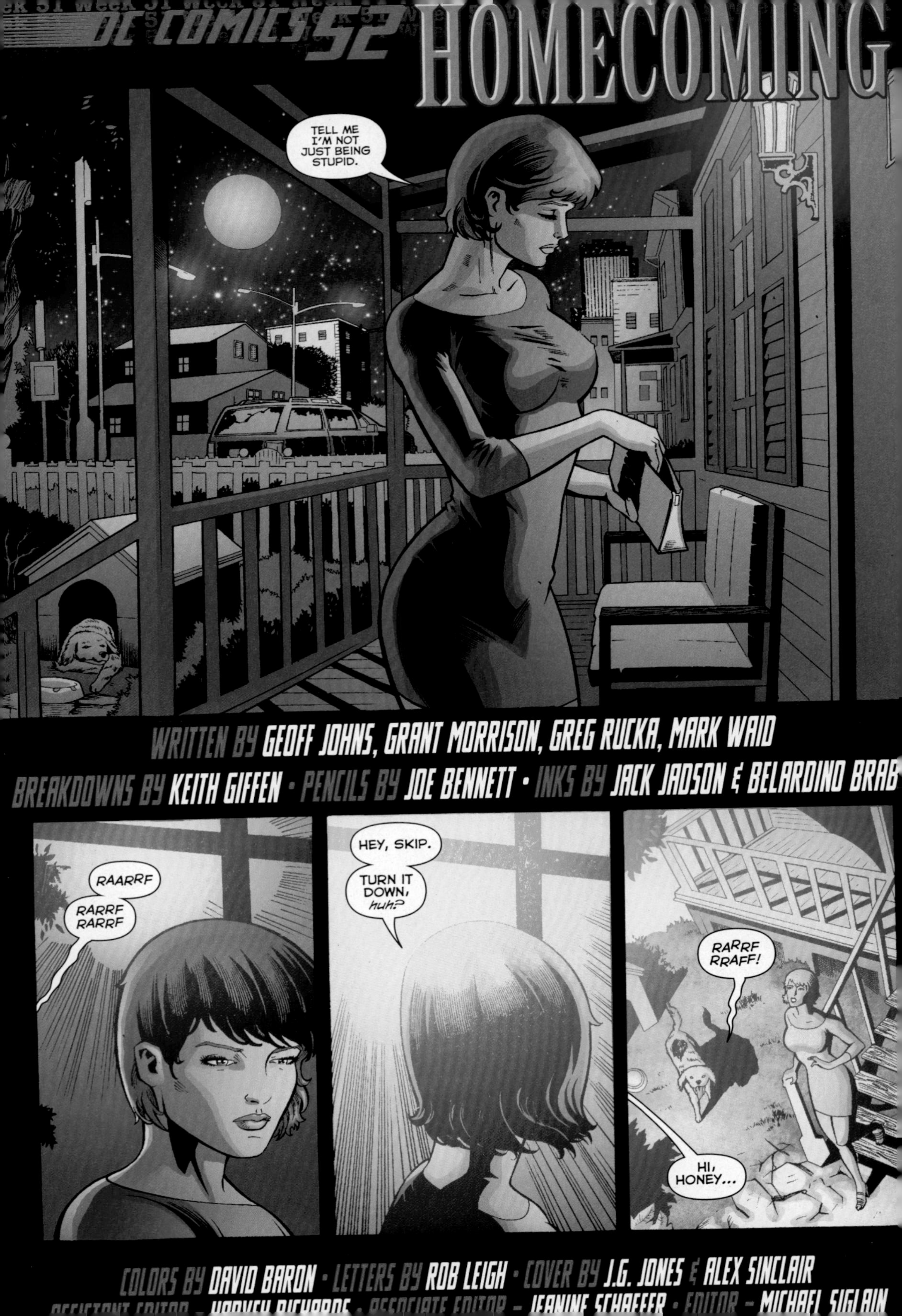

DC COMICS 52
HOMECOMING
TELL ME I'M NOT JUST BEING STUPID.
WRITTEN BY GEOFF JOHNS, GRANT MORRISON, GREG RUCKA, MARK WAID
BREAKDOWNS BY KEITH GIFFEN • PENCILS BY JOE BENNETT • INKS BY JACK JADSON & BELARDINO BRAB
RAARRF
RARRF RARRF
HEY, SKIP.
TURN IT DOWN, huh?
RARRF RRAFF!
HI, HONEY...
COLORS BY DAVID BARON • LETTERS BY ROB LEIGH • COVER BY J.G. JONES & ALEX SINCLAIR
ASSISTANT EDITOR – HARVEY RICHARDS – ASSOCIATE EDITOR – JEANINE SCHAEFER – EDITOR – MICHAEL SIGLAIN

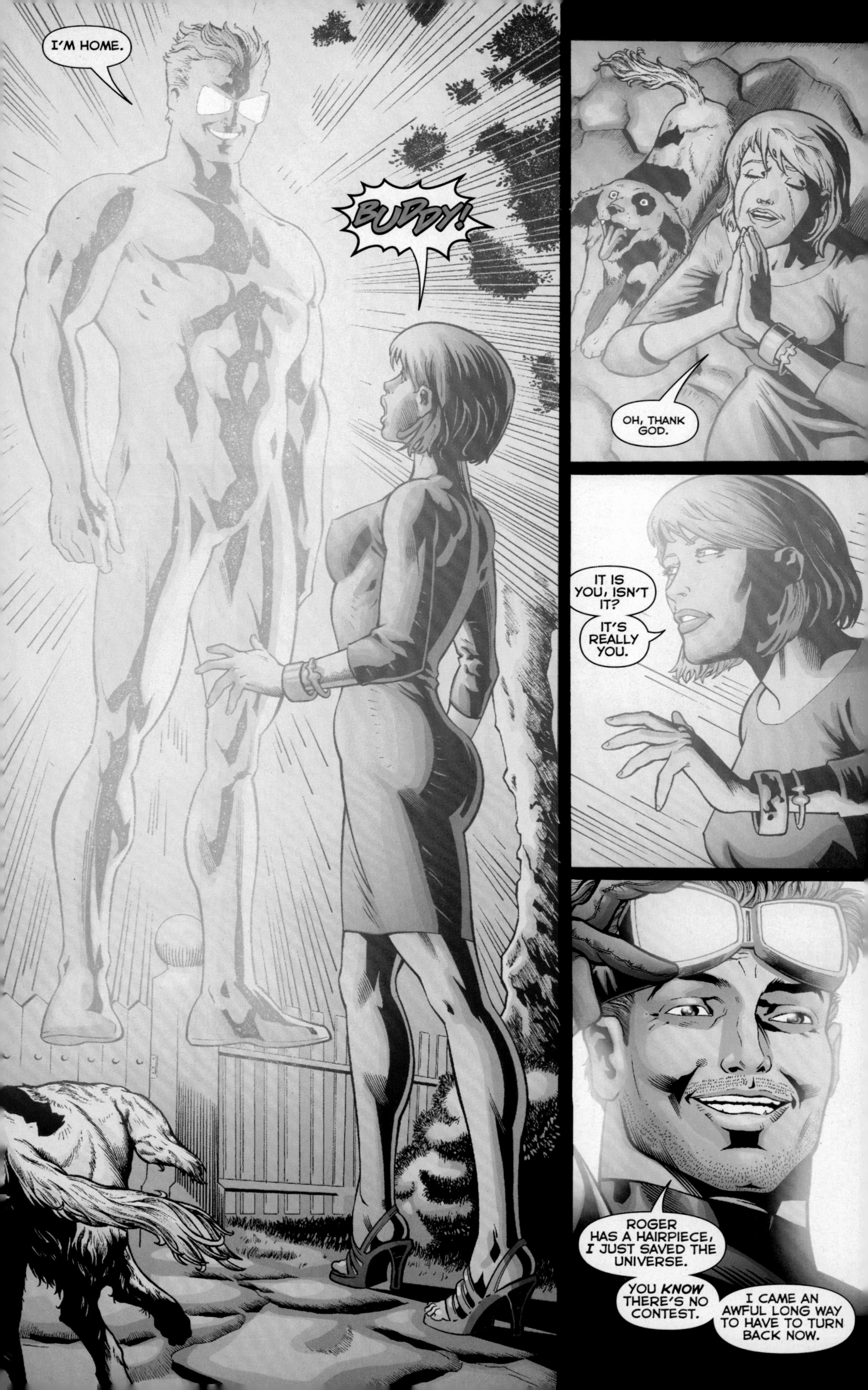
I'M HOME.
BUDDY!
OH, THANK GOD.
IT IS YOU, ISN'T IT?
IT'S REALLY YOU.
ROGER HAS A HAIRPIECE, I JUST SAVED THE UNIVERSE.
YOU KNOW THERE'S NO CONTEST.
I CAME AN AWFUL LONG WAY TO HAVE TO TURN BACK NOW.

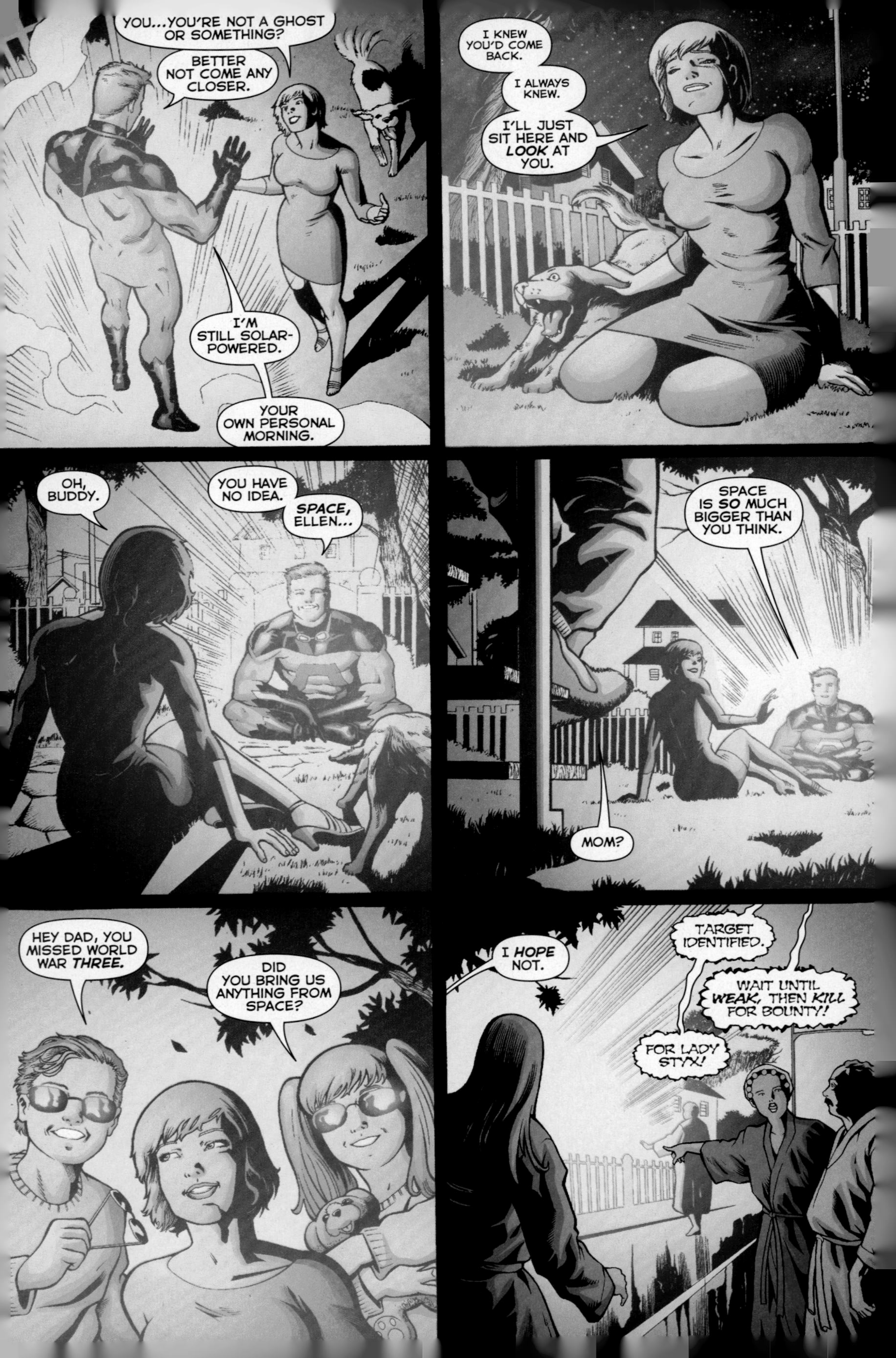

YOU...YOU'RE NOT A GHOST OR SOMETHING?
BETTER NOT COME ANY CLOSER.
I'M STILL SOLAR-POWERED.
YOUR OWN PERSONAL MORNING.
I KNEW YOU'D COME BACK.
I ALWAYS KNEW.
I'LL JUST SIT HERE AND LOOK AT YOU.
OH, BUDDY.
YOU HAVE NO IDEA.
SPACE, ELLEN...
SPACE IS SO MUCH BIGGER THAN YOU THINK.
MOM?
HEY DAD, YOU MISSED WORLD WAR THREE.
DID YOU BRING US ANYTHING FROM SPACE?
I HOPE NOT.
TARGET IDENTIFIED.
WAIT UNTIL WEAK, THEN KILL FOR BOUNTY!
FOR LADY STYX!

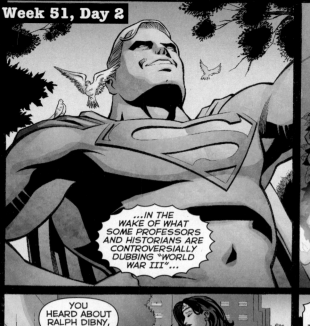

...IN THE WAKE OF WHAT SOME PROFESSORS AND HISTORIANS ARE CONTROVERSIALLY DUBBING "WORLD WAR III"...

...DOZENS OF MASKED MEN AND WOMEN HAVE ARRIVED TO JOIN THOUSANDS PAYING THEIR RESPECTS TO A YOUNG BOY WHO SACRIFICED HIMSELF FOR US ONE YEAR AGO...

YOU HEARD ABOUT RALPH DIBNY, DONNA.

FIRE TOLD ME.

THERE'S SOMETHING SO STRANGE ABOUT IT ALL AND...NOW I'LL NEVER BE ABLE TO SAY I'M SORRY.

...AND TO HONOR THOSE WHO GAVE THEIR LIVES TO HALT THE RAMPAGE OF THE WORLD'S MOST WANTED MORTAL, BLACK ADAM.

YOU'LL FIND A WAY, CASSIE.

AGENT PRINCE.

THE DEPARTMENT OF METAHUMAN AFFAIRS IS HERE TO SECURE THE AREA, NOT OGLE THE "NEW" WONDER WOMAN.

JUST GETTING A LIST OF WHO'S IN ATTENDANCE, SARGE.

263

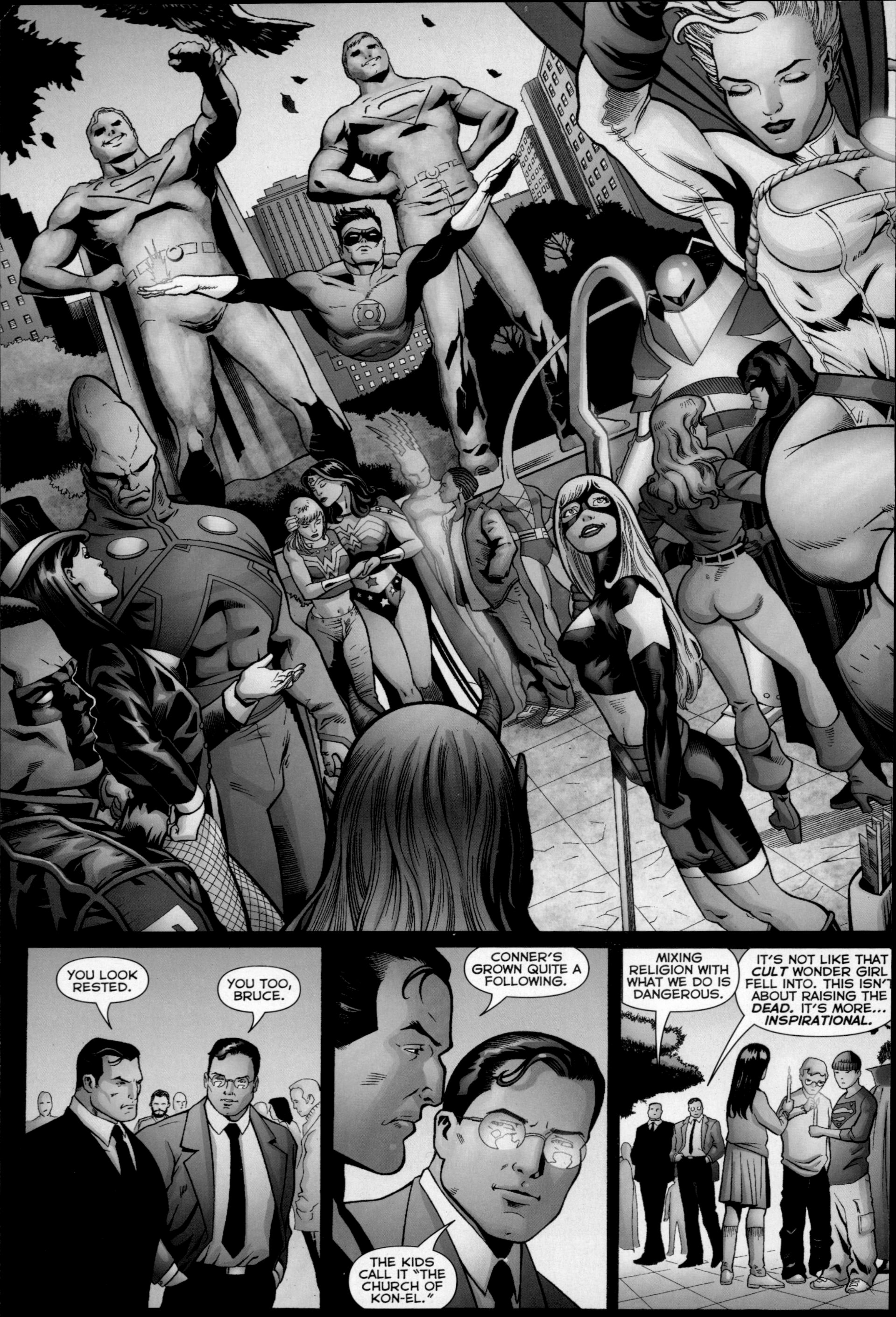
YOU LOOK RESTED.
YOU TOO, BRUCE.
CONNER'S GROWN QUITE A FOLLOWING.
THE KIDS CALL IT "THE CHURCH OF KON-EL."
MIXING RELIGION WITH WHAT WE DO IS DANGEROUS.
IT'S NOT LIKE THAT CULT WONDER GIRL FELL INTO. THIS ISN'T ABOUT RAISING THE DEAD. IT'S MORE... INSPIRATIONAL.

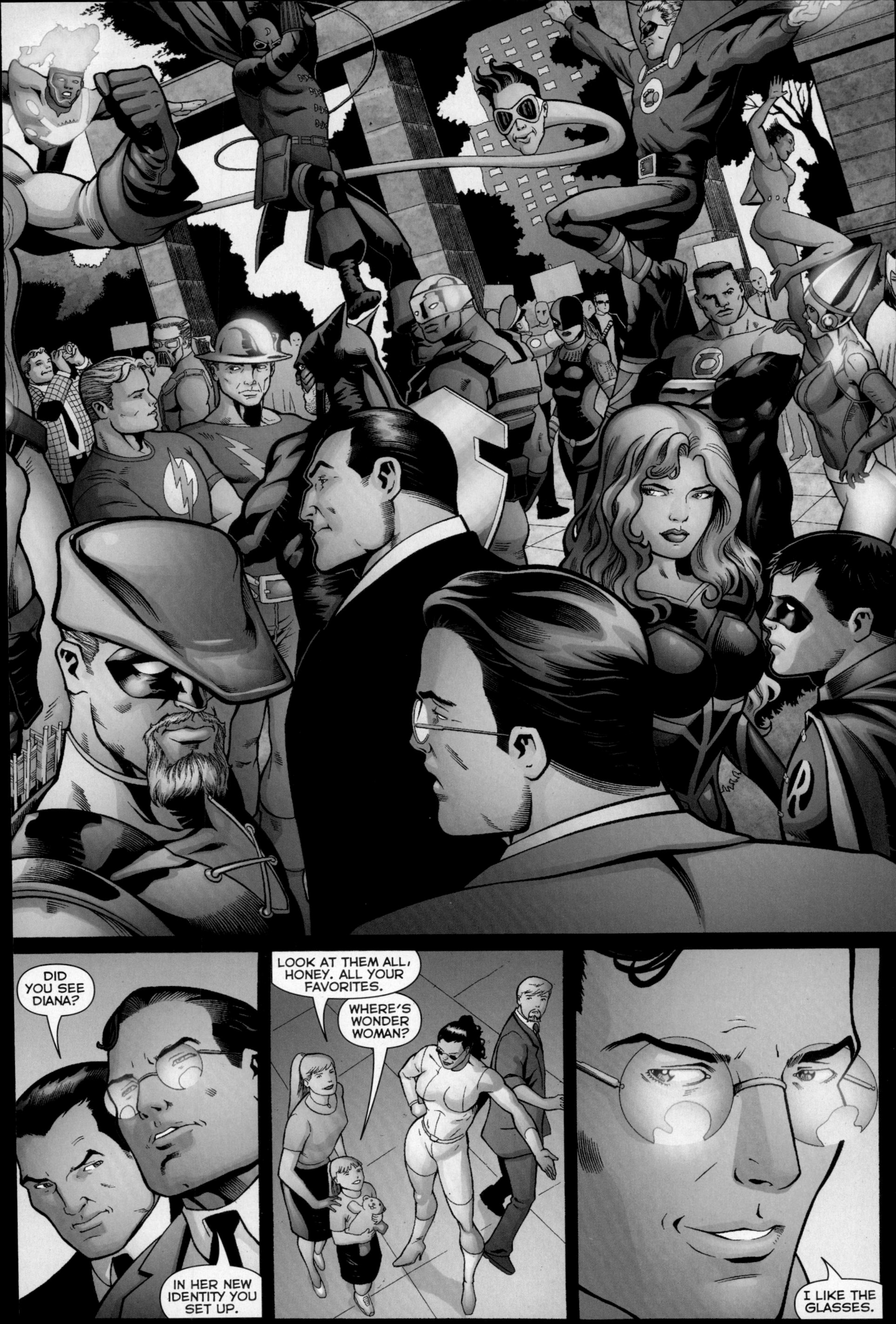
DID YOU SEE DIANA?
IN HER NEW IDENTITY YOU SET UP.
LOOK AT THEM ALL, HONEY. ALL YOUR FAVORITES.
WHERE'S WONDER WOMAN?
I LIKE THE GLASSES.

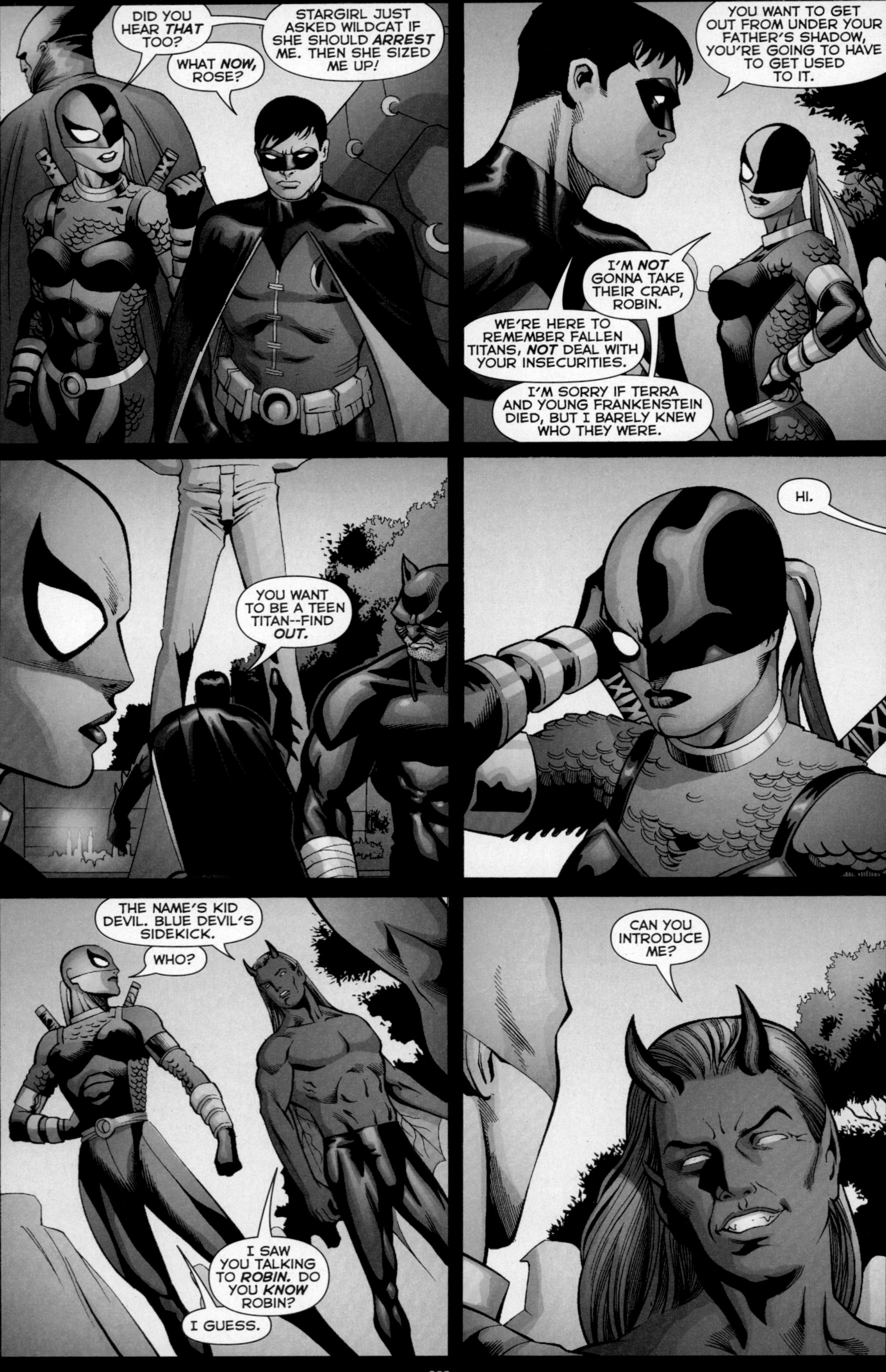
DID YOU HEAR THAT TOO?
STARGIRL JUST ASKED WILDCAT IF SHE SHOULD ARREST ME. THEN SHE SIZED ME UP!
WHAT NOW, ROSE?
YOU WANT TO GET OUT FROM UNDER YOUR FATHER'S SHADOW, YOU'RE GOING TO HAVE TO GET USED TO IT.
I'M NOT GONNA TAKE THEIR CRAP, ROBIN.
WE'RE HERE TO REMEMBER FALLEN TITANS, NOT DEAL WITH YOUR INSECURITIES.
I'M SORRY IF TERRA AND YOUNG FRANKENSTEIN DIED, BUT I BARELY KNEW WHO THEY WERE.
YOU WANT TO BE A TEEN TITAN--FIND OUT.
HI.
THE NAME'S KID DEVIL. BLUE DEVIL'S SIDEKICK.
WHO?
I SAW YOU TALKING TO ROBIN. DO YOU KNOW ROBIN?
I GUESS.
CAN YOU INTRODUCE ME?

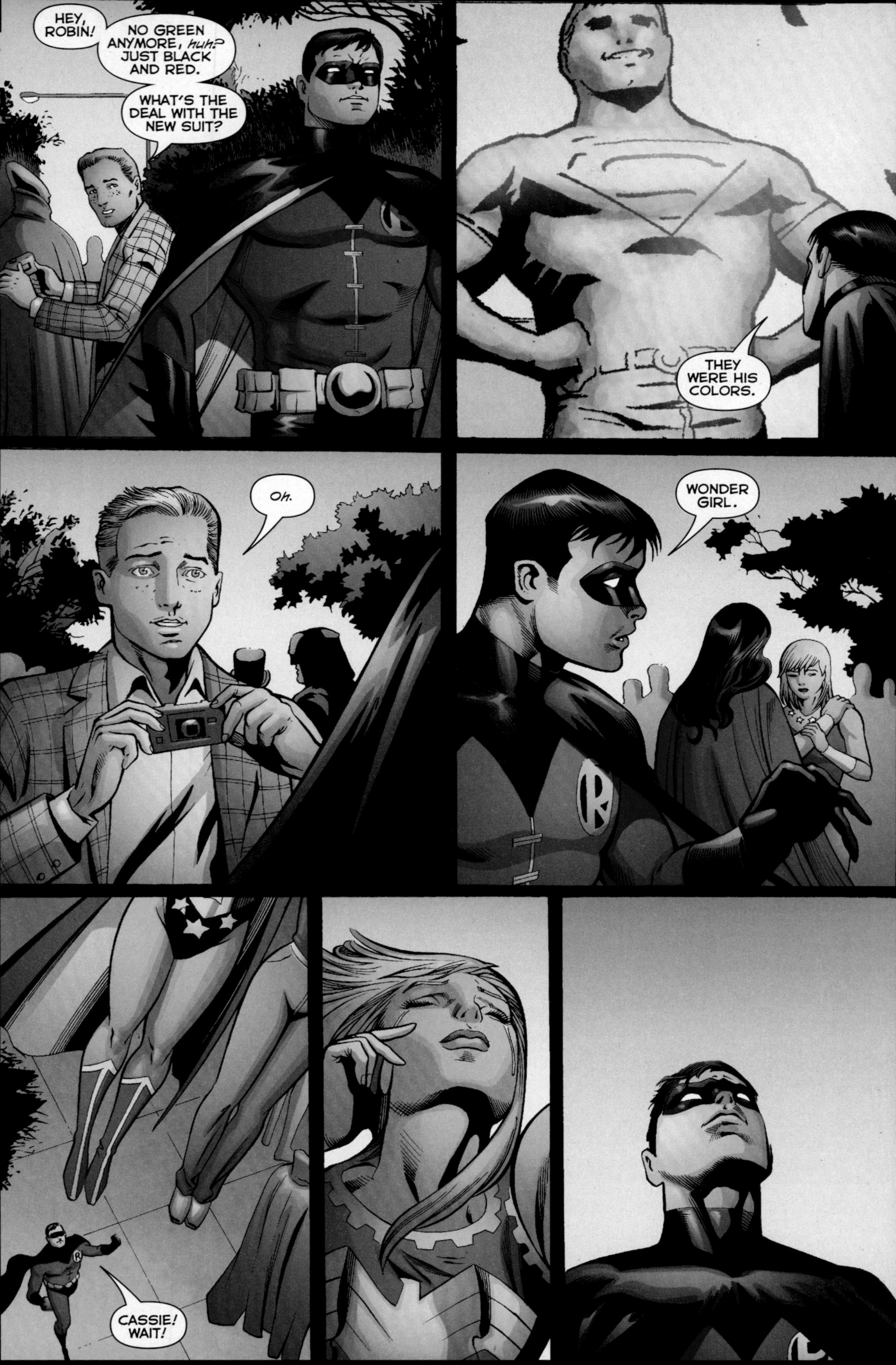
HEY, ROBIN!
NO GREEN ANYMORE, *huh?* JUST BLACK AND RED.
WHAT'S THE DEAL WITH THE NEW SUIT?
THEY WERE HIS COLORS.
Oh.
WONDER GIRL.
CASSIE! WAIT!

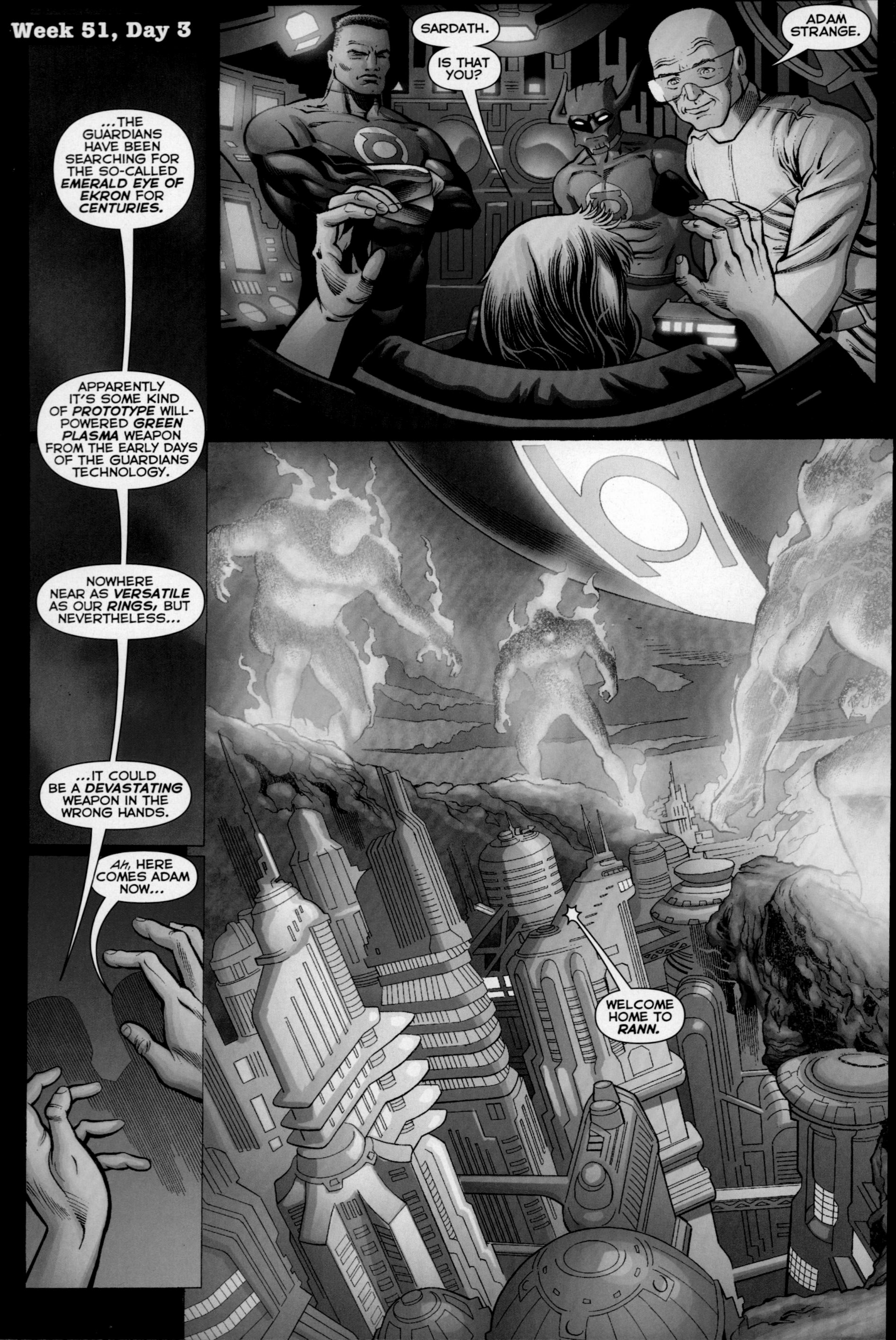
Week 51, Day 3
...THE GUARDIANS HAVE BEEN SEARCHING FOR THE SO-CALLED EMERALD EYE OF EKRON FOR CENTURIES.
SARDATH.
IS THAT YOU?
ADAM STRANGE.
APPARENTLY IT'S SOME KIND OF PROTOTYPE WILL-POWERED GREEN PLASMA WEAPON FROM THE EARLY DAYS OF THE GUARDIANS TECHNOLOGY.
NOWHERE NEAR AS VERSATILE AS OUR RINGS, BUT NEVERTHELESS...
...IT COULD BE A DEVASTATING WEAPON IN THE WRONG HANDS.
Ah, HERE COMES ADAM NOW...
WELCOME HOME TO RANN.

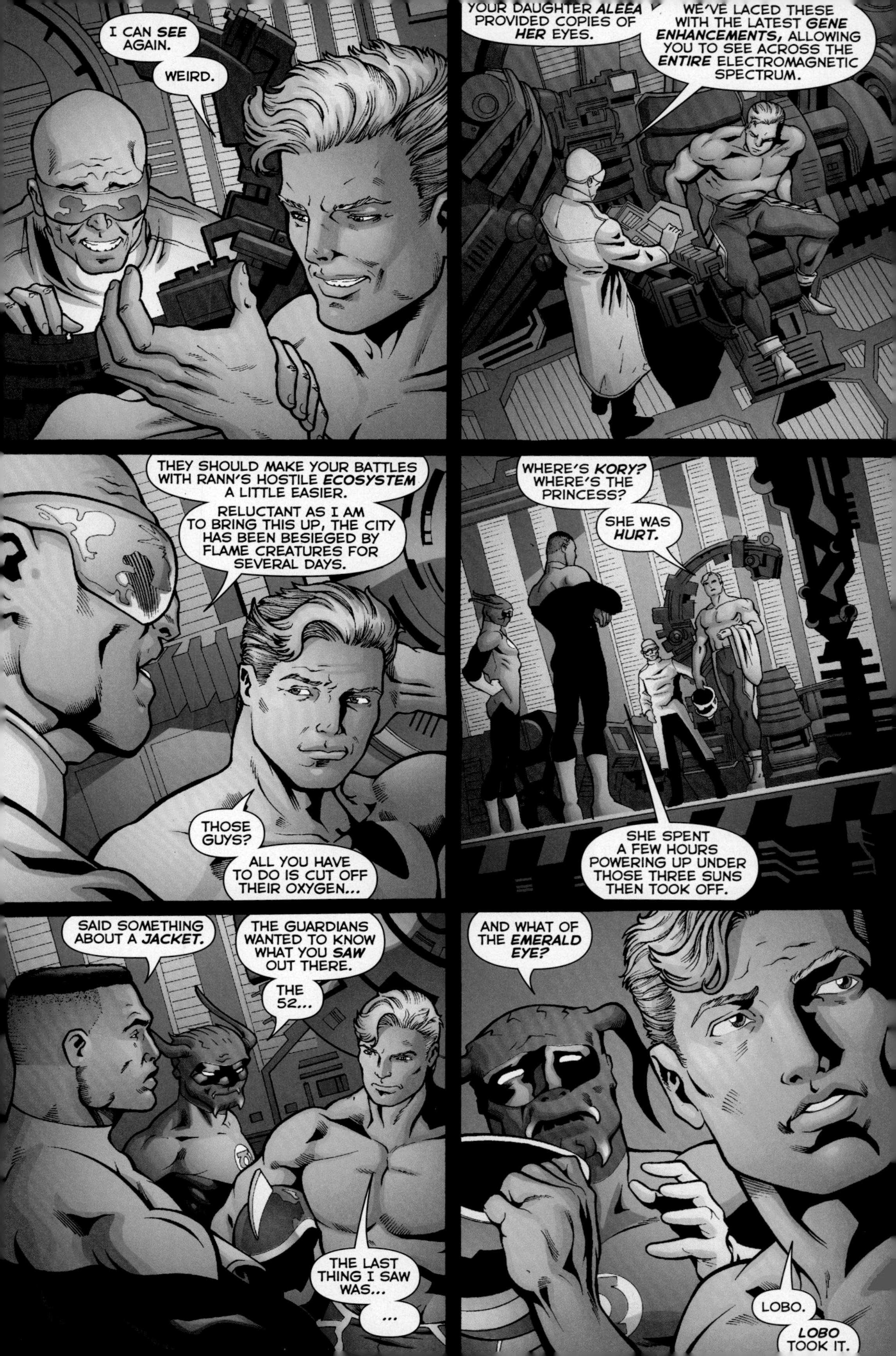

I CAN SEE AGAIN.
WEIRD.
YOUR DAUGHTER ALEEA PROVIDED COPIES OF HER EYES.
WE'VE LACED THESE WITH THE LATEST GENE ENHANCEMENTS, ALLOWING YOU TO SEE ACROSS THE ENTIRE ELECTROMAGNETIC SPECTRUM.
THEY SHOULD MAKE YOUR BATTLES WITH RANN'S HOSTILE ECOSYSTEM A LITTLE EASIER.
RELUCTANT AS I AM TO BRING THIS UP, THE CITY HAS BEEN BESIEGED BY FLAME CREATURES FOR SEVERAL DAYS.
THOSE GUYS?
ALL YOU HAVE TO DO IS CUT OFF THEIR OXYGEN...
WHERE'S KORY? WHERE'S THE PRINCESS?
SHE WAS HURT.
SHE SPENT A FEW HOURS POWERING UP UNDER THOSE THREE SUNS THEN TOOK OFF.
SAID SOMETHING ABOUT A JACKET.
THE GUARDIANS WANTED TO KNOW WHAT YOU SAW OUT THERE.
THE 52...
THE LAST THING I SAW WAS...
...
AND WHAT OF THE EMERALD EYE?
LOBO.
LOBO TOOK IT.

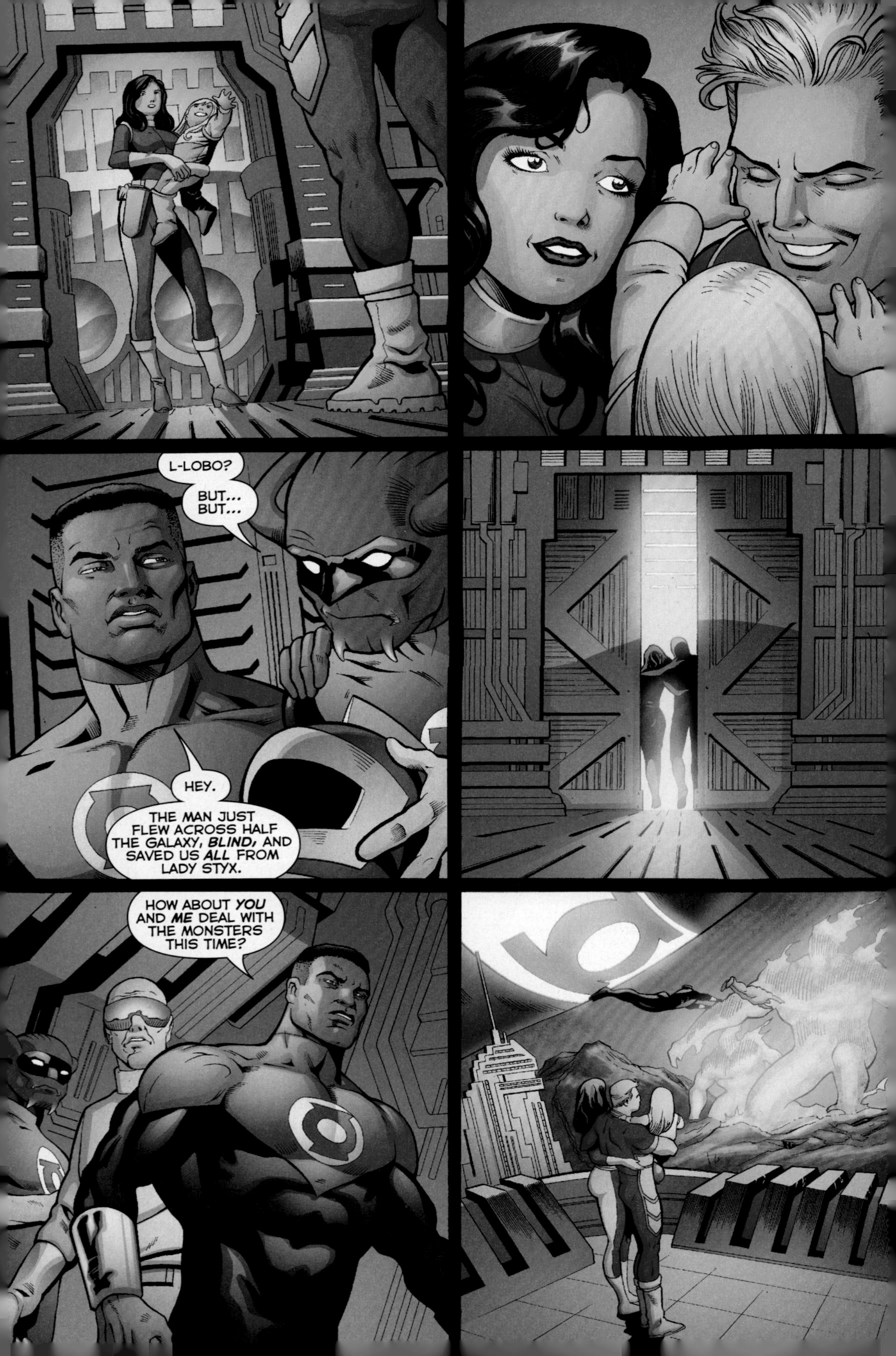

L-LOBO?
BUT... BUT...
HEY.
THE MAN JUST FLEW ACROSS HALF THE GALAXY, *BLIND*, AND SAVED US *ALL* FROM LADY STYX.
HOW ABOUT *YOU* AND *ME* DEAL WITH THE MONSTERS THIS TIME?

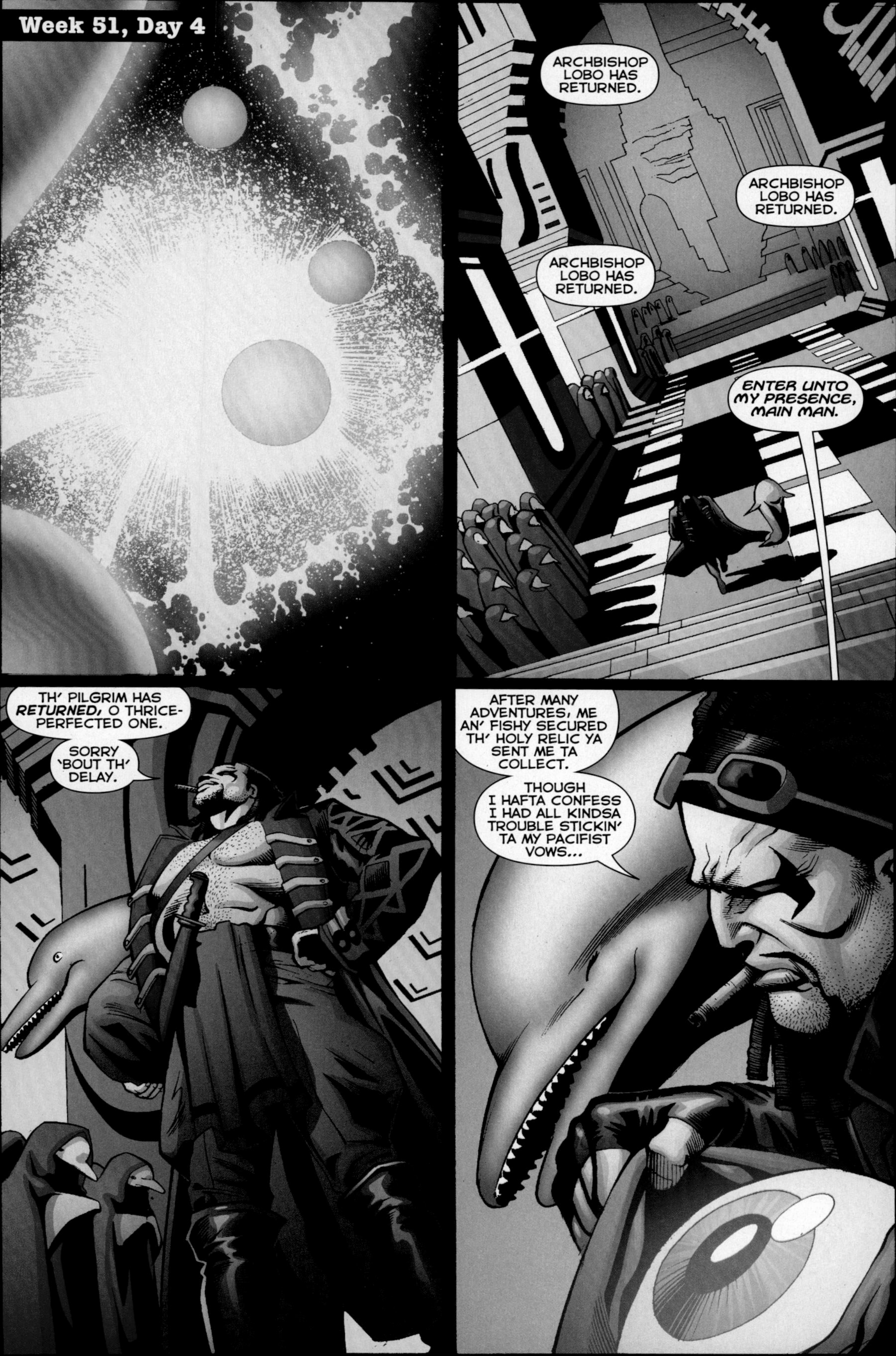
Week 51, Day 4
ARCHBISHOP LOBO HAS RETURNED.
ARCHBISHOP LOBO HAS RETURNED.
ARCHBISHOP LOBO HAS RETURNED.
ENTER UNTO MY PRESENCE, MAIN MAN.
TH' PILGRIM HAS RETURNED, O THRICE-PERFECTED ONE.
SORRY 'BOUT TH' DELAY.
AFTER MANY ADVENTURES, ME AN' FISHY SECURED TH' HOLY RELIC YA SENT ME TA COLLECT.
THOUGH I HAFTA CONFESS I HAD ALL KINDSA TROUBLE STICKIN' TA MY PACIFIST VOWS...

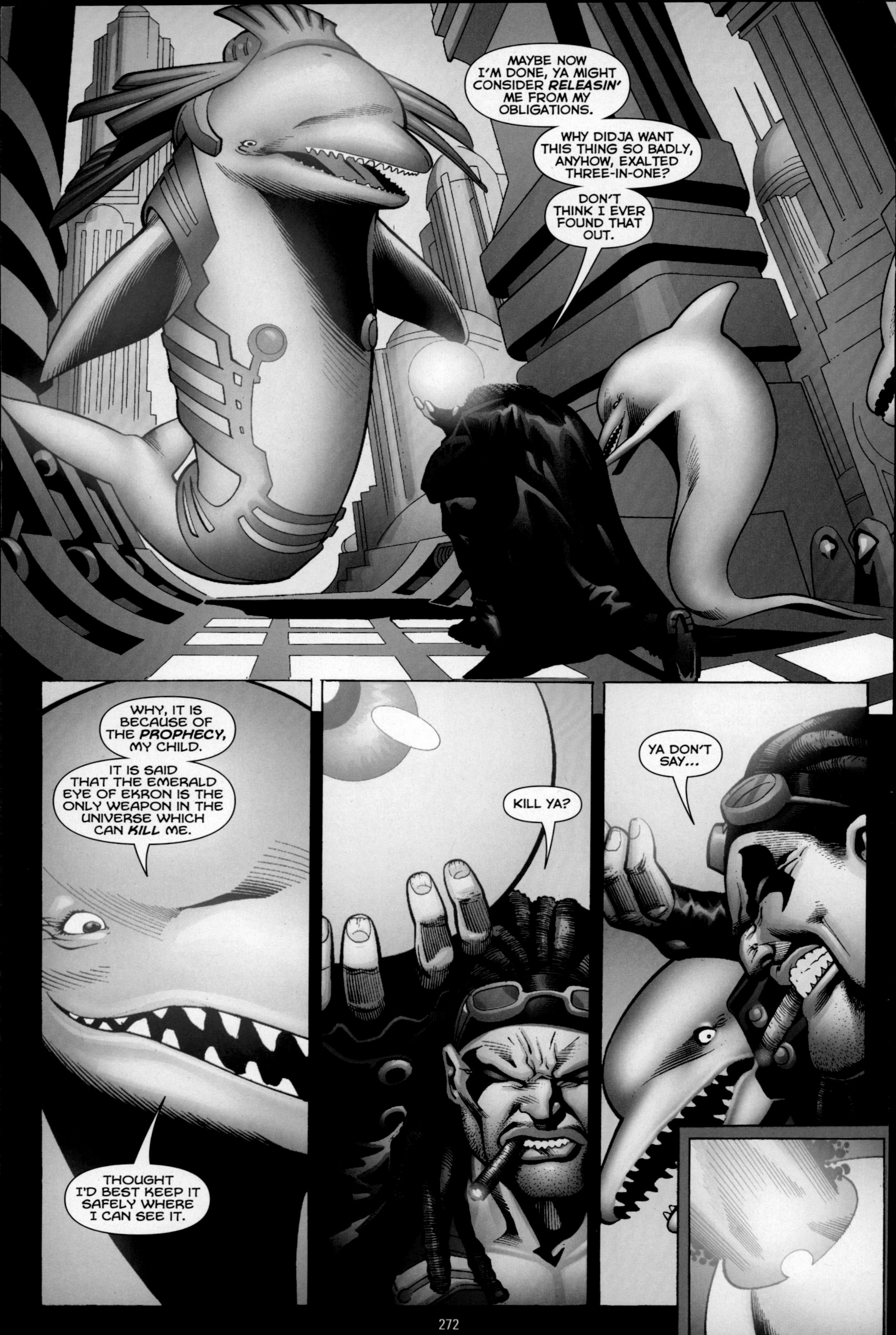
MAYBE NOW I'M DONE, YA MIGHT CONSIDER *RELEASIN'* ME FROM MY OBLIGATIONS.
WHY DIDJA WANT THIS THING SO BADLY, ANYHOW, EXALTED THREE-IN-ONE?
DON'T THINK I EVER FOUND THAT OUT.
WHY, IT IS BECAUSE OF THE *PROPHECY*, MY CHILD.
IT IS SAID THAT THE EMERALD EYE OF EKRON IS THE ONLY WEAPON IN THE UNIVERSE WHICH CAN *KILL* ME.
THOUGHT I'D BEST KEEP IT SAFELY WHERE I CAN SEE IT.
KILL YA?
YA DON'T SAY...

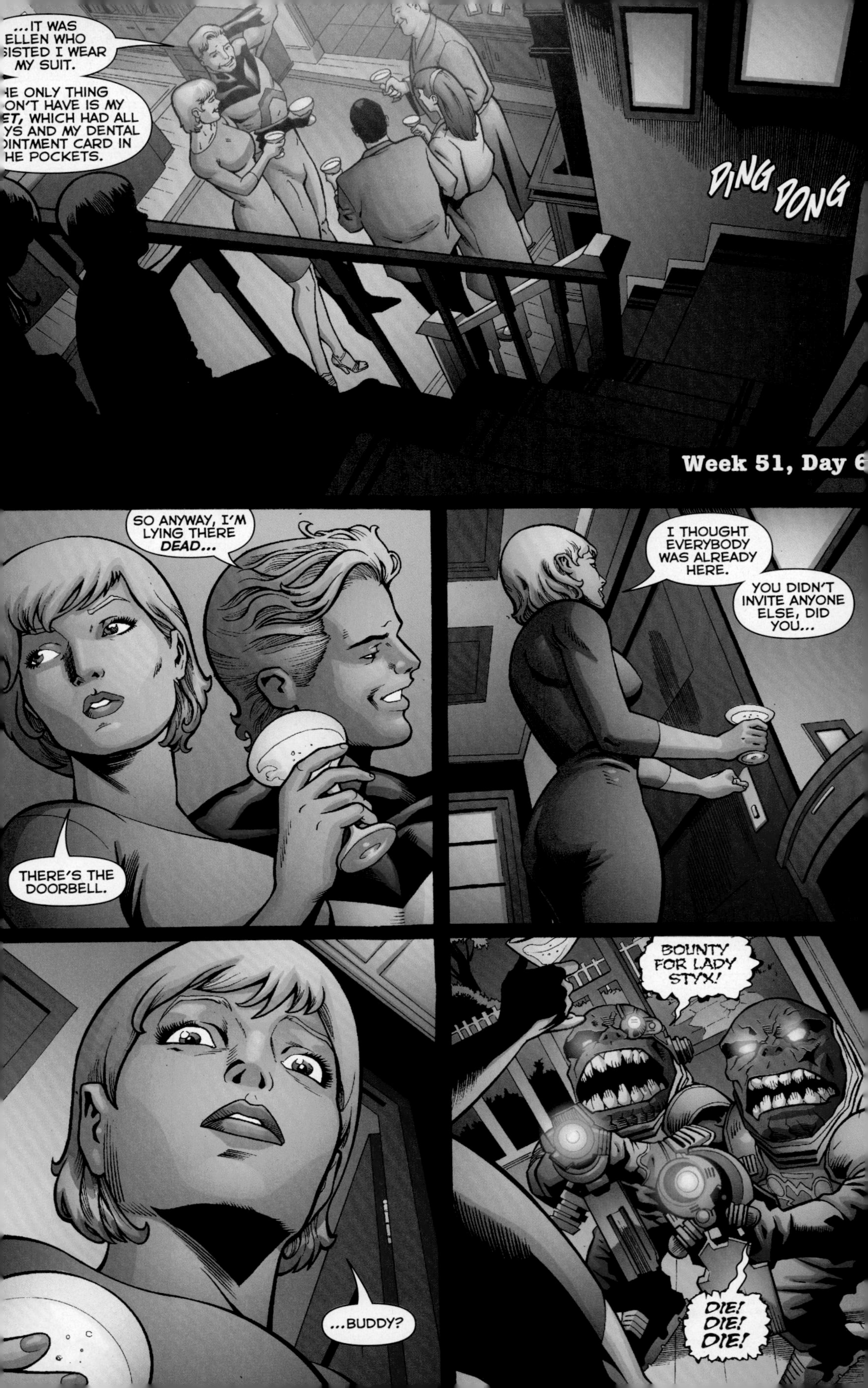
...IT WAS
ELLEN WHO
SISTED I WEAR
MY SUIT.
HE ONLY THING
ON'T HAVE IS MY
ET, WHICH HAD ALL
YS AND MY DENTAL
OINTMENT CARD IN
HE POCKETS.
DING DONG
Week 51, Day 6
SO ANYWAY, I'M LYING THERE *DEAD*...
THERE'S THE DOORBELL.
I THOUGHT EVERYBODY WAS ALREADY HERE.
YOU DIDN'T INVITE ANYONE ELSE, DID YOU...
...BUDDY?
BOUNTY FOR LADY STYX!
DIE! DIE! DIE!

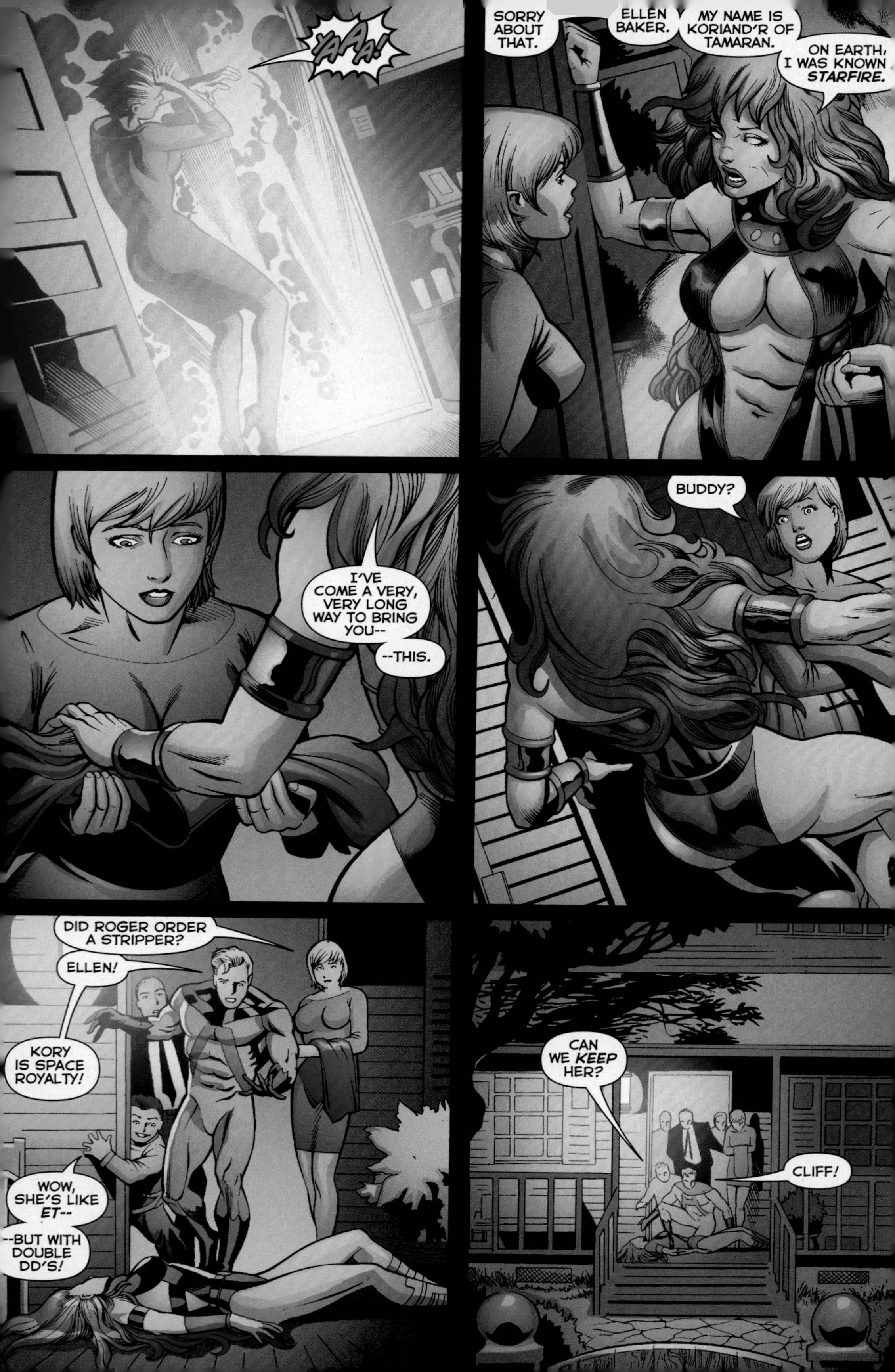
YAAA!
SORRY ABOUT THAT.
ELLEN BAKER.
MY NAME IS KORIAND'R OF TAMARAN.
ON EARTH, I WAS KNOWN STARFIRE.
I'VE COME A VERY, VERY LONG WAY TO BRING YOU--
--THIS.
BUDDY?
DID ROGER ORDER A STRIPPER?
ELLEN!
KORY IS SPACE ROYALTY!
WOW, SHE'S LIKE ET--
--BUT WITH DOUBLE DD'S!
CAN WE KEEP HER?
CLIFF!

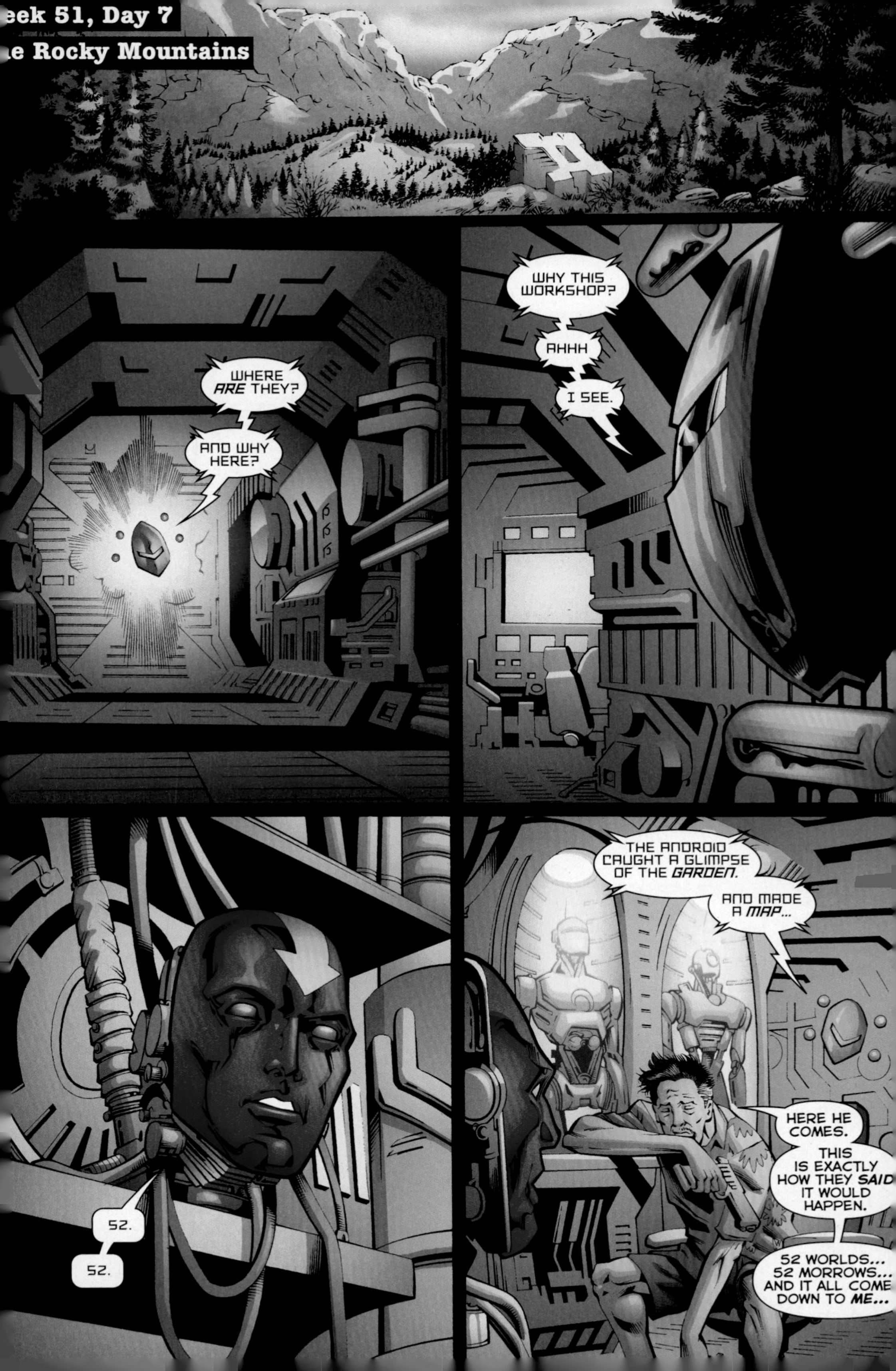

eek 51, Day 7
e Rocky Mountains
WHERE ARE THEY?
AND WHY HERE?
WHY THIS WORKSHOP?
AHHH
I SEE.
52.
52.
THE ANDROID CAUGHT A GLIMPSE OF THE GARDEN.
AND MADE A MAP...
HERE HE COMES.
THIS IS EXACTLY HOW THEY SAID IT WOULD HAPPEN.
52 WORLDS... 52 MORROWS... AND IT ALL COME DOWN TO ME...

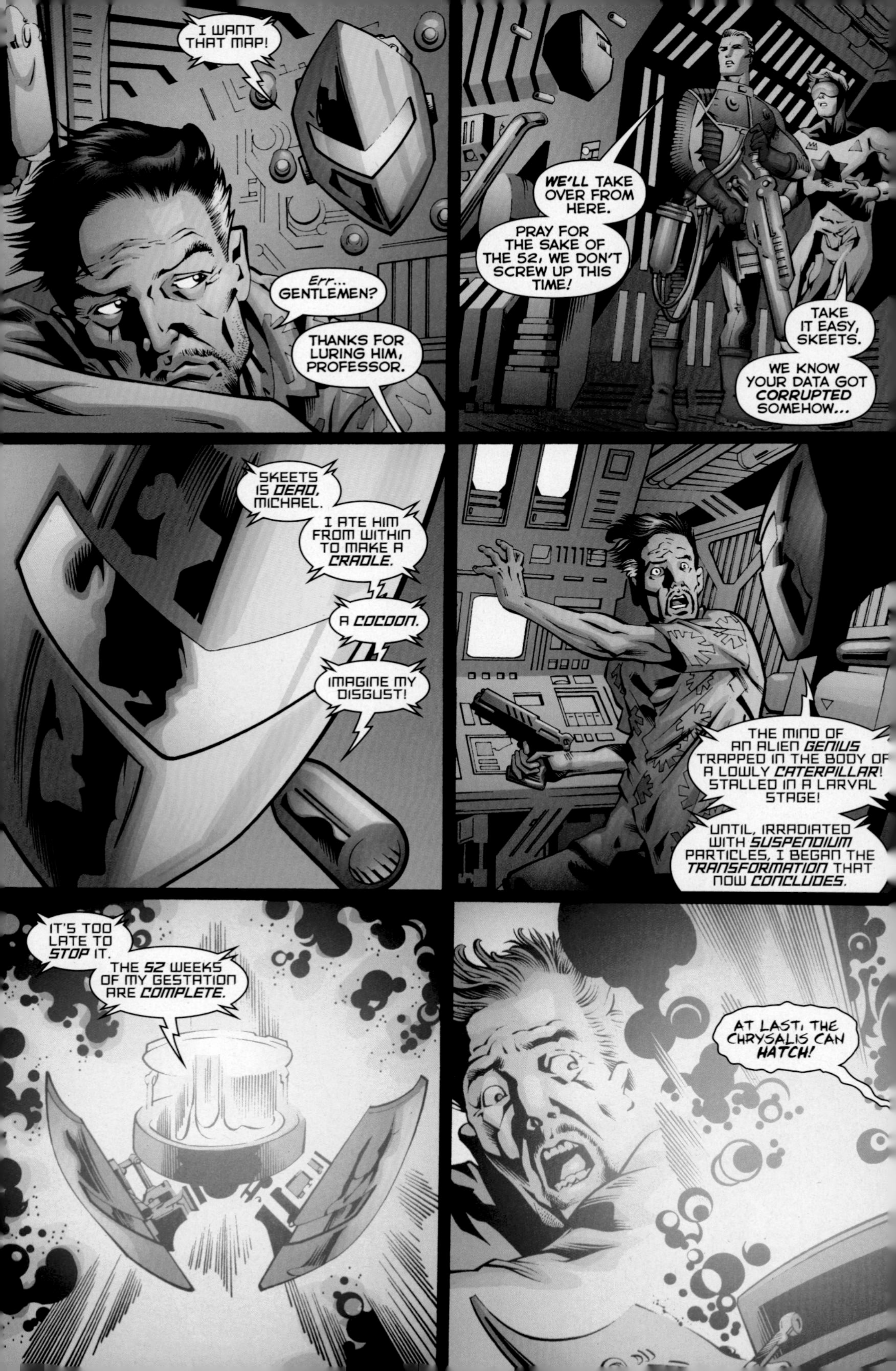
I WANT THAT MAP!
Err... GENTLEMEN?
THANKS FOR LURING HIM, PROFESSOR.
WE'LL TAKE OVER FROM HERE.
PRAY FOR THE SAKE OF THE 52, WE DON'T SCREW UP THIS TIME!
TAKE IT EASY, SKEETS.
WE KNOW YOUR DATA GOT CORRUPTED SOMEHOW...
SKEETS IS DEAD, MICHAEL.
I ATE HIM FROM WITHIN TO MAKE A CRADLE.
A COCOON.
IMAGINE MY DISGUST!
THE MIND OF AN ALIEN GENIUS TRAPPED IN THE BODY OF A LOWLY CATERPILLAR! STALLED IN A LARVAL STAGE!
UNTIL, IRRADIATED WITH SUSPENDIUM PARTICLES, I BEGAN THE TRANSFORMATION THAT NOW CONCLUDES.
IT'S TOO LATE TO STOP IT.
THE 52 WEEKS OF MY GESTATION ARE COMPLETE.
AT LAST, THE CHRYSALIS CAN HATCH!

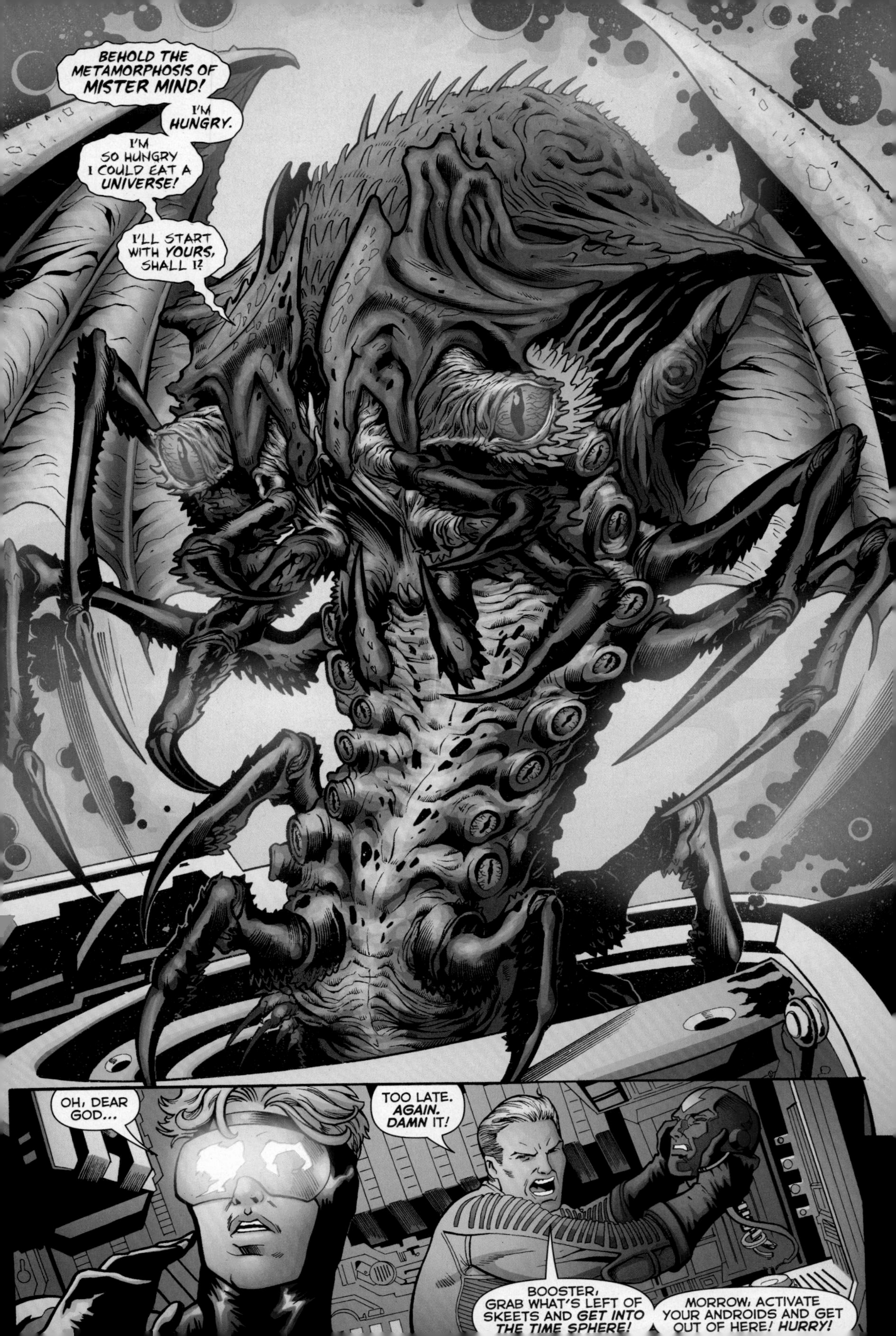
BEHOLD THE METAMORPHOSIS OF MISTER MIND!
I'M HUNGRY.
I'M SO HUNGRY I COULD EAT A UNIVERSE!
I'LL START WITH YOURS, SHALL I?
OH, DEAR GOD...
TOO LATE. AGAIN. DAMN IT!
BOOSTER, GRAB WHAT'S LEFT OF SKEETS AND GET INTO THE TIME SPHERE!
MORROW, ACTIVATE YOUR ANDROIDS AND GET OUT OF HERE! HURRY!

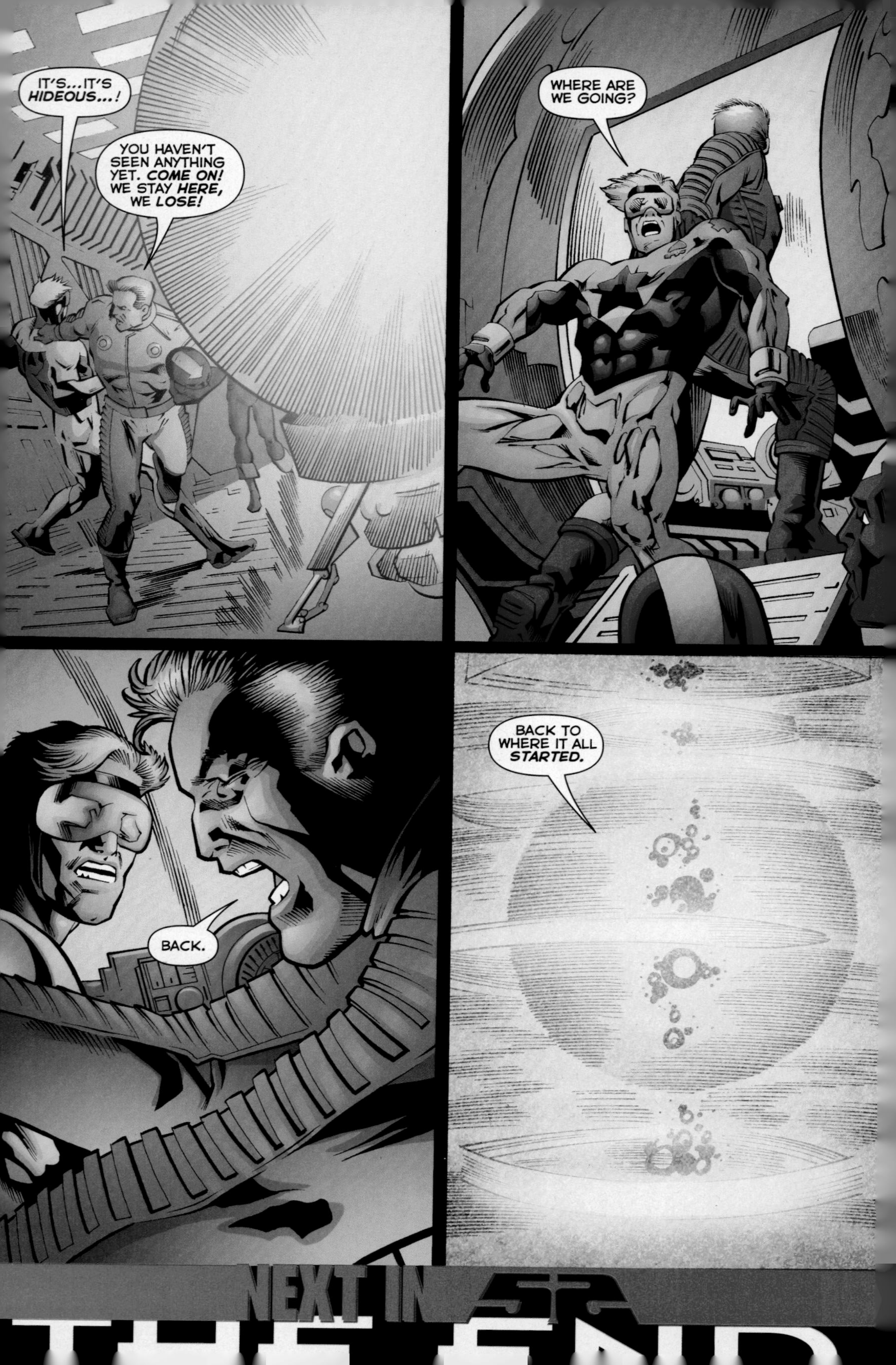
IT'S...IT'S HIDEOUS...!
YOU HAVEN'T SEEN ANYTHING YET. COME ON! WE STAY HERE, WE LOSE!
WHERE ARE WE GOING?
BACK.
BACK TO WHERE IT ALL STARTED.
NEXT IN 52
THE END

WEEK FIFTY-ONE NOTES

MARK WAID

The mechanics and reveal behind Animal Man's return to Earth were pitched by Grant at one of our earliest meetings, and it was a moment we were all eagerly anticipating. The further adventures of Near-Naked Alien Girl Staying With The Baker Family can be found in the spinoff series COUNTDOWN TO ADVENTURE, on sale now.

One of the best, the very best, things about being a comic book writer by trade is that you get to confess to things that insurance salesmen and stock brokers never dream of; specifically, in this case, that the editor and the 52 writers went around and around and around for about a week trying to decide whether or not the super-mutated Mr. Mind, minuscule worm grown to giant size and possessing the ability to rend the universe asunder with each flap of his monstrous wings, would still be wearing his trademark eyeglasses. If you don't like the choice we eventually made, feel free to marker in your own specs. Recently, a fan asked me if the reason all the Phantom Zone villains that Mr. Mind-as-Skeets ate back in week 37 were wearing goggles was a clue to Mind's true identity. I didn't have the heart to tell him that, no, that never occurred to us, that's just how Phantom Zone prisoners dress; instead, I congratulated him on his remarkable insight.

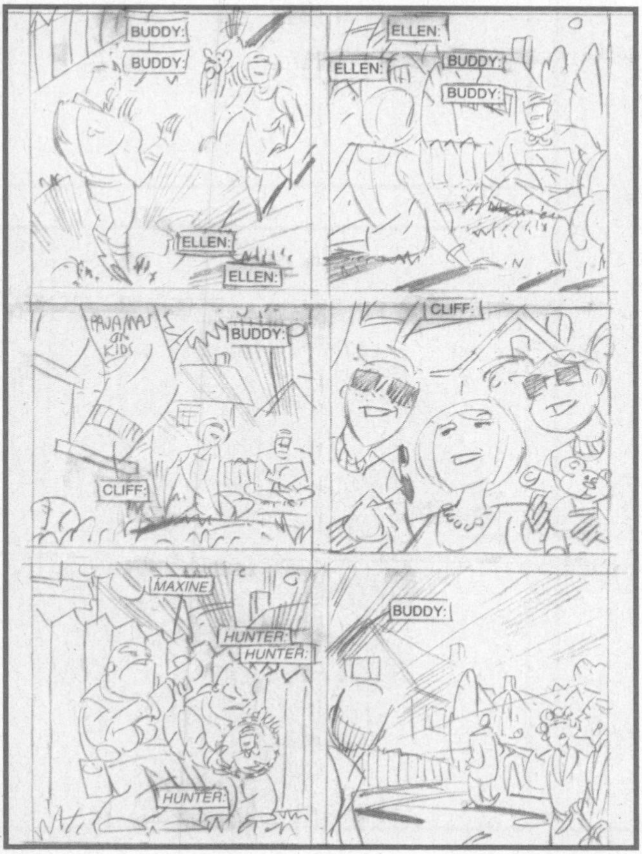

BUDDY:
BUDDY:
ELLEN:
ELLEN:
ELLEN:
ELLEN:
BUDDY:
BUDDY:
PAJAMAS ON KIDS
BUDDY:
CLIFF:
CLIFF:
MAXINE:
HUNTER:
HUNTER:
HUNTER:
BUDDY:

Breakdown
by **Keith Giffen**

The final version of this scene is shown on page 262.

Note the tiny bounty hunter aliens on lower left. In the printed version, they were only heard here — and physically revealed later in the issue.

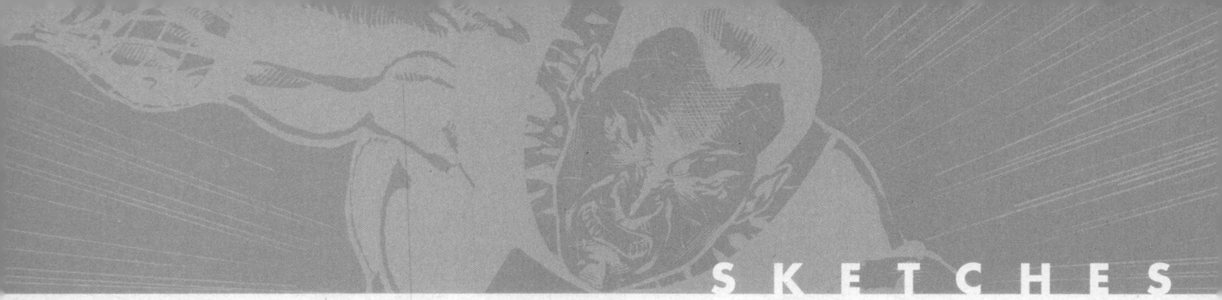

SKETCHES

BY **JUSTINIANO**

In order to safely travel the timestream, Rip Hunter uses a space diving suit. Artist Justiniano provides the design of the suit, which makes its debut in the next (and last) chapter.

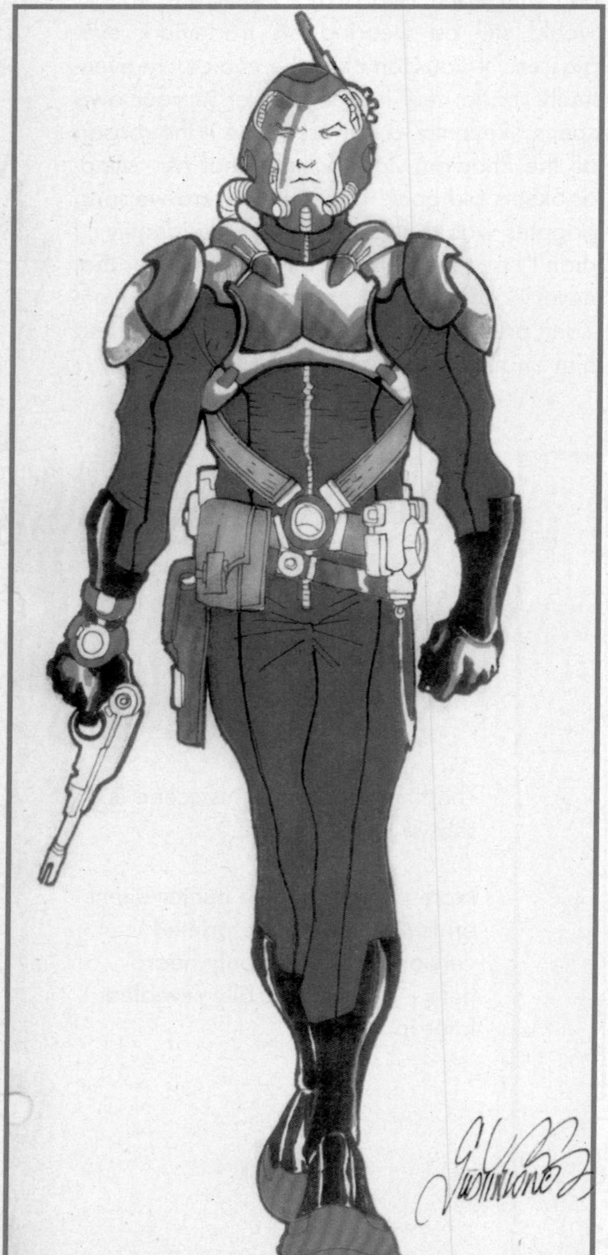

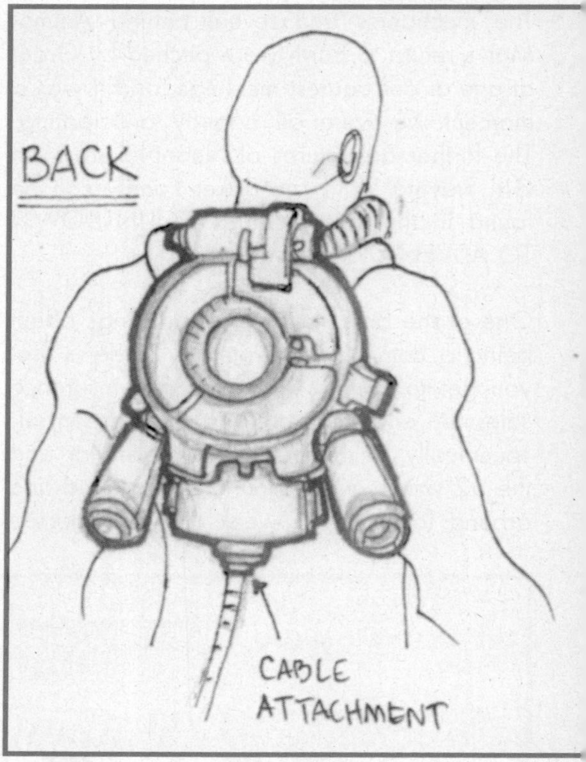
BACK
CABLE ATTACHMENT

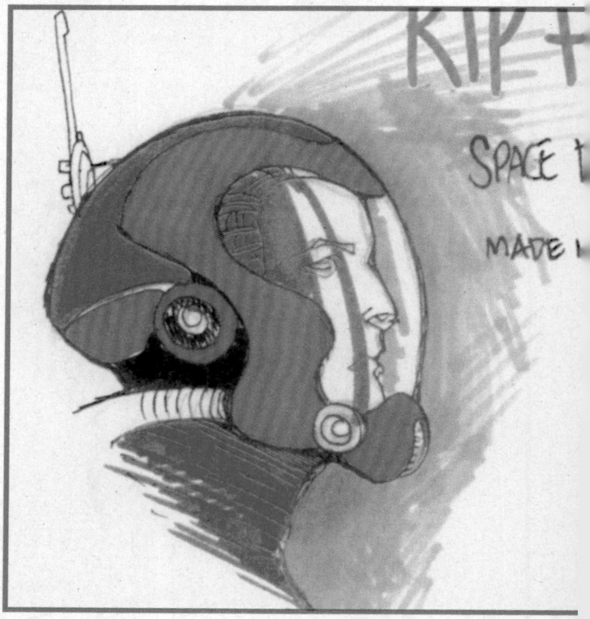
RIP
SPACE
MADE

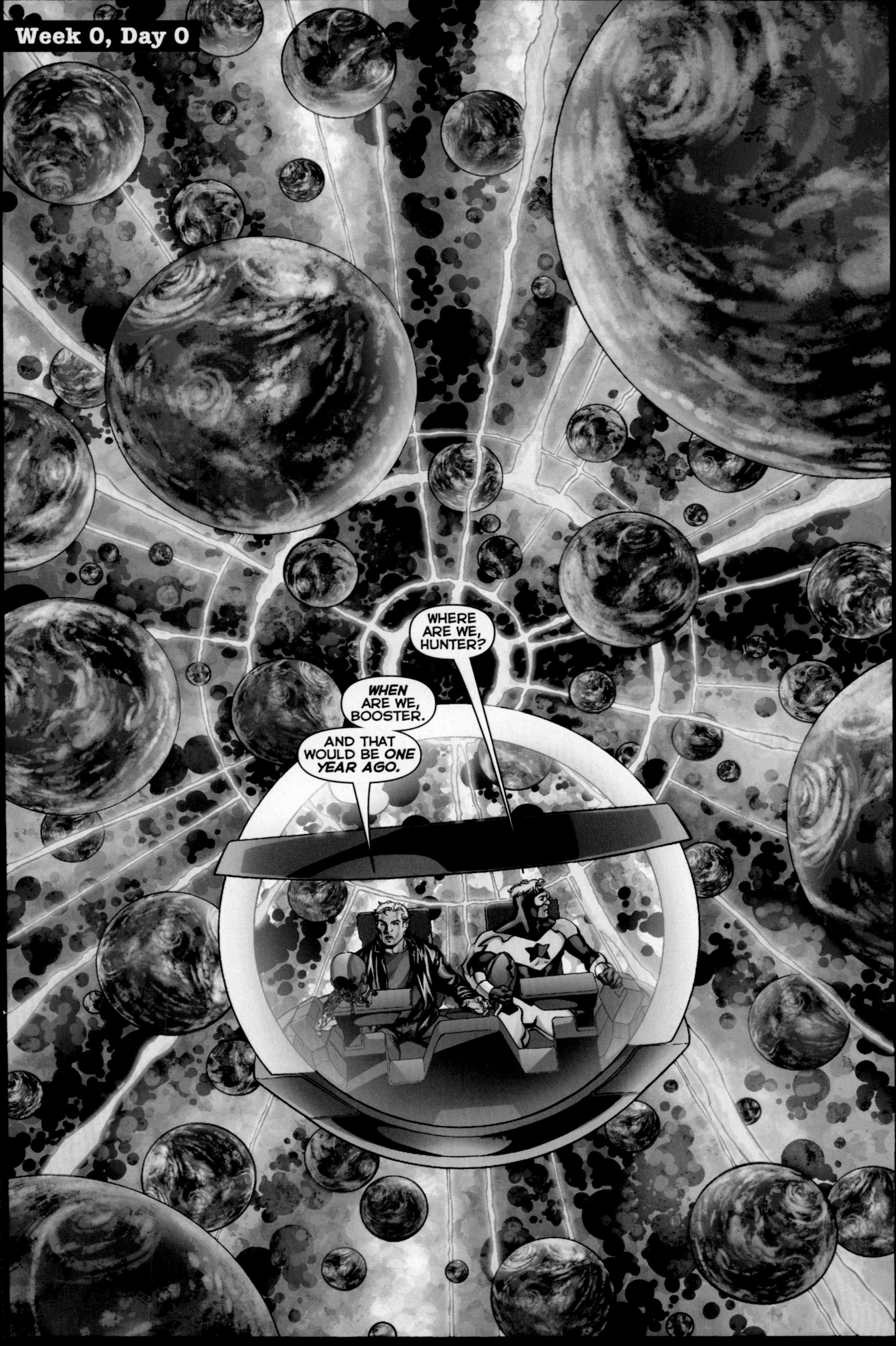
Week 0, Day 0
WHERE ARE WE, HUNTER?
WHEN ARE WE, BOOSTER.
AND THAT WOULD BE ONE YEAR AGO.

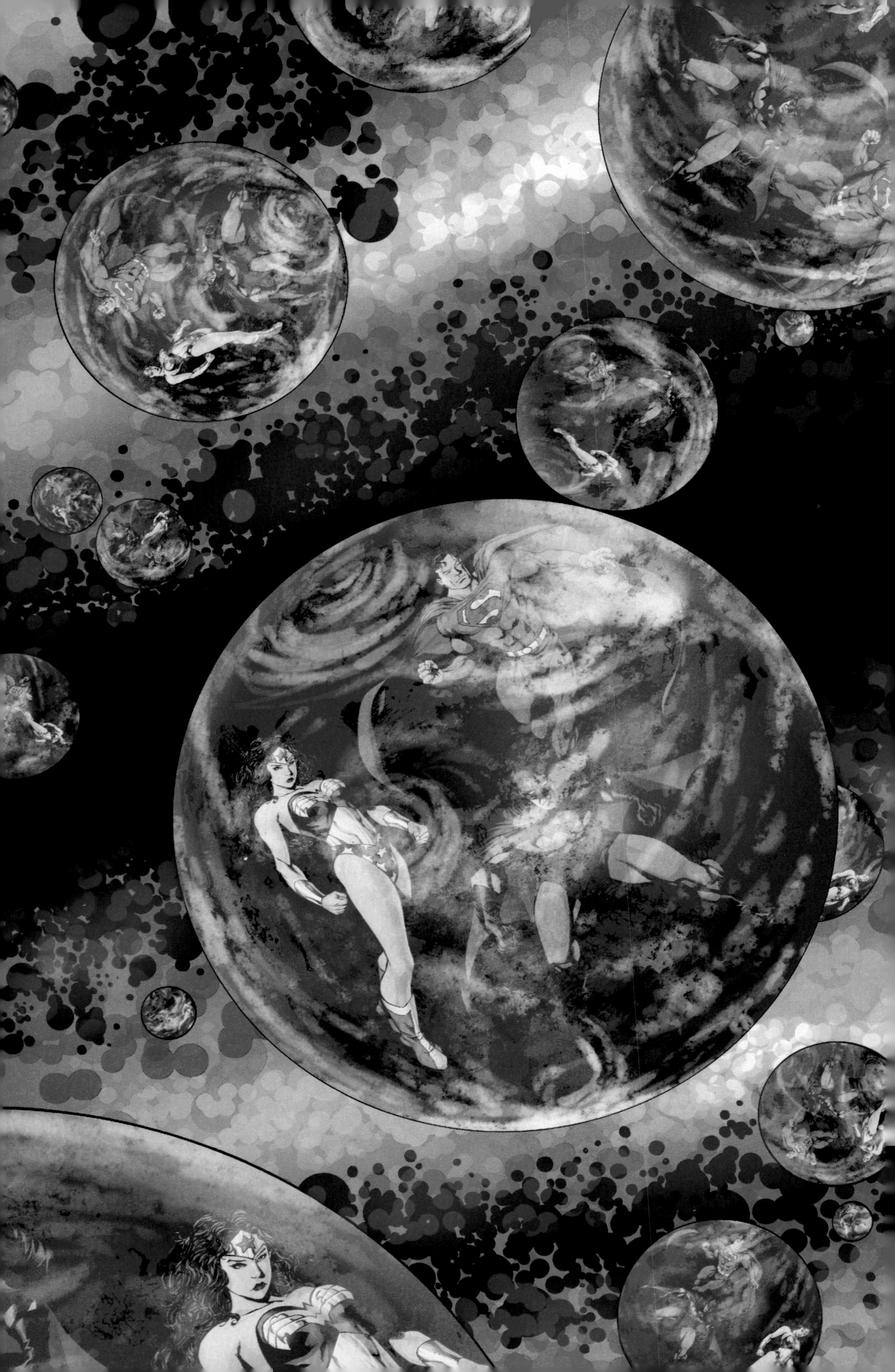

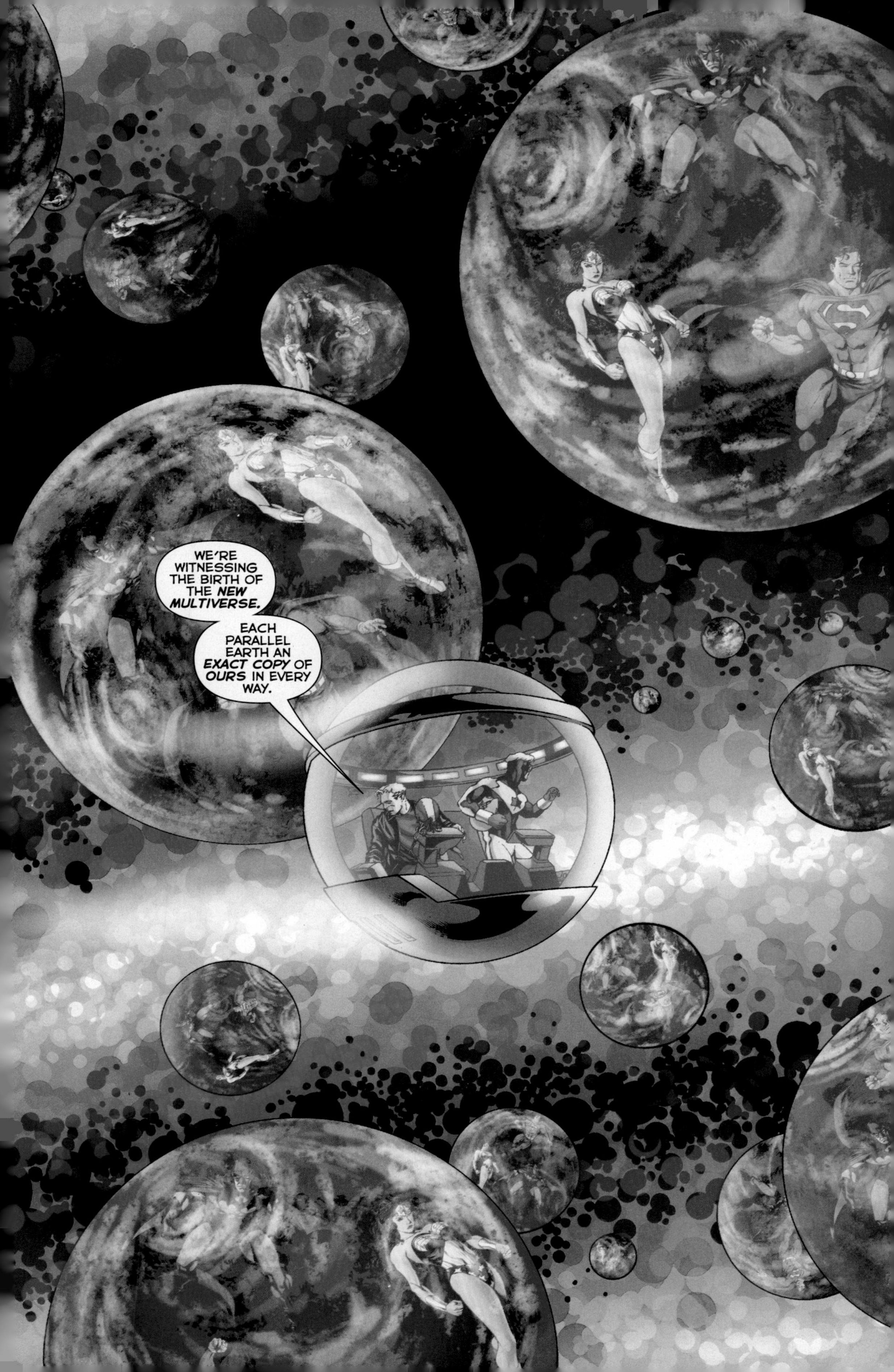
WE'RE WITNESSING THE BIRTH OF THE *NEW MULTIVERSE.*
EACH PARALLEL EARTH AN *EXACT COPY* OF *OURS* IN EVERY WAY.

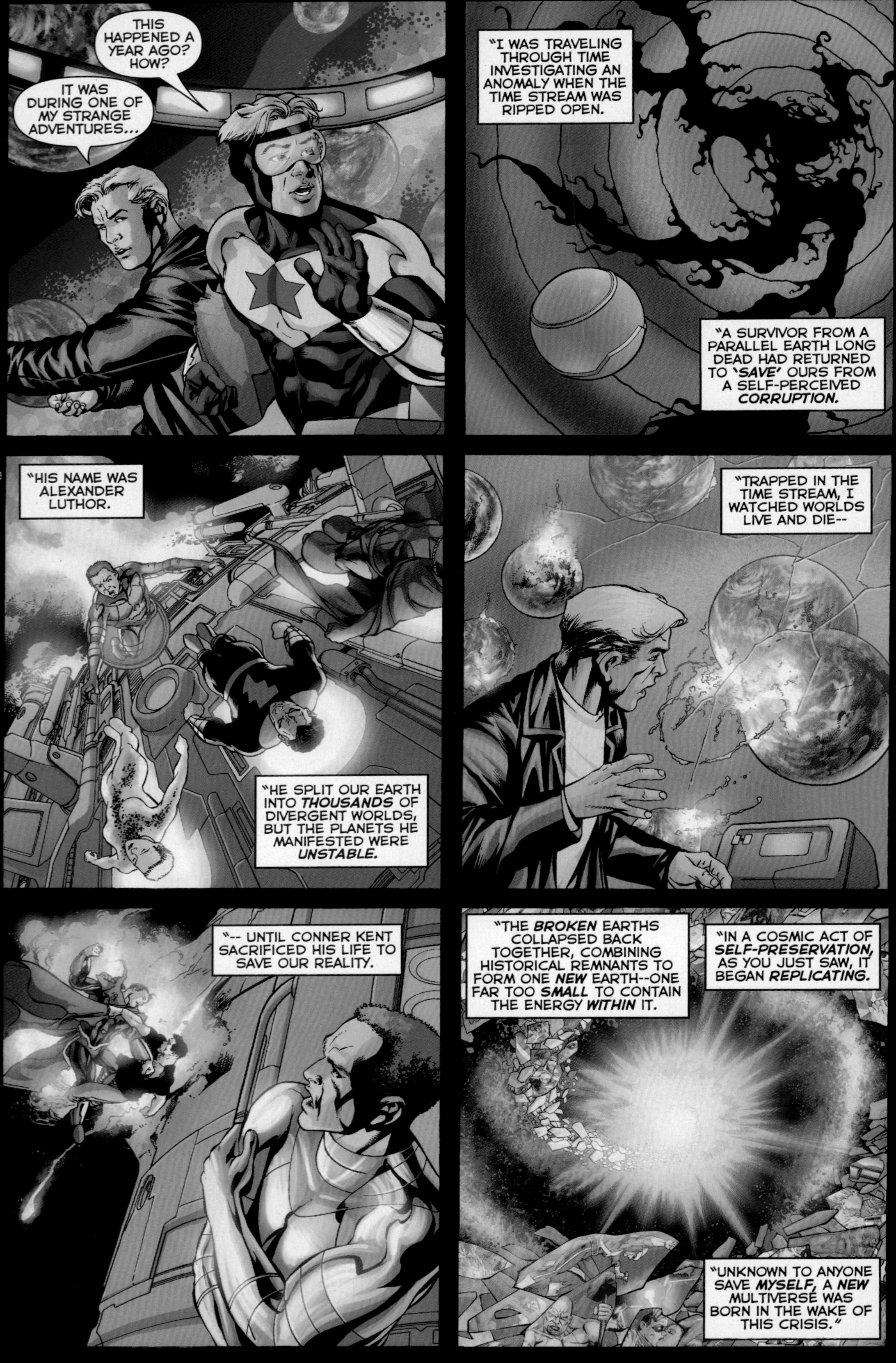

THIS HAPPENED A YEAR AGO? HOW?
IT WAS DURING ONE OF MY STRANGE ADVENTURES...
"I WAS TRAVELING THROUGH TIME INVESTIGATING AN ANOMALY WHEN THE TIME STREAM WAS RIPPED OPEN.
"A SURVIVOR FROM A PARALLEL EARTH LONG DEAD HAD RETURNED TO 'SAVE' OURS FROM A SELF-PERCEIVED CORRUPTION.
"HIS NAME WAS ALEXANDER LUTHOR.
"HE SPLIT OUR EARTH INTO THOUSANDS OF DIVERGENT WORLDS, BUT THE PLANETS HE MANIFESTED WERE UNSTABLE.
"TRAPPED IN THE TIME STREAM, I WATCHED WORLDS LIVE AND DIE--
"-- UNTIL CONNER KENT SACRIFICED HIS LIFE TO SAVE OUR REALITY.
"THE BROKEN EARTHS COLLAPSED BACK TOGETHER, COMBINING HISTORICAL REMNANTS TO FORM ONE NEW EARTH--ONE FAR TOO SMALL TO CONTAIN THE ENERGY WITHIN IT.
"IN A COSMIC ACT OF SELF-PRESERVATION, AS YOU JUST SAW, IT BEGAN REPLICATING.
"UNKNOWN TO ANYONE SAVE MYSELF, A NEW MULTIVERSE WAS BORN IN THE WAKE OF THIS CRISIS."

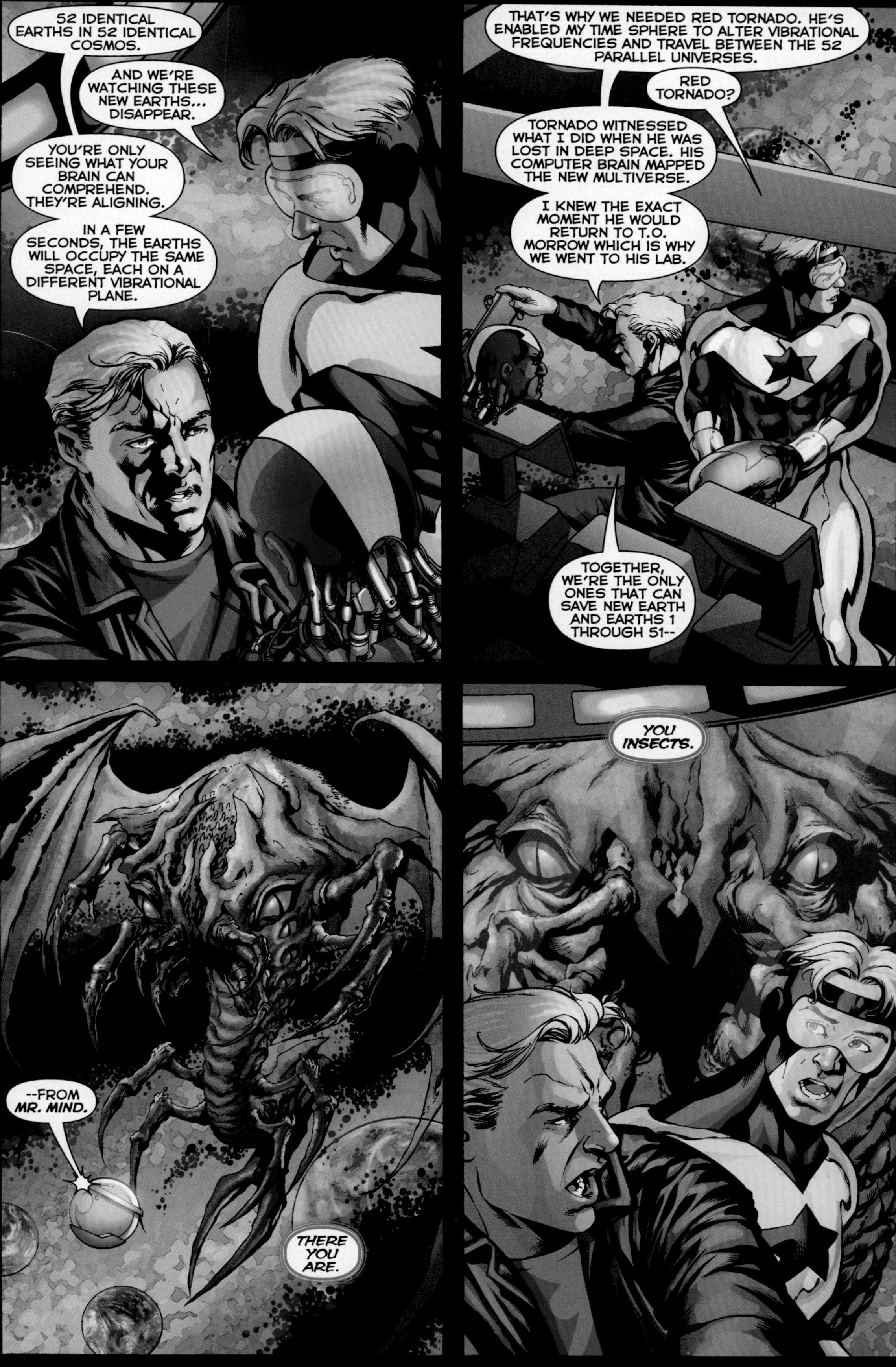
52 IDENTICAL EARTHS IN 52 IDENTICAL COSMOS.
AND WE'RE WATCHING THESE NEW EARTHS... DISAPPEAR.
YOU'RE ONLY SEEING WHAT YOUR BRAIN CAN COMPREHEND. THEY'RE ALIGNING.
IN A FEW SECONDS, THE EARTHS WILL OCCUPY THE SAME SPACE, EACH ON A DIFFERENT VIBRATIONAL PLANE.
THAT'S WHY WE NEEDED RED TORNADO. HE'S ENABLED MY TIME SPHERE TO ALTER VIBRATIONAL FREQUENCIES AND TRAVEL BETWEEN THE 52 PARALLEL UNIVERSES.
RED TORNADO?
TORNADO WITNESSED WHAT I DID WHEN HE WAS LOST IN DEEP SPACE. HIS COMPUTER BRAIN MAPPED THE NEW MULTIVERSE.
I KNEW THE EXACT MOMENT HE WOULD RETURN TO T.O. MORROW WHICH IS WHY WE WENT TO HIS LAB.
TOGETHER, WE'RE THE ONLY ONES THAT CAN SAVE NEW EARTH AND EARTHS 1 THROUGH 51--
--FROM MR. MIND.
THERE YOU ARE.
YOU INSECTS.

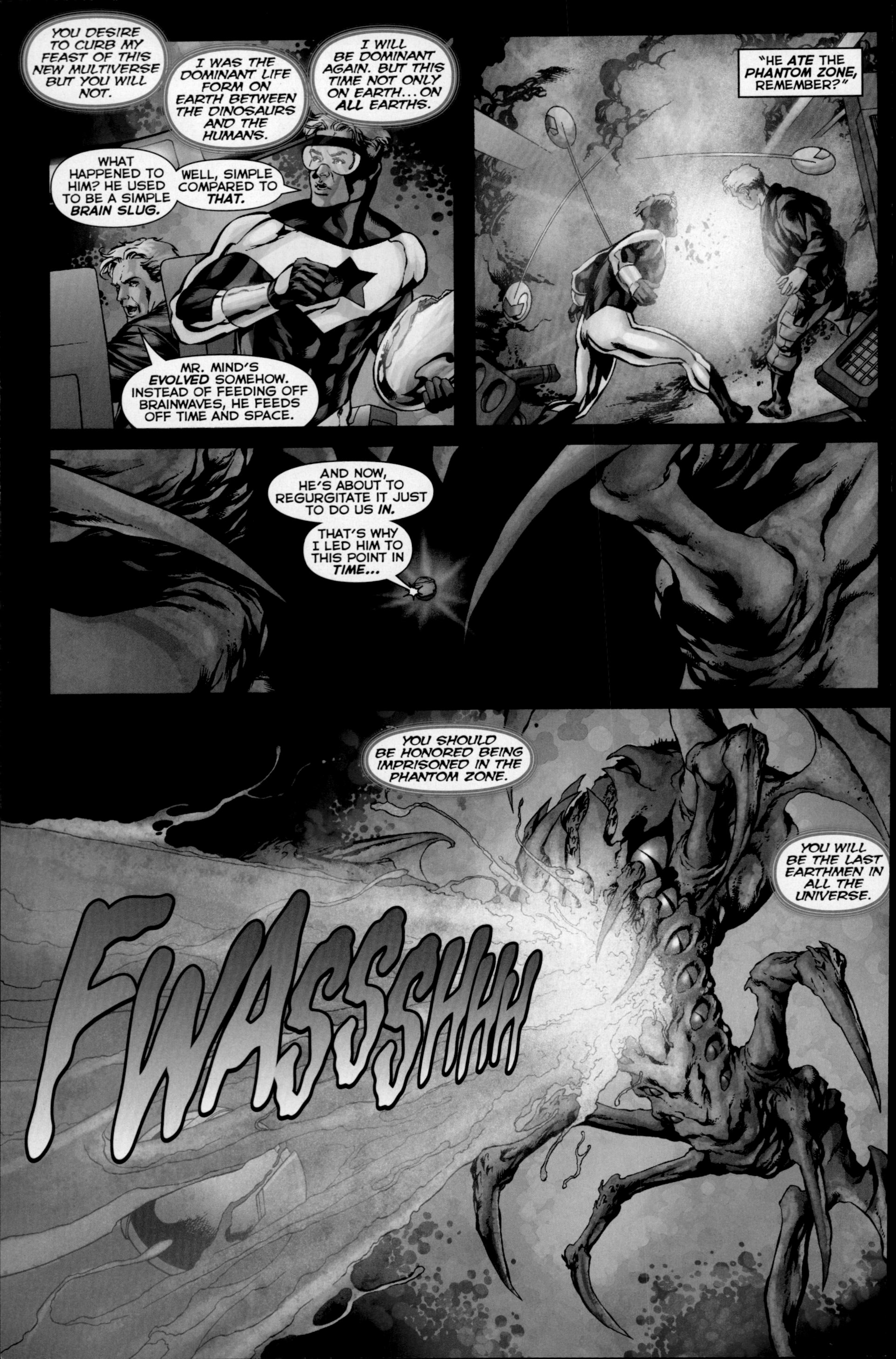
YOU DESIRE TO CURB MY FEAST OF THIS NEW MULTIVERSE BUT YOU WILL NOT.
I WAS THE DOMINANT LIFE FORM ON EARTH BETWEEN THE DINOSAURS AND THE HUMANS.
I WILL BE DOMINANT AGAIN. BUT THIS TIME NOT ONLY ON EARTH... ON ALL EARTHS.
WHAT HAPPENED TO HIM? HE USED TO BE A SIMPLE BRAIN SLUG.
WELL, SIMPLE COMPARED TO THAT.
MR. MIND'S EVOLVED SOMEHOW. INSTEAD OF FEEDING OFF BRAINWAVES, HE FEEDS OFF TIME AND SPACE.
"HE ATE THE PHANTOM ZONE, REMEMBER?"
AND NOW, HE'S ABOUT TO REGURGITATE IT JUST TO DO US IN.
THAT'S WHY I LED HIM TO THIS POINT IN TIME...
YOU SHOULD BE HONORED BEING IMPRISONED IN THE PHANTOM ZONE.
YOU WILL BE THE LAST EARTHMEN IN ALL THE UNIVERSE.
FWASSSHHH

I GOT IT! I GOT IT!

SUPERNOVA?

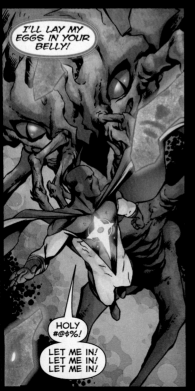

I'LL LAY MY EGGS IN YOUR BELLY!

HOLY #@$%!

LET ME IN! LET ME IN! LET ME IN!

SUPERNOVA?

THANKS TO THE PHANTOM ZONE TECH LACED IN HIS UNIFORM, IT'S ABLE TO DEFLECT AND RESTORE THE PHANTOM ZONE TO ITS PROPER DIMENSIONAL PLANE.

WAIT A SECOND. I WAS SUPERNOVA.

OKAY... OKAY, I DID WHAT YOU ASKED...

...NOW TAKE ME HOME.

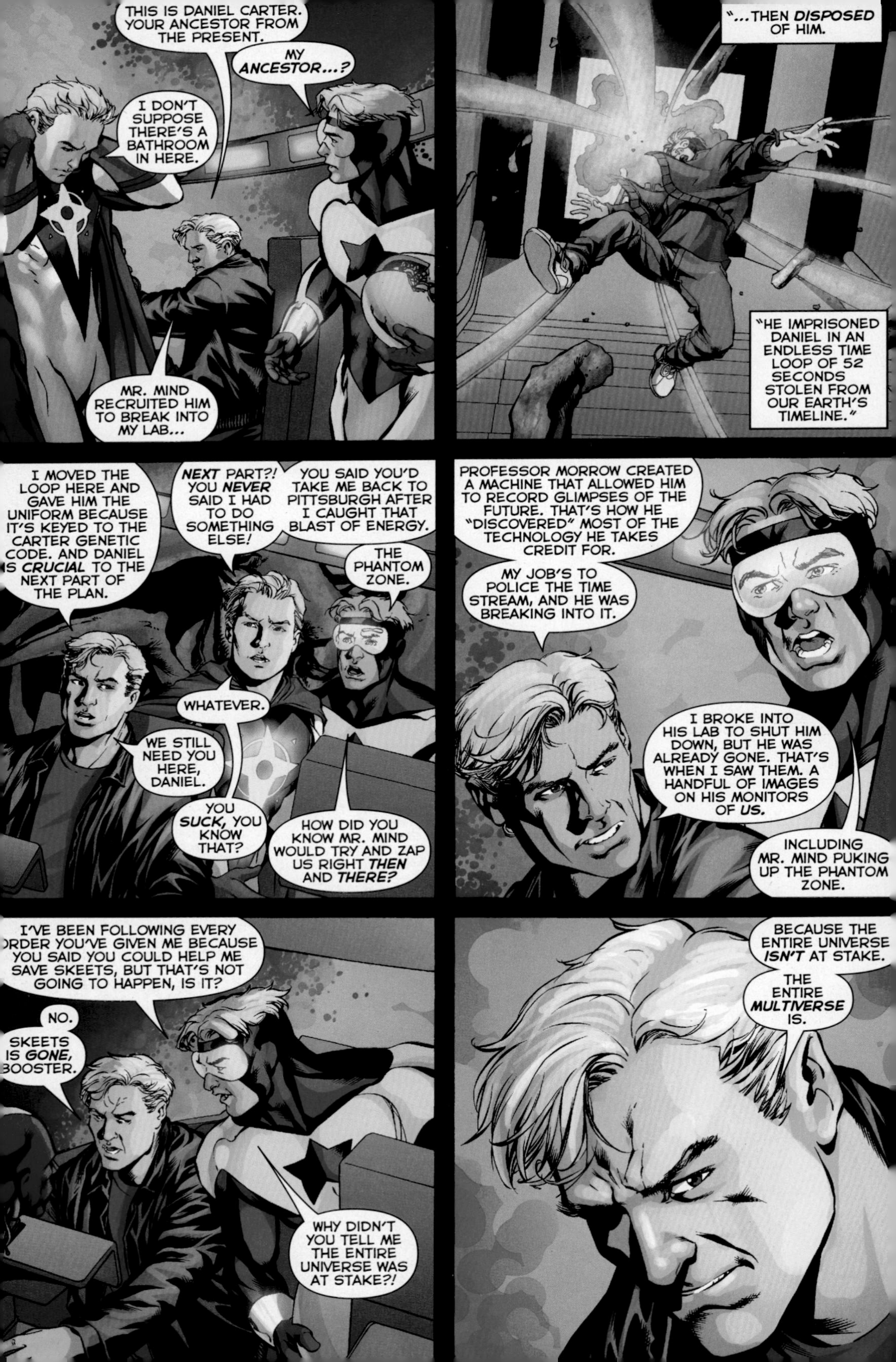
THIS IS DANIEL CARTER. YOUR ANCESTOR FROM THE PRESENT.
MY ANCESTOR...?
I DON'T SUPPOSE THERE'S A BATHROOM IN HERE.
MR. MIND RECRUITED HIM TO BREAK INTO MY LAB...
"...THEN DISPOSED OF HIM.
"HE IMPRISONED DANIEL IN AN ENDLESS TIME LOOP OF 52 SECONDS STOLEN FROM OUR EARTH'S TIMELINE."
I MOVED THE LOOP HERE AND GAVE HIM THE UNIFORM BECAUSE IT'S KEYED TO THE CARTER GENETIC CODE. AND DANIEL IS CRUCIAL TO THE NEXT PART OF THE PLAN.
NEXT PART?! YOU NEVER SAID I HAD TO DO SOMETHING ELSE!
YOU SAID YOU'D TAKE ME BACK TO PITTSBURGH AFTER I CAUGHT THAT BLAST OF ENERGY.
THE PHANTOM ZONE.
WHATEVER.
WE STILL NEED YOU HERE, DANIEL.
YOU SUCK, YOU KNOW THAT?
HOW DID YOU KNOW MR. MIND WOULD TRY AND ZAP US RIGHT THEN AND THERE?
PROFESSOR MORROW CREATED A MACHINE THAT ALLOWED HIM TO RECORD GLIMPSES OF THE FUTURE. THAT'S HOW HE "DISCOVERED" MOST OF THE TECHNOLOGY HE TAKES CREDIT FOR.
MY JOB'S TO POLICE THE TIME STREAM, AND HE WAS BREAKING INTO IT.
I BROKE INTO HIS LAB TO SHUT HIM DOWN, BUT HE WAS ALREADY GONE. THAT'S WHEN I SAW THEM. A HANDFUL OF IMAGES ON HIS MONITORS OF US.
INCLUDING MR. MIND PUKING UP THE PHANTOM ZONE.
I'VE BEEN FOLLOWING EVERY ORDER YOU'VE GIVEN ME BECAUSE YOU SAID YOU COULD HELP ME SAVE SKEETS, BUT THAT'S NOT GOING TO HAPPEN, IS IT?
NO.
SKEETS IS GONE, BOOSTER.
WHY DIDN'T YOU TELL ME THE ENTIRE UNIVERSE WAS AT STAKE?!
BECAUSE THE ENTIRE UNIVERSE ISN'T AT STAKE.
THE ENTIRE MULTIVERSE IS.

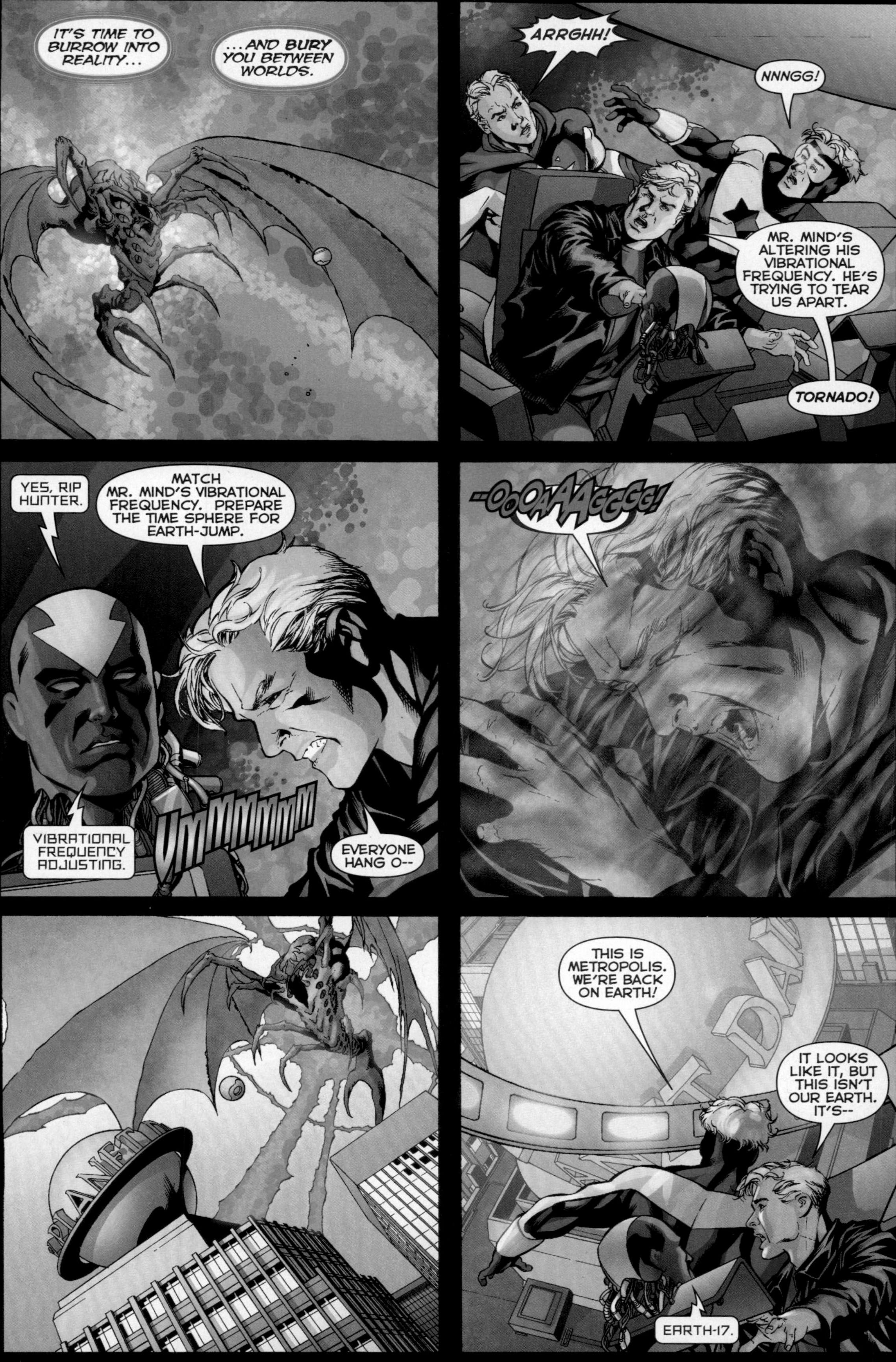
IT'S TIME TO BURROW INTO REALITY...
...AND BURY YOU BETWEEN WORLDS.
ARRGHH!
NNNGG!
MR. MIND'S ALTERING HIS VIBRATIONAL FREQUENCY. HE'S TRYING TO TEAR US APART.
TORNADO!
YES, RIP HUNTER.
MATCH MR. MIND'S VIBRATIONAL FREQUENCY. PREPARE THE TIME SPHERE FOR EARTH-JUMP.
VIBRATIONAL FREQUENCY ADJUSTING.
VMMMMMM
EVERYONE HANG O--
--OOOAAAGGGG!
THIS IS METROPOLIS. WE'RE BACK ON EARTH!
IT LOOKS LIKE IT, BUT THIS ISN'T OUR EARTH. IT'S--
EARTH-17.

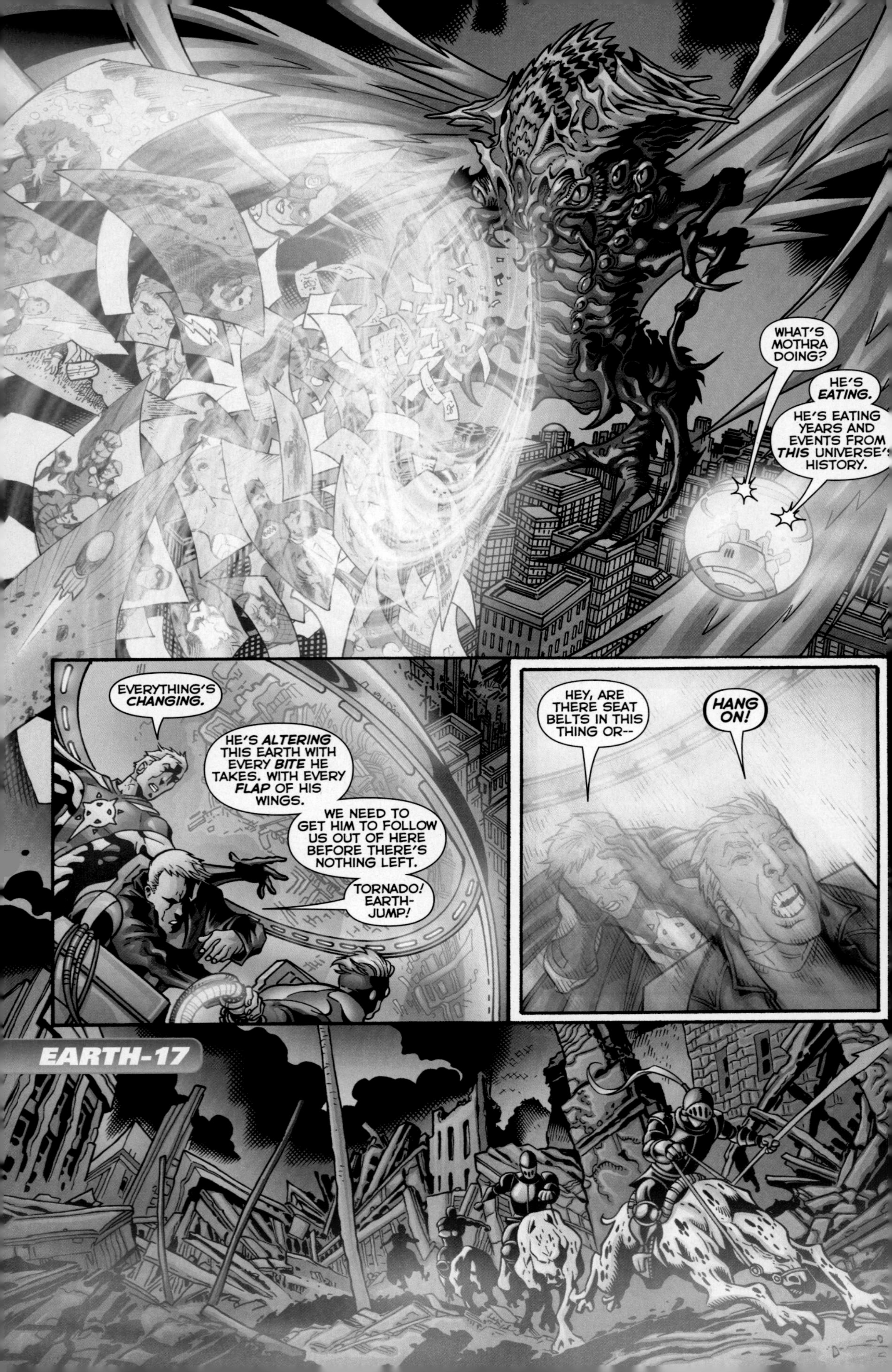
WHAT'S MOTHRA DOING?
HE'S EATING.
HE'S EATING YEARS AND EVENTS FROM THIS UNIVERSE'S HISTORY.
EVERYTHING'S CHANGING.
HE'S ALTERING THIS EARTH WITH EVERY BITE HE TAKES. WITH EVERY FLAP OF HIS WINGS.
WE NEED TO GET HIM TO FOLLOW US OUT OF HERE BEFORE THERE'S NOTHING LEFT.
TORNADO! EARTH-JUMP!
HEY, ARE THERE SEAT BELTS IN THIS THING OR--
HANG ON!
EARTH-17

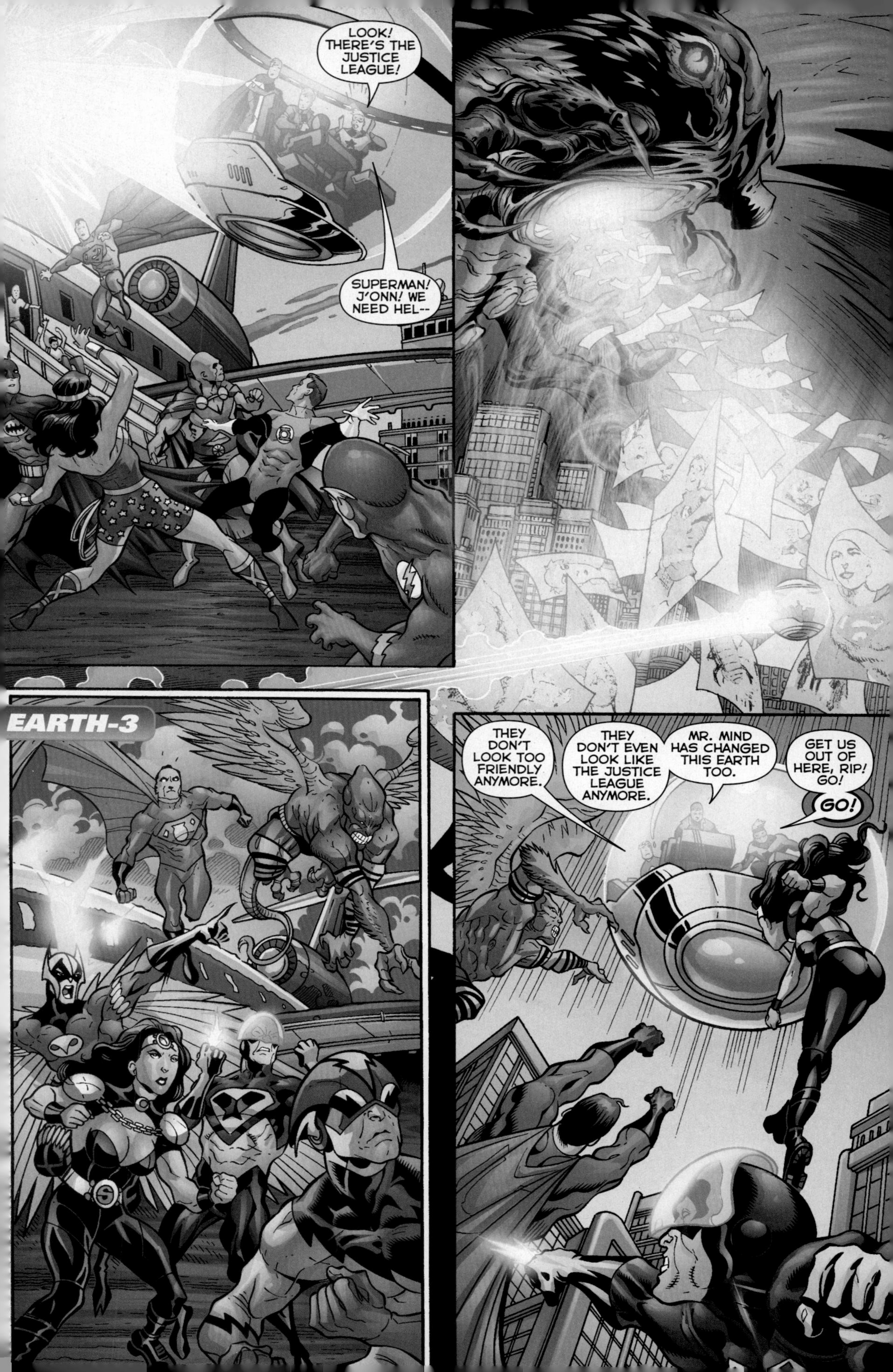
LOOK! THERE'S THE JUSTICE LEAGUE!
SUPERMAN! J'ONN! WE NEED HEL--
EARTH-3
THEY DON'T LOOK TOO FRIENDLY ANYMORE.
THEY DON'T EVEN LOOK LIKE THE JUSTICE LEAGUE ANYMORE.
MR. MIND HAS CHANGED THIS EARTH TOO.
GET US OUT OF HERE, RIP! GO!
GO!

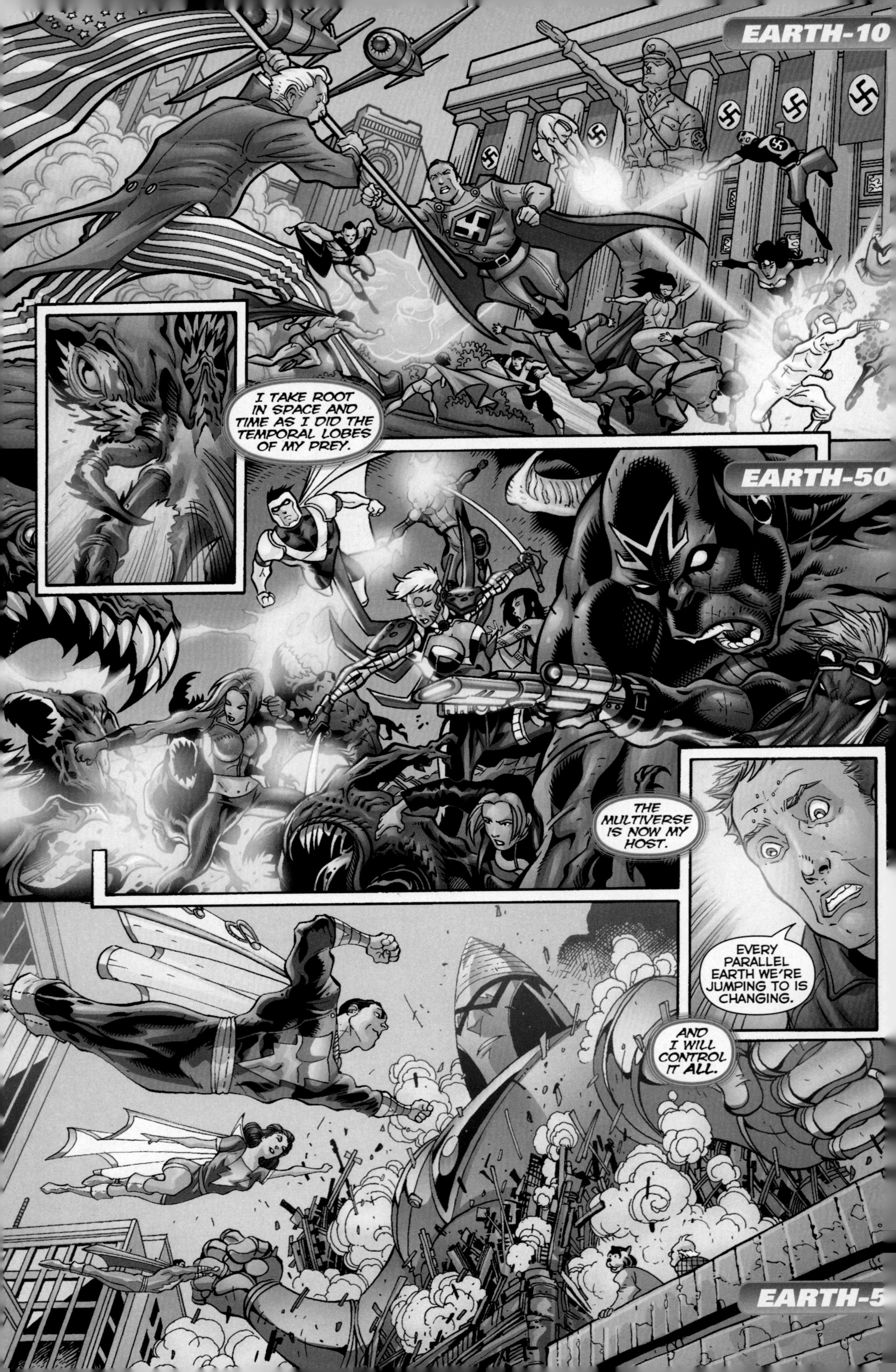

EARTH-10
I TAKE ROOT IN SPACE AND TIME AS I DID THE TEMPORAL LOBES OF MY PREY.
EARTH-50
THE MULTIVERSE IS NOW MY HOST.
EVERY PARALLEL EARTH WE'RE JUMPING TO IS CHANGING.
AND I WILL CONTROL IT ALL.
EARTH-5

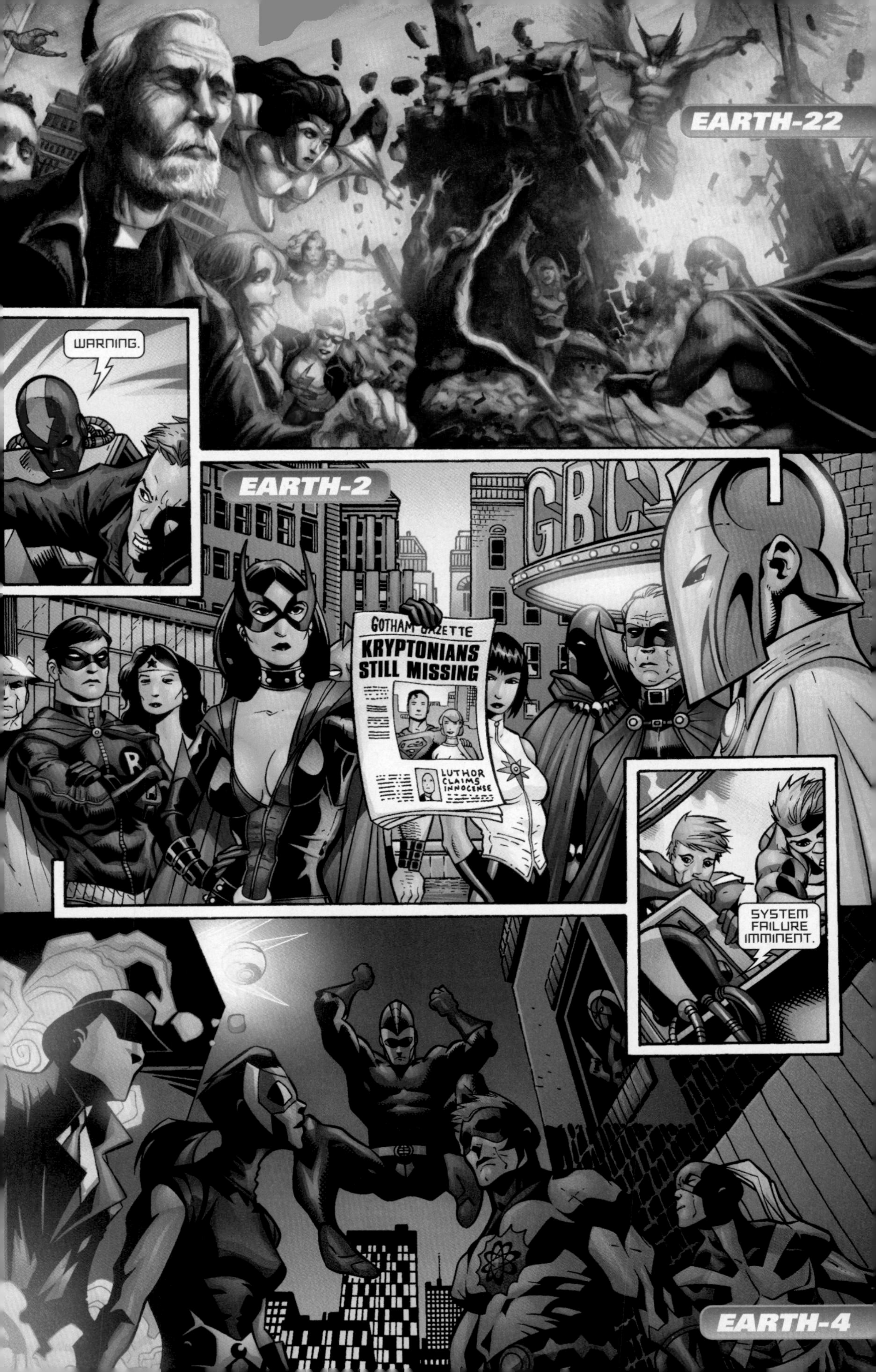
EARTH-22
WARNING.
EARTH-2
GBC
GOTHAM GAZETTE
KRYPTONIANS STILL MISSING
LUTHOR CLAIMS INNOCENSE
SYSTEM FAILURE IMMINENT.
EARTH-4

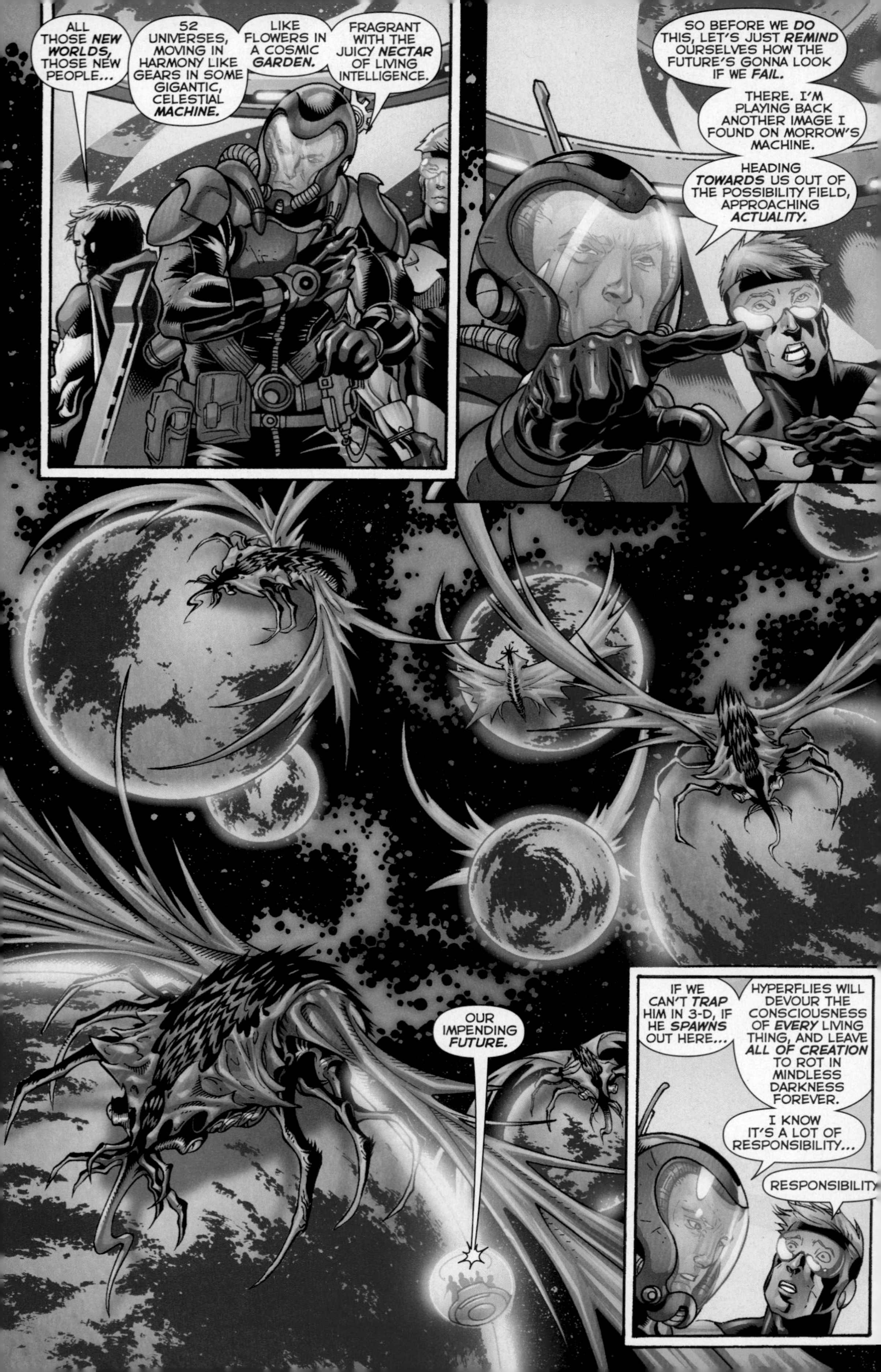
ALL THOSE NEW WORLDS, THOSE NEW PEOPLE...
52 UNIVERSES, MOVING IN HARMONY LIKE GEARS IN SOME GIGANTIC, CELESTIAL MACHINE.
LIKE FLOWERS IN A COSMIC GARDEN.
FRAGRANT WITH THE JUICY NECTAR OF LIVING INTELLIGENCE.
SO BEFORE WE DO THIS, LET'S JUST REMIND OURSELVES HOW THE FUTURE'S GONNA LOOK IF WE FAIL.
THERE. I'M PLAYING BACK ANOTHER IMAGE I FOUND ON MORROW'S MACHINE.
HEADING TOWARDS US OUT OF THE POSSIBILITY FIELD, APPROACHING ACTUALITY.
OUR IMPENDING FUTURE.
IF WE CAN'T TRAP HIM IN 3-D, IF HE SPAWNS OUT HERE...
HYPERFLIES WILL DEVOUR THE CONSCIOUSNESS OF EVERY LIVING THING, AND LEAVE ALL OF CREATION TO ROT IN MINDLESS DARKNESS FOREVER.
I KNOW IT'S A LOT OF RESPONSIBILITY...
RESPONSIBILITY

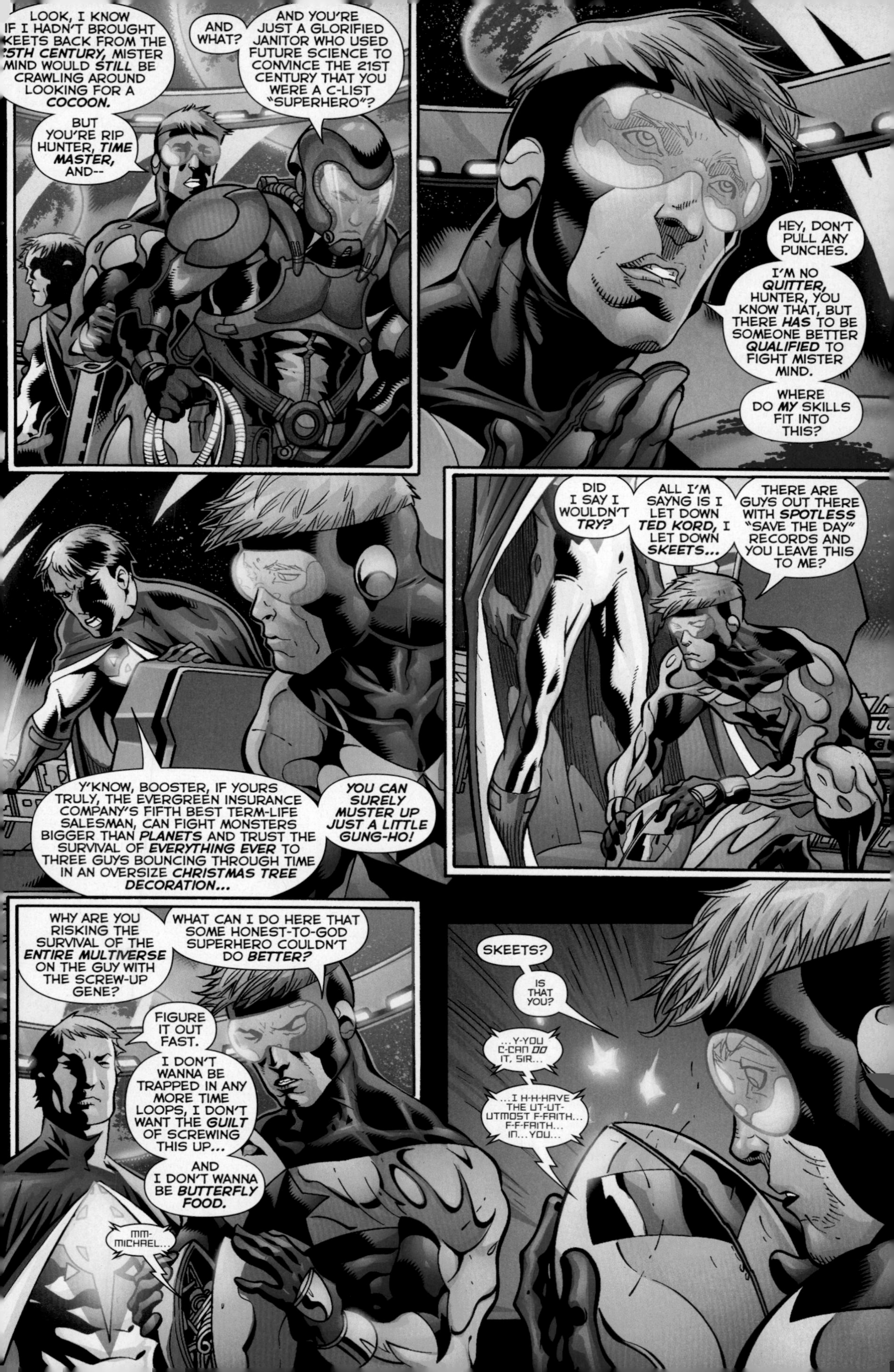
LOOK, I KNOW IF I HADN'T BROUGHT SKEETS BACK FROM THE 25TH CENTURY, MISTER MIND WOULD STILL BE CRAWLING AROUND LOOKING FOR A COCOON.
BUT YOU'RE RIP HUNTER, TIME MASTER, AND--
AND WHAT?
AND YOU'RE JUST A GLORIFIED JANITOR WHO USED FUTURE SCIENCE TO CONVINCE THE 21ST CENTURY THAT YOU WERE A C-LIST "SUPERHERO"?
HEY, DON'T PULL ANY PUNCHES.
I'M NO QUITTER, HUNTER, YOU KNOW THAT, BUT THERE HAS TO BE SOMEONE BETTER QUALIFIED TO FIGHT MISTER MIND.
WHERE DO MY SKILLS FIT INTO THIS?
Y'KNOW, BOOSTER, IF YOURS TRULY, THE EVERGREEN INSURANCE COMPANY'S FIFTH BEST TERM-LIFE SALESMAN, CAN FIGHT MONSTERS BIGGER THAN PLANETS AND TRUST THE SURVIVAL OF EVERYTHING EVER TO THREE GUYS BOUNCING THROUGH TIME IN AN OVERSIZE CHRISTMAS TREE DECORATION...
YOU CAN SURELY MUSTER UP JUST A LITTLE GUNG-HO!
DID I SAY I WOULDN'T TRY?
ALL I'M SAYNG IS I LET DOWN TED KORD, I LET DOWN SKEETS...
THERE ARE GUYS OUT THERE WITH SPOTLESS "SAVE THE DAY" RECORDS AND YOU LEAVE THIS TO ME?
WHY ARE YOU RISKING THE SURVIVAL OF THE ENTIRE MULTIVERSE ON THE GUY WITH THE SCREW-UP GENE?
WHAT CAN I DO HERE THAT SOME HONEST-TO-GOD SUPERHERO COULDN'T DO BETTER?
FIGURE IT OUT FAST.
I DON'T WANNA BE TRAPPED IN ANY MORE TIME LOOPS, I DON'T WANT THE GUILT OF SCREWING THIS UP...
AND I DON'T WANNA BE BUTTERFLY FOOD.
MM-MICHAEL...
SKEETS?
IS THAT YOU?
...Y-YOU C-CAN DO IT, SIR...
...I H-H-HAVE THE UT-UT-UTMOST F-FAITH... F-F-FAITH... IN... YOU...

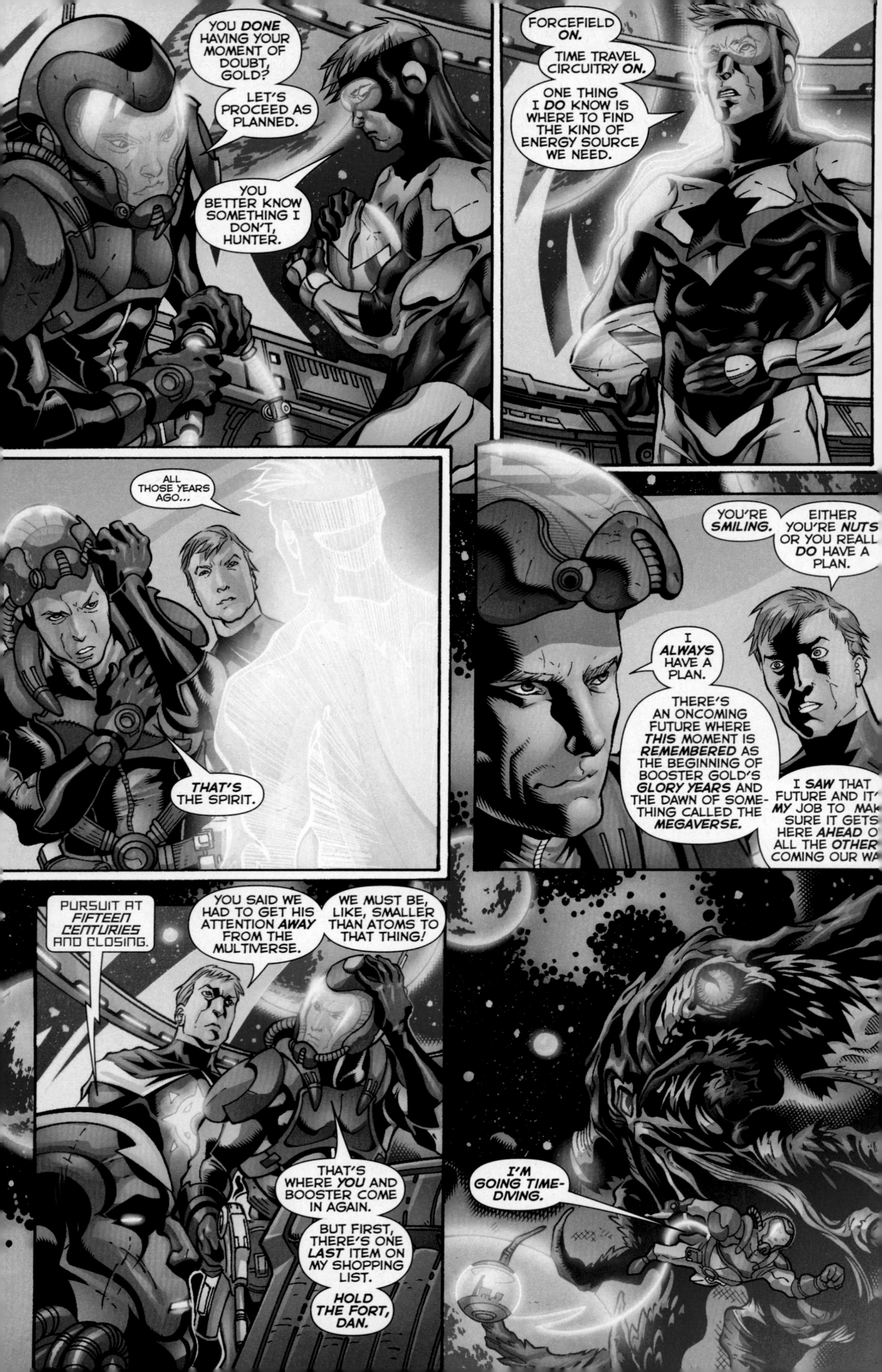
YOU DONE HAVING YOUR MOMENT OF DOUBT, GOLD?
LET'S PROCEED AS PLANNED.
YOU BETTER KNOW SOMETHING I DON'T, HUNTER.
FORCEFIELD ON.
TIME TRAVEL CIRCUITRY ON.
ONE THING I DO KNOW IS WHERE TO FIND THE KIND OF ENERGY SOURCE WE NEED.
ALL THOSE YEARS AGO...
THAT'S THE SPIRIT.
YOU'RE SMILING.
EITHER YOU'RE NUTS OR YOU REALL DO HAVE A PLAN.
I ALWAYS HAVE A PLAN.
THERE'S AN ONCOMING FUTURE WHERE THIS MOMENT IS REMEMBERED AS THE BEGINNING OF BOOSTER GOLD'S GLORY YEARS AND THE DAWN OF SOMETHING CALLED THE MEGAVERSE.
I SAW THAT FUTURE AND IT' MY JOB TO MAK SURE IT GETS HERE AHEAD O ALL THE OTHER COMING OUR WA
PURSUIT AT FIFTEEN CENTURIES AND CLOSING.
YOU SAID WE HAD TO GET HIS ATTENTION AWAY FROM THE MULTIVERSE.
WE MUST BE, LIKE, SMALLER THAN ATOMS TO THAT THING!
THAT'S WHERE YOU AND BOOSTER COME IN AGAIN.
BUT FIRST, THERE'S ONE LAST ITEM ON MY SHOPPING LIST.
HOLD THE FORT, DAN.
I'M GOING TIME-DIVING.

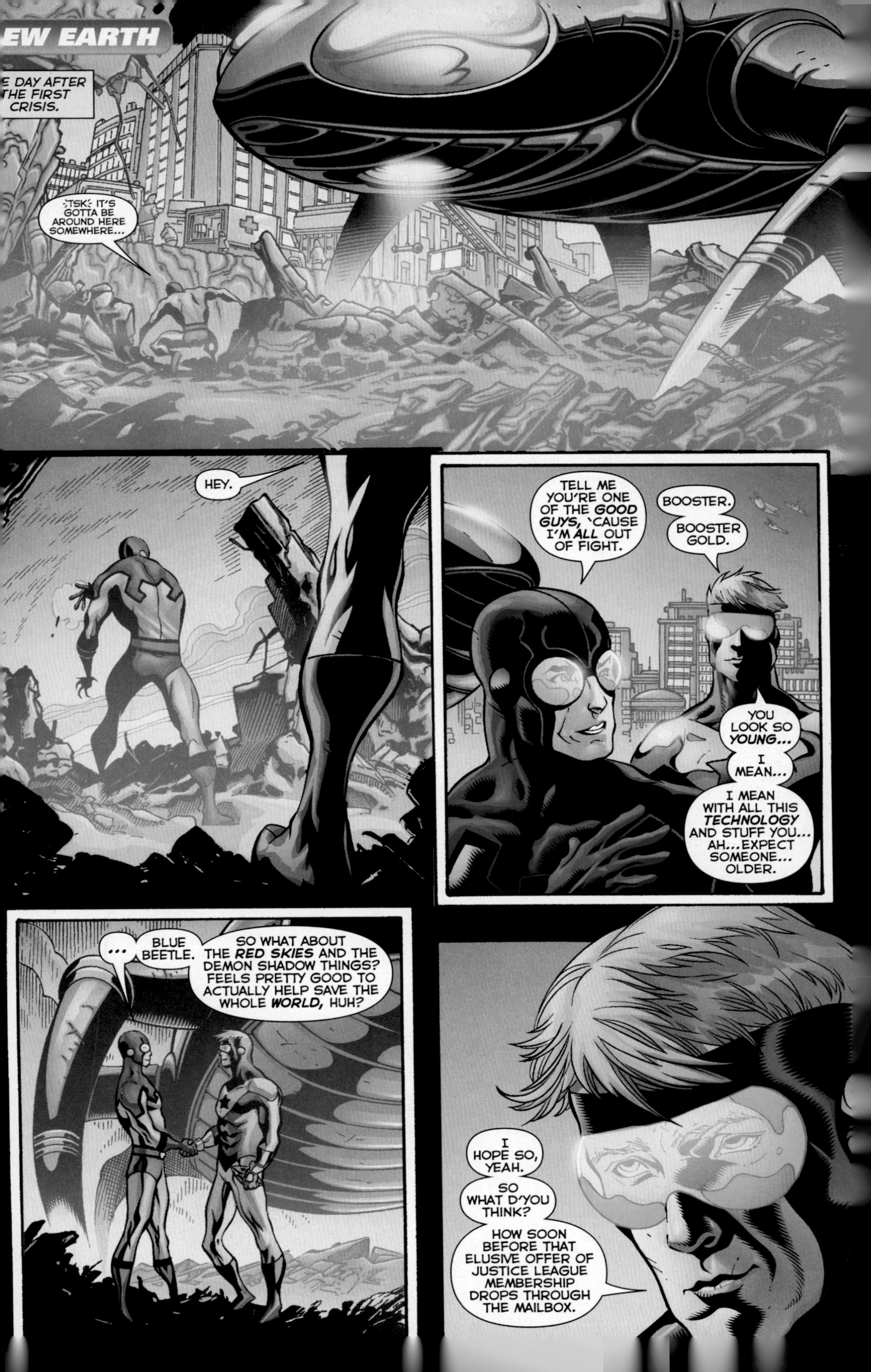

EW EARTH
E DAY AFTER THE FIRST CRISIS.
-TSK- IT'S GOTTA BE AROUND HERE SOMEWHERE...
HEY.
TELL ME YOU'RE ONE OF THE GOOD GUYS, 'CAUSE I'M ALL OUT OF FIGHT.
BOOSTER.
BOOSTER GOLD.
YOU LOOK SO YOUNG...
I MEAN...
I MEAN WITH ALL THIS TECHNOLOGY AND STUFF YOU... AH...EXPECT SOMEONE... OLDER.
...
BLUE BEETLE.
SO WHAT ABOUT THE RED SKIES AND THE DEMON SHADOW THINGS? FEELS PRETTY GOOD TO ACTUALLY HELP SAVE THE WHOLE WORLD, HUH?
I HOPE SO, YEAH.
SO WHAT D'YOU THINK?
HOW SOON BEFORE THAT ELUSIVE OFFER OF JUSTICE LEAGUE MEMBERSHIP DROPS THROUGH THE MAILBOX.

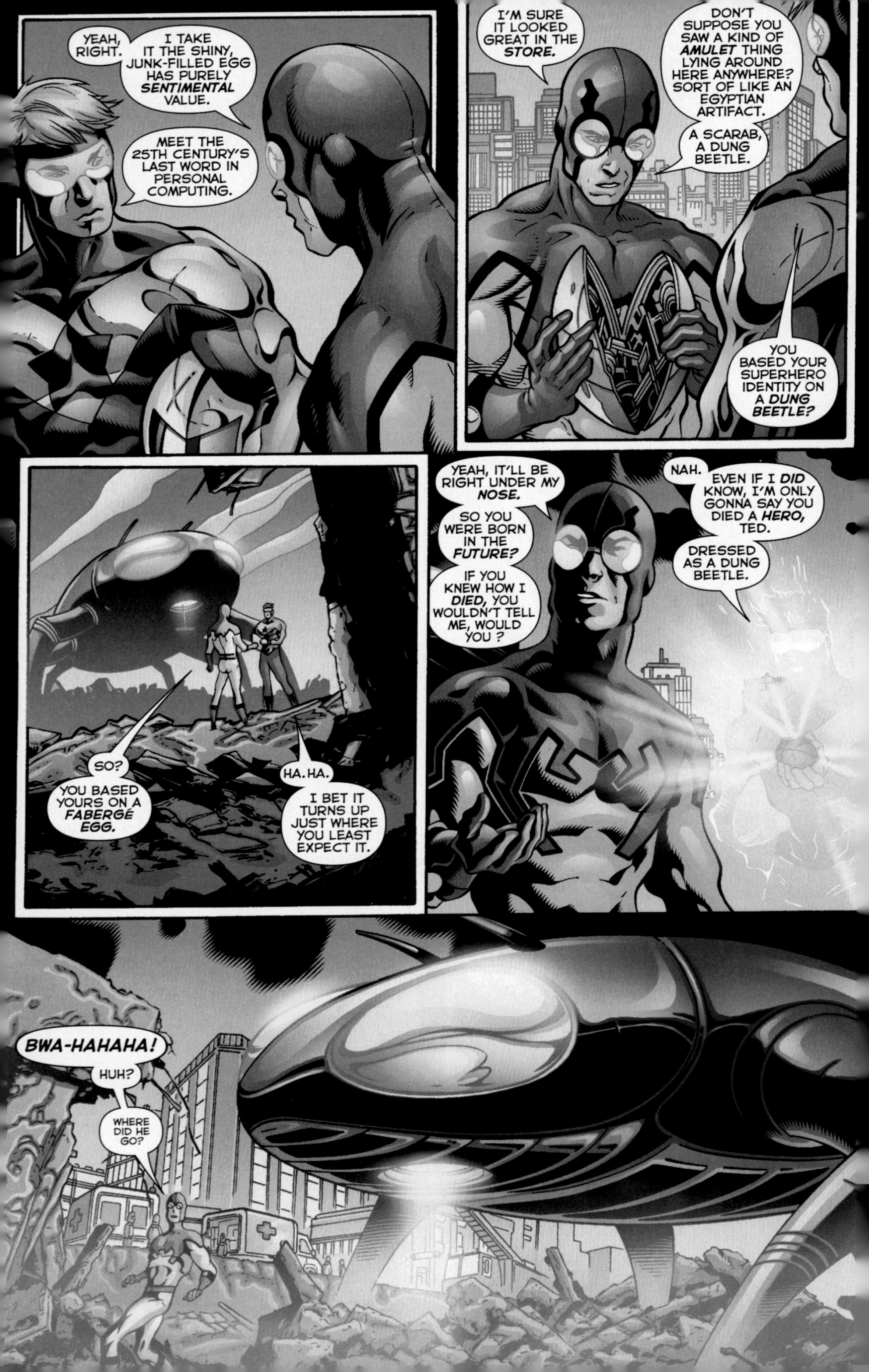
YEAH, RIGHT.
I TAKE IT THE SHINY, JUNK-FILLED EGG HAS PURELY SENTIMENTAL VALUE.
MEET THE 25TH CENTURY'S LAST WORD IN PERSONAL COMPUTING.
I'M SURE IT LOOKED GREAT IN THE STORE.
DON'T SUPPOSE YOU SAW A KIND OF AMULET THING LYING AROUND HERE ANYWHERE? SORT OF LIKE AN EGYPTIAN ARTIFACT.
A SCARAB, A DUNG BEETLE.
YOU BASED YOUR SUPERHERO IDENTITY ON A DUNG BEETLE?
SO?
YOU BASED YOURS ON A FABERGÉ EGG.
HA. HA.
I BET IT TURNS UP JUST WHERE YOU LEAST EXPECT IT.
YEAH, IT'LL BE RIGHT UNDER MY NOSE.
SO YOU WERE BORN IN THE FUTURE?
IF YOU KNEW HOW I DIED, YOU WOULDN'T TELL ME, WOULD YOU ?
NAH.
EVEN IF I DID KNOW, I'M ONLY GONNA SAY YOU DIED A HERO, TED.
DRESSED AS A DUNG BEETLE.
BWA-HAHAHA!
HUH?
WHERE DID HE GO?

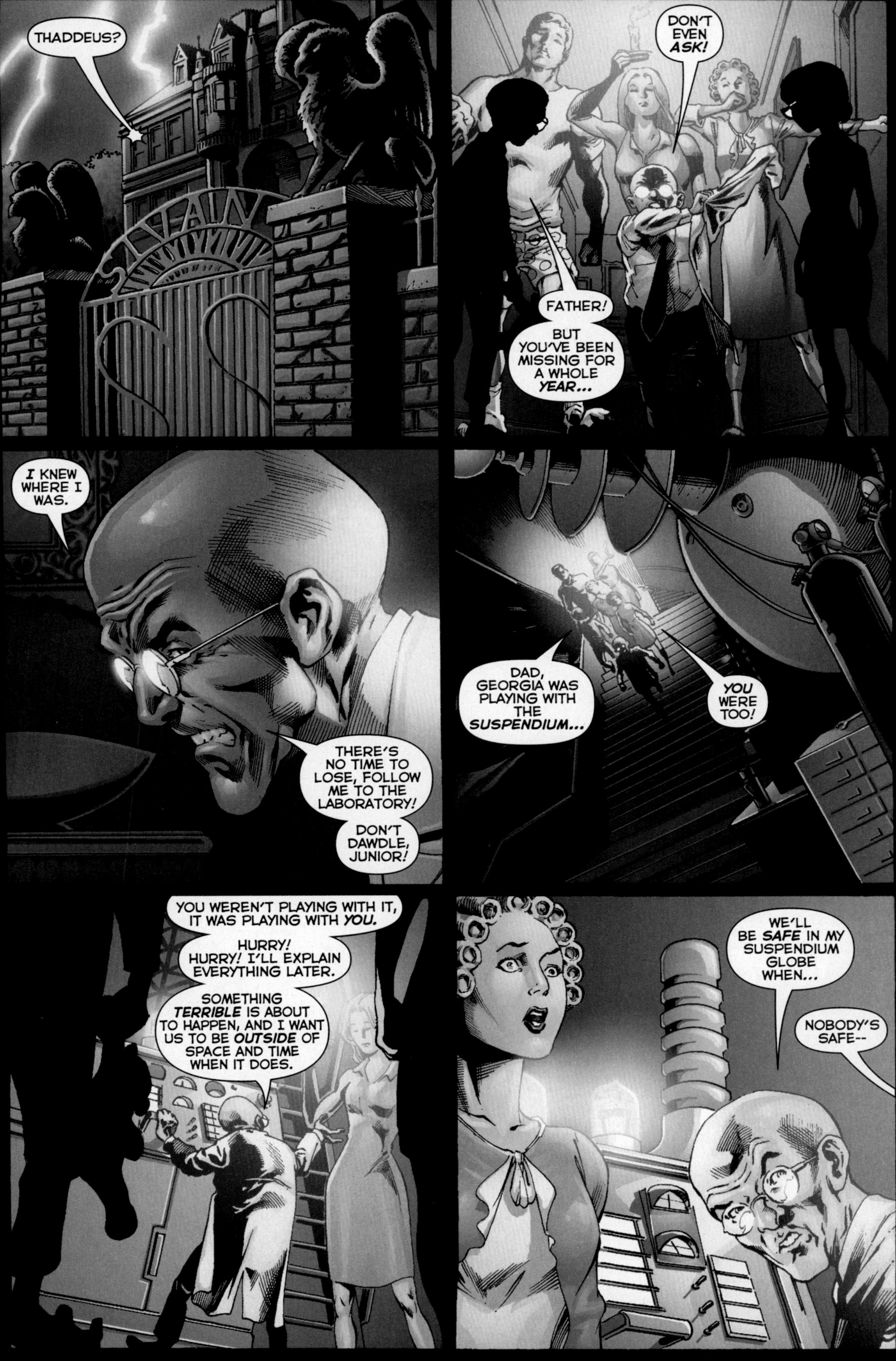
THADDEUS?
SINTAIN
DON'T EVEN ASK!
FATHER!
BUT YOU'VE BEEN MISSING FOR A WHOLE YEAR...
I KNEW WHERE I WAS.
THERE'S NO TIME TO LOSE, FOLLOW ME TO THE LABORATORY!
DON'T DAWDLE, JUNIOR!
DAD, GEORGIA WAS PLAYING WITH THE SUSPENDIUM...
YOU WERE TOO!
YOU WEREN'T PLAYING WITH IT, IT WAS PLAYING WITH YOU.
HURRY! HURRY! I'LL EXPLAIN EVERYTHING LATER.
SOMETHING TERRIBLE IS ABOUT TO HAPPEN, AND I WANT US TO BE OUTSIDE OF SPACE AND TIME WHEN IT DOES.
WE'LL BE SAFE IN MY SUSPENDIUM GLOBE WHEN...
NOBODY'S SAFE--

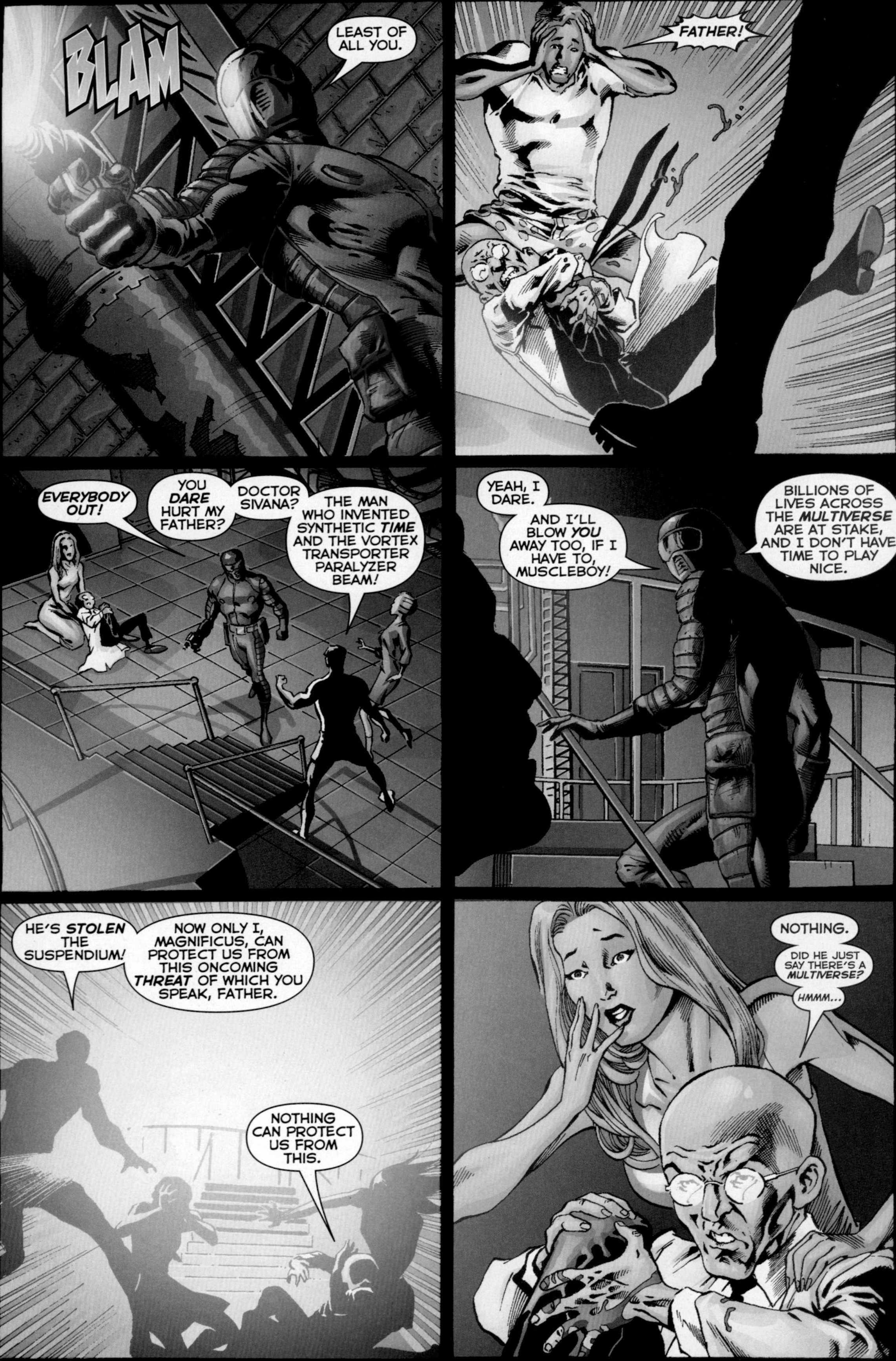
BLAM
LEAST OF ALL YOU.
FATHER!
EVERYBODY OUT!
YOU DARE HURT MY FATHER?
DOCTOR SIVANA?
THE MAN WHO INVENTED SYNTHETIC TIME AND THE VORTEX TRANSPORTER PARALYZER BEAM!
YEAH, I DARE.
AND I'LL BLOW YOU AWAY TOO, IF I HAVE TO, MUSCLEBOY!
BILLIONS OF LIVES ACROSS THE MULTIVERSE ARE AT STAKE, AND I DON'T HAVE TIME TO PLAY NICE.
HE'S STOLEN THE SUSPENDIUM!
NOW ONLY I, MAGNIFICUS, CAN PROTECT US FROM THIS ONCOMING THREAT OF WHICH YOU SPEAK, FATHER.
NOTHING CAN PROTECT US FROM THIS.
NOTHING.
DID HE JUST SAY THERE'S A MULTIVERSE?
HMMM...

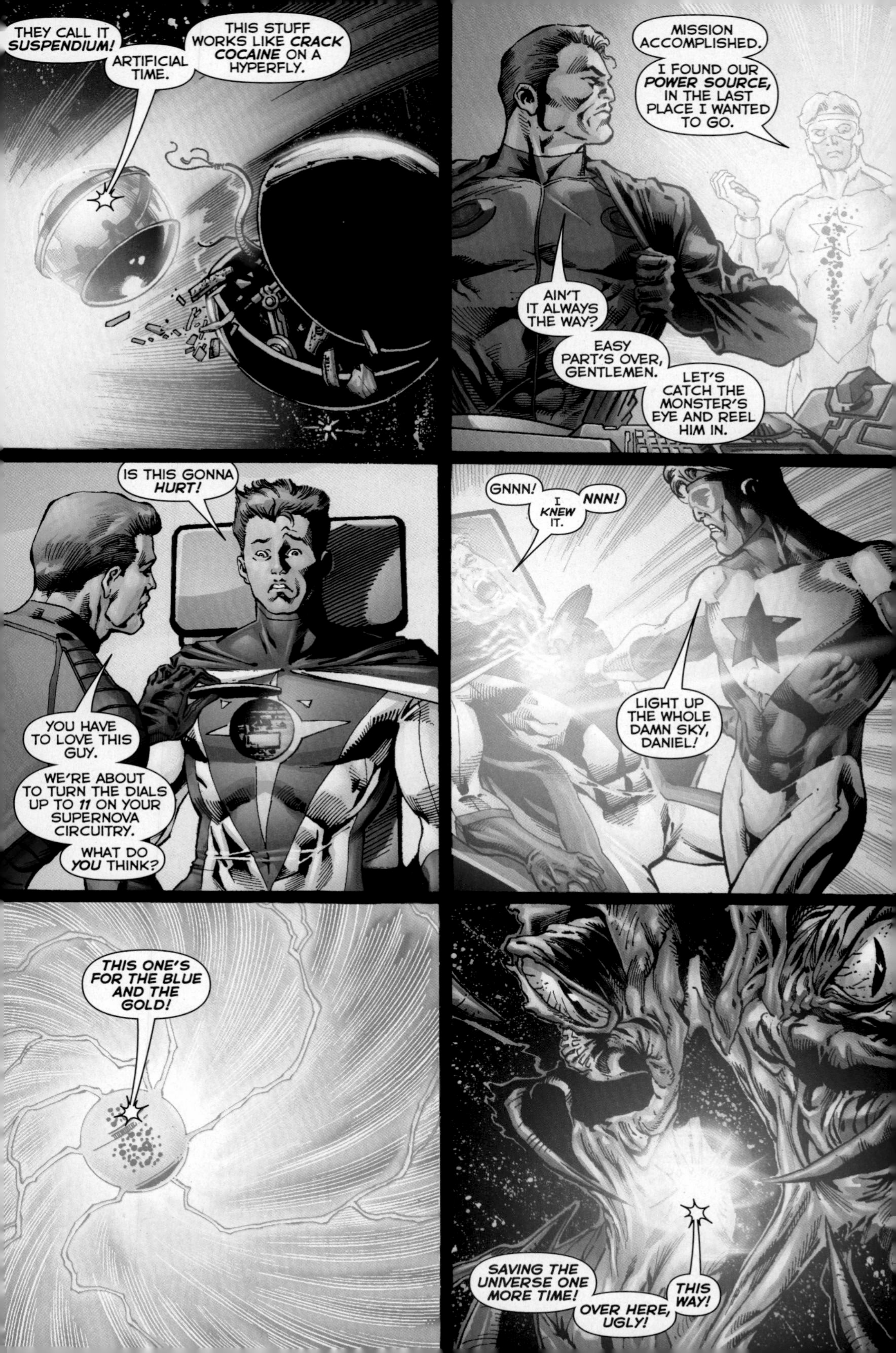
THEY CALL IT SUSPENDIUM!
ARTIFICIAL TIME.
THIS STUFF WORKS LIKE CRACK COCAINE ON A HYPERFLY.
MISSION ACCOMPLISHED.
I FOUND OUR POWER SOURCE, IN THE LAST PLACE I WANTED TO GO.
AIN'T IT ALWAYS THE WAY?
EASY PART'S OVER, GENTLEMEN.
LET'S CATCH THE MONSTER'S EYE AND REEL HIM IN.
IS THIS GONNA HURT!
YOU HAVE TO LOVE THIS GUY.
WE'RE ABOUT TO TURN THE DIALS UP TO 11 ON YOUR SUPERNOVA CIRCUITRY.
WHAT DO YOU THINK?
GNNN!
I KNEW IT.
NNN!
LIGHT UP THE WHOLE DAMN SKY, DANIEL!
THIS ONE'S FOR THE BLUE AND THE GOLD!
SAVING THE UNIVERSE ONE MORE TIME!
OVER HERE, UGLY!
THIS WAY!

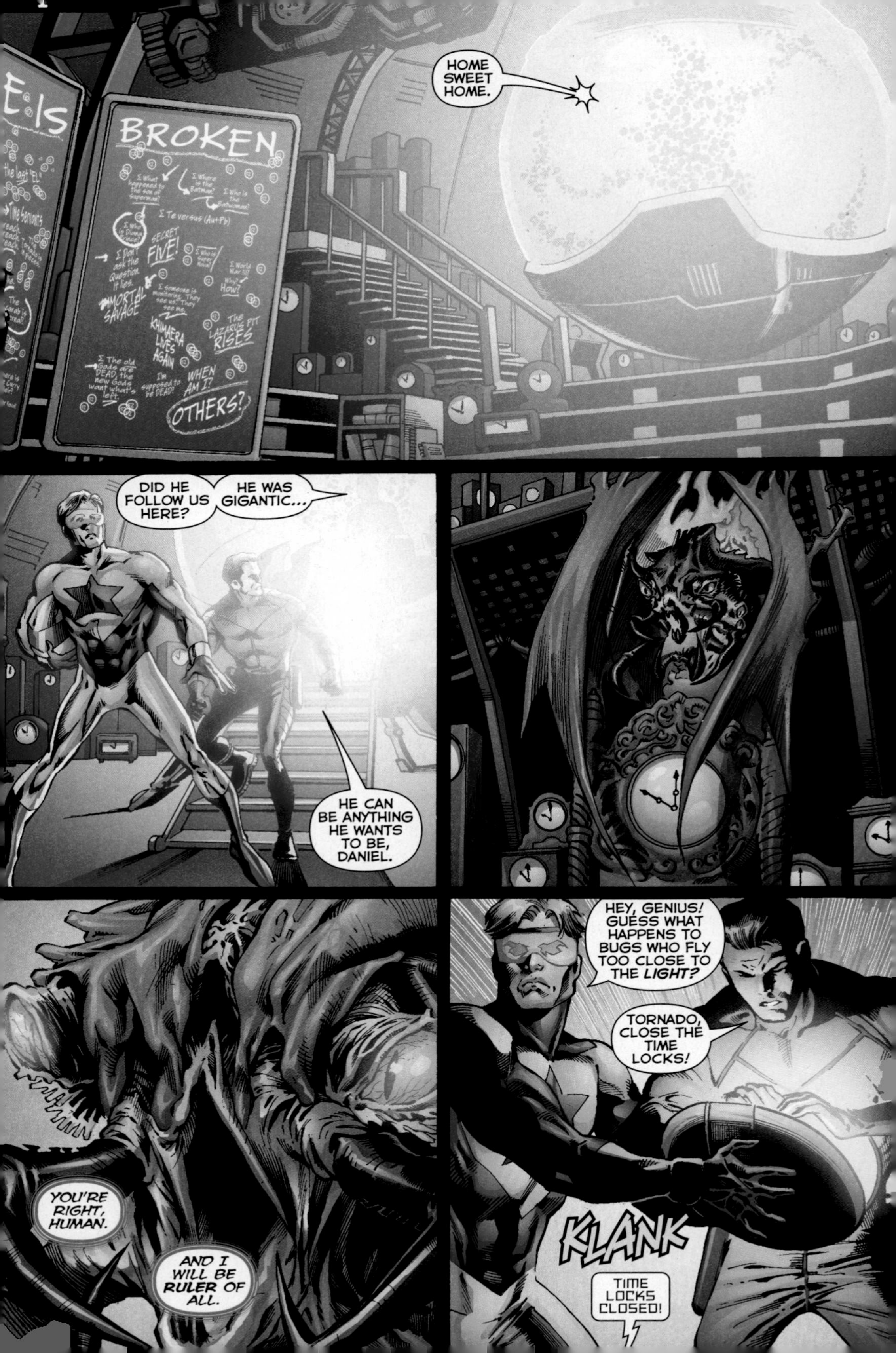
E IS
BROKEN
SECRET FIVE!
KHIMAERA LIVES AGAIN
WHEN AM I?
OTHERS?
HOME SWEET HOME.
DID HE FOLLOW US HERE?
HE WAS GIGANTIC...
HE CAN BE ANYTHING HE WANTS TO BE, DANIEL.
YOU'RE RIGHT, HUMAN.
AND I WILL BE RULER OF ALL.
HEY, GENIUS! GUESS WHAT HAPPENS TO BUGS WHO FLY TOO CLOSE TO THE LIGHT?
TORNADO, CLOSE THE TIME LOCKS!
KLANK
TIME LOCKS CLOSED!

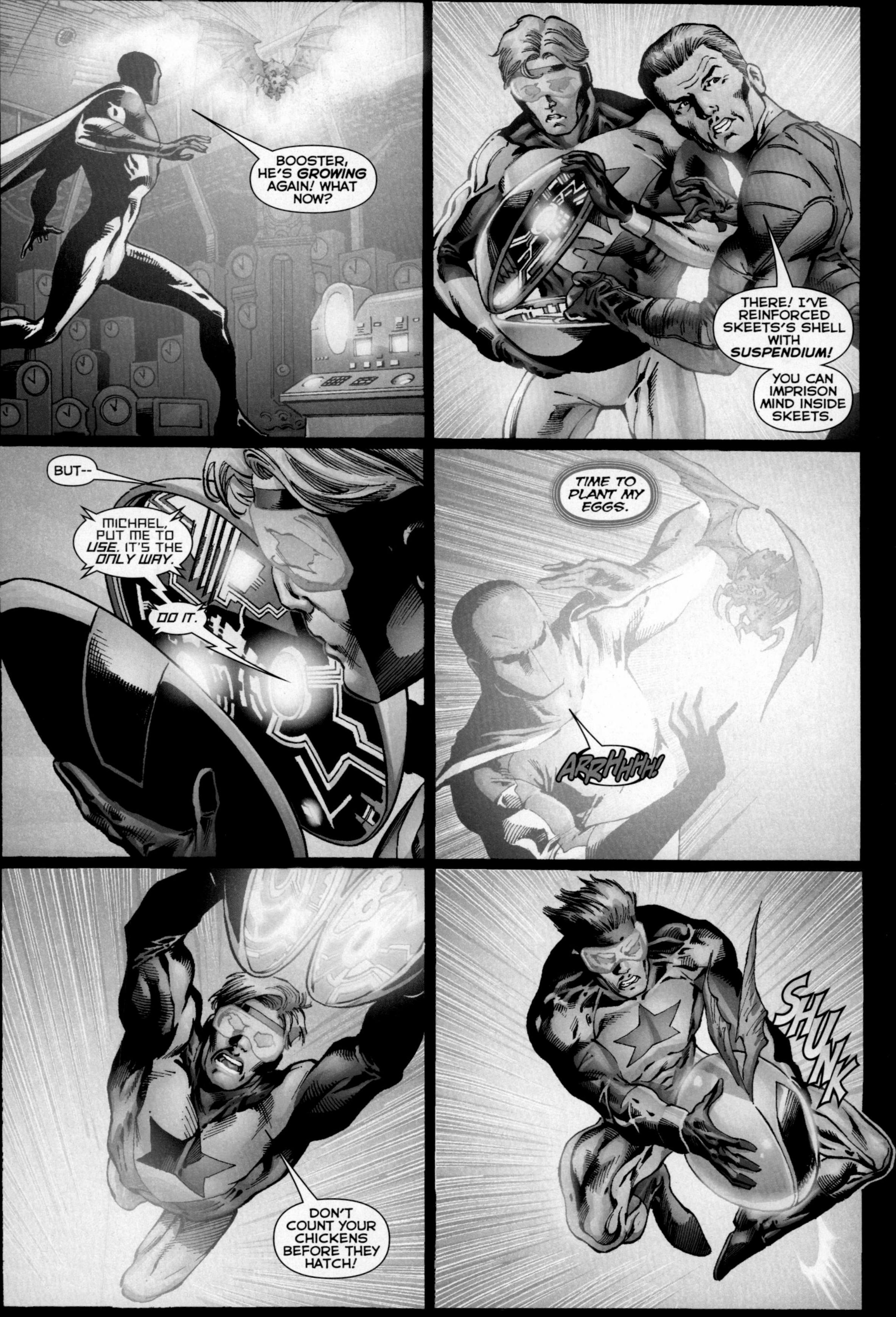

BOOSTER, HE'S GROWING AGAIN! WHAT NOW?
THERE! I'VE REINFORCED SKEETS'S SHELL WITH SUSPENDIUM!
YOU CAN IMPRISON MIND INSIDE SKEETS.
BUT--
MICHAEL, PUT ME TO USE. IT'S THE ONLY WAY.
DO IT.
TIME TO PLANT MY EGGS.
ARRHHHH!
DON'T COUNT YOUR CHICKENS BEFORE THEY HATCH!
SHUNK

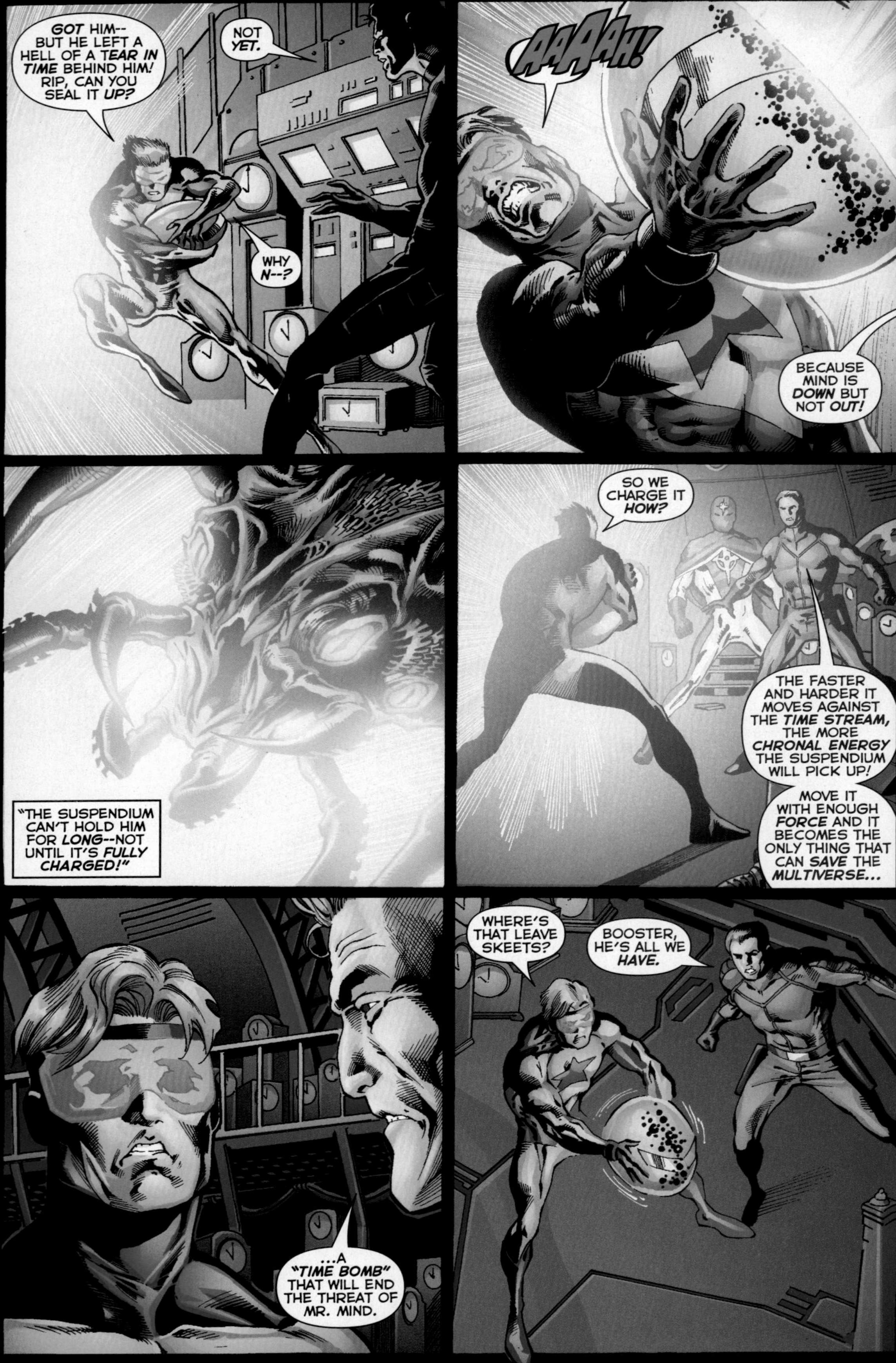

GOT HIM-- BUT HE LEFT A HELL OF A TEAR IN TIME BEHIND HIM! RIP, CAN YOU SEAL IT UP?
NOT YET.
WHY N--?
AAAAH!
BECAUSE MIND IS DOWN BUT NOT OUT!
"THE SUSPENDIUM CAN'T HOLD HIM FOR LONG--NOT UNTIL IT'S FULLY CHARGED!"
SO WE CHARGE IT HOW?
THE FASTER AND HARDER IT MOVES AGAINST THE TIME STREAM, THE MORE CHRONAL ENERGY THE SUSPENDIUM WILL PICK UP!
MOVE IT WITH ENOUGH FORCE AND IT BECOMES THE ONLY THING THAT CAN SAVE THE MULTIVERSE...
...A "TIME BOMB" THAT WILL END THE THREAT OF MR. MIND.
WHERE'S THAT LEAVE SKEETS?
BOOSTER, HE'S ALL WE HAVE.

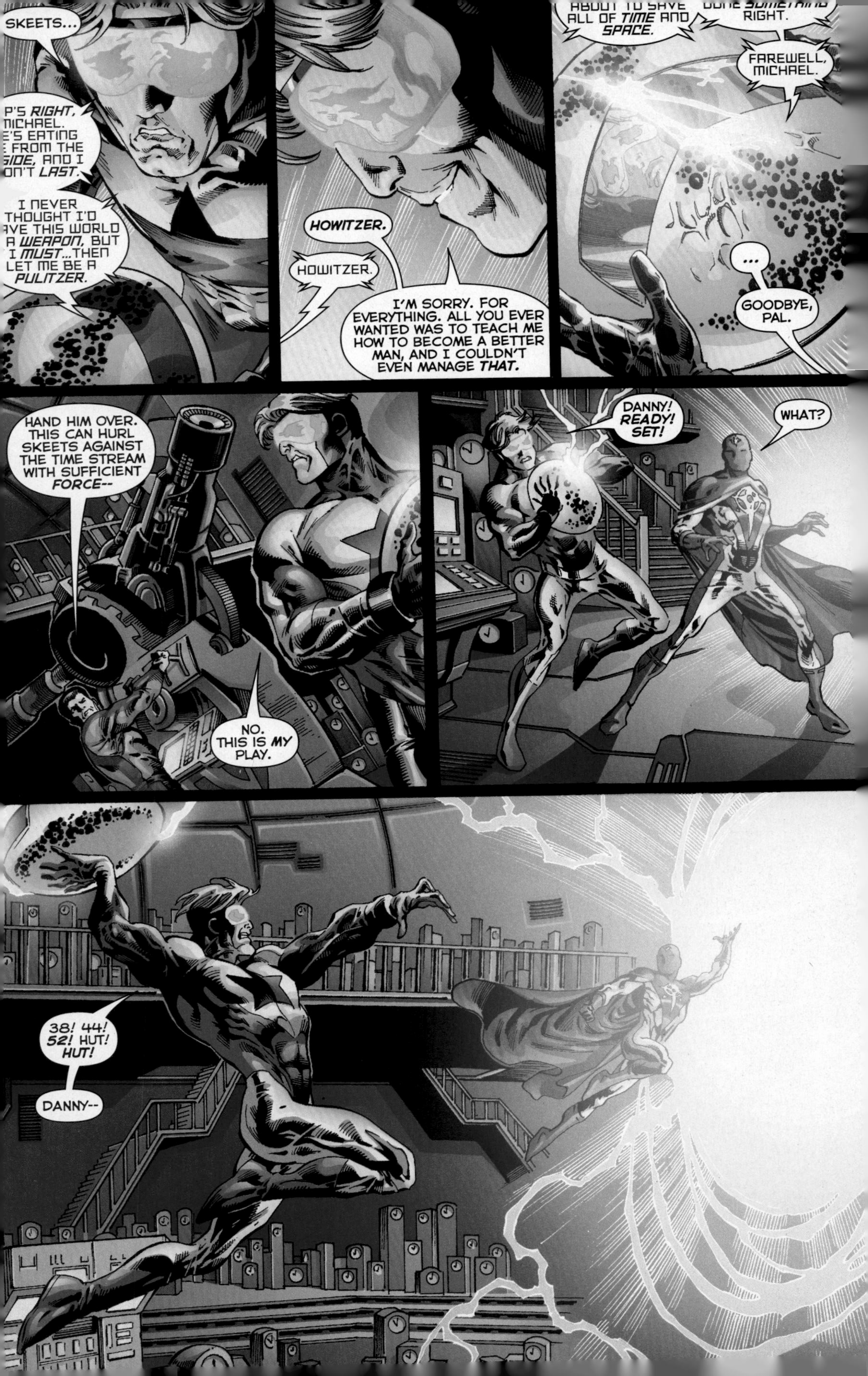
SKEETS...
...'S RIGHT, MICHAEL. ...'S EATING ... FROM THE ...SIDE, AND I ...ON'T LAST.
I NEVER THOUGHT I'D ...AVE THIS WORLD ...A WEAPON, BUT I MUST...THEN LET ME BE A PULITZER.
HOWITZER.
HOWITZER.
I'M SORRY. FOR EVERYTHING. ALL YOU EVER WANTED WAS TO TEACH ME HOW TO BECOME A BETTER MAN, AND I COULDN'T EVEN MANAGE THAT.
...ABOUT TO SAVE ALL OF TIME AND SPACE.
...RIGHT.
FAREWELL, MICHAEL.
...
GOODBYE, PAL.
HAND HIM OVER. THIS CAN HURL SKEETS AGAINST THE TIME STREAM WITH SUFFICIENT FORCE--
NO. THIS IS MY PLAY.
DANNY! READY! SET!
WHAT?
38! 44! 52! HUT! HUT!
DANNY--

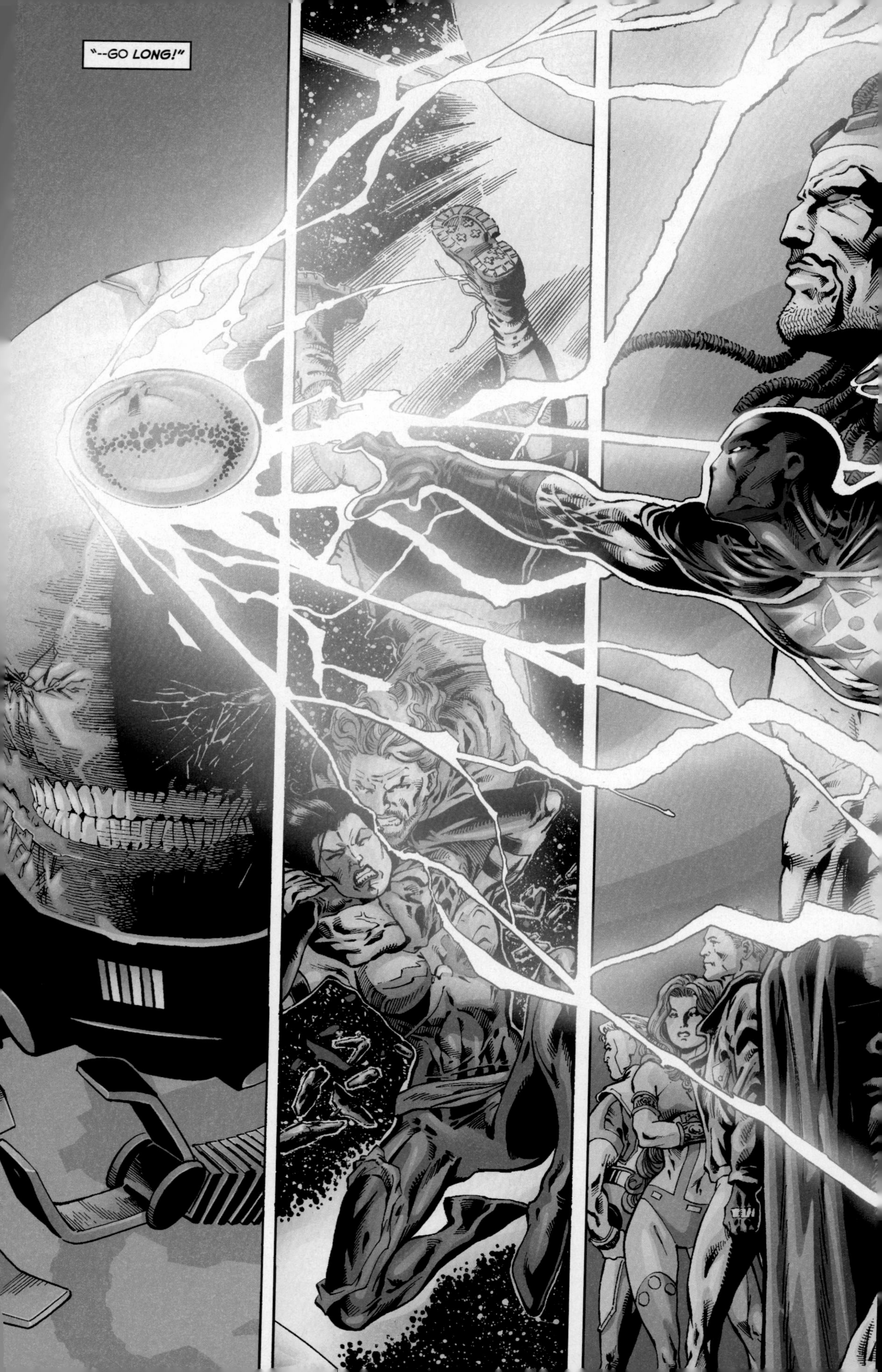
"--GO LONG!"

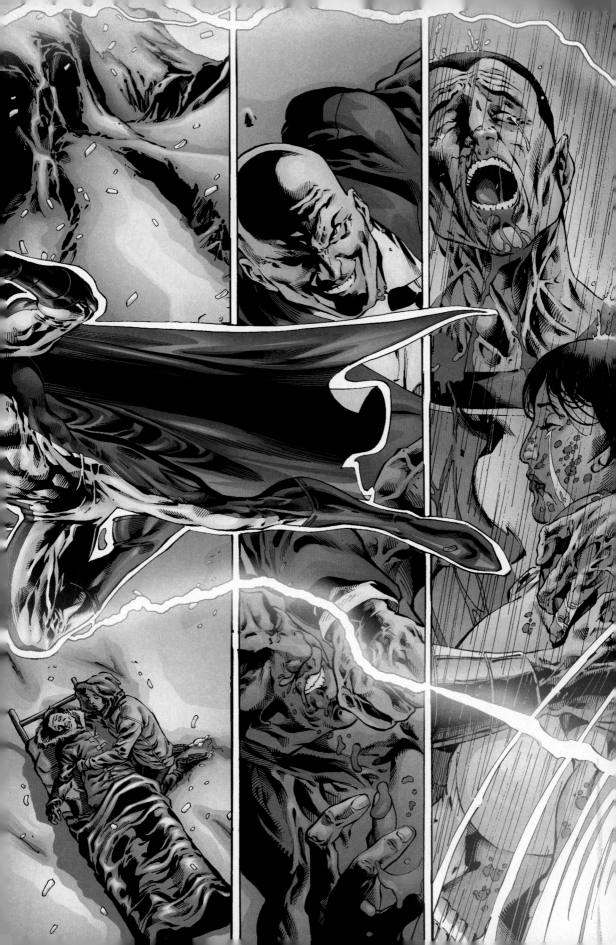

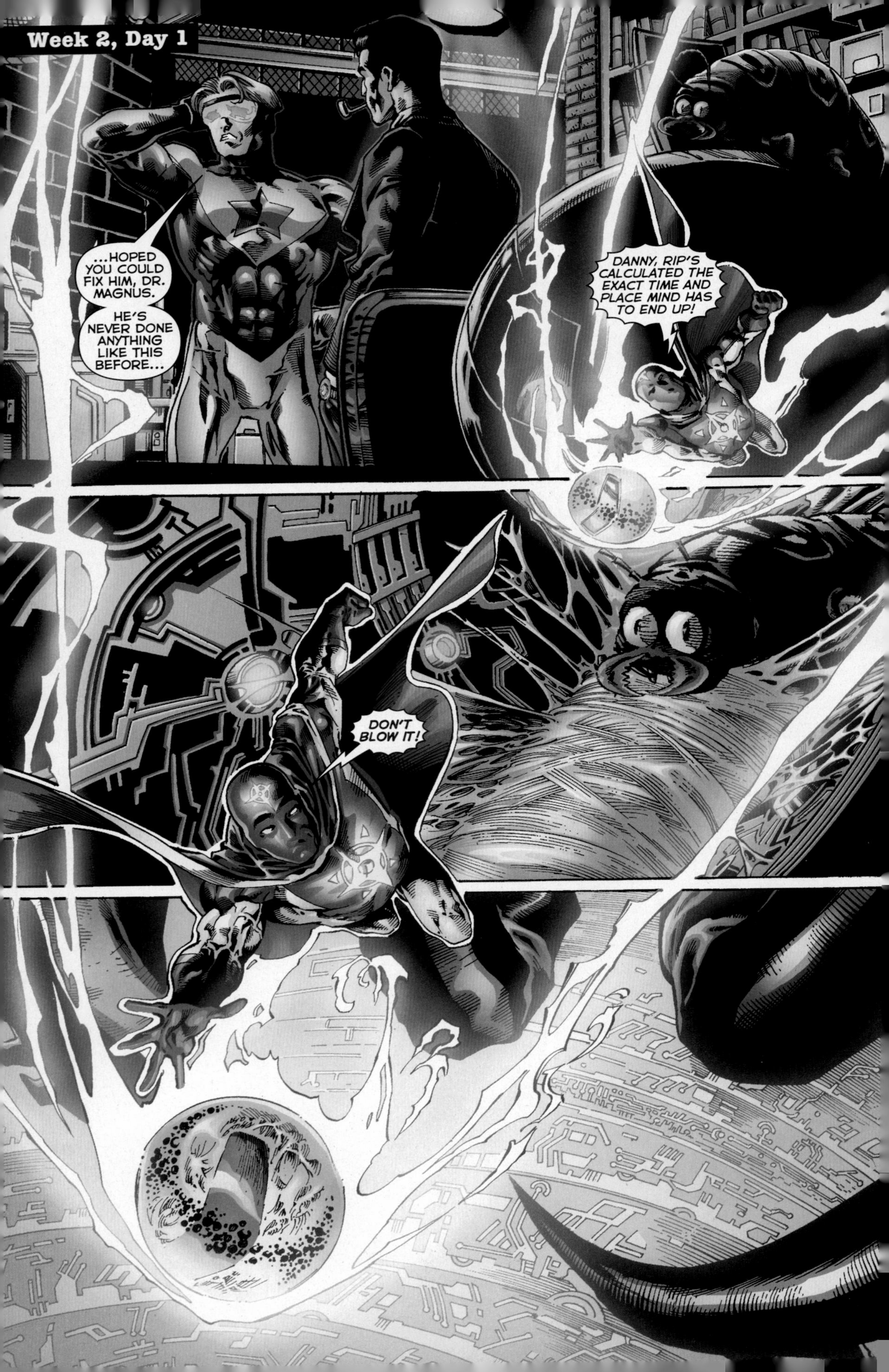
Week 2, Day 1
...HOPED YOU COULD FIX HIM, DR. MAGNUS.
HE'S NEVER DONE ANYTHING LIKE THIS BEFORE...
DANNY, RIP'S CALCULATED THE EXACT TIME AND PLACE MIND HAS TO END UP!
DON'T BLOW IT!

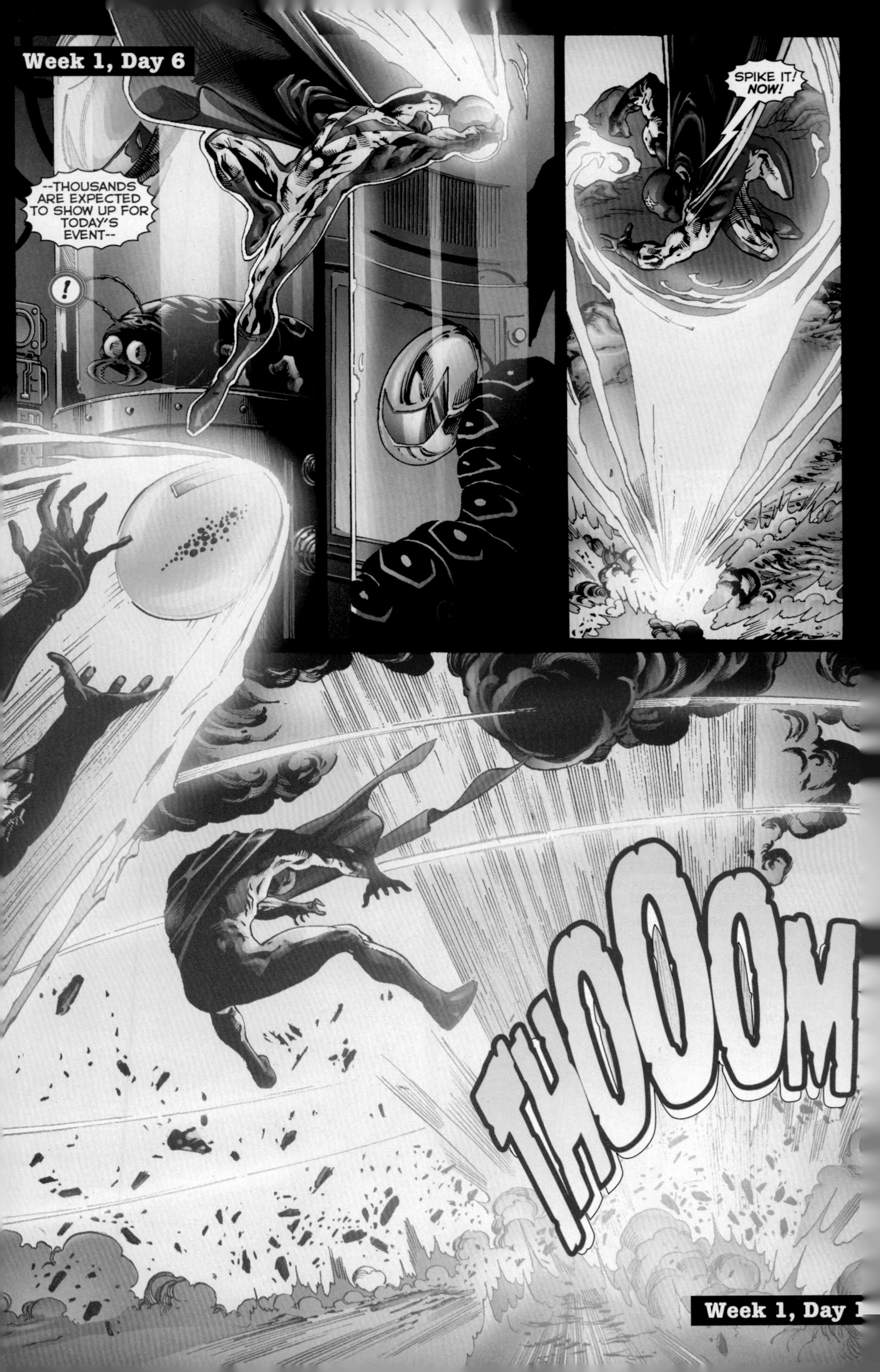

Week 1, Day 6
--THOUSANDS ARE EXPECTED TO SHOW UP FOR TODAY'S EVENT--
!
SPIKE IT! NOW!
THOOOM
Week 1, Day

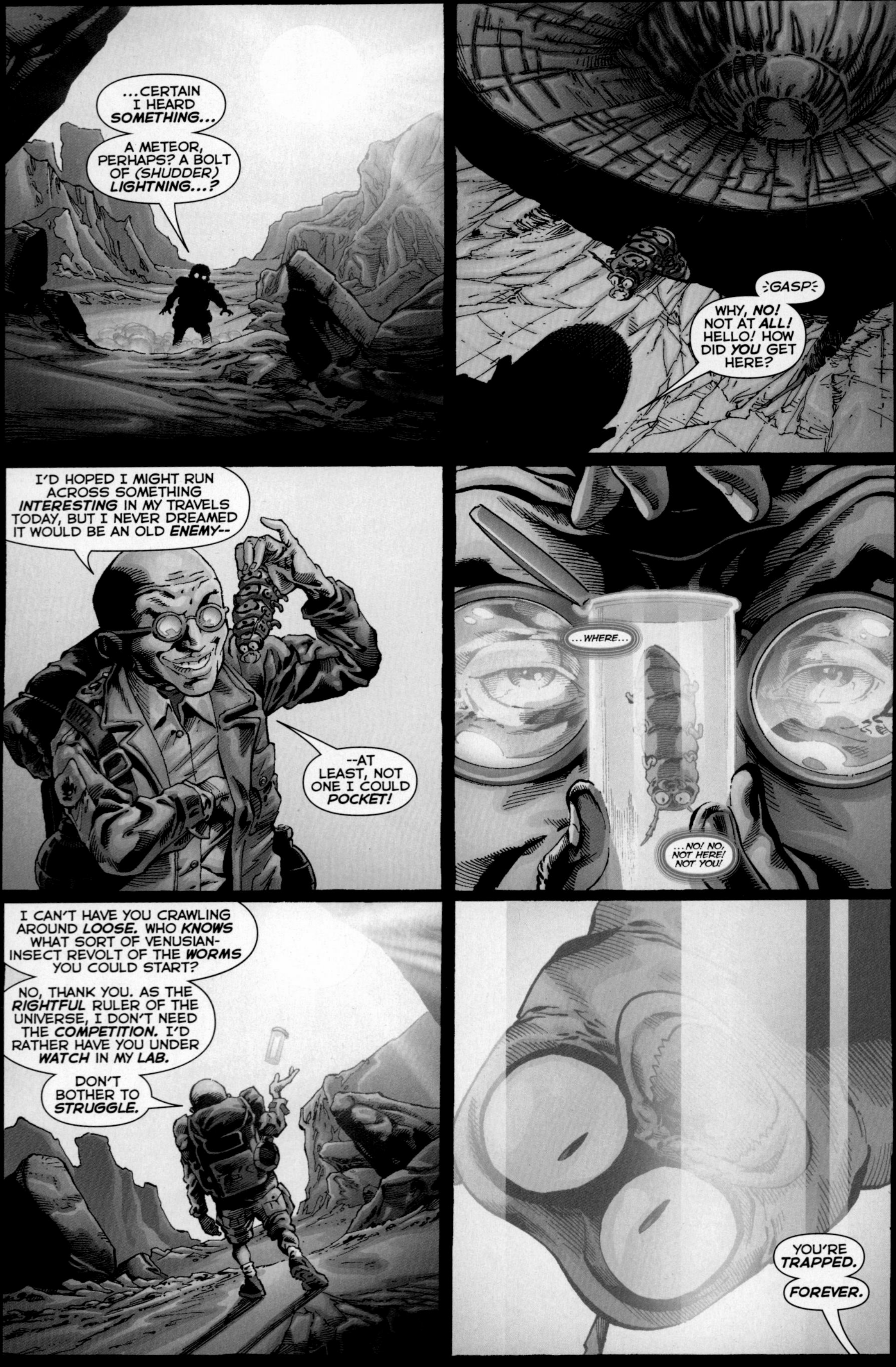
...CERTAIN I HEARD SOMETHING...
A METEOR, PERHAPS? A BOLT OF (SHUDDER) LIGHTNING...?
GASP
WHY, NO! NOT AT ALL! HELLO! HOW DID YOU GET HERE?
I'D HOPED I MIGHT RUN ACROSS SOMETHING INTERESTING IN MY TRAVELS TODAY, BUT I NEVER DREAMED IT WOULD BE AN OLD ENEMY--
--AT LEAST, NOT ONE I COULD POCKET!
...WHERE...
...NO! NO, NOT HERE! NOT YOU!
I CAN'T HAVE YOU CRAWLING AROUND LOOSE. WHO KNOWS WHAT SORT OF VENUSIAN-INSECT REVOLT OF THE WORMS YOU COULD START?
NO, THANK YOU. AS THE RIGHTFUL RULER OF THE UNIVERSE, I DON'T NEED THE COMPETITION. I'D RATHER HAVE YOU UNDER WATCH IN MY LAB.
DON'T BOTHER TO STRUGGLE.
YOU'RE TRAPPED.
FOREVER.

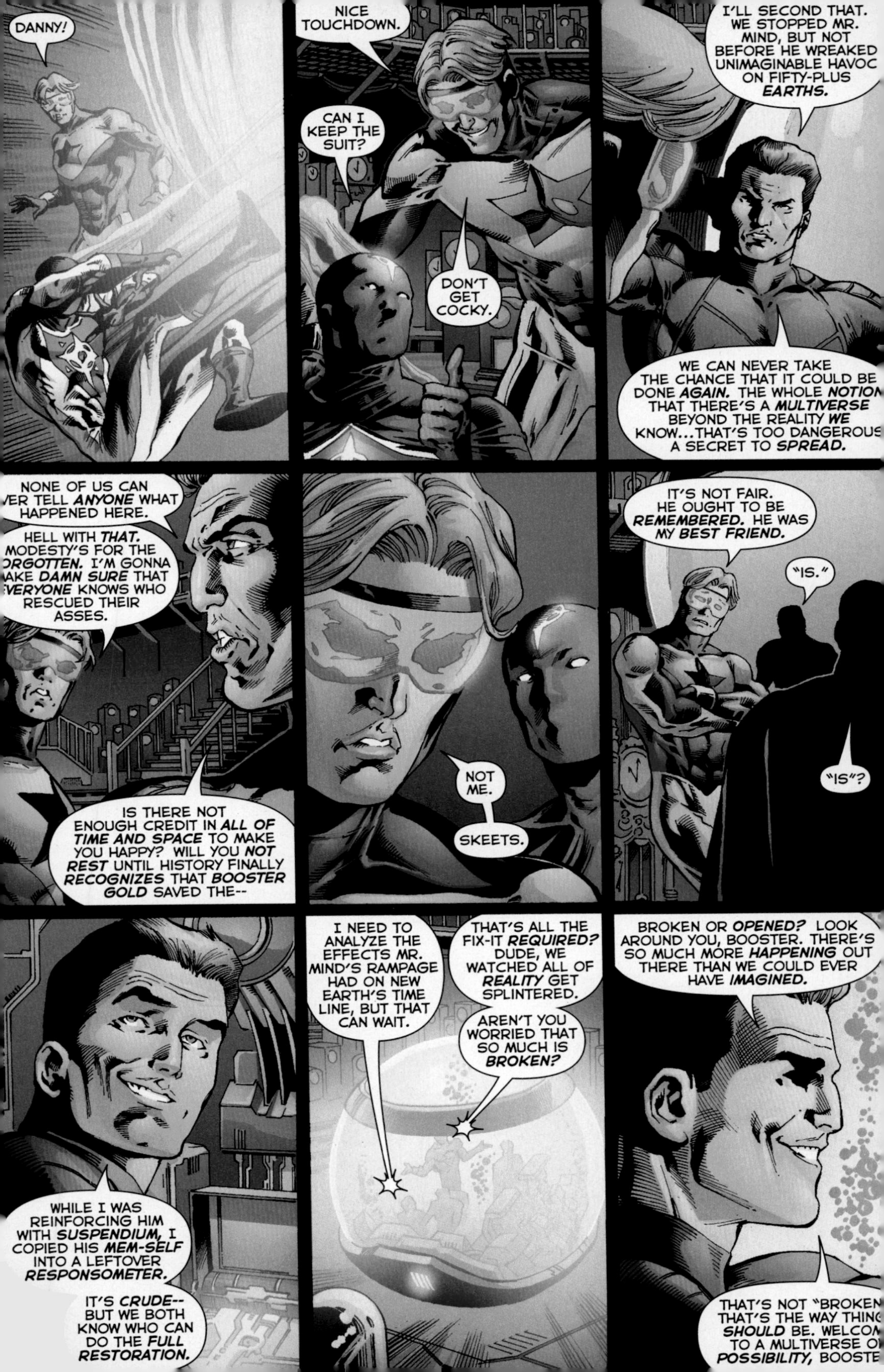
DANNY!
NICE TOUCHDOWN.
CAN I KEEP THE SUIT?
DON'T GET COCKY.
I'LL SECOND THAT. WE STOPPED MR. MIND, BUT NOT BEFORE HE WREAKED UNIMAGINABLE HAVOC ON FIFTY-PLUS EARTHS.
WE CAN NEVER TAKE THE CHANCE THAT IT COULD BE DONE AGAIN. THE WHOLE NOTION THAT THERE'S A MULTIVERSE BEYOND THE REALITY WE KNOW...THAT'S TOO DANGEROUS A SECRET TO SPREAD.
NONE OF US CAN EVER TELL ANYONE WHAT HAPPENED HERE.
HELL WITH THAT. MODESTY'S FOR THE FORGOTTEN. I'M GONNA MAKE DAMN SURE THAT EVERYONE KNOWS WHO RESCUED THEIR ASSES.
IS THERE NOT ENOUGH CREDIT IN ALL OF TIME AND SPACE TO MAKE YOU HAPPY? WILL YOU NOT REST UNTIL HISTORY FINALLY RECOGNIZES THAT BOOSTER GOLD SAVED THE--
NOT ME.
SKEETS.
IT'S NOT FAIR. HE OUGHT TO BE REMEMBERED. HE WAS MY BEST FRIEND.
"IS."
"IS"?
WHILE I WAS REINFORCING HIM WITH SUSPENDIUM, I COPIED HIS MEM-SELF INTO A LEFTOVER RESPONSOMETER.
IT'S CRUDE-- BUT WE BOTH KNOW WHO CAN DO THE FULL RESTORATION.
I NEED TO ANALYZE THE EFFECTS MR. MIND'S RAMPAGE HAD ON NEW EARTH'S TIME LINE, BUT THAT CAN WAIT.
THAT'S ALL THE FIX-IT REQUIRED? DUDE, WE WATCHED ALL OF REALITY GET SPLINTERED.
AREN'T YOU WORRIED THAT SO MUCH IS BROKEN?
BROKEN OR OPENED? LOOK AROUND YOU, BOOSTER. THERE'S SO MUCH MORE HAPPENING OUT THERE THAN WE COULD EVER HAVE IMAGINED.
THAT'S NOT "BROKEN THAT'S THE WAY THING SHOULD BE. WELCOM TO A MULTIVERSE O POSSIBILITY, BOOSTE

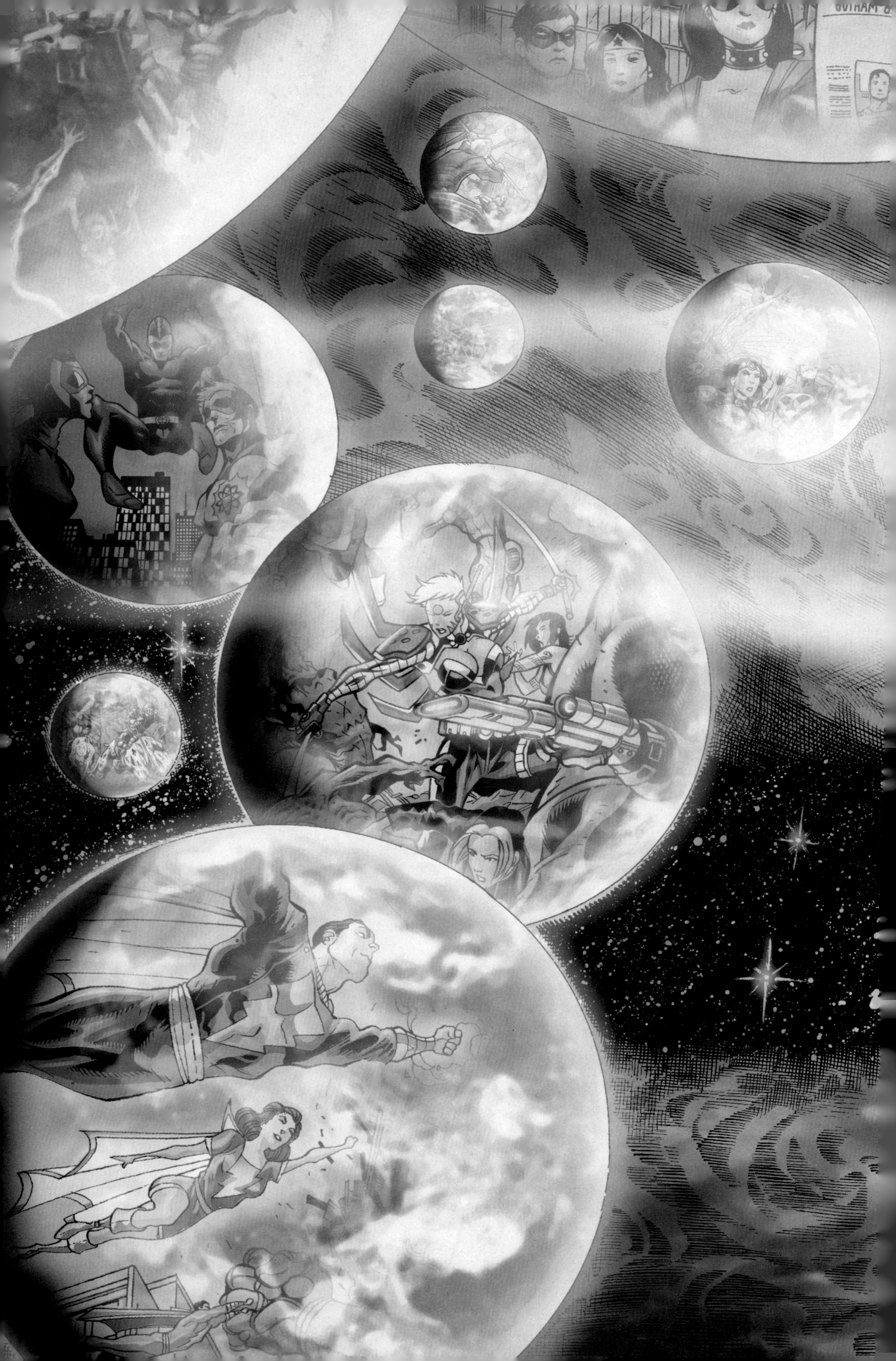

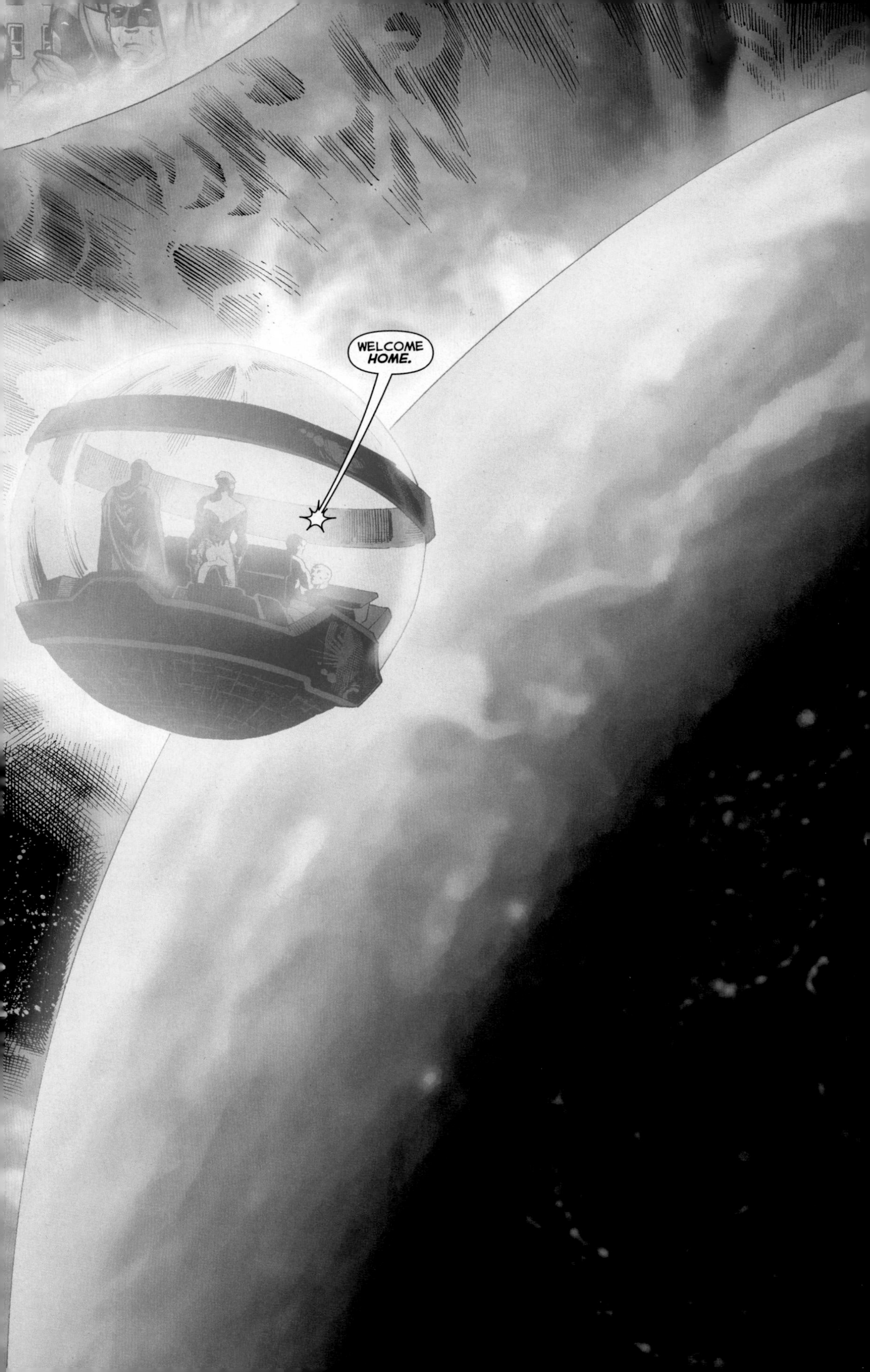
WELCOME HOME.

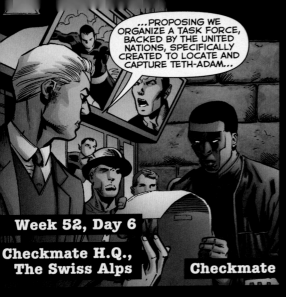

...PROPOSING WE ORGANIZE A TASK FORCE, BACKED BY THE UNITED NATIONS, SPECIFICALLY CREATED TO LOCATE AND CAPTURE TETH-ADAM...

Week 52, Day 6

Checkmate H.Q., The Swiss Alps

Checkmate

...INTERNATIONAL AID CONTINUES TO POUR IN AND THE THREAT OF INVASION IS NON-EXISTENT. THOUGH MISSING, BLACK ADAM'S SHADOW STILL HANGS OVER KAHNDAQ.

THE REST OF THE WORLD REMAINS EVER-VIGILANT THAT IT WILL CAPTURE AND PROSECUTE KAHNDAQ'S FORMER LEADER...

KZZZZT

Metropolis

Steelworks

UNCLE JOHN?

DID THEY SAY WHAT HAPPENED TO INFINITY INC.? NO ONE'S SEEN THEM...

YOU ASK ME, NAT--

"--THEY'RE LONG GONE."

Kahndaq

The Amulet of Isis

...THEY'RE TAGGING HIM "THE MOST WANTED *MORTAL* IN THE WORLD." SOMEONE *WILL* FIND BLACK ADAM...

Washington, D.C.

The Department of Metahuman Affairs

"...BUT I PRAY THAT SOMEONE ISN'T US."

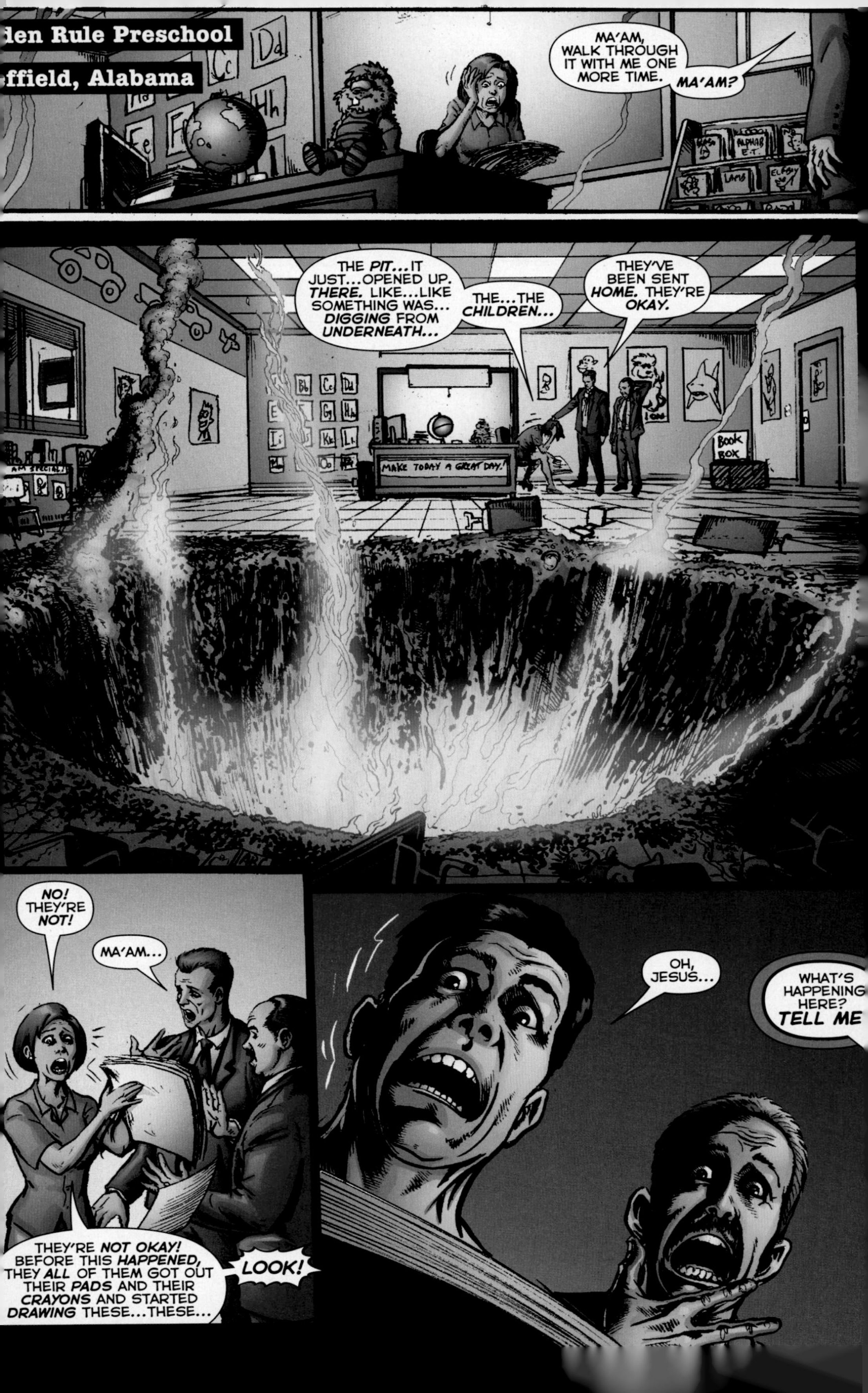

den Rule Preschool
ffield, Alabama
MA'AM, WALK THROUGH IT WITH ME ONE MORE TIME. MA'AM?
THE PIT...IT JUST...OPENED UP. THERE. LIKE...LIKE SOMETHING WAS... DIGGING FROM UNDERNEATH...
THE...THE CHILDREN...
THEY'VE BEEN SENT HOME. THEY'RE OKAY.
MAKE TODAY A GREAT DAY!
BOOK BOX
NO! THEY'RE NOT!
MA'AM...
THEY'RE NOT OKAY! BEFORE THIS HAPPENED, THEY ALL OF THEM GOT OUT THEIR PADS AND THEIR CRAYONS AND STARTED DRAWING THESE...THESE...
LOOK!
OH, JESUS...
WHAT'S HAPPENING HERE? TELL ME

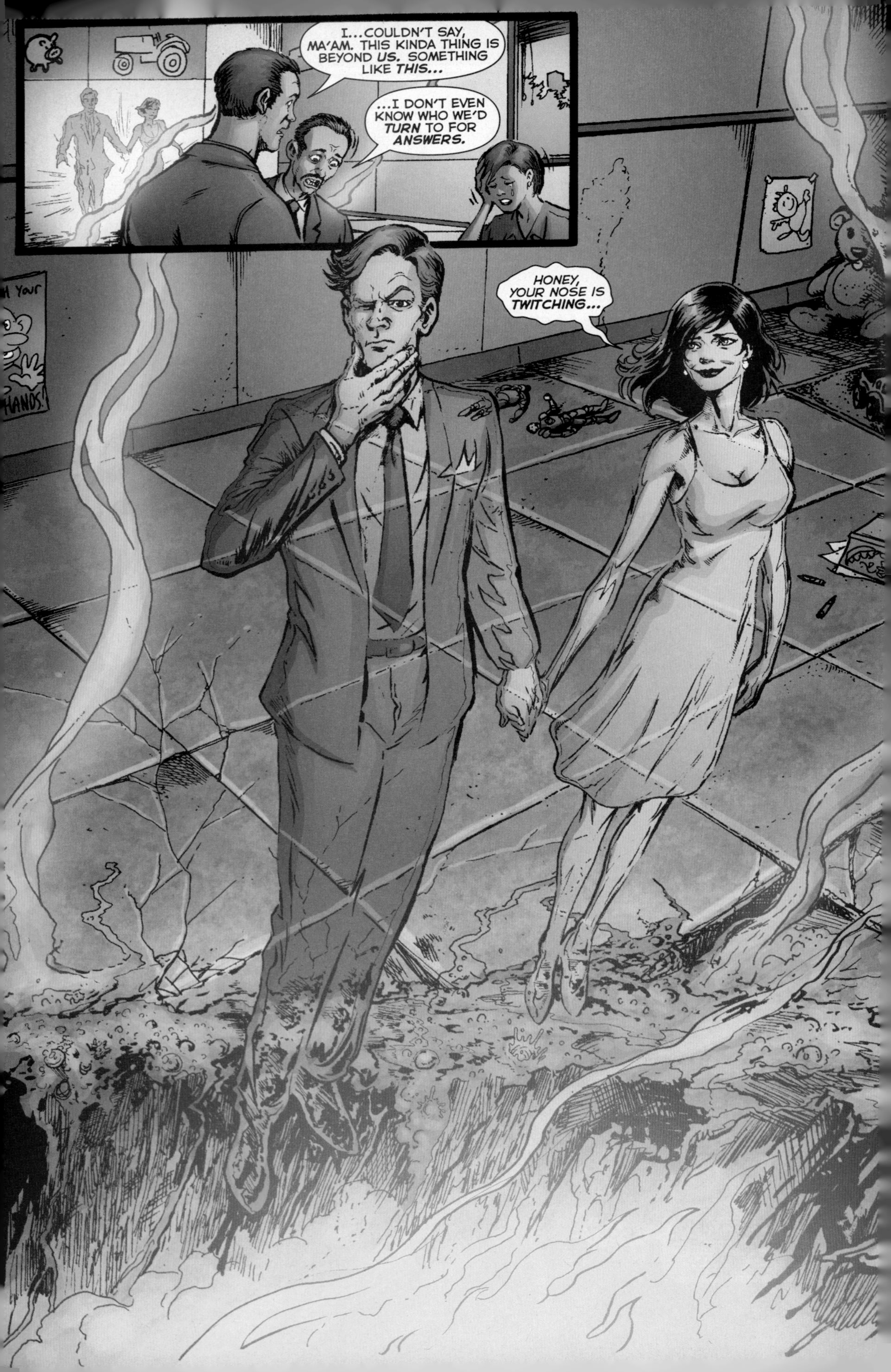
I...COULDN'T SAY, MA'AM. THIS KINDA THING IS BEYOND *US.* SOMETHING LIKE *THIS...*
...I DON'T EVEN KNOW WHO WE'D *TURN* TO FOR *ANSWERS.*
HONEY, YOUR NOSE IS ***TWITCHING...***

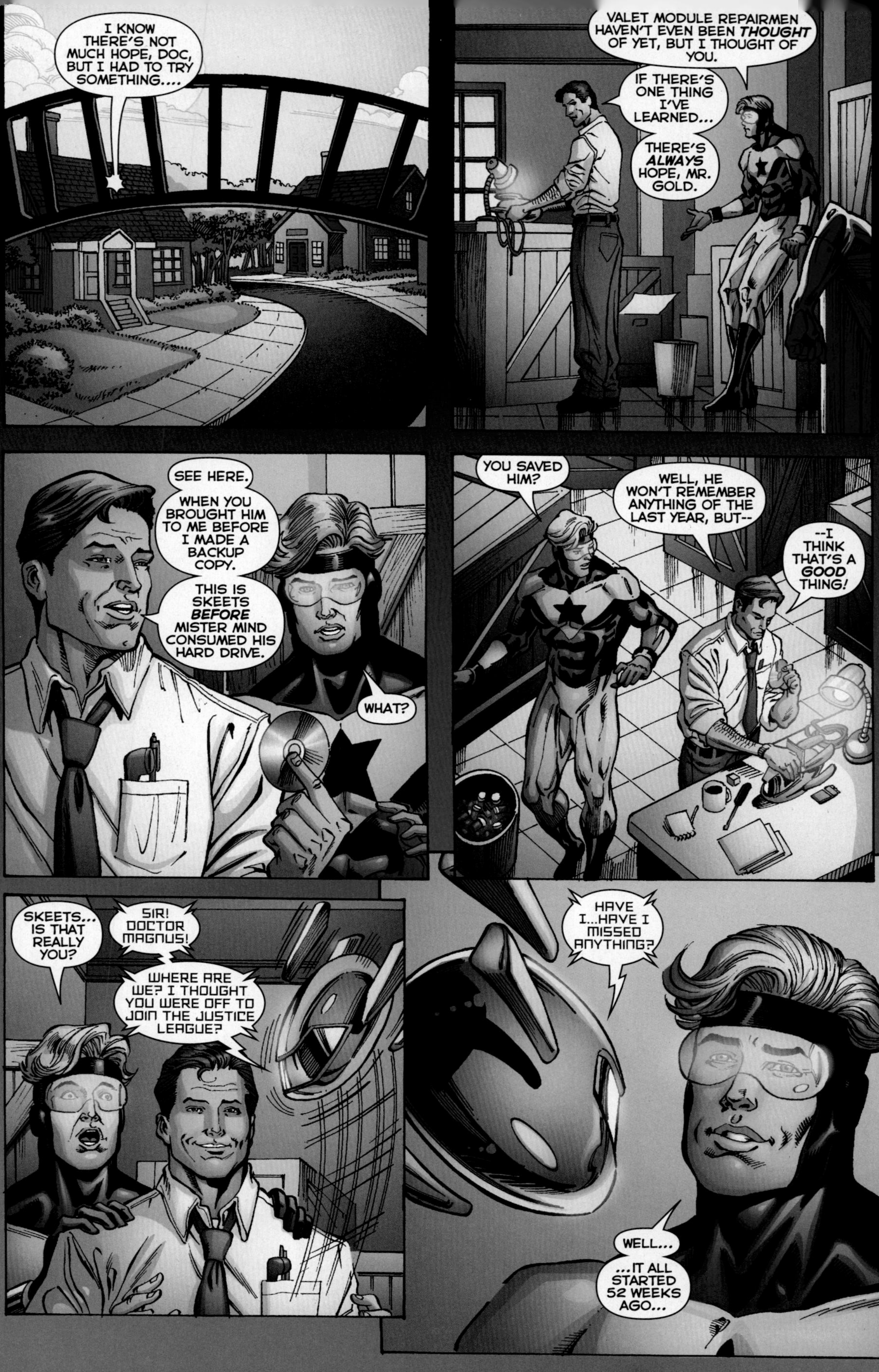
I KNOW THERE'S NOT MUCH HOPE, DOC, BUT I HAD TO TRY SOMETHING....
VALET MODULE REPAIRMEN HAVEN'T EVEN BEEN THOUGHT OF YET, BUT I THOUGHT OF YOU.
IF THERE'S ONE THING I'VE LEARNED...
THERE'S ALWAYS HOPE, MR. GOLD.
SEE HERE.
WHEN YOU BROUGHT HIM TO ME BEFORE I MADE A BACKUP COPY.
THIS IS SKEETS BEFORE MISTER MIND CONSUMED HIS HARD DRIVE.
WHAT?
YOU SAVED HIM?
WELL, HE WON'T REMEMBER ANYTHING OF THE LAST YEAR, BUT--
--I THINK THAT'S A GOOD THING!
SKEETS... IS THAT REALLY YOU?
SIR! DOCTOR MAGNUS!
WHERE ARE WE? I THOUGHT YOU WERE OFF TO JOIN THE JUSTICE LEAGUE?
HAVE I...HAVE I MISSED ANYTHING?
WELL...
...IT ALL STARTED 52 WEEKS AGO...

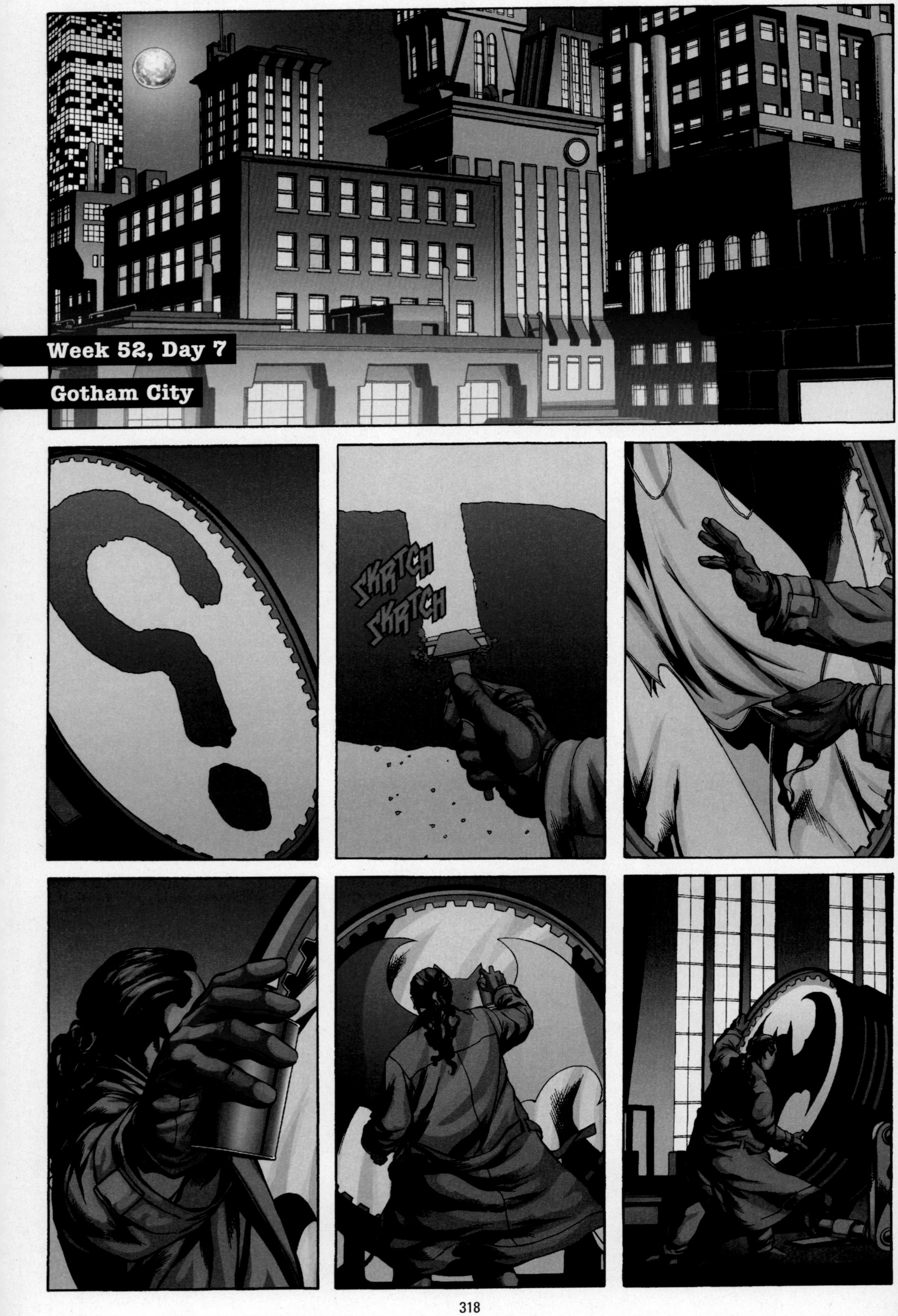
Week 52, Day 7
Gotham City
SKRTCH
SKRTCH

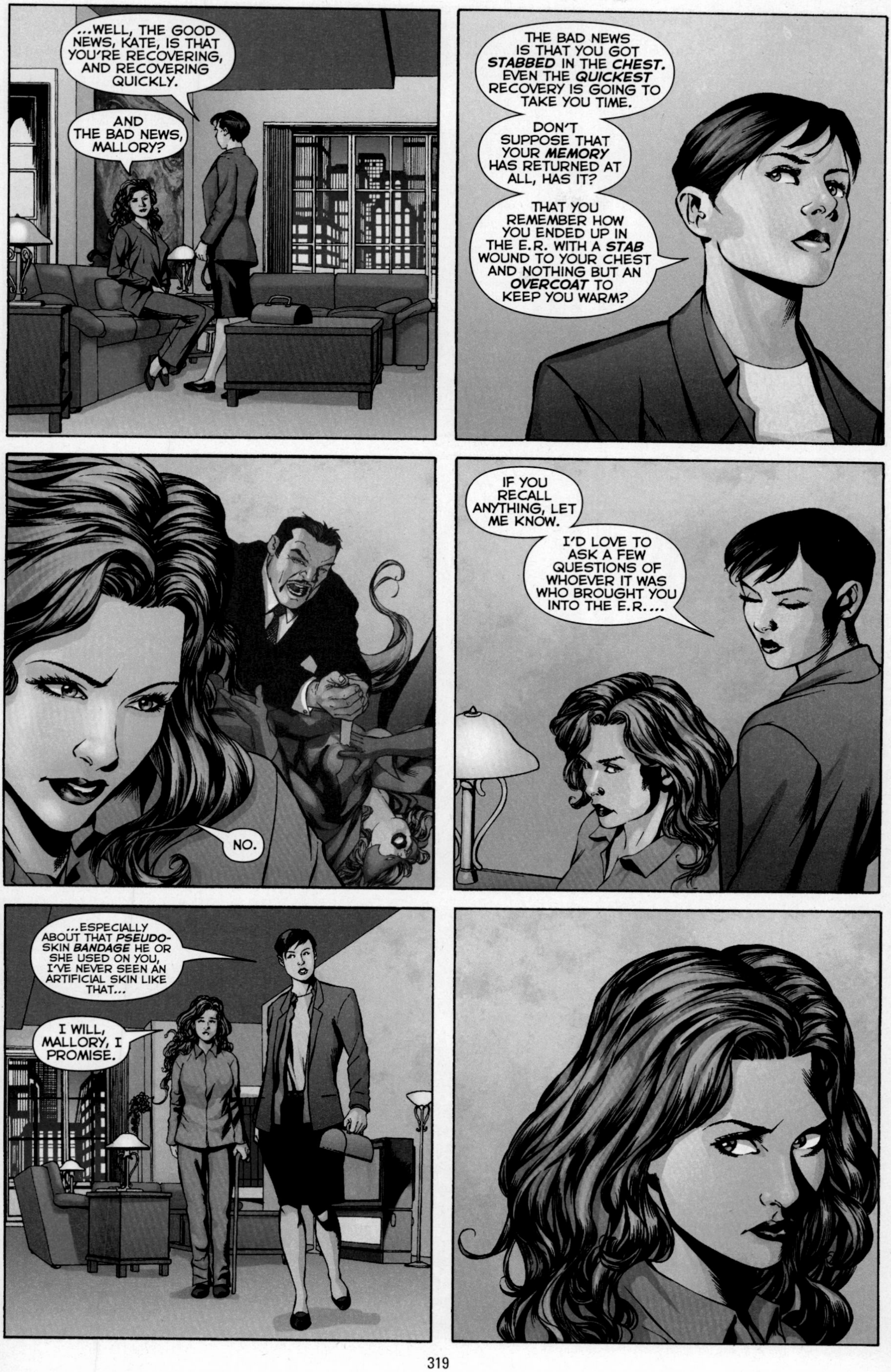
...WELL, THE GOOD NEWS, KATE, IS THAT YOU'RE RECOVERING, AND RECOVERING QUICKLY.
AND THE BAD NEWS, MALLORY?
THE BAD NEWS IS THAT YOU GOT *STABBED* IN THE *CHEST.* EVEN THE *QUICKEST* RECOVERY IS GOING TO TAKE YOU TIME.
DON'T SUPPOSE THAT YOUR *MEMORY* HAS RETURNED AT ALL, HAS IT?
THAT YOU REMEMBER HOW YOU ENDED UP IN THE E.R. WITH A *STAB* WOUND TO YOUR CHEST AND NOTHING BUT AN *OVERCOAT* TO KEEP YOU WARM?
NO.
IF YOU RECALL ANYTHING, LET ME KNOW.
I'D LOVE TO ASK A FEW QUESTIONS OF WHOEVER IT WAS WHO BROUGHT YOU INTO THE E.R....
...ESPECIALLY ABOUT THAT *PSEUDO-SKIN BANDAGE* HE OR SHE USED ON YOU, I'VE NEVER SEEN AN ARTIFICIAL SKIN LIKE THAT...
I WILL, MALLORY, I PROMISE.

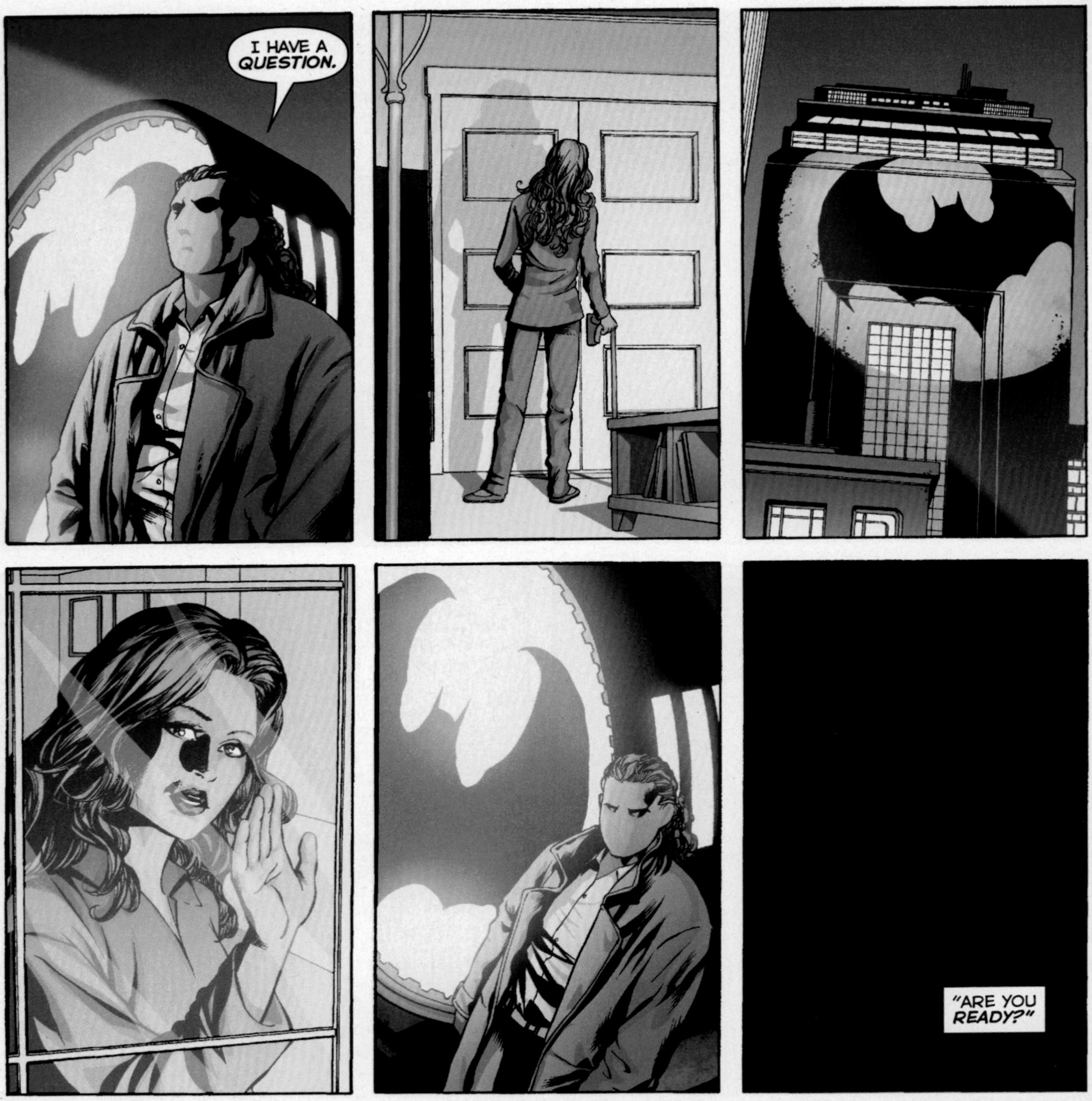
I HAVE A QUESTION.
"ARE YOU READY?"

Week 52

A YEAR IN THE LIFE

Written by **GEOFF JOHNS, GRANT MORRISON, GREG RUCKA, MARK WAID**
Art Breakdowns by **KEITH GIFFEN**
Pencils by **MIKE McKONE, JUSTINIANO, EDDY BARROWS, CHRIS BATISTA, PAT OLLIFFE,** and **DARICK ROBERTSON**
Inks by **ANDY LANNING, WALDEN WONG, RODNEY RAMOS, DREW GERACI** and **DARICK ROBERTSON**

Colors by **ALEX SINCLAIR, DAVID BARON** and **HI-FI** Letters by **KEN LOPEZ**
Assistant Edited by **HARVEY RICHARDS** Associate Edited by **JEANINE SCHAEFER**
Edited by **MICHAEL SIGLAIN**
Cover by **J.G. JONES** & **ALEX SINCLAIR**
Special Thanks to **STEPHEN WACKER**

WEEK FIFTY-TWO NOTES

MARK WAID

I will never, ever tell what the whole, cosmic significance of the number "52" was originally conceived to be, but this wasn't it. This was better. Fifty-two parallel Earths, each created in the "big bang" moment of INFINITE CRISIS, each corrupted and twisted by the timefight with Mr. Mind as his wingflaps rippled through history and altered their individual timestreams. My recollection is that Geoff came up with the former and I came up with the latter, but both sprang from Grant's original suggestion that Skeets had been inhabited by Mr. Mind and all the ideas were vetted by the inestimable Rucka, making the finale a true team effort. (Greg often served as our logic barometer and grounded us when we went too far too wildly.)

When it came time to map the alternate Earths, we elected to invent new ones rather than simply reestablish familiar ones from old DC comics. That said, many are designed to deliberately resemble DC worlds of yore, such as Earth-22 (home of the KINGDOM COME miniseries) and Earth-5 (formerly "Earth-S," the "S" standing for "Shazam"). Exec Editor Dan DiDio gave our editor a great deal of guidance in the look of some of these worlds.

"Welcome home" is my favorite line in the entire series. "Home," both to us as writers and to our characters, is not a constriction of rules and regulations in which only one "definitive" interpretation of the DC heroes can exist and everything not currently in vogue is "wrong"; it's a multiverse of possibility where absolutely anything can happen and where imagination has no limits. From the time a caveman told the first bedtime story to today, no good fiction ever came out of worrying first and foremost whether its events fit into "continuity."

Of all the things we accomplished in 52 weeks, reuniting Ralph and Sue Dibny is the one of which I'm, by miles, the proudest. Ralph and Sue, Ghost Detectives, was probably the first big idea that the writers as a group came up with, and I still think it's the single best notion we had because it so perfectly fits those characters and gives Ralph a happy, but not schmaltzy, ending. If DC had gotten cold feet and backed out of this event, if our entire series had somehow been only two pages long, they would have been the Ralph and Sue pages.

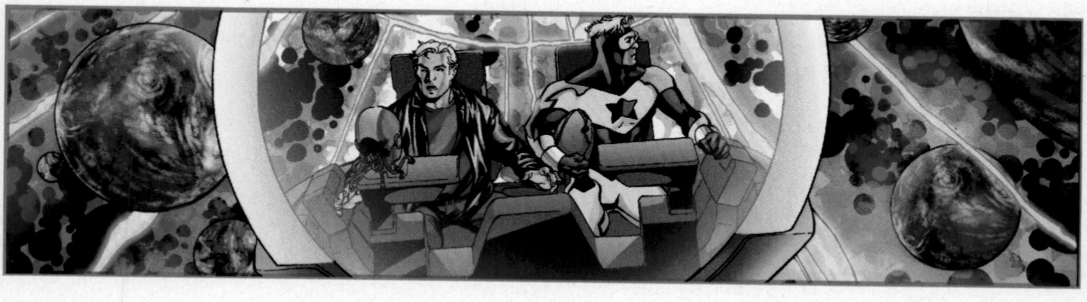

MICHAEL SIGLAIN

Well, we did it. We took it right down to the wire, but we did it. It was a Herculean task at times, but we proved the naysayers wrong and delivered a good story on a weekly basis. And we did it despite a million little hurdles (like lost packages, and late scripts and artwork) and a couple big hurdles (like an editorial switch midway through), but we pulled it off.

52 was the most intimidating and monstrous job of my career. It was also one of the greatest editorial experiences of my career. The amount of work that goes into a weekly comic is unbelievable. I even had to work from home on the day of my wedding to make sure that the last book got to the printer in time (thanks, sweetie!). Yes, it was a ridiculous amount of work, but not for one second did anyone think that we'd miss a beat, either in story or shipping.

Geoff, Grant, Greg, and Mark did an absolutely amazing job and it was an honor and a pleasure to work with each and every one of them. Add Keith Giffen, J.G. Jones, Alex Sinclair and a stellar list of artists and colorists to the mix, and you've got pure gold. Thanks, guys. Ya done good.

I'd also like to thank my predecessor, Stephen Wacker, who did a truly remarkable job on the book. Steve's a great guy and an even better editor, and I'm proud to have my name alongside his.

A very big THANK YOU also goes out to Nick Napolitano, Hank Manfra, and Paul Moore (from DC's Production and Editorial Administration departments). This book would not have looked so damn good, or have come out every week, were it not for these three men. Well done, gentlemen. We got this.

And let's not forget Corey Breen, Dezi Sienty, Cherie King, Chris Burns, Kenny Lopez, David Ng, Arlene Lo, Fred Haynes, Lauren Kestner, Steve Wands, Robert Clark, Jared K. Fletcher, Travis Lanham, Pat Brosseau, Phil Balsman, Rob Leigh, Jack Mahan, Scott Wilson, Valerie Reupert, Chris Conroy, Mike Zagari, Dave McCullough, John Morgan, David Hyde, and last but certainly not least, Alex Segura. These guys and girls behind the scenes are the unsung heroes of 52, and the series wouldn't have been what it was without them.

Assistant Editor Harvey Richards and Associate Editor Jeanine Schaefer were with me on the battlefield day in, and day out, and to this day I'm still in their debt. Thanks for everything, guys.

Finally, the biggest thank-you must be saved for Dan DiDio and Paul Levitz, not only for the idea of the series (thanks, Mr. Levitz!), but for their faith, dedication, and encouragement.

And that's it. Thanks for reading, gang. Hope everyone enjoyed the series, be it in single issues or as collected editions. It was a helluva ride!

BREAKDOWNS

BY **KEITH GIFFEN**

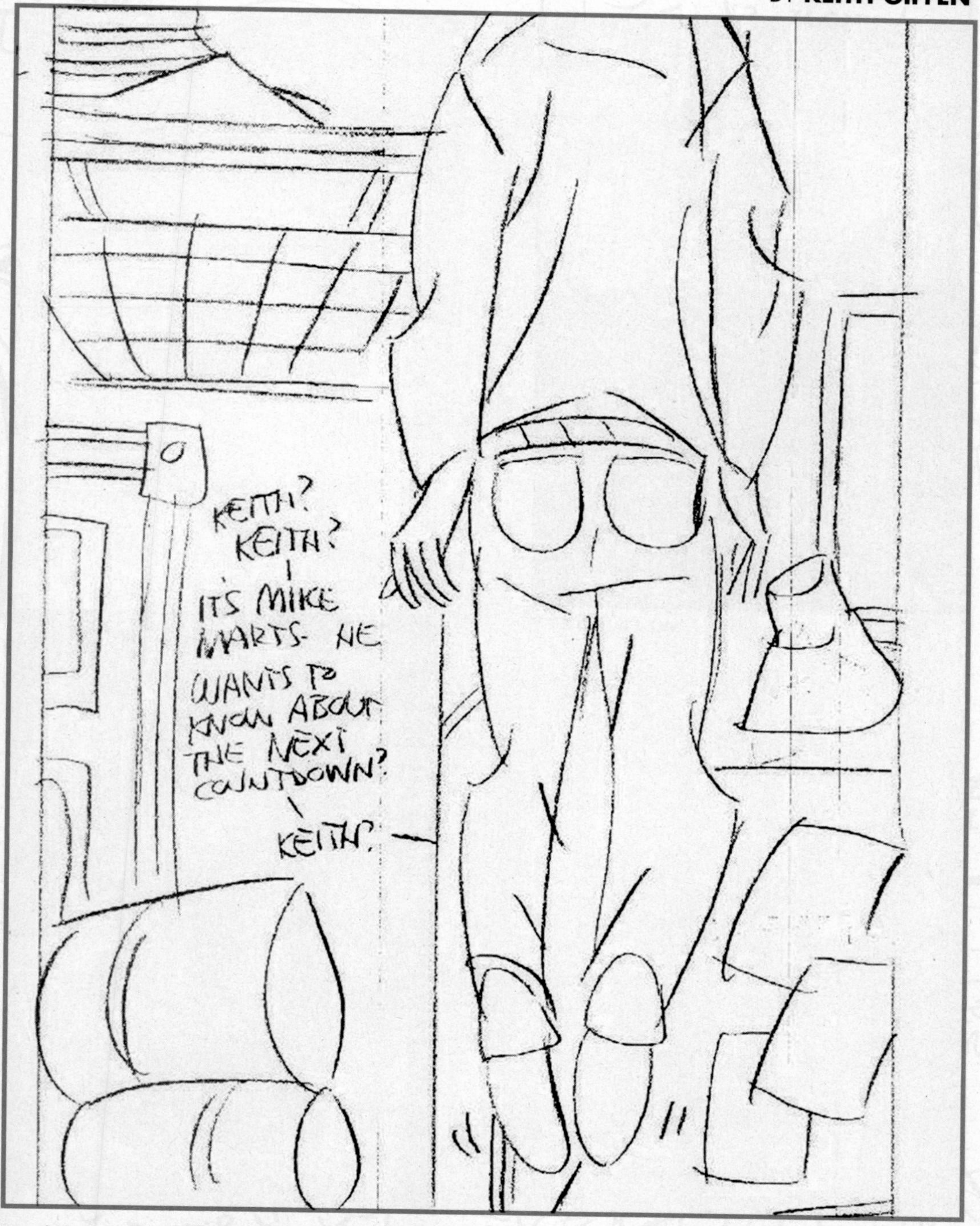
KEITH?
KEITH?
IT'S MIKE MARTS- HE WANTS TO KNOW ABOUT THE NEXT COUNTDOWN?
KEITH?

Breakdown artist Keith Giffen drew an epilogue to "52," before starting work on the next weekly series, COUNTDOWN.

COVER GALLERY

ART BY **J.G. JONES** WITH **ALEX SINCLAIR**

WEEK **FORTY**

WEEK **FORTY-ONE**

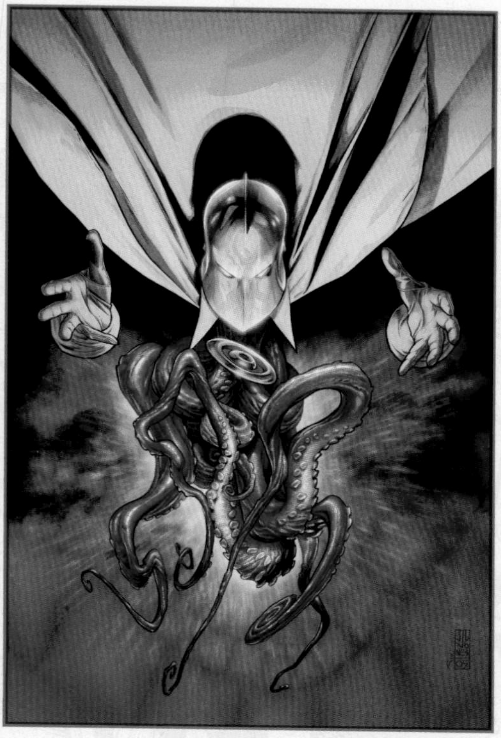

WEEK **FORTY-TWO**

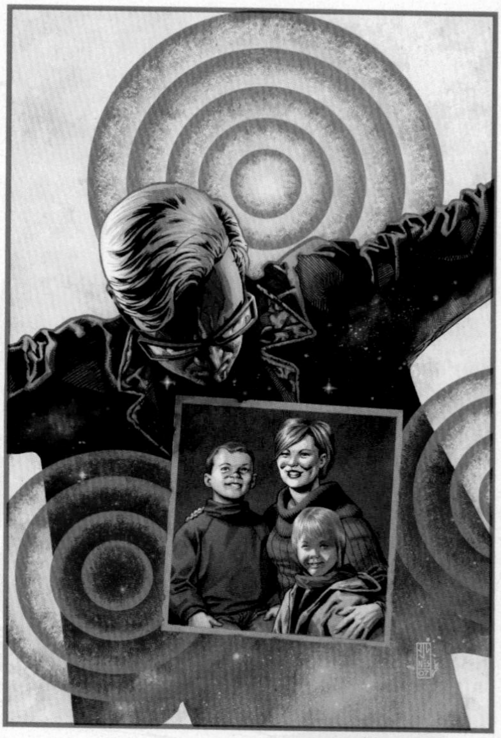

WEEK **FORTY-THREE**

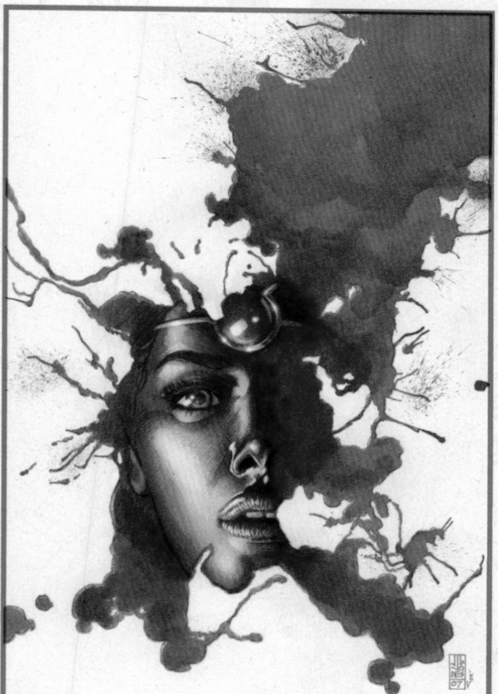

WEEK **FORTY-FOUR**

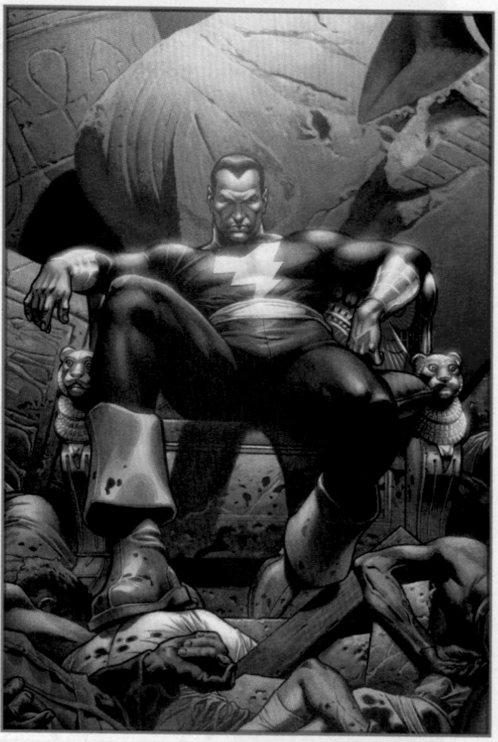

WEEK **FORTY-FIVE**

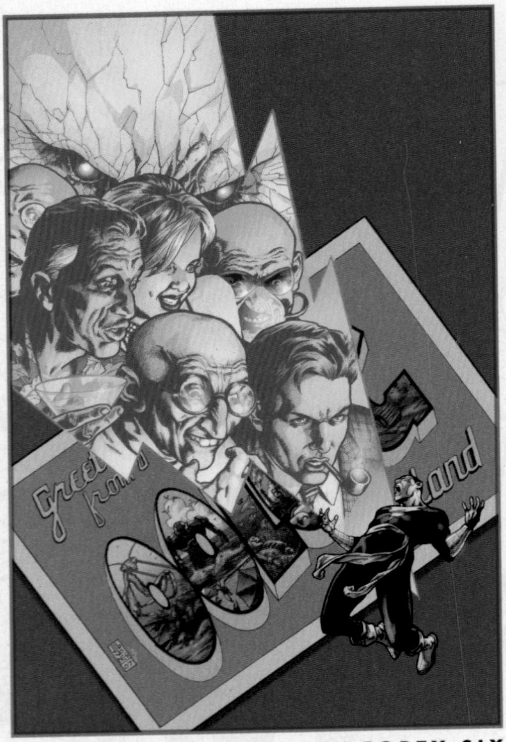

WEEK **FORTY-SIX**

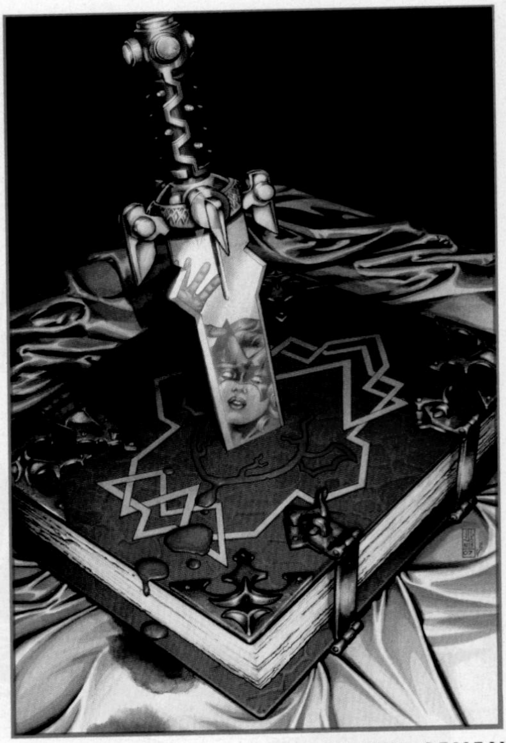

WEEK **FORTY-SEVEN**

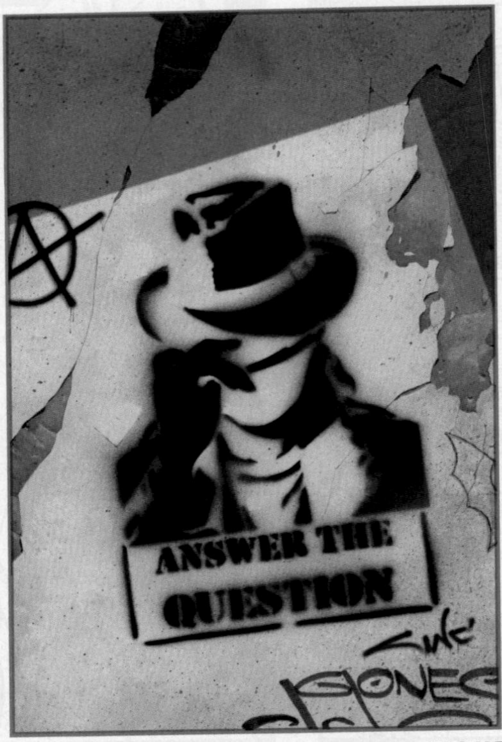
ANSWER THE
QUESTION

WEEK **FORTY-EIGHT**

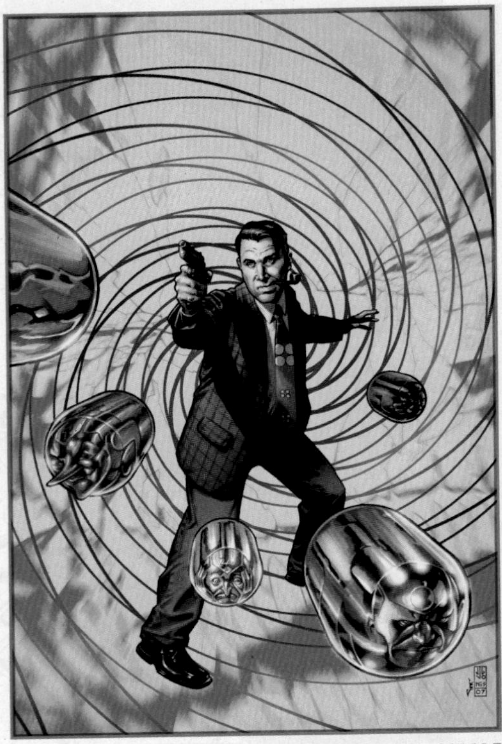

WEEK **FORTY-NINE**

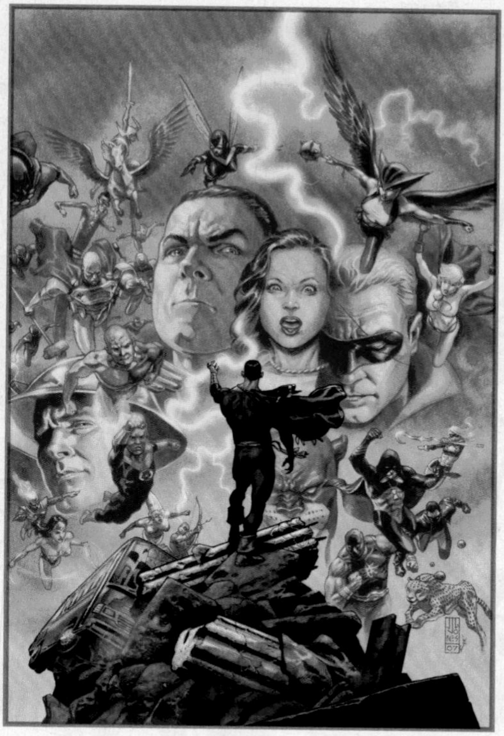

WEEK **FIFTY**

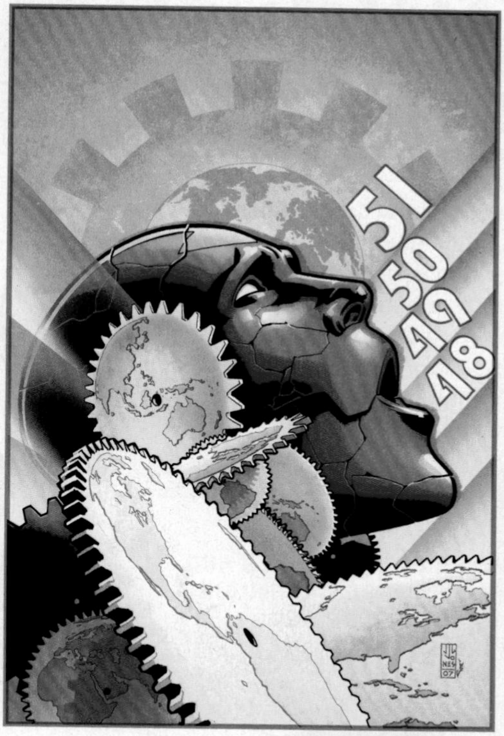
51
50
49
48

WEEK **FIFTY-ONE**

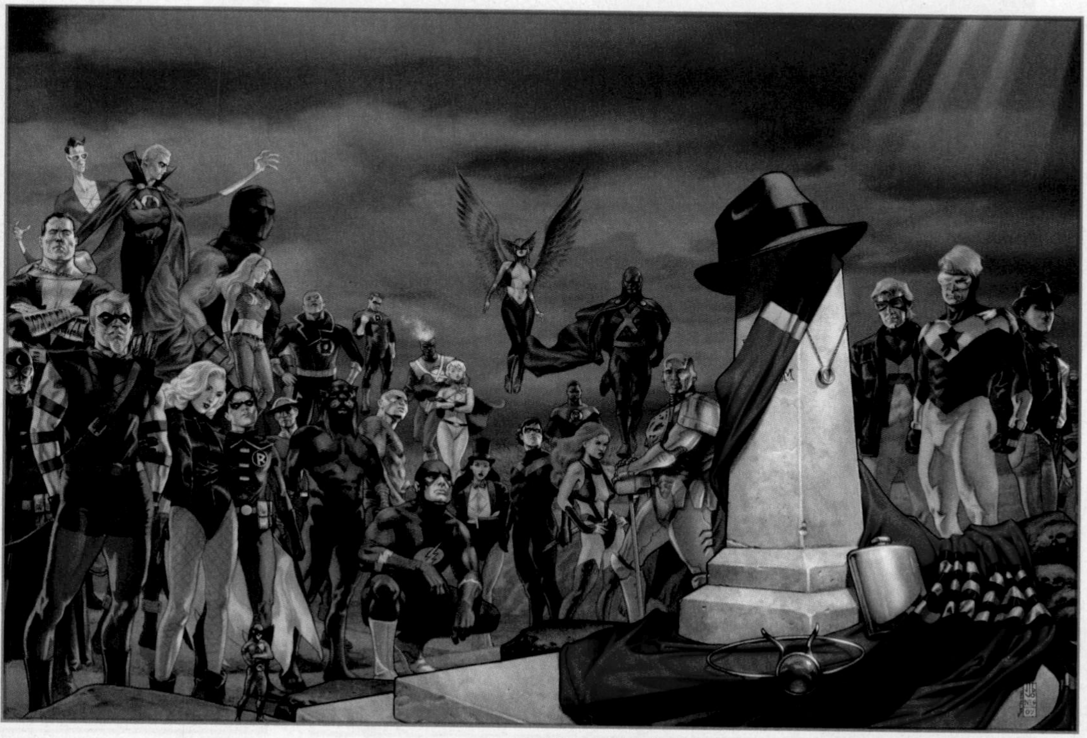

WEEK **FIFTY-TWO**

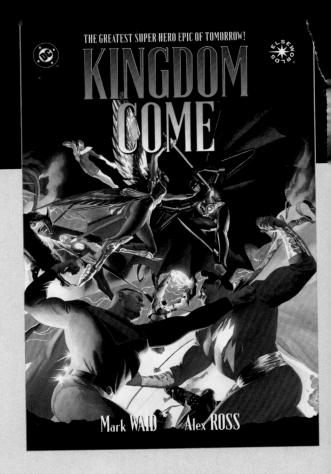
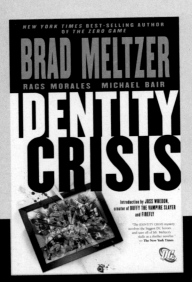